REAL ESTATE PRINCIPLES

TWELFTH EDITION

CHARLES J. JACOBUS

DREI, CREI

OnCourse Learning

United States

Real Estate Principles, Twelfth Edition

Charles J. Jacobus

Executive Editor: Sara Glassmeyer

Developmental Editor: Arlin Kauffmann

Rights Acquisition Director: Audrey Pettengill

Rights Acquisition Specialist, Text and Image: Amber Hosea

Senior Manufacturing Planner: Charlene Taylor

Art and Cover Direction, Production Management, and Composition: Cenveo Publisher Services

Cover & Internal Images: © Brand X Pictures/ Getty Images, © Jupiterimages/Photos.com/

For product information and technology assistance, contact us at
www.oncourselearning.com

Library of Congress Control Number: 2013935512

ISBN-13: 978-1-62980-030-1

ISBN-10: 1-62980-030-9

OnCourse Learning
3100 Cumberland Blvd., Suite 1450
Atlanta, GA 30339
USA

Visit our website at **www.oncoursepublishing.com**

Printed in the United States of America
3 4 5 6 7   17 16 15

I wish to thank the following individuals who, through their thoughtful comments, have helped to shape and improve this book: Barney Fletcher, Richard T. Fryer, Joe Goeters, John Hamilton, Barry Hoy, F. Jeffrey Keil, Edith Lank, Don Moseley, Susan Moseley, L.K. ODrudy, Larry Outlaw, Katherine Pancak, Kimberly Possert, Marie Spodek, Prof. Michael Sumoo, John A. Tirone, John P. Torbush, Skip Weber, Judy Wolk, and Mary Alford.

BRIEF CONTENTS

CONTENTS

Chapter 3   RIGHTS AND INTERESTS IN LAND   33

Chapter 4   **FORMS OF OWNERSHIP**   55

Chapter 5   **TRANSFERRING TITLE**   71

Chapter 6 **RECORDATION, ABSTRACTS, AND TITLE INSURANCE** 89

Chapter 9   **MORTGAGE AND NOTE**   143

Chapter 11   LENDING PRACTICES   181

Chapter 14   TYPES OF FINANCING   245

Chapter 17   **REAL ESTATE LEASES**   303

Chapter 19   **LICENSING LAWS AND PROFESSIONAL AFFILIATION**   351

Chapter 20 **THE PRINCIPAL–BROKER
RELATIONSHIP: EMPLOYMENT   385**

Chapter 21 | THE PRINCIPAL–BROKER RELATIONSHIP: AGENCY 399

Chapter 22   FAIR HOUSING, ADA, EQUAL CREDIT, AND COMMUNITY REINVESTMENT   419

Chapter 23   CONDOMINIUMS, COOPERATIVES, PUDS, AND TIME-SHARES   433

Chapter 24   **PROPERTY INSURANCE**   449

Chapter 25   **LAND-USE CONTROL**   459

In the Beginning

Real estate has always been one of the more interesting topics to discuss. The age of consumerism (and highly motivated and informed consumers) has changed the real estate business forever. There are important consumer protection statutes in every state. The law of agency has changed dramatically. Real estate agents now represent buyers, negotiate their commissions, and offer limited service agreements.

The Internet has made information (once limited to the industry) available to all consumers. The information highway has forced the business to adapt to a new way of thinking, being more open and flexible to consumers' needs and desires. VA and FHA, once a benchmark of available financing, is now overshadowed by new financing vehicles from private sources; affordable housing loans have made the American dream more attainable. Not surprisingly, the need for education has grown too.

Government has recently become so involved in every aspect of real estate that it is becoming unpredictable at all levels. The free market used to have free reign, and people worked through the cycles of the economy as the market fluctuated. Should the government attempt to eliminate these cycles by forgiving debt, forcing "affordable loans" into the market place, or creating more government agencies to oversee the market? Who has these answers? You do. Students today will set the pace for tomorrow.

This Is Why

This book was written by teachers. Now in its 12th edition, it was originated by my good friend, Dr. Bruce Harwood, with whom I co-authored another text. After his untimely death, I continued our efforts to revise this book to reflect our dedication to teach those who want to learn this subject. I've kept the easy-to-read style and the straightforward, transaction-oriented approach to the subject, which, as a teacher, I've found very effective. I've tried to keep the language simple and not as "stilted" as many academic applications tend to be. This subject can be presented accurately and correctly, without being boring.

The basics of real estate have stayed the same for hundreds of years, being based on the English common law. These fundamentals are discussed in different ways in different chapters, each reinforcing what was learned in prior topics. Ownership and estates in land, for instance, can be revisited when discussing contracts and mortgages. All of this information, then, is again revisited when the student begins learning the more complicated topics of recording, appraising, financing, fair housing, and land use control. Most of those who read this book will move on to become licensed as a real estate professional, so I've tried to cover all pertinent topics to prepare the reader for the license examination and provide a good base of more education.

Here's How

The special features of this book include the following:

- **Additional Study Material!** At the end of each chapter there is a vocabulary review of key terms, questions and problems, and additional readings for deeper research. These are designed to help readers focus on the chapter's important terms and concepts. The questions will help students review the material and pinpoint areas that may need more study when preparing for the licensing examination. Answers to these questions are found in Appendix E, thus making this book a self-contained study tool.

- **Easy Review!** Beginning with Chapter 2, each chapter offers learning objectives and a list of key terms and their definitions. Key terms are also boldfaced when first used in a chapter, as well as listed in the combined Glossary/Index at the back of the book. To aid students in reviewing terms and topics, this book combines the glossary with the index, allowing the reader to look up a term and find not only the definition, but also the page references to where the topic is discussed throughout the book.

- **Useful Appendices!** These appendices offer the reader comprehensive study tools for the field of real estate. They include the following:
  - Construction Illustrations and Terminology
  - Real Estate Math Review
  - Interest and Present Value Tables
  - Measurement Conversion Table
  - Answers to Chapter Questions and Problems

New to This Edition

Chapter 1 – New topic on Title Insurance
Chapter 3 – New topic on Wind Energy
Chapter 4 – New topic on Series LLC
Chapter 5 – Table 5.1 updated to correct number of years of occupancy required to claim title
Chapter 9 – New Figures added on Federal National Mortgage Association (FNMA) Uniform Note, The Modified FNMA Master Form Mortgage; Updated content on Deficiency Judgment topic
Chapter 10 – New Deed of Trust figure provided.
Chapter 11 – Updated content on Current FHA Coverage, Mortgage Insurance, Construction Regulations
Chapter 12 – Updated content on Truth-in-Lending Act; New topics added on Identity Theft and Fake Check/Fast Closing
Chapter 13 – Updated content on Mortgage Brokers topic
Chapter 14 – Updated content on Reverse Mortgage and Overly Creative Financing topics
Chapter 15 – Updated content on Capital Gains topic
Chapter 16 – Updated content on New RESPA Regulations; New HUD-1 Settlement Statement

Chapter 18 – Updated content on Sales Comparison Approach; New topic on New Appraisal Regulations

Chapter 19 – Updated Table 19.1 to reflect new Real Estate Education and Experience Requirements; Updated Examination Services, Bonds Recovery Funds and E & O Insurance and REALTOR sections; Updated Code of Ethics figure

Chapter 21 – New topic added "Is Non-Agency the Answer?"

Chapter 26 – Updated content for Age Distribution, Watching the Fed and Types of Inflation

Chapter 27 – New topic added on Real Estate Investment Trusts

We Can Help

Important study aids and instructional material complete this package for the principles course.

- *For the Student:*
  - **Study Guide:** This excellent learning tool offers basic test-taking tips, reinforces the learning objectives from each chapter, and provides objective quizzes for every chapter. In the back are the answers and rationale for further explanation!
  - **Online Tool:** We have posted our PowerPoint^{TM} online to offer students an additional study option! Visit this textbook's support site at www.oncourselearning.com.

- *For the Instructor:*
  - **Instructor's Manual/Test Item File:** All in one, this supplement is a must-have. The instructor's manual is available with adoption of this text and includes chapter outlines, teaching tips, a bank of test questions beginning with Chapter 2, and nearly 100 masters to be made into transparencies of figures, tables, and notes from the book.
  - **Online Tool:** The files for the instructor's manual can be found on our site at www.oncoursepublishing.com.

Looking Ahead

As a publisher, we understand that learning does not stop after the pre-license exam, and neither do our products. From pre-license to brokerage, or principles to graduate degrees, we provide learning solutions that address continuing education, professional development, and advanced study needs. To learn more about OnCourse Learning's complete list of real estate education resources, visit us online at www.oncoursepublishing.com.

ABOUT THE AUTHOR

Charles J. Jacobus received a Bachelor of Science degree from the University of Houston in 1970 and a Doctor of Jurisprudence degree from the University of Houston Law Center in 1973. He is board certified by the State Bar of Texas Board of Legal Specialization in both residential and commercial real estate law. He is a member of the American College of Lawyers and the Houston Real Estate Lawyer's Council, and he has served as president of the Real Estate Educators' Association, chairman of the Real Estate Section of the Houston Bar Association, and chairman of the American Bar Association Committee on Real Estate Brokers and Brokerage. He has served on the Board of Editors for the American Bar Association Committee on Books and Publications, was Mayor of his hometown, Bellaire, Texas, and served on the Real Estate, Probate, and Trust Law Council of the State Bar of Texas as chairman of the State Bar of Texas Committee on Title Insurance.

He is currently serving on the Texas Real Estate Commission's Broker-Lawyer Committee, and the Texas Real Estate Center's MCE Advisory Committee. He is also an adjunct professor at the University of Houston Law Center and the University Of Houston Bauer School of Business MBA program in Real Estate.

CHAPTER 1

Introduction to Real Estate

LEARNING OBJECTIVES

After reading this chapter, you should be able to:

‹ Understand different career paths in the profession of real estate.

‹ Recognize different characteristics of those careers.

‹ Recognize personal traits which may make one career path more interesting to you.

‹ Recognize fundamental forms of licensing in the various states.

Real estate is a unique subject, and because it is unique, real estate has spawned complex legal theories and very unusual fact situations. No two situations are ever exactly alike, and the subject never ceases to be intellectually stimulating. Everyone has a favorite story about real estate, and it has remained a fascinating topic for centuries. This fascination is what makes real estate such a fun, interesting business.

As a new real estate student, one must be prepared to learn a lot of new concepts and be willing to commit the time and effort to that end. There are some who say that the only way to learn real estate is by experience. Many years ago this was the traditional concept. Real estate was then considered to be a "marketing" or "salesmanship" business, and experience was the best teacher. Recent years, however, have seen the development of extensive academic and technological applications in real estate education. Real estate has come to the academic forefront—undergraduate degrees in real estate are becoming more common, and graduate-level degree programs are proliferating. There is also a resulting emphasis on the professionalism and ethics of these new real estate professionals. Technological advances in all phases of the real estate industry have placed both real estate education and real estate practice on a new level of competition and efficiency. Unlike many other academic subjects, however, real estate continues to emphasize experience in the "people-oriented" aspects of the business. Experience has a high correlation with success in the real estate business.

With these combinations in mind, this book has been written to provide you with an understanding of the basic principles and business fundamentals of real estate. Emphasis is placed on an easily readable presentation that combines explanations of the basic principles of the subject with "why" things are done and "how" these principles apply to everyday activities.

How to Read This Book

At the beginning of each chapter (2 through 27) there is a list of key terms that you will learn, along with brief definitions, and an introduction of topics to be covered. Read these before starting the chapter. In the body of the chapter, these terms, as well as other terms important to real estate, are set in **Boldface type** and are given a more in-depth discussion. At the end of each chapter is a vocabulary review plus questions and problems. These are designed to help you test yourself on your comprehension of the material in the chapter you've just read. The answers are given in the back of the book.

Also at the back of this book is a combined index and glossary, meant to reinforce your familiarity with the language of real estate. Terms in the index and glossary receive a short definition, followed by a page reference for more detailed discussion.

Another feature of this book is its simplified documents. Contracts and title policies, for example, are sometimes written in legal language, which may be confusing to anyone except a lawyer. In the chapters ahead, you will find simplified versions of these documents, written in plain English and set in standard-size type. The intention is to give you a clearer understanding of these important real estate documents.

In this edition, I have also added topics in various chapters to show real, up-to-date, practical applications of the topics.

Transaction Overview

Figure 1.1 provides a visual summary of the real estate transaction cycle. It is included here to give you an overview of the different steps involved in the sale of real property and to show how these steps are related to one another. The chapter in which each step is discussed is shown in parentheses. Whether your point of view is that of a real estate agent, owner, buyer, or seller, you will find the chapters that follow to be informative and valuable.

Chapter Organization

Great care has been taken to organize this text in a manner that will build your knowledge of real estate. For example, land description methods and rights and interests in land are necessary to sales contracts, abstracts, deeds, mortgages, and listings and therefore are discussed early in the text. In Chapter 2, you will find such topics as metes and bounds and tract maps. You will also find a discussion of what is real estate and what is not, and how land is physically and economically different from other commodities. You will then look at the various rights and interests that exist in a given parcel of land. In Chapter 3, you will see that there is much more to ownership of land than meets the eye! In Chapter 4, we look at how a given right or interest in land can be held by an individual, by two or more persons, or by a business entity. Included in this chapter are discussions of joint tenancy, tenancy in common, and community property. Chapters 5 and 6 deal with the process by which the ownership of real estate is transferred from one person to another. In particular, Chapter 5 discusses deeds and wills, and Chapter 6 deals with how a person gives evidence to the world that he possesses a given right or interest in land. Abstracts and title insurance are among the topics included. In Chapters 7 and 8, we turn to contract law and its application to offers and acceptances. Because so much

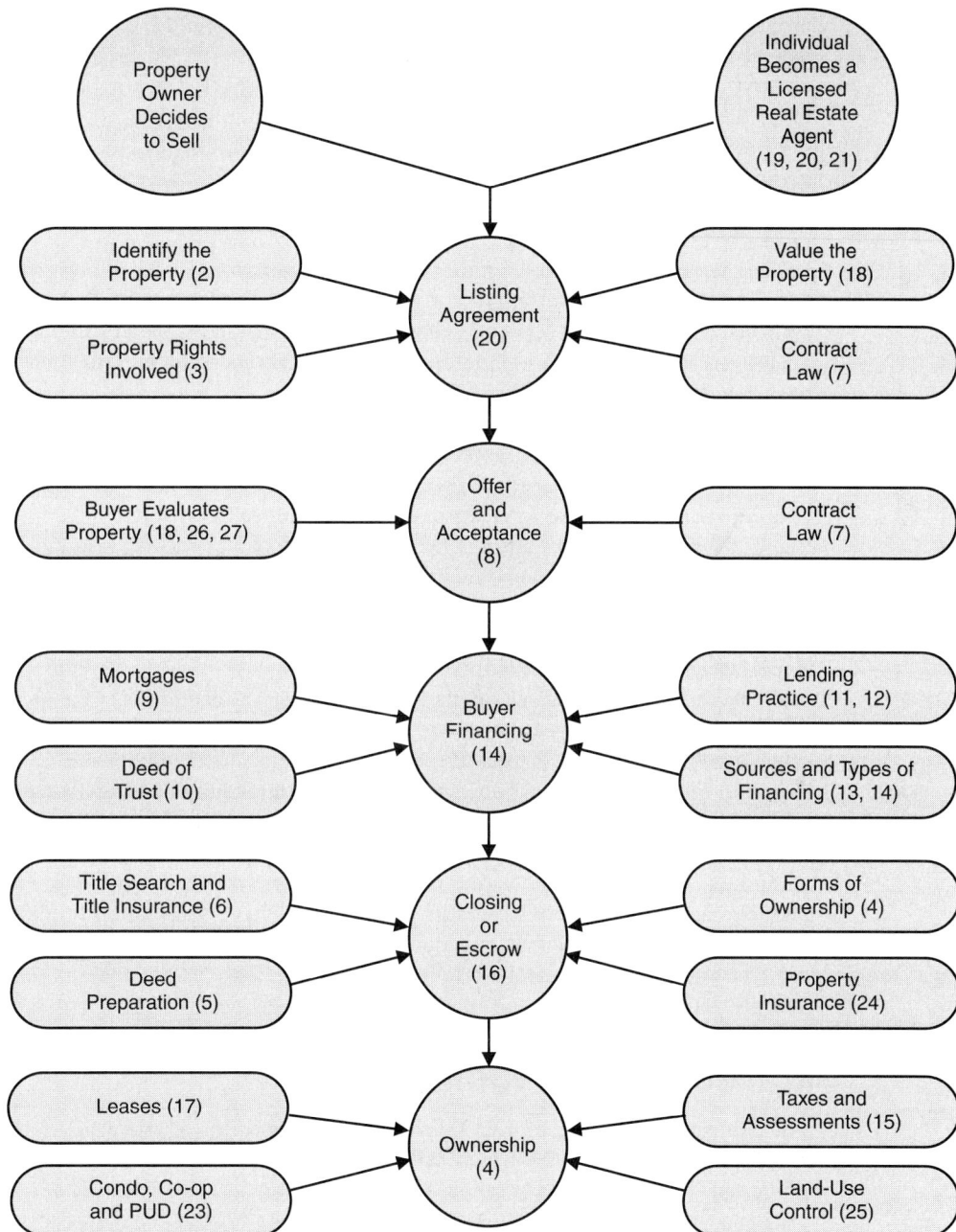

FIGURE 1.1   An Overview of a Real Estate Transaction

Property Owner Decides to Sell

Individual Becomes a Licensed Real Estate Agent (19, 20, 21)

Identify the Property (2)

Value the Property (18)

Property Rights Involved (3)

Contract Law (7)

Listing Agreement (20)

Buyer Evaluates Property (18, 26, 27)

Contract Law (7)

Offer and Acceptance (8)

Mortgages (9)

Lending Practice (11, 12)

Deed of Trust (10)

Sources and Types of Financing (13, 14)

Buyer Financing (14)

Title Search and Title Insurance (6)

Forms of Ownership (4)

Deed Preparation (5)

Property Insurance (24)

Closing or Escrow (16)

Leases (17)

Taxes and Assessments (15)

Condo, Co-op and PUD (23)

Land-Use Control (25)

Ownership (4)

NOTE: Numbers in parentheses refer to chapter numbers.

Source: © 2014 OnCourse Learning

of what takes place in real estate is in the form of contracts, you will want to have a solid understanding of what makes a contract legally binding and what doesn't. Chapters 9 through 14 are devoted to real estate finance. In Chapter 9, mortgages and the laws regarding their use are explained. Chapter 10 covers the deed of trust and is intended for readers in those states in which the deed of trust is used in place of a mortgage. Amortized loans, points, Federal Housing Administration (FHA) and Veterans Affairs (VA) programs, and mortgage insurance are discussed in Chapter 11. Loan applications and federal truth-in-lending issues are discussed in Chapter 12. Mortgage lenders, the secondary mortgage market, and due-on-sale clauses are covered in Chapter 13. Adjustable rate mortgages and financing alternatives are discussed in Chapter 14. In Chapter 15 we see how property taxes and assessments are calculated, and Chapter 16 explains title closing and escrow. Chapter 17 deals with leasing real estate and includes a sample lease document with discussion. Chapter 18 explores the language, principles, and techniques of real estate appraisal.

Chapter 19 deals with real estate license law requirements, how a salesperson chooses a broker, and professional ethics. In Chapter 20 we examine the relationship between real estate agents and buyers and sellers. Chapter 21 concentrates on the law of agency. Special emphasis is placed on the duties and obligations of brokers to their clients and on fair housing laws in Chapter 22.

The remaining chapters of this book deal with a number of individual and specialized real estate topics. Chapter 23 explores the condominium, cooperative, and planned unit development forms of real estate ownership. Included is a look at how they are created and the various rights and interests in land that are created by them, including timesharing. In Chapter 24 we take a brief and informative look at property insurance. An owner of real property should know how to insure against financial loss due to property damage and public liability.

Zoning, land planning, and deed restrictions are covered in Chapter 25. These are important topics because any limitation on a landowner's right to develop and use land can have a substantial effect on its value. Chapter 26 explores several pertinent and timely relationships between the value of real estate and the condition of the U.S. economy. The final chapter, Chapter 27, is an introduction to the opportunities available to you as a real estate investor. Topics include tax shelter, equity build-up, what to buy, and when to buy.

Following the final chapter are several appendixes that you will find useful. There are compound interest, present value, and measurement conversion tables. (Amortization and loan balance tables are located in Chapter 11.) There is also an appendix containing construction illustrations to help acquaint you with construction terminology. Additionally, you will find a short real estate math review section plus the answers to the quizzes and problems found at the end of Chapters 2 through 27.

Career Opportunities

The contents and organization of this book are designed for people who are interested in real estate because they now own or plan to own real estate and for people who are interested in real estate as a career. It is to those who are considering real estate as a profession that the balance of this chapter is devoted.

In practice, there is not a job or career that doesn't somehow involve a knowledge of real estate. Most people who are considering a career in real estate think of becoming a real estate agent who specializes in selling homes. This is quite natural because home selling is the most visible segment of the real estate industry. It is the area of the business most people enter, and the one in which most practicing real estate licensees make their living. Selling residential property is a good experience. Entry-level positions are more available, and it can help you to decide whether real estate sales appeals to you.

RESIDENTIAL BROKERAGE

Residential brokerage requires a broad knowledge of the community and its neighborhoods; an understanding of real estate principles, law, and practice; and an ability to work well with people. Working hours will often include nights and weekends, as these times are usually most convenient to buyers and sellers. A residential agent must also supply an automobile that is suitable for taking clients to see properties.

Some real estate offices are now giving new residential salespersons a minimum guaranteed salary or a draw against future commissions. However, this is not always the case, so a newcomer should have enough capital to survive until the first commissions are earned—and that can take four to six months. Additionally, the salesperson must be capable of developing and handling a personal budget that will withstand the feast-or-famine cycles that can occur in real estate selling.

A person who is adept at interpersonal relations, who can identify clients' motives, and who can find the property to fit will probably be quite successful in this business.

COMMERCIAL BROKERAGE

Commercial brokers specialize in income-producing properties such as apartment and office buildings, retail stores, and warehouses. In this specialty, the salesperson is primarily selling monetary benefits. These benefits are the income, appreciation, mortgage reduction, and tax shelter that a property can reasonably be expected to produce.

To be successful in income property brokerage, one must be very competent in mathematics, know how to finance transactions, and keep abreast of current tax laws. One must also have a sense for what makes a good investment, what makes an investment salable, and what the growth possibilities are in the neighborhood where a property is located.

Commission income from commercial brokerage is likely to be less frequent, but in larger amounts than from residential brokerage. The time required to break into the business is longer, but once in the business, agent turnover is low. The working hours of a commercial broker are much closer to regular business hours than for those in residential selling, although appearances can be deceiving. Commercial brokers often spend nights and weekends "networking," as that is a primary source of their business. One almost always finds commercial brokers actively involved in charitable activities, fundraisers, golf tournaments, and similar activities, as it gives them a lot of time to work with community leaders and expand these networks.

INDUSTRIAL BROKERAGE

Similar to commercial brokers, industrial brokers specialize in finding suitable land and buildings for industrial concerns. This includes leasing and developing industrial property as well as listing and selling it. An industrial broker must be familiar with industry requirements such as proximity to raw materials, water and power, labor supplies, and transportation. An industrial broker must also know about local building, zoning, and tax laws as they pertain to possible sites, and about the schools, housing, cultural, and recreational facilities that would be used by future employees of the plant.

Commissions are irregular, but usually substantial. Working hours are regular business hours and sales efforts are primarily aimed at locating facts and figures and presenting them to clients in an orderly fashion. Industrial clients are usually sophisticated businesspeople. Gaining entry to industrial brokerage and acquiring a client list can be slow.

FARM BROKERAGE

With the rapid disappearance of the family farm, the farm broker's role is changing. Today a farm broker must be equally capable of handling the 160-acre spread of farmer Jones and the 10,000-acre operation owned by an agribusiness corporation. College training in agriculture is an advantage and on-the-job training is a must. Knowledge of soils, seeds, plants, fertilizers, production methods, new machinery, government subsidies, and tax laws is vital to success. Farm brokerage offers as many opportunities to earn commissions and fees from leasing and property management as from listing and selling property.

PROPERTY MANAGEMENT

For an investment property, the property manager's job is to supervise every aspect of a property's operation so as to produce the highest possible financial return over the longest period of time. The manager's tasks include renting, tenant relations, building repair and maintenance, accounting, advertising, and supervision of personnel and tradesmen.

The expanding development of condominiums has resulted in a growing demand for property managers to maintain them. In addition, large businesses that own property for their own use hire property managers. Property managers are usually paid a salary and, if the property is a rental, a bonus for keeping the building fully occupied. To be successful, a property manager should be not only a public relations expert and a good bookkeeper, but also at ease with tenants, handy with tools, and knowledgeable about laws applicable to rental units.

RENTAL LISTING SERVICES

In some cities there are rental listing services that help tenants find rental units and landlords find tenants. Most compile lists of available rentals and sell this information to persons looking for rentals. A few also charge the landlord for listing the property. The objective is to save a person time and gasoline by providing pertinent information on a large number of rentals. Each property on the list is accompanied by information regarding location, size, rent, security deposit, pet policy, and so on.

Especially popular in cities with substantial numbers of single persons are roommate listing services. These maintain files on persons with space to share (such as the second bedroom in a two-bedroom apartment) and those looking for space. The files contain such information as location, rent, gender, smoking preference, etc. Most roommate and rental listing services have been started by individual entrepreneurs and are not affiliated with real estate offices. A majority of states now require a real estate license for rental listing services.

REAL ESTATE APPRAISING

The job of the real estate appraiser is to gather and evaluate all available facts affecting a property's value. Appraisal is a real estate career opportunity that does not require property selling; however, it does demand a special set of skills of its own. The job requires practical experience, technical education, and good judgment. If you have an analytical mind and like to collect and interpret data, you might consider becoming a real estate appraiser. The job combines office work and field work, and the income of an expert appraiser can match that of a top real estate salesperson. One can be an independent appraiser, or there are numerous opportunities to work as a salaried appraiser for local tax authorities or lending institutions. The appraisal process is now becoming more complex, however. Most lenders and taxing authorities require that their appraisers have some advanced credential designation. Appraisers must be licensed in all 50 states and Washington DC. By 2014, appraisers will be required to have a college degree.

GOVERNMENT SERVICE

Approximately one-third of the land in the United States is government owned. This includes vacant and forested lands, office buildings, museums, parks, zoos, schools, hospitals, public housing, libraries, fire and police stations, roads and highways, subways, airports, and courthouses. All of these are real estate, and all of these require government employees who can negotiate purchases and sales, appraise, finance, manage, plan, and develop. Cities, counties, and state governments all have extensive real estate holdings. At the federal level, the Forest Service, Park Service, Department of Agriculture, Army Corps of Engineers, Bureau of Land Management, and General Services Administration are all major landholders. In addition to outright real estate ownership, government agencies such as the Federal Housing Administration, VA, and Federal Home Loan Bank employ thousands of real estate specialists to operate their real estate lending programs.

LAND DEVELOPMENT

Most new homes in the United States are built by developers who in turn sell them to homeowners and investors. Some homes are built by small-scale developers who produce only a few a year. Others are part of 400-home subdivisions and 40-story condominiums that are developed and constructed by large corporations that have their own planning, appraising, financing, construction, and marketing personnel. There is equal opportunity for success in development whether you build 4 houses per year or work for a firm that builds 400 per year.

URBAN PLANNING

Urban planners work with local governments and civic groups for the purpose of anticipating future growth and land-use changes. The urban planner makes recommendations for new streets, highways, sewer and water lines, schools, parks, and libraries. Emphasis on environmental protection and controlled growth has made urban planning one of real estate's most rapidly expanding specialties. An urban planning job is usually a salaried position and does not emphasize sales ability.

MORTGAGE FINANCING

Specialists in mortgage financing have a dual role: (1) to find economically sound properties for lenders, and (2) to locate money for borrowers. A mortgage specialist can work independently, receiving a fee from the borrower for locating a lender, or as a salaried employee of a lending institution. The ease with which mortgages can be bought and sold has encouraged many individuals to open their own mortgage companies in competition with established lending institutions. Some mortgage specialists also offer real estate loan consulting for a fee. They will help a borrower choose from among the numerous mortgage loan formats available today, find the best loan for the client, and assist in filling out and processing the loan application.

SECURITIES AND SYNDICATIONS

Limited partnerships and other forms of real estate syndications that combine the investment capital of a number of investors to buy large properties number in the thousands. The investment opportunities and professional management offered by syndications are eagerly sought after by people with money to invest in real estate. As a result, there are job opportunities in creating, promoting, and managing real estate syndications.

CONSULTING

Real estate consulting involves giving others advice about real estate for a fee. A consultant must have a very broad knowledge about real estate including financing, appraising, brokerage, management, development, construction, investing, leasing, zoning, taxes, title, economics, and law. To remain in business as a consultant, one must develop a good track record of successful suggestions and advice.

TITLE INSURANCE

The title insurance business offers an abundance of job opportunities and a wide range of varieties. A person who is very good at simple accounting procedures, preparing closing statements, and has an outgoing personality, could be an excellent escrow officer. One who is more inclined to the technical side, research, or document review could be a title examiner. There are also opportunities available in administration and management. These positions require a variety of skills. It can be very rewarding. It's interesting to note that most people who go into the title insurance business very seldom leave it. There are different challenges every day.

RESEARCH AND EDUCATION

A person interested in real estate research can concentrate on such matters as improved construction materials and management methods, or on finding answers to economic questions such as "What is the demand for homes going to be next year in this community (state, country)?"

Opportunities abound in real estate education. Nearly all states require the completion of specified real estate courses before a real estate license can be issued. All states require continued education for license renewal (mandatory continuing education, or "MCE"). As a result, persons with experience in the industry and an ability to effectively teach the subject are much sought after as instructors. Most states require a state approved instructor for teaching these classes.

FULL-TIME INVESTOR

One of the advantages of the free enterprise system is that you can choose to become a full-time investor solely for yourself. A substantial number of people have quit their jobs to work full time with their investment properties, and have done quite well at it. A popular and successful route for many has been to purchase, inexpensively and with a low down payment, a small apartment building that has not been maintained but is in a good neighborhood. The property is then thoroughly reconditioned, and rents are raised. This process increases the value of the property. The increase is parlayed into a larger building—often through a tax-deferred exchange—and the process is repeated. Alternatively, the investor can increase the mortgage loan on the building, and take the cash he receives as a "salary" or use it as a down payment on another not-too-well-maintained apartment building in a good neighborhood. This can also be done with single-family houses. It is not unusual for an investor to acquire several dozen rental houses over a period of years.

Other individual investors have done well financially by searching newspaper ads and regularly visiting real estate brokerage offices looking for underpriced properties that can be sold at a markup. A variation of this is to write to out-of-town property owners in a given neighborhood to see if there is any wish to sell at a bargain price. Another approach is to become a small-scale developer and contractor. (No license is needed if you work with your own property.) Through your own personal efforts, you create value in your projects, and then hold them as investments.

License Requirements

As previously stated, property owners who deal only with their own property are not required to hold a real estate license. However, any person who, for compensation or the promise of compensation, lists or offers to list, sells or offers to sell, buys or offers to buy, negotiates or offers to negotiate, either directly or indirectly for the purpose of bringing about a sale, purchase, or option to purchase, exchange, auction, lease, or rental of real estate, or any interest in real estate, is required to hold a valid real estate license. Some states also require persons offering their services as real estate appraisers, property managers, syndicators, counselors, mortgage bankers, or rent collectors to hold real estate licenses.

If your real estate plans are such that you may need a license, you should skip ahead to Chapter 19 and read the material there regarding real estate licensing.

Additional Readings

At the end of each chapter you will find a list of additional readings. These are included to give you a cross-section of written materials you may find valuable in furthering your real estate education. Because of space limitations, not all real estate books, booklets, and periodicals currently available are listed in the additional readings. A visit to your local library, bookstores, and the World Wide Web will undoubtedly produce additional real estate material not listed here, and each year brings new titles.

"Goals Help Your Career in Focus" by Amy R. Dillman (*Real Estate Today*, June 1994, vol. 27, number 6, p. 40).

"If You're Not a Good Negotiator, You're Not a Salesperson" by Ethel Green (*Today's Realtor*, June 1996, vol. 29, number 6, p. 39).

"Real Estate Principles for the Retail Industry" by Ann Berrigan (*Chain Store Age Executive with Shopping Center Age*, September 2001, vol. 77, issue 9, p. S5).

Your Successful Real Estate Career by Kenneth W. Edwards (Amacom, 2003).

CHAPTER 2

Nature and Description of Real Estate

What is real estate? **Real estate**, or **real property**, is land and the improvements made to land, and the rights to use them. In this chapter, you will be introduced to the terminology used to define and describe real estate. Real estate is defined, and rights to land are also described. Other topics include fixtures, appurtenances, water rights, and land descriptions. The metes and bounds description of land and the rectangular survey system of describing land are also covered, as are other land survey systems. This chapter includes the coverage of the physical and economic characteristics of land. Key terms such as *scarcity*, *fixity*, and *situs* are also defined. These and other terms defined within this second chapter should be studied thoroughly and be remembered to enhance your understanding of material in subsequent chapters.

real estate
Land and improvements in a physical sense, as well as the rights to own or use them; also known as **real property**.

Land

Often we think of land as only the surface of the earth. But, it is substantially more than that. As Figure 2.1 illustrates, land starts at the center of the earth, passes through the earth's surface, and continues on into space. An understanding of this concept is important because, given a particular parcel of land, it is possible for one person to own the rights to use its surface (**surface rights**), another to own the rights to drill or dig below its surface (**subsurface rights**), and still another to own the rights to use the airspace above it (**air rights**).

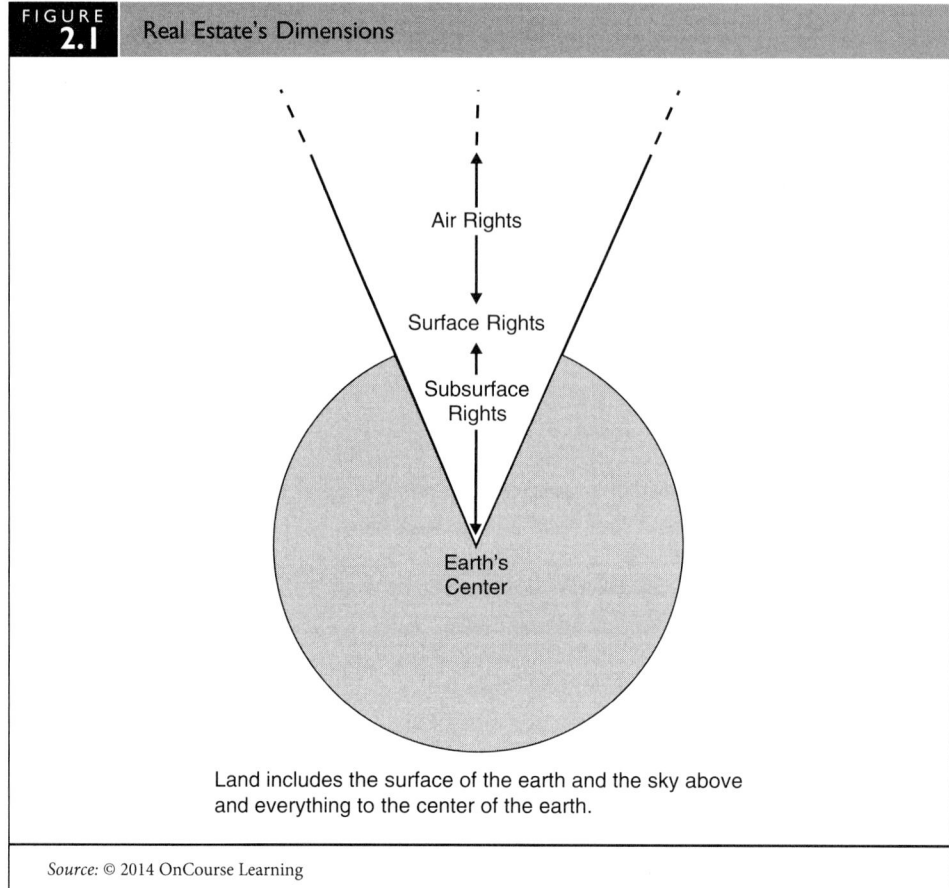

FIGURE 2.1   Real Estate's Dimensions

Air Rights

Surface Rights

Subsurface Rights

Earth's Center

Land includes the surface of the earth and the sky above and everything to the center of the earth.

Source: © 2014 OnCourse Learning

Improvements

improvements

Any form of land development, such as buildings, roads, fences, and pipelines.

Anything affixed to land with the intent of being permanent is considered to be part of the land and therefore real estate. Thus, houses, schools, factories, barns, fences, roads, pipelines, and landscaping are real estate. As a group, these are referred to as **improvements** because they improve or develop land.

Being able to identify what is real estate and what is not is important. In conveying ownership to a house, only the lot is described in the deed. It is not necessary to describe the dwelling unit itself, or landscaping, driveways, or sidewalks. They are all part of the lot itself. Items that are not a part of the land, such as tables, chairs, beds, desks, automobiles, and farm machinery, are classified as **personal property**, or **personalty**; if the right to use them is to be transferred to the buyer, the seller should sign a separate **bill of sale** in addition to the deed.

personal property

A right or interest in things of a temporary or movable nature; anything not classified as real property.

Fixtures

fixture

An object that has been attached to land so as to become real estate.

When an object that was once personal property is attached to land (or a building thereon) so as to become part of the real estate, it is called a **fixture**. As a rule, a fixture is the property of the landowner, and when the land is conveyed to a new owner, it is automatically included with the land. The question of whether an item is a fixture also arises with regard to property taxes, mortgages, lease terminations, and hazard insurance policies. Specifically, real estate taxes are based on real property valuation. Real estate mortgages are secured by real property. Objects attached to a building by a tenant may become real property and hence belong to the building's owner. Hazard insurance policies treat real property differently than personal property.

Whether an object becomes real estate depends on whether the object was affixed or installed with the *intention* of permanently improving the land. Intention is evidenced by four tests: (1) the manner of attachment, (2) the adaptation of the object, (3) the existence of an agreement, and (4) the relationship of the parties involved.

MANNER OF ATTACHMENT

The first test, *manner of attachment*, refers to how the object is attached to the land. Ordinarily, when an object that was once personal property is attached to land by virtue of its being imbedded in the land or affixed to the land by means of cement, nails, bolts, and so on, it becomes a fixture. To illustrate, when asphalt and concrete for driveways and sidewalks are still on the delivery truck, they are movable and therefore personal property. But once they are poured into place, the asphalt and concrete become part of the land. Similarly, lumber, wiring, pipes, doors, toilets, sinks, water heaters, furnaces, and other construction materials change from personal property to real estate when they become part of a building. Items brought into the house that do not become permanently affixed to the land remain personal property; for example, furniture, clothing, cooking utensils, radios, and television sets.

ADAPTATION OF THE OBJECT

Historically, the manner of attachment was the only method of classifying an object as personal property or real estate, but as time progressed, this test alone was no longer adequate. For example, how would you classify custom-made drapes made for an unusual window? For the answer, we must apply a second test: *How is the article adapted to the building?* If the drapes are specifically made for the window, they are automatically included in the purchase or rental of the building. Another example is the key to a house. Although it spends most of its useful life in a pocket or purse, it is nonetheless quite specifically adapted to the house and therefore a part of it.

EXISTENCE OF AN AGREEMENT

The third test is the *existence of an agreement* between the parties involved. For example, a seller can clarify in advance and in writing to the broker what he considers personal property, and thus will be removed, and what he does not consider personal property, and thus will transfer to the buyer. Common items that can cause confusion are garage door openers, satellite dishes, remote controls, swimming pool equipment, keyless entry systems, surround sound systems, plasma TVs, and controls for burglar alarm systems. Many of these items can be uniquely adapted to the premises, but the seller considers them personal property as they might be able to be recoded or utilized for another residence.

RELATIONSHIP OF THE PARTIES

The fourth test in determining whether an item of personal property has become a fixture is to look at the *relationship of the parties*. For example, a supermarket moves into a rented building, then buys and bolts to the floor various **trade fixtures** such as display shelves, meat and dairy coolers, frozen food counters, and checkout stands. When the supermarket later moves out, do these items, by virtue of their attachment, become the property of the building owner? Modern courts rule that tenant-owned trade fixtures do not become the property of the landlord. However, they must be removed before the expiration of the lease and without seriously damaging the building.

Prior Liens against Fixtures

In addition to the misunderstandings that often arise between buyer and seller in determining the intention of the parties regarding fixtures, there are also priorities given in the law that can create a lien on fixtures if that lien is timely and properly recorded. For instance, if one finances a new air-conditioning unit from a vendor, the vendor has a right to file a lien on that item that will become a fixture, and will show up as a lien on the real estate in the real property records. Many homeowners are surprised when they have a lien from a department store on an item that they thought they put on their charge account, when in fact, it was a lien created for a home improvement (air conditioners, roofs, gutters, or other major repairs that had been financed through a local department store).

Ownership of Plants, Trees, and Crops

Trees, cultivated perennial plants, and uncultivated vegetation of any sort are considered part of the land. For example, landscaping is included in the sale or rental of a house. If a tenant plants a tree or plant in the ground while renting, the tree or plant stays when the lease expires unless both landlord and tenant agree otherwise. Plants and trees in movable pots are personal property and are not generally included in a sale or lease.

Annual cultivated crops are called **emblements**, and most courts of law regard them as personal property even though they are attached to the soil. For example, a tenant farmer is entitled to the fruits of his labor even though the landlord terminates the lease part way through the growing season. When property with harvestable plants, trees, or crops is offered for sale or lease, it is good practice to make clear in any listing, sale, or lease agreement who will have the right to harvest the crop that season. This is particularly true of farm property, where the value of the crop can be quite substantial.

Appurtenances

The conveyance of land carries with it any appurtances to the land. An **appurtenance** is a right or privilege or improvement that belongs to and passes with land but is not necessarily a part of the land. Examples of appurtances are easements and rights-of-way (discussed in Chapter 3), condominium parking stalls, and shares of stock in a mutual water company that services the land.

Water Rights

Water rights vary greatly across the country. Some have noted the "30-inch" rule. This concept divides the country from north to south between the eastern areas that receive more than 30 inches of annual rainfall and the western areas that receive less than 30 inches of annual rainfall (roughly paralleling Interstate Highway 35, from Texas to Minnesota). Eastern areas generally have an ample supply of water; so, their water laws are largely the law of surface waters and are modeled after the English riparian system.

Western areas regularly experience varying degrees of water shortages and drought conditions, resulting in water law rules being based on the concept that the state is the owner of the water (in fee or in trust for the public) and allowing a person to establish a state-permitted right to use the water by putting it to beneficial use.

The ownership of land that borders on a river or stream carries with it the right to use that water in common with the other landowners whose lands border the same watercourse. This is known as a **riparian right**. The landowner does not have absolute ownership of the water that flows past his land but may use it in a reasonable manner. In western states, riparian rights have been modified by the **doctrine of prior appropriation**: The first owner to divert water for his own use may continue to do so, even though it is not equitable to the other landowners along the watercourse. Some estates have a right to the use of property as a prior appropriation. Where land borders on a lake or sea, it is said to carry **littoral rights** rather than riparian rights. Littoral rights allow a landowner to use and enjoy the water touching his land provided he does not alter the water's position by artificial means. A lakefront lot owner would be an example of this.

Ownership of land normally includes the right to drill for and remove water found below the surface. The first to use the water (even underground water) has a prior right to its use. This is called the **doctrine of capture**. Where water is not confined to a defined underground waterway, it is known as **percolating water**. In some states, a landowner has the right, in conjunction with neighboring owners, to draw her share of percolating water. Other states subscribe to the doctrine of prior appropriation. When speaking of underground water, the term *water table* refers to the upper limit of percolating water below the earth's surface. It is also called the groundwater level. This may be only a few feet below the surface or hundreds of feet down.

riparian right
The right of a landowner whose land borders a river or stream to use and enjoy that water.

Land Descriptions

There are six commonly used methods of describing the location of land: (1) metes and bounds, (2) rectangular survey system, (3) recorded plat, (4) reference to documents other than maps, (5) informal reference, and (6) assessor's parcel number. Methods (1) through (4) are generally considered to be **legal descriptions**. That is, they sufficiently identify the land so that it cannot be confused with another tract. Methods (5) and (6) are informal references. While commonly used, they are not sufficient for legally identifying the land. For instance, if a home is located on Pine, it could be Pine Street, Pine Avenue, Pine Lane, or Pine Court. They are often confused with each other when a person lives "on Pine." Finally, some houses have one address but are located on two lots; some single-family lots have two houses with different addresses; or tax assessors misidentify tracts (their employees identify tracts for tax purposes only and can make mistakes). This is why a proper legal description is so important. Let's look at each in detail.

METES AND BOUNDS

Early land descriptions in the United States depended heavily on convenient natural or man-made objects called **monuments**. A stream might serve to mark one side of a parcel, an old oak tree to mark a corner, a road another side, a pile of rocks a second corner, a fence another side, and so forth. This survey method was handy, but it had two major drawbacks: there might not be a convenient corner or boundary marker where one was needed, and, over time, oak trees died, stone heaps were moved, streams and rivers changed course, stumps rotted, fences were removed, and unused roads became overgrown with vegetation. The following description, excerpted from the Hartford, Connecticut,

monuments
An iron pipe, stone, tree, or other fixed point used in making a survey.

probate court records for 1812, illustrates just how difficult it can be to try to locate a parcel's boundaries precisely using only convenient natural or man-made objects:

Commencing at a heap of stone about a stone's throw from a certain small clump of alders, near a brook running down off from a rather high part of said ridge; thence, by a straight line to a certain marked white birch tree, about two or three times as far from a jog in a fence going around a ledge nearby; thence by another straight line in a different direction, around said ledge, and the Great Swamp, so called; thence...to the "Horn," so called, and passing around the same as aforesaid, as far as the "Great Bend," so called, and...to a stake and stone not far off from the old Indian trail; thence, by another straight line...to the stump of the big hemlock tree where Philo Blake killed the bear; thence, to the corner begun at by two straight lines of about equal length, which are to be run by some skilled and competent surveyor, so as to include the area and acreage as herein before set forth.

PERMANENT MONUMENTS. The drawbacks of the previous outmoded method of land description are resolved by setting a permanent man-made monument at one corner of the parcel. This monument will typically be an iron pin or pipe, one to two inches in diameter, driven several feet into the ground. Sometimes concrete or stone monuments are used. To guard against the possibility that the monument might later be destroyed or removed, it is referenced by means of a **connection line** to a nearby permanent reference mark established by a government survey agency. Other parcels in the vicinity will also be referenced to the same permanent reference mark.

The surveyor then describes the parcel in terms of distance and direction from that point. This is called **metes and bounds** surveying, which means distance (metes) and direction (bounds). From the monument, the surveyor runs the parcel's outside lines by compass and distance so as to take in the land area being described. Distances are measured in feet, usually to the nearest one-tenth or one-hundredth of a foot. Direction is shown in degrees, minutes, and seconds. There are 360 degrees (°) in a circle, 60 minutes (′) in each degree, and 60 seconds (″) in each minute. The abbreviation 29°14′52″ would be read as 29 degrees, 14 minutes, and 52 seconds. Figure 2.2 illustrates a simple modern metes and bounds land description. Note that at each corner a coordinate system is superimposed. This may help you better understand how the bounds are set from each point.

With a metes and bounds description, you start from a permanent reference mark and travel to the nearest corner of the property. This is where the parcel survey begins and is called the **point of beginning** or **point of commencement**. From this point in Figure 2.2, we travel clockwise along the parcel's perimeter, reaching the next corner by going in the direction 80 degrees east of south for a distance of 180 feet. We then travel in a direction 15 degrees west of south for 160 feet, thence 85 degrees west of south for 151 feet, and thence 4 degrees, 11 minutes, and 8 seconds east of north for 199.5 feet back to the point of beginning. In mapping shorthand, this parcel would be described by first identifying the monument, then the county and state within which it lies, and "thence S80°0′0″E, 180.0′; thence S15°0′0″W, 160.0′; thence S85°0′0″E, 151.0″; thence N4°11′8″E, 199.5′ back to the p.o.b." Although one can successfully describe a parcel by traveling around it either clockwise or counterclockwise, it is customary to travel clockwise.

The job of taking a written land description (such as the one just described) and locating it on the ground is done by a two-person survey team. The survey team drives a wooden or metal stake into the ground at each corner of the parcel. If a corner lies on a sidewalk, a nail through a brass disc about one-half inch wide is used. (Look closely for these the next time you are out walking. At construction sites you will see that corner stakes often have colored streamers on them.) The basic equipment of a survey team includes a compass, a transit, a sight pole or rod, a steel tape, and a computation book.

metes and bounds

A detailed method of land description that identifies a parcel by specifying its shape and boundaries.

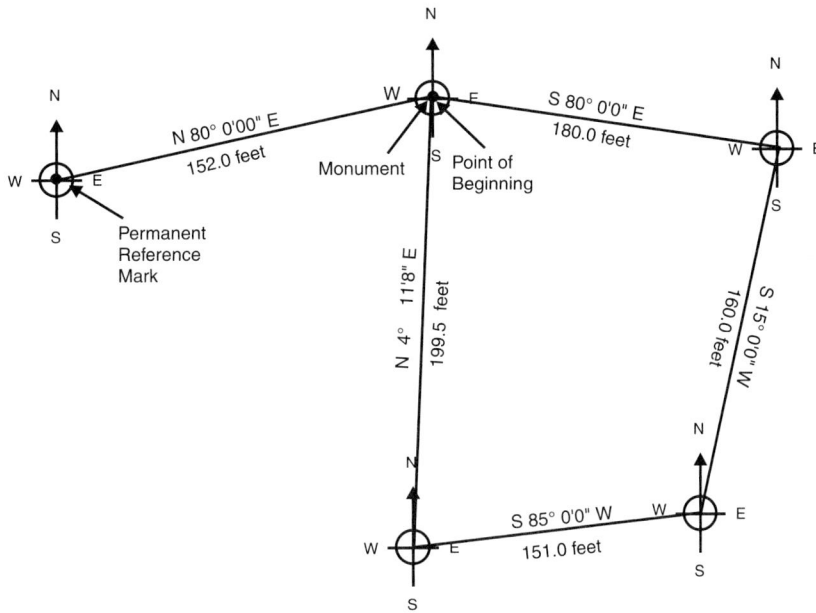

FIGURE 2.2 Describing Land by Metes and Bounds

Source: © 2014 OnCourse Learning

A transit consists of a very accurate compass plus a telescope with crosshairs that can be rotated horizontally and vertically. It will measure angles accurately to one second of a degree. The sight pole is about eight feet high and held by the rodman, the second member of the survey team. Marks on the sight pole are aligned by the surveyor with the crosshairs in the telescope. A 100-foot steel tape, made of a special alloy that resists expansion on hot days, is used to measure distances. For longer distances, and especially distances across water, canyons, heavy brush, and so on, surveyors use laser beam equipment. The beam is aimed at a mirror on the sight pole, bounced back, and electronically converted to a digital readout that shows the distance to the pole. Handheld computers now perform many of the angle and distance computations necessary to a survey.

COMPASS DIRECTIONS. The compass illustrated in Figure 2.3A shows how the direction of travel along each side of the parcel in Figure 2.2 is determined. Note that the same line can be labeled two ways, depending on which direction you are traveling. To illustrate, look at the line from *P* to *Q*. If you are traveling toward *P* on the line, you are going N45°W. But, if you are traveling toward point *Q* on the line, you are going S45°E.

Curved boundary lines are produced by using arcs of a circle. The length of the arc is labeled *L* or *A*; the radius of the circle producing the arc is labeled *R*. The symbol Δ (delta) indicates the angle used to produce the arc (see Figure 2.3B). Where an arc connects to a straight boundary or another arc, the connection is indicated by a small circle or by a dot, as shown in Figure 2.3B.

Bench marks are commonly used as permanent reference marks. A **bench mark** is a fixed mark of known location and elevation. It may be as simple as an iron post or as elaborate as an engraved 3¾″ brass disc set into concrete. The mark is usually set in place by a government survey team from the United States Geological Survey (USGS)

FIGURE 2.3	Metes and Bounds Mapping

(A) Naming Directions for a Metes and Bounds Survey

(B) Mapping a Curve

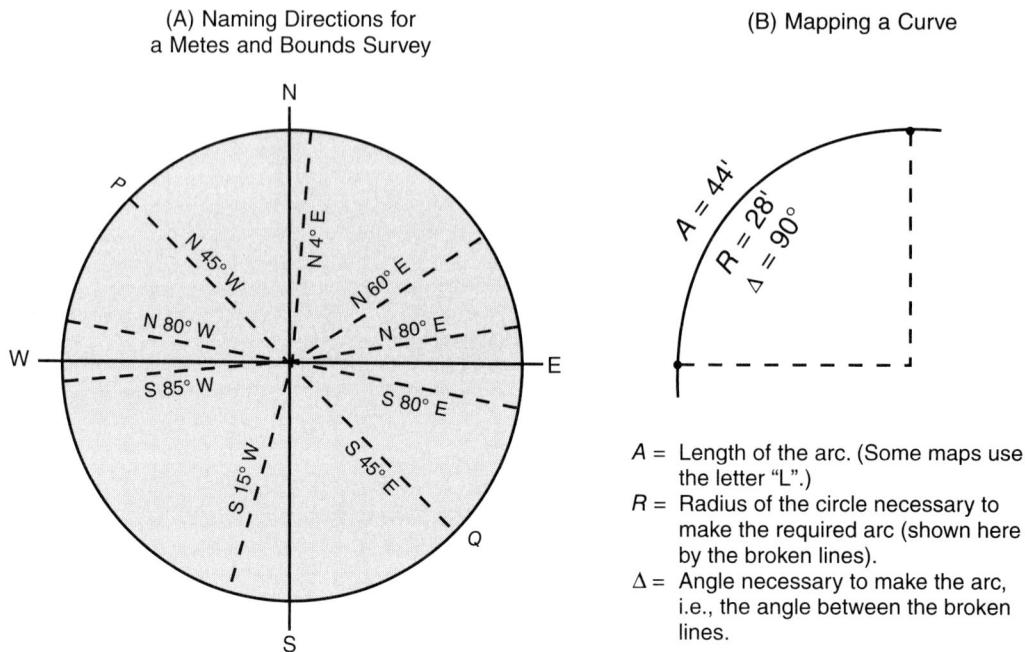

A = Length of the arc. (Some maps use the letter "L".)

R = Radius of the circle necessary to make the required arc (shown here by the broken lines).

Δ = Angle necessary to make the arc, i.e., the angle between the broken lines.

Moving in a clockwise direction from the point of beginning, set the center of a circle compass (like the one shown above) on each corner of the parcel to find the direction of travel to the next corner.

Source: © 2014 OnCourse Learning

or the United States Coast and Geodetic Survey (USCGS). Bench marks are referenced to each other by distance and direction. The advantages of this type of reference point, compared to stumps, trees, rocks, and the like, are permanence and accuracy to within a fraction of an inch. Additionally, even though it is possible to destroy a reference point or monument, it can be replaced in its exact former position because the location of each is related to other reference points. In states using the rectangular survey system or a grid system (discussed shortly), a section corner or a grid intersection is often used as a permanent reference mark. As a convenience to surveyors, it will be physically marked with an iron post or a brass disc set in concrete.

Even with good surveyors, there is potential for mistakes because ground levels change and permanent monuments established by prior surveyors may not be exactly correct. The use of global positioning systems is now making metes and bounds descriptions very accurate. The new satellite positioning systems are exact, and therefore are constantly finding errors, mostly minor, which need to be constantly corrected as the technology is improving.

RECTANGULAR SURVEY SYSTEM

The **rectangular survey system** was authorized by Congress in May 1785. It was designed to provide a faster and simpler method than metes and bounds for describing land in newly annexed territories and states. Rather than using available physical monuments, the rectangular survey system, also known as the **government survey system** or

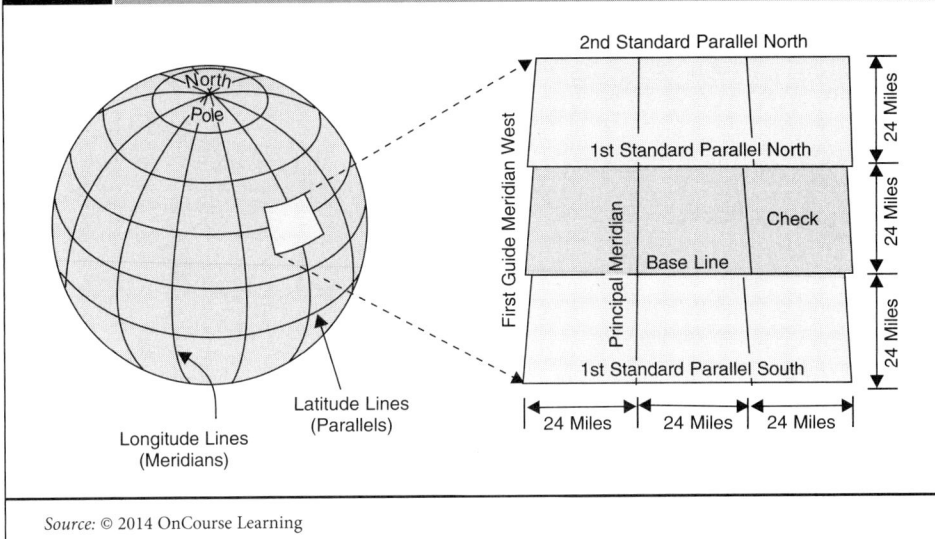

FIGURE 2.4   Selected Latitude and Longitude Lines Serve as Base Lines and Meridians

Source: © 2014 OnCourse Learning

U.S. Public Lands Survey system, is based on imaginary lines. These lines are the east-west **latitude lines** and the north-south **longitude lines** that encircle the earth, as illustrated in Figure 2.4. A helpful way to remember this is that longitude lines (**meridians**) run the long way around the earth.

Certain longitude lines were selected as **principal meridians**. For each of these an intercepting latitude line was selected as a **base line**. Every 24 miles north and south of a base line, **correction lines** or **standard parallels** were established. Every 24 miles east and west of a principal meridian, **guide meridians** were established to run from one standard parallel to the next. These are needed because the earth is a sphere, not a flat surface. As one travels north in the United States, longitude (meridian) lines come closer together—that is, they converge. Figure 2.4 shows how guide meridians and correction lines adjust for this problem. Each 24-by-24-mile area created by the guide meridians and correction lines is called a **check** or **quadrangle**.

There are 36 principal meridians and their intersecting base lines in the U.S. Public Lands Survey system. Figure 2.5 shows the states in which this system is used and the land area for which each principal meridian and base line act as a reference. For example, the Sixth Principal Meridian is the reference point for land surveys in Kansas, Nebraska, and portions of Colorado, Wyoming, and South Dakota. In addition to the U.S. Public Lands Survey system, a portion of western Kentucky was surveyed into townships by a special state survey. Also, the state of Ohio contains eight public land surveys that are rectangular in design but which use state boundaries and major rivers rather than latitude and longitude as reference lines.

RANGE. Figure 2.6 (on page 21) shows how land is referenced to a principal meridian and a base line. Every six miles east and west of each principal meridian, parallel imaginary lines are drawn. The resulting six-mile-wide columns are called **ranges** and are numbered consecutively east and west of the principal meridian. For example, the first range west is called Range 1 West and is abbreviated R1W. The next range west is R2W, and so forth. The fourth range east is R4E.

TOWNSHIP. Every six miles north and south of a base line, township lines are drawn. They intersect with the range lines and produce six-by-six-mile imaginary

meridians

Imaginary lines running north and south, used as references in mapping land.

FIGURE 2.5   The Public Land Survey System of the United States

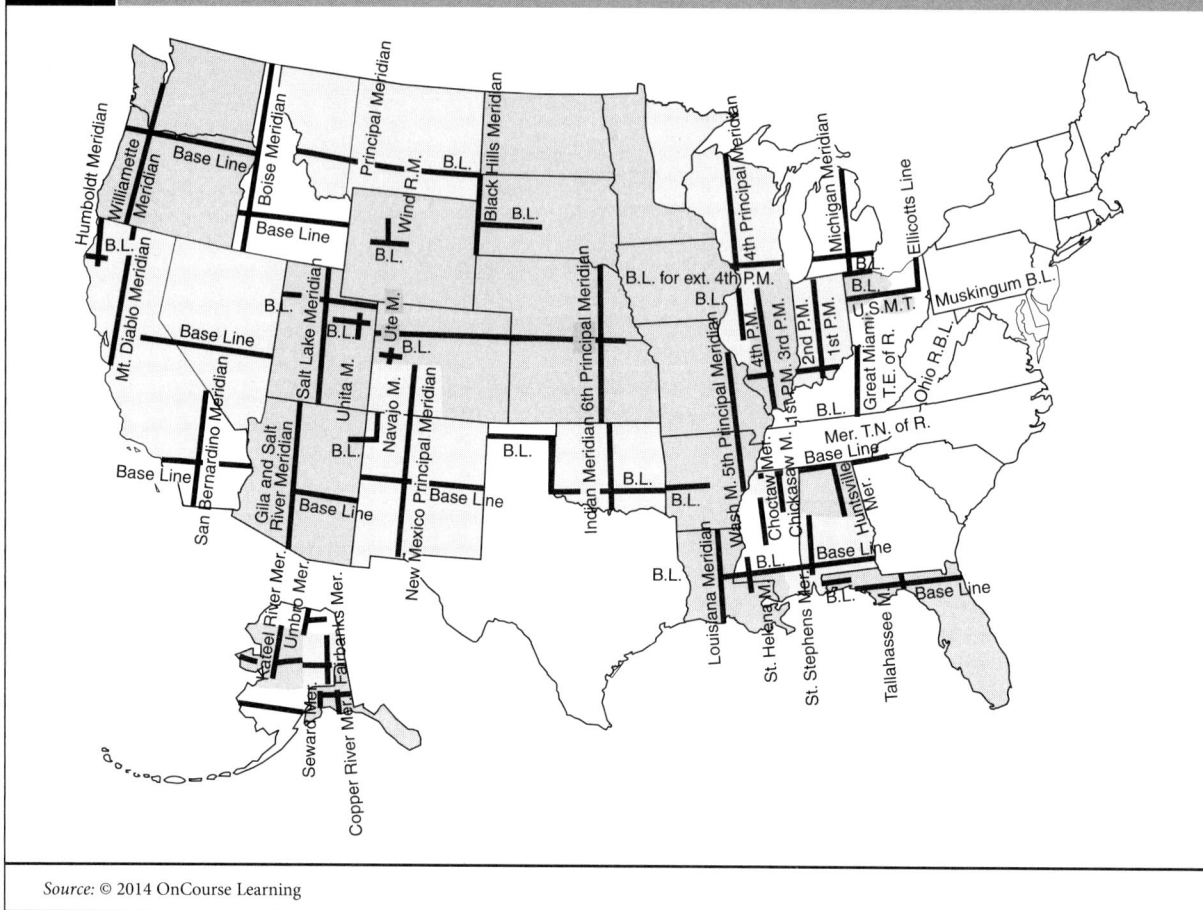

Source: © 2014 OnCourse Learning

squares called **townships** (not to be confused with the word *township* as applied to political subdivisions). Each tier or row of townships thus created is numbered with respect to the base line. Townships lying in the first tier north of a base line all carry the designation Township 1 North, abbreviated T1N. Townships lying in the first tier south of the base line are all designated T1S, and in the second tier south, T2S. By adding a range reference, an individual township can be identified. Thus, T2S, R2W would identify the township lying in the second tier south of the base line and the second range west of the principal meridian. T14N, R52W would be a township 14 tiers north of the base line and 52 ranges west of the principal meridian.

SECTION. Each 36-square-mile township is divided into 36 one-square-mile units called **sections**. When one flies over farming areas, particularly in the Midwest, the checkerboard pattern of farms and roads that follow section boundaries can be seen. Sections are numbered 1 through 36, starting in the upper-right corner of the township. With this numbering system, any two sections with consecutive numbers share a common boundary. The section numbering system is illustrated in Figure 2.6 where the shaded section is described as Section 32, T2N, R3E, Sixth Principal Meridian.

ACRE. Each square-mile **section** contains 640 acres, and each **acre** contains 43,560 square feet. Any parcel of land smaller than a full 640-acre section is identified by its

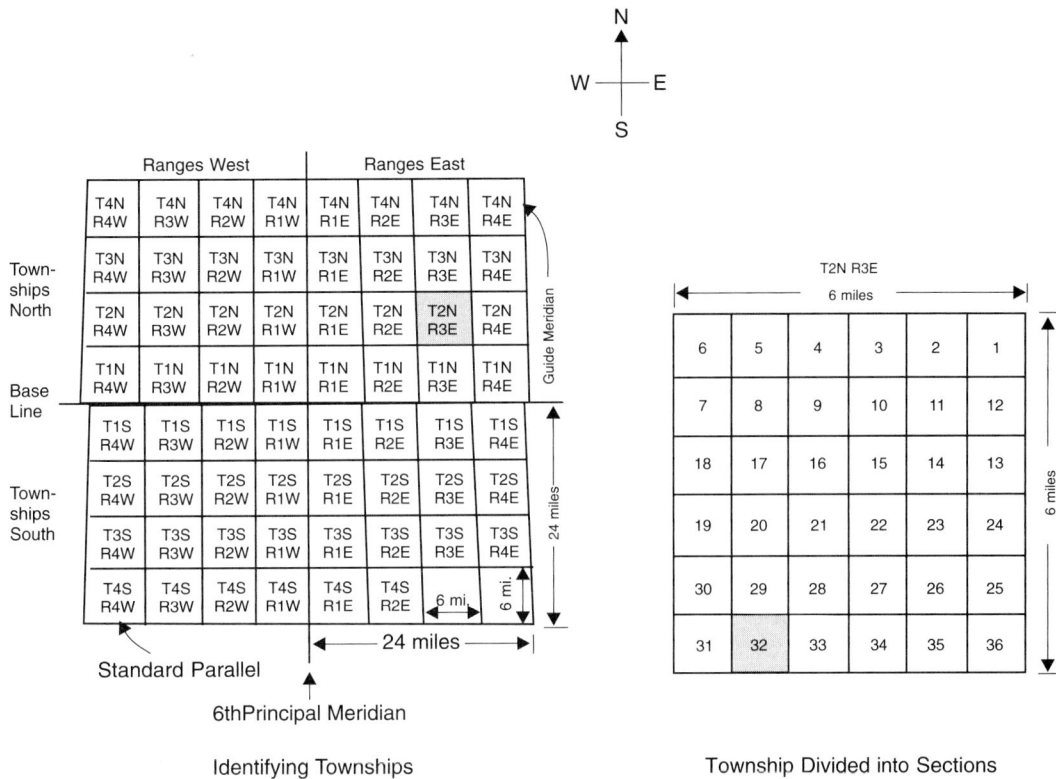

FIGURE 2.6 Identifying Townships and Sections

	Ranges West			Ranges East			

Identifying Townships

Township Divided into Sections

Source: © 2014 OnCourse Learning

position in the section. This is done by dividing the section into quarters and halves as shown in Figure 2.7. For example, the shaded parcel shown at A is described as the NW¼ of the SW¼ of Section 32, T2N, R3E, Sixth Principal Meridian. Additionally, it is customary to name the county and state in which the land lies. How much land does the NW¼ of the SW¼ of a section contain? A section contains 640 acres; therefore, a **quarter-section** contains 160 acres. Dividing a quarter-section again into quarters results in four 40-acre parcels. Thus, the northwest quarter of the southwest quarter contains 40 acres.

The rectangular survey system is not limited to parcels of 40 or more acres. To demonstrate this point, the SE¼ of Section 32 is exploded in the right half of Figure 2.7. Parcel Ⓑ is described as the SE¼ of the SE¼ of the SE¼ of the SE¼ of Section 32 and contains 2½ acres. Parcel Ⓒ is described as the west 15 acres of the NW¼ of the SE¼ of Section 32. Parcel Ⓓ would be described in metes and bounds using the northeast corner of the SE¼ of Section 32 as the starting point. When locating or sketching a rectangular survey on paper, many people find it helpful to start at the end of the description and work to the beginning—that is, work backwards. Try it.

Not all sections contain exactly 640 acres. Some are smaller because the earth's longitude lines converge toward the North Pole. Also, a section may be larger or smaller than 640 acres due to historical accommodations or survey errors dating back a hundred years or more. For the same reason, not all townships contain exactly 36 square miles. Between

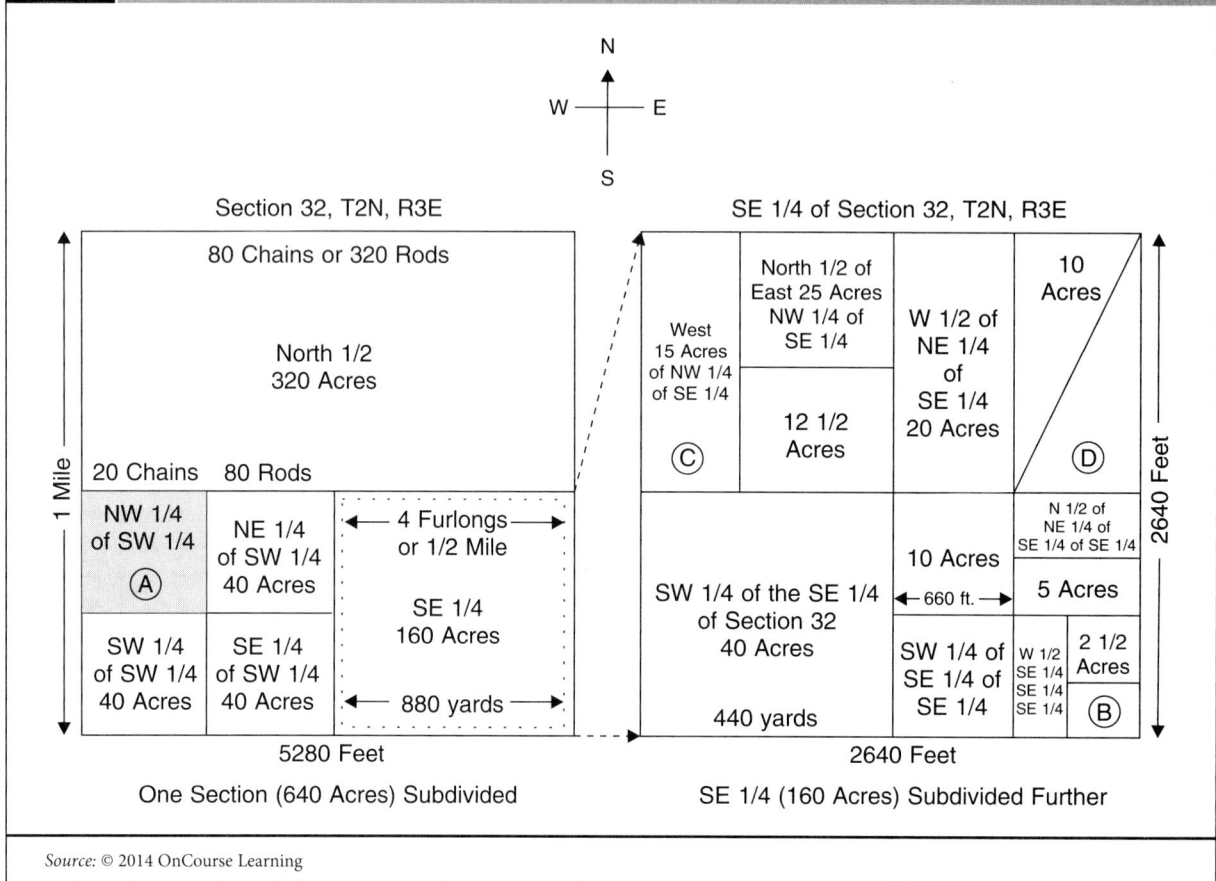

FIGURE 2.7 Subdividing a Section

Source: © 2014 OnCourse Learning

1785 and 1910, the U.S. government paid independent surveyors by the mile. The job was often accomplished by tying a rag to one spoke of the wheel of a buckboard wagon. A team of horses was hitched to the wagon and the surveyor, compass in hand, headed out across the prairie. Distance was measured by counting the number of wheel turns and multiplying by the circumference of the wheel. Today, large area surveys are made with the aid of aerial photographs, sophisticated electronic equipment, and earth satellites.

In terms of surface area, more land in the United States is described by the rectangular survey system than by any other survey method. But in terms of number of properties, the recorded plat is the most important survey method.

RECORDING PLAT

recorded plat

A subdivision map filed in the county recorder's office that shows the location and boundaries of individual parcels of land.

When a tract of land is ready for subdividing into lots for homes and businesses, reference by **recorded plat** provides the simplest and most convenient method of land description. A **plat** is a map that shows the location and boundaries of individual properties. Also known as the **lot-block-tract system**, **recorded map**, or **recorded survey**, this method of land description is based on the filing of a surveyor's plat in the public recorder's office of the county where the land is located. Figure 2.8 illustrates a plat. Notice that a metes and bounds survey has been made, and a map prepared to show in detail

FIGURE 2.8 Land Description by Recorded Plat

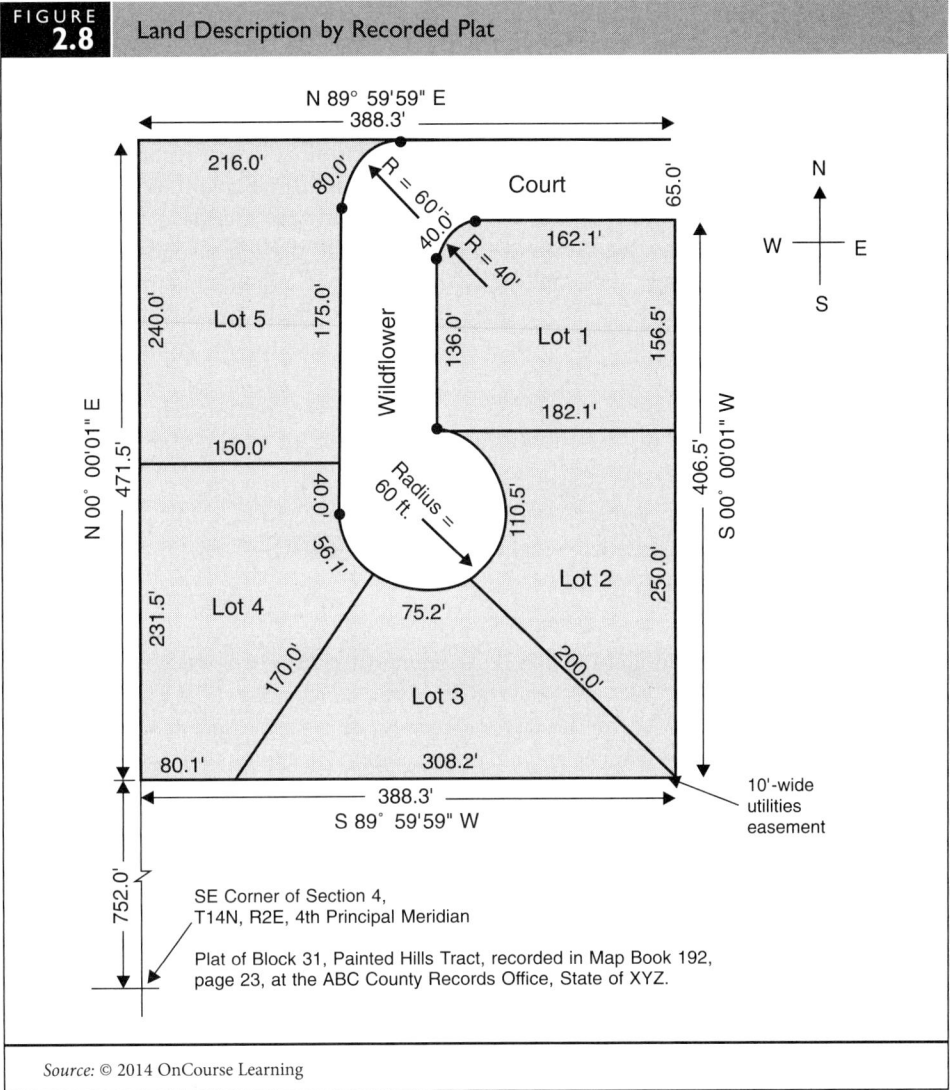

Source: © 2014 OnCourse Learning

the boundaries of each parcel of land. Each parcel is then assigned a lot number. Each block in the tract is given a block number, and the tract itself is given a name or number. A plat showing all the blocks in the tract is delivered to the county recorder's office, where it is placed in **map books** or **survey books**, along with plats of other subdivisions in the county.

Each plat is given a book and page reference number, and all map books are available for public inspection. From that point on, it is no longer necessary to give a lengthy metes and bounds description to describe a parcel. Instead, one need provide only the lot and block number, tract name, map book reference, county, and state. To find the location and dimensions of a recorded lot, one simply looks in the map book at the county recorder's office.

Note that the plat in Figure 2.8 combines both of the land descriptions just discussed. The boundaries of the numbered lots are in metes and bounds. These, in turn, are referenced to a section corner in the rectangular survey system.

REFERENCE TO DOCUMENTS OTHER THAN MAPS

Land can also be described by referring to another publicly recorded document, such as a deed or a mortgage, which contains a full legal description of the parcel in question. For example, suppose that several years ago Baker received a deed from Adams that contained a long and complicated metes and bounds description. Baker recorded the deed in the public records office, where a photocopy was placed in Book 1089, page 456. If Baker later wants to deed the same land to Cooper, Baker can describe the parcel in his deed to Cooper by saying, "all the land described in the deed from Adams to Baker recorded in Book 1089, page 456, county of ABC, state of XYZ, at the public recorder's office for said county and state." Since these books are open to the public, Cooper (or anyone else) could go to Book 1089, page 456, and find a detailed description of the parcel's boundaries.

The key test of a land description is: "Can another person, reading what I have written or drawn, understand my description and go out and locate the boundaries of the parcel?"

INFORMAL REFERENCES—STREET NUMBERS AND COMMON NAMES

Street numbers and place names are informal references: the house located at 7216 Maple Street; the apartment identified as Apartment 101, 875 First Street; the office identified as Suite 222, 3570 Oakview Boulevard; or the ranch known as the Rocking K Ranch—in each case followed by the city (or county) and state where it is located—are informal references. The advantage of an informal reference is that it is easily understood. The disadvantage from a real estate standpoint is that it is not a precise method of land description. A street number or place name does not provide the boundaries of the land at that location, and these numbers and names change over the years. Consequently, in real estate, the use of informal references is limited to situations in which convenience is more important than precision. Thus, in a rental contract, Apartment 101, 875 First Street, city and state, is sufficient for a tenant to find the apartment unit. However, if you were buying the apartment building, you would want a more precise land description.

ASSESSOR'S PARCEL NUMBERS

In many counties in the United States, the tax assessor assigns an **assessor's parcel number** to each parcel of land in the county. The primary purpose is to aid in the assessment of property for tax collection purposes. However, these parcel numbers are public information, and real estate brokers, appraisers, and investors can and do use them extensively to assist in identifying real properties.

A commonly used system is to divide the county into map books. Each book is given a number and covers a given portion of the county. On every page of the map book are parcel maps, each with its own number. For subdivided lots, these maps are based on the plats submitted by the subdivider to the county records office when the subdivision was made. For unsubdivided land, the assessor's office prepares its own maps.

Each parcel of land on the map is assigned a parcel number by the assessor. The assessor's parcel number may or may not be the same as the lot number assigned by the subdivider. To reduce confusion, the assessor's parcel number is either circled or underlined. Figure 2.9 illustrates a page out of an assessor's map book. The assessor also produces an assessment roll that lists every parcel in the county by its assessor's

FIGURE 2.9 Assessor's Map

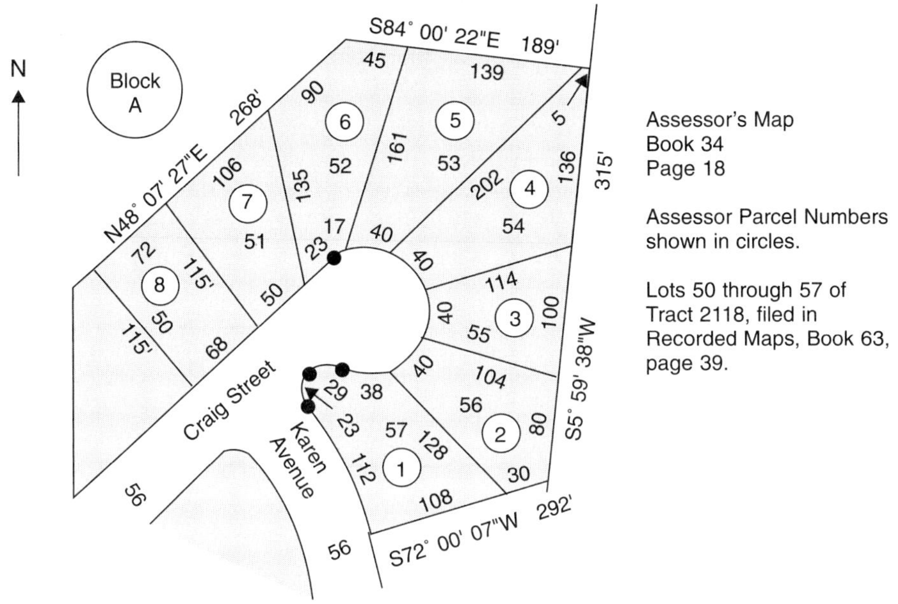

The tax assessor assigns every parcel of land in the county its own parcel number. For example, the westernmost parcel (Lot 50) in the map would carry the number 34-18-8, meaning Book 34, Page 18, Parcel 8.

Source: © 2014 OnCourse Learning

parcel number. Stored and printed by computer now, this roll shows the current owner's name and address and the assessed value of the land and buildings.

The assessor's maps are open to viewing by the public at the assessor's office. In many counties, private firms reproduce the maps and the accompanying list of property owners, and make them available to real estate brokers, appraisers, and lenders for a fee.

Before leaving the topic of assessor's maps, a word of caution is in order. These maps should not be relied upon as the final authority for the legal description of a parcel. That can come only from a title search that includes looking at the current deed to the property and the recorded copy of the subdivider's plat. Note also that an assessor's parcel number is never used as a legal description in a deed.

Grid Systems

Several states, such as North Carolina and Connecticut, have developed their own state-wide systems of reference points for land surveying. The North Carolina system, for example, divides that state into a grid of 84 blocks, each side of which corresponds to 30 minutes (one-half of one degree) of latitude or longitude. This establishes a **grid system** of intersecting points throughout the state to which metes and bounds surveys can be referenced. State-sponsored grid systems (also called coordinate systems) are especially helpful for surveying large parcels of remote area land.

Vertical Land Description

In addition to surface land descriptions, land may also be described in terms of vertical measurements. This type of measurement is necessary when air rights or subsurface rights need to be described—as for multistory condominiums or oil and mineral rights.

A point, line, or surface from which a vertical height or depth is measured is called a **datum**. The most commonly used datum plane in the United States is mean sea level, although a number of cities have established other data surfaces for use in local surveys. Starting from a datum, bench marks are set at calculated intervals by government survey teams; thus, a surveyor need not travel to the original datum to determine an elevation. These same bench marks are used as reference points for metes and bounds surveys.

In selling or leasing subsurface drilling or mineral rights, the chosen datum is often the surface of the parcel. For example, an oil lease may permit the extraction of oil and gas from a depth greater than 500 feet beneath the surface of a parcel of land. (Subsurface rights are discussed in Chapter 3.)

An **air lot** (a space over a given parcel of land) is described by identifying both the parcel of land beneath the air lot and the elevation of the air lot above the parcel (see Figure 2.10A). Multistory condominiums use this system of land description.

Contour maps (topographic maps) indicate elevations. On these maps, **contour lines** connect all points having the same elevation. The purpose is to show hills and valleys, slopes, and water runoff. If the land is to be developed, the map shows where soil will have to be moved to provide level building lots. Figure 2.10B illustrates how vertical distances are shown using contour lines.

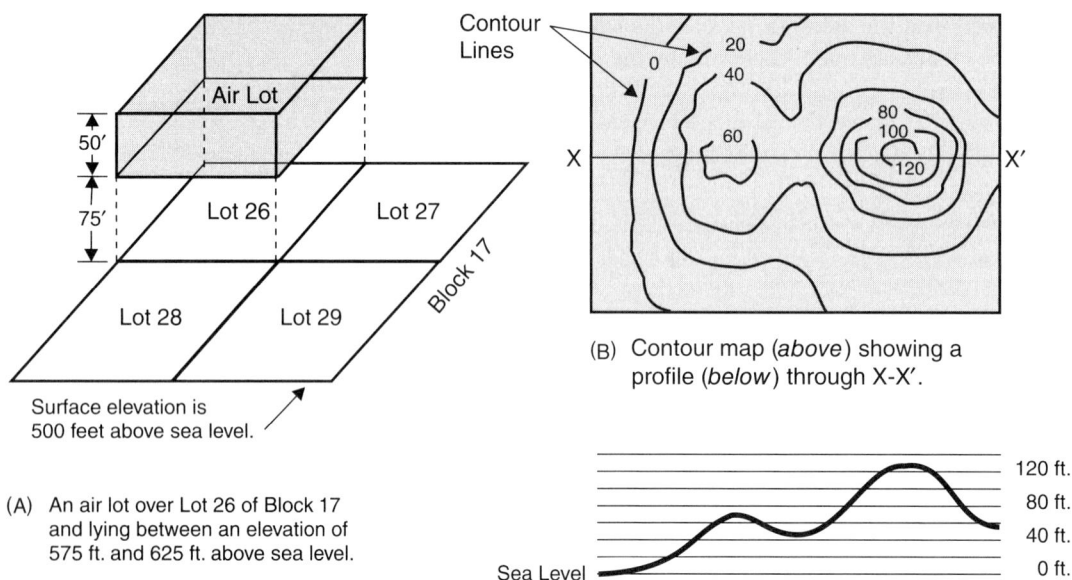

FIGURE 2.10   Air Lot and Contour Lines

(A) An air lot over Lot 26 of Block 17 and lying between an elevation of 575 ft. and 625 ft. above sea level.

(B) Contour map (*above*) showing a profile (*below*) through X-X'.

Surface elevation is 500 feet above sea level.

Source: © 2014 OnCourse Learning

Lot Types

In talking about subdivisions, there are several terms with which you should be familiar. All of these are illustrated in Figure 2.11. A **cul-de-sac** is a street that is closed at one end with a circular turnaround. The pie-shaped lots fronting on the turnaround are called **cul-de-sac lots**. A **flag lot** is a lot shaped like a flag on a flagpole. It's a popular method of creating a buildable lot out of the land at the back of a larger lot. A **corner lot** is a lot that fronts on two or more streets. Because of added light and access, a corner lot is usually worth more than an **inside lot**—that is, a lot with only one side on a street. A **key lot** is a lot that adjoins the side or rear property line of a corner lot. The key lot has added value if it is needed by the corner lot for expansion. A **T lot** is a lot at the end of a **T intersection** as shown in Figure 2.11.

Physical Characteristics of Land

The physical characteristics of land are immobility, indestructibility, and nonhomogeneity. This combination of characteristics makes land different from other commodities and directly and indirectly influences man's use of it.

IMMOBILITY

A parcel of land cannot be moved. It is true that soil, sand, gravel, and minerals can be moved by the action of nature (erosion) or man (digging); however, the parcel itself still retains its same geographical position on the globe. Because land is *immobile*, a person

FIGURE 2.11	Lot Types

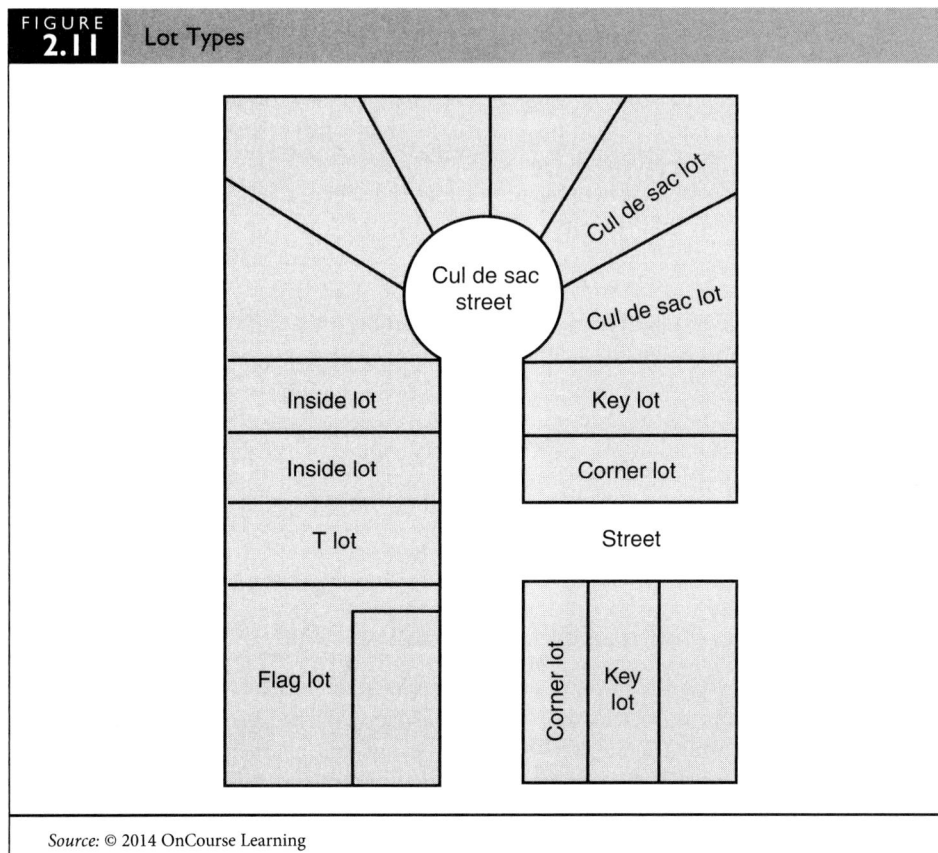

Source: © 2014 OnCourse Learning

must go to the land; it cannot be brought to him. When land is sold, the seller cannot physically deliver his land to the buyer. Instead, the seller gives the buyer a document called a deed that transfers to the buyer the right to go onto that land and use it. Because land is immobile, real estate offices nearly always limit their sales activities to nearby properties. Even so, a great deal of a salesperson's effort is used in traveling to show properties to clients. Immobility also creates a need for property management firms, because unless an owner of rental property lives on it or nearby, neither land nor buildings can be effectively managed.

INDESTRUCTIBILITY

Land is *indestructible*, that is, durable. Today one can travel to the Middle East and walk on the same land that was walked on in Biblical days. Most of the land that we use in the United States today is the same land used by the Native Americans a thousand years ago.

The characteristic of physical durability encourages many people to buy land as an investment because they feel that stocks and bonds and paper money may come and go, but land will always be here. Although this is true in a physical sense, whether a given parcel has and will have economic value depends on one's ability to protect his or her ownership, and on subsequent demand for that land by others. Physical durability must not be confused with economic durability.

NONHOMOGENEITY

The fact that no two parcels of land are exactly alike, because no two parcels can occupy the same position on the globe, is known as **nonhomogeneity** (heterogeneity). Courts of law recognize this characteristic of land, and treat land as a **nonfungible** (pronounced non•fun′je′ble) commodity; that is, nonsubstitutable. Thus, in a contract involving the sale or rental of land (and any improvement to that land), the courts can be called upon to enforce specific performance of the contract. For example, in a contract to sell a home, if the buyer carries out his obligations and the seller fails to convey ownership to the buyer, a court of law will force the seller to convey ownership of *that* specific home to the buyer. The court will not require the buyer to accept a substitute home. This is different from a homogeneous or **fungible** commodity that is freely substitutable in carrying out a contract. For example, one bushel of number one grade winter wheat can be freely replaced by another bushel of the same grade, and one share of General Motors common stock can be substituted for another, as all are identical.

Although land is nonhomogeneous, there can still be a high degree of physical and economic similarity. For example, in a city block containing 20 house lots of identical size and shape, there will be a high degree of similarity even though the lots are still nonhomogeneous. Finding similar properties is, in fact, the basis for the market-comparison approach to appraising real estate.

Economic Characteristics of Land

The dividing line between the physical and economic characteristics of land is sometimes difficult to define. This is because the physical aspects of land greatly influence man's economic behavior toward land. However, four economic characteristics are generally recognized: scarcity, modification, permanence of investment (fixity), and area preference (situs, pronounced si′tus).

SCARCITY

The shortage of land in a given geographical area where there is great demand for land is referred to as **scarcity**. It is a man-made characteristic. For example, land is scarce in Miami Beach, Florida, because a relatively large number of people want to use a relatively small area of land. Another well-known example is 2-mile-wide, 13-mile-long Manhattan Island in New York City, where more than a million people live and twice that number work. Yet one need only travel 25 miles west of Miami Beach or into central New York state to find plenty of uncrowded land available for purchase at very reasonable prices. The sheer quantity of undeveloped land in the United States as seen from an airplane on a cross-country flight is staggering.

Land scarcity is also influenced by our ability to use land more efficiently. To illustrate, in agricultural areas, production per acre of land has more than doubled for many crops since 1940. This is not due to any change in the land, but is the result of improved fertilizers and irrigation systems, better seeds, and modern crop management. Likewise, in urban areas, an acre of land that once provided space for five houses can be converted to high-rise apartments to provide homes for 100 or more families.

Thus, although there is a limited physical amount of land on the earth's surface, scarcity is chiefly a function of demand for land in a given geographical area and the ability of man to make land more productive. The persistent notion that all land is scarce has led to periodic land sale booms in undeveloped areas, followed by a collapse in land prices when it becomes apparent that that particular land is not economically scarce.

scarcity
Shortage of land in a given geographical area where there is great demand for land.

MODIFICATION

Land use and value are greatly influenced by **modification**—that is, improvements made by man to surrounding parcels of land. For example, the construction of an airport will increase the usefulness and value of land parallel to runways but will have a negative effect on the use and value of land at the ends of runways because of noise from landings and takeoffs. Similarly, land subject to flooding will become more useful and valuable if government-sponsored flood control dams are built upriver.

One of the most widely publicized cases of land modification occurred near Orlando, Florida, when Disney World was constructed. Nearby land previously used for agricultural purposes suddenly became useful as motel, gas station, restaurant, house, and apartment sites and increased rapidly in value.

FIXITY

The fact that land and buildings and other improvements to land require long periods of time to pay for themselves is referred to as **fixity** or **investment permanence**. For example, it may take 20 or 30 years for the income generated by an apartment or office building to repay the cost of the land and building plus interest on the money borrowed to make the purchase. Consequently, real estate investment and land-use decisions must consider not only how the land will be used next month or next year, but also the usefulness of the improvements 20 years from now. There is no economic logic in spending money to purchase land and improvements that will require 20 to 30 years to pay for themselves if their usefulness is expected to last only 5 years.

Fixity also reflects the fact that land cannot be moved from its present location to another location where it will be more valuable. With very few exceptions, improvements to land are also fixed. Even with a house, the cost of moving it, plus building a foundation at the new site, can easily exceed the value of the house after the move. Thus, when an investment is made in real estate, it is regarded as a **fixed** or **sunk cost**.

fixity
Refers to the fact that land and buildings require long periods of time to pay for themselves.

SITUS

situs

Refers to the preference by people for a given location.

Situs or **location preference** refers to location from an economic rather than a geographic standpoint. It has often been said that the single most important word in real estate is *location*. This refers to the preference of people for a given area. For a residential area, these preferences are the result of *natural* factors, such as weather, air quality, scenic views, and closeness to natural recreation areas, and of *man-made* factors, such as job opportunities, transportation facilities, shopping, and schools. For an industrial area, situs depends on such things as an available labor market, adequate supplies of water and electricity, nearby rail lines, and highway access. In farming areas, situs depends on soil and weather conditions, water and labor availability, and transportation facilities.

Situs is the reason that house lots on street corners sell for more than identically sized lots not on corners. This reflects a preference for open space. The same is true in apartments; corner units usually rent for more than similar-sized noncorner units. In a high-rise apartment building, units on the top floors, if they offer a view, command higher prices than identical units on lower floors. On a street lined with stores, the side of the street that is shaded in the afternoon will attract more shoppers than the unshaded side. Consequently, buildings on the shaded side will generate more sales and, as a result, be worth more.

It is important to realize that, since situs is a function of people's preferences, and preferences can change with time, situs can also change. For example, the freeway and expressway construction boom that started in the 1950s and accelerated during the 1960s increased the preference for suburban areas. This resulted in declining property values in inner city areas and increasing land values in the suburbs. Today, historic rehabilitation and a desire to live closer to work are drawing people back to downtown areas.

Vocabulary Review

Match terms a–v with statements 1–22.

a. Acre
b. Appurtenance
c. Assessor's parcel number
d. Base line
e. Bill of sale
f. Contour line
g. Cul-de-sac
h. Datum
i. Emblements
j. Fixture
k. Flag lot
l. Government survey
m. Lot-block-tract
n. Meridian
o. Metes and bounds
p. Monument

_____ 1. An object that has been attached to land so as to become real estate.

_____ 2. Contains 36 sections of land.

_____ 3. The depth below the surface at which water-saturated soil can be found.

_____ 4. A survey line running east and west from which townships are established.

_____ 5. Contains 640 acres of land.

_____ 6. The right of a landowner to use water flowing past his or her land.

_____ 7. An iron pipe or other object set in the ground to establish land boundaries.

_____ 8. A survey line that runs north and south in the rectangular survey system.

_____ 9. Annual crops produced by man.

_____ 10. A horizontal plane from which height and depth are measured.

_____ 11. A numbering system to aid in the assessment of property for tax collection purposes.

q. Quarter-section
r. Riparian right
s. Section
t. Subsurface right
u. Township
v. Water table

_____12. A system of land description that identifies a parcel by specifying its shape and boundaries.

_____13. A land survey system based on imaginary latitude and longitude lines.

_____14. Includes the right to mine minerals and drill for oil.

_____15. Lines on a map that connect points having the same elevation.

_____16. Land description by reference to a recorded map.

_____17. 43,560 square feet.

_____18. Contains 160 acres of land.

_____19. A right or privilege or improvement that passes with land.

_____20. A document that transfers title to personal property.

_____21. A street that is closed at one end with a circular turnaround.

_____22. A lot shaped like a flag on a pole.

Questions and Problems

1. Is the land upon which you make your residence described by metes and bounds, lot-block-tract, or the rectangular survey system?

2. On a sheet of paper, sketch the following parcels of land in Section 6, T1N, R3E: (a) the NW¼; (b) the SW¼ of the SW¼; (c) the W½ of the SE¼; (d) the N17 acres of the E½ of the NE¼; (e) the SE¼ of the SE¼ of the SE¼ of the NE¼.

3. How many acres are there in each parcel described in number 2?

4. Describe the parcels labeled A, B, C, D, and E in the section shown below.

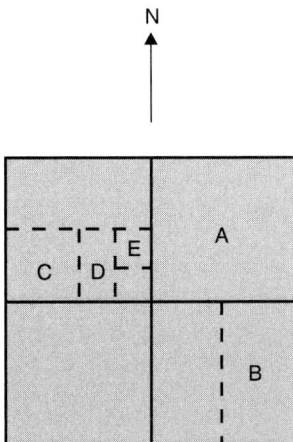

5. Using an ordinary compass and ruler, sketch the following parcel of land: "Beginning at monument M, thence due east for 40 feet, thence south 458 east for 14.1 feet, thence due south for 40 feet, thence north 458 west for 70.7 feet back to the point of beginning."

6. If a landowner owns from the center of the earth to the limits of the sky, are aircraft that pass overhead trespassers?

7. Would you classify the key to the door of a building as personal property or real property?

8. With regard to your own residence, itemize what you consider to be real property and what you consider to be personal property.

9. With regard to riparian rights, does your state follow the doctrine of prior appropriation or the right to a reasonable share?

10. What effects do you think changes in the location of the magnetic north pole would have on surveys over a long period of time? How would earthquakes affect bench marks?

Additional Readings

Dividing the Land: Early American Beginnings of Our Private Property by Edward T. Price (University of Chicago Press, 1995).

"Land for All: A History of U.S. Real Estate to 1900" by John McMahan (*Real Estate Review*, Winter 76, p. 78). A fascinating four-part history of American real estate speculation and development before the year 1900.

Property Rights in American History: From the Colonial Era to the Present by James W. Ely, Jr. (Routledge Publishing, Inc., 1997).

Real Estate Law, 11th ed. by Charles J. Jacobus (OnCourse Learning, 2013).

CHAPTER 3

Rights and Interests in Land

This chapter provides general and legal information concerning rights and interest in land. It begins with a brief discussion of government rights and land, individual rights, easements, encroachments, deed restrictions, and types of liens. Other topics covered in this chapter include various types of estates, homestead rights, chattels, and subsurface rights.

Feudal and Allodial Systems

Early man was nomadic and had no concept of real estate. Roaming bands followed game and the seasons and did not claim the exclusive right to use a given area. When man began to cultivate crops and domesticate animals, the concept of an exclusive right to the use of land became important. This right was claimed for the tribe as a whole, and each family in the tribe was given the right to the exclusive use of a portion of the tribe's land. In turn, each family was obligated to aid in defending the tribe's claim against other tribes.

FEUDAL SYSTEM

As time passed, individual tribes allied with each other for mutual protection; eventually these alliances resulted in political states. In the process, land ownership went to the head of the state, usually a king. The king, in turn, gave the right (called a feud) to use large tracts of land to select individuals, called lords. The lords did not receive ownership. They were tenants of the king, and were required to serve and pay duties to the king and to help fight the king's wars. It was customary for the lords to remain tenants for life, subject, of course, to the defeat of their king by

LEARNING OBJECTIVES

After reading this chapter, you should be able to:

❮ Understand the history of feudal and allodial systems.

❮ Define government rights in land and the effect of those rights.

❮ Understand and define the term *fee simple ownership.*

❮ Discuss the two types of easements and how to create and terminate easement rights.

❮ Understand various lien issues involving real property.

❮ Understand the concept of life estates and leasehold estates.

KEY TERMS

Chattel • Easement • Eminent domain • Encroachment • Encumbrance • Estate • Fee simple • Lien • Title another king. This system, wherein all land ownership rested in the name of the king, became known as the **feudal system**.

The lords gave their subjects the right to use small tracts of land. For this, the subjects owed their lord a share of their crops and their allegiance in time of war. The subjects (vassals) were, in effect, tenants of the lord and subtenants of the king. Like the lord, the vassal could neither sell his rights nor pass them to his heirs.

ALLODIAL SYSTEM

The first major change in the feudal system occurred in 1285 when King Edward I of England gave his lords the right to pass their tenancy rights to their heirs. Subsequently, tenant vassals were permitted to convey their tenancy rights to others. By the year 1650, the feudal system had come to an end in England; in France, it ended with the French Revolution in 1789. In its place arose the **allodial system** of land ownership under which individuals were given the right to own land. Initially, lords became owners and the peasants remained tenants of the lords. As time passed, the peasants became landowners either by purchase or by gift from the lords.

When the first European explorers reached North American shores, they claimed the land in the name of the king or queen whom they represented. When the first settlers later came to America from England, they claimed the land in the name of their mother country. However, since the feudal system had been abolished in the meantime, the king of England granted the settlers private ownership of the land upon which they settled, while retaining the claim of ownership to the unsettled lands.

Claims by the king of England to land in the 13 colonies were ended with the American Revolution. Subsequently, the U.S. government acquired the ownership right to additional lands by treaty, wars, and purchase, resulting in the borders of the United States as we know them today. The United States adopted the allodial system of ownership, and not only permits, but encourages its citizens to own land within its borders.

Government Rights in Land

Under the feudal system, the king was responsible for organizing defense against invaders, making decisions on land use, and providing services such as roads and bridges, and for the general administration of the land and his subjects. An important aspect of the transition from feudal to allodial ownership was that the need for these services did not end. Consequently, even though ownership could now be held by private citizens, it became necessary for the government to retain the rights of taxation, eminent domain, police power, and escheat. Let's look at each of these more closely.

PROPERTY TAXES

Under the feudal system, governments financed themselves by requiring lords and vassals to share a portion of the benefits they received from the use of the king's lands. With the change to private ownership, the need to finance governments did not end. Thus, the government retained the right to collect **property taxes** from landowners. Before the advent of income taxes, the taxes levied against land were the main source of government revenues. Taxing land was a logical method of raising revenue for two reasons: (1) until the Industrial Revolution, which started in the mid-eighteenth century, land and agriculture were the primary sources of income; the more land one owned, the wealthier one was considered to be, and therefore, the better able to pay taxes to support the government; (2) land is impossible to hide, making it easily identifiable for taxation. This is not true of other valuables such as gold or money.

The real property tax has endured over the centuries, and today it is still a major source of government revenue. The major change in real estate taxation is that initially it was used to support all levels of government, including defense. Today, defense is supported by the income tax, and real estate taxes are sources of city, county, and, in some places, state revenues. At state and local government levels, the real property tax provides money for such things as schools, fire and police protection, parks, and libraries. To encourage property owners to pay their taxes in full and on time, the right of taxation also enables the government to seize ownership of real estate upon which taxes are delinquent and to sell the property to recover the unpaid taxes.

EMINENT DOMAIN

The right of government to take ownership of privately held real estate regardless of the owner's wishes is called **eminent domain**. Land for schools, freeways, streets, parks, urban renewal, public housing, public parking, and other social and public purposes is obtained this way. Quasi-public organizations, such as utility companies and railroads, are also permitted to obtain land needed for utility lines, pipes, and tracks by state and federal laws. The legal proceeding involved in eminent domain is **condemnation**, and the property owner must be paid the fair market value of the property taken from him. The actual condemnation is usually preceded by negotiations between the property owner and an agent of the public body wanting to acquire ownership. If the agent and the property owner can arrive at a mutually acceptable price, the property is purchased outright. If an agreement cannot be reached, a formal proceeding in eminent domain is filed against the property owner in a court of law. The court hears expert opinions from appraisers brought by both parties and then sets the price the property owner must accept in return for the loss of ownership.

When only a portion of a parcel of land is being taken, **severance damages** may be awarded in addition to payment for land actually being taken. For example, if a new highway requires a 40-acre strip of land through the middle of a 160-acre farm, the farm owner will not only be paid for the 40 acres, but will also receive severance damages to compensate for the fact that the farm will be more difficult to work because it is no longer in one piece.

An **inverse condemnation** is a proceeding brought about by a property owner demanding that his land be purchased from him. In a number of cities, homeowners at the end of airport runways have forced airport authorities to buy their homes because of the deafening noise of jet aircraft during takeoffs. Damage awards may also be made when land itself is not taken but its usefulness is reduced because of a nearby condemnation. These are **consequential damages** and might be awarded, for instance, when land is taken for a sewage treatment plant and privately owned land downwind from the plant suffers a loss in value owing to foul odors.

POLICE POWER

The right of government to enact laws and enforce them for the order, safety, health, morals, and general welfare of the public is called **police power**. Examples of police power applied to real estate are zoning laws, planning laws, building, health and fire codes, and rent control. A key difference between police power and eminent domain is that, although police power restricts how real estate may be used, there is no legally

eminent domain
The right of government to take privately held land for public use, provided fair compensation is paid.

recognized "taking" of property. Consequently, there is no payment to an owner who suffers a loss of value through the exercise of police power. A government may not utilize police power in an offhand or capricious manner; any law that restricts how an owner may use his real estate must be deemed in the public interest and applied evenhandedly to be valid. The breaking of a law based upon police power results in either a civil or criminal penalty rather than in the seizing of real estate, as in the case of unpaid property taxes. Of the various rights government holds in land, police power has the most impact on land value.

ESCHEAT

When a person dies and leaves no heirs and no instructions as to how to dispose of her real and personal property, or when property is abandoned, the ownership of that property reverts to the government (state or county). This reversion to the state is called **escheat** from the Anglo-French word meaning to *fall back*. Escheat solves the problem of property becoming ownerless.

Protecting Ownership

It cannot be overemphasized that, to have real estate, there must be a system or means of protecting rightful claims to the use of land and the improvements thereon. In the United States, the federal government is given the task of organizing a defense system to prevent confiscation of those rights by a foreign power. The federal government, in combination with state and local governments, also establishes laws and courts within the country to protect the ownership rights of one citizen in relation to another citizen. Whereas the armed forces protect against a foreign takeover within a country, deeds, public records, contracts, and other documents have replaced the need for brute force to prove and protect ownership of real estate.

Fee Simple

fee simple

The largest, most complete bundle of rights one can hold in land; land ownership.

estate

Legal interest or rights in land.

title

The right to or ownership of something; also the evidence of ownership, such as a deed or bill of sale.

The concept of real estate ownership can be more easily understood when viewed as a collection or bundle of rights. Under the allodial system, the rights of taxation, eminent domain, police power, and escheat are retained by the government. The remaining bundle of rights, called **fee simple**, is available for private ownership. The fee simple bundle of rights can be held by a person and his heirs forever, or until his government can no longer protect those rights. Figure 3.1 illustrates the fee simple bundle of rights concept.

The word *estate* is synonymous with bundle of rights. Stated another way, **estate** refers to one's legal interest or rights in land, not the physical quantity of land as shown on a map. A fee simple is the largest estate one can hold in land. Most real estate sales are for the fee simple estate. When a person says he or she "owns" or has "title" to real estate, it is usually the fee simple estate that is being discussed. The word **title** refers to the ownership of something. All other lesser estates in land, such as life estates and leaseholds, are created from the fee simple estate.

As shown in Figure 3.1, real estate is concerned with the "sticks" in the bundle: how many are there, how useful they are, and who possesses the sticks not in the bundle. With that in mind, let us describe what happens when sticks are removed from the bundle.

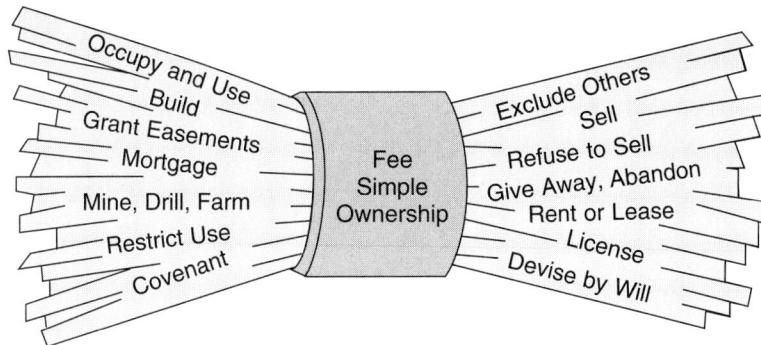

FIGURE 3.1   The Fee Simple Bundle of Rights

Occupy and Use
Build
Grant Easements
Mortgage
Mine, Drill, Farm
Restrict Use
Covenant

Fee Simple Ownership

Exclude Others
Sell
Refuse to Sell
Give Away, Abandon
Rent or Lease
License
Devise by Will

Real estate ownership is, in actuality, the ownership of rights to land. The largest bundle available for private ownership is called "fee simple."

Source: © 2014 OnCourse Learning

Encumbrances

Whenever a stick is removed from the fee simple bundle, it creates an impediment to the free and clear ownership and use of that property. These impediments to title are called encumbrances. An **encumbrance** is defined as any claim, right, lien, estate, or liability that limits the fee simple title to property. An encumbrance is, in effect, a stick that has been removed from the bundle. Commonly found encumbrances are easements, encroachments, deed restrictions, liens, leases, and air and subsurface rights. In addition, qualified fee estates are encumbered estates, as are life estates.

encumbrance

Any impediment to a clear title, such as a lien, lease, or easement.

The party holding a stick from someone else's fee simple bundle is said to hold a claim to or a right or interest in that land. In other words, what is one person's encumbrance is another person's right or interest or claim. For example, a lease is an encumbrance from the standpoint of the fee simple owner. But from the tenant's standpoint, it is an interest in land that gives the tenant the right to the exclusive use of land and buildings. A mortgage is an encumbrance from the fee owner's viewpoint but a right to foreclose from the lender's viewpoint. A property that is encumbered with a lease and a mortgage is called "a fee simple subject to a lease and a mortgage." Figure 3.2 illustrates how a fee simple bundle shrinks as rights are removed from it. Meanwhile, let us turn our attention to a discussion of individual sticks found in the fee simple bundle.

EASEMENTS

An **easement** is a right or privilege one party has to the use of land of another for a special purpose consistent with the general use of the land. The landowner is not dispossessed from his land but rather coexists side by side with the holder of the easement. Examples of easements are those given to telephone and electric companies to erect poles and run lines over private property, easements given to people to drive or walk across someone else's land, and easements given to gas and water companies to run pipelines to serve their customers. Figure 3.3 on page 39 illustrates several examples of easements.

easement

The right or privilege one party has to use land belonging to another for a special purpose not inconsistent with the owner's use of the land.

There are several different ways an easement can come into being. One is for the landowner to use a written document to specifically grant an easement to another

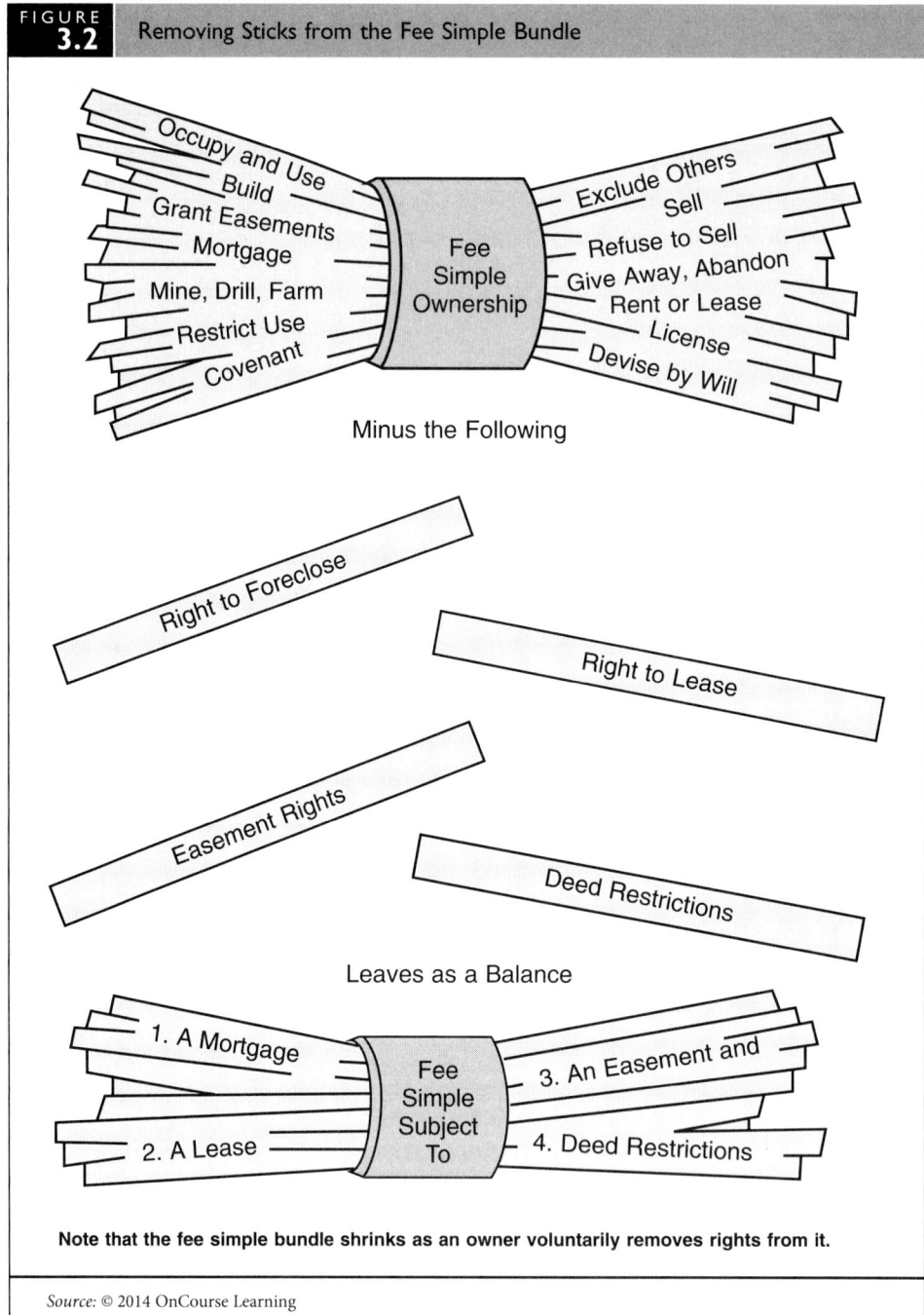

FIGURE 3.2   Removing Sticks from the Fee Simple Bundle

Occupy and Use
Build
Grant Easements
Mortgage
Mine, Drill, Farm
Restrict Use
Covenant

Fee Simple Ownership

Exclude Others
Sell
Refuse to Sell
Give Away, Abandon
Rent or Lease
License
Devise by Will

Minus the Following

Right to Foreclose

Right to Lease

Easement Rights

Deed Restrictions

Leaves as a Balance

1. A Mortgage

2. A Lease

Fee Simple Subject To

3. An Easement and

4. Deed Restrictions

Note that the fee simple bundle shrinks as an owner voluntarily removes rights from it.

Source: © 2014 OnCourse Learning

party. A second way is for an owner to reserve (withhold) an easement in the deed when granting the property to another party. For example, a land developer may reserve easements for utility lines when selling the lots and then grant the easements to the utility companies that will service the lots. Another way for an easement to be created is by government condemnation, such as when a government flood control district purchases an easement to run a drainage pipe under someone's land.

It is also possible for an easement to arise without a written document. For example, a parcel of land fronts on a road, and the owner sells the back half of the parcel. If the only access to the back half is by crossing over the front half, even if the seller did not expressly grant an easement, the law will generally protect the buyer's right to travel over the front half to get to his land. The buyer cannot be landlocked by the seller. This is known as an **easement by necessity**. Another method of acquiring an easement without a written document is by constant use, or **easement by prescription**: if a person acts as though he owns an easement long enough, and the use is open, obvious, and without permission of the property owner, that person will have a legally recognized easement. One using a private road without permission for a long enough period of time can acquire a legally recognized easement by this method.

EASEMENT APPURTENANT. In Figure 3.3, the driveway from the road to the back lot is called an **easement appurtenant**. This driveway is automatically included with the back lot whenever the back lot is sold or otherwise conveyed. This is so because this easement is legally connected (appurtenant) to the back lot. Please note that just as the back lot benefits from this easement, the front lot is burdened by it. Whenever the front lot is sold or otherwise conveyed, the new owners must continue to respect the easement to the back lot. The owner of the front lot owns all the front lot, but cannot

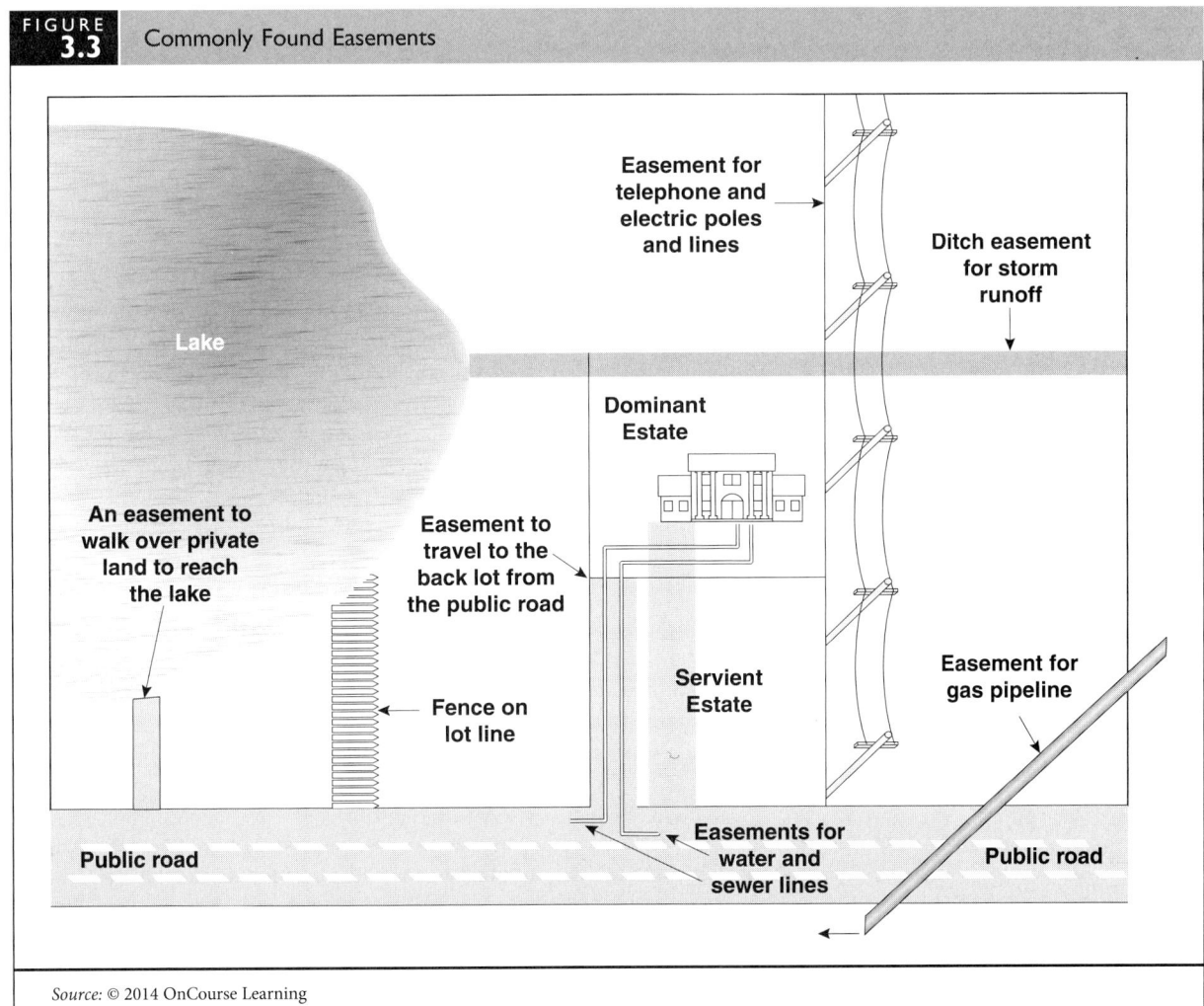

FIGURE 3.3   Commonly Found Easements

Source: © 2014 OnCourse Learning

put a fence across the easement, plant trees on it, grow a garden on it, or otherwise hamper access to the back lot. Because the front lot serves the back lot, the front lot is called the **servient estate** and the back lot is called the **dominant estate**. When one party has the right or privilege, by usage or contract, to travel over a designated portion of another person's land, it is called a **right-of-way**.

Although the law may protect the first purchaser through the doctrine of easement by necessity, it is nonetheless critical that any subsequent purchaser of back lots and back acreage carefully inspect the public records and the property to make certain there is both legal and actual means of access from a public road to the parcel. It is also important for anyone purchasing land to inspect the public records and the property for evidence of the rights of others to pass over that land, for example, a driveway or private road to a back lot or a pathway used by the public to get from a road to a beach.

EASEMENT IN GROSS. An **easement in gross** differs from an easement appurtenant because there is a servient estate but no dominant estate. Some examples will illustrate this: telephone, electricity, and gas line easements are all easements in gross. These easements belong to the telephone, electric, and gas companies, respectively, not to a parcel of land. The servient estate is the parcel on which the telephone, electric, and gas companies have the right to run their lines. All future owners of the parcel are bound by these easements.

Although utility easements are the most common examples of easements in gross, the ditch easement for storm runoff in Figure 3.3 is also one. It will most likely be owned by a flood control district. Note that utility and drainage easements, although legally a burden on a parcel, are consistent with the use of a parcel if the purpose of the easement is to provide utility service or flood control for the parcel. In fact, without these services, a parcel would be less useful and hence less valuable.

PARTY WALL EASEMENT. **Party wall** easements exist when a single wall is located on the lot line that separates two parcels of land. The wall may be either a fence or the wall of a building. In either case, each lot owner owns that portion of the wall on his land, plus an easement in the other half of the wall for physical support. Party walls are common where stores and office buildings are built right up to the lot line. Such a wall can present an interesting problem when the owner of one lot wants to demolish his building. Since the wall provides support for the building next door, the owner must leave the wall and provide special supports for the adjacent building during demolition and until another building is constructed on the lot. A party wall is an easement appurtenant.

EASEMENT TERMINATION. Easements may be terminated when the necessity for the easement no longer exists (for example, a public road is built adjacent to the back half of the lot mentioned earlier), or when the dominant and servient estates are combined (merged) with the intent of extinguishing the easement, or by release from the easement holder to the servient estate, or by lack of use (abandonment).

ENCROACHMENTS

encroachment

The unauthorized intrusion of a building or other improvement onto another person's land.

The unauthorized intrusion of a building or other form of real property onto another person's land is called an **encroachment**. A tree that overhangs into a neighbor's yard or a building or eave of a roof that crosses a property line are examples of encroachments. The owner of the property being encroached upon has the right to force the removal of the encroachment.

FIGURE 3.4	Commonly Found Encroachments

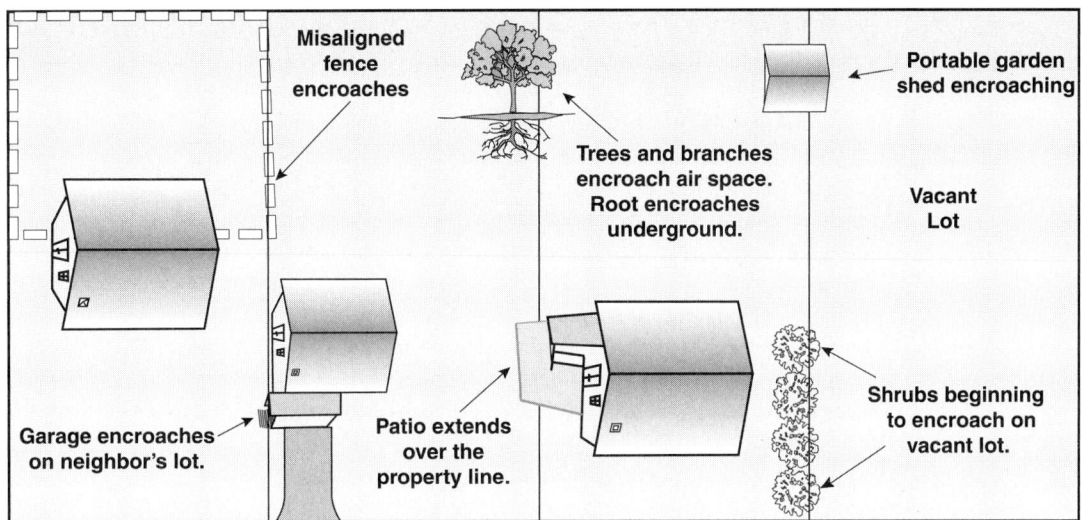

Misaligned fence encroaches

Portable garden shed encroaching

Trees and branches encroach air space. Root encroaches underground.

Vacant Lot

Garage encroaches on neighbor's lot.

Patio extends over the property line.

Shrubs beginning to encroach on vacant lot.

Source: © 2014 OnCourse Learning

Failure to do so may eventually injure his title and make the land more difficult to sell. Ultimately, inaction may result in the encroaching neighbor claiming a legal right to continue the use. Figure 3.4 illustrates several commonly found encroachments.

DEED RESTRICTIONS

Private agreements that govern the use of land are known as **deed restrictions** or **deed covenants**. For example, a land subdivider can require that persons who purchase lots from him build only single-family homes containing 1,200 square feet or more. The purpose would be to protect those who have already built houses from an erosion in property value due to the construction of nearby buildings not compatible with the neighborhood. Where scenic views are important, deed restrictions may limit the height of buildings and trees to 15 feet. A buyer would still obtain fee simple ownership, but, at the same time, would voluntarily give up some of his rights to do as he pleases. As a buyer, he is said to receive a fee simple title subject to deed restrictions. The right to enforce the restrictions is usually given by the developer to the subdivision's homeowner association. Violation of a deed restriction can result in a civil court action brought by other property owners who are bound by the same deed restriction.

LIENS

A hold or claim that one person has on the property of another to secure payment of a debt or other obligation is called a **lien**. Common examples are property tax liens, mechanic's liens, judgment liens, and mortgage liens. From the standpoint of the property owner, a lien is an encumbrance on her title. Note that a lien does not transfer title to property. In most states, the debtor retains title unless the lien is foreclosed. When there is more than one lien against a property, the lien that was recorded first usually has the highest priority in the event of foreclosure. Property tax liens are, however, always superior to other liens.

lien
A hold or claim that one person has on the property of another to secure payment of a debt or other obligation.

PROPERTY TAX LIEN. **Property tax liens** result from the right of government to collect taxes from property owners. At the beginning of each tax year, a tax lien is placed on taxable property. It is removed when the property taxes are paid. If they are not paid, the lien gives the government the right to force the sale of the property in order to collect the unpaid taxes.

MECHANIC'S LIEN. **Mechanic's lien** laws give anyone who has furnished labor or materials for the improvement of land, the right to place a lien against those improvements and the land if payment has not been received. A sale of the property can then be forced to recover the money owed. To be entitled to a mechanic's lien, the work or materials must have been provided pursuant to contract with the landowner or his representative. For example, if a landowner hires a contractor to build a house or add a room to his existing house and then fails to pay the contractor, the contractor may file a mechanic's lien against the land and its improvements. Furthermore, if the landowner pays the contractor but the contractor does not pay his subcontractors, the subcontractors are entitled to file a mechanic's lien against the property. In this situation, the owner may have to pay twice.

The legal theory behind mechanic's lien rights is that the labor and materials supplied enhance the value of the property. Therefore, the property should be security for payment. If the property owner does not pay voluntarily, the lien can be enforced with a court-supervised foreclosure sale.

Mechanics (contractors), materialmen, architects, surveyors, and engineers are among those who may be entitled to the protection of mechanic's lien laws. All mechanic's liens attach and take effect at the time the first item of labor or material is furnished, even though no document has been filed with the county recorder. To preserve the lien, a lien statement must be filed in the county where the property is located and within 20 to 120 days (depending on the state) after labor or material has been furnished. This is called **perfecting the lien**.

Whenever improvements are made to the land, all persons (including sellers under a contract for deed and landlords) may be held to have authorized the improvements. As protection, an owner can serve or post notice that the improvements are being made without the owner's authority.

A lender planning to finance a property will be particularly alert for the possibility of mechanic's liens. If work has commenced or material has been delivered before the mortgage is recorded, the mechanic's lien may be superior to the mortgage in the event of foreclosure.

JUDGMENT LIEN. **Judgment liens** arise from lawsuits for which money damages are awarded. The law permits a hold to be placed against the real and personal property of the debtor until the judgment is paid. Usually the lien created by the judgment covers only property in the county where the judgment was awarded. However, the creditor can extend the lien to property in other counties by filing a **notice of lien** in each of those counties. If the debtor does not repay the lien voluntarily, the creditor can (although this can vary from state to state) ask the court to issue a **writ of execution** that directs the county sheriff to seize and sell a sufficient amount of the debtor's property to pay the debt and expenses of the sale.

MORTGAGE LIEN. A mortgage lien is created when property is offered by its owner as security for the repayment of a debt. If the debt secured by the mortgage lien is not repaid, the creditor can foreclose and sell the property. If this is insufficient to repay the debt, some states allow the creditor to petition the court for a judgment lien for the balance due. (Mortgage law is covered in more detail in Chapter 9.)

VOLUNTARY AND INVOLUNTARY LIENS. A **voluntary lien** is a lien created by the property owner. A mortgage lien is an example of a voluntary lien: The owner voluntarily creates a lien against his/her property in order to borrow money. An **involuntary lien** is created by operation of law. Examples are property tax liens, judgment liens, and mechanic's liens.

SPECIAL AND GENERAL LIENS. A **special lien** is a lien on a specific property. A property tax lien is a special lien because it is a lien against a specific property and no other. Thus, if a person owns five parcels of land scattered throughout a given county and fails to pay the taxes on one of those parcels, the county can force the sale of just that one parcel; the others cannot be touched. Mortgages and mechanic's liens are also special liens in that they apply to only the property receiving the materials or labor. In contrast, a **general lien** is a lien on all the property of a person in a given jurisdiction. For example, a judgment lien is a lien on all the debtor's property in the county or counties where the judgment has been filed. Federal and state liens for taxes are also general liens.

LIENOR, LIENEE. The party holding the lien is called the **lienor**. Examples of lienors are mortgage lenders, judgment holders, and tax authorities. The party whose property is subject to the lien is called a **lienee**. The terms *lienor* and *lienee* apply whether the lien is voluntary or involuntary, specific or general.

Qualified Fee Estates

A **qualified fee estate** is a fee estate that is subject to certain limitations imposed by the person creating the estate. Qualified fee estates fall into three categories: determinable, condition subsequent, and condition precedent. They will be discussed only briefly as they are rather uncommon.

A **fee simple determinable estate** indicates that the duration of the estate can be determined from the deed itself. For example, Mr. Smith donates a parcel of land to a church so long as the land is used for religious purposes. The key words are *so long as*. So long as the land is used for religious purposes, the church has all the rights of fee simple ownership. But if some other use is made of the land, it reverts to the grantor (Mr. Smith) or someone else named by Mr. Smith (called a **remainderman**). Note that the termination of the estate is automatic if the land is used contrary to the limitation stated in the deed.

A **fee simple subject to condition subsequent** gives the grantor the *right* to terminate the estate. Continuing the above example, Mr. Smith would have the right to reenter the property and take it back if it was no longer being used for religious purposes.

With a **fee simple upon condition precedent**, title will not take effect until a condition is performed. For example, Mr. Smith could deed his land to a church with the condition that the deed will not take effect until a religious sanctuary is built.

Occasionally, qualified fees have been used by land developers in lieu of deed restrictions or zoning. For example, the buyer has fee title so long as he uses the land for a single-family residence. In another example, a land developer might use a condition precedent to encourage lot purchasers to build promptly. This would enhance the value of his unsold lots. From the standpoint of the property owner, a qualification is an encumbrance to his title.

Life Estates

A **life estate** conveys an estate for the duration of someone's life. The duration of the estate can be tied to the life of the **life tenant** (the person holding the life estate) or to a third party. In addition, someone must be named to acquire the estate upon its termination. The following example will illustrate the life estate concept. Suppose you have an aunt who needs financial assistance and you have decided to grant her, for the rest of her life, a house to live in. When you create the life estate, she becomes the life tenant. Additionally, you must decide who gets the house upon her death. If you want it back, you would want a **reversion** for yourself. This way the house reverts to you, or if you predecease her, to your heirs. If you want the house to go to someone else, your son or daughter for example, you could name him or her as the remainderman. Alternatively, you could name a friend, relative, or charity as the remainderman. Sometimes a life estate is used to avoid the time and expense of probating a will and to reduce estate taxes. For example, an aging father could deed his real estate to his children but retain a life estate for himself.

A life estate can also be created for the life of another. For example, I will deed this property to Jim Bob for the life of his mother (anticipating that Jim Bob will maintain control over the property for the purpose of taking care of his mother—perhaps given the opportunity to live there at no cost). Then, upon the death of his mom, the life estate would revert to the grantor or vest in the remainderman, depending on the terms that created the life estate. In legal terms, this is called a life estate **pur autre vie**.

PROHIBITION OF WASTE

Since a life estate arrangement is temporary, the life tenant must not commit **waste** by destroying or harming the property. Furthermore, the life tenant is required to keep the property in reasonable repair and to pay any property taxes, assessments, and interest on debt secured by the property. The life tenant is entitled to income generated by the property, and may sell, lease, rent, or mortgage his or her interest.

Although the life estate concept offers intriguing gift and estate planning possibilities, the uncertainty of the duration of the estate makes it rather unmarketable. Thus, you will rarely see a life estate advertised for sale in a newspaper or listed for sale at a real estate brokerage office.

Statutory Estates

Statutory estates are created by state law. They include dower, which gives a wife rights in her husband's real property; curtesy, which gives a husband rights in his wife's real property; and community property, which gives each spouse a one-half interest in marital property. Additionally, there is homestead protection, which is designed to protect the family's home from certain debts and, upon the death of one spouse, provide the other with a home for life.

DOWER

Historically, **dower** came from old English common law in which the marriage ceremony was viewed as merging the wife's legal existence into that of her husband's. From this viewpoint, property bought during marriage belongs to the husband, with both husband and wife sharing the use of it. As a counterbalance, the dower right recognizes the wife's efforts in marriage and grants her legal ownership to one-third (in some states one-half) of the family's real property for the rest of her life. This prevents the husband from conveying ownership of the family's real estate without the wife's permission and protects her even if she is left out of her husband's will.

In real estate sales, the effect of dower laws is such that when a husband and wife sell their property, the wife must relinquish her dower rights. This is usually accomplished by the wife signing the deed with her husband or by signing a separate quitclaim deed. If she does not relinquish her dower rights, the buyer (or even a future buyer) may find that, upon the husband's death, the wife may return to legally claim an undivided ownership in the property. This is important if you buy real estate. Have the property's ownership researched by an abstracter, and have the title insured by a title insurance company.

CURTESY

Roughly the opposite of dower, **curtesy** gives the husband benefits in his deceased wife's property as long as he lives. However, unlike dower, the wife can defeat those rights in her will. Furthermore, state law may require the couple to have had a child in order for the husband to qualify for curtesy.

Because dower and curtesy rights originally were unequal, some states interpret dower and curtesy so as to give equal rights, while other states have enacted additional legislation to protect spousal rights. To summarize, the basic purpose of dower and curtesy (and community property laws) is to require both spouses to sign any deed or mortgage or other document affecting title to their lands, and to provide legal protection for the property rights of a surviving spouse.

COMMUNITY PROPERTY

Ten states (Alaska, Arizona, California, Idaho, Louisiana, Nevada, New Mexico, Texas, Washington, and Wisconsin) recognize the legal theory that each spouse has an equal interest in all property acquired by their joint efforts during the marriage. This jointly produced property is called **community property**. Upon the death of one spouse, their community property passes to the heirs and/or the surviving spouse. When community property is sold or mortgaged, both spouses must sign the document. Community property rights arise upon marriage (either formal or common law) and terminate upon divorce or death. Community property is discussed at greater length in Chapter 4.

HOMESTEAD PROTECTION

Nearly all states have passed **homestead protection** laws, usually with two purposes in mind: (1) to provide some legal protection for the homestead claimants from debts and judgments against them that might result in the forced sale and loss of the home, and (2) to provide a home for a widow, and sometimes a widower, for life. Homestead laws also restrict one spouse from acting without the other when conveying the homestead or using it as collateral for a loan. Although dower, curtesy, and community property rights are automatic in those states that have them, the homestead right may require that a written declaration be recorded in the public records. As referred to here, homestead is not the acquiring of title to state or federally owned lands by filing and establishing a residence (see Chapter 5). Additionally, *homestead protection* should not be confused with the *homestead exemption* some states grant to homeowners in order to reduce their property taxes (see Chapter 15).

A homeowner is also protected by the Federal Bankruptcy Reform Act. While more protective state statutes may control, the Reform Act provides that a person who seeks protection under this act is entitled to an exemption of up to $20,200 of the equity in his /her residence. Also exempt is any household item that does not exceed $525 in value.

Freehold Estates

In a carryover from the old English court system, estates in land are classified as either **freehold estates** or **leasehold estates**. The main difference is that freehold estate cases are tried under real property laws, whereas leasehold (also called nonfreehold or less-than-freehold) estates are tried under personal property laws.

The two distinguishing features of a freehold estate are: (1) there must be actual ownership of the land, and (2) the estate must be of unpredictable duration. Fee estates, life estates, and estates created by statute are freehold estates.

Leasehold Estates

The distinguishing features of a leasehold estate are: (1) although there is possession of the land, there is no ownership, and (2) the estate is of definite duration. Stated another way, freehold means ownership and less-than-freehold means rental.

As previously noted, the user of a property need not be its owner. Under a leasehold estate, the user is called the **lessee** or **tenant**, and the person from whom he leases is the **lessor** or **landlord**. As long as the tenant has a valid lease, abides by it, and pays the rent on time, the owner, even though he owns the property, cannot occupy it until the lease has expired. During the lease period, the freehold estate owner is said to hold a *reversion*. This is his right to recover possession at the end of the lease period. Meanwhile, the lease is an encumbrance against the property.

There are four categories of leasehold estates: estate for years, periodic estate, estate at will, and tenancy at sufferance. Note that in this chapter we will be examining leases primarily from the standpoint of estates in land. Leases as financing tools are discussed in Chapter 14, and lease contracts are covered in Chapter 17.

ESTATE FOR YEARS

Also called a tenancy for years, the **estate for years** is somewhat misleadingly named as it implies that a lease for a number of years has been created. Actually, the key criterion is that the lease have a specific starting time and a specific ending time. It can be for any length of time, ranging from less than a day to many years. An estate for years does not automatically renew itself. Neither the landlord nor the tenant must act to terminate it, as the lease agreement itself specifies a termination date.

Usually the lessor is the freehold estate owner. However, the lessee could also be a lessor. To illustrate, a fee owner leases to a lessee, who in turn leases to another person. By doing this, this first lessee has become a **sublessor**. The person who leases from him is a **sublessee**. It is important to realize that in no case can a sublessee acquire from the lessee any more rights than the lessee has. Thus, if a lessee has a five-year lease with three years remaining, he can assign to a sublessee only the remaining three years or a portion of it.

PERIODIC ESTATE

Also called an estate from year-to-year, or a periodic tenancy, a **periodic estate** has an original lease period with fixed length; when it runs out, unless the tenant or the landlord acts to terminate it, renewal is automatic for another like period of time. A month-to-month apartment rental is an example of this arrangement. To avoid last-minute confusion, rental agreements usually require that advance notice be given if either the landlord or the tenant wishes to terminate the tenancy.

ESTATE AT WILL

Also called a tenancy at will, an **estate at will** is a landlord-tenant relationship with all the normal rights and duties of a lessor-lessee relationship, except that the estate may be terminated by either the lessor or the lessee at any time. However, most states recognize the inconvenience a literal interpretation of *anytime* can cause and require that reasonable advance notice be given. What is considered "reasonable" notice is often specified by state law.

TENANCY AT SUFFERANCE

A **tenancy at sufferance** occurs when a tenant stays beyond his legal tenancy without the consent of the landlord. In other words, the tenant wrongfully holds the property against the owner's wishes. In a tenancy at sufferance, the tenant is commonly called a **holdover tenant**, although once the stay exceeds the terms of the lease or rental agreement, he is not actually a tenant in the normal landlord-tenant sense. The landlord is entitled to evict him and recover possession of the property, provided the landlord does so in a timely manner. A tenant at sufferance differs from a trespasser only in that the original entry was rightful. If during the holdover period the tenant pays and the landlord accepts rent, the tenancy at sufferance changes to a periodic estate.

Overview

Figure 3.5 on the next page provides an overview of the various rights and interests in land that are discussed in this chapter and the previous chapter. This chart is designed to give you an overall perspective of what real estate includes.

LICENSE

A **license** is not a right or an estate in land, but a personal privilege given to someone to use land (the *license*). It is nonassignable, and can be canceled by the person who issues it. A license to park is typically what an automobile parking lot operator provides for persons parking in his lot. The contract creating the license is usually written on the stub that the lot attendant gives the driver, or it is posted on a sign on the lot. Tickets to theaters and sporting events also fall into this category. Because it is a personal privilege, a license is not an encumbrance against land.

CHATTELS

A **chattel** is an article of personal property. The word comes from the old English word for cattle, which, of course, were (and still are) personal property. *Chattel* is a word more often heard in a law office than in a real estate office. Occasionally you will see it used in legal documents, such as in the case of a **chattel mortgage**, which is a mortgage against personal property.

chattel
An article of personal property.

LAW SOURCES

You will better understand real estate law when you understand its roots. Most U.S. law originally came from early English law through English colonization of America.

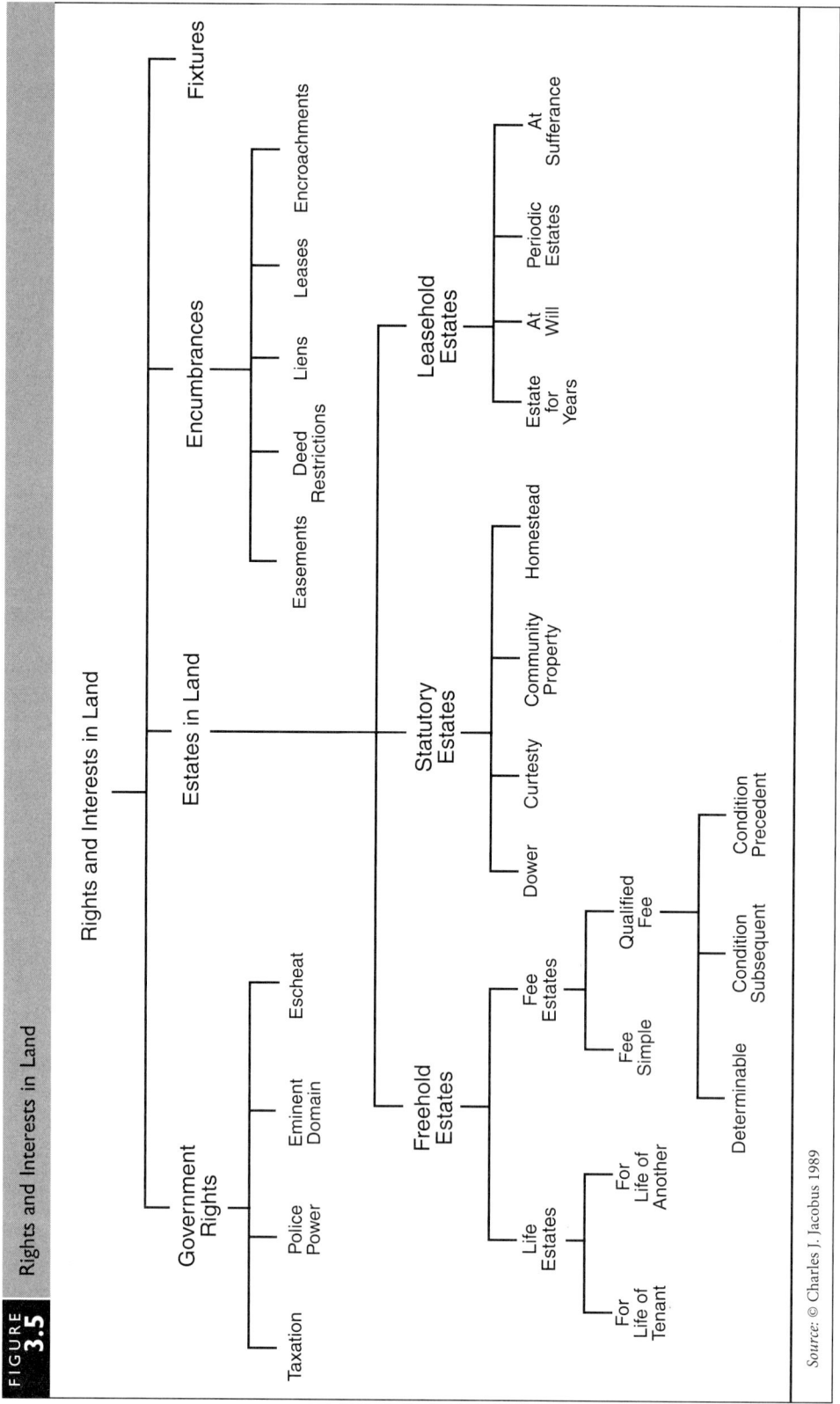

FIGURE **3.5** Rights and Interests in Land

Source: © Charles J. Jacobus 1989

Additionally, Spanish law, via Spain's colonization of Mexico, can be found in Arizona, California, Idaho, Nevada, New Mexico, Texas, and Washington. Lastly, old French civil law, by way of the French ownership of Louisiana, is the basis for that state's law. In all three of these, the law that took root in the United States originated in predominantly agricultural economies. Consequently, there has been a great deal of legal modification over the years by legislatures and courts.

COMMON LAW

You will also find it helpful to understand the difference between common law and statutory law. **Common law** derives its authority from usage and custom over long periods of time. Thus, the concepts of fee simple estates, qualified fee estates, life estates, leasehold estates, mortgages, air rights, and subsurface rights, for example, grew out of usage over hundreds of years. Individual court decisions (called **case law**) also contributed to the development of common law in England and the United States.

STATUTORY LAW

Statutory law is created by the enactment of legislation. Examples of statutory laws are laws enacted by state legislatures that require the licensing of real estate agents. Zoning laws and building codes are also statutory laws as they have their source in legislative enactment. Federal and state income tax and local property tax laws are statutory laws.

Sometimes common law concepts are enacted into statutory law. For example, many statutory laws pertaining to leasehold estates and the rights and obligations of landlords and tenants have come directly from common law. Additionally, statutory laws have been passed where common law was held to be unclear or unreasonable. For example, old English law did not provide equality in property rights for both spouses. Modern statutory laws do provide equality.

Pictorial Summary

Let's conclude this chapter by combining what has been discussed in Chapter 2 regarding the physical nature of land with what has been covered in this chapter regarding estates and rights in land. The results, diagrammed in Figures 3.6 and 3.7 (on pages 50–51), show why real estate is both complicated and exciting. A single parcel of land can be divided into subsurface, surface, and air space components. Each of these carries its own fee simple bundle of rights, which, in turn, can be divided into the various estates and rights we discussed in this chapter.

To more clearly convey this idea, let us turn our attention to Figure 3.6. In parcel A, the fee landowner has leased to a farmer the bulk of the surface and air rights, plus the right to draw water from the wells, for the production of crops and livestock. This leaves the fee owner with the right to lease or sell subterranean rights for mineral, oil, and gas extraction. With a single parcel of land, the fee owner has created two estates, one for farming and another for oil and gas production. This is referred to as **lateral severance**. With the minor exception of the placement of the well platforms, pumps, and pipes, neither use interferes with the other and both bring income to the landowners. The subsurface owner is the dominant estate, though. The farmer, in turn, can personally utilize the leasehold estate he possesses or he can sublease it to another farmer. The oil company, if it has leased its rights, can sublease them; if it has purchased them, it can sell or lease them.

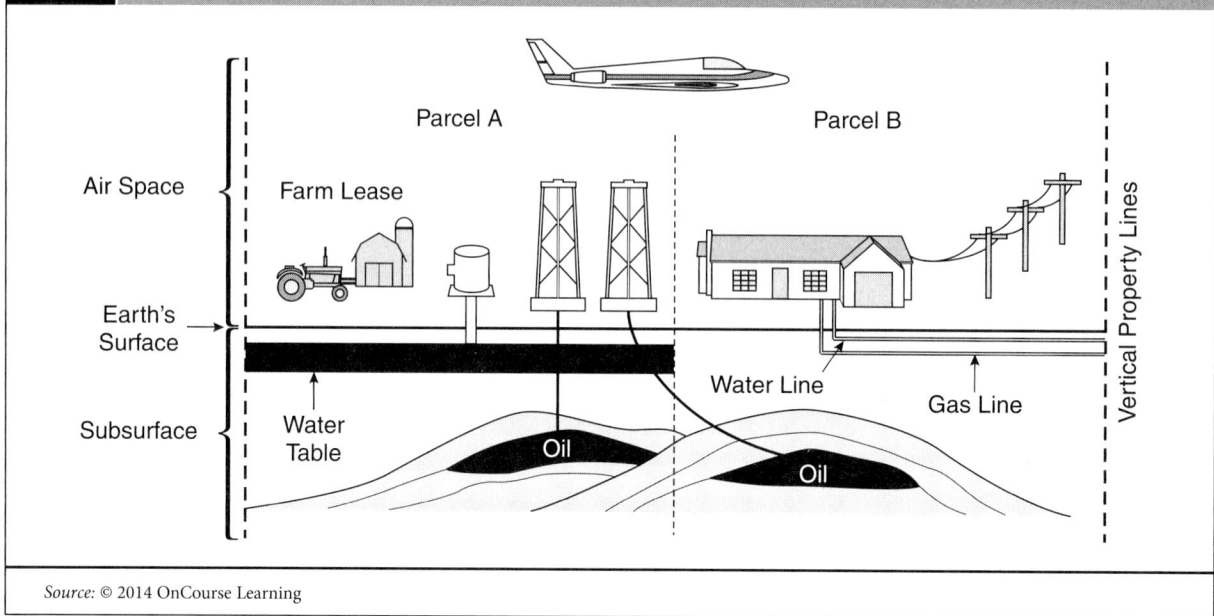

FIGURE 3.6   Cross-Section of Estates and Rights in Land

Air Space
Parcel A
Parcel B
Farm Lease
Vertical Property Lines
Earth's Surface
Subsurface
Water Table
Oil
Water Line
Gas Line
Oil

Source: © 2014 OnCourse Learning

This has become a key issue in residential real estate in some areas. Oil and gas reserves have been discovered in paying quantities (the price of oil and gas has increased dramatically) in areas that may be under existing subdivisions. In those cases, the oil company must contact every owner in the subdivision regarding their respective interest in the oil rights. Oil and gas rights are complicated.

In the public interest, the government has claimed the right to allow aircraft to fly over the land. Although a landowner technically owns from the center of the earth out to the heavens, the right given aircraft by the government to fly overhead creates a practical limit on that ownership, as does the use of air waves for cellular phones and computers.

WIND

Wind has become a source of energy. Wind energy leases usually pay a royalty fee that is based on the percentage of the gross revenue generated from the sale of the electricity. Wind by itself, however, does not seem to be susceptible to ownership, so its value must be based on the value after the investment has been made by harnessing that power.

This is a brand new area of the law, and it is evolving very quickly. We have always subscribed to the theory that we own the fee simple interest up through the earth and the sky. Can one own the wind? Can the rights to the wind be separated similar to mineral rights and water rights? There are areas of the country that are very conducive to sustained high wind. Most of these areas are remote and sparsely populated. The mechanics of getting the wind-generated power to populated areas without a significant loss of power is a challenging concept. Could an adjacent owner build anything that would hinder the free flow of wind through that wind farm? Do wind farms constitute a nuisance because they diminish the scenic beauty of the surrounding land? One issue which has been litigated is the unsightliness of the turbines. Most courts seem to hold that wind turbines are not unsightly. These and many other questions are on the horizon for this new source of energy. There will be a lot of new law in this area over the next few years.

SURFACE RIGHT OF ENTRY

In parcel B, the fee simple landowner has leased or sold the right to extract oil and gas from beneath the land. However, no surface right for the purpose of entering and drilling has been leased or sold. Thus, the oil company must slant drill from a nearby property where it does have a **surface right of entry**. The remaining rights amount to a full fee estate in the surface and air space. However, use of those rights is subject to zoning laws and building codes that restrict what can be built. Deed restrictions may include additional limitations on the type of structure that can be built. Also, the government claims air space rights for passing aircraft, as it does over all land within its borders. Just above and beneath the surface, easement rights have been granted to utility companies for electric, telephone, water, and gas lines.

Despite the fact that this homeowner's bundle of rights is not complete, what she does have is quite suitable for a home site. Recognizing this, lenders will accept the owner's offer of this house and lot as collateral for a loan. This might not be the case if the oil company had a surface right of entry. The noise, odor, and fire hazard of a working oil well next to a house would considerably reduce its value as a residence.

LAND LEASE

In parcel C shown in Figure 3.7, the fee owner has created an estate for years by a long-term lease of his land to an investor, who has subsequently constructed an apartment building on the land. This estate gives the building owner or lessee the right to occupy and use the land for a fixed period of time, most often between 55 and 99 years. In turn, the building owner rents out apartment units on a monthly or yearly basis. The rights to any mineral, oil, or gas deposits can either be included in the lease or reserved by the landowner. At the end of the lease period, the reversion held by the owner of the fee estate entitles the owner to retake possession of the land, including the buildings and other improvements thereon.

FIGURE 3.7   Cross-Section of Estates and Rights in Land

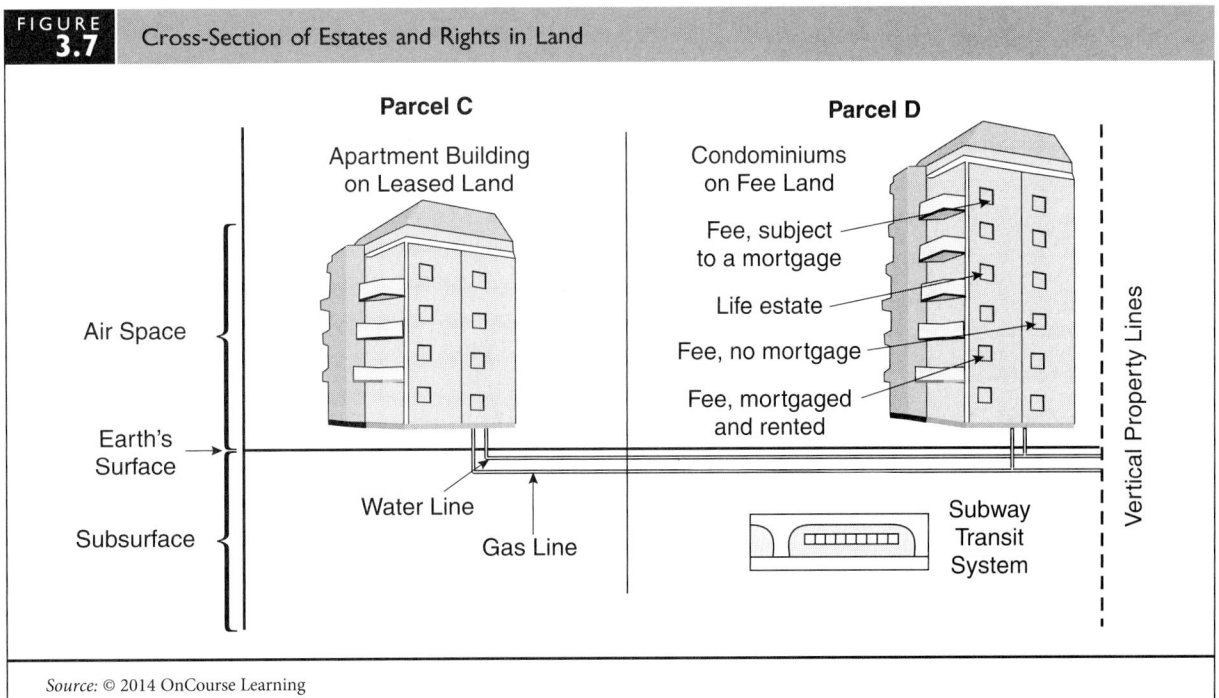

Parcel C

Apartment Building on Leased Land

Parcel D

Condominiums on Fee Land

Fee, subject to a mortgage

Life estate

Fee, no mortgage

Fee, mortgaged and rented

Air Space

Earth's Surface

Subsurface

Water Line

Gas Line

Subway Transit System

Vertical Property Lines

Source: © 2014 OnCourse Learning

CONDOMINIUM LOTS

In parcel D, fee simple air lots have been sold to individual apartment owners in a condominium apartment building. The owner of each air lot has a fee simple bundle of rights and is free to mortgage it by taking the foreclosure "stick" out of the bundle and giving it to a lender in exchange for a loan. Also, the owner can lease the unit to a tenant, thereby creating a leasehold estate and a reversion.

Condominium owners as a group usually own the surface of the land upon which the building rests, any air space not used as air lots, and the subsurface. In parcel D, the owners have either sold, leased, or granted to a transit authority the right to build a subway line under this parcel. Underground rights of this type are very important in cities with subsurface transportation networks and will continue to be so as more cities open underground mass transit systems.

An alternative to fee owners granting a subsurface right for underground transportation lines is for the line owner to own the fee interest in the entire parcel, use the subsurface portion for its tracks, and sell or lease the use of the surface and air space above. In Chicago and New York City, for instance, railroads have sold or leased surface and air rights above their downtown tracks for the purpose of constructing office buildings and convention halls. Passenger trains run just below the surface, while new buildings occupy the space above.

Vocabulary Review

Match terms a–x with statements 1–24.

a. Allodial
b. Chattel
c. Common law
d. Dominant estate
e. Easement
f. Easement appurtenant
g. Eminent domain
h. Encroachment
i. Encumbrance
j. Escheat
k. Estate
l. Estate for years
m. Freehold estate
n. Inverse condemnation
o. Lessor
p. Lien
q. Life estate
r. Mechanic's lien
s. Party wall
t. Periodic tenancy

_____ 1. A lease with a specific starting and ending date and no automatic renewal provision.

_____ 2. A charge or hold against property to use it as debt security.

_____ 3. A leasehold estate that automatically renews itself unless canceled.

_____ 4. An article of personal property.

_____ 5. The unauthorized intrusion of a building or other improvement upon the land of another.

_____ 6. Any impediment to clear title.

_____ 7. The right of government to take property from private owners, who in turn must be compensated.

_____ 8. A real property ownership system that allows land to be owned by individuals.

_____ 9. One's legal interest or rights in land.

_____ 10. A lawsuit by a property owner demanding that a public agency purchase his property.

_____ 11. The reversion of property to the state when the owner dies without leaving a will or heirs.

_____ 12. One who holds title and leases out property; the landlord.

_____ 13. A right or privilege one party has in the use of land belonging to another.

u. Right-of-way

v. Specific lien

w. Statutory law

x. Voluntary lien

_____14. Law based on custom and court decisions.

_____15. Law created by the enactment of legislation.

_____16. A lien purposely created by a property owner.

_____17. A lien on a specific property.

_____18. Lien rights for suppliers of labor or materials.

_____19. The parcel that benefits from an easement across another person's land.

_____20. An easement attached to a parcel of land and included with that parcel whenever it is conveyed.

_____21. An estate indicating actual ownership of land.

_____22. An estate for the duration of someone's life.

_____23. A wall located on a property boundary line.

_____24. The right to travel over a portion of another's land.

Questions and Problems

1. Distinguish between freehold and leasehold estates in land.

2. Under what conditions is it possible for an easement to be created without there being specific mention of it in writing?

3. What steps have been taken by your state legislature to recognize the legal equality of married women in real estate ownership?

4. Which three European countries provided the basis for real estate law in the United States?

5. From the standpoint of possession, what is the key difference between an easement and a lease?

6. What is an encumbrance? Give three examples.

7. In your community, name specific examples of the application of police power to the rights of landowners.

8. If your state has a homestead protection law, how much protection does it offer and what must a person do to qualify?

9. Technically speaking, a 99-year lease on a parcel of land is personal property. However, from a practical standpoint, the exclusive right to use a parcel of land for such a long period of time seems more like real property. Do the laws of your state treat a 99-year lease as real or personal property?

Additional Readings

American Law of Real Estate by J. David Reitzel, Robert B. Bennett, and Michael S. Garrison (OnCourse Learning, 2002).

"Can Eminent Domain Be Wielded against Developers?" by Beth Wade (*National Law Journal*, February 18, 2002, vol. 24, issue 24).

Cases and Material on Modern Property Law by Jon W. Bruce and James W. Ely, Jr. (Thomson West, 2007).

"Constitutional Questions about Tax Lien Foreclosures" by Frank S. Alexander (*Government Finance Review*, June 2000, vol. 16, issue 3, pp. 27–31).

Land Rights: The 1990's Property Rights Rebellion by Bruce Yandle (Rowman & Littlefield Publishers, Inc., 1995).

The Law of Easements and Licenses in Land by Jon W. Bruce and James Ely (Warren, Gorham & Lamont, 1992). Entire book provides information on measurements, land utilization, land ownership, and real estate law.

Forms of Ownership

In Chapter 2, we looked at the land from a physical standpoint: the size and shape of a parcel, where it is located, and what was affixed to it. In Chapter 3, we explored various legal rights of interest that can be held in land. In Chapter 4, we will look at how a given right or interest in land is held by one or more individuals. It covers such topics as sole ownership, tenants in common, joint tenancy, tenancy by the entirety, and community property.

Sole Ownership

When title to property is held by one person, it is called an **estate in severalty**, or **sole ownership**. Although the word *severalty* seems to imply that several persons own a single property, the correct meaning can be easily remembered by thinking of "severed" ownership. Sole ownership is available to single and married persons, although the nature of ownership can vary, depending on an individual state's marital property laws. Businesses usually hold title to property in severalty. It is from the estate in severalty that all other tenancies are created.

The major advantage of sole ownership for an individual is flexibility. As a sole owner you can make all the decisions regarding a property without having to get the agreement of co-owners. You can decide what property or properties to buy, when to buy, and how much to offer. You can decide whether to pay all cash or to seek a loan by using the property as collateral. Once bought, you control (within the bounds of the law) how the property will be used, how much will be charged if it is rented, and how it will be managed. If you decide to sell, you alone decide when to offer the property for sale and at what price and terms.

LEARNING OBJECTIVES

After reading this chapter, you should be able to:

❮ Recognize the different types of ownership recognized in the law and differences between each.

❮ Understand the difference between individual ownerships in property versus those of business entities in property.

❮ Understand the difference in liability issues between the various ownership theories and the ability to insulate some of those liabilities by choosing a proper ownership entity.

❮ Understand the role of various entities and controlling business ownership (i.e., who has the authority to sign documents, etc.).

KEY TERMS

Concurrent ownership • Estate in severalty • Joint tenancy • Limited liability company • Limited partnership • Partnership • Right of survivorship • Tenancy by the entirety • Tenants in common • Undivided interest

estate in severalty
Owned by one person; sole ownership.

But freedom and responsibility go together. For example, if you purchase a rental property, you must determine the prevailing rents, find tenants, prepare contracts, collect the rent, and keep the property in repair; or, you must hire and pay someone else to manage the property. Another deterrent to sole ownership is the high entry cost. This form of real estate ownership is usually not possible for someone with only a few hundred dollars to invest.

Let's now turn to methods of **concurrent ownership**—that is, ownership by two or more persons at the same time.

Tenants in Common

When two or more persons wish to share the ownership of a single property, they may do so as **tenants in common**. As tenants in common, each owns an **undivided interest** in the whole property. This means that each owner has a right to possession of the entire property. None can exclude the others nor claim any specific portion for himself. In a tenancy in common, these interests need not be the same size, and each owner can independently sell, mortgage, give away, or devise his individual interest. This independence is possible because each tenant in common has a separate legal title to his undivided interest.

Suppose that you invest $20,000 along with two of your friends, who invest $30,000 and $50,000, respectively; together you buy 100 acres of land as tenants in common. Presuming that everyone's ownership interest is proportional to his or her cash investment, you will hold a 20% interest in the entire 100 acres and your two friends will hold 30% and 50%. You cannot pick out 20 acres and exclude the other co-owners from them, nor can you pick out 20 acres and say, "These are mine and I'm going to sell them"; nor can they do that to you. You do, however, have the legal right to sell or otherwise dispose of your 20% interest (or a portion of it) without the permission of your two friends. Your friends have the same right. If one of you sells, the purchaser becomes a new tenant in common with the remaining co-owners.

WORDING OF CONVEYANCE

As a rule, a tenancy in common is indicated by naming the co-owners in the conveyance and adding the words *as tenants in common*. For example, a deed might read, "Samuel Smith, John Jones, and Robert Miller, as tenants in common." If nothing is said regarding the size of each co-owner's interest in the property, the law presumes that all interests are equal. Therefore, if the co-owners intend their interests to be unequal, the size of each co-owner's undivided interest must be stated as a percent or a fraction, such as 60% and 40% or one-third and two-thirds.

In nearly all states, if two or more persons are named as owners, and there is no specific indication as to how they are taking title, they are presumed to be tenants in common. Thus, if a deed is made out to "Donna Adams and Barbara Kelly," the law would consider them to be tenants in common, each holding an undivided one-half interest in the property. An important exception to this presumption is when the co-owners are married to each other. In this case, they may be automatically considered to be taking ownership as joint tenants, tenants by the entirety, or community property, depending on state law.

NO RIGHT OF SURVIVORSHIP

When a tenancy in common exists, if a co-owner dies, his interest passes to his heirs or devisees, who then become tenants in common with the remaining co-owners. There is no **right of survivorship**—that is, the remaining co-owners do not acquire the deceased's

concurrent ownership

Ownership by two or more persons at the same time.

tenants in common

Shared ownership of a single property among two or more persons; interests need not be equal, and no right of survivorship exists.

undivided interest

Ownership by two or more persons that gives each the right to use the entire property.

right of survivorship

A feature of joint tenancy whereby the surviving joint tenants automatically acquire all the rights, title, and interest of the deceased joint tenant.

interest unless they are named in the deceased's last will and testament to do so. When a creditor has a claim on a co-owner's interest and forces its sale to satisfy the debt, the new buyer becomes a tenant in common with the remaining co-owners. If one co-owner wants to sell (or give away) only a portion of his undivided interest, he may; the new owner becomes a tenant in common with the other co-owners.

CO-OWNER RESPONSIBILITIES

Any income generated by the property belongs to the tenants in common in proportion to the size of their interests. Similarly, each co-owner is responsible for paying his proportionate share of property taxes, repairs, upkeep, and so on, plus interest and debt repayment, if any. If any co-owner fails to contribute his proportionate share, the other co-owners can pay on his behalf and then sue him for that amount. If co-owners find that they cannot agree as to how the property is to be run and cannot agree on a plan for dividing or selling it, it is possible to request a court-ordered partition. A **partition** divides the property into distinct portions so that each person can hold his proportionate interest in severalty. If this is physically impossible, such as when three co-owners each have a one-third interest in a house, the court will order the property sold and the proceeds divided among the co-owners.

"WHAT IFS"

The major advantage of tenancy in common is that it allows two or more persons to achieve goals that one person could not accomplish alone. However, prospective co-owners should give advance thought to what they will do (short of going to court): (1) if a co-owner fails to pay his share of ownership expenses, (2) if differences arise regarding how the property is to be operated, (3) if agreement cannot be reached as to when to sell, for how much, and on what terms, and (4) if a co-owner dies and those who inherit his interest have little in common with the surviving co-owners. The counsel of an attorney experienced in property ownership can be very helpful when considering the co-ownership of property.

Joint Tenancy

Another form of concurrent ownership is **joint tenancy**. The most distinguishing characteristic of joint tenancy is the right of survivorship. Upon the death of a joint tenant, his interest does not descend to his heirs or pass by his will. Rather, the entire ownership remains in the surviving joint tenant(s). In other words, there is simply one less owner.

joint tenancy
A form of property co-ownership that features the right of survivorship.

FOUR UNITIES

To create a joint tenancy, **four unities** must be present. They are the unities of time, title, interest, and possession.

Unity of time means that each joint tenant must acquire his or her ownership interest at the same moment. Once a joint tenancy is formed, it is not possible to add new joint tenants later unless an entirely new joint tenancy is formed among the existing co-owners and the new co-owner. To illustrate, suppose that A, B, and C own a parcel of land as joint tenants. If A sells her interest to D, then B, C, and D must sign documents to create a new joint tenancy among them. If this is not done, D automatically becomes a tenant in common with B and C who, between themselves, remain joint tenants. D will then own an undivided one-third interest in common with B and C, who will own an undivided two-thirds interest as joint tenants.

Unity of title means that the joint tenants acquire their interests from the same source—that is, the same deed or will. (Some states allow a property owner to create a valid joint tenancy by conveying to himself, or herself, and another without going through a third party.)

Unity of interest means that the joint tenants own one interest together and each joint tenant has exactly the same right in that interest. (This, by the way, is the foundation upon which the survivorship feature rests.) If the joint tenants list individual interests, they lack unity of interest and will be treated as tenants in common. Unity of interest also means that if one joint tenant holds a fee simple interest in the property, the others cannot hold anything but a fee simple interest.

Unity of possession means that the joint tenants must enjoy the same undivided possession of the whole property. All joint tenants have the use of the entire property, and no individual owns a particular portion of it. By way of contrast, unity of possession is the only unity essential to a tenancy in common.

RIGHT OF SURVIVORSHIP

The feature of joint tenancy ownership that is most widely recognized is its right of survivorship. Upon the death of a joint tenant, that interest in the property is extinguished. In a two-person joint tenancy, when one person dies, the other immediately becomes the sole owner. With more than two persons as joint tenants, when one dies, the remaining joint tenants are automatically left as owners. Ultimately, the last survivor becomes the sole owner. The legal philosophy is that the joint tenants constitute a single owning unit. The death of one joint tenant does not destroy that unit—it only reduces the number of persons owning the unit. For the public record, a copy of the death certificate and an affidavit of death of the joint tenant are recorded in the county where the property is located. The property must also be released from any estate tax liens.

It is the right of survivorship that has made joint tenancy a popular form of ownership among married couples. Married couples often want the surviving spouse to have sole ownership of the marital property. Any property held in joint tenancy goes to the surviving spouse without the delay of probate and usually with less legal expense.

"POOR MAN'S WILL"

Because of the survivorship feature, joint tenancy has loosely been labeled a "poor man's will." However, it cannot replace a properly drawn will as it affects only that property held in joint tenancy. Moreover, a will can be changed if the persons named therein are no longer in one's favor. But once a joint tenancy is formed, title is permanently conveyed and there is no further opportunity for change. As a joint tenant, you cannot will your joint tenancy interest to someone because your interest ends upon your death. Also, be aware that ownership in joint tenancy may result in additional estate taxes.

Another important aspect of joint tenancy ownership is that it can be used to defeat dower or curtesy rights. If a married man forms a joint tenancy with someone other than his wife (such as a business partner) and then dies, his wife has no dower rights in that joint tenancy. As a result, courts have begun to look with disfavor upon the right of survivorship. Louisiana, Ohio, and Oregon either do not recognize joint tenancy or have abolished it. Of the remaining states that recognize joint tenancy ownership (see Table 4.1), 14 have abolished the automatic presumption of survivorship. In these states, if the right of survivorship is desired in a joint tenancy, it must be clearly stated in the conveyance. For example, a deed might read, "Karen Carson and Judith Johnson, as joint tenants with the right of survivorship and not as tenants in common." Even in those states not requiring

TABLE 4.1	Concurrent Ownership by States

	L.L.P.*	L.L.C.**	Tenancy in common	Joint tenancy	Tenancy by the entirety	Community property		L.L.P.*	L.L.C.**	Tenancy in common	Joint tenancy	Tenancy by the entirety	Community property
Alabama	X	X	X	X			Missouri	X	X	X	X	X	
Alaska	X	X	X		X	X	Montana	X	X	X	X		
Arizona	X	X	X	X		X	Nebraska	X	X	X	X		
Arkansas	X	X	X	X	X		Nevada	X	X	X	X		X
California	X	X	X	X		X	New Hampshire	X	X	X	X		
Colorado	X	X	X	X			New Jersey	X	X	X	X	X	
Connecticut	X	X	X	X			New Mexico	X	X	X	X		X
Delaware	X	X	X	X	X		New York	X	X	X	X	X	
District of Columbia	X	X	X	X	X		North Carolina	X	X	X	X	X	
							North Dakota	X	X	X	X		
							Ohio	X	X	X			
Florida	X	X	X	X	X		Oklahoma	X	X	X	X	X	
							Oregon	X	X	X		X	
Georgia	X	X	X	X									
							Pennsylvania	X	X	X	X	X	
Hawaii	X	X	X	X	X								
							Rhode Island	X	X	X	X	X	
Idaho	X	X	X	X		X							
Illinois	X	X	X	X	X		South Carolina	X	X	X	X		
Indiana	X	X	X	X	X		South Dakota	X	X	X	X		
Iowa	X	X	X	X	X								
							Tennessee	X	X	X	X	X	
Kansas	X	X	X	X			Texas	X	X	X	X		X
Kentucky	X	X	X	X	X								
							Utah	X	X	X	X		
Louisiana	X	X				X							
							Vermont	X	X	X	X	X	
Maine	X	X	X	X			Virginia	X	X	X	X	X	
Maryland	X	X	X	X	X								
Massachusetts	X	X	X	X	X		Washington	X	X	X	X		X
Michigan	X	X	X	X	X		West Virginia	X	X	X	X		
Minnesota	X	X	X	X			Wisconsin	X	X	X	X		X
Mississippi	X	X	X	X	X		Wyoming	X	X	X	X	X	

*Limited Liability Partnership
**Limited Liability Company

In Ohio and Oregon, other means are available to achieve rights of survivorship between nonmarried persons. When two or more persons own property together in Louisiana, it is termed an "ownership in indivision" or a "joint ownership." Louisiana law is based on an old French civil law.

Source: © 2014 OnCourse Learning

it, this wording is often used to ensure that the right of survivorship is intended. In community property states, one spouse cannot take community funds and establish a valid joint tenancy with a third party.

There is a popular misconception that a debtor can protect himself from creditors' claims by taking title to property as a joint tenant. It is generally true that in a joint tenancy, the surviving joint tenant(s) acquire(s) the property free and clear of any liens against the deceased. However, this can happen only if the debtor dies before the creditor seizes the debtor's interest.

Only a human being can be a joint tenant. A corporation cannot be a joint tenant. This is because a corporation is an artificial legal being and can exist in perpetuity—that is, never die. Joint tenancy ownership is not limited to the ownership of land; any estate in land and any chattel interest may be held in joint tenancy.

Tenancy by the Entirety

tenancy by the entirety

A form of joint ownership reserved for married persons; right of survivorship exists, and neither spouse has a disposable interest during the lifetime of the other.

Tenancy by the entirety (also called *tenancy by the entireties*) is a form of joint tenancy specifically for married persons. To the four unities of a joint tenancy is added a fifth: **unity of person**. The basis for this is the legal premise that a husband and wife are an indivisible legal unit. Two key characteristics of a tenancy by the entirety are: (1) the surviving spouse becomes the sole owner of the property upon the death of the other, and (2) neither spouse has a disposable interest in the property during the lifetime of the other. Thus, while both are alive and married to each other, both signatures are necessary to convey title to the property. With respect to the first characteristic, tenancy by the entirety is similar to joint tenancy because both feature the right of survivorship. They are quite different, however, with respect to the second characteristic. Whereas a joint tenant can convey to another party without approval of the other joint tenant(s), a tenancy by the entirety can be terminated only by joint action of (or joint judgment against) husband and wife.

States that recognize tenancy by the entirety are listed in Table 4.1. Some of these states automatically assume that a tenancy by the entirety is created when married persons buy real estate. However, it is best to use a phrase such as "John and Mary Smith, husband and wife as tenants by the entirety with the right of survivorship" on deeds and other conveyances. This avoids later questions as to whether their intention might have been to create a joint tenancy or a tenancy in common.

ADVANTAGES AND DISADVANTAGES

There are several important advantages to tenancy by the entirety ownership: (1) it protects against one spouse conveying or mortgaging the couple's property without the consent of the other, (2) it provides, in many states, some protection from the forced sale of jointly held property to satisfy a debt judgment against one of the spouses, and (3) it features automatic survivorship. Disadvantages are that: (1) tenancy by the entirety provides for no one except the surviving spouse, (2) it may create estate tax problems, and (3) it does not replace the need for a will to direct how the couple's personal property shall be disposed.

EFFECT OF DIVORCE

In the event of divorce, the parting spouses become tenants in common. This change is automatic, as tenancy by the entirety can exist only when the co-owners are husband and wife. If the ex-spouses do not wish to continue co-ownership, either can sell his or her individual interest. If a buyer cannot be found for a partial interest, nor an amicable agreement can be reached for selling the interests of both ex-spouses simultaneously, either may seek a court action to partition the property.

Note that severalty, tenancy in common, joint tenancy, and tenancy by the entirety are called English common law estates because of their historical roots in English common law.

Community Property

Laws and customs acquired from Spain and France, when vast areas of the United States were under their control, are the basis for the community property system of ownership for married persons. Table 4.1 identifies the ten states that recognize community property. The laws of each community property state vary slightly, but the underlying concept is that the husband and wife contribute jointly and equally to their marriage, and should share equally in any property purchased during marriage. Whereas English law is based on the merging of husband's and wife's interests upon marriage, community property law treats husband and wife as equal partners, with each owning a one-half interest.

SEPARATE PROPERTY

Property owned before marriage and property acquired after marriage by gift, inheritance, or purchase with separate funds, can be exempted from the couple's community property. Such property is called **separate property**, and can be conveyed or mortgaged without the signature of the owner's spouse. The owner of separate property also has full control over naming someone in his or her will to receive the property. All other property acquired by the husband or wife during marriage is considered community property, and requires the signature of both spouses before it can be conveyed or mortgaged. Each spouse can name in his or her will the person to receive his or her one-half interest. It does not have to go to the surviving spouse. If death occurs without a will, in six states (California, Idaho, Nevada, New Mexico, Texas, and Washington) the deceased spouse's interest goes to the surviving spouse. In Arizona and Louisiana, the descendants of the deceased spouse are the prime recipients. Texas also allows community property to be held with a right of survivorship. Neither dower nor curtesy exists in community property states.

PHILOSOPHY

The major advantage of the community property system is found in its philosophy: It treats the spouses as equal partners in property acquired through their mutual efforts during marriage. Even if the wife elects to be a full-time homemaker and all the money brought into the household is the result of her husband's job (or vice versa), the law treats them as equal co-owners in any property bought with that money. This is true even if only one spouse is named as the owner.

In the event of divorce, if the parting couple cannot amicably decide how to divide their community property, the courts will do so. If the courts do not, the ex-spouses will become tenants in common with each other. If it later becomes necessary, either can file suit for partition.

CAVEAT TO AGENTS

Often, while preparing a real estate purchase contract, the buyers will ask the real estate agent how to take title. This is an especially common question posed by married couples purchasing a home. If the agent attempts to answer with a specific recommendation, the agent is practicing law, and that requires a license to practice law. The agent can describe the ownership methods available in the state, but should then refer the buyers to their lawyer for a specific recommendation. This is important because the choice of ownership method cannot be made in the vacuum of a single purchase. It must be made in the light of the buyers' total financial picture and estate plans, by someone well-versed in federal, state estate, and tax laws.

Partnership

partnership

Two or more persons engaged in a business for profit.

A **partnership** exists when two or more persons, as partners, unite their property, labor, and skill as a business to share the profits and losses created by it. The agreement between the partners need not be formal and may be oral or written.

The partners may hold the partnership property either in their own names or in the name of the partnership (which would hold title in severalty). For convenience, especially in a large partnership, the partners may designate two or three of their group to make contracts and sign documents on behalf of the entire partnership. There are three types of partnerships: general partnerships made up entirely of general partners, limited partnerships composed of general and limited partners, and joint ventures.

GENERAL PARTNERSHIP

The **general partnership** is an outgrowth of common law. However, to introduce clarity and uniformity into general partnership laws across the United States, 49 states and the District of Columbia have adopted the **Uniform Partnership Act**, either in total or with local modifications. (The exception is Louisiana.) Briefly, the highlights of the act are that: (1) title to partnership property may be held in the partnership's name, (2) each partner has an equal right of possession of partnership property—but only for partnership purposes, (3) upon the death of one partner, his rights in the partnership property go to the surviving partners—but the deceased's estate must be reimbursed for the value of his interest in the partnership, (4) a partner's right to specific partnership property is not subject to dower or curtesy, and (5) partnership property can only be attached by creditors for debts of the partnership, not for debts of a partner.

As a form of property ownership, the partnership is a method of combining the capital and expertise of two or more persons. It is equally important to note that the profits and losses of the partnership are taxable directly to each individual partner in proportion to his or her interest in the partnership. Although the partnership files a tax return, it is only for informational purposes. The partnership itself does not pay taxes. Negative aspects of this form of ownership center around financial liability, illiquidity, and, in some cases, management.

Financial liability means that each partner is personally responsible for all the debts of the partnership. Thus, each general partner can lose not only what he has invested in the partnership, but more, up to the full extent of his personal financial worth. In addition, each partner is an agent of, and can bind, the partnership in the normal course of business. If one partner makes a commitment on behalf of the partnership, all partners are responsible for making good on that commitment. If the partnership is sued, each partner is fully responsible. **Illiquidity** refers to the possibility that it may be very difficult to sell one's partnership interest on short notice in order to raise cash. **Management** means that each general partner is expected to take an active part in the operation of the partnership.

LIMITED PARTNERSHIP

Because of the potential for unlimited financial liability and management responsibility, an alternative partnership form, the **limited partnership**, has developed. Forty-nine states, plus the District of Columbia, have adopted the **Revised Uniform Limited Partnership Act**. The only exception is Louisiana, which has its own general and limited partnership laws. The limited partnership acts recognize the legality of limited partnerships and require that a limited partnership be formed by a written document.

A limited partnership is composed of general and limited partners. The **general partners** organize and operate the partnership, contribute some capital, and agree to accept the full financial liability of the partnership. The **limited partners** provide the bulk of the investment capital, have little say in the day-to-day management of the partnership, share in the profits and losses, and contract with their general partners to limit the financial liability of each limited partner to the amount he or she invests. Additionally, a well-written partnership agreement will allow for the continuity of the partnership in the event of the death of a general or limited partner.

The advantages of limited liability, minimum management responsibility, and direct pass-through of profits and losses for taxation purposes have made this form of ownership popular. However, being free of management responsibility is only advantageous to the investors if the general partners are capable and honest. If they are not, the only control open to the limited partners is to vote to replace the general partners. A limited partner should be cautioned, however, not to get too involved in the management of a limited partnership. If a limited partner becomes so involved, he may become a general partner by operation of law and have more liability than he bargained for!

Before investing in a limited partnership, one should investigate the past record of the general partners, for this is usually a good indication of how the new partnership will be managed. The investigation should include their previous investments, checking court records for any legal complaints brought against them, and talking to past investors. Additionally, the prospective partner should be prepared to stay in for the duration of the partnership, as the resale market for limited partnership interests is small.

Limited partnerships are a popular method of investing in real estate. The general partners find property, organize and promote the partnership, and invite people to invest money to become limited partners. Such a partnership can be as small as a dozen or so investors, or as large as the multimillion-dollar partnerships marketed nationally by major stock brokerage firms. If a limited partnership consists of more than a few close friends, registration with state and federal securities agencies is required before it can be sold to investors.

> **limited partnership**
> Composed of general partners who mainly organize and operate the partnership, and limited partners who provide the capital.

LIMITED LIABILITY PARTNERSHIPS

In response to the owners' joint and several liability of general partnerships, the majority of state legislatures have now enacted another form of partnership called the **limited liability partnership (LLP)**. This form of ownership attempts to limit the liability of its general partner from the misconduct of other general partners. For instance, in a law firm or a brokerage firm organized as a general partnership, all the general partners have the right to bind the partnership and all the general partners have a 100% liability for partnership obligations. The limited liability partnership, however, limits the liability of a partner, so that if one partner commits malfeasance or malpractice (for example, a partner in the tax section of the law firm), it would not create liability for a partner in the real estate section of that law firm. Only the partners who have direct supervisory control over the conduct will have the liability for it. Note that many large law firms now have LLP behind their names. In the states that have enabled LLP, the partnership must register with the secretary of state and carry a specified amount of professional liability insurance coverage.

JOINT VENTURE

A **joint venture** is a partnership to carry out a single business project. A joint venture is treated as a partnership for tax purposes. Examples of joint ventures in real estate are the purchase of land by two or more persons with the intent of grading it and selling it as lots, the association of a landowner and builder to build and sell, and the association of a lender and builder to purchase land and develop buildings on it to sell to investors. Each member of the joint venture makes a contribution in the form of capital or talent, and all have a strong incentive to make the joint venture succeed. If more than one project is undertaken, the relationship becomes more like a general partnership than a joint venture.

Corporations

Each state has passed laws to permit groups of people to create **corporations** that can buy, sell, own, and operate in the name of the corporation. The corporation, in turn, is owned by stockholders who possess shares of stock as evidence of their ownership.

Because the corporation is an entity (or legal being) in the eyes of the law, the corporation must pay income taxes on its profits. What remains after taxes can be used to pay dividends to the stockholders, who in turn pay personal income taxes on their dividend income. This double taxation of profits is the most important negative factor in the corporate form of ownership. On the positive side, the entity aspect shields the investor from unlimited liability. Even if the corporation falls on the hardest of financial times and owes more than it owns, the worst that can happen to the stockholder is that the value of his stock will drop to zero. Another advantage is that shares of stock are much more liquid than any previously discussed form of real estate ownership, even sole ownership. Stockbrokers who specialize in the purchase and sale of corporate stock usually complete a sale in a week or less. Furthermore, shares of stock in most corporations sell for less than $100, thus enabling an investor to operate with small amounts of capital. In a corporation, the stockholders elect a board of directors, who in turn hire the management needed to run the day-to-day operations of the company. As a practical matter, however, unless a person is a major shareholder in a corporation, there is little control over management. The alternative is to buy stock in firms where one likes the management and sell where one does not.

S CORPORATIONS

Several large real estate corporations are traded on the New York Stock Exchange, and the corporation is a popular method of organization for real estate brokers and developers. Nevertheless, most real estate investors shun corporations because of the double taxation feature and because the tax benefits of owning real estate are trapped inside the corporation.

In 1958, the Internal Revenue Code first allowed **Subchapter S** corporations that provided the liability protection of a corporation with the profit-and-loss pass-through of a partnership. Although the original 10-stockholder maximum was a drawback, the real problem for real estate investors was that no more than 20% of a Subchapter S's gross receipts could come from passive income. Rent is also passive income. In October 1982, Congress revised the rules and eliminated the passive income restriction, increased the maximum number of shareholders to 75, and changed the name to **S corporations**. (Regular corporations are now called C corporations.)

CAVEAT

A caution should be noted in utilizing the corporate entity. While the foregoing discussion generally presumes a typical publicly held corporation, the laws in various states have enabled certain creditors to pierce corporate veils (find individual liability for owners, directors, and shareholders) when the corporation has been fraudulently created, was undercapitalized, or has been involved in dishonest activities. Simply incorporating, by itself, does not insulate all forms of liability, and legal counsel should be consulted, as general presumptions do not apply in every circumstance.

Trusts

In all states, the trust form of ownership can be used to provide for the well-being of another person. Basically, this is an arrangement whereby title to real and/or personal property is transferred by its owner (the **trustor**) to a trustee. The **trustee** holds title and manages the property for the benefit of another (the **beneficiary**) in accordance with instructions given by the trustor. Trust forms include the inter vivos trust (also called a living trust), the testamentary trust, land trusts, and real estate investment trusts.

INTER VIVOS AND TESTAMENTARY TRUSTS

An **inter vivos trust** takes effect during the life of its creator. For example, you can transfer property to a trustee with instructions that it be managed and that income from the trust assets be paid to your children, spouse, relatives, or a charity.

A **testamentary trust** takes effect after death. For example, you could place instructions in your will that upon your death, your property is to be placed into a trust. You can name whomever you want as trustee (a bank or trust company or friend, for example) and whom you want as beneficiaries. You can also give instructions as to how the assets are to be managed and how much (and how often) to pay the beneficiaries. Because trusts provide property management and financial control, as well as a number of tax and estate planning advantages, this form of property ownership is growing in popularity.

LAND TRUSTS

In several states, an owner of real estate may create a trust wherein he is both the trustor and the beneficiary. Called a **land trust**, the landowner conveys his real property to a trustee, who in turn manages the property according to the beneficiary's (owner's) instructions. Since the beneficial interest created by the trust is considered personal property, the land trust effectively converts real property to personal property. Originally, the land trust gained popularity because true ownership could be cloaked in secrecy behind the name of a bank's trust department. Today, however, its popularity is also due to the simplified probate procedures available to a person who lives in one state and owns land in another. The land trust is also a useful vehicle for group ownership and is not subject to legal attachment like real property.

REAL ESTATE INVESTMENT TRUSTS

The idea of creating a trust that in turn carries out the investment objectives of its investors is not new. In 1961, Congress passed a law allowing trusts that specialize in real estate investments to avoid double taxation by following strict rules. These **real estate investment trusts** (REITs) pool the money of many investors for the purchase of real estate, much as mutual funds do with stocks and bonds. Investors in a REIT are called **beneficiaries**, and they purchase **beneficial interests** somewhat similar to shares of corporate stock. The trust officers, with the aid of paid advisors, buy, sell, mortgage, and operate real estate investments on behalf of the beneficiaries. If a REIT confines its activities to real estate investments, and if the REIT has at least 100 beneficiaries and distributes at least 95% of its net income every year, the Internal Revenue Service will collect tax on the distributed income only once—at the beneficiaries' level. Failure to follow the rules results in double taxation.

The REIT is an attempt to combine the advantages of the corporate form of ownership with single taxation status. Like stock, the beneficial interests are freely transferable and usually sell for $100 each or less, a distinct advantage for the investor with a small amount of money to invest in real estate. Beneficial interests in the larger REITs are sold on a national basis, thus enabling a REIT to have thousands of beneficiaries and millions of dollars of capital for real estate purchases.

Limited Liability Companies

There has been legitimate, and probably justified, concern over liabilities of defendants in a business environment. One understands that if a person is harmed, there should be an ability to recover from the wrongdoer, yet many juries are awarding significant sums of money, and attempt to pursue personal liability for officers and directors of corporations because of their duties of care in the business entity (including real estate brokers!). At this time, at least 30 states have adopted legislation of historical significance by passing laws providing for the existence of a **limited liability company** (LLC). There will be a lot of case law and perhaps amendments to the statutes forthcoming in the next few years.

limited liability company

Organization of members or managers with little formal organization and limited liability.

Any person who is 18 years of age or older can act as an organizer of a limited liability company by signing the articles of organization of such limited liability company and giving the original copy of the articles to the department of the state responsible for company registrations. The state then issues a certificate of organization, and the existence of the limited liability company begins at that time.

The limited liability company name must include the word *limited* or the abbreviation *Ltd.* or *LC.* It must maintain a registered office and registered agent (similar to a corporation), and all real or personal property owned or purchased by the limited liability company shall be held and owned, and the conveyance shall be made, in the name of the limited liability company. All instruments and documents providing for the acquisition, mortgage, or disposition of the limited liability company shall be valid and binding upon the company if they are executed by one or more persons acting as manager or member (if the management of the limited liability company is retained by the members).

In general terms, a member or manager of a limited liability company is not liable for debts, obligations, or liabilities of a limited liability company. A membership interest is considered to be personal property and the member has no interest in specific limited liability company property. Please note that the limited liability companies are not corporations, partnerships, or limited partnerships. They are a totally new theory of ownership, and, as stated previously, there is a lot of law yet to be made in this area. Figure 4.1 provides a visual summary of the various forms of ownership described in this chapter.

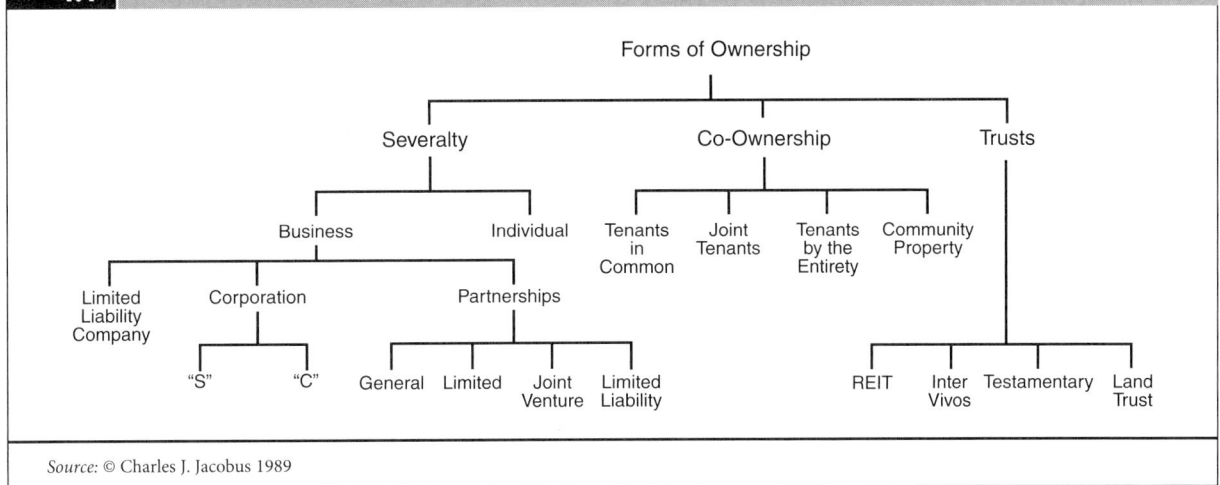

FIGURE 4.1 Holding Title

Source: © Charles J. Jacobus 1989

SERIES LLC

There has been a frequent concern by investors as to whether or not they should put each of their investments in a separate LLC to get the maximum insulation of liability, allowing each investment to stand on its own, such that if one investment is bad it doesn't affect the other investment. Forming a limited liability company for each investment may be very expensive in the long run.

Many states have addressed this issue by creating a new form of LLC called a "Series LLC." It allows an investor to hold assets and liabilities within separate investments as a separate "series" under the umbrella of one LLC. It is similar to a corporate structure with several subsidiaries, but the investor only has to incur the expense of setting up one LLC. If the investor chooses to be a series company, it must be specifically established in the formation documents with the secretary of state. This concept is similar to the limited liability partnership, which was previously discussed.

Syndication

Although you will often hear the word *syndication* used in such a way as to imply it is a form of ownership, it is not. In other words, there is no such thing as "tenancy by syndication." Rather, **syndication** is a broad term that simply refers to two or more individuals who have combined to pursue an investment enterprise too large for any of them to undertake individually. The form of ownership might be a tenancy in common, joint tenancy, general or limited partnership, joint venture, or a corporation. When people talk about a syndication in the context of real estate investing, it most likely refers to the real estate limited partnership.

Caution

The purpose of this chapter has been to acquaint you with the fundamental aspects of the most commonly used forms of real estate ownership in the United States. You undoubtedly saw instances where you could apply these. Unfortunately, it is not possible in a real estate principles book to discuss each detail of every state's law (many of which change frequently), nor to take into consideration the specific characteristics of a particular transaction. In applying the principles in this book to a particular transaction, you should obtain competent legal advice regarding your state's legal interpretation of these principles.

Vocabulary Review

Match terms a–q with statements 1–17.

a. Community property

b. Estate in severalty

c. Financial liability

d. General partnership

e. Joint tenancy

f. Joint venture

g. Limited partnership

h. Partition

i. Real estate investment trust (REIT)

j. Right of survivorship

k. Separate property

l. Syndication

m. Tenancy by the entirety

n. Tenants in common

o. Undivided interest

p. Unity of interest

q. Unity of time

_____ 1. Owned by only one person; sole ownership.

_____ 2. Each owner has a right to use the entire property.

_____ 3. Undivided ownership by two or more persons without right of survivorship; interests need not be equal.

_____ 4. The remaining co-owners automatically acquire the deceased's undivided interest.

_____ 5. A form of co-ownership in which the most widely recognized feature is the right of survivorship.

_____ 6. All co-owners have an identical interest in the property; a requirement for joint tenancy.

_____ 7. All co-owners acquired their ownership interests at the same time. A requirement for joint tenancy.

_____ 8. Spouses are treated as equal partners with each owning a one-half interest; French and Spanish law origin.

_____ 9. An English law form of ownership reserved for married persons. Right of survivorship exists and neither spouse has a disposable interest during the lifetime of the other.

_____ 10. Each partner is fully liable for all the debts and obligations of the partnership.

_____ 11. A member of a limited partnership whose financial liability is limited to the amount invested.

_____ 12. Two or more persons joining together on a single project as partners.

_____ 13. Property acquired before marriage in a community property state.

_____ 14. A type of mutual fund for real estate investment and ownership wherein a trustee holds property for the benefit of the beneficiaries.

_____ 15. A general term that refers to a group of persons who organize to pool their money.

_____ 16. Refers to the amount of money a person can lose.

_____ 17. To divide jointly held property so that each owner can hold a sole ownership.

Questions and Problems

1. What is the key advantage of sole ownership? What is the major disadvantage?

2. Explain what is meant by the term *undivided interest* as it applies to joint ownership of real estate.

3. Name the four unities of a joint tenancy. What requirements do they impose on the joint tenants?

4. What does the term *right of survivorship* mean in real estate ownership?

5. Suppose that a deed was made out to "John and Mary Smith, husband and wife" with no mention as to how they were taking title. Which would your state assume: joint tenancy, tenancy in common, tenancy by the entirety, or community property?

6. Does your state permit the right of survivorship among persons who are not married?

7. If a deed is made out to three women as follows: "Susan Miller, Rhoda Wells, and Angela Lincoln," with no mention as to the form of ownership or the interest held by each, what can we presume regarding the form of ownership and the size of each woman's ownership interest?

8. In a community property state, if a deed names only the husband (or the wife) as the owner, can we assume that only that person's signature is necessary to convey title? Why or why not?

9. List two ways in which a general partnership differs from a limited partnership.

10. What advantages does a real estate investment trust offer a person who wants to invest in real estate?

Additional Readings

The Edges of the Field: Lessons on the Obligations of Ownership by Joseph William Singer (Beacon Press, 2001).

"House Fight" by Jay Akasie (*Forbes*, June 14, 1999, vol. 163, issue 12, pp. 358–359).

Land Ownership and the Social System by Leland G. Stauber (Four Willows Press, 2002).

"Legacies of Possessions: Passing Property at Death" by Lawrence A. Frolik (*Generations*, Fall 1996, vol. 20, issue 3, pp. 9–12).

Property and Values: Alternatives to Public and Private Ownership by Charles C. Geisler and Gail Daneker (Island Press, 2000).

Trespassing: An Inquiry into the Private Ownership of Land by John Hanson Mitchell (DIANE Publishing Company, 2000).

Transferring Title

In this chapter, you will learn how the ownership of real estate is conveyed from one owner to another. Voluntary conveyance of real estate by deed, conveyance after death, conveyance by occupancy, accession, public grant, dedication, and forfeiture are covered. An important part of this chapter, and the part that you should review very carefully, is the coverage of the central elements of the deed. Likewise, the various covenants and warranties should be reviewed. In the previous three chapters we emphasized how real estate is described, the rights and interests available for ownership, and how title can be held. In this chapter, we shall discuss how ownership of real estate is conveyed from one owner to another.

LEARNING OBJECTIVES

After reading this chapter, you should be able to:

❮ Recognize the different types of deeds.

❮ Recognize the requirements of deeds.

❮ Determine the difference in types of deeds.

❮ Understand how conveyances made upon the death of a party by will.

❮ Understand the fundamentals of involuntary transfer such as adverse possession and easements by prescription.

❮ Understand the principles behind dedication of interests in real property.

KEY TERMS

Adverse possession • Bargain and sale deed • Cloud on the title • Color of title • Consideration • Covenant • Deed • Grantee • Grantor • Quitclaim deed • Special warranty deed • Warranty

Deeds

A **deed**, when properly executed and delivered, is a written legal document by which ownership of real property is conveyed from one party to another. Deeds were not always used to transfer real estate. In early England, when land was sold, its title was conveyed by inviting the purchaser onto the land. In the presence of witnesses, the seller picked up a clod of earth and handed it to the purchaser. Simultaneously, the seller stated that he was delivering ownership of the land to the purchaser. In times when land sales were rare, because ownership usually passed from generation to generation, and when witnesses seldom moved from the towns or farms where they were born, this method worked well. However, as transactions became more common and people more mobile, this method of title transfer became less reliable. Furthermore, it was susceptible to fraud if enough people could be bribed or forced to make false

deed
A written document that, when properly executed and delivered, conveys title to land.

statements. In 1677, England passed a law known as the **Statute of Frauds**. This law, subsequently adopted by each of the American states, requires that transfers of real estate ownership be in writing and signed in order to be enforceable in a court of law. Thus, the need for a deed was created.

ESSENTIAL ELEMENTS OF A DEED

grantor
The person named in a deed who conveys ownership.

grantee
The person named in a deed who acquires ownership.

consideration
Anything of value given to induce another to enter into a contract.

What makes a written document a deed? What special phrases, statements, and actions are necessary to convey the ownership rights one has in land and buildings? First, a deed must identify the **grantor**, who is the person giving up ownership; and the **grantee**, the person who is acquiring that ownership. The actual act of conveying ownership is known as a grant. To be legally enforceable, the grantor must be of legal age (18 years in most states) and of sound mind.

Second, the deed must state that **consideration** was given by the grantee to the grantor. It is common to see the phrase, *for ten dollars ($10) and other good and valuable consideration*, or the phrase, *for valuable consideration*. These meet the legal requirement that consideration be shown but retain privacy regarding the exact amount paid.

If the conveyance is a gift, the phrase *For natural love and affection* may be used, provided the gift is not for the purpose of defrauding the grantor's creditors. In these situations, consideration is not required in a deed, and the conveyance is still valid.

WORDS OF CONVEYANCE. Third, the deed must contain **words of conveyance**. With these words the grantor: (1) clearly states that he is making a grant of real property to the grantee, and (2) identifies the quantity of the estate being granted. Usually the estate is fee simple, but it may also be a lesser estate (such as a life estate) or an easement.

A **land description** that cannot possibly be misunderstood is the fourth requirement. Acceptable legal descriptions are made by the metes and bounds method, by the government survey system, by recorded plat, or by reference to another recorded document that, in turn, uses one of these methods. Street names and numbers are not used because they do not identify the exact boundaries of the land and because street names and numbers can change over time. Assessor parcel numbers are not used either. They are subject to change by the assessor, and the maps they refer to are for the purpose of collecting taxes. If the deed conveys only an easement or air right, the deed states that fact along with the legal description of the land. The key point is that a deed must clearly specify what the grantor is granting to the grantee.

SIGNATURE. Fifth, the grantor executes the deed by signing it. Some states require that the grantor's signature be witnessed and that the witnesses sign the deed. If the grantor is unable to write his name, he may make a mark, usually an X, in the presence of witnesses. They, in turn, print the grantor's name next to the X and sign as witnesses. If the grantor is a corporation, the corporation's seal may be affixed to the deed and the corporation's authorized officer signs it. More states are now also adopting their own versions of the federal "esign" legislation, which allows signatures or marks to be electronically encoded on the documents. Yes, this does supercede the Statute of Frauds when it requires an original signature.

Figure 5.1 illustrates the essential elements that combine to form a deed. Notice that the example includes an identification of the grantor and grantee; fulfills the requirement for consideration; and has words of conveyance, a legal description of the land involved, and the grantor's signature. The words of conveyance are *grant and release,* and the phrase *to have and to hold forever* says that the grantor is conveying all future benefits, not just a life estate or a tenancy for years. Ordinarily, the grantee does not sign the deed.

FIGURE 5.1	Essential Elements of a Deed

Witnesseth, <u>John Stanley</u>, grantor, for valuable consideration given by <u>Robert Brenner</u>, grantee, does hereby grant and release unto the grantee, his heirs and assigns to have and to hold forever, the following described land: [insert legal description here].

John Stanley
Grantor's signature

Source: © 2014 OnCourse Learning

DELIVERY AND ACCEPTANCE. For a deed to convey ownership, there must also be **delivery and acceptance**. Although a deed may be completed and signed, it does not transfer title to the grantee until the grantor voluntarily delivers it to the grantee and the grantee willingly accepts it. At that moment title passes. As a practical matter, the grantee is presumed to have accepted the deed if the grantee retains the deed, records the deed, encumbers the title, or performs any other act of ownership. This includes the grantee's appointment of someone else to accept and/or record the deed on the grantee's behalf. Once delivery and acceptance have occurred, the deed is evidence that the title transfer has taken place.

COVENANTS AND WARRANTIES

Although legally adequate, a deed meeting the preceding requirements can still leave a very important question unanswered in the grantee's mind: "Does the grantor possess all the right, title, and interest he is purporting to convey by this deed?" As a protective measure, the grantee can ask the grantor to include certain **covenants** and **warranties** in the deed. These are written promises by the grantor that the condition of title is as stated in the deed, together with the grantor's guarantee that if title is not as stated, he will compensate the grantee for any loss suffered. Five covenants and warranties have evolved over the centuries for use in deeds; and a deed may contain none, some, or all of them, in addition to the essential elements already discussed. They are seizin, quiet enjoyment, against encumbrances, further assurance, and warranty forever.

Under the **covenant of seizin** (sometimes spelled *seisin*), the grantor warrants (guarantees) that he is the owner and possessor of the property being conveyed and that he has the right to convey it. Under the **covenant of quiet enjoyment**, the grantor warrants to the grantee that the grantee will not be disturbed, after he takes possession, by someone else claiming an interest in the property.

In the **covenant against encumbrances**, the grantor guarantees to the grantee that the title is not encumbered with any easements, restrictions, unpaid property taxes, assessments, mortgages, judgments, and so on, except as stated in the deed. If the grantee later discovers an undisclosed encumbrance, he can sue the grantor for the cost of removing it. The **covenant of further assurance** requires the grantor to procure and deliver to the grantee any subsequent documents that might be necessary to make good the grantee's title. **Warranty forever** is a guarantee to the grantee that the grantor will bear the expense of defending the grantee's title. If at any time in the future someone else can prove that he

covenant
A written agreement or promise.

warranty
An assurance or guarantee that something is true as stated.

is the rightful owner, the grantee can sue the grantor for damages up to the value of the property at the time of the sale. Because these warranties and covenants are a formidable set of promises, grantors often back them up with title insurance (see Chapter 6). The grantee is also more comfortable if the deed is backed by title insurance.

DATE AND ACKNOWLEDGMENT. Although it is customary to show on the deed the *date* it is executed by the grantor, it is not essential to the deed's validity. Remember that title passes upon *delivery* of the deed to the grantee, and that this may not necessarily be the date it is signed.

It is standard practice to have the grantor appear before a notary public or other public officer and formally declare that he signed the deed as a voluntary act. This is known as an **acknowledgment**. Most states consider a deed to be valid even though it is not witnessed or acknowledged, but very few states will allow such a deed to be recorded in the public records. Acknowledgments and the importance of recording deeds will be covered in more detail in Chapter 6. Meanwhile, let us turn our attention to examples of the most commonly used deeds in the United States.

FULL COVENANT AND WARRANTY DEED

The **full covenant and warranty deed**, also known as the **general warranty deed** or **warranty deed**, contains all five covenants and warranties. It is thus considered to be the best deed a grantee can receive and is used extensively in most states.

Figure 5.2 illustrates in plain language the essential parts of a warranty deed. Beginning at [1], it is customary to identify at the top of the document that it is a warranty deed. At [2] the wording begins with *this deed....* These words are introductory in purpose. The fact that this is a deed depends on what it contains, not on what it is labeled. A commonly found variation starts with *this indenture* (meaning this agreement or contract) and is equally acceptable. The place the deed was made [3] and the date it was signed [4] are customarily included, but are not necessary to make the deed valid.

At [5] and [6] the grantor is identified by name and, to avoid confusion with other persons having the same name, by address. Marital status is also stated: husband and wife, single man, single woman, widow, or widower. To avoid the inconvenience of repeating the grantor's name each time it is needed, the wording at [7] states that in the balance of the deed the word *Grantor* will be used instead. Next appears the name and marital status of the *Grantee* [8] and the method by which title is being taken (severalty, tenants in common, joint tenants, etc.). The grantee's address appears at [9], and the wording at [10] states that the word *Grantee* will now be used instead of the grantee's name.

GRANTING CLAUSE. The legal requirement that consideration be shown is fulfilled at [11]. Next we come to the **granting clause** at [12]. Here the grantor states that the intent of this document is to pass ownership to the grantee, and at [13] the grantor describes the extent of the estate being granted. The phrase *The grantee's heirs and assigns forever* indicates a fee simple estate. The word *assigns* refers to anyone the grantee may later convey the property to, such as by sale or gift.

The legal description of the land involved is then shown at [14]. When a grantor is unable or does not wish to convey certain rights of ownership, he can list the exceptions here. For example, a grantor either not having or wishing to hold back oil and gas rights may convey to the grantee the land described, "except for the right to explore and recover oil and gas at a depth below 200 feet beneath the surface." The separate mention at numbers [15] and [16] of buildings, estate, and rights is not an essential requirement as the definition of land already includes these items. Some deed forms add the word

<table>
<tr><td>FIGURE
5.2</td><td>Example of a Warranty Deed</td></tr>
</table>

WARRANTY DEED [1]

[2]THIS DEED, made in the city of [3] <u>Exeter</u>, state of <u>XY</u> on the [4] <u>4th</u> day of <u>April</u>, 20 <u>xx</u>, between [5] <u>Adam Baum a single man</u>, residing at [6] <u>1234 Pleasant Rd., Exeter, XY</u>, herein called the GRANTOR, [7] and [8] <u>Ben A. Mandalay and wife, Anita Mandalay, husband and wife as tenants by the entirety</u>, residing at [9] <u>567 Friendly Lane, Exeter, XY</u>, herein called the GRANTEE. [10]

WITNESSETH that in consideration [11] of ten dollars ($10.00) and other valuable consideration, paid by the Grantee to the Grantor, the Grantor does hereby grant [12] and convey unto the Grantee, the Grantee's [13] heirs and assigns forever, the following described parcel of land:

[legal description of land][14]

together with the buildings [15] and improvements thereon and all the estate [16] and rights pertaining thereto, [17] TO HAVE AND TO HOLD the premises herein granted unto the Grantee, the Grantee's heirs [18] and assigns forever.

The premises are free from encumbrances except as stated herein:[19]

[note exceptions here]

The Grantee shall not:[20]

[list restrictions imposed by Grantor on the Grantee]

The Grantor is lawfully seized [21] of a good, absolute, and indefeasible estate in fee simple and has good right, full power, and lawful authority to convey the same by this deed.

The Grantee, the Grantee's heirs and assigns, shall peaceably [22] and quietly have, hold, use, occupy, possess, and enjoy the said premises.

The Grantor shall execute or procure any further [23] necessary assurance of the title to said premises, and the Grantor will forever [24] warrant and defend the title to said premises.

IN WITNESS WHEREOF, the Grantor has duly executed this deed the day and year first written above.[25]

[26] *Adam Baum*
   (Grantor's signature)

                              [location of the
                              acknowledgment:
[27](SEAL)   see Chapter 6][28]

appurtenances at [16]. Again, this is not essential wording as appurtenances by definition belong to and pass with the conveyance of the land unless specifically withheld by the grantor. Examples of real estate appurtenances are rights-of-way and other easements, water rights, condominium parking stalls, and improvements to land.

HABENDUM CLAUSE. The **habendum clause**, sometimes called the "To have and to hold clause," begins at [17] and continues through [18]. This clause, together with the statements at [12] and [13], forms the deed's words of conveyance. For this reason, the words at [18] must match those at [13]. Number [19] identifies the covenant against encumbrances. The grantor warrants that there are no encumbrances on the property except as listed here. The most common exceptions are property taxes, mortgages, and assessment (improvement district) bonds. For instance, a deed may recite, "Subject to an existing mortgage...," and name the mortgage holder and the original amount of the loan, or "Subject to a city sewer improvement district levy in the amount of $1,500."

At [20] the grantor may impose restrictions as to how the grantee may use the property. For example, "The grantee hereby agrees that grantee shall not build upon this land a home with less than 1,500 square feet of living space." If obligations are imposed on the grantee, the grantor may want the grantee to execute the deed, to acknowledge grantee's acceptance and agreement with its terms.

SPECIAL WORDING. The covenants of seizin and quiet enjoyment are located at [21] and [22], respectively. Number [23] identifies the covenant of further assurance, and at [24] the grantor agrees to warrant and defend forever the title he is granting. The order of grouping of the five covenants is not critical, and in some states there are laws that permit the use of two or three special words to imply the presence of all five covenants. For example, in Alaska, Illinois, Kansas, Michigan, Minnesota, and Wisconsin, if the grantor uses the words *convey and warrant*, he implies the five covenants even though the grantor does not list them in the deed. The words *warrant generally* accomplish the same purpose in Pennsylvania, Vermont, Virginia, and West Virginia, as do *grant*, *bargain*, and *sell* in the states of Arkansas, Florida, Idaho, Missouri, and Nevada.

At [25] the grantor states that he signed this deed on the date noted at [4]. This is the **testimony clause**; although customarily included in deeds, it is redundant and could be left out as long as the grantor signs the deed at [26]. Historically, a seal made with hot wax was essential to the validity of a deed. Today, those few states that require a seal [27] accept a hot wax seal, a glued paper seal, an embossed seal, or the word *seal* or *LS* The letters *LS* are an abbreviation for the Latin words *locus sigilli* (place of the seal). The acknowledgment is placed at [28], the full wording of which is given in Chapter 6. If an acknowledgment is not used, this space is used for the signatures of witnesses to the grantor's signature. Their names would be preceded by the words *In the presence of.*

DEED PREPARATION. The exact style or form of a deed is not critical as long as it contains all the essentials clearly stated and in conformity with state law. For example, one commonly used warranty deed format begins with the words *Know all men by these presents*, is written in the first person, and has the date at the end. Although a person may prepare his own deed, the writing of deeds should be left to experts in the field. In fact, some states permit only attorneys to write deeds for other persons. Even the preparation of preprinted deeds from stationery stores and title companies should be left to knowledgeable persons. Preprinted deeds contain several pitfalls for the unwary. First, the form may have been prepared and printed in another state and, as a result, may not meet the laws of your state. Second, if the blanks are incorrectly filled in, the deed may not accomplish its intended purpose. This is a particularly difficult problem when neither the grantor nor grantee realizes it until several years after the deed's delivery. Third, the use of a form deed presumes that the grantor's situation can be fitted to the form and that the grantor will be knowledgeable enough to select the correct form.

GRANT DEED

Some states, notably California, Idaho, and North Dakota, use a grant deed instead of a warranty deed. In a **grant deed**, the grantor covenants and warrants that: (1) he has not previously conveyed the estate being granted to another party, (2) he has not encumbered the property except as noted in the deed, and (3) he will convey to the grantee any title to the property he may later acquire. These covenants are fewer in number and narrower in coverage than those found in a warranty deed, particularly the covenant regarding encumbrances. In the warranty deed, the grantor makes himself responsible for the encumbrances of prior owners as well as his own. The grant deed limits the grantor's responsibility to the period of time he owned the property. Figure 5.3 summarizes the key elements of a California grant deed.

Referring to the numbers in Figure 5.3, [1] labels the document, [2] fulfills the requirement that consideration be shown, and [3] is for the name and marital status of the grantor. By California statutory law, the single word *GRANT(S)* at [4] is both the granting clause *and* habendum, *and* it implies the covenants and warranties of possession, prior encumbrances, and further title. Thus, they need not be individually listed.

Number [5] is for the name and marital status of the grantee and the method by which title is being taken. Numbers [6] and [7] identify the property being conveyed. Easements, property taxes, conditions, reservations, restrictions, and so on, are noted at [8]. The deed is dated at [9], signed at [10], and acknowledged at [11].

Why have grantees, in states with more than one-tenth of the total U.S. population, been willing to accept a deed with fewer covenants than a warranty deed? The primary reason is the early development and extensive use of title insurance in these states, whereby the grantor and grantee acquire an insurance policy to protect themselves if a

FIGURE 5.3 Example of a Grant Deed

GRANT DEED[1]

For a valuable [2] consideration, receipt of which is hereby acknowledged,

_____[3]_____ hereby GRANT(S) [4] to _____[5]_____
(name of grantor)   (name of the grantee)

the following described real property in _____[6]_____ ,
(city, town, etc.)

County of _____ , State of California:

[legal description of land here][7]

Subject to:

[note exceptions and restrictions here][8]

Dated _____[9]_____   _____[10]_____
(Grantor's signature)

[11] [location of the acknowledgment]

Source: © 2014 OnCourse Learning

flaw in ownership is later discovered. Title insurance is now available in all parts of the United States and is explained in Chapter 6.

SPECIAL WARRANTY DEED

**special
warranty deed**

Grantor warrants title only against defects occurring during the grantor's ownership.

In a **special warranty deed**, the grantor warrants the property's title only against defects occurring during the grantor's ownership and not against defects existing before that time. The special warranty deed is typically used by executors and trustees who convey on behalf of an estate or principal because the executor or trustee has no authority to warrant and defend the acts of previous holders of title. The grantee can protect against this gap in warranty by purchasing title insurance. The special warranty deed is also known in some states as a bargain and sale deed with a covenant against only the grantor's acts.

BARGAIN AND SALE DEED

**bargain and
sale deed**

A deed that contains no covenants but does imply that the grantor owns the property being conveyed.

The basic **bargain and sale deed** contains no covenants and only the minimum essentials of a deed (see Figure 5.4). It has a date, identifies the grantor and grantee, recites consideration, describes the property, contains words of conveyance, and has the grantor's signature. But lacking covenants, what assurance does the grantee have that he is

---

FIGURE 5.4   Example of a Bargain and Sale Deed

BARGAIN AND SALE DEED

THIS DEED made _____ , between _____ residing at
                    (date)

_____ , herein called the Grantor, and _____

residing at _____ , herein called the Grantee.

WITNESSETH, that the Grantor, in consideration of _____ ,
does hereby grant and release unto the Grantee, the Grantee's heirs, successors, and assigns forever, all that parcel of land described as

[legal description of land]

TOGETHER WITH the appurtenances and all the estate and rights of the Grantor in and to said property.

TO HAVE AND TO HOLD the premises herein granted together with the appurtenances unto the Grantee. This conveyance is made however, without any warranties, express, implied, or statutory.

IN WITNESS WHEREOF, the Grantor sets his hand and seal the day and year first written above.

_____ L.S.
        (Grantor)

[location of the acknowledgment]

Source: © 2014 OnCourse Learning

acquiring title to anything? Actually, none. In this deed, the grantor only implies that he owns the property described in the deed and that he is granting it to the grantee. Logically, then, a grantee will much prefer a warranty deed over a bargain and sale deed, or require title insurance.

QUITCLAIM DEED

A **quitclaim deed** has no covenants or warranties (see Figure 5.5). Moreover, the grantor makes no statement, nor does he even imply that he owns the property he is quitclaiming to the grantee. Whatever rights the grantor possesses at the time the deed is delivered are conveyed to the grantee. If the grantor has no interest, right, or title to the property described in the deed, none is conveyed to the grantee. However, if the grantor possesses fee simple title, fee simple title will be conveyed to the grantee.

The critical wording in a quitclaim deed is the grantor's statement that he *does hereby remise, release, and quitclaim forever. Quitclaim* means to renounce all possession, right, or interest. **Remise** means to give up any existing claim one may have, as does the word *release*. If the grantor subsequently acquires any right or interest in the property, he is not obligated to convey it to the grantee.

quitclaim deed
A legal instrument used to convey whatever title the grantor has; it contains no covenants, warranties, or implication of the grantor's ownership.

FIGURE 5.5   Example of Aquitclaim Deed

QUITCLAIM DEED

THIS DEED, made the _____ day of _____ , 20 _____ , BETWEEN

_____ of _____ , party of the first part, and

_____ of _____ , party of the second part.

WITNESSETH, that the party of the first part, in consideration of ten dollars ($10.00) and other valuable consideration, paid by the party of the second part, does hereby remise, release, and quitclaim unto the party of the second part, the heirs, successors, and assigns of the party of the second part forever.

ALL that certain parcel of land, with the buildings and improvements thereon, described as follows:

[legal description of land]

TOGETHER WITH the appurtenances and all the estate and rights of the Grantor in and to said property.

TO HAVE AND TO HOLD the premises herein granted unto the party of the second part, the heirs or successors and assigns of the party of the second part, forever.

IN WITNESS WHEREOF, the party of the first part has duly executed this deed the day and year first above written.

_____
(Grantor)

[location of the acknowledgment]

Source: © 2014 OnCourse Learning

At first glance it may seem strange that such a deed should even exist, but it does serve a very useful purpose. Situations often arise in real estate transactions when a person claims to have a partial or incomplete right or interest in a parcel of land. Such a right or interest, known as a **title defect** or **cloud on the title**, may have been due to an inheritance, dower, curtesy, or community property right, or to a mortgage or right of redemption because of a court-ordered foreclosure sale. By releasing that claim to the fee simple owner through the use of a quitclaim deed, the cloud on the fee owner's title is removed. A quitclaim deed can also be used to create an easement as well as release (extinguish) an easement. It can also be used to release remainder and reversion interests. It cannot be used to perpetuate a fraud, however.

cloud on the title

Any claim, lien, or encumbrance that impairs title to property.

OTHER TYPES OF DEEDS

A **gift deed** is created by simply replacing the recitation of money and other valuable consideration with the statement *in consideration of his [her, their] natural love and affection*. This phrase may be used in a warranty, special warranty, or grant deed. However, it is most often used in quitclaim or bargain and sale deeds, as these permit the grantor to avoid being committed to any warranties regarding the property.

A **guardian's deed** is used to convey a minor's interest in real property. It contains only one covenant, that the guardian and minor have not encumbered the property. The deed must state the legal authority (usually a court order) that permits the guardian to convey the minor's property.

Sheriff's deeds and **referee's deeds in foreclosure** are issued to the new buyer when a person's real estate is sold as the result of a mortgage or other court-ordered foreclosure sale. The deed should state the source of the sheriff's or referee's authority and the amount of consideration paid. Such a deed conveys only the foreclosed party's title, and, at the most, carries only one covenant: that the sheriff or referee has not damaged the property's title.

A **correction deed**, also called a deed of confirmation, is used to correct an error in a previously executed and delivered deed. For example, a name may have been misspelled or an error found in the property description. A quitclaim deed containing a statement regarding the error is used for this purpose. A **cession deed** is a form of a quitclaim deed wherein a property owner conveys street rights to a county or municipality. An **interspousal deed** is used in some states to transfer real property between spouses. A **tax deed** is used to convey title to real estate that has been sold by the government because of the nonpayment of taxes. A **deed of trust** may be used to convey real estate to a third party as security for a loan and is discussed in Chapter 10.

Conveyance after Death

If a person dies without leaving a last will and testament (or leaves one that is subsequently ruled void by the courts because it was improperly prepared), she is said to have died **intestate**, which means without a testament. When this happens, state law directs how the deceased's assets shall be distributed. This is known as a **title by descent**, or **intestate succession**. The surviving spouse and children are the dominant recipients of the deceased's assets. The deceased's grandchildren receive the next largest share, followed by the deceased's parents, brothers and sisters, and their children. These are known as the deceased's **heirs**, or, in some states, **distributees**. The amount each heir receives, if anything, depends on individual state law and on how many persons with superior positions in the succession are alive. If no heirs can be found, the deceased's property escheats (reverts) to the state.

TESTATE, INTESTATE

A person who dies and leaves a valid will is said to have died **testate**, which means that a testament with instructions for property disposal was left behind. The person who made the will is the **testator** (masculine) or **testatrix** (feminine). In the will, the testator names the persons or organizations who are to receive the testator's real and personal property. Real property that is willed is known as a **devise**, and the recipient, a **devisee**. Personal property that is willed is known as a **bequest** or **legacy**, and the recipient, a **legatee**. In the will, the testator usually names an **executor** (masculine) or **executrix** (feminine) to carry out the instructions. If one is not named, the court appoints an **administrator** or **administratrix**. In some states the person named in the will or appointed by the court to settle the estate is called a **personal representative**.

Notice an important difference between the transfer of real estate ownership by deed and by will: once a deed is made and delivered, the ownership transfer is permanent, the grantor cannot have a change of mind and take back the property. With respect to a will, the devisees, although named, have no rights to the testator's property until the testator dies. Until that time the testator is free to have a change of mind, revoke the old will, and write a new one.

PROBATE OR SURROGATE COURT

Upon death, the deceased's will must be filed with a court having power to admit and certify wills, usually called a **probate court** or **surrogate court**. This court determines whether the will meets all the requirements of law: in particular, that it is genuine, properly signed and witnessed, and that the testator was of sound mind when the will was made. At this time anyone may step forward and contest the validity of the will. If the court finds the will to be valid, the executor is permitted to carry out its terms. If the testator owned real property, its ownership is conveyed using an **executor's deed** prepared and signed by the executor. The executor's deed is used both to transfer title to a devisee and to sell real property to raise cash. It contains only one covenant, a covenant that the executor has not encumbered the property. An executor's deed is a special warranty deed.

PROTECTING THE DECEASED'S INTENTIONS

Because the deceased is not present, state laws attempt to ensure that fair market value is received for the deceased's real estate by requiring court approval of proposed sales, and, in some cases, by sponsoring open bidding in the courtroom. As protection, a purchaser should ascertain that the executor has the authority to convey title.

For a will to be valid, it must meet specific legal requirements. All states recognize the **formal** or **witnessed** will, a written document prepared in most cases by an attorney. The testator must declare it to be his or her will and sign it in the presence of two to four witnesses (depending on the state), who, at the testator's request and in the presence of each other, sign the will as witnesses. A formal will prepared by an attorney is the preferred method, as the will then conforms explicitly to the law. This greatly reduces the likelihood of its being contested after the testator's death. Additionally, an attorney may offer valuable advice on how to word the will to reduce estate and inheritance taxes.

HOLOGRAPHIC WILL

A **holographic will** is a will that is entirely handwritten, with no typed or preprinted words. The will is dated and signed by the testator, but there are no witnesses. Nineteen states recognize holographic wills as legally binding. Persons selecting this form of will generally do so because it saves the time and expense of seeking professional legal aid and because it is entirely private. Besides the fact that holographic wills are considered to have no effect in 31 states, they often result in much legal argument in states that do accept them. This can occur when the testator is not fully aware of the law as it pertains to the making of wills. Many otherwise happy families have been torn apart by dissension when a relative dies and they read the will, only to find that there is a question as to whether it was properly prepared and, hence, valid. Unfortunately, what follows is not what the deceased intended; those who would receive more from intestate succession will request that the will be declared void and of no effect; those with more to gain if the will stands as written will muster legal forces to argue for its acceptance by the probate court.

ORAL WILL

An **oral will**, more properly known as a **nuncupative will**, is a will spoken by a person who is very near death. The witness must promptly put in writing what was heard and submit it to probate. An oral will can only be used to dispose of personal property. Any real estate belonging to the deceased is disposed of by intestate succession. Some states limit the use of oral wills to those serving in the armed forces.

CODICIL

A **codicil** is a written supplement or amendment made to a previously existing will. It is used to change some aspect of the will or to add a new instruction, without the work of rewriting the entire will. The codicil must be dated, signed, and witnessed in the same manner as the original will. The only way to change a will is with a codicil or by writing a completely new will. The law will not recognize cross-outs, notations, or other alterations made on the will itself.

Adverse Possession

adverse possession

Acquisition of land through prolonged and unauthorized occupation.

Through the unauthorized occupation of another person's land for a long enough period of time, it is possible under certain conditions to acquire ownership by **adverse possession**. The historical roots of adverse possession go back many centuries to a time before written deeds were used as evidence of ownership. At that time, in the absence of any claims to the contrary, a person who occupied a parcel of land was presumed to be its owner. Today, adverse possession is, in effect, a statute of limitations that bars a legal owner from claiming title to land when he has done nothing to oust an adverse occupant during the statutory period. From the adverse occupant's standpoint, adverse possession is a method of acquiring title by possessing land for a specified period of time under certain conditions.

Courts of law are quite demanding of proof before they will issue a decree in favor of a person claiming title by virtue of adverse possession. The claimant must have maintained actual, visible, continuous, hostile, exclusive, and notorious possession and be publicly claiming ownership to the property. These requirements mean that the claimant's use must have been visible and obvious to the legal owner, continuous and not just occasional, and exclusive enough to give notice of the claimant's individual claim. Furthermore, the use must have been without permission (hostile), and the claimant must have acted as though he were the owner, even in the presence of the actual owner. Finally, the adverse claimant must be able to prove that he has met these requirements for a period ranging from 3 to 30 years, as shown in Table 5.1.

TABLE 5.1	Adverse Possession: Number of Years of Occupancy Required to Claim Title*				
	Adverse occupant lacks color of title and does not pay the property taxes	Adverse occupant has color of title and/or pays the property taxes		Adverse occupant lacks color of title and does not pay the property taxes	Adverse occupant has color of title and/or pays the property taxes
Alabama	20	10	Missouri	10	10
Alaska	10	7	Montana		5
Arizona	10	5	Nebraska	10	10
Arkansas	7	7	Nevada	15	5
California		5	New Hampshire	20	20
Colorado	18	7	New Jersey	30–60	30–60
Connecticut	15	15	New Mexico	10	10
Delaware	20	20	New York	10	10
District of Columbia	15	15	North Carolina	20–30	7–20
			North Dakota	20	10
Florida		7	Ohio	21	21
Georgia	20	7	Oklahoma	15	15
Hawaii	20	20	Oregon	10	10
Idaho	20	20	Pennsylvania	21	21
Illinois	20	7	Rhode Island	10	10
Indiana		10	South Carolina	10	10
Iowa	40	10	South Dakota	20	20
Kansas	15	15	Tennessee	7	7
Kentucky	15	15	Texas	10–25	3–5
Louisiana	30	10	Utah	7	7
Maine	20	20	Vermont	15	15
Maryland	20	20	Virginia	15	15
Massachusetts	20	20	Washington	10	7
Michigan	15	5–10	West Virginia	10	10
Minnesota	15	15	Wisconsin	20	7–10
Mississippi	10	10	Wyoming	10	10

*As may be seen, in a substantial number of states, the waiting period for title by adverse possession is shortened if the adverse occupant has color of title and/or pays the property taxes. In California, Florida, Indiana, Montana, Nevada, and Utah, the property taxes must be paid to obtain the title. Generally speaking, adverse possession does not work against minors and other legal incompetents. However, when the owner becomes legally competent, the adverse possession must be broken within the time limit set by each state's law (the range is 1 to 10 years). In the states of Louisiana, Oklahoma, and Tennessee, adverse possession is referred to as **title by prescription**.

Source: © 2014 OnCourse Learning

COLOR OF TITLE

The required occupancy period is shortened and the claimant's chances of obtaining legal ownership are enhanced in many states if he has been paying the property taxes and the possession has been under "color of title." **Color of title** suggests some plausible appearance of ownership interest, such as an improperly prepared deed that purports to transfer title to the claimant or a claim of ownership by inheritance. In accumulating the required number of years, an adverse claimant may tack on his

color of title

Some plausible but not completely clear-cut indication of ownership rights.

period of possession to that of a prior adverse occupant, commonly called **tacking**. This could be done through the purchase of that right. The current adverse occupant could in turn sell his claim to a still later adverse occupant until enough years were accumulated to present a claim in court.

Although the concept of adverse possession often creates the mental picture of a trespasser moving onto someone else's land and living there long enough to acquire title in fee, this is not the usual application. More often, adverse possession is used to extinguish weak or questionable claims to title. For example, if a person buys property at a tax sale, takes possession, and pays the property taxes each year afterward, adverse possession laws act to cut off claims to title by the previous owner. Another source of successful adverse possession claims arises from encroachments. If a building extends over a property line and nothing is said about it for a long enough period of time, the building will be permitted to stay.

Easement by Prescription

An easement can also be acquired by prolonged adverse use. This is known as acquiring an easement by prescription. As with adverse possession, the laws are strict: The usage must be openly visible, continuous, and exclusive, as well as hostile and adverse to the owner. Additionally, the use must have occurred over a period of 5 to 20 years, depending on the state. All of these facts must be proved in a court of law before the court will issue the claimant a document legally recognizing his ownership of the easement. As an easement is a right to use land for a specific purpose and not ownership of the land itself, courts rarely require the payment of property taxes to acquire a prescriptive easement.

As may be seen from the foregoing discussion, a landowner must be given obvious notification *at the location* of his land that someone is attempting to claim ownership or an easement. Since an adverse claim must be continuous and hostile, an owner can break it by ejecting the trespassers, by preventing them from trespassing, or by simply giving them permission to be there. Any of these actions would demonstrate the landowner's superior title. Owners of stores and office buildings with private sidewalks or streets used by the public can take action to break claims to a public easement by either periodically barricading the sidewalk or street or by posting signs giving permission to pass. These signs are often seen in the form of brass plaques embedded in the sidewalk or street. In certain states, a landowner may record with the public records office a **notice of consent**. This is evidence that subsequent uses of his land for the purposes stated in the notice are permissive and not adverse. The notice may later be revoked by recording a **notice of revocation**. Federal, state, and local governments protect themselves against adverse claims to their lands by passing laws making themselves immune.

Ownership by Accession

The extent of one's ownership of land can be altered by **accession**. This can result from natural or man-made causes. With regard to natural causes, the owner of land fronting on a lake, river, or ocean may acquire additional land because of the gradual accumulation of rock, sand, and soil. This process is called **accretion** and the results are referred to as *alluvion* and *reliction*. **Alluvion** is the increase of land that results when waterborne soil is gradually deposited to produce firm, dry ground. **Reliction** (or dereliction) results when a lake, sea, or river permanently recedes, exposing dry land. When land is rapidly washed away by the action of water, it is known as **avulsion**. Man-made accession occurs through **annexation** of personal property to real estate. For example, when lumber, nails, and cement are used to build a house, they alter the extent of one's land ownership.

Public Grant

A transfer of land by a government body to a private party is called a **public grant**. Since 1776, the federal government has granted millions of acres of land to settlers, land companies, railroads, state colleges, mining and logging promoters, and any war veteran from the American Revolution through the Mexican War. Most famous was the **Homestead Act** passed by the U.S. Congress in 1862. That act permitted persons wishing to settle on otherwise unappropriated federal land to acquire fee simple ownership by paying a small filing charge and occupying and cultivating the land for five years. Similarly, for only a few dollars, a person may file a mining claim to public land for the purpose of extracting whatever valuable minerals can be found. To retain the claim, a certain amount of work must be performed on the land each year. Otherwise, the government will consider the claim abandoned and another person may claim it. If the claim is worked long enough, a public grant can be sought and fee simple title obtained. In the case of both the homestead settler and the mining claim, the conveyance document that passes fee title from the government to the grantee is known as a **land patent**. In 1976, the U.S. government ended the homesteading program in all states except Alaska.

Dedication

When an owner makes a voluntary gift for the use of land to the public, it is known as **dedication**. Dedication is not a transfer of title, only a dedication of use for the benefit of the public. To illustrate, a land developer buys a large parcel of vacant land and develops it into streets and lots. The lots are sold to private buyers, but what about the streets? In all probability they will be dedicated to the town, city, or county. By doing this, the developer, and later the lot buyers, will not have to pay taxes on the streets, and the public will be responsible for maintaining them. The fastest way to accomplish the dedication is by either statutory dedication or dedication by deed. In **statutory dedication**, the developer prepares a map showing the streets, has the map approved by local government officials, and then records it as a public document. In **dedication by deed**, the developer prepares a deed that identifies the streets and grants them to the city.

Common law dedication takes place when a landowner, by his acts or words, shows that he intends part of his land to be dedicated, even though he has never officially made a written dedication. For example, a landowner may encourage the public to travel on his roads in an attempt to convince a local road department to take over maintenance.

Forfeiture

Forfeiture of title can occur when a deed contains a condition or limitation. For example, a grantor states in the deed that the land conveyed may be used for residential purposes only. If the grantee constructs commercial buildings, the grantor can reacquire title on the grounds that the grantee did not use the land for the required purpose.

Alienation

A change in ownership of any kind is known as an **alienation of title**. In addition to the forms of alienation discussed in this chapter, alienation can result from court action in connection with escheat, eminent domain, partition, foreclosure, execution sales, quiet title suits, and marriage. These topics are discussed in other chapters.

Vocabulary Review

Match terms a–z with statements 1–26.

a. Accretion
b. Adverse possession
c. Alienation of title
d. Alluvion
e. Bargain and sale deed
f. Cloud on the title
g. Codicil
h. Color of title
i. Consideration
j. Correction deed
k. Covenants and warranties
l. Dedication
m. Deed
n. Easement by prescription
o. Executor
p. Grant
q. Grantor
r. Holographic will
s. Intestate
t. Land patent
u. Probate
v. Quitclaim deed
w. Special warranty deed
x. Statute of Frauds
y. Warranty deed
z. Will

_____ 1. A written document that, when properly executed and delivered, conveys title to land.

_____ 2. Requires that transfers of real estate be in writing to be enforceable.

_____ 3. Person named in a deed who conveys ownership.

_____ 4. The act of conveying ownership.

_____ 5. Anything of value given to produce a contract.

_____ 6. Promises and guarantees found in a deed.

_____ 7. Any claim, lien, or encumbrance that impairs title to property.

_____ 8. A deed that contains the covenants of seizin, quiet enjoyment, encumbrances, further assurance, and warranty forever.

_____ 9. A deed that contains no covenants; it only implies that the grantor owns the property described in the deed.

_____ 10. A deed with no covenants and no implication that the grantor owns the property she is deeding to the grantee.

_____ 11. To die without a will.

_____ 12. A will written entirely in one's own handwriting and signed but not witnessed.

_____ 13. The process of verifying the legality of a will and carrying out its instructions.

_____ 14. A supplement or amendment to a previous will.

_____ 15. Acquisition of real property through prolonged and unauthorized occupation.

_____ 16. Some plausible but not completely clear-cut indication of ownership rights.

_____ 17. Acquisition of an easement by prolonged use.

_____ 18. Waterborne soil deposited to produce firm, dry ground.

_____ 19. A document for conveying government land in fee.

_____ 20. Private land voluntarily donated for use by the public.

_____ 21. The process of land build-up due to the gradual accumulation of rock, sand, and soil.

_____ 22. A change in ownership of any kind.

_____ 23. Used to correct an error in a previously executed and delivered deed.

_____ 24. A person named in a will to carry out its instructions.

_____ 25. Grantor warrants title only against defects occurring during the grantor's ownership.

_____ 26. Instructions stating how a person wants his property disposed of after death.

Questions and Problems

1. Is it possible for a document to convey fee title to land even though it does not contain the word deed? If so, why?

2. In the process of conveying real property from one person to another, at what instant in time does title actually pass from the grantor to the grantee?

3. What legal protections does a full covenant and warranty deed offer a grantee?

4. As a real estate purchaser, which deed would you prefer to receive: warranty, special warranty, or bargain and sale? Why?

5. What are the hazards of preparing your own deeds?

6. Name at least five examples of title clouds.

7. What is meant by the term *intestate succession*?

8. With regard to probate, what is the key difference between an executor and an administrator?

9. Does your state consider holographic wills to be legal? How many witnesses are required by your state for a formal will?

10. Can a person who has rented the same building for 30 years claim ownership by virtue of adverse possession? Why or why not?

11. Cite examples from your own community or state where land ownership has been altered by alluvion, reliction, or avulsion.

Additional Readings

American and English Law on Title of Record: Practice and Procedure by Alfred Bonito Cosey (Gaunt, Inc., 1999).

"Deed Warranties and Surveys" by Jerry R. Broadus (*Point of Beginning*, November 2001, vol. 27, issue 2, pp. 56–59).

"Estate-Planning Lessons I Learned the Hard Way" by William G. Porter (*Medical Economics*, October 14, 1996, vol. 73, number 19, pp. 119–121).

"A Friend in Deeds" by Peter J. G. Williams (*Estates Gazette*, May 19, 2001, issue 120, p. 224).

Treatise on the Deeds and Forms Used in the Constitution Transmission and Extinction of Feudal Rights by Alexander Duff (Gale, 2010).

CHAPTER 6

Recordation, Abstracts, and Title Insurance

LEARNING OBJECTIVES

After reading this chapter, you should be able to:

❮ Discuss the rationale of recording systems.

❮ Understand and define the different types of notice.

❮ Understand the difference between "abstract indices," and "grantor and grantee indices."

❮ Recognize the significance of a chain of title.

❮ Understand the purpose and perimeters of title insurance.

❮ Define "marketable title."

KEY TERMS

Abstract of title • Acknowledgment • Actual notice • Chain of title • Constructive notice • Marketable title • Public recorder's office • Quiet title suit • Title insurance • Torrens system

In this chapter we shall focus on: (1) the need for a method of determining real property ownership, (2) the process by which current and past ownership is determined from public records, (3) the availability of insurance against errors made in determining ownership, (4) the Torrens system of land title registration, and (5) the Uniform Marketable Title Act.

Need for Public Records

Until the enactment of the Statute of Frauds in England in 1677, determining who owned a parcel of land was primarily a matter of observing who was in physical possession. A landowner gave notice to the world of his claim to ownership by visibly occupying the land. When land changed hands, the old owner moved off the land and the new owner moved onto the land. After 1677, written deeds were required to show transfers of ownership. The problem then became one of finding the person holding the most current deed to the land. This was easy if the deedholder also occupied the land, but was more difficult if he did not. The solution was to create a government-sponsored public recording service where a person could record his deed. These records would then be open free of charge to anyone. In this fashion, an owner could post notice to all that he claimed ownership of a parcel of land.

CONSTRUCTIVE NOTICE

There are two ways a person can give notice of a claim or right to land. One is by recording documents in the public records that give written notice to that effect. The other is by visibly occupying or otherwise visibly making use of the land (**possession**). The law holds interested parties responsible for examining the public records and looking at the land for this notice of right or claim. This is called constructive notice. **Constructive notice** (also sometimes referred to as **legal notice**) charges the public with the responsibility of looking in the public records and at the property itself to obtain knowledge of all who are claiming a right or interest. In other words, our legal system provides an avenue by which a person can give notice (recording and occupancy) and makes the presumption that anyone interested in the property has inspected the records *and* the property.

constructive notice

Notice given by the public records and by visible possession, coupled with the legal presumption that all persons are thereby notified.

INQUIRY NOTICE

A person interested in a property is also held by law to be responsible for making further inquiry of anyone giving visible or recorded notice. This is referred to as **inquiry notice**, in which the law presumes a reasonably diligent person would obtain by making further inquiry. For example, suppose you are considering the purchase of vacant acreage and, upon inspecting it, see a dirt road cutting across the land that is not mentioned in the public records. The law expects you to make further inquiry. The road may be a legal easement across the property. Another example is that any time you buy rental property, you are expected to make inquiry as to the rights of the occupants. They may hold substantial rights (such as an option to purchase) you would not know about without asking them.

ACTUAL NOTICE

actual notice

Knowledge gained from what one has actually seen, heard, read, or observed.

Actual notice is knowledge that one has actually gained based on what one has seen, heard, read, or observed. For example, if you read a deed from Jones to Smith, you have actual notice of the deed and Smith's claim to the property. If you go to the property and you see someone in possession, you have actual notice of that person's claim to be there. Remember that anyone claiming an interest or right is expected to make it known either by recorded claim or visible use of the property. Anyone acquiring a right or interest is expected to look in the public records and go to the property to make a visual inspection to determine who has possession, and inquire as to the extent of those claims.

RECORDING ACTS

public recorder's office

A government-operated facility wherein documents are entered in the public records.

All states have passed **recording acts** to provide for the recording of every instrument (i.e., document) by which an estate, interest, or right in land is created, transferred, or encumbered. Within each state, each county has a **public recorder's office**, known variously as the County Recorder's Office, County Clerk's Office, Circuit Court Clerk's Office, County Registrar's Office, or Bureau of Conveyances. The person in charge is called the recorder, clerk, or registrar. Located at the seat of county government, each public recorder's office will record documents submitted to it that pertain to real property in that county. Thus, a deed to property in XYZ county is recorded with the public recorder in XYZ county. Similarly, anyone seeking information regarding ownership of land in XYZ county would go to the recorder's office in XYZ county. Some cities also maintain record rooms where deeds are recorded. The recording process itself involves photocopying the documents and filing them for future reference. To encourage people to use public recording facilities, laws in each state provide that: (1) a deed, mortgage, or other instrument affecting real

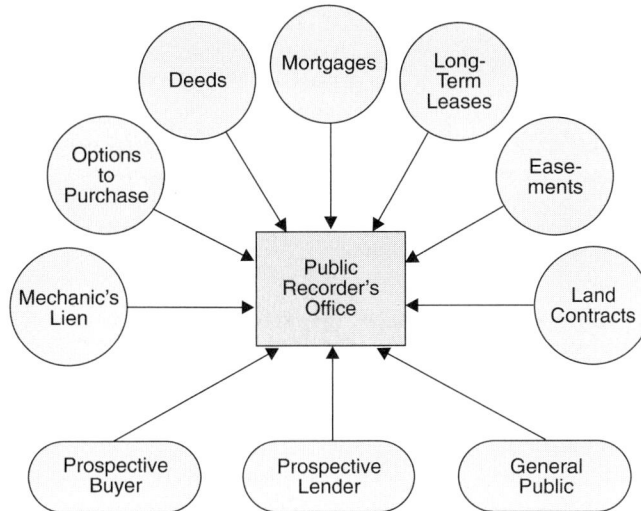

FIGURE 6.1 The Recorder's Role

The public recorder's office serves as a central information station for changes in rights, estates, and interests in land.

Source: © 2014 OnCourse Learning

estate is not effective as far as subsequent purchasers and lenders (without actual notice) are concerned if it is not recorded, and (2) prospective purchasers, mortgage lenders, and the public at large are presumed notified when a document is recorded. Figure 6.1 illustrates the concept of public recording.

MORTGAGE ELECTRONIC REGISTRATION SYSTEM

The mortgage electronic registration system, commonly known as MERS, is a computerized book registration system of tracking the beneficial interests or "bundle of rights" connected with both residential and commercial real estate loans. Formally known as the "MERS®," it records all of the beneficial interests connected to a mortgage electronically. The 20 largest mortgage banking organizations in the United States, as well as the secondary market (discussed in Chapter 13), and all Wall Street rating agencies automatically register notes and security interests in accordance with the Uniform Electronic Transactions Act (UETA). The Federal Electronic Signatures and Global and National Commerce Act (esign) system also provide payoff information to title industry members. Theoretically, MERS will be the mortgagee of record for all security instruments registered whether in the form of the original mortgage, deed of trust, or recorded assignment. Regardless of the number of times a beneficial interest or a mortgage is bought or sold between MERS members, no transfer or assignment need be recorded in the real property records. In a lending market that drowns in a sea of paper, MERS is an efficient method of keeping track of loan data on a national basis.

UNRECORDED INTERESTS

Although recording acts permit the recording of any estate, right, or interest in land, many lesser rights are rarely recorded. Month-to-month rentals and leases for a year or less fall into this category. Consequently, only an on-site inspection would reveal their existence, or the existence of any developing adverse possession or prescriptive easement claim.

SUMMARY

To summarize, if you are a prospective purchaser (or lessee or lender), you are presumed by law to have inspected both the land itself and the public records to determine the present rights and interests of others. If you receive a deed, mortgage, or other document relating to an estate, right, or interest in land, have it recorded *immediately* in the county in which the land is located. If you hold an unrecorded rental or lease, you should visibly occupy the property.

Requirements for Recording

Nearly all states require that a document be *acknowledged* before it is eligible to be recorded. A few states will permit proper witnessing as a substitute. Some states require both. The objective of these requirements is to make certain that the person who signs the document is the same person named in the document and that the signing was a free and voluntary act. This is done to reduce the possibility that forged or fraudulently induced documents will enter the public records.

WITNESSES

In states that accept witnesses, the person executing the document signs in the presence of at least two witnesses, who in turn sign the document indicating that they are witnesses. To protect themselves, witnesses should not sign unless they know that the person named in the document is the person signing. In the event the witnessed signature is contested, the witnesses would be summoned to a court of law and, under oath, testify to the authenticity of the signature. An example of a witness statement is shown in Figure 6.2.

ACKNOWLEDGMENT

acknowledgment

Formal declaration by a person signing a document that he or she, in fact, did sign the document.

An **acknowledgment** is a formal declaration by a person signing a document that he or she, in fact, did sign the document. Persons authorized to take acknowledgments include **notaries public**, recording office clerks, commissioners of deeds, judges of courts of record, justices of the peace, and certain others as authorized by state law. Commissioned military officers are authorized to take the acknowledgments of persons in the

---

FIGURE 6.2   Witness Statement

IN WITNESS whereof, the grantor has duly executed this deed in the presence of:

_____   _____
Witness   Grantor

_____
Witness

Source: © 2014 OnCourse Learning

military; foreign ministers, foreign notaries public, and consular agents can take acknowledgments abroad. If an acknowledgment is taken outside the state where the document will be recorded, either the recording county must already recognize the out-of-state official's authority or the out-of-state official must provide certification that he or she is qualified to take acknowledgments. The official seal or stamp of the notary on the acknowledgment normally fulfills this requirement.

An acknowledgment is illustrated in Figure 6.3. Notice the words; the person signing the document must personally appear before the notary, and the notary must state that he or she knows that person to be the person described in the document. If they are strangers, the notary will require proof of identity. The person acknowledging the document does so by acknowledging to the notary that they signed it. Note that it is the signer who does the acknowledging, not the notary. The notary takes the acknowledgment. At the completion of the signing, a notation of the event is made in a permanent record book kept by the notary. This record is later given to the state government for safekeeping.

Public Records Organization

Each document brought to a public recorder's office for recordation is photocopied and then returned to its owner. The photocopy is placed in chronological order with photocopies of other documents. These are stamped with consecutive page numbers and bound into a book. These books are placed in chronological order on shelves that are open to the public for inspection. Before modern-day photocopying machines, public recorders' offices used large cameras with light-sensitive paper (from roughly 1920 to 1955). Before that, documents were copied by hand using typewriters (from roughly 1900 to 1920), and before that, copying was done in longhand. One current trend is toward entirely paperless systems wherein documents are recorded directly onto microfilm and then returned to

FIGURE 6.3 Acknowledgment

ACKNOWLEDGMENT FOR AN INDIVIDUAL

STATE OF _____

COUNTY OF _____

On this _____ day of _____ , 20 _____ , before me, the undersigned, a Notary Public in and for said State, personally appeared [name of person exe-cuting document] known to me to be the person whose name is subscribed to the within instrument and acknowledged that he (she) executed the same [in some states, the words "by his (her) free act and deed" are added here]. Witness my hand and official seal.

[space for seal or stamp of the notary public]

_____
Signature of notary public

My commission expires _____

Date

Source: © 2014 OnCourse Learning

their owners. Each document is assigned a book and page number or a reel and frame number. Microfilm readers are made available to anyone wanting to read the microfilms. New recording systems are being established that will provide for electronic recording, with electronic signatures, and the documents will be kept in a computer bank at the courthouse where the real property records are maintained. At some time in the near future, all of this information will be accessible from a personal computer.

Filing incoming documents in chronological order is necessary to establish the chronological priority of documents; however, it does not provide an easy means for a person to locate all the documents relevant to a given parcel of land. Suppose that you are planning to purchase a parcel of land and want to make certain that the person selling it is the legally recognized owner. Without an index to guide you, you might have to inspect every document in every volume. Consequently, recording offices have developed systems of indexing. The two most commonly used are the grantor and grantee indexes, used by all states; and the tract index, used by nine states.

TRACT INDEXES

Of the two indexing systems, the **tract index** is the simplest to use. In it, one page is allocated to either a single parcel of land or to a group of parcels, called a *tract*. On that page you will find listed all the recorded deeds, mortgages, and other documents at the recorder's office that relate to that parcel. A few words describing each document are given, together with the book and page where a photocopy of the document can be found.

GRANTOR AND GRANTEE INDEXES

Grantor and grantee indexes are alphabetical indexes and are usually bound in book form. There are several variations in use in the United States, but the basic principle is the same. For each calendar year, the **grantor index** lists in alphabetical order all grantors named in the documents recorded that year. Next to each grantor's name is the name of the grantee named in the document, the book and page where a photocopy of the document can be found, and a few words describing the document. The **grantee index** is arranged by grantee names and gives the name of the grantor and the location and description of the document.

EXAMPLE OF TITLE SEARCH

As an example of the application of the grantor and grantee indexes to a title search, suppose Robert T. Davis states that he is the owner of Lot 2, Block 2, in the Hilldale Tract in your county, and you would like to verify that statement in the public records. You begin by looking in the grantee index for his name, starting with this year's index and working backward in time. The purpose of this first step is to determine whether the property was ever granted to Davis. If it was, you will find his name in the grantee index and, next to his name, a book and page reference to a photocopy of his deed to that parcel.

THE NEXT STEP

The next step is to look through the grantor index for the period of time starting from the moment he received his deed up to the present. If he has granted the property to someone else, Davis's name will be noted in the grantor index with a reference to the book and page where you can see a copy of the deed. (Davis could have reduced your efforts by showing you the actual deed conveying the lot to him. However, you would still have to inspect the grantor index for all dates subsequent to his taking title to see if he has conveyed title to a new grantee. If you do not have the name of the property owner, you would first have to go to the property tax office.)

Suppose your search shows that on July 1, 1999, in Book 2324, page 335, a warranty deed from John S. Miller to Davis, for Lot 2, Block 2, of the Hilldale Tract was recorded. Furthermore, you find that no subsequent deed showing Davis as grantor of this land has been recorded. Based on this, it would appear that Davis is the fee owner. However, you must inquire further to determine if Miller was the legally recognized owner of the property when he conveyed it to Davis. In other words, on what basis did Miller claim his right of ownership and, subsequently, the right to convey that ownership to Davis? The answer is that Miller based his claim to ownership on the deed he received from the previous owner.

Chain of Title

By looking for Miller's name in the 1999 grantee index and then working backward in time through the yearly indexes, you will eventually find his name and a reference to Lot 2, Block 2, in the Hilldale Tract. Next to Miller's name you will find the name of the grantor and a reference to the book and page where the deed was recorded.

By looking for that name in the grantee index, you will locate the next previous deed. By continuing this process, you can construct a chain of title. A **chain of title** shows the linkage of property ownership that connects the present owner to the original source of title. In most cases, the chain starts with the original sale or grant of the land from the government to a private citizen. It is used to prove how title came to be **vested** in (i.e., possessed by) the current owner. Figure 6.4 illustrates the chain-of-title concept.

chain of title
The linkage of property ownership that connects the present owner to the original source of title.

Sometimes, while tracing (running) a chain of title back through time, an apparent break or dead end can occur. This can happen because the grantor is an administrator, executor, sheriff, or judge, or because the owner died, or because a mortgage against the land was foreclosed. To regain the title sequence, one must search outside the recorder's office by checking probate court records in the case of a death, or by checking civil court actions in the case of a foreclosure. The chain must be complete from the original source of title to the present owner. If there is a missing link, the current "owner" does not have valid title to the property.

In addition to looking for grantors and grantees, a search must be made for any outstanding mortgages, judgments, actions pending, liens, and unpaid taxes that may affect the title. With regard to searching for mortgages, states again differ slightly. Some place mortgages in the general grantor and grantee indexes, listing the borrower (mortgagor) as the grantor and the lender (mortgagee) as the grantee. Other states have separate index books for mortgagors and mortgagees. The process involves looking for the name of each owner in each annual **mortgagor index** published while that owner owned the land. If a mortgage is found, a further check will reveal whether it has been satisfied and released. If it has been released, the recorder's office will have noted on the margin of the recorded mortgage the book and page where the release is located. When one knows the lender's name, the mortgage location and its subsequent release can also be found by searching the **mortgagee index**.

Title may be clouded by judgments against recent owners, or there may be lawsuits pending that might later affect title. This information is found, respectively, on the **judgment rolls** and in the **lis pendens index** at the office of the county clerk. The term *lis pendens* is Latin for "pending lawsuits." A separate search is made for mechanic's liens against the property by workmen and material suppliers. This step includes both a search of the public records and an on-site inspection of the land for any recent construction activity or material

FIGURE 6.4	Chain of Title

United States Government
to Isaiah Adams
by Homestead Act
    Recorded 4/2/1880, Bk. 29, pg. 37

Isaiah Adams
to Samuel Brady and wife Anne
by warranty deed
    Recorded 5/18/1908, Bk. 133, pg. 145

Samuel Brady and wife Anne
to Samuel Brady, Jr.
by bargain and sale deed reserving
a life estate for the grantors
    Recorded 3/3/1924, Bk. 272, pg. 238

Samuel Brady dies on
    6/30/1935
Anne Brady dies on
    12/21/1938

James Potter, executor of
the estate of Samuel Brady, Jr.
to Anna Cummings
by will
    Probated 7/15/1955

Anna Cummings
to John S. Miller
by warranty deed
    Recorded 6/6/1982, Bk. 1716, pg. 158

John S. Miller
to Robert T. Davis
by warranty deed
    Recorded 7/1/1999, Bk. 2324, pg. 335

Source: © 2014 OnCourse Learning

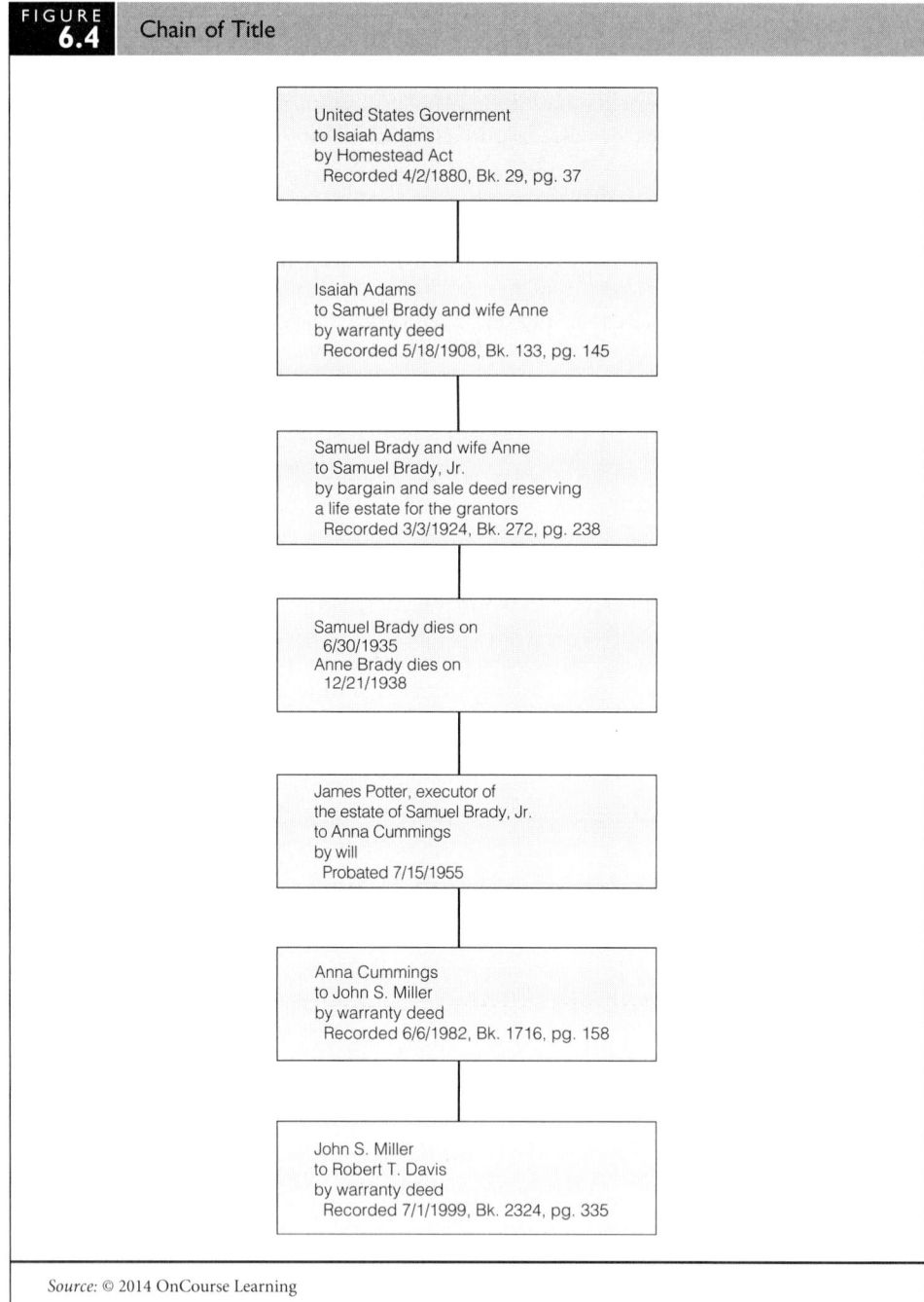

deliveries. A visit is made to the local tax assessor's office to check the tax rolls for unpaid property taxes and to check the county map records to determine changes in deed restriction or subdivision plats. This does not exhaust all possible places that must be visited to do a thorough title search. A title searcher may also be found researching birth, marriage, divorce, and adoption records, probate records, military files, and federal tax liens in an effort to identify all the parties with an interest or potential interest in a given parcel of land and its improvements.

Abstract of Title

Although it is useful for the real estate practitioner to be able to find a name or document in the public records, full-scale title searching should be left to professionals. In a sparsely populated county, title searching is usually done on a part-time basis by an attorney. In more heavily populated counties, a full-time **abstracter** will search the records. These persons are experts in the field of title search, and, for a fee, will prepare an abstract of title for a parcel of land.

An **abstract of title** is a complete historical summary of all recorded documents affecting the title of a property. It recites in chronological order all recorded grants and conveyances and recorded easements, mortgages, wills, tax liens, judgments, pending lawsuits, marriages, divorces, and so on, that might affect title. The abstracter will summarize each document, note the book and page (or other source) where it was found, and give the date it was recorded or entered. In the case of a deed, for example, the abstracter identifies the grantor, grantee, and type of deed, and gives a brief description of the property, any conditions or restrictions found in the deed, the date on the deed, the recording date, and the book and page. For a mortgage, the abstracter identifies the borrower and lender, gives a brief description of the mortgage contents, and if repaid, the book and page location of the mortgage release document and its date of recordation. The abstract also includes a list of the public records searched, and not searched, in preparing the abstract.

abstract of title
A summary of all recorded documents affecting title to a given parcel of land.

The abstract is next sent to an attorney. On the basis of the attorney's knowledge of law and the legal history presented in the abstract, the attorney renders an **opinion of title** as to who the fee owner is and names anyone else with a legitimate right or interest in the property. This opinion, when written, signed by the attorney, and attached to the abstract, is known in many states as a **certificate of title**. In some parts of the United States, this certified abstract is so valuable that it is brought up-to-date each time the property is sold and passed from seller to buyer. Generally speaking, the seller pays the cost of updating the abstract and getting a current attorney's opinion and certificate.

"WHAT IFS"

Despite the diligent efforts of abstracters and attorneys to give as accurate a picture of land ownership as possible, there is no guarantee that the finished abstract, or its certification, is completely accurate. Persons preparing abstracts and opinions are liable to mistakes due to their own negligence, and they can be sued if that negligence results in a loss to a client. But what if a recorded deed in the title chain is a forgery? Or what if a married person represented himself on a deed as a single person, thus resulting in unextinguished dower rights? Or what if a deed was executed by a minor or an otherwise legally incompetent person? Or what if a deed contained an erroneous land description? Or what if a document was misfiled, or there were undisclosed heirs, or a missing will later came to light, or there was confusion because of similar names on documents? These situations can result in substantial losses to a property owner; yet the fault may not lie with the abstracter or attorney. Nor is the recorder's office responsible for verifying the contents of a deed, just that it shows an acceptable acknowledgment. The solution has been the organization of private companies to sell insurance against losses arising from title defects such as these, as well as from errors in title examination.

Title Insurance

Efforts to insure titles date back to the last century and were primarily organized by and for the benefit of attorneys who wanted protection from errors that they might make in

title insurance

An insurance policy against defects in title not listed in the title report or abstract.

the interpretation of abstracts. As time passed, **title insurance** became available to anyone wishing to purchase it. The basic principle of title insurance is similar to any form of insurance: Many persons pay a small amount into an insurance pool that is then available if any one of them should suffer a loss. In some parts of the United States, it is customary to purchase the title insurance policy through the attorney who reads and certifies the abstract. Elsewhere it is the custom to purchase it from a title company that combines the search and policy in one fee.

TITLE COMMITMENT

When a title company receives a request for a title insurance policy, the first step is an examination of the public records. This is usually done by an abstracter or **title searcher** employed by the title company. A company attorney then reviews the findings and renders an opinion as to who the fee owner is and lists anyone else with a legitimate right or interest in the property, such as a mortgage lender or easement holder. This information is typed and becomes the **title commitment**. An example of a title commitment is illustrated in plain language in Figure 6.5. The title commitment commits the title company to insure the property. Note that it commits to the proposed insured that the title company will issue a policy in the future provided certain conditions are met. Most of these conditions are predictable (i.e., required payoff of certain liens or other defects so the title will be clear).

Notice how a title commitment differs from an abstract. Whereas an abstract is a chronologically arranged summary of all recorded events that have affected the title to a given parcel of land, a title commitment is more like a snapshot that shows the condition of title at a specific moment in time. A title commitment does not tell who the previous owners were; it only tells who the current owner is. A title report does not list all mortgage loans ever made against the land, but only those that have not been removed. The title commitment in Figure 6.5 states that a search of the public records shows Barbara Baker to be the fee owner of Lot 17, Block M, at the time the search was conducted.

In Schedule C, the report lists all recorded objections that could be found to Baker's fee estate, in this case, county property taxes, a mortgage, and two easements. In Schedule B, the title company states that there may be certain unrecorded matters that either could not be or were not researched in preparing the report. Note in particular that the title company does not make a visual inspection of the land nor does it make a boundary survey. The buyer is responsible for making the on-site inspection and for hiring a surveyor if uncertain as to the land's boundaries. It is also the buyer's responsibility to check the zoning of the land and any other governmental restrictions on the land.

Although an owner may purchase a title insurance policy on his property at any time, it is most often purchased when real estate is sold. In connection with a sale, the title commitment is used to verify that the seller is indeed the owner. Additionally, the title commitment alerts the buyer and seller as to what needs to be done to bring title to the condition called for in the sales contract. For example, referring to Figure 6.5, the present owner (Barbara Baker) may have agreed to remove the existing mortgage so that the buyer can get a new and larger loan. Once this is done and the seller has delivered her deed to the buyer, the title company issues a title policy that deletes the old mortgage, adds the new mortgage, and shows the buyer as the owner. Note that title policies are often required by long-term lessees (10 years or more). They, too, want to know who has property rights superior to theirs.

TITLE COMMITMENT

The title insurance company agrees to issue to you our title insurance policy when the provisions of Schedule B and C have been complied with.

Schedule A

LAND DESCRIPTION: Lot 17, Block M, Atwater's Addition, Jefferson County, State of _____ .

PROPOSED INSURED: George W. Bush

DATE AND TIME OF SEARCH: March 3, 20xx at 9:00 A.M.

TITLE APPEARS TO BE VESTED IN: Barbara Baker, a single woman

ESTATE OR INTEREST: Fee simple

EXCEPTIONS:

Schedule B

1. Taxes or assessments not shown by the records of any taxing authority or by the public records.

2. Any facts, rights, interests, or claims that, although not shown by the public records, could be determined by inspection of the land and inquiry of persons in possession.

3. Discrepancies or conflicts in boundary lines or area or encroachments that would be shown by a survey, but which are not shown by the public records.

4. Easements, liens, or encumbrances not shown by the public records.

5. Zoning and governmental restrictions.

6. Unpatented mining claims and water rights or claims.

Schedule C

1. A lien in favor of Jefferson County for property taxes, in the amount of $645.00, due on or before April 30, 19xx.

2. A mortgage in favor of the First National Bank in the amount of $30,000.00, recorded June 2, 1974, in Book 2975, Page 245 of the Official County Records.

3. An easement in favor of the Southern Telephone Company along the eastern five feet of said land for telephone poles and conduits. Recorded on June 15, 1946, in Book 1210, Page 113 of the Official County Records.

4. An easement in favor of Coastal States Gas and Electric Company along the north ten feet of said land for underground pipes. Recorded on June 16, 1946, in Book 1210, Page 137 of the Official County Records.

Source: © 2014 OnCourse Learning

POLICY PREMIUM

In some parts of the United States, it is customary for the seller to pay the cost of both the title search and the insurance. In other parts, the seller pays for the search and the buyer pays for the insurance. In a relatively few instances, the buyer pays for both. Customarily, when a property is sold, it is insured for an amount equal to the purchase price. This insurance remains effective as long as the buyer (owner) or his heirs have an interest in the property.

The insurance premium consists of a single payment. On the average-priced home, the combined charge for a title report and title insurance amounts to about one-half of 1% of the amount of insurance purchased. Each time the property is sold, a new policy must be purchased. The old policy cannot be assigned to the new owner. Some title insurance companies offer reduced **reissue rates** if the previous owner's policy is available for updating.

LENDER'S POLICY

Thus far our discussion of title insurance has centered on what is called an **owner's policy**. In addition, title insurance companies also offer what is called a **lender's policy**. This gives title protection to a lender who has taken real estate as collateral for a loan. There are three significant differences between an owner's title policy and a lender's title policy. First, the owner's policy is good for the full amount of coverage stated on the policy for as long as the insured or the insured's heirs have an interest in the property. In contrast, the lender's policy protects only for the amount owed on the mortgage loan. Thus, the coverage on a lender's policy declines and finally terminates when the loan is fully repaid. The second difference is that the lender's policy does not make exceptions for claims to ownership that could have been determined by physically inspecting the property. The third difference is that the lender's policy is assignable to subsequent holders of that same loan; an owner's policy is not.

The cost of a lender's policy (also known as a mortgagee's title policy or a loan policy) is similar to an owner's policy. Although the insurance company takes added risks by eliminating some exceptions found in the owner's policy, this is balanced by the fact that the liability decreases as the loan is repaid. When an owner's and a lender's policy are purchased at the same time, as in the case of a sale with new financing, the combined cost is only a few dollars more than the cost of the owner's policy alone. Note that the lender's policy covers only title problems. It does not insure that the loan will be repaid by the borrower.

CLAIMS FOR LOSSES

The last item in a title policy is a statement as to how the company will handle claims. Although this "Conditions and Stipulations Section" is too lengthy to reproduce here, its key aspects can be summarized as follows. When an insured defect arises, the title insurance company reserves the right to either pay the loss or fight the claim in court. If it elects to fight, any legal costs the company incurs are in addition to the amount of coverage stated in the policy. If a loss is paid, the amount of coverage is reduced by that amount and any unused coverage is still in effect. If the company pays a loss, it acquires the right to collect from the party who caused the loss.

In comparing title insurance to other forms of insurance (e.g., life, fire, automobile), note that title insurance protects against something that has already happened but has not been discovered. A forged deed may result in a disagreement over ownership: The forgery is a fact of history, the insurance is in the event of its discovery. But in some cases the problem will never be discovered. For example, a married couple may be totally unaware of dower and curtesy rights, and fail to extinguish them when they sell their property. If neither later claims them, when they die, the rights extinguish themselves, and the intervening property owners will have been unaffected.

Only a small part of the premiums collected by title insurance companies are used to pay claims. This is largely because title companies take great pains to maintain on their own premises complete photographic copies (often computer indexed) of the public records for each county in which they do business. These are called **title plants**. In many cases they are actually more complete and better organized than those available at the public recorder's office. The philosophy is that the better the quality of the title search, the fewer the claims that must be paid.

THE GROWTH OF TITLE INSURANCE

Four important factors have caused the title insurance business to mushroom. First, in a warranty deed the grantor makes several strongly worded covenants. As you will recall, the grantor covenants that he is the owner, that the grantee will not be disturbed in his possession, that there are no encumbrances except as stated in the deed, that the grantor will procure any necessary further assurance of title for the grantee, and that the grantor will bear the expense of defending the grantee's title and possession. Thus, signing a warranty deed places a great obligation on the grantor. By purchasing title insurance, the grantor can transfer that obligation to an insurance company.

Second, a grantee is also motivated to have title insurance. Even with a warranty deed, there is always the lingering question of whether the seller would be financially capable of making good on his covenants and warranties. They are useless if one cannot enforce them. Moreover, title insurance typically provides a grantee broader assurance than a warranty deed. For example, an outsider's claim must produce physical dispossession of the grantee before the covenant of quiet enjoyment is considered broken. Yet the same claim would be covered by title insurance before dispossession took place.

Third, the broad use of title insurance has made mortgage lending more attractive and borrowing a little easier and cheaper for real property owners. This is because title insurance has removed the risk of loss due to defective titles. As a result, lenders can charge a lower rate of interest. Secondary market purchasers of loans such as FNMA and FHLMC (Chapter 14) require title insurance on every loan they buy.

MARKETABLE TITLE. Fourth, title insurance has made titles to land much more marketable. In nearly all real estate transactions, the seller agrees to deliver marketable title to the buyer. **Marketable title** is title that is free from reasonable doubt as to who the owner is. Even when the seller makes no mention of the quality of the title, courts ordinarily require that marketable title be conveyed. To illustrate, a seller orders an abstract prepared and it is read by an attorney who certifies it as showing marketable title. The buyer's attorney feels that certain technical defects in the title chain contradict certification as marketable. The attorney advises the buyer to refuse to complete the sale. The line between what is and what is not marketable title can be exceedingly thin and differences of legal opinion are quite possible. One means of breaking the stalemate is to locate a title insurance company that will insure the title as being marketable. If the defect is not serious, the insurance company will accept the risk. If it is a serious risk, the company may either accept the risk and increase the insurance fee, or recommend a quiet title suit.

marketable title

Title that is free from reasonable doubt as to who is the owner.

QUIET TITLE SUIT

When a title defect (also called a cloud on the title or a **title cloud**) must be removed, it is logical to remove it by using the path of least resistance. For example, if an abstract or title report shows unpaid property taxes, the buyer may require the seller to pay them in full before the deal is completed. A cloud on the title as a result of pending foreclosure proceedings can be halted by either bringing the loan payments up-to-date or negotiating with the lender for a new loan repayment schedule. Similarly, a distant relative with ownership rights might be willing, upon negotiation, to quit-claim them for a price.

Sometimes a stronger means is necessary to remove title defects. For example, the distant relative may refuse to negotiate, the lender may refuse to remove a mortgage lien, despite

quiet title suit

Court-ordered hearings held to determine land ownership.

pleas from the borrower that it has been paid, or there may be a missing link in a chain of title. The solution is a **quiet title suit** (also called a *quiet title action*). Forty-seven states have enacted legislation that permits a property owner to ask the courts to hold hearings on the ownership of his land. At these hearings, anyone claiming to have an interest or right to the land in question may present verbal or written evidence of that claim. A judge, acting on the evidence presented and the laws of his state, rules on the validity of each claim. The result is to recognize legally those with a genuine right or interest and to "quiet" those without a genuine interest.

The Torrens System

torrens system

A state-sponsored method of registering land titles.

Over a century ago, Sir Robert Torrens, a British administrator in Australia, devised an improved system of identifying landownership. He was impressed by the relative simplicity of the British system of sailing-ship registration. The government maintained an official ships' registry that listed on a single page a ship's name, its owner, and any liens or encumbrances against it. Torrens felt land titles might be registered in a similar manner. The system he designed, known as the **Torrens system** of land title registration, starts with a landowner's application for registration and the preparation of an abstract. This is followed by a quiet title suit at which all parties named in the abstract and anyone else claiming a right or interest to the land in question may attend and be heard.

TORRENS CERTIFICATE OF TITLE

Based on the outcome of the suit, a government-appointed **registrar of titles** prepares a certificate of title. This certificate names the legally recognized fee owner and lists any legally recognized exceptions to that ownership, such as mortgages, easements, long-term leases, or life estates. The registrar keeps the original certificate of title and issues a duplicate to the fee owner. (Although they sound similar, a Torrens certificate of title is not the same as an attorney's certificate of title. The former shows ownership and claims against that ownership as established by a court of law. The latter is strictly an opinion of the condition of title.)

Once a title is registered, any subsequent liens or encumbrances against it must be entered on the registrar's copy of the certificate of title in order to give constructive notice. When a lien or encumbrance is removed, its notation on the certificate is canceled. In this manner, the entire concept of constructive notice for a given parcel of land is reduced to a single-page document open to public view at the registrar's office. This, Torrens argued, would make the whole process of title transfer much simpler and cheaper.

When registered land is conveyed, the grantor gives the grantee a deed. The grantee takes the deed to the registrar of titles, who transfers the title by canceling the grantor's certificate and issuing a new certificate in the name of the grantee. With a Torrens property, this is the point in time when title is conveyed, not when the deed is delivered by the grantor to the grantee. Any liens or other encumbrances not removed at the same time are carried over from the old to the new certificate. The deed and certificate are kept by the registrar; the grantee receives a duplicate of the certificate. If the conveyance is accompanied by a new mortgage, it is noted on the new certificate and a copy of the mortgage is retained by the registrar. Except for the quiet title suit aspect, the concept of land title registration is quite similar to that used in the United States for registering ownership of motor vehicles.

ADOPTION

In the United States, Illinois was the first state to have a land registration act in 1895. Other states slowly followed, but often their laws were vague and cumbersome to the point of being useless. At one point, 19 states had land title registration acts, but since then 9 states have repealed their acts and only 10 remain. They are Hawaii, Massachusetts, Minnesota, New York, Colorado, Georgia, North Carolina, Ohio, Virginia, and Washington.

In all 10 states, Torrens coexists with the regular recording procedures described earlier in this chapter. Thus, it is possible for a house on one side of a street to be Torrens registered, and a house across the street to be recorded the regular way. Also, it may be customary to use Torrens in just certain areas of the state. In Minnesota, it's used in the Minneapolis area; in Massachusetts, the Boston area; and in New York, Suffolk County (eastern Long Island). In Hawaii, Torrens is used statewide, but primarily by large landowners and subdivision developers who want to clear up complex title problems. In the remaining six states, the public has made relatively little use of land title registration. This limited adoption of Torrens is because of, among other things, the promotion, widespread availability, and lower short-run cost of title insurance. (The quiet title suit can be costly.) Note, too, that although a state-run insurance fund is usually available to cover registration errors, some lenders feel this is not adequate protection and require title insurance.

Marketable Title Acts

At least 18 states have a **marketable title act**. This is *not* a system of title registration. Rather, it is legislation aimed at making abstracts easier to prepare and less prone to error. This is done by cutting off claims to rights or interests in land that have been inactive for longer than the act's statutory period. In Connecticut, Michigan, Utah, Vermont, and Wisconsin, this period is 40 years. Thus, in these states, a person who has an unbroken chain of title with no defects for at least 40 years is regarded by the law as having marketable title. Any defects more than 40 years old are outlawed. The result is to concentrate the title search process on the immediate past 40 years. Thus, abstracts can be produced with less effort and expense, and the chance for an error, either by the abstracter or in the documents themselves is greatly reduced. This is particularly true in view of the fact that record-keeping procedures in the past were not as sophisticated as they are today.

The philosophy of a marketable title act is that a person has 40 years to come forward and make his claim known; if the person does not, then he apparently does not consider it worth pursuing. As protection for a person actively pursuing a claim that is about to become more than 40 years old, the claim can be renewed for another 40 years by again recording notice of the claim in the public records. In certain situations, a title must be searched back more than 40 years (e.g., when there is a lease of more than a 40-year duration or when no document affecting ownership has been recorded in over 40 years). In Nebraska, the statutory period is 22 years; in Florida, North Carolina, and Oklahoma, it is 30 years; in Indiana, 50 years.

Marketable title acts do not eliminate the need for legal notice, nor do they eliminate the role of adverse possession.

Vocabulary Review

Match terms of a–v with statements 1–22.

a. Abstract of title
b. Acknowledgment
c. Actual notice
d. Chain of title
e. Constructive notice
f. Grantor-grantee indexes
g. Inquiry notice
h. Lender's policy
i. Lis pendens index
j. Marketable title
k. Marketable Title Act
l. Notary public
m. Opinion of title
n. Owner's policy
o. Public recorder's office
p. Quiet title suit
q. Title cloud
r. Title insurance
s. Title report
t. Title searcher
u. Torrens system
v. Vested

_____ 1. Knowledge gained from what one has seen, heard, read, or observed.

_____ 2. Notice given by the public records or by visible possession coupled with the legal presumption that all persons are thereby notified.

_____ 3. A formal declaration, made in the presence of a notary public or other authorized individual, by a person affirming that he signed a document.

_____ 4. A person authorized to take acknowledgments.

_____ 5. A place where a person can enter documents affecting title to real estate.

_____ 6. A book at the public recorder's office that lists grantors alphabetically by name.

_____ 7. The linkage of ownership that connects the present owner to the original source of title.

_____ 8. A publicly available index whereby a person can learn of any pending lawsuits that may affect title.

_____ 9. A title defect.

_____ 10. A complete summary of all recorded documents affecting title to a given parcel of land.

_____ 11. Insurance to protect a property owner against monetary loss if his title is found to be imperfect.

_____ 12. A report made by a title insurance company showing current title condition.

_____ 13. A title policy written to protect a real estate lender.

_____ 14. Title that is free from reasonable doubt as to who the owner is.

_____ 15. Court-ordered hearings held to determine land ownership.

_____ 16. Laws that automatically cut off inactive claims to rights or interests in land.

_____ 17. A method of registering land titles that is similar to that of automobile ownership registration.

_____ 18. Claims to property rights the law presumes a reasonably diligent person would find through further investigation.

_____ 19. A statement as to the ownership of a property that is made by an attorney after reading the abstract.

_____ 20. An insurance policy against loss due to errors in title report preparation and inaccuracies in the public records.

_____ 21. A person trained and employed to examine the public records.

_____ 22. Possessed by; owned by.

Questions and Problems

1. How much does your public recorder's office charge to record a deed? A mortgage? What requirements must a document meet before it will be accepted for recording?

2. Where is the public recorder's office for your community located?

3. Explain constructive notice.

4. What is the purpose of grantor and grantee indexes?

5. Why is it important that a title search be carried out in more places than just the county recorder's office?

6. What is the difference between a certificate of title issued by an attorney and a Torrens certificate of title?

7. How does a title report differ from an abstract?

8. What is the purpose of title insurance?

9. Thorsen sells his house to Williams. Williams moves in, but, for some reason, does not record his deed. Thorsen discovers this and sells the house to an out-of-state investor who orders a title search, purchases an owner's title policy, and records his deed. Thorsen then disappears with the money he received from both sales. Who is the loser when this scheme is discovered: Williams, the out-of- state investor, or the title company? Why?

10. Go to the public recorder's office for your county, examine the records for a parcel of land (such as your home), and trace its ownership back through three owners.

Additional Readings

"The Case for Personal Property Lien Priority Insurance" by James D. Prendergast (*Uniform Commercial Code Law Journal*, Winter 2001, vol. 34, issue 3, pp. 252–268).

"The Dynamic Effects of Land Title Systems" by Thomas J. Miceli, C. F. Sirmans, and Geoffrey K. Turnbull (*Journal of Urban Economics*, May 2000, vol. 47, issue 3, pp. 370–389).

"New Advances and Tools for Lenders and Counsel in Title Insurance" by James M. Orphanides and S. H. Spencer

Compton (*Real Estate Finance Journal*, Fall 2001, vol. 17, issue 2, pp. 10–14).

Title Insurance: A Comprehensive Overview, 3rd ed. by James L. Gosdin, American Bar Association, 2008.

Title Insurance 101: Principles and Fundamentals of the Title Insurance Process by Abilio Perez-Salva (Leathers Publishing, 1999).

Contract Law

A **contract** is a legally enforceable agreement to do (or not to specific thing. In this chapter we shall see how a contract is created and what makes it legally binding. Topics covered include offer and acceptance, fraud, mistake, lawful objective, consideration, performance, and breach of contract. In Chapter 8, we will turn our attention to the purchase contract, installment contract, lease with option to buy, first right of refusal, and trade agreement.

How a Contract Is Created

A contract may be either expressed or implied. An **expressed contract** occurs when the parties to the contract declare their intentions either orally or in writing. (The word *party* is a legal term that refers to a person or group involved in a legal proceeding.) A lease or rental agreement, for example, is an expressed contract. The lessor (landlord) expresses the intent to permit the lessee (tenant) to use the premises, and the lessee agrees to pay rent in return. A contract to purchase real estate is also an expressed contract.

An **implied contract** is created by actions of the parties indicating that they intend to create a contract. For example, when you step into a taxicab, you imply that you will pay the fare. The cab driver, by allowing you in the cab, implies that you will be taken where you want to go. The same thing occurs at a restaurant. The presence of tables, silverware, menus, waiters, and waitresses implies that you will be served food. When you order, you imply that you are going to pay when the bill is presented.

BILATERAL CONTRACT

A contract may be either bilateral or unilateral. A **bilateral contract** results when a promise is exchanged for a promise. For example, in a typical real estate sale, the buyer promises to pay the agreed price and the seller promises to deliver title to the

LEARNING OBJECTIVES

After reading this chapter, you should be able to:

‹ Understand how a contract is created.

‹ Define and list the essentials of a valid contract.

‹ Define each of the elements that make a valid contract.

‹ Understand the process of offer and acceptance.

‹ Understand the multiple meanings of the word "consideration".

‹ Develop an understanding of the effective contractual remedies.

KEY TERMS

Breach of contract • Competent party • Consideration • Contract • Counteroffer • Duress • Fraud • Liquidated damages • Power of attorney • Specific performance • Void contract • Voidable contract

contract
A legally enforceable agreement to do (or not to do) a particular thing.

buyer. In a lease contract, the lessor promises the use of the premises to the lessee and the lessee promises to pay rent in return. A bilateral contract is basically an "I will do this *and* you will do that" arrangement.

UNILATERAL CONTRACT

A **unilateral contract** results when a promise is exchanged for performance. For instance, during a campaign to get more listings, a real estate office manager announces to the firm's sales staff that an extra $1,000 bonus will be paid for each new listing. No promises or agreements are necessary from the salespersons. The offer is accepted by the salesperson's performance. Each time the salesperson performs by bringing in a listing, he or she is entitled to the promised $1,000 bonus. An option to purchase is also a unilateral contract. It is an offer by the optionor to sell his property in the future in return for an option fee. At the time the option is exercised (and the optionee has the obligation to close), it becomes a bilateral contract for sale (i.e., the optionor has agreed to the conveyance and the optionee has agreed to purchase at some time in the very near future). Similarly, a listing can be structured as a unilateral contract. The seller agrees to pay a commission if the broker finds a buyer. When the broker starts to perform, the contract becomes more bilateral, as the agent has expended time and money and would be entitled to reimbursement. When the broker produces the buyer, the broker has completed the performance. The commission is earned and the seller's promise to pay the commission is enforceable. The broker has accepted the offer (discussed later) and the agreement to pay the commission becomes a valid, binding contract because of the broker's performance. A unilateral contract is basically an "I will do this *if* you will do that" arrangement. The offer is made and it is accepted by performance.

FORBEARANCE

Most contract agreements are based on promises by the parties involved to act in some manner (pay money, provide services, or deliver title). However, a contract can contain a promise to **forbear** (not to act) by one or more of its parties. For example, a lender may agree not to foreclose on a delinquent mortgage loan if the borrower agrees to a new payment schedule.

LEGAL EFFECT

A **valid contract** is one that meets all the requirements of law. It is binding upon its parties and legally enforceable in a court of law. A **void contract** has no legal effect, and, in fact, is not a contract at all. Even though the parties may have gone through the motions of attempting to make a contract, no legal rights are created and any party thereto may ignore it at his pleasure. A **voidable contract** binds one party but not the other. An **unenforceable contract** is one that may have been valid, but its enforcement is now barred by the statute of limitations or the doctrine of laches (unreasonable delay). For instance, if you try to sue on a contract six years after the other party stops performing, the suit would be barred by a four-year statute of limitations. Examples of valid, void, and voidable contracts are included throughout this chapter. Let us turn our attention to the requirements of a valid contract.

void contract

A contract that has no binding effect on the parties who made it.

voidable contract

A contract that is able to be voided by one of its parties.

Essentials of a Valid Contract

For a contract to be legally valid, and hence binding and enforceable, the following five requirements must be met:

1. Legally competent parties
2. Mutual agreement

3. Lawful objective

4. Consideration or cause

5. Contract in writing when required by law

If these conditions are met, any party to the contract may, if the need arises, call upon a court of law to either enforce the contract as written or award money damages for nonperformance. In reality, a properly written contract seldom ends up in court because each party knows it will be enforced as written. It is the poorly written contract or the contract that borders between enforceable and unenforceable that ends up in court. A judge must then decide if a contract actually exists and the obligations of each party. Using the courts, however, is an expensive and time-consuming method of interpreting an agreement. It is much better to have a correctly prepared contract in the first place. Let's look more closely at the five requirements of an enforceable contract.

COMPETENT PARTIES

For a contract to be legally enforceable, all parties entering into it must be legally **competent**. In deciding competency, the law provides a mixture of objective and subjective standards. The most objective standard is that of age. A person must reach the age of majority to be legally capable of entering into a contract. **Minors** do not have contractual capability. The minimum age for entering into legally binding contracts is 18 years. The purpose of those laws is to protect minors from entering into contracts that they may not be old enough to understand. Most contracts made with minors, except those contracts for necessities such as food and clothing, are voidable by the minor at the minor's option. For example, a lease signed by a minor is voidable by the minor, although it could be enforced against the other party. A minor wishing to disaffirm a contract must do so while still a minor, or within a reasonable time after reaching majority. If not, the contract becomes valid. In some cases, a contract with a minor is void. For example, a minor does not have the capacity to appoint someone to sell his property. Any contract to do so (called a power of attorney) is void from the outset. If a contract with a minor is required, it is still possible to obtain a binding contract by working through the minor's legal guardian.

Regarding intoxicated persons, if there was a deliberate attempt to intoxicate a person for the purpose of approving a contract, the intoxicated person, upon sobering up, can call upon the courts to cancel the contract. If the contracting party was voluntarily drunk to the point of incompetence, when he is sober he may ratify or deny the contract if he does so promptly. However, some courts look at the matter strictly from the standpoint of whether the intoxicated person had the capability of formulating the intent to enter into a contract. Obviously, there are some fine and subjective distinctions here, and a judge may interpret them differently than the parties to the contract do. The points made in this paragraph also apply to a person who contracts while under the influence of other legal or illegal drugs.

Persons of unsound mind who have been declared incompetent by a judge may not make a valid contract, and any attempt to do so results in a void contract. The solution is to contract through the person appointed to act on behalf of the incompetent. If a person has not been judged legally incompetent but nonetheless appears incapable of understanding the transaction in question, he has no legal power to contract. In some states, persons convicted of felonies may not enter into valid contracts without the prior approval of the parole board.

competent party
Persons considered legally capable of entering into a binding contract.

POWER OF ATTORNEY. An individual can give another person the power to act on her behalf: for example, to buy or sell land or sign a lease. The document that accomplishes this is called a **power of attorney**. The person holding the power of attorney is called an **attorney-in-fact**. With regard to real estate, a power of attorney must be in writing because the real estate documents to be signed must be in writing. Any document signed with a power of attorney should be executed as follows: "Paul Jones, principal, by Samuel Smith, agent, his attorney-in-fact." If the attorney-in-fact is to convey title to land, then the power of attorney must be acknowledged by the principal and recorded. The attorney-in-fact is legally competent to the extent of the powers granted to him by the principal as long as the principal remains legally competent, and as long as both of them are alive. The power of attorney can, of course, be terminated by the principal at any time. A recorded notice of revocation is needed to revoke a recorded power of attorney.

CORPORATIONS, ETC. Corporations are considered legally competent parties. However, the individual contracting on behalf of the corporation must have authority from the board of directors. Some states also require that the corporate seal be affixed to contracts. A partnership can contract either in the name of the partnership or in the name of any of its general partners. Executors and administrators with court authorization can contract on behalf of estates, and trustees on behalf of trusts.

MUTUAL AGREEMENT

The requirement of **mutual agreement** (also called **mutual consent**, or **mutual assent**, or **meeting of the minds**) means that there must be agreement to the provisions of the contract by the parties involved. In other words, there must be a mutual willingness to enter into a contract. The existence of mutual agreement is evidenced by the words and acts of the parties indicating that there is a valid offer and an unqualified acceptance. In addition, there must be no fraud, misrepresentation, or mistake, and the agreement must be genuine and freely given. Let's consider each of these points in more detail.

OFFER AND ACCEPTANCE. **Offer and acceptance** requires that one party (the **offeror**) makes an offer to another party (the **offeree**). If the offer is acceptable, the offeree must then communicate the acceptance to the offeror. The means of communication may be spoken or written or an action that implies acceptance. To illustrate, suppose that you own a house and want to sell it. You tell your listing broker that you will accept $100,000 and that you will deliver a general warranty deed and pay the normal closing costs for the area. Within a few days, the broker submits a signed document from a prospective buyer. This constitutes an offer, and the buyer (the offeror) has just communicated it to you (the offeree). One requirement of a valid offer is that the offer be specific in its terms. Mutual agreement cannot exist if the terms of the offer are vague or undisclosed and/or the offer does not clearly state the obligations of each party involved. If the seller were to say to a prospective purchaser "Do you want to buy this house?" without stating the price, and the prospective purchaser said "Yes," the law would not consider this to be a valid offer.

COUNTEROFFER. Upon receiving the offer, the offeree has three options: to agree to it, to reject it, or to make a counteroffer. If the offeree agrees, he must agree to every item of the offer. An offer is considered by law to be rejected not only if the offeree rejects it outright but also if any change is made in the terms. *Any* change in the terms is considered a **counteroffer**. Although it may appear that the offeree is only amending the offer before he accepts it, the offeree has actually rejected it, and is making a new offer. This now makes the seller the offeror. To illustrate, suppose the prospective purchaser submits an offer to the listing broker to purchase the property for $95,000, but instead of accepting the $95,000 offer, the seller amends the contract to reflect a selling price of $100,000. This is a rejection of the original offer and creates a counteroffer to the purchaser. The purchaser now has the right to accept or reject this counteroffer. If, however, the original $95,000 offer is agreeable to the offeree (seller), he must communicate the acceptance to the purchaser. While a spoken "Yes, I'll take it," would be legally adequate, prudent real estate brokers should obtain the signature of the seller on a contract, without any further changes.

It should also be pointed out that an offer can be revoked by the offeror at any time prior to the offeror hearing of its acceptance. For example, if you tell a prospective tenant that she can rent the property for $495 per month, and, while waiting for her response, you find another prospective tenant who is willing to pay more, you can revoke your first offer at any time prior to hearing of its acceptance, then make your contract with the second prospective tenant. An offeror should be strongly advised, however, not to initiate more than one offer at a time, since considerable confusion can be caused by multiple offers, revocations, and acceptances in one transaction.

FRAUD. Mutual agreement requires that there be no fraud, misrepresentation, or mistake in the contract if it is to be valid. A **fraud** is an act intended to deceive for the purpose of inducing another to part with something of value. It can be as blatant as knowingly telling a lie or making a promise with no intention of performance. For example, you are showing your apartment and a prospective tenant asks if there is frequent bus service nearby. There isn't, but you say yes as you sense this is important and want to rent the apartment. The prospective tenant rents the apartment, relying on this information from you, and moves in. The next day he calls and says there is no public transportation and he wants to break the rental agreement immediately. Because mutual agreement was lacking, the tenant can **rescind** (cancel) the contract and get his money back.

Fraud can also result from failing to disclose important information, thereby inducing someone to accept an offer. For example, the day you show your apartment to a prospective tenant the weather is dry. But you know that during every rainstorm the tenant's automobile parking stall becomes a lake of water six inches deep. This would qualify as a fraud if the prospective tenant was not made aware of the problem before agreeing to the rental contract. Once again, the law will permit the aggrieved party to rescind the contract. However, the tenant does not have to rescind the contract. If he likes the other features of the apartment enough, he can elect to live with the flooded parking stall.

If a real estate agent commits a fraud to make a sale and the deceived party later rescinds the sales contract, not only is the commission lost, but explanations will be necessary to the other parties of the contract. In addition to the civil liability a brokerage firm may incur, state license laws provide for suspension or revocation of a real estate license for fraudulent acts.

INNOCENT MISREPRESENTATION. Innocent misrepresentation differs from fraud (intentional misrepresentation) in that the party providing the wrong information is not doing so to deceive another for the purpose of reaching an agreement. To illustrate, suppose that over the past year you have observed that city buses stop near your apartment building. If you tell a prospective tenant that there is bus service, only to learn the day after the tenant moves in that service stopped last week, this is innocent

counteroffer
An offer made in response to an offer.

fraud
An act intended to deceive for the purpose of inducing another to give up something of value.

misrepresentation. Although there was no dishonesty involved, the tenant still has the right to rescind the contract. If performance has not begun on the contract (in this case the tenant has not moved in), the injured party may give notice that she **disaffirms** (revokes) the contract. However, if the tenant wants to break the contract, she must do so in a timely manner; otherwise, the law will presume that the situation is satisfactory to the tenant.

MISTAKE. Mistake as applied in contract law has a very narrow meaning. It does not include innocent misrepresentation, nor does it include ignorance, inability, or poor judgment. If a person enters into a contract that he later regrets because he did not investigate it thoroughly enough, or because it did not turn out to be beneficial, the law will not grant relief to him on the grounds of mistake, even though he may now consider it was a "mistake" to have made the contract in the first place. Mistake, as used in contract law, arises from ambiguity in negotiations and mistake of material fact. For example, you offer to sell your mountain cabin to an acquaintance. He has never seen your cabin, and you give him instructions on how to get there to look at it. He returns and accepts your offer. However, he made a wrong turn and the cabin he looked at was not your cabin. A week later he discovers his error. The law considers this ambiguity in negotiations. In this case the buyer, in his mind, was purchasing a different cabin from the one the seller was selling; therefore, there is no mutual agreement and any contract signed is void.

To illustrate a mistake of fact, suppose that you show your apartment to a prospective tenant and tell him that he must let you know by the next day if he wants to rent it. The next day he visits you and together you enter into a rental contract. Although neither of you is aware of it, there has just been a serious fire in the apartment. Since a fire-gutted apartment is not what the two of you had in mind when the rental contract was signed, there is no mutual agreement.

Occasionally, "mistake of law" will be claimed as grounds for relief from a contract. However, mistake as to one's legal rights in a contract is not generally accepted by courts of law unless it is coupled with a mistake of fact. Ignorance of the law is not considered a mistake.

CONTRACTUAL INTENT. Mutual agreement also requires that the parties express **contractual intent**. This means that their intention is to be bound by the agreement, thus precluding jokes or jests from becoming valid contracts.

duress

The application of force to obtain an agreement.

DURESS. The last requirement of mutual agreement is that the offer and acceptance be genuine and freely given. **Duress** (use of force), **menace** (threat of violence), or **undue influence** (unfair advantage) cannot be used to obtain agreement. The law permits a contract made under any of these conditions to be revoked by the aggrieved party.

LAWFUL OBJECTIVE

To be enforceable, a contract cannot call for the breaking of laws. This is because a court of law cannot be called upon to enforce a contract that requires that a law be broken. Such a contract is void, or if already in operation, it is unenforceable in a court of law. For example, a debt contract requiring an interest rate in excess of that allowed by state law would be void. If the borrower had started repaying the debt and then later stopped, the lender would not be able to look to the courts to enforce collection of the balance. Contracts contrary to general public policy are also unenforceable.

CONSIDERATION

For an agreement to be enforceable it must be supported by **consideration**. The purpose of requiring consideration is to demonstrate that a bargain has been struck between the parties to the contract. The size, quantity, nature, or amount of what is being exchanged is irrelevant as long as it is present. Consideration is usually something of value such as a promise to do something, money, property, or personal services. For example, there can be an exchange of a promise for a promise, money for a promise, money for property, goods for services, and so on. Forbearance also qualifies as consideration.

consideration

An act or promise given in exchange for something.

EXCHANGE OF PROMISES. In a typical offer to purchase a home, the consideration is the mutual exchange of promises by the buyer and seller to obligate themselves to do something they were not previously required to do. In other words, the seller agrees to sell on the terms agreed and the buyer agrees to buy the property on those same terms. The earnest money the buyer may put down is not the consideration necessary to make the contract valid. Rather, earnest money is a tangible indication of the buyer's intent and may become a source of compensation (damages) to the seller in the event the buyer does not carry out his promises.

In a deed, the consideration requirement is usually met with a statement such as "For ten dollars and other good and valuable consideration." Also, the purchase contract is part of the consideration and is legally merged into the deed. In a lease, the periodic payment of rent is the consideration for the use of the premises.

VALUABLE CONSIDERATION. A contract fails to be legally binding if consideration is lacking from any party to the contract. The legal philosophy is that a person cannot promise to do something of value for someone else without receiving in turn some form of consideration. Stated another way, each party must give up something—that is, each must suffer a detriment. For example, if I promise to give you my car, the consideration requirement is not met since you promise nothing in return. But if I promise to give you my car when you take me to Hawaii, the consideration requirement is met. As a group, money, plus promises, property, legal rights, services, and forbearance, if they are worth money, are classified as **valuable consideration**.

GOOD CONSIDERATION. What about outright gifts such as the gift of real property from a parent to a child based solely on love and affection? Although this is not valuable consideration, it is nonetheless **good consideration** and, as such, fulfills the legal requirement that consideration be present. The law generally will not inquire as to the adequacy of the consideration unless there is evidence of fraud, mistake, duress, threat, or undue influence. For instance, if a man gave away his property or sold it very cheaply to keep it from his creditors, the creditors could ask the courts to set aside those transfers.

MULTIPLE MEANINGS OF THE WORD *CONSIDERATION*. If the word *consideration* continues to be confusing to you, it is because the word has three meanings in real estate. The first is consideration from the standpoint of a legal requirement for a valid contract. You may wish to think of this form of consideration as **legal consideration** or **cause**. The second meaning is money. For example, the consideration upon which conveyance taxes are charged is the amount of money exchanged in the transaction. The third meaning is acknowledgment. Thus, the phrase "in consideration of ten dollars" means "in acknowledgment of" or "in receipt of."

CONTRACT IN WRITING

In each state there is a law that is commonly known as a *Statute of Frauds*. Its purpose is to prevent frauds by requiring that all contracts for the sale of land, or an interest in land, be in writing and signed to be enforceable in a court of law. This includes such things as offers, acceptances, binders, land contracts, deeds, escrows, and options to purchase. Mortgages and trust deeds (and their accompanying bonds and notes) and leases for more than one year must also be in writing to be enforceable. In addition, most states have adopted the **Uniform Commercial Code** that requires, among other things, that the sale of personal property with value in excess of $500 be in writing. Most states also require that real estate listing contracts be expressed in writing.

PURPOSE. The purpose of requiring that a contract be written and signed is to prevent perjury and fraudulent attempts to seek legal enforcement of a contract that never existed. It is not necessary that a contract be a single formal document. It can consist of a series of signed letters or memoranda as long as the essentials of a valid contract are present. Note that the requirement for a written contract relates only to the enforceability of the contract. Thus, if Mr. Colby orally agrees to sell his land to Mr. Conan and they carry out the deal, neither can come back after the contract was performed and ask a court to rescind the deal because the agreement to sell was oral.

The most common real estate contract that does not need to be in writing to be enforceable is a month-to-month rental agreement that can be terminated by either landlord or tenant on one month's notice. Nonetheless, most are in writing because people tend to forget oral promises. While the unhappy party can go to court, the judge may have a difficult time determining what oral promises were made, particularly if there were no witnesses other than the parties to the agreement. Hence, it is advisable to put all important contracts in writing and for each party to recognize the agreement by signing it. If a party is a corporation, most states require the signatures of two corporate officers plus the corporate seal. It is also customary to date written contracts, although most can be enforced without showing the date the agreement was reached.

A written contract will supersede an oral one. Thus, if two parties orally promise one thing and then write and sign something else, the written contract will prevail. This has been the basis for many complaints against overzealous real estate agents who make oral promises that do not appear anywhere in the written sales contract.

PAROL EVIDENCE RULE. Under certain circumstances, the **parol evidence rule** permits oral evidence to complete an otherwise incomplete or ambiguous written contract. However, the application of this rule is quite narrow. If a contract is complete and clear in its intent, the courts presume that what the parties put into writing is what they agreed upon.

EXECUTORY, EXECUTED, EXECUTE

A contract that is in the process of being carried out is said to be **executory**—that is, in the process of being performed. Once completed, it is said to be **executed**—that is, performance has taken place. This may refer to the signing of the contract or to its completed performance depending on what the contract requires. The word *execute*, a much more frequently used term, refers to the process of completing, performing, or carrying out something. Thus, you execute a document when you sign it, and this is the most common use of the term. Once signed, you execute the terms of the contract by carrying out its terms.

"esign"

The federal government has preempted all of the foregoing rules somewhat by authorizing electronic signatures and documents. The Electronic Records in Global and National Commerce Act was signed on October 1, 2000, and became effective on March 1, 2001.

The primary purpose of this act, popularly referred to as "esign," is to repeal state law requirements for written instruments as they apply to electronic agreements. The operative language is quite clear and succinct:

> "Notwithstanding any statute, regulation, or other rule of law [other than subsequent parts of this same statute], with respect to any transaction in or affecting interstate or foreign commerce-
>
> (1) a signature, contract, or other record relating to such transaction may not be denied legal effect, validity or enforceability solely because it is in electronic form; and
>
> (2) a contract relating to such transaction may not be denied legal effect, validity or enforceability solely because an electronic signature or electronic record was used in its formation."

The operative term is "transaction." The esign legislation provides a very broad definition:

> "The term 'transaction' means an action or set of actions relating to the conduct of business, consumer or commercial affairs between two or more persons, including any of the following types of conduct-
>
> (A) the sale, lease, exchange, licensing or other disposition of [personal property, services, and intangibles]
>
> (B) the sale, lease, exchange, or other disposition of any interest in real property, or any combination thereof."

Congress has provided that almost anything can be an electronic signature rendering a party bound to agreement. The statutory language states:

> "The term 'electronic signature' means an electronic sound, symbol, or process, attached to or logically associated with a contract or other record and executed or adopted by a person with the intent to sign the record."

For instance, if you were sent an e-mail from John Jones that said: "I'll buy your property at 450 W. Meyer in Chicago for $50,000," and you typed at the top of this message "OK" and hit return, we might have a binding real estate contract. All John Jones would have to show is that the typing of the word "OK" indicated my intent to express agreement. The fact that I didn't even type out my name would not matter, since I "attached" an "electronic symbol" to the contract. The parties must agree to an electronic transaction, but the use of e-mail is arguably an implied consent. The contract would still have to meet standards of clarity and certainty. And perhaps an exchange this informal would not meet those standards in some jurisdictions. The point is that a relatively simple and perhaps thoughtless act arguably could result in the formation of a contract.

Note that the act applies to only transactions in "interstate commerce." An e-mail message, when it leaves a computer, could conceivably bounce to Detroit, then to Geneva, then to Mexico City, all on its way to another computer, even if the other computer was located in the building next door. Further, it was carried on a variety of communications media commonly associated with interstate transactions. The likelihood is quite strong that even the Supreme Court will have difficulty interpreting around the conclusion that e-mail transactions are interstate commerce. There is a provision that allows states to supercede this legislation with their own version of the Uniform Electronic Transactions Act (UETA), so check your own state's legislation.

Performance and Discharge of Contracts

Most contracts are discharged by being fully performed by the contracting parties in accordance with the contract terms. However, alternatives are open to the parties of the contract. One is to sell or otherwise **assign the contract to another party**. Unless prohibited by the contract, rights, benefits, and obligations under a contract can be assigned to someone else. The original party to the contract, however, still remains ultimately liable for its performance. Note, too, that an assignment is a contract in itself and must meet all the essential contract requirements to be enforceable. A common example of an assignment occurs when a lessee wants to move out and sells his lease to another party. When a contract creates a personal obligation, such as a listing agreement with a broker, an assignment may not be made.

NOVATION

A contract can also be performed by novation. **Novation is the substitution** of a new contract between the same or new parties. For example, novation occurs when a buyer assumes a seller's loan *and* the lender releases the seller from the loan contract. With novation, the departing party is released from the obligation to complete the contract.

If the objective of a contract becomes legally impossible to accomplish, the law will consider the contract discharged. For example, a new legislative statute may forbid what the contract originally intended. If the parties mutually agree to cancel their contract before it is executed, this too is a form of discharge. For instance, you sign a five-year lease to pay $900 per month for an office. Three years later you find a better location and want to move. Meanwhile, rents for similar offices in your building have increased to $1,000 per month. Under these conditions, the landlord might be happy to agree to cancel your lease.

DECEASED PARTY

If one of the contracting parties dies, a contract is considered discharged if it calls for some specific act that only the deceased person could have performed. For example, if you hired a freelance gardener to tend your landscaping and he died, the contract would be discharged. However, if your contract is with a firm that employs other gardeners who can do the job, the contract would still be valid.

If there is a valid purchase contract and one party dies, the contract is usually enforceable against the estate because the estate has the authority to carry out the deceased's affairs. Similarly, if a person mortgages his or her property and dies, the estate must continue the payments or lose the property.

Breach of Contract

breach of contract
Failure, without legal excuse, to perform as required by a contract.

When one party fails to perform as required by a contract, and the law does not recognize the reason for failure to be a valid excuse, there is a **breach of contract**. The wronged or innocent party has six alternatives: (1) to accept partial performance, (2) to rescind the contract unilaterally, (3) to sue for money damages, (4) to sue for specific performance, (5) to accept liquidated money damages, or (6) to mutually rescind the contract. Let us consider each of these.

PARTIAL PERFORMANCE

Partial performance may be acceptable to the innocent party because there may not be a great deal at stake or because the innocent party feels that the time and effort to sue would not be worth the rewards. Suppose that you contracted with a roofing repairman to fix your roof for $400. When he was finished, you paid him. A week later, you discover a spot that he had agreed to fix but missed. After many futile phone calls, you accept the breach and consider the contract discharged because it is easier to fix the spot yourself than to keep pursuing the repairman.

UNILATERAL RESCISSION

Under certain circumstances, the innocent party can **unilaterally rescind** a contract. That is, the innocent party can take the position that if the other party is not going to perform his obligations, then the innocent party will not either. An example would be a rent strike in retaliation to a landlord who fails to keep the premises habitable. Unilateral rescission should be resorted to only after consulting an attorney.

LAWSUIT FOR MONEY DAMAGES

If the damages to the innocent party can be reasonably expressed in terms of money, the innocent party can sue for **money damages**. For example, you rent an apartment to a tenant. As part of the rental contract, you furnish the refrigerator and freezer unit. While the tenant is on vacation, the unit breaks down and $200 worth of frozen meat and other perishables spoil. Since your obligation under the contract is to provide the tenant with a working refrigerator-freezer, the tenant can sue you for $200 in money damages. He can also recover interest on the money awarded to him from the day of the loss to the day you reimburse him.

LAWSUIT FOR SPECIFIC PERFORMANCE

A lawsuit for **specific performance** is an action in court by the innocent party to force the breaching party to carry out the remainder of the contract according to the precise terms, price, and conditions agreed upon. For example, you make an offer to purchase a parcel of land and the seller accepts. A written contract is prepared and signed by both of you. If you carry out all your obligations under the contract, but the seller has a change of mind and refuses to deliver title to you, you may bring a lawsuit against the seller for specific performance. In reviewing your suit, the court will determine whether the contract is valid and legal, whether you have carried out your duties under the contract, and whether the contract is just and reasonable. If you win your lawsuit, the court will force the seller to deliver title to you as specified in the contract.

specific performance
Contract performance according to the precise terms agreed upon.

COMPARISON

Note the difference between suing for money damages and suing for specific performance. When money can be used to restore one's position (as in the case of the tenant who can buy $200 worth of fresh food), a suit for money damages is appropriate.

In situations in which money cannot provide an adequate remedy, and this is often the case in real estate because no two properties are exactly alike, specific performance is appropriate. Notice, too, that the mere existence of the legal rights of the wronged party is often enough to gain cooperation. In the case of the spoiled food, you would give the tenant the value of the lost food before spending time and money in court to hear a judge tell you to do the same thing. A threat of a lawsuit will often bring the desired results if the defendant knows that the law will side with the wronged party. The cases that do go to court are usually those in which the identity of the wronged party and/or the extent of the damages is not clear.

LIQUIDATED DAMAGES

liquidated damages

An amount of money specified in a contract as compensation to be paid if the contract is not satisfactorily completed.

The parties to a contract may decide in advance the amount of damages to be paid in the event either party breaches the contract. An example is an offer to purchase real estate that includes a statement to the effect that, once the seller accepts the offer, if the buyer fails to complete the purchase, the seller may keep the buyer's deposit (the earnest money) as **liquidated damages**. If a broker is involved, seller and broker usually agree to divide the damages, thus compensating the seller for damages and the broker for time and effort. Another case of liquidated damages occurs when a builder promises to finish a building by a certain date or pay the party that hired him a certain number of dollars per day until it is completed. This impresses upon the builder the need for prompt completion and compensates the property owner for losses due to the delay.

MUTUAL RESCISSION

Specific performance, money damages, and liquidated damages are all designed to aid the innocent party in the event of a breach of contract. However, as a practical matter, the time and cost of pursuing a remedy in a court of law may sometimes exceed the benefits to be derived. Moreover, there is the possibility the judge for your case may not agree with your point of view. Therefore, even though you are the innocent party and you feel you have a legitimate case that can be pursued in the courts, you may find it more practical to agree with the other party (or parties) to simply rescind (i.e., cancel or annul) the contract. To properly protect everyone involved, the agreement to cancel must be in writing and signed by the parties to the original contract. Properly executed, **mutual rescission** relieves the parties to the contract from their obligations to each other.

An alternative to mutual rescission is novation. As noted earlier, this is the substitution of a new contract for an existing one. Novation provides a middle ground between suing and rescinding. Thus, the breaching party may be willing to complete the contract, provided the innocent party will voluntarily make certain changes in it. If this is acceptable, the changes should be put into writing (or the contract redrafted) and then signed by the parties involved.

Statute of Limitations

The **statute of limitations** limits by law the amount of time a wronged party has to seek the aid of a court in obtaining justice. The aggrieved party must start legal proceedings within a certain period of time or the courts will not help him. The amount of time varies from state to state and by type of legal action involved. However, time limits of three to seven years are typical for breach of contract.

Implied Obligations

As was pointed out at the beginning of this chapter, one can incur contractual obligations by implication, as well as by oral or written contracts. Home builders and real estate agents provide two timely examples. For many years, if a homeowner discovered poor design or workmanship after she had bought a new home, it was her problem. The philosophy was *caveat emptor*—let the buyer beware *before* he or she buys. Today, courts of law find that in building a home and offering it for sale, the builder simultaneously implies that it is fit for living. Thus, if a builder installs a toilet in a bathroom, the implication is that it will work. In fact, many states have now passed legislation that makes builders liable for their work for one year.

Similarly, real estate agent trade organizations, such as the National Association of REALTORS® and state and local REALTOR® associations, are constantly working to elevate the status of real estate brokers and salespersons to that of a competent professional in the public's mind. But as professional status is gained, there is an implied obligation to dispense professional-quality service. Thus, an individual agent is not only responsible for acting in accordance with written laws, but is also responsible for being competent and knowledgeable. Once recognized as a professional by the public, the real estate agent will not be able to plead ignorance.

In view of the present trend toward consumer protection, the concept of "Let the buyer beware" is being replaced with "Let the seller beware" and "Let the agent beware."

Vocabulary Review

Match terms a–z with statements 1–26.

a. Assign
b. Attorney-in-fact
c. Breach of contract
d. Competent party
e. Consideration
f. Contract
g. Counteroffer
h. Disaffirm
i. Duress
j. Execute
k. Forbear
l. Fraud
m. Liquidated damages
n. Minor
o. Money damages
p. Mutual agreement
q. Novation
r. Offeror
s. Party

_____F_____ 1. A legally enforceable agreement to do (or not to do) something.

_____ 2. A contract in which one party makes a promise or begins performance without first receiving any promise to perform from the other.

_____ 3. An act intended to deceive for the purpose of inducing another to part with something of value.

_____ 4. A person who is considered legally capable of entering into a contract.

_____ 5. A person who is not old enough to enter into legally binding contracts.

_____ 6. A contract that is not legally binding on any of the parties that made it.

_____ 7. The party who makes an offer.

_____ 8. An offer made in response to an offer.

_____ 9. To cancel a contract and restore the parties involved to their respective positions before the contract was made.

_____10. Use of force to obtain contract agreement.

_____11. Not to act.

_____12. To transfer one's rights in a contract to another person.

_____13. Damages that can be measured in and compensated by money.

_____14. Failure, without legal excuse, to perform any promise called for in a contract.

_____15. Contract performance according to the precise terms agreed upon.

t. Rescind

u. Specific performance

v. Statute of Frauds

w. Statute of limitations

x. Unilateral contract

y. Void contract

z. Voidable contract

_____16. A sum of money called for in a contract that is to be paid if the contract is breached.

_____17. Laws that set forth the period of time within which a lawsuit must be filed.

_____18. A person or group involved in a legal proceeding.

_____19. A contract that is able to be voided by one of its parties.

_____20. The person holding a power of attorney on behalf of another.

_____21. A meeting of the minds.

_____22. To revoke.

_____23. An act or promise given in exchange for something.

_____24. Requires all contracts for the sale of land to be in writing to be enforceable in a court of law.

_____25. To complete, perform, or carry out something.

_____26. The substitution of a new contract for an existing one.

Questions and Problems

1. What is the difference between an expressed contract and an implied contract? Give an example of each.

2. Name the five requirements of a legally valid contract.

3. What is the difference between a void contract and a voidable contract?

4. Give four examples of persons not considered legally competent to enter into contracts.

5. How can an offer be terminated prior to its acceptance?

6. What does the word *mistake* mean when applied to contract law?

7. Why must consideration be present for a legally binding contract to exist? Give examples of three types of consideration.

8. If a contract is legally unenforceable, are the parties to the contract stopped from performing it? Why or why not?

9. If a breach of contract occurs, what alternatives are open to the parties to the contract?

10. Assume that a breach of contract has occurred and the wronged party intends to file a lawsuit over the matter. What factors would he consider in deciding whether to sue for money damages or for specific performance?

Additional Readings

"Code of Federal Regulations, Title 41, Public Contracts and Property Management" by the United States Government Printing Office (Revised as of July 1, 2001).

Doing the Right Thing: A Real Estate Practitioner's Guide to Ethical Decision Making, 4th ed. by Deborah H. Long (OnCourse Learning, 2007).

"The Emergency of Dynamic Contract Law" by Melvin A. Eisenberg (*California Law Review*, December 2000, vol. 88, issue 6, pp. 1743–1816).

The Failure of Contracts: Contract, Restitutionary, and Proprietary Consequences by Francis D. Rose (Hart Publishing, 1997).

Good Faith in Contract and Property Law by Angelo D. M. Forte (Hart Publishing, 1999).

Real Estate Law, 11th ed. by Charles Jacobus (OnCourse Learning, 2013). A guide to the legal aspects of sales, mortgages, conveyances, exchanges, and leasing. Examines broker-lawyer relationship, and identifies various legal entanglements and methods to avoid them.

CHAPTER 8

Real Estate Sales Contracts

The present chapter focuses on contracts used to initiate the sale of real estate. Chiefly we will look at the purchase contract, the installment contract, and the lease with option to buy. There will also be brief discussions of a real estate binder, letter of intent, right of first refusal, and real estate exchange.

Purpose of Sales Contracts

What is the purpose of a real estate sales contract? If a buyer and a seller agree on a price, why can't the buyer hand the seller the necessary money, and the seller simultaneously hand the buyer a deed? The main reason is that the buyer needs time to ascertain that the seller is, in fact, legally capable of conveying title. For protection, the buyer enters into a written and signed contract with the seller, promising that the purchase price will be paid only after title has been searched and found to be in satisfactory condition. The seller, in turn, promises to deliver a deed to the buyer when the buyer has paid his money. This exchange of promises forms the legal consideration of the contract. A contract also gives the buyer time to arrange financing and to specify how such matters as taxes, existing debts, leases, and property inspections will be handled.

A properly prepared contract commits each party to its terms. Once a sales contract is in writing and signed, the seller cannot change his mind and sell to another person. The seller is obligated to convey title to the buyer when the buyer has performed as required by the contract. Likewise, the buyer must carry out his promises, including paying for the property, provided the seller has done everything required by the contract.

LEARNING OBJECTIVES

After reading this chapter, you should be able to:

❮ Understand the purpose of real estate sales contracts.

❮ Define at least three contingencies that are common in most real estate sales contracts.

❮ Understand common provisions of real estate sales contracts.

❮ Define federal laws that effect contracts for the sale of real estate.

❮ Define and understand the use of installment land contracts.

❮ Understand the concept of "equitable title."

❮ Determine the difference with "options" and "rights of first refusal."

❮ Discuss real estate exchange agreements under Section 1031 of the Internal Revenue Code.

KEY TERMS

Binder • Default • Earnest money deposit • Equitable title • Installment contract • Lease-option • Qualified intermediary • Right of first refusal • Tax-deferred exchange • "Time is of the essence"

Purchase Contracts

Variously known as a purchase contract, deposit receipt, offer and acceptance, purchase offer, or purchase and sales agreement, these preprinted forms contain four key parts: (1) provision for the buyer's earnest money deposit, (2) the buyer's offer to purchase, (3) the acceptance of the offer by the seller, and (4) provisions for the payment of a brokerage commission.

Figure 8.1 illustrates in simplified language the highlights of a real estate purchase contract. The purchase contract begins at [1] and [2] by identifying the location and date of the deposit and offer. At [3], the name of the buyer is written, and at [4], the name of the property owner (seller). At [5], the property for which the buyer is making his offer is described. Although the street address and type of property (in this case a house) are not necessary to the validity of the contract, this information is often included for convenience in locating the property. The legal description that follows is crucial. Care must be taken to make certain that it is correct.

EARNEST MONEY DEPOSIT

earnest money deposit

Money that accompanies an offer to purchase as evidence of good faith.

The price that the buyer is willing to pay, along with the manner in which he proposes to pay it, is inserted at [6]. Of particular importance in this paragraph is the earnest money deposit that the buyer submits with his offer. With the exception of court-ordered sales, no laws govern the size of the deposit or even the need for one. Generally speaking though, the seller and his agent will want a reasonably substantial deposit to show the buyer's earnest intentions and to have something for their trouble if the seller accepts and the buyer fails to follow through. The buyer will prefer to make as small a deposit as possible, as a deposit ties up his capital, and there is the possibility of losing it. However, the buyer also recognizes that the seller may refuse even to consider the offer unless accompanied by a reasonable deposit. The amount of earnest money, therefore, is always negotiable. In most parts of the country, a deposit of $2,000 to $5,000 on a $120,000 offer would be considered acceptable. In court-ordered sales, the required deposit is usually 10% of the offering price.

Note that earnest money, by itself, is not consideration. The consideration in a bilateral contract for sale is the mutual promises the parties make to each other. The earnest money can be agreed-upon liquidated damages (note the discussion in the previous chapter) in the event of a buyer's default.

default

Failure to perform a legal duty, such as failure to carry out the terms of a contract.

DEED AND CONDITION OF TITLE

At [7], the buyer requests that the seller convey title by means of a warranty deed, and provide and pay for a policy of title insurance showing the condition of title to be as described here. Before the offer is made, the broker and seller will have told the buyer about the condition of title. However, the buyer has no way of verifying that information until the title is actually searched. To protect himself, the buyer states at [7] the condition of title that he is willing to accept. If title to the property is not presently in this condition, the seller is required by the contract to take whatever steps are necessary to place title in this condition before title is conveyed. If, for example, there is an existing mortgage or judgment lien against the property, the seller must have it removed. If there are other owners, their interests must be extinguished. If anyone has a right to use the property (such as a tenant under a lease), or controls the use of the property (such as a deed restriction), or has an easement, other than what is specifically mentioned, the seller must remove these before conveying title to the buyer.

FIGURE
8.1   Sample Purchase Contract

REAL ESTATE PURCHASE CONTRACT

[1] City of _Riverdale_ , State of _____ , _October 10, 20xx_ .[2]

[3] _Ben Thayer_ (herein called the Buyer) agrees to purchase and [4] _Cliff Dweller and Sandy Dweller_ (herein called the Seller) agree to sell the following described real property located in the City of [5] _Riverdale_ , County of _Lakeside_ , State of _____ , _a single-family dwelling commonly known as 1704 Main Street_ , and legally described as _Lot 21, Block C of Madison's Subdivision as per map in Survey Book 10, page 51, in the Office of the County Recorder of said County_ .

[6] The total purchase price is _one hundred twenty thousand_ dollars _($120,000.00)_ , payable as follows: _Three thousand dollars ($3,000.00) is given today as an earnest money deposit, receipt of which is hereby acknowledged. An additional $21,000.00 is to be placed into escrow by the Buyer before the closing date. The remaining $96,000.00 is to be by way of a new mortgage on said property_ .

[7] Seller will deliver to the Buyer a _warranty_ deed to said property. Seller will furnish to the Buyer at the _Seller's_ expense a standard American Land Title Association title insurance policy issued by _First Security Title Company_ showing title vested in the Buyer and that the Seller is conveying title free of liens, encumbrances, easements, rights, and conditions except as follows: _People's Gas and Electric Company utility easement along eastern five feet of said lot_ .

[8] The escrow agent shall be _Tidal Title Company_ and escrow instructions shall be signed by the Buyer and Seller and delivered to escrow within five days upon receipt thereof. The close of escrow shall be _45_ days after the date of mutual agreement to this contract.

[9] Property taxes, property insurance, mortgage interest, income and expense items shall be prorated as of _the close of escrow_ .

[10] Any outstanding bonds or assessments on the property shall be _paid by the Seller_ .

[11] Any existing mortgage indebtedness against the property is to be _paid by the Seller_ .

[12] Seller will provide Buyer with a report from a licensed pest control inspector that the property is free of termites and wood rot. The cost of the report and any corrective work deemed necessary by the report are to be paid for by the _Seller_ .

[13] Possession of the property is to be delivered to the Buyer _upon close of escrow_ .

[14] Escrow expenses shall be _shared equally by the Buyer and Seller_ .

[15] Conveyance tax to be paid by _Seller_ .

[16] The earnest money deposit to be held _in escrow_ .

[17] All attached floor coverings, attached television antenna, window screens, screen doors, storm windows, storm doors, plumbing and lighting fixtures (except floor, standing and swag lamp), curtain rods, shades, venetian blinds, bathroom fixtures, trees, plants, shrubbery, water heaters, awnings, built-in heating, ventilating, and cooling systems, built-in stoves and ranges, and fences now on the premises shall be included unless otherwise noted. Any leased fixtures on the premises are not included unless specifically stated.

[18] Other provisions: _the purchase of this property is contingent upon the Buyer obtaining a mortgage loan on this property in the amount of $96,000.00 or more, with a maturity date of at least 25 years, at an interest rate no higher than 8% per year and loan fees not to exceed two points. Purchase price to include the refrigerator currently on the premises. Purchase is subject to buyer's approval of a qualified building inspector's report. Said report to be obtained within 7 days at Buyer's expense_ .

(continued)

FIGURE 8.1   Sample Purchase Contract (continued)

[19] If the improvements on the property are destroyed or materially damaged prior to the close of escrow, or if the Buyer is unable to obtain financing as stated herein, or if the Seller is unable to deliver title as promised, then the Buyer, at his option, may terminate this agreement and the deposit made by him shall be returned to him in full. If the Seller fails to fulfill any of the other agreements made herein, the Buyer may terminate this agreement with full refund of deposit, accept lesser performance, or sue for specific performance.

[20] If this purchase is not completed by reason of the Buyer's default, the Seller is released from his obligation to sell to the Buyer and shall retain the deposit money as his sole right to damages.

[21] Upon the signature of the Buyer, this document becomes an offer to the Seller to purchase the property described herein. The Seller has until __11:00 P.M., October 13, 20xx__ to indicate acceptance of this offer by signing and delivering it to the Buyer. If acceptance is not received by that time, this offer shall be deemed revoked and the deposit shall be returned in full to the Buyer.

[22] Time is of the essence in this contract.

Real Estate Broker __Riverdale Realty Company__. By [23] __Shirley Newhouse__.

Address __1234 Riverdale Blvd__. Telephone __333-1234__.

[24] The undersigned offers and agrees to buy the above described property on the terms and conditions stated herein and acknowledges receipt of a copy hereof.

Buyer __Ben Thayer__

Address __2323 Cedar Ave. Riverdale__

Telephone __666-2468__

ACCEPTANCE

[25] The undersigned accepts the foregoing offer and agrees to sell the property described above on the terms and conditions set forth.

[26] The undersigned has employed __Lakeside Realty Company__ as Broker and for Broker's services agrees to pay said Broker as commission the sum of __fifty-seven hundred sixty --- dollars ($5760.00)__ upon recordation of the deed or if completion of this sale is prevented by the Seller. If completion of this contract is prevented by the Buyer, Broker shall share equally in any damages collected by the Seller, not to exceed the above stated commission.

[27] The undersigned acknowledges receipt of a copy hereof.

Seller __Sandy Dweller__

Seller __Cliff Dweller__

Address __1704 Tenth St. Riverdale__

Telephone __333-3579__ Date __10/10/xx__

NOTIFICATION OF ACCEPTANCE

[28] Receipt of a copy of the foregoing agreement is hereby acknowledged.

Buyer *Ben Thayer* Date __10/10/xx__

Note: This illustration has been prepared for discussion purposes only and not as a form to copy and use in a real estate sale. For that purpose, you must use a contract specifically legal in your state.

Source: © 2014 OnCourse Learning

CLOSING AGENT

In a growing number of states, escrow agents (described in more detail in Chapter 16) handle the closing. Number [8] names the escrow agent, states that the escrow instructions must be signed promptly, and sets the closing date for the transaction. It is on that date that the seller will receive his money and the buyer his deed. The selection of a closing date is based on the estimated length of time necessary to carry out the conditions of the purchase contract. Normally, the most time-consuming item is finding a lender to make the necessary mortgage loan. Typically, this takes from 30 to 60 days, depending on the lender and the availability of loan money. The other conditions of the contract, such as the title search and arrangements to pay off any existing liens, take less time and can be done while arranging for a new mortgage loan. Once a satisfactory loan source is found, the lender makes a commitment to the buyer that the needed loan money will be placed into escrow on the closing date.

In regions of the United States where the custom is to use a closing meeting rather than an escrow, this section of the contract would name the attorney, broker, or other person responsible for carrying out the paperwork and details of the purchase agreement. A date would also be set for the closing meeting at which the buyer and seller and their attorneys, the lender, and the title company representative would be present to conclude the transaction.

PRORATING

Number [9] deals with the question of how certain ongoing expenses, such as property taxes, insurance, and mortgage interest, will be divided between the buyer and the seller. For example, if the seller pays $220 in advance for a one-year fire insurance policy and then sells his house halfway through the policy year, what happens to the remaining six months of coverage that the seller paid for but will not use? One solution is to transfer the remaining six months of coverage to the buyer for $110. Income items are also prorated. Suppose that the seller has been renting the basement of his house to a college student for $90 per month. The student pays the $90 rent in advance on the first of each month. If the property is sold part way through the month, the buyer is entitled to the portion of the month's rent that is earned while he owns the property. This process of dividing ongoing expenses and income items is known as **prorating**. More information and examples regarding the prorating process are included in Chapter 16.

At [10], the buyer states that, if there are any unpaid assessments or bonds currently against the property, the seller shall pay them as a condition of the sale. Alternatively, the buyer could agree to assume responsibility for paying them off. Since the buyer wants the property free of mortgages so that he can arrange for his own loan, at [11] he asks the seller to remove any existing indebtedness. On the closing date, part of the money received from the buyer is used to clear the seller's debts against the property. Alternatively, the buyer could agree to assume responsibility for paying off the existing debt against the property as part of the purchase price.

TERMITE INSPECTION

At [12], the buyer asks that the property be inspected at the seller's expense for signs of termites and rotted wood (**dry rot**), and that the seller pay for extermination and repairs. If the property is offered for sale as being in sound condition, a termite and wood rot clause is reasonable. If the property is being offered for sale on an "**as is**" basis in its present condition with no guarantee or warranty of quality and if it has a price to match, then the clause is not reasonable. If the seller is quite sure that there are no termites or wood rot, this condition would not be a major negotiating point, as the cost of an inspection without corrective work is a minor cost in a real estate transaction.

POSSESSION

The day on which possession of the property will be turned over to the buyer is inserted at [13]. As a rule, this is the same day as the closing date. If the buyer needs possession sooner or the seller wants possession after the closing date, the usual procedure is to arrange for a separate rental agreement between the buyer and seller. Such an agreement produces fewer problems if the closing date is later changed or if the transaction falls through and the closing never occurs.

At [14], the purchase contract calls for the buyer and seller to share escrow expenses equally. The buyer and seller could divide them differently if they mutually agreed. Most states charge a conveyance tax when a deed is recorded. At [15], the seller agrees to pay this tax. This is in addition to the fee the buyer pays to have the deed recorded in the public records. At [16], the buyer and seller agree as to where the buyer's deposit money is to be held pending the close of the transaction. It could be held by the escrow agent, the broker, the seller, or an attorney.

The paragraph at [17] is not absolutely essential to a valid real estate purchase contract, since what is considered real estate (and is therefore included in the price) and what is personal property (and is not included in the price) is a matter of law. However, because the buyer and seller may not be familiar with the differences between real property and personal property, this statement is often included to avoid misunderstandings. Moreover, such a statement can clarify whether an item like a storm window or trash compactor, which may or may not be real property depending on its design, is included in the purchase price. If it is the intention of the buyer and seller that an item mentioned here not be included, that item is crossed out and initialed by all of them.

LOAN CONDITIONS

At [18], space is left to add conditions and agreements not provided for elsewhere in the preprinted contract. To complete his purchase of this property, the buyer must obtain a $96,000 loan. However, what if he agrees to the purchase but cannot get a loan? Rather than risk losing his deposit money, the buyer makes his offer subject to obtaining a $96,000 loan on the property. To further protect himself against having to accept a loan "at any price," he states the terms on which he must be able to borrow. The seller, of course, takes certain risks in accepting an offer subject to obtaining financing. If the buyer is unable to obtain financing on these terms, the seller will have to return the buyer's deposit and begin searching for another buyer. Meanwhile, the seller may have lost anywhere from a few days to a few weeks of selling time. But without such a condition, a buyer may hesitate to make an offer at all. The solution is for the seller to accept only those loan conditions that are reasonable in the light of current loan availability. For example, if lenders are currently quoting 9% interest for loans on similar properties, the seller would not want to accept an offer subject to the buyer obtaining a 7% loan. The possibility is too remote. If the buyer's offer is subject to obtaining a loan at current interest rates, the probability of the transaction collapsing on this condition is greatly reduced. The same principle applies to the amount of loan needed, the number of years to maturity, and loan fees: They must be reasonable in light of current market conditions.

In Figure 8.1, the buyer has until the closing date, a period of 45 days, to find the required loan. However, to move things along and release the property sooner if the required loan is unavailable, the contract could contain wording that calls for the buyer to obtain within 30 days a letter from a lender stating that the lender will make the required loan at the closing. If this **loan commitment letter** is not obtained, the seller is released from the deal.

ADDITIONAL CONDITIONS

In the paragraph at [18], we also find that the buyer is asking the seller to include an item of personal property in the selling price. While technically a bill of sale is used for the sale of personal property, such items are often included in the real estate purchase contract if the list is not long. If the refrigerator were real property rather than personal, no mention would be required, as all real property falling within the descriptions at [5] and [17] is automatically included in the price. The third item in the paragraph at [18] gives the buyer an opportunity to have the property inspected by a professional building inspector. Most home buyers do not know what to look for in the way of structural deterioration or defects that may soon require expensive repairs. Consequently, in the past several years, property inspection clauses in purchase contracts have become more common. The cost of this inspection is borne by the buyer. The inspector's report should be completed as soon as possible so that the property can be returned to the market if the buyer does not approve of the findings.

PROPERTY DAMAGE

The paragraph at [19] sets forth conditions under which the buyer can free himself of his obligations under this contract and recover his deposit in full. It begins by addressing the question of property destruction between the contract signing and the closing date. Fire, wind, rain, earthquake, or other damage does occasionally occur during that period of time. Whose responsibility would it be to repair the damage, and could the buyer point to the damage as a legitimate reason for breaking the contract? It is reasonable for the buyer to expect that the property will be delivered to him in as good a condition as when he offered to buy it. Consequently, if there is major damage or destruction, the wording here gives the buyer the option of rescinding the contract and recovering his deposit in full. Note, however, that this clause does not prevent the buyer from accepting the damaged property or the seller from negotiating with the buyer to repair any damage in order to preserve the transaction.

Under the Uniform Vendor and Purchaser Risk Act, if neither possession nor title has passed and there is material destruction to the property, the seller cannot enforce the contract and the purchaser is entitled to his money back. If damage is minor and promptly repaired by the seller, the contract would still be enforceable. If either title or possession has passed and destruction occurs, the purchaser is not relieved of his duty to pay the price, nor is he entitled to a refund of money already paid.

Paragraph [19] also states that, if the buyer is unable to obtain financing as outlined at [18] or the seller is unable to convey title as stated at [7], the buyer can rescind the contract and have his deposit refunded. However, if the buyer is ready to close the transaction and the seller decides he does not want to sell, perhaps because the value of the property has increased between the signing of the contract and the closing date, the buyer can force the seller to convey title through use of a lawsuit for specific performance.

BUYER DEFAULT

Once the contract is signed by all parties involved, if the buyer fails to carry out his obligations, the standard choices for the seller are: (1) release the buyer and return his deposit in full, (2) sue the buyer for specific performance, or (3) sue the buyer for damages suffered. Returning the deposit does not compensate for the time and effort the seller and his broker spent with the buyer, nor for the possibility that, while the seller was committed to the buyer, the real estate market turned sour. Yet the time, effort, and cost of suing for specific performance or damages may be uneconomical. Consequently, it has become common practice in many parts of the country to insert a clause in the purchase contract whereby the buyer agrees in advance to forfeit his deposit if he defaults on the contract, and the seller agrees to accept the deposit as his sole right to damages. Thus, the seller gives up the right to sue the buyer and accepts instead the buyer's deposit. The buyer knows in advance how much it will cost if he defaults, and the cost of default is limited to that amount. This is the purpose of paragraph [20].

TIME LIMITS

At [21], the buyer clearly states that he is making an offer to buy and gives the seller a certain amount of time to accept. If the seller does not accept the offer within the time allotted, the offer is void. This feature is automatic: The buyer does not have to contact the seller to tell him that the offer is no longer open. The offer must be open long enough for the seller to physically receive it, make a decision, sign it, and return it to the buyer. If the seller lives nearby, the transaction is not complicated, and the offer can be delivered in person, three days is reasonable. If the offer must be mailed to an out-of-town seller, seven to ten days is appropriate.

If the buyer wants to make an offer on another property should the first offer not be accepted, the first offer can be made valid for only a day, or even a few hours. A short offer life also limits the amount of time the seller has to hold out for a better offer. If a property is highly marketable, a buyer will want his offer accepted before someone else makes a better offer. Some experienced real estate buyers argue that a purposely short offer life has a psychological value. It motivates the seller to accept before the offer expires. Note, too, a buyer can withdraw and cancel his offer at any time before the seller has accepted and the buyer is aware of that acceptance.

"TIME IS OF THE ESSENCE"

"time is of the essence"

A phrase that means that the time limits of a contract must be faithfully observed or the contract is voidable.

"Time is of the essence" at [22] means that the time limits set by the contract must be faithfully observed or the contract is voidable by the nondefaulting party. Moreover, lateness may give cause for an action for damages. Neither buyer nor seller should expect extensions of time to complete their obligations. This clause does not prohibit the buyer or seller from voluntarily giving the other an extension. But extensions are neither automatic nor mandatory.

"Time is of the essence" is a very difficult issue to litigate in court, and courts interpret it inconsistently. Generally speaking, courts disfavor automatic cancellation and forfeiture of valuable contract rights after "slight" or "reasonable" delays in performance. This is because unexpected delays are commonplace, and buyers and sellers customarily overlook delays in order to allow a deal to close. As a practical matter, the phrase, when used without additional supporting language, seems to be a firm reminder to all parties to keep things moving toward completion. If time is truly an important issue (as in an option contract, for example), the parties must be very explicit in the contract regarding their intentions.

SIGNATURES

The real estate agency and salesperson responsible for producing this offer to buy are identified at [23]. At [24], the buyer clearly states that this is an offer to purchase. If the buyer has any doubts or questions regarding the legal effect of the offer, he should take it to an attorney for counsel before signing it. After he signs, the buyer retains one copy, and the rest of the copies are delivered to the seller for his decision. By retaining one copy, the buyer has a written record to remind him of his obligations under the offer. Equally important, the seller cannot forge a change on the offer, as he does not have all the copies. Regarding delivery, the standard procedure is for the salesperson who obtained the offer to make an appointment with the agent who obtained the listing, and together they call upon the seller and present the offer.

ACCEPTANCE

For an offer to become binding, the seller must accept everything in it. The rejection of even the smallest portion of the offer is a rejection of the entire offer. If the seller wishes to reject the offer but keep negotiations alive, the seller can make a counteroffer. This is a written offer to sell to the buyer at a new price and with terms that are closer to the buyer's offer than the seller's original asking price and terms. The agent prepares the counteroffer by either filling out a fresh purchase contract identical in all ways to the buyer's offer except for these changes, or by amending the offer (or on another sheet of paper) so that the seller offers to sell at the terms the buyer had offered except for the stated changes. The changes are initialed by the seller. The counteroffer is then dated and signed by the seller, and a time limit is given to the buyer to accept. Note that the seller has created a new offer and is now the counter offeror. The seller keeps a copy, and the counteroffer is delivered to the buyer for his decision. If the counteroffer is acceptable to the buyer, he initials the changes, signs and dates it, and the contract is complete.

NOTIFICATION

Returning to Figure 8.1, suppose that the sellers accept the offer as presented to them. At [25], they indicate acceptance; at [26], they state that they employed the Lakeside Realty Company and agree on a commission of $5,760 for brokerage services, to be paid upon closing and recordation of the deed. Provisions are also included as to the amount of the commission if the sale is not completed. At [27], the sellers sign and date the contract and acknowledge receipt of a copy. The last step is to notify the buyer that his offer has been accepted, give him a copy of the completed agreement, and at [28] have him acknowledge receipt of it. If a party to a purchase contract dies after it has been signed, the deceased's heirs are, as a rule, required to fulfill the agreement. Thus, if a husband and wife sign a purchase contract and one of them dies, the sellers can look to the deceased's estate and the survivor to carry out the terms of the contract. Similarly, if a seller dies, the buyer is still entitled to receive the property as called for in the contract.

If an offer is rejected, it is good practice to have the sellers write the word *rejected* on the offer, followed by their signatures.

FEDERAL CLAUSES

In two instances the government requires that specific clauses be included in real estate sales contracts. First, an **amendatory language** clause must be included whenever a sales contract is signed by a purchaser prior to the receipt of a Federal Housing Administration (FHA) Appraised Value or a Veterans Affairs (VA) Certificate of Reasonable Value on the property. The purpose is to assure that the purchaser may terminate the contract without loss when it appears that the agreed purchase price may be significantly above the appraised value. The specific clauses, which must be used verbatim, are available from FHA and VA approved lenders. Second, the Federal Trade Commission (FTC)

LEAD-BASED PAINT

Lead-based paint and its required disclosure are beginning to come under scrutiny. The incidence of lead poisoning has dropped dramatically, with just 0.4% of young children reported as having lead poisoning, according to the Centers for Disease Control and Prevention. This drop seems to have occurred because we have eliminated lead from gasoline products, solder, food and beverage cans, and water supply pipes, which makes one wonder why lead-based paint is an issue today. In a recent court case in Illinois, a buyer sued for failure to receive the lead-based paint disclosure form. The court rejected the buyer's claim for damages because lead-based paint was never discovered on the property, and the couple did not incur any clean up or damages. Therefore, the case did not move forward. If the industry is no longer producing lead-based paint (since 1978), how applicable is this legislation today?

---

requires that builders and sellers of new homes include **insulation disclosures** in all purchase contracts. Disclosures, which may be based upon manufacturer claims, must cite the type, thickness, and R-value of the insulation installed in the home. The exact clause will be provided by the builder or seller of the home based on model clauses provided by the National Association of Homebuilders, as modified by local laws.

LEAD-BASED PAINT DISCLOSURES

Federal law requires that before a buyer or tenant becomes obligated under a contract for sale or lease, the sellers and landlords must disclose known lead-based paint and lead-based paint hazards and provide available reports to buyers or tenants. Sellers and landlords must give the buyer a pamphlet entitled "Protect Your Family from Lead in Your Home." Unless otherwise agreed to, the homebuyers are entitled to a 10-day period to conduct a lead-based paint inspection or risk assessment at their own expense. Sales contracts and lease arrangements must include certain language to ensure the disclosure notification actually takes place. This law places a special burden on real estate agents, who must ensure that sellers and landlords are aware of their obligations that they disclose the proper information to buyers and tenants. The agent must comply with the law if the seller or landlord fails to do so.

PREPRINTED CLAUSES

The purchase contract in Figure 8.1 is designed to present and explain the basic elements of a purchase contract for a house. One popular preprinted purchase contract presently for sale to real estate agents consists of four legal-size pages that contain dozens of preprinted clauses. The buyer, seller, and agent select and fill in those clauses pertinent to their transaction. For example, if the home is a condominium, there are clauses that pertain to the condominium documents and maintenance reserves. If the home is in a flood zone, there is a clause for disclosing that fact to the buyer and the requirement of flood insurance by lenders. There are four different pest inspection and repair clauses from which the buyer and seller can choose. There are smoke detector clauses and roof inspection clauses, as well as detailed contingency and default clauses. There are clauses for personal property included in the sale and guarantees by the seller that electrical, heating, cooling, sewer, plumbing, built-in appliances, and so on are all in normal working order at the closing. Additionally, there may be state-mandated clauses. For example, some states require specific, due-on-sale balloon payment and insulation disclosures.

The benefit of preprinted clauses is that much of the language of the contract has already been written for the buyer, seller, and agent. But the buyer, seller, and agent must read all the clauses and choose those appropriate to the transaction.

RIDERS

A **rider** is any addition annexed to a document and made a part of the document by reference. A rider is usually written, typed, or printed on a separate piece of paper and stapled to the document. There will be a reference in the document that the rider is a part of the document and a statement in the rider to that effect. The parties to the document should place their initials on the rider. Riders are also known as **addendums** or **attachments**.

NEGOTIATION

One of the most important principles of purchase contracts (and real estate contracts in general) is that nearly everything is negotiable, and nearly everything has a price. In preparing or analyzing any contract, consider what the advantages and disadvantages of each condition are to each party to the contract. A solid contract results when the buyer and seller each feel that they have gained more than they have given up. The prime example is the sale price of the property itself. The seller prefers the money over the property, while the buyer prefers the property over the money. Each small negotiable item in the purchase contract has its price too. For example, the seller may agree to include the refrigerator for $200 more. Equally important in negotiating is the relative bargaining power of the buyer and seller. If the seller is confident of having plenty of buyers at the asking price, he can elect to refuse offers for less money, and reject those with numerous conditions or insufficient earnest money. However, if the owner is anxious to sell and has received only one offer in several months, he may be quite willing to accept a lower price and numerous conditions.

The Binder

Throughout most of the United States, the real estate agent prepares the purchase contract as soon as the agent is about to (or has) put a deal together. Using preprinted forms available from real estate trade associations, title companies, and stationery stores, the agent fills in the purchase price, down payment, and other details of the transaction and has the buyer and seller sign it as soon as they reach an agreement.

In a few communities, particularly in the northeastern United States, the practice is for the real estate agent to prepare a short-form contract called a **binder**. The purpose of a binder is to hold a deal together until a more formal purchase contract can be drawn by an attorney, and signed by the buyer and seller. In the binder, the buyer and seller agree to the purchase price, the down payment, and how the balance will be financed. The brokerage commission (to whom and how much) is stated, along with an agreement to meet again to draw up a more formal contract that will contain all the remaining details of the sale. The agent then arranges a meeting at the office of the seller's attorney. In attendance are the seller and his attorney, the buyer and his attorney, and the real estate agents responsible for bringing about the sale. Together they prepare a written contract, which the buyer and seller sign. When the seller's attorney writes the formal contract, the contract will favor the seller, because the seller's attorney is expected to protect the seller's best interests at all times. The purchaser, to protect his interests, should bring his own attorney.

binder
A short purchase contract used to secure a real estate transaction until a more formal contract can be signed.

WHAT THE BINDER DOES NOT SAY

While it is easy to minimize the importance of a binder because it is replaced by another contract, it does, nonetheless, meet all the requirements of a legally binding contract. In the absence of another contract, it can be used to enforce completion of a sale by a buyer or seller. The major weakness of a binder is in what it *does not say*. For example, the binder will probably make no mention of a termite inspection, the type of deed the seller is expected to use, or the closing date. Unless the buyer and seller can agree on these matters at the formal contract meeting, a dilemma results. Certainly, the buyer will wonder if his refusal to meet all the seller's demands at the contract meeting will result in the loss of his deposit money. If a stalemate develops, the courts may be asked to decide the termite question, deed type, closing date, and any other unresolved points. However, because this is costly and time consuming for all involved, there is give-and-take negotiation at the contract meeting. If a completely unnegotiable impasse is reached, as a practical matter, the binder is usually rescinded by the buyer and seller, and the buyer's deposit returned.

Letter of Intent

If two or more parties want to express their mutual intention to buy, sell, lease, develop, or invest, and wish to do so without creating any firm, legal obligation, they may use a **letter of intent**. Generally, such a letter contains an outline of the proposal and concludes with language to the effect that the letter is only an expression of mutual intent and that no liability or obligation is created by it. In other words, a letter of intent is neither a contract nor an agreement to enter into a contract. However, it is expected, and usually stipulated in the letter, that the parties signing the letter will proceed promptly and in good faith to conclude the deal proposed in the letter. The letter of intent is usually found in connection with more complex transactions such as commercial leases, real estate development, and construction projects, and with multimillion-dollar real estate sales.

Practicing Law

Historically in the United States, the sale of real estate was primarily a legal service. Lawyers matched buyers with sellers, wrote the sales contract, and prepared the mortgage and deed. When persons other than lawyers began to specialize in real estate brokerage, the question of who should write the sales contract became important. The lawyer was more qualified in matters of contract law, but the broker wanted something that could be signed the moment the buyer and seller were in agreement. For many years the solution was a compromise. The broker had the buyer and seller sign a binder, and they agreed to meet again in the presence of a lawyer to draw up and sign a more formal contract. The trend today, however, is for the real estate agent to prepare a complete purchase contract as soon as there is a meeting of the minds.

The preparation of contracts by real estate agents for their clients has not gone unnoticed by lawyers. The legal profession maintains that preparing contracts for clients is practicing law, and state laws restrict the practice of law to lawyers. This has been, and continues to be, a controversial issue between brokers and lawyers. Resolution of the matter has come in the form of **accords** between the real estate brokerage industry and the legal profession. In nearly all states, courts have ruled that a real estate agent is permitted to prepare purchase, installment, and rental contracts provided the agent uses a preprinted form approved by a lawyer or the state's real estate department, and provided the agent is limited to filling in only the blank spaces on the form. (Figure 8.1 illustrates this concept.)

If the preprinted form requires extensive cross-outs, changes, and riders, the contract should be drafted by a lawyer. A real estate license is *not* a license to practice law.

Installment Contracts

An **installment contract** (also known as a **land contract**, **conditional sales contract**, **contract for deed**, or **agreement of sale**) combines features from a sales contract, a deed, and a mortgage. An installment contract contains most of the provisions of the purchase contract described in Figure 8.1, plus wording familiar to the warranty deed described in Chapter 5, plus many of the provisions of the mortgage described in the next chapter.

installment contract
A method of selling and financing property whereby the seller retains title but the buyer takes possession while making the payments.

The most important feature of an installment contract is that the seller does not deliver a deed to the buyer at the closing. Rather, the seller promises to deliver the deed at some future date. Meanwhile, the purchaser is given the right to occupy the property (the magic word is *possession*) and have, for all practical purposes, the rights, obligations, and privileges of ownership.

The widest use of the installment contract occurs when the buyer does not have the full purchase price in cash or is unable to borrow it from a lender. To sell under these conditions, the seller must accept a down payment plus monthly payments. To carry this out, the seller can choose to either: (1) deliver a deed to the buyer at the closing and at the same moment take back from the buyer a promissory note and a mortgage secured by the property (a mortgage carryback), or (2) enter into an installment contract wherein the buyer makes the required payments to the seller before the seller delivers a deed to the buyer.

VENDOR, VENDEE

Historically, installment contracts were most commonly used to sell vacant land where the buyer put only a modest amount of money down and the seller agreed to receive the balance as installment payments. When all the installments were made, the seller delivered a deed to the purchaser. The terms of these contracts were usually weighted in favor of the seller. For example, if the buyer (called the **vendee**) failed to make all the payments on time, the seller (called the **vendor**) could rescind the contract, retain payments already made as rent, and retake possession of the land. Additionally, the seller might insert a clause in the installment contract prohibiting the buyer from recording it. The public records would continue to show the seller as owner and the seller could use the land as collateral for loans. That such a one-sided contract would exist may seem surprising. But, if a buyer was unable to obtain financing from another source, the buyer was stuck with accepting what the seller offered or not buying the property. Sellers took the position that if they were selling to buyers who were unwilling or unable to find their own sources of financing, then sellers wanted a quick and easy way of recovering the property if the payments were not made. By selling on an installment contract and not allowing it to be recorded, the seller could save the time and expense of regular foreclosure proceedings. The seller would simply notify the buyer in writing that the contract was in default and thereby rescind it. Meanwhile, as far as the public records were concerned, title was still in the seller's name.

PUBLIC CRITICISM

Such strongly worded agreements received much public criticism, as did the possibility that even if the buyer made all the payments, the seller might not be capable of delivering good title. For example, the buyer could make all payments, yet find that the seller had encumbered the property with debt, had gone bankrupt, had become legally incapacitated, or had died.

Then, in the late 1970s, interest rates rose sharply. In order to sell their properties, sellers looked for ways of passing along the benefits of their fixed-rate, low-interest loans to buyers. The installment contract was rediscovered, and it moved from being used primarily to sell land to being used to sell houses and apartment buildings, and even office buildings and industrial property. Basically, the seller kept the property and mortgage in the seller's name and made the mortgage payments out of the buyer's monthly payments. This continued until the buyer found alternative financing, at which time the seller delivered the deed.

PROTECTIONS

With its increased popularity, the need for more sophisticated and more protective installment contracts was created. Simultaneously, courts and legislatures in various states were listening to consumer complaints and finding existing installment contract provisions too harsh. One by one, states began requiring that a buyer be given a specified period to cure any default before the seller could rescind. Some states began requiring that installment contracts be foreclosed like regular mortgages. And most states now require that installment contracts be recorded and/or prohibit a seller from enforcing nonrecording clauses.

Buyers, too, have become much more sophisticated. For example, it is common practice today to require the seller to place the deed (usually a warranty deed) in an escrow at the time the installment contract is made. This relieves a number of problems regarding the unwillingness or inability of the seller to prepare and deliver the deed later. Also, the astute buyer will require that a collection account be used to collect the buyer's payments and make the payments on the underlying mortgage. This is done using a neutral third party such as the escrow holder of the deed, a bank, or a trust company. The seller will probably insist that the buyer place one-twelfth of the annual property taxes and hazard insurance in the escrow account each month to pay for these items. The buyer will want to record the contract to establish the buyer's rights to the property. The buyer may also want to include provisions whereby the seller delivers a deed to the buyer and takes back a mortgage from the buyer once the buyer has paid, say, 30% or 40% of the purchase price.

If an installment contract is used for the purchase of real estate, it should be done with the help of legal counsel to make certain that it provides adequate safeguards for the buyer as well as the seller. In Chapter 14, the installment contract is discussed as a tool to finance the sale of improved property.

Equitable Title

equitable title

The right to demand that title be conveyed upon payment of the purchase price.

Between the moment that a buyer and seller sign a valid purchase contract and the moment the seller delivers a deed to the buyer, who holds title to the property? Similarly, under an installment contract, until the seller delivers a deed to the buyer, who holds title to the property? The answer, in both cases, is the seller. But this is only technically true because the buyer is entitled to receive a deed (and thereby title) once the buyer has completed the terms of the purchase or installment contract. During the period beginning with the buyer and seller signing the contract and the seller delivering the deed, the buyer is said to hold **equitable title** to the property. The concept of equitable title stems from the fact that a buyer has the exclusive right to purchase and can enforce specific performance of the contract to get title. Meanwhile, the seller holds bare or naked title (i.e., title in name only and without full ownership rights).

The equitable title that a purchaser holds under a purchase or installment contract is transferable by subcontract, assignment, or deed. Equitable title can be sold, given away, or mortgaged, and it passes to the purchaser's heirs and devisees upon the purchaser's death.

It is not unusual to see a property offered for sale wherein the vendee under an installment contract is offering those rights for sale. Barring any due-on-sale clause in the installment contract, this can be done. The buyer receives from the vendee an assignment of the contract, and with it, the vendee's equitable title. The buyer then takes possession and continues to make the payments called for by the contract. When the payments are completed, the deed and title transfer can be handled in one of two ways. One way is for the original seller to agree to deliver a deed to the new buyer. The other, most common, way is for the vendee to place a deed to the new buyer in escrow. When the last payment is made, the deed from the original seller to the vendee is recorded, and immediately after it, the deed from the vendee to the new buyer.

Option Contracts

Recall that an earnest money contract is an executory, bilateral contract. In contrast to this, the option contract is a unilateral, executed contract. Once the contract is executed, the buyer then has a right to purchase the property but with no obligation to do so. Therefore, the remedy of specific performance against the buyer doesn't exist. The buyer has the right (not the obligation) to buy, but the seller does have the obligation to sell. In return for granting the option to purchase, the buyer must pay consideration to the seller in order for the contract to be enforceable. In most cases, this is a cash payment directly to the seller in lieu of earnest money. In return for the cash payment, the seller takes the property off the market for the term of the option agreement. The buyer does not have to give the seller any reason for the termination, nor give the seller copies of any reports, studies, or other investigated matters.

In commercial real estate, it is common for large companies wanting to select sites in a given area to option five or ten sites, knowing that they will never have the obligation to purchase any of the sites. This gives them the opportunity to investigate the sites in more detail, do whatever studies are required, and then purchase them should they choose to do so. Many feel that this makes the transaction much cleaner and eliminates disputes over repairs, inspections, and financing contingencies. At the end of the option, the contract terminates at the option of the buyer. Note that some contracts require the buyer to send a notice of termination to the seller, or the contract converts into an earnest money contract and the buyer becomes obligated to purchase. However, this is not true in all option contracts. Many option contracts simply have an option period (e.g., 60 days), and if the option is not exercised, the contract terminates by its own terms.

Exercising the option converts the option contract to an earnest money contract. At that point, the buyer has the duty to perform.

Lease with Option to Buy

Another popular option contract in real estate is the **lease with option to buy**. Often simply referred to as a **lease-option**, it allows the tenant to buy the property at a preset price and terms during the option period. For a residential property, the lease is typically for one year, and the option to buy must be exercised during that time. Let's look more closely.

In a lease-option contract, all the normal provisions of a lease are present, such as those shown in Figure 17.1. All the normal provisions of a purchase contract are present, such as

lease-option

Allows the tenant to buy the property at a preset price and terms for a given period of time.

those shown in Figure 8.1. In addition, there will be wording stating that the tenant has the option of exercising the purchase contract, provided the tenant notifies the landlord in writing of that intent during the option period. All terms of the purchase contract must be negotiated and in writing when the lease is signed. Both the tenant and the landlord must sign the lease. Only the landlord must sign the purchase contract and option agreement, although both parties often do so. If the tenant wants to buy during the option period, the tenant notifies the landlord in writing that the tenant wishes to exercise the purchase contract. Together they proceed to carry out the purchase contract as in a normal sale.

If the tenant does not exercise the option within the option period, the option expires and the purchase contract is null and void. If the lease also expires at the end of the option period, the tenant must either arrange with the landlord to continue renting or move out. Alternatively, they can negotiate a new purchase contract or a new lease-option contract.

POPULARITY

Lease-options are particularly popular in soft real estate markets in which a home seller is having difficulty finding a buyer. One solution is to lower the asking price and/or make the financing terms more attractive. However, the seller may wish to hold out in hopes that prices will rise within a year. In the meantime, the seller needs someone to occupy the property and provide some income.

The lease-option is attractive to a tenant because the tenant has a place to rent plus the option of buying any time during the option period for the price in the purchase contract. In other words, the tenant can wait a year and see if he or she likes the property and if values rise to or above the price in the purchase contract. If the tenant does not like the property and/or the property does not rise in value, the tenant is under no obligation to buy. Once the lease expires, the tenant is also under no obligation to continue renting.

EXAMPLES

To encourage a tenant to exercise the option to buy, the contract may allow the tenant to apply part or all of the rent paid to the purchase price. In fact, quite a bit of flexibility and negotiation can take place in creating a lease-option. For example, take a home that would rent for $1,250 per month and sell for $125,000 on the open market. Suppose the owner wants $140,000 and won't come down to the market price. Meanwhile, the home is vacant and there are mortgage payments to be made. The owner could offer a one-year lease-option with a rental charge of $1,250 each month and an exercise price of $140,000. Within a year, $140,000 may look good to the tenant, especially if the market value of the property has risen significantly above $140,000. The tenant can exercise the option or, if not prohibited by the contract, sell it to someone who intends to exercise it. The owner receives $15,000 more for the property than he would have received the previous year, and the tenant has the benefit of any value increase above that.

Continuing the example, what if the property rises to $130,000 in value? There is no economic incentive for the tenant to exercise the option at $140,000. The tenant can simply disregard the option and make an offer of $130,000 to the owner. The owner's choice is to sell at that price or continue renting the home, perhaps with another one-year lease-option.

OPTION FEE

The owner can also charge the tenant extra for the privilege of having the option, but it must make economic sense to the tenant. Suppose in the previous example the purchase price is set equal to the current market value—that is, $125,000. This would be a valuable benefit to the tenant, and the owner could charge an up-front cash fee for the option and/or charge above-market rent. The amounts would depend on the market's expectations regarding the value of this home a year from now. There is nothing special about a one-year option period, although it is a very popular length of time. The owner and tenant can agree to a three-month, six-month, or nine-month option if it fits their needs, and the lease can run longer than the option period. Options for longer than one year are generally reserved for commercial properties. For example, a businessperson just starting out, or perhaps expanding, wants to buy a building but needs one or two years to see how successful the business will be and how much space it will need.

CAVEATS

Be aware that lease-options may create income-tax consequences that require professional tax counseling. Legal advice is also very helpful in preparing and reviewing the lease-option papers. This is because the entire deal (lease, option, and purchase contract) must be watertight from the beginning. One cannot wait until the option is exercised to write the purchase contract or even a material part of it. If a real estate agent puts a lease-option together, the agent is entitled to a leasing commission at the time the lease is signed. If the option is exercised, the agent is due a sales commission on the purchase contract.

Evidence that the option to buy exists should be recorded to establish not only the tenant's rights to purchase the property, but also to establish those rights back to the date the option was recorded. An option is an example of a unilateral contract. When it is exercised, it becomes bilateral. The lease portion of a lease-option is a bilateral contract. The party giving the option is called the **optionor** (owner in a lease-option). The party receiving the option is the **optionee** (tenant in a lease-option). Sometimes an option to buy is referred to as a **call**. You will see how an option can be used by a home builder to buy land in Chapter 14 and how options can be used to renew leases in Chapter 17.

Right of First Refusal

Sometimes a tenant will agree to rent a property only if given an opportunity to purchase it before someone else does. In other words, the tenant is saying, "Mr. Owner, if you get a valid offer from someone else to purchase this property, show it to me and give me an opportunity to match the offer." This is called a **right of first refusal**. If someone presents the owner with a valid offer, the owner must show it to the tenant before accepting it. If the tenant decides not to match it, the owner is free to accept it.

right of first refusal
The right to match or better an offer before the property is sold to someone else.

A right of first refusal protects a tenant from having the property sold out from under him when, in fact, if the tenant knew about the offer, he would have been willing to match it. The owner usually does not care who buys.

It is important to note, however, that under these conditions an owner can never seriously negotiate with the potential purchaser because every facet of the negotiation has to be transmitted to the tenant, effectively giving the tenant a veto power. It is only in the unlikely event that the potential purchaser will either: (1) pay the seller more money, or (2) offer better terms than the tenant that the transaction turns out to be beneficial to the seller. In most circumstances, the right of first refusal is not beneficial to the owner except during a very strong sellers' market.

Exchange Agreements

Most real estate transactions involve the exchange of real estate for monetary consideration. However, among sophisticated real estate investors, exchanging real property for real property has become popular for two important reasons. First, real estate trades can be accomplished without large amounts of cash by trading a property you presently own for one you want. This sidesteps the intermediate step of converting real estate to cash and then converting cash back to real estate. Second, by using an exchange, you can dispose of one property and acquire another without paying income taxes on the profit in the first property at the time of the transaction. As a result, the phrase *tax-free exchange* is often used when talking about trading.

To illustrate, suppose that you own an apartment building as an investment. The value on your accounting books is $500,000, but its market value today is $750,000. If you sell for cash, you will have to pay income taxes on the difference between the value of the property on your accounting books, and the amount you receive for it. If instead of selling for cash you find another building that you want and can arrange a trade, then for income tax purposes, the new building acquires the accounting book value of the old and no income taxes are due at the time of the trade. Taxes will be due, however, if and when you finally sell rather than trade. The **tax-deferred exchange** rules apply to investment properties only. Owner-occupied dwellings are treated differently. The Internal Revenue Service (IRS) permits a homeowner to sell and exclude all gains within the specified limits (see Chapter 15).

tax-deferred exchange

A sale of real property in exchange for another parcel of real estate to effect a nontaxable gain.

TRADING UP

Real estate exchanges need not involve properties of equal value. For example, if you own, debt free, a small office building worth $100,000, you could trade it for a building worth $500,000 with $400,000 of mortgage debt against it. Alternatively, if the building you wanted was priced at $600,000 with $400,000 in debt against it, you could offer your building plus $100,000 in cash.

qualified intermediary

The third-party escrow agent used in a tax-deferred exchange.

The vast majority of tax-deferred exchanges today consist of three transactions: the two conveyances and an escrow agreement with a **qualified intermediary (QI)**. The qualified intermediary can be a title company, attorney, or, in some cases, an

NEW FEDERAL REGULATIONS

New federal regulations announced by the Internal Revenue Service allow for second homes that have personal use to qualify for 1031 tax-free like-kind exchanges. To qualify for the like-kind exchange, both the relinquished property and the replacement property must meet certain requirements. The relinquished property must be owned by the taxpayer for at least 24 months before the exchange, and at each of the two 12-month periods immediately preceding the exchange, the taxpayer must rent the dwelling unit to another person or persons at a fair market rental for 14 days or more, and the taxpayer's personal use of the dwelling must not exceed the greater of 14 days or 10 percent of the number of rental days of the 12-month period. Similarly, the replacement dwelling must be owned by the taxpayer for at least 24 months after the exchange, with the same rental requirement for those two years. This rule applies to transactions occurring on or after March 10, 2008.

independent company providing this service as tax advisors. The QI maintains control over the funds and the closing documents pursuant to the instructions contained in the escrow agreement. This allows the various parties to deposit documents and funds with the QI (often by mail), which makes it much more convenient. As a practical matter, the QI signs all documents relevant to the closing other than the conveyancing documents. The IRS rules allow the conveyancing documents to be executed by the parties to the transaction without involving the formality of the QI's execution. This prevents the QI from becoming "in the chain of title," which could further complicate the transaction.

Assume the party who wants to do the tax-deferred exchange is Seller 1, who signs a contract to convey real estate to Buyer 1. After executing a contract of sale, Seller 1 assigns his interest in the contract to the QI, then executes an **escrow agreement** with the QI that defines the QI's role. Seller 1 then locates the property he is interested in purchasing, and enters into a purchase contract to acquire that property; he then sends notice of designation of property to the QI, then assigns his interest in the contract as purchaser to the QI. In both transactions, the deed is drafted from Seller to Buyer (so the QI owner never takes title to either tract). The QI, who has escrowed the funds from transaction #1, then uses these proceeds to pay Seller 2 to complete transaction #2.

The key factor is that Seller 1 (taxpayer) has no control over the funds held by the QI and cannot be deemed to be in receipt of those funds. In effect, the transaction results in Seller 1 conveying his property to the QI and the QI conveying the exchange property to the seller. Note Figure 8.2.

Although trading is a complicated business, it can also be very lucrative for real estate agents. Whereas an ordinary sale results in one brokerage commission, a two-party exchange results in two commissions and a four-party exchange in four commissions.

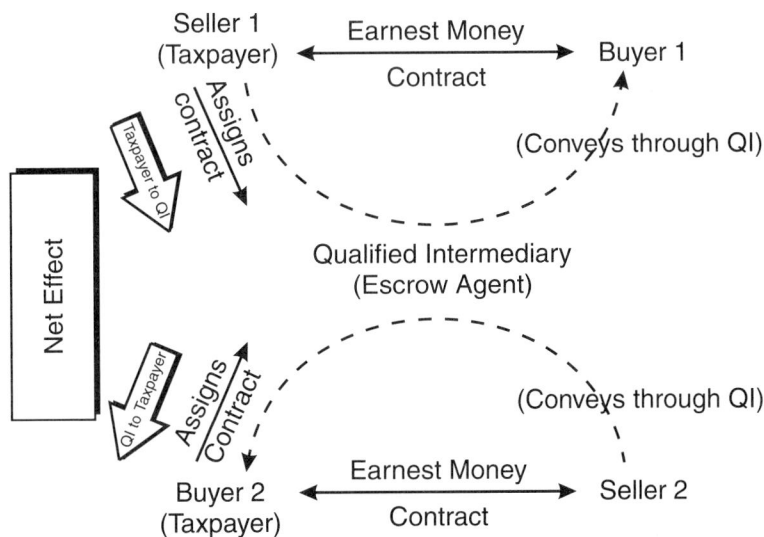

FIGURE 8.2 Possible Trading Combinations

Source: © 2014 OnCourse Learning

DELAYED EXCHANGES

The Internal Revenue Code allows nonsimultaneous exchanges to be tax-deferred under certain circumstances. Such an exchange, commonly called a **delayed exchange**, occurs when property is exchanged for a right to receive property at a future date. It is a helpful technique when one party is willing to exchange out of a property but has not yet chosen a property to exchange into. Meanwhile the other parties to the exchange are ready and want to close. The delayed exchange allows the closing to take place by giving the party that has not chosen a property the right to designate a property and take title after the closing. The 1984 act specifically allows this, provided: (1) the designated property is identified within 45 days of the original closing, (2) the title to the designated property is acquired within 180 days of the original closing, and (3) the designated property is received before the designating party's tax return is due. If these rules are not met, the transaction will be treated as a sale for the designating party, not an exchange.

REVERSE EXCHANGES

What if a party signed the exchange contracts, but the sale of the exchange property is delayed and the seller has to acquire the replacement property before selling the existing property? Because of the nature of real estate contracts, this is not an uncommon occurrence. To deal with this issue, the Internal Revenue Code established a procedure in 2000. The criteria requires that the qualified intermediary, pursuant to a specified arrangement between the taxpayers and the QI, become an Exchange Accommodation Titleholder (EAT). The taxpayer transfers the ownership of the replacement property to the accommodation titleholder (either paying cash or by getting a loan sufficient to pay the sale price to the seller of the replacement property), and then the accommodation titleholder holds title until the exchange property can be sold. The seller, in effect, "parks" the replacement property with the accommodation titleholder until a buyer can be found for the exchange property. Then the same rules apply as the conveyance of the relinquished property must occur within 180 days after the property is parked with the accommodation titleholder. This has been deemed by the IRS as an "exchange last" reverse like kind exchange. The reverse exchange can also be used to acquire the replacement property first, before values go up, or to take advantage of a timely "good buy."

Typical Trade Contract

Space does not permit a detailed review of a trade contract. However, very briefly, a typical trade contract identifies the traders involved and their respective properties; names the type of deed and quality of title that will be conveyed; names the real estate brokers involved and how much they are to be paid; discusses prorations, personal property, rights of tenants, and damage to the property; provides a receipt for the deposit that each trader makes; requires each trader to provide an abstract of title; and sets forth the consequences of defaulting on the contract. If the same broker represents more than one trader, he must disclose this to each trader whom he represents.

Vocabulary Review

Match terms a–s with statements 1–19.

a. "As is"

b. Bill of sale

c. Binder

d. Closing date

e. Delayed exchange

f. Dry rot

g. Earnest money deposit

h. Equitable title

i. Installment contract

j. Lease-option

k. Letter of intent

l. Loan commitment letter

m. Optionee

n. Option fee

o. Purchase contract

p. Qualified intermediary (QI)

q. Right of first refusal

r. "Time is of the essence"

s. Vendee

_____ 1. A written and signed agreement specifying the terms at which a buyer will purchase and an owner will sell.

_____ 2. A short-form purchase contract to hold a real estate transaction together until a more formal contract can be prepared and signed.

_____ 3. Money that accompanies an offer to purchase as evidence of good faith; also called the deposit.

_____ 4. Property offered for sale in its present condition with no guarantee or warranty of quality provided by the seller.

_____ 5. Rotted wood; usually the result of alternate soaking and drying over a long period of time.

_____ 6. The day on which the buyer pays the money and the seller delivers title.

_____ 7. Written evidence of the sale of personal property.

_____ 8. A phrase meaning that all parties to a contract are expected to perform on time as a condition of the contract.

_____ 9. Also known as a conditional sales contract, land contract, contract for deed, or agreement of sale.

_____ 10. The buyer under a contract for deed.

_____ 11. The right to demand that title be conveyed upon payment of the purchase price.

_____ 12. Allows the tenant to buy the property at a preset price for a given period of time.

_____ 13. The right to match or better an offer before the property is sold to someone else.

_____ 14. Expresses a mutual intention to buy, sell, lease, develop, or invest without creating any firm, legal obligation.

_____ 15. The party receiving an option.

_____ 16. An agreement by a lender to make a loan.

_____ 17. Money paid for the privilege of having an option.

_____ 18. A nonsimultaneous real estate trade.

_____ 19. A third-party escrow agent used in tax-deferred exchanges.

Questions and Problems

1. Why is it necessary to include the extra step of preparing and signing a purchase contract when it would seem much easier if the buyer simply paid the seller the purchase price and the seller handed the buyer a deed?

2. Why is it preferable to prepare a purchase contract that contains all the terms and conditions of sale at the outset rather than to leave some items to be "ironed out" later?

3. What are the advantages and the disadvantages of using preprinted real estate purchase contract forms?

4. Is it legal for a seller to accept an offer that is not accompanied by a deposit? Why or why not?

5. If a purchase contract for real property describes the land, is it also necessary to mention the fixtures? Why or why not?

6. How will the relative bargaining strengths and weaknesses of the buyer and seller affect the contract negotiation process?

7. Under an installment contract, what is the advantage to the seller if he does not have to deliver title to the buyer until all required payments are made?

8. What position does your state take toward payment forfeiture and nonrecording clauses in land contracts?

9. What are the advantages of trading real estate rather than selling it? What do you consider the disadvantages to be?

10. What is a letter of intent?

Additional Readings

"The Contract for Deed as a Mortgage: The Case for the Restatement Approach" by Grant S. Nelson (*Brigham Young University Law Review*, vol. 1998, issue 3, pp. 1111–1168).

"Equitable Conversion: The Effects of a Hurricane on Real Estate Sales Contracts" by Gary S. Gaffney (*Nova Law Review*, Spring 1993, vol. 17, number 3).

Sales Contracts for the Real Estate Professional by Virginia L. Lawson (OnCourse Learning, 2002).

CHAPTER 9

Mortgage and Note

There are two documents involved in a mortgage loan. The first is the promissory note and the second is the mortgage. In 16 states, it is customary to use a deed of trust in preference to a mortgage. We begin by describing the promissory note because it is common to both the mortgage and deed of trust. Then we shall discuss the mortgage document at length. This will be followed by an explanation of foreclosure and brief descriptions of the deed of trust, equitable mortgage, security deed, and chattel mortgage. (If you either live in or deal with property in a state where the deed of trust is the customary security instrument, you will also want to read Chapter 10, as it deals exclusively with the deed of trust.) Meanwhile, let's begin with the promissory note.

Promissory Note

The **promissory note**, or **real estate lien note**, is a contract between a borrower and a lender. It establishes the amount of the debt, the terms of repayment, and the interest rate. A sample promissory note, usually referred to simply as a **note**, is shown in Figure 9.1. Some states use a **bond** to accomplish the same purpose as the promissory note. What is discussed here regarding promissory notes also applies to bonds.

To be valid as evidence of debt, a note must: (1) be in writing, (2) be between a borrower and lender, both of whom have contractual capacity, (3) state the borrower's promise to pay a certain sum of money, (4) show the terms of payment, (5) be signed by the borrower, and (6) be voluntarily delivered by the borrower and accepted by the lender. If the note is secured by a mortgage

LEARNING OBJECTIVES

After reading this chapter, you should be able to:

❮ Understand the difference between a "promissory note" and a lien securing the payments of that note.

❮ Discuss covenants generally contained in mortgage documents.

❮ Define the foreclosure process and the difference between nonjudicial foreclosures and judicial foreclosures.

❮ Define "deed in lieu of foreclosure," and the effects of the document.

❮ Understand the concept of "strict foreclosure."

KEY TERMS

Acceleration clause • Deficiency judgment • First mortgage • Foreclosure • Junior mortgage • Mortgage • Mortgagee • Power of sale • Promissory note • Subordination

promissory note
A written promise to repay a debt.

FIGURE 9.1   Federal National Mortgage Association (FNMA) Uniform Note

NOTE

[2] March 31, 20xx   _____, _____
      [Date]   [City]   [State]

[Property Address]

1. BORROWER'S PROMISE TO PAY

[3]   In return for a loan that I have received, I promise to pay U.S. $96,000.00 [5] (this amount is called "Principal"), plus interest, to the order of the Lender. The Lender is <u>Pennywise Mortgage Company.</u> [4] I will make all payments under this Note in the form of cash, check or money order.

I understand that the Lender may transfer this Note. The Lender or anyone who takes this Note by transfer and who is entitled to receive payments under this Note is called the "Note Holder."

2. INTEREST

Interest will be charged on unpaid principal until the full amount of Principal has been paid. I will pay interest at a yearly rate of <u>7%.</u> [6]

The interest rate required by this Section 2 is the rate I will pay both before and after any default described in Section 6(B) of this Note.

3. PAYMENTS
(A) Time and Place of Payments

I will pay principal and interest by making a payment every month.

I will make my monthly payment on the <u>1st</u> day of each month beginning on <u>May 1, 20xx.</u> [8] I will make these payments every month until I have paid all of the principal and interest and any other charges described below that I may owe under this Note. Each monthly payment will be applied as of its scheduled due date and will be applied to interest before Principal. If, on _____, 20_____, I still owe amounts under this Note, I will pay those amounts in full on that date, which is called the "Maturity Date."

I will make my monthly payments at <u>2242 National Blvd., [City, State]</u> or at a different place if required by the Note Holder.

(B) Amount of Monthly Payments

My monthly payment will be in the amount of U.S. <u>$639.36.</u> [7]

[9] 4. BORROWER'S RIGHT TO PREPAY

I have the right to make payments of Principal at any time before they are due. A payment of Principal only is known as a "Prepayment." When I make a Prepayment, I will tell the Note Holder in writing that I am doing so. I may not designate a payment as a Prepayment if I have not made all the monthly payments due under the Note.

[11]   I may make a full Prepayment or partial Prepayments without paying a Prepayment charge. The Note Holder will use my Prepayments to reduce the amount of Principal that I owe under this Note. However, the Note Holder may apply my Prepayment to the accrued and unpaid interest on the Prepayment amount, before applying my Prepayment to reduce the Principal amount of the Note. If I make a partial Prepayment, there will be no changes in the due date or in the amount of my monthly payment unless the Note Holder agrees in writing to those changes.

(continued)

5. LOAN CHARGES

If a law, which applies to this loan and which sets maximum loan charges, is finally interpreted so that the interest or other loan charges collected or to be collected in connection with this loan exceed the permitted limits, then: (a) any such loan charge shall be reduced by the amount necessary to reduce the charge to the permitted limit; and (b) any sums already collected from me which exceeded permitted limits will be refunded to me. The Note Holder may choose to make this refund by reducing the Principal I owe under this Note or by making a direct payment to me. If a refund reduces Principal, the reduction will be treated as a partial Prepayment.

6. BORROWER'S FAILURE TO PAY AS REQUIRED

(A) Late Charge for Overdue Payments

If the Note Holder has not received the full amount of any monthly payment by the end of 10 [10] calendar days after the date it is due, I will pay a late charge to the Note Holder. The amount of the charge will be 5% of my overdue payment of principal and interest. I will pay this late charge promptly but only once on each late payment.

(B) Default

If I do not pay the full amount of each monthly payment on the date it is due, I will be in default.

(C) Notice of Default

[12]   If I am in default, the Note Holder may send me a written notice telling me that if I do not pay the overdue amount by a certain date, the Note Holder may require me to pay immediately the full amount of Principal which has not been paid and all the interest that I owe on that amount. That date must be at least 30 days after the date on which the notice is mailed to me or delivered by other means.

(D) No Waiver By Note Holder

Even if, at a time when I am in default, the Note Holder does not require me to pay immediately in full as described above, the Note Holder will still have the right to do so if I am in default at a later time.

(E) Payment of Note Holder's Costs and Expenses

[13]   If the Note Holder has required me to pay immediately in full as described above, the Note Holder will have the right to be paid back by me for all of its costs and expenses in enforcing this Note to the extent not prohibited by applicable law. Those expenses include, for example, reasonable attorneys' fees.

7. GIVING OF NOTICES

Unless applicable law requires a different method, any notice that must be given to me under this Note will be given by delivering it or by mailing it by first class mail to me at the Property Address above or at a different address if I give the Note Holder a notice of my different address.

Any notice that must be given to the Note Holder under this Note will be given by delivering it or by mailing it by first class mail to the Note Holder at the address stated in Section 3(A) above or at a different address if I am given a notice of that different address.

8. OBLIGATIONS OF PERSONS UNDER THIS NOTE

If more than one person signs this Note, each person is fully and personally obligated to keep all of the promises made in this Note, including the promise to pay the full amount owed. Any person who is a guarantor, surety or endorser of this Note is also obligated to do these things. Any person who takes over these obligations, including the obligations of a guarantor, surety or endorser of this Note, is also obligated

(continued)

FIGURE
9.1   Federal National Mortgage Association (FNMA) Uniform Note (continued)

to keep all of the promises made in this Note. The Note Holder may enforce its rights under this Note against each person individually or against all of us together. This means that any one of us may be required to pay all of the amounts owed under this Note.

9. WAIVERS

I and any other person who has obligations under this Note waive the rights of Presentment and Notice of Dishonor. "Presentment" means the right to require the Note Holder to demand payment of amounts due. "Notice of Dishonor" means the right to require the Note Holder to give notice to other persons that amounts due have not been paid.

10. UNIFORM SECURED NOTE

[14]   This Note is a uniform instrument with limited variations in some jurisdictions. In addition to the protections given to the Note Holder under this Note, a Mortgage, Deed of Trust, or Security Deed (the "Security Instrument"), dated the same date as this Note, protects the Note Holder from possible losses which might result if I do not keep the promises which I make in this Note. That Security Instrument describes how and under what conditions I may be required to make immediate payment in full of all amounts I owe under this Note. Some of those conditions are described as follows:

If all or any part of the Property or any Interest in the Property is sold or transferred (or if Borrower is not a natural person and a beneficial interest in Borrower is sold or transferred) without Lender's prior written consent, Lender may require immediate payment in full of all sums secured by this Security Instrument. However, this option shall not be exercised by Lender if such exercise is prohibited by Applicable Law.

If Lender exercises this option, Lender shall give Borrower notice of acceleration. The notice shall provide a period of not less than 30 days from the date the notice is given in accordance with Section 15 within which Borrower must pay all sums secured by this Security Instrument. If Borrower fails to pay these sums prior to the expiration of this period, Lender may invoke any remedies permitted by this Security Instrument without further notice or demand on Borrower.

WITNESS THE HAND(S) AND SEAL(S) OF THE UNDERSIGNED.

_____ (Seal) [15]
- Borrower

_____ (Seal)
- Borrower

_____ (Seal)
- Borrower

[Sign Original Only]

or trust deed, it must say so. Otherwise, it is solely a personal obligation of the borrower. Although interest is not required to make the note valid, most loans do carry an interest charge; when they do, the rate of interest must be stated in the note. Finally, in some states it is necessary for the borrower's signature on the note to be acknowledged and/or witnessed.

OBLIGOR, OBLIGEE

Figure 9.1 is a Federal National Mortgage Association (FNMA) Uniform Note, commonly used throughout the United States. Number [1] identifies the document as a promissory note, and [2] gives the location and date of the note's execution (signing). As with any contract, the location stated in the contract establishes the applicable state laws. For example, a note that says it was executed in Virginia will be governed by the laws of the state of Virginia. At [3], the borrower states that he has received something of value, and, in turn, promises to pay the debt described in the note. Typically, the "value received" is a loan of money in the amount described in the note; it could, however, be services or goods or anything else of value.

The section of the note at [4] identifies to whom the obligation is owed, sometimes referred to as the **obligee**, or **payee**, and where the payments are to be sent.

THE PRINCIPAL

The **principal** or amount of the obligation, $96,000, is shown at [5]. The rate of interest on the debt and the date from which it will be charged is given at [6]. The amount of the periodic payment at [7] is calculated from the loan tables discussed in Chapter 11. In this case, $639.36 each month for 30 years will return the lender's $96,000 plus interest at the rate of 7% per year on the unpaid portion of the principal. When payments will begin and when subsequent payments will be due are outlined at [8]. In this example, they are due on the first day of each month until the full $96,000 and interest have been paid. The clause at [9] is a **prepayment privilege** for the borrower. It allows the borrower to pay more than the required $639.36 per month and to pay the loan off early without penalty. Without this very important privilege, the note requires the borrower to pay $639.36 per month, no more and no less, until the $96,000 plus interest has been paid. On some note forms, the prepayment privilege is created by inserting the words *or more* after the word *dollars* where it appears between [7] and [9]. The note would then read "six hundred thirty nine and 36/100 dollars or more...." The "or more" can be any amount from $639.36 up to and including the entire balance remaining.

ACCELERATION CLAUSE

At [10], the lender gives the borrower a 10-day grace period to accommodate late payments. For payments made after that, the borrower agrees to pay a late charge of $25.00. The clause at [11] states that, whenever a payment is made, any interest due on the loan is first deducted, and then the remainder is applied to reducing the loan balance. Also, if interest is not paid, it too will earn interest at the same rate as the principal, in this example 7% per year. The provision at [12] allows the lender to demand immediate payment of the entire balance remaining on the note if the borrower misses any of the individual payments. This is called an **acceleration clause**, as it "speeds up" the remaining payments due on the note. Without this clause, the lender can only foreclose on the payments that have come due and have not been paid. In this example, that could take as long as 30 years. This clause also has a certain psychological value: Knowing that the lender has the option of calling the entire loan balance due upon default makes the borrower think twice about being late with the payments.

acceleration clause

Allows the lender to demand immediate payment of the entire loan if the borrower defaults.

SIGNATURE

At [13], the borrower agrees to pay any collection costs incurred by the lender if the borrower falls behind in his payments. At [14], the promissory note is tied to the mortgage that secures it, making it a mortgage loan. Without this reference, it would be a personal loan. At [15], the borrower signs the note. If two or more persons sign the note, it is common to include a statement in the note that the borrowers are "jointly and severally liable" for all provisions in the note. This means that the terms of the note and the obligations it creates are enforceable upon the makers as a group and upon each maker individually. If the borrower is married, lenders generally require both husband and wife to sign.

The Mortgage Instrument

The mortgage is a separate agreement from the promissory note. Whereas the note is evidence of a debt and a promise to pay, the **mortgage** provides security (collateral) that the lender can sell if the note is not paid. The technical term for this is hypothecation. **Hypothecation** means the borrower retains the right to possess and use the property while it serves as collateral. In contrast, **pledging** means to give up possession of the property to the lender while it serves as collateral. An example of pledging is the loan made by a pawn shop. The shop holds the collateral until the loan is repaid. The modified FNMA Mortgage in Figure 9.2 illustrates the key provisions most commonly found in real estate mortgages used in the United States. Let's look at these provisions.

The mortgage begins at [1] with the date of its making and the names of the parties involved. In mortgage agreements, the person or party who hypothecates his property and gives the mortgage is the **mortgagor**. The person or party who receives the mortgage (the lender) is the **mortgagee**. For the reader's convenience, we shall refer to the mortgagor as the borrower and the mortgagee as the lender.

At [2], the debt for which this mortgage provides security is identified. Only property named in the mortgage is security for that mortgage. At [3], the borrower conveys to the lender the property described at [4]. This will most often be the property that the borrower purchased with the loan money, but this is not a requirement. The mortgaged property need only be something of sufficient value in the eyes of the lender; it could just as easily be some other real estate the borrower owns. At [5], the borrower states that the property is his and that he will defend its ownership. The lender will, of course, verify this with a title search before making the loan.

As you may have already noticed, the wording of [3], [4], and [5] is strikingly similar to that found in a warranty deed. In states taking the **title theory** position toward mortgages, the wording at [3] is interpreted to mean that the borrower is deeding his property to the lender. Sometimes you will see the words *Mortgage Deed* printed at the top of a mortgage because, in fact, a mortgage does technically deed the property to the lender, at least in title theory states. In **lien theory** states, the wording at [3] gives only a lien right to the lender, and the borrower (mortgagor) retains title. In **intermediate theory** states, a mortgage is a lien unless the borrower defaults, at which time it conveys title to the lender. No matter which legal philosophy prevails, the borrower retains possession of the mortgaged property, and when the loan is repaid in full, the mortgage is defeated as stated in the defeasance clause.

COVENANTS

After [6], there is a list of covenants (promises) that the borrower makes to the lender. They are the covenants of taxes, removal, insurance, and repair. These covenants protect the security for the loan.

In the **covenant to pay taxes** at [7], the borrower agrees to pay the taxes on the mortgaged property even though the title may be technically with the lender. This is

mortgage

A document that makes property security for the repayment of a debt.

mortgagee

The party receiving the mortgage; the lender.

FIGURE 9.2 The Modified FNMA Master Form Mortgage

After Recording Return To:

_____

_____

_____

_____

_____   _____

MORTGAGE

WORDS USED OFTEN IN THIS DOCUMENT

Words used in multiple sections of this document are defined below. Other words are defined in Sections 3, 5, 8, 10, 11, 13, 18, 20 and 21. Certain rules about the usage of words used in this document are also provided in Section 16.

(A) "Security Instrument" means this document, which is dated _____, _____. The term "Security Instrument" includes any Riders recorded with the Security Instrument.

[1] **(B) "Borrower"** means _____, who sometimes will be called "Borrower" and sometimes simply "I" or "me." "Borrower" is granting a mortgage under this Security Instrument. "Borrower" is not necessarily the same as the Person or Persons who signed the Note. The obligations of Borrowers who did not sign the Note are explained further in Section 13.

(C) "Lender" means _____. Lender is a corporation or association which exists under the laws of _____. Lender's address is _____. Except as provided in Sections 13 and 20, the term "Lender" may include any Person who takes ownership of the Note and this Security Instrument.

[2] **(D) "Note"** means the note signed by _____ and dated _____, _____. The Note shows that its signer or signers owe Lender _____ Dollars (U.S. $ _____) plus interest and promise to pay this debt in Periodic Payments and to pay the debt in full by _____, _____.

(E) "Property" means the property that is described below in the section titled "Description of the Property" or any portion of the Property.

(F) "Sums Secured" means the unpaid balance of amounts described below in the section titled "Borrower's Transfer to Lender of Rights in the Property."

BORROWER'S TRANSFER TO LENDER OF RIGHTS IN THE PROPERTY

[3] I mortgage, grant and convey the Property to Lender, with mortgage covenants, subject to the terms of this Security Instrument, to have and to hold all of the Property to Lender, and to its successors and assigns, forever. This means that, by signing this Security Instrument, I am giving Lender those rights that are stated in this Security Instrument and also those rights that Applicable Law gives to Lenders who hold mortgages on real property. Those rights that Applicable Law gives to Lenders who hold mortgages on real property include those rights known as "Mortgage Covenants." I am giving Lender these rights to protect Lender from possible losses that might result if:

(A) Some or all of the Loan is not paid when due;

(B) I fail to pay, with interest, any amounts that Lender spends under Section 9 of this Security Instrument to protect the value of the Property and Lender's rights in the Property; or

(C) I fail to keep any of my other promises and agreements under this Security Instrument.

These amounts are the "Sums Secured."

(continued)

FIGURE
9.2   The Modified FNMA Master Form Mortgage (continued)

DESCRIPTION OF THE PROPERTY

[4] I grant and mortgage to Lender the Property described in (A) through (G) below:

(A) The Property which is located at _____,

[Street]

_____, Maine _____ ("Property Address"). This

[City]   [Zip Code]

Property is in _____ County. It has the following legal description:

(B) All buildings and other improvements that are located on the Property described in subsection (A) of this section;

(C) All rights in other property that I have as owner of the Property described in subsection (A) of this section. These rights are known as "easements and appurtenances attached to the Property;"

(D) All rights that I have in the land which lies in the streets or roads in front of, or next to, the Property described in subsection (A) of this section;

(E) All fixtures that are now or in the future will be on the Property described in subsections (A) and (B) of this section;

(F) All of the rights and property described in subsections (B) through (E) of this section that I acquire in the future; and

(G) All replacements of or additions to the Property described in subsections (B) through (F) of this section.

BORROWER'S RIGHT TO MORTGAGE THE PROPERTY AND BORROWER'S OBLIGATION TO DEFEND OWNERSHIP OF THE PROPERTY

[5] I promise that: (A) I lawfully own the Property; (B) I have the right to mortgage, grant and convey the Property to Lender; and (C) there are no outstanding claims or charges against the Property, except for those which are of public record.

I give a general warranty of title to Lender. This means that I will be fully responsible for any losses which Lender suffers because someone other than myself has some of the rights in the Property which I promise that I have. I promise that I will defend my ownership of the Property against any claims of such rights.

PLAIN LANGUAGE SECURITY INSTRUMENT

This Security Instrument contains promises and agreements that are used in real property security instruments all over the country. It also contains promises and agreements that vary, to a limited extent, in different parts of the country. My promises and other agreements are stated in "plain language."

[6] ## COVENANTS

I promise and I agree with Lender as follows:

1. Borrower's Promise to Pay. If I signed the Note, I will pay to Lender when due principal and interest due under the Note and any prepayment charges and late charges due under the Note. Regardless of whether I signed the Note, I will pay funds for Escrow Items as described in Section 3. I will make all payments in U.S. currency. If any Borrower makes any Loan payment to Lender with a check or other instrument that is returned for any reason (*i.e.*, the check bounces), except when prohibited by Applicable Law, the Lender may require that any subsequent payment be made by: (a) cash; (b) money order; (c) certified check, bank check, treasurer's check or cashier's check (all of which must be drawn on an institution

(continued)

FIGURE 9.2 The Modified FNMA Master Form Mortgage (continued)

whose deposits are insured by a federal agency, instrumentality, or entity); or (d) Electronic Funds Transfer. Lender may reasonably specify which payment form is required.

Payments are only considered received when they reach the Lender's address specified in the Note, or a different address specified by Lender under Section 15 of this Security Instrument. Lender may return any payments or partial payments if the payments are insufficient to bring the Loan current. Lender may accept any payments or partial payments insufficient to bring the Loan current, but doing so will not affect Lender's rights under this Security Instrument, and Lender may still refuse such late, partial payments in the future.

I agree that no claim or legal right I may have against the Lender will excuse my obligation to make timely payments under the Loan or to keep my other promises in this Security Instrument.

2. Application of Payments or Proceeds. Except as otherwise described in this Section 2, all payments accepted and applied by Lender will be applied in the following order of priority: (a) interest due under the Note; (b) principal due under the Note; (c) amounts payable under Section 3. Such payments will be applied to each Periodic Payment in the order in which it became due. Any remaining amounts will be applied first to late charges, second to any other amounts due under this Security Instrument, and then to reduce the principal balance of the Note.

If Lender receives a payment from me for a delinquent Periodic Payment which includes a sufficient amount to pay any late charge due, the payment may be applied to the delinquent Periodic Payment and the late charge. If more than one Periodic Payment is outstanding, Lender may apply any payment received from me to the repayment of the Periodic Payments if, and to the extent that, each payment can be paid in full. To the extent that any excess exists after the payment is applied to the full payment of one or more Periodic Payments, such excess may be applied to any late charges due. Voluntary extra payments must be applied first to any charges for making voluntary extra payments and then as described in the Note.

If voluntary extra payments I may make or the crediting of insurance proceeds or Miscellaneous Proceeds to the Note are enough to pay principal ahead of schedule, I must still make my regularly scheduled Periodic Payments under the Note, when scheduled, without any delay or reduction of amount.

[7] **3. Monthly Payments for Taxes and Insurance.**

(a) Borrower's Obligations. I will pay to Lender all amounts necessary to pay for taxes, assessments, ground leasehold payments or rents (if any), hazard or property insurance covering the Property, flood insurance (if any), and any required Mortgage Insurance, or a loss reserve as described in Section 10 in the place of Mortgage Insurance. Each Periodic Payment will include an amount to be applied toward the payment of the following items, which are called "Escrow Items:"

[7.5] (1) The taxes, assessments and other items which under the Applicable Law may be or become superior to this Security Instrument as a lien on the Property. Any claim, demand or charge that is made against property because an obligation has not been fulfilled is known as a "lien;"

(2) The leasehold payment or Ground Rents on the Property (if any);

(3) The premium for insurance covering the Property required under Section 5;

(4) The premium for Mortgage Insurance (if any);

(5) The amount I may be required to pay Lender under Section 10 below instead of the payment of the premium for Mortgage Insurance (if any); and

(6) If Lender requires, Community Association Dues, Fees, and Assessments.

After signing of the Note, or at any time during its term, Lender may include these amounts as Escrow Items. The monthly payment that I will make for Escrow Items will be based on Lender's estimate of the annual amount required.

I will pay all of these amounts to Lender unless Lender tells me, in writing, that I do not have to do so, or unless Applicable Law requires otherwise. I will make these payments on the same day that my Periodic Payments of principal and interest are due under the Note.

(continued)

FIGURE 9.2   The Modified FNMA Master Form Mortgage (continued)

I will promptly send Lender a copy of all notices of amounts to be paid under this Section. I must pay Lender for Escrow Items as part of my regular Periodic Payments, unless Lender excuses this requirement in writing. If Lender excuses me in writing, I will pay all Escrow Items covered by the excuse, directly and on time. I will provide receipts proving my direct payments of Escrow Items on request and in the time period Lender requires. If Lender excuses me from paying Escrow Items to Lender and if I fail to pay any amount due for an Escrow Item directly, Lender may pay such amount under Section 9, and I will be obligated to repay Lender, plus interest at the Note rate. Lender may revoke the excuse regarding any or all Escrow Items at any time by a notice given in accordance with Section 15 and, upon such revocation, I will pay to Lender all Funds (defined below), and in such amounts, that are then required under this Section 3.

The amounts that I pay to Lender for Escrow Items under this Section 3 will be called the "Funds." The Funds are pledged as additional security for all Sums Secured.

Lender may, at any time, collect and hold Funds in an amount (1) sufficient to permit Lender to apply the Funds at the time specified under RESPA, but (2) not to exceed the maximum amount a lender can require under RESPA. Lender will estimate the amount of Funds due on the basis of current data and reasonable estimates of expenditures of future Escrow Items or otherwise in accordance with Applicable Law.

[8] **5. Borrower's Obligation to Maintain Hazard Insurance or Property Insurance; Use of Insurance Proceeds.** I will obtain hazard or property insurance to cover all buildings and other improvements that now are or in the future will be located on the Property. The insurance must cover loss or damage caused by: (a) fire; (b) hazards normally covered by "extended coverage" hazard insurance policies; and (c) other hazards for which Lender requires coverage, including floods and earthquakes. The insurance must be in the amounts (including deductibles) and for the periods of time required by Lender. Lender's requirements can change during the term of the Loan. I may choose the insurance company, but my choice is subject to Lender's approval. Lender may not refuse to approve my choice unless the refusal is reasonable. If I do not maintain any of the insurance coverages described above, Lender may obtain insurance coverage at its option and charge me in accordance with Section 9 below.

[9] **7. Borrower's Obligation to Maintain and Protect the Property; Inspections.** I will keep the Property in good repair. I will not destroy, damage or harm the Property, and I will not allow the Property to deteriorate or diminish in value due to its condition whether or not I am residing in the Property. In addition, I will promptly repair the Property, if damaged, to avoid further deterioration or damage unless it is determined pursuant to Section 5 that repair or restoration is not economically feasible. If insurance or condemnation proceeds are paid in connection with damage to, or the taking of, the Property, I will be responsible for repairing or restoring the Property only if Lender has released Proceeds for such purposes. Lender may disburse Proceeds for the repairs and restoration in a single payment or in a series of progress payments as the work is completed. If the insurance or condemnation proceeds are not sufficient to repair or restore the Property, I will not be relieved of my obligation to complete such repair or restoration.

[10] Lender or its agents may enter and inspect the Property at reasonable times. If it has reasonable cause, Lender may inspect the interior of the improvements on the Property. Lender will give me notice prior to an interior inspection specifying such reasonable cause.

[11] **9. Lender's Right to Protect its Rights in the Property.** If: (a) I do not keep my promises and agreements made in this Security Instrument; (b) someone, including me, begins a legal proceeding that may significantly affect Lender's interest in the Property or rights under this Security Instrument (such as a legal proceeding in bankruptcy, in probate, for Condemnation or Forfeiture, for enforcement of a lien which may become superior to this Security Instrument or to enforce laws or regulations); or (c) I abandon the Property, then Lender may do and pay for whatever is necessary to protect the value of the Property and Lender's rights in the Property. Lender's actions to protect its interest in the Property and/or rights under this Security Instrument, including

(continued)

FIGURE
9.2   The Modified FNMA Master Form Mortgage (continued)

its secured position in a bankruptcy proceeding, may include appearing in court, paying reasonable attorneys' fees, paying superior liens on the Property, protecting and/or assessing the value of the Property, and securing and/or repairing the Property. Securing the Property includes, for example, entering the Property to make repairs, change locks, replace or board up doors and windows, drain water from pipes, eliminate building or other code violations or dangerous conditions, and have utilities turned on or off. Although Lender may take action under this Section 9, Lender does not have to do so and is not under any duty or obligation to do so. I agree that Lender incurs no liability for not taking any or all actions authorized under this Section 9.

I will pay to Lender any amounts, with interest, which Lender spends under this Section 9. I will pay those amounts to Lender when Lender sends me a notice requesting that I do so. I will also pay interest on those amounts at the Note rate. Interest on each amount will begin on the date that the amount is spent by Lender.

If I do not own but am a tenant on the Property, I will fulfill all my obligations under my lease. I also agree that, if I subsequently purchase or otherwise become the owner of the Property, my interest as the tenant and my interest as the owner will remain separate unless Lender agrees in writing.

[13]   **11. Agreements about Miscellaneous Proceeds and Condemnation of the Property.** I assign to Lender all Miscellaneous Proceeds (as defined above in subsection (M) of the section entitled "Words Used Often In This Document"). All Miscellaneous Proceeds will be paid to Lender. Miscellaneous Proceeds include, among other things, awards or claims for damages for Condemnation. A taking of property by any governmental authority by eminent domain is known as "Condemnation."

[12]   **18. Agreements about Lender's Rights If the Property Is Sold or Transferred.** As used in this Section 18, "Interest in the Property" means any interest in the Property recognized or protected by Applicable Law including, for example, those interests transferred in a bond for deed, contract for deed, installment sales contract or escrow agreement, if the intent is the transfer of title by Borrower at a future date to a purchaser.

Lender may require immediate payment in full of all Sums Secured by this Security Instrument if all or any part of the Property, or if any interest in the Property, is sold or transferred without Lender's prior written permission. If Borrower is not a natural Person and a beneficial interest in Borrower is sold or transferred without Lender's prior written permission, Lender also may require immediate payment in full. However, Lender will not require immediate payment in full if prohibited by Applicable Law.

If Lender requires immediate payment in full under this Section 18, Lender will give me a notice which states this requirement, following the procedures in Section 15. The notice will give me at least 30 days to make the required payment. The 30-day period will begin on the date the notice is mailed or delivered. If I do not make the required payment during that period, Lender may act to enforce its rights under this Security Instrument without giving me any further notice or demand for payment.

[13] BY SIGNING BELOW, I accept and agree to the promises and agreements contained in this Security Instrument and in the Rider signed by me and recorded with it.

WITNESSES:

_____   _____ (Seal) [14]

                                                          - Borrower

_____   _____ (Seal)

                                                          - Borrower

_____   _____

Source: © 2014 OnCourse Learning

important to the lender, because if the taxes are not paid, they become a lien on the property that is superior to the lender's mortgage.

Lenders often require an impound account where the lender collects monthly amounts for the tax and insurance escrows to make sure they are timely paid. In that event, an **escrow clause** is often used as an additional covenant, shown as [7.5].

The **covenant of insurance** at [8] requires the borrower to carry adequate insurance against damage or destruction of the mortgaged property. This protects the value of the collateral for the loan, because without insurance, if buildings or other improvements on the mortgaged property are damaged or destroyed, the value of the property might fall below the amount owed on the debt. With insurance, the buildings can be repaired or replaced, thus restoring the value of the collateral.

The **covenant of good repair** at [9], also referred to as the **covenant of preservation and maintenance**, requires the borrower to keep the mortgaged property in good condition. The clause at [10] gives the lender permission to inspect the property to make sure that it is being kept in good repair, and has not been damaged or demolished.

If the borrower breaks any of the mortgage covenants or note agreements, the lender wants the right to terminate the loan. Thus, an acceleration clause at [11] is included to permit the lender to demand the balance be paid in full immediately. If the borrower cannot pay, foreclosure takes place and the property is sold.

ALIENATION CLAUSE

When used in a mortgage, an **alienation clause** (also called a **due-on-sale clause**) gives the lender the right to call the entire loan balance due if the mortgaged property is sold or otherwise conveyed (alienated) by the borrower. An example is shown at [12]. The purpose of an alienation clause is twofold. If the mortgaged property is put up for sale and a buyer proposes to assume the existing loan, the lender can refuse to accept that buyer as a substitute borrower if the buyer's credit is not good. In times of escalating interest rates, lenders have used it as an opportunity to eliminate old loans with low rates of interest. This issue, from both borrower and lender perspectives, is discussed in Chapter 13.

CONDEMNATION CLAUSE

Number [13] is a **condemnation clause**. If all or part of the property is taken by action of eminent domain, any money so received is used to reduce the balance owing on the note.

At [14], the mortgagor states that he has made this mortgage. Actually, the execution statement is more a formality than a requirement; the mortgagor's signature alone indicates his execution of the mortgage and agreement to its provisions. At [15], the mortgage is acknowledged and/or witnessed as required by state law for placement in the public records. Like deeds, mortgages must be recorded if they are to be effective against any subsequent purchaser, mortgagee, or lessee. The reason the mortgage, but not the promissory note, is recorded is that the mortgage deals with rights and interests in real property, whereas the note represents a personal obligation. Moreover, most people do not want the details of their promissory notes in the public records.

Mortgage Satisfaction

By far, most mortgage loans are paid in full either on or ahead of schedule. When the loan is paid, the standard practice is for the lender to return the promissory note to the borrower, along with a document called a **satisfaction of mortgage** or a **release of mortgage**. Issued by the lender, this document states that the promissory note or bond has been paid in full, and the accompanying mortgage may be discharged from the public records. It is extremely important that this document be promptly recorded by the public recorder in the same county where the mortgage is recorded. Otherwise, the records will continue to indicate that the property is mortgaged. When a satisfaction or release is recorded, a recording office employee makes a note of its book and page location on the margin of the recorded mortgage. This is done to assist title searchers, and is called a **marginal release**.

PARTIAL RELEASE

Occasionally, the situation arises where the borrower wants the lender to release a portion of the mortgaged property from the mortgage after part of the loan has been repaid. This is known as asking for a **partial release**. For example, a land developer purchases 40 acres of land for a total price of $1,000,000 and finances his purchase with $250,000 in cash plus a mortgage and note for $750,000 to the seller. In the mortgage agreement, he might ask that the seller release 10 acres free and clear of the mortgage encumbrance for each $200,000 paid against the loan.

This would allow the subdivider to develop and sell those 10 acres without first paying the entire $750,000 remaining balance. The seller gives up part of the security, but usually sees an increased value on the remainder of the property because of the new development.

"Subject To"

If an existing mortgage on a property does not contain a due-on-sale clause, the seller can pass the benefits of that financing along to the buyer. (This can occur when the existing loan carries a lower rate of interest than currently available on new loans.) One method of doing this is for the buyer to purchase the property **subject to** the existing loan. In the purchase contract, the buyer states that he is aware of the existence of the loan and the mortgage that secures it, but takes no personal liability for it. Although the buyer pays the remaining loan payments as they come due, the seller continues to be personally liable to the lender for the loan. As long as the buyer faithfully continues to make the loan payments, which he would normally do as long as the property is worth more than the debts against it, this arrangement presents no problem to the seller. However, if the buyer stops making payments before the loan is fully paid, even though it may be years later, in most states, the lender can require the seller to pay the balance due plus interest. This is true even though the seller thought she was free of the loan because she sold the property.

Assumption

The seller is on safer ground if the buyer assumes the loan (**assumption**). Under this arrangement, the buyer promises in writing to the seller that he will pay the loan, thus personally obligating himself to the seller. In the event of default on the loan, the lender will look to both the buyer and the seller because the seller's name is still on the original promissory note. The seller may have to make the payments, but can file suit against the buyer for the money.

Novation

The safest arrangement for the seller is to ask the lender to **substitute** the buyer's liability for his. This **novation** releases the seller from the personal obligation created by his promissory note, and the lender can now require only the buyer to repay the loan. The lender will require the buyer to prove financial capability to repay by having the buyer fill out a loan application and by running a credit check on the buyer. The lender may also adjust the rate of interest on the loan to reflect current market interest rates. The seller is also on safe ground if the mortgage agreement or state law prohibits deficiency judgments, a topic that will be explained shortly.

Estoppel

When a buyer is to continue making payments on an existing loan, he will want to know exactly how much is still owing. A **certificate of reduction** is prepared by the lender to show how much of the loan remains to be paid. If a recorded mortgage states that it secures a loan for $135,000, but the borrower has reduced the amount owed to $50,000, the certificate of reduction will show that $50,000 remains to be paid. Roughly, the mirror image of a certificate of reduction is the **estoppel certificate**. In it, the borrower is asked to verify the amount still owed and the rate of interest. The most common application of an estoppel certificate is when the holder of a loan sells the loan to another investor. It avoids future confusion and litigation over misunderstandings as to how much is still owed on a loan. The word *estoppel* comes from the Latin "to stop up."

Debt Priorities

The same property can usually be used as collateral for more than one mortgage. This presents no problems to the lenders involved as long as the borrower makes the required payments on each note secured by the property. The difficulty arises when a default occurs on one or more of the loans and the price the property brings at its foreclosure sale does not cover all the loans against it. As a result, a priority system is necessary. The debt with the highest priority is satisfied first from the foreclosure sale proceeds, then the next highest priority debt is satisfied, then the next, and so on until either the foreclosure sale proceeds are exhausted or all debts secured by the property are satisfied.

FIRST MORTGAGE

In the vast majority of foreclosures, the sale proceeds are not sufficient to pay all the outstanding debt against the property; thus, it becomes extremely important that a lender know his priority position before making a loan. Unless there is a compelling reason otherwise, a lender will want to be in the most senior position possible. This is normally accomplished by being the first lender to record a mortgage against a property that is otherwise free and clear of mortgage debt; this lender is said to hold a **first mortgage** on the property. If the same property is later used to secure another note before the first is fully satisfied, the new mortgage is a **second mortgage**, and so on. The first mortgage is also known as the **senior mortgage**. Any mortgage with a lower priority is known as a **junior mortgage**. As time passes and higher priority mortgages are satisfied, the lower priority mortgages move up in priority. Thus, if a property is secured by a first and a second mortgage and the first is paid off, the second becomes a first mortgage. Note that nothing is stamped or written on a mortgage document to indicate if it is a

first mortgage

The mortgage loan with highest priority for repayment in the event of foreclosure.

junior mortgage

Any mortgage on a property that is subordinate to the first mortgage in priority.

first or second or third, and so on. That can only be determined by searching the public records for mortgages recorded against the property that have not been released.

SUBORDINATION

Sometimes a lender will voluntarily take a lower-priority position than the lender would otherwise be entitled to by virtue of recording date. This is known as **subordination** and it allows a junior loan to move up in priority. For example, the holder of a first mortgage can volunteer to become a second mortgagee and allow the second mortgage to move into the first position. Although it seems irrational that a lender would actually volunteer to lower his priority position, it is sometimes done by landowners to encourage developers to buy their land.

subordination
Voluntary acceptance of a lower mortgage priority than one would otherwise be entitled to.

CHATTEL LIENS

As we discussed in the earlier topic of fixtures, an interesting situation regarding priority occurs when chattels are bought on credit and then affixed to land that is already mortgaged. If the chattels are not paid for, can the chattel lienholder come onto the land and remove them? If there is default on the mortgage loan against the land, are the chattels sold as fixtures? The solution is for the chattel lienholder to record a *chattel mortgage* or a **financing statement**. This protects the lienholder even though the chattel becomes a fixture when it is affixed to land. A **chattel mortgage** is a mortgage secured by personal property. If the borrower defaults, the lender is permitted to take possession and sell the mortgaged goods. A more streamlined approach, and one used by most states today, is to file a financing statement as provided by the Uniform Commercial Code to establish lien priority regarding personal property.

The Foreclosure Process

Although relatively few mortgages are foreclosed, it is important to have a basic understanding of what happens when foreclosure takes place. First, knowledge of what causes **foreclosure** can help in avoiding it; second, if foreclosure does occur, one should know the rights of the parties involved. As you read the following material, keep in mind that to *foreclose* simply means to cut off. What the lender is saying is, "Mr. Borrower, you are not keeping your end of the bargain. We want you out so the property can be put into the hands of someone who will keep the agreements." (What is often unsaid is that the lender has commitments to its investors that must be met. Can you imagine going to the bank and asking for the interest on your savings account and hearing the teller say they don't have it because their borrowers have not been making payments?)

foreclosure
The procedure by which a person's property can be taken and sold to satisfy an unpaid debt.

DELINQUENT LOAN

Although noncompliance with any part of the mortgage agreement by the borrower can result in the lender calling the entire balance immediately due, in most cases foreclosure occurs because the note is not being repaid on time. When a borrower runs behind in his payments, the loan is said to be a **delinquent loan**. At this stage, rather than presuming that foreclosure is automatically next, the borrower and lender usually meet and attempt to work out an alternative payment program. Contrary to early motion picture plots in which lenders seemed anxious to foreclose their mortgages, today's lender considers foreclosure to be the last resort. This is because the foreclosure process is time consuming, expensive, and unprofitable. The lender would much rather have the borrower make regular payments. Consequently, if a borrower is behind in loan payments, the lender prefers to arrange a new, stretched-out payment schedule, rather than to immediately declare the acceleration clause in effect, and move toward foreclosing the borrower's rights to the property.

If a borrower realizes that stretching out payments is not going to solve his financial problem, instead of presuming foreclosure to be inevitable, he can seek a buyer for the property who can make the payments. This, more than any other reason, is why relatively few real estate mortgages are foreclosed. The borrower, realizing the financial trouble, sells his property. It is only when the borrower cannot find a buyer and when the lender sees no further sense in stretching the payments that the acceleration clause is invoked, and the path toward foreclosure taken.

FORECLOSURE ROUTES

Basically, there are two foreclosure routes: judicial and nonjudicial. **Judicial foreclosure** means taking the matter to a court of law in the form of a lawsuit that asks the judge to foreclose (cut off) the borrower. A **nonjudicial foreclosure** does not go to court and is not heard by a judge. It is conducted by the lender (or by a trustee) in accordance with provisions in the mortgage and in accordance with state law pertaining to nonjudicial foreclosures. Comparing the two, a judicial foreclosure is more costly and more time consuming, but it does carry the approval of a court of law, and it may give the lender rights to collect the full amount of the loan if the property sells for less than the amount owed. It is also the preferred method when the foreclosure case is complicated and involves many parties and interests. The nonjudicial route is usually faster, simpler, and cheaper, and it is preferred by lenders when the case is simple and straightforward. Let's now look at foreclosure methods for standard mortgages. (Deed of trust foreclosure will be discussed in greater detail in Chapter 10.)

Judicial Foreclosure

The judicial foreclosure process begins with a title search. Next, the lender files a lawsuit naming as defendants the borrower and anyone who acquired a right or interest in the property after the lender recorded his mortgage. In the lawsuit, the lender identifies the debt and the mortgage securing it and states that it is in default. The lender then asks the court for a judgment directing that: (1) the defendants' interests in the property be cut off in order to return the condition of title to what it was when the loan was made, (2) the property be sold at a public auction, and (3) the lender's claim be paid from the sale proceeds.

SURPLUS MONEY ACTION

A copy of the complaint along with a summons is delivered to the defendants. This officially notifies them of the pending legal action against their interests. A junior mortgage holder who has been named as a defendant has basically two choices. One choice is to allow the foreclosure to proceed and file a **surplus money action**. By doing this, the junior mortgage holder hopes that the property will sell at the foreclosure sale for enough money to pay all senior claims, as well as his own claim against the borrower. The other choice is to halt the foreclosure process by making the delinquent payments on behalf of the borrower, and then adding them to the amount the borrower owes the junior mortgage holder. To do this, the junior mortgage holder must use cash out of his own pocket and decide whether this is a case of "good money chasing bad." In making this decision, the junior mortgage holder must consider whether he will have any better luck being paid than did the holder of the senior mortgage.

NOTICE OF LIS PENDENS

At the same time that the lawsuit to foreclose is filed with the court, a **notice of lis pendens** is filed with the county recorder's office where the property is located. This notice informs the public that a legal action is pending against the property. If the borrower attempts to sell the property at this time, the prospective buyer, upon making a title search, will learn of the pending litigation. The buyer can still proceed to purchase the property, but is now informed of the unsettled lawsuit.

PUBLIC AUCTION

The borrower, or any other defendant named in the lawsuit, may now reply to the suit by presenting his side of the issue to the court judge. If no reply is made, or if the issues raised by the reply are found in favor of the lender, the judge will order that the interests of the borrower and other defendants in the property be foreclosed and the property sold. The sale is usually a **public auction**. The objective is to obtain the best possible price for the property by inviting competitive bidding, and conducting the sale in full view of the public. To announce the sale, the judge orders a notice to be posted on the courthouse door and advertised in local newspapers.

EQUITY OF REDEMPTION

The sale is conducted by the county sheriff or by a referee or master appointed by the judge. At the sale, which is held at either the property or at the courthouse, the lender and all parties interested in purchasing the property are present. If the borrower should suddenly locate sufficient funds to pay the judgment, the borrower can, up to the minute the property goes on sale, step forward and redeem the property. This privilege to redeem property anytime between the first sign of delinquency and the moment of foreclosure sale is the borrower's **equity of redemption**. If no redemption is made, the bidding begins. Anyone with adequate funds can bid. Typically, a cash deposit of 10% of the successful bid must be made at the sale, with the balance of the bid price due upon closing, usually 30 days later.

While the lender and borrower hope that someone at the auction will bid more than the amount owed on the defaulted loan, the probability is not high. If the borrower was unable to find a buyer at a price equal to or higher than the loan balance, the best cash bid will probably be less than the balance owed. If this happens, the lender usually enters a bid of his own. The lender is in the unique position of being able to "bid the loan"— that is, the lender can bid up to the amount owed without having to pay cash. All other bidders must pay cash, as the purpose of the sale is to obtain cash to pay the defaulted loan. In the event the borrower bids at the sale and is successful in buying back the property, the junior liens against the property are not eliminated. Note however, that no matter who is the successful bidder, the foreclosure does not cut off property tax liens against the property; they remain.

DEFICIENCY JUDGMENT

If the property sells for more than the claims against it, including any junior mortgage holders, the borrower receives the excess. For example, if a property with $150,000 in

deficiency judgment

A judgment against a borrower if the foreclosure sale does not bring enough to pay the balance owed.

claims against it sells for $155,000, the borrower will receive the $5,000 difference, less unpaid property taxes and expenses of the sale. However, if the highest bid is only $40,000, how is the $110,000 deficiency treated? The laws of the various states differ on this question. Forty states allow the lender to pursue a **deficiency judgment** for the $110,000, with which the lender can proceed against the borrower's other unsecured assets. In other words, the borrower is still personally obligated to the lender for $110,000 and the lender is entitled to collect it. This may require the borrower to sell other assets.

Only a judge can award a lender a deficiency judgment. If the property sells for an obviously depressed price at its foreclosure sale, a deficiency judgment may be allowed only for the difference between the court's estimate of the property's fair market value and the amount still owing against it. Note that if a borrower is in a strong enough bargaining position, it is possible to add wording in the promissory note that the note is *without recourse* or with *no personal liability*, this generally prohibits the lender from seeking a deficiency judgment, but this must be done before the note is signed.

A new federal law has also been passed to protect consumers. The general rule is that any deficiency that is forgiven becomes taxable income to the borrower. So, while the lender may not pursue a deficiency, they may file a 1099 with the Internal Revenue Service declaring that they gave you income during the year of the foreclosure when they did not pursue a deficiency. This is often termed "phantom income." The new Mortgage Debt Relief Act of 2007, however, allows the taxpayer to exclude from income any gain on cancelled debt due on the principal residence. It applies only to the taxpayer's principal residence. It applies to all loans to buy, build, or substantially improve that residence. The act is effective from 2007 through 2012.

The purchaser at the foreclosure sale receives either a referee's deed in foreclosure or a sheriff's deed. These are usually special warranty deeds that convey the title the borrower had at the time the foreclosed mortgage was originally made. The purchaser may take immediate possession, and the court will assist him in removing anyone in possession who was cut off in the foreclosure proceedings.

STATUTORY REDEMPTION

In states with **statutory redemption** laws, the foreclosed borrower has, depending on the state, from one month to one year or more after the foreclosure sale to pay in full the judgment and retake title. This leaves the high bidder at the foreclosure auction in the dilemma of not knowing if he will get the property for certain until the statutory redemption period has run out. Meanwhile, the high bidder receives a **certificate of sale** entitling him to a referee's or sheriff's deed if no redemption is made. Depending on the state, the purchaser may or may not get possession until then. If not, the foreclosed borrower may allow the property to deteriorate and lose value. Knowing this, bidders tend to offer less than what the property would be worth if title and possession could be delivered immediately after the foreclosure sale. In this respect, statutory redemption works against the borrower as well as the lender. This problem can be made less severe if the court appoints a **receiver** (manager) to take charge of the property during the redemption period. Judicial foreclosure with public auction is the predominant method in 21 states, and 9 of them allow a statutory redemption period.

Strict Foreclosure

Strict foreclosure is a judicial foreclosure without a judicial sale and usually without a statutory redemption period. The lender files a lawsuit requesting that the borrower be given a period of time to exercise the equitable right of redemption or lose all rights to the property with title vesting irrevocably to the lender. Although this conjures up visions of a greedy lender foreclosing on a borrower who has nearly paid for the property and misses a payment or two, the court will give the borrower time to make up the back payments or sell the property on the open market. Much more likely is the situation in which the debt owed clearly exceeds the property's value. In this case, there is little to be gained by conducting a judicial sale. Strict foreclosure is the predominant method of foreclosure in two states and is occasionally used in others. Where the debt exceeds the property's value and the foreclosure prohibits a deficiency judgment, this method may be advantageous to the borrower.

Power of Sale

In 27 states, the predominant method of foreclosure is by **power of sale**, also known as **sale by advertisement**. This clause, which must be placed in the mortgage before it is signed, gives the lender the power to conduct the foreclosure and sell the mortgaged property without taking the issue to court. The procedure begins when a lender files a **notice of default** with the public recorder. Next is a waiting period that is the borrower's equity of redemption. The property is then advertised at an auction held by the lender and open to the public. The precise procedures the lender must follow are set by state statutes. After the auction, the borrower can still redeem the property if his state offers statutory redemption. The deed the purchaser receives is prepared and signed by the lender or trustee.

> **power of sale**
> Allows a mortgagee to conduct a foreclosure sale without first going to court.

A lender foreclosing under power of sale cannot award himself a deficiency judgment. If there is a deficiency as a result of the sale, and the lender wants a deficiency judgment, the lender must go to court for it. Because power of sale foreclosures take place outside the jurisdiction of a courtroom, it is said that courts watch them with a careful eye. If a borrower feels mistreated by power of sale proceedings, the borrower can appeal the issue to a court. Wise lenders know this and keep scrupulous records and follow foreclosure rules carefully. The wise junior mortgage holder will already have filed a **request for notice of default** with the public records office when the junior mortgage was recorded. This requires anyone holding a more senior lien to notify the junior mortgagee if a default notice has been filed. (Usually, the junior mortgagee is aware of the problem because if the borrower is not making payments to the holder of the first mortgage, the borrower probably is not making payments to any junior mortgage holders.)

Entry and Possession

Used as the predominant method of foreclosure in one state, and to a lesser degree in three others, **entry and possession** is based on the lender giving notice to the borrower that the lender wants possession of the property. The borrower moves out and the lender takes possession, and this is witnessed and recorded in the public records. If the borrower does not peacefully agree to relinquish possession, the lender will have to use a judicial method of foreclosure.

Deed in Lieu of Foreclosure

To avoid the hassle of foreclosure proceedings and possible deficiency judgment, a borrower may want to voluntarily deed the mortgaged property to the lender. In turn, the borrower should demand cancellation of the unpaid debt and a letter to that effect from the lender. This method relieves the lender of foreclosing and waiting out any required redemption periods, but it also presents the lender with a sensitive situation. With the borrower in financial distress and about to be foreclosed, it is quite easy for the lender to take advantage of the borrower. As a result, a court of law will usually side with the borrower if he complains of any unfair dealings. Therefore, the lender must be prepared to prove conclusively that the borrower received a fair deal by deeding the property voluntarily to the lender in return for cancellation of the debt. A word of caution, though: The debt cancellation may be taxable as income! If the property is worth more than the balance due on the debt, the lender must pay the borrower the difference in cash. A **deed in lieu of foreclosure** is a voluntary act by both borrower and lender, and is sometimes called a "friendly foreclosure." Nonetheless, if either feels he will fare better in regular foreclosure proceedings, he need not agree to it. Note also that, depending on local state law, a deed in lieu of foreclosure may not cut off the rights of junior mortgage holders. This means the lender may have to make those payments or be foreclosed by the junior mortgage holder(s). Figure 9.3 summarizes through illustration the five methods of mortgage foreclosure that have just been discussed.

Installment Contract Foreclosure

An installment contract (discussed in Chapter 8) is both a purchase contract and a debt instrument. In years past, if the buyer (vendee) stopped making the payments called for by the contract, the seller (vendor) simply rescinded the contract. The buyer gave up possession, the seller kept all the payments to date, and there was no deficiency judgment. (This effectively is a strict foreclosure without the protection of a court.)

State legislatures found installment contracts too often one-sided in favor of the seller, especially where the buyer had made a substantial number of payments and/or the property had appreciated in value. The need for added consumer protection became even more urgent with increased use of installment contracts in connection with house sales. As a result, many states have enacted legislation that requires installment contracts to be foreclosed like regular mortgages.

Deed of Trust

In some states, debts are often secured by trust deeds. Whereas a mortgage is a two-party arrangement with a borrower and a lender, the **trust deed**, also known as a *deed of trust*, is a three-party arrangement consisting of the borrower (the trustor), the lender (the beneficiary), and a neutral third party (a trustee). The key aspect of this system is that the borrower executes a deed to the trustee rather than to the lender. If the borrower pays the debt in full and on time, the lender instructs the trustee to reconvey title back to the borrower. If the borrower defaults on the loan, the lender instructs the trustee to sell the property, at an out of court foreclosure, to pay off the debt. Trust deeds are covered in more detail in Chapter 10.

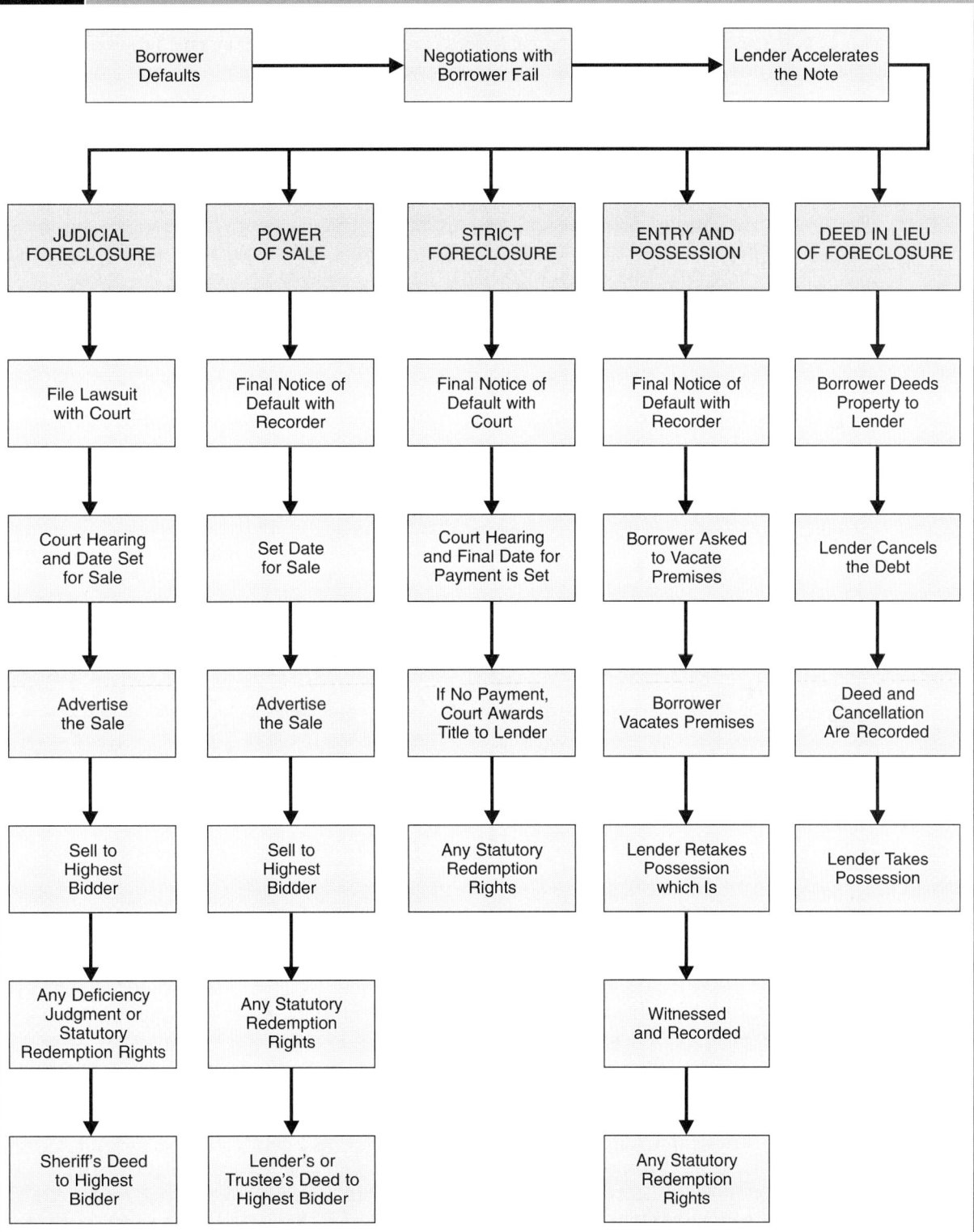

FIGURE 9.3 An overview of Mortgage Foreclosure

| Borrower Defaults | → | Negotiations with Borrower Fail | → | Lender Accelerates the Note |

JUDICIAL FORECLOSURE	POWER OF SALE	STRICT FORECLOSURE	ENTRY AND POSSESSION	DEED IN LIEU OF FORECLOSURE
File Lawsuit with Court	Final Notice of Default with Recorder	Final Notice of Default with Court	Final Notice of Default with Recorder	Borrower Deeds Property to Lender
Court Hearing and Date Set for Sale	Set Date for Sale	Court Hearing and Final Date for Payment is Set	Borrower Asked to Vacate Premises	Lender Cancels the Debt
Advertise the Sale	Advertise the Sale	If No Payment, Court Awards Title to Lender	Borrower Vacates Premises	Deed and Cancellation Are Recorded
Sell to Highest Bidder	Sell to Highest Bidder	Any Statutory Redemption Rights	Lender Retakes Possession which Is	Lender Takes Possession
Any Deficiency Judgment or Statutory Redemption Rights	Any Statutory Redemption Rights		Witnessed and Recorded	
Sheriff's Deed to Highest Bidder	Lender's or Trustee's Deed to Highest Bidder		Any Statutory Redemption Rights	

Source: © 2014 OnCourse Learning

Equitable Mortgage

An **equitable mortgage** is a written agreement that, although it does not follow the form of a regular mortgage, is considered by the courts to be one. For example, Black sells his land to Green, with Green paying part of the price now in cash and promising to pay the balance later. Normally, Black would ask Green to execute a regular mortgage as security for the balance due. However, instead of doing this, Black makes a note of the balance due him on the deed before handing it to Green. The laws of most states would regard this notation as an equitable mortgage. For all intents and purposes, it is a mortgage, although not specifically called one. Another example of an equitable mortgage can arise from the deposit money accompanying an offer to purchase property. If the seller refuses the offer and refuses to return the deposit, the courts will hold that the purchaser has an equitable mortgage in the amount of the deposit against the seller's property.

Deed as Security

Occasionally, a borrower will give a bargain and sale or warranty **deed as security** for a loan. On the face of it, the lender (grantee) would appear to own the property. However, if the borrower can prove that the deed was, in fact, security for a loan, the lender must foreclose like a regular mortgage if the borrower fails to repay. If the loan is repaid in full and on time, the lender is obligated to convey the land back to the borrower. Like the equitable mortgage, a deed used as security is treated according to its intent, not its label.

In one state, Georgia, the standard mortgage instrument is the **security deed**. This is a warranty deed with a reconveyance clause. The security deed transfers title to the lender and, when all payments have been made on the accompanying note, the lender executes the reconveyance (or cancellation) clause on the reverse of the deed and it is recorded. If the borrower defaults, a power of sale clause in the deed allows the lender to advertise and sell the property without going through judicial foreclosure.

Choice of Security Instrument

Generally speaking, a lender will choose, and ask the borrower to sign, whatever security instrument provides the smoothest foreclosure in that state. To illustrate, some states require a statutory redemption period for a mortgage foreclosure but not for a deed of trust foreclosure. Some will allow power of sale for a deed of trust but not for a mortgage. All states allow the use of a deed of trust, but some require that it be foreclosed like a mortgage. More and more states require installment contracts to be foreclosed like mortgages. An analogy for the development of security instrument law is that of a plant growing up through a pile of rocks. Its path up may be twisted and curved, but it reaches its goal—the sunlight. Security instruments follow many paths, but always with one goal in mind—to get money to the borrower who uses it and then returns it to the lender.

Lastly, take a look at Figures 10.1 and 10.5 in the next chapter. These illustrations will help you visualize the differences between a mortgage, deed of trust, and land contract at the time of creation, repayment, and foreclosure.

Vocabulary Review

Match terms a–z with statements 1–26.

a. Acceleration clause
b. Alienation clause
c. Assumption
d. Chattel mortgage
e. Covenant of insurance
f. Deed of trust
g. Defeasance clause
h. Deficiency judgment
i. Delinquent loan
j. Equitable mortgage
k. Equity of redemption
l. First mortgage
m. Foreclosure
n. Junior mortgage
o. Maker
p. Mortgage
q. Mortgagor
r. Partial release
s. Power of sale
t. Prepayment privilege
u. Promissory note
v. Public auction
w. Satisfaction of mortgage
x. Statutory redemption
y. Subject to
z. Subordination

_____ 1. A document by which property secures the repayment of a debt.

_____ 2. A clause in a mortgage stating that the mortgage is defeated if the borrower repays the accompanying note on time.

_____ 3. The borrower's right, prior to the day of foreclosure, to repay the balance due on a delinquent loan.

_____ 4. A lawsuit filed by a lender that asks a court to set a time limit on how long a borrower has to redeem her property.

_____ 5. An agreement that is considered to be a mortgage in its intent even though it may not follow the usual mortgage wording.

_____ 6. A document wherein personal property is used as security for a promissory note.

_____ 7. The evidence of debt; contains amount owed, interest rate, repayment schedule, and a promise to repay.

_____ 8. One who gives a mortgage; the borrower.

_____ 9. A clause in a mortgage that allows the lender to call the loan due if the property changes ownership; also known as a due-on-sale clause.

_____ 10. A clause in a mortgage whereby the borrower agrees to keep mortgaged property adequately insured against destruction.

_____ 11. Discharge of a mortgage upon payment of the debt owed.

_____ 12. Release of a portion of a property from a mortgage.

_____ 13. The buyer personally obligates himself to repay an existing mortgage loan as a condition of the sale.

_____ 14. The buyer of an already mortgaged property makes the payments but does not take personal responsibility for the loan.

_____ 15. Any mortgage lower than a first mortgage in priority.

_____ 16. A loan on which the borrower is behind in his payments.

_____ 17. A clause in a mortgage that gives the mortgagee the right to conduct a foreclosure sale without first going to court.

_____ 18. A judgment against a borrower if the sale of mortgaged property at foreclosure does not bring in enough to pay the balance owed.

_____ 19. The right of a borrower, after a foreclosure sale, to reclaim the property by repaying the defaulted loan.

_____ 20. Voluntary acceptance of a lower mortgage priority position than one would otherwise be entitled to.

_____ 21. A deed given to a trustee as security for a loan.

_____ 22. The mortgage loan with highest priority for repayment in the event of foreclosure.

_____ 23. A person who signs a promissory note.

_____ 24. Allows the borrower to pay more than the required payment.

_____ 25. The usual procedure by which foreclosed properties are sold.

_____ 26. Allows the lender to declare the loan due if the borrower defaults.

Questions and Problems

1. Is a prepayment privilege to the advantage of the borrower or the lender?

2. What are the legal differences between lien theory and title theory?

3. How does strict foreclosure differ from foreclosure by sale? Which system does your state use?

4. A large apartment complex serves as security for a first, a second, and a third mortgage. Which of these are considered junior mortgage(s)? Senior mortgage(s)?

5. Describe the procedure in your county that is used in foreclosing delinquent real estate loans.

6. What do the laws of your state allow real estate borrowers in the way of equitable and statutory redemption?

7. Do the laws of your state allow a delinquent borrower adequate opportunity to recover his mortgaged real estate? Do you advocate more or less borrower protection than is presently available?

8. In a promissory note, who is the obligor? Who is the obligee?

9. Why does a mortgage lender insist on including mortgage covenants pertaining to insurance, property taxes, and removal?

10. What roles do a certificate of reduction and an estoppel certificate play in mortgage lending?

Additional Readings

Financing Residential Real Estate by David L. Rockwell and Megan Dorsey (Rockwell Publishing Company, 1997).

Real Estate Finance: Theory & Practice by Terrence M. Clauretie and G. Stacy Sirmans (OnCourse Learning, 2014). A clearly written introduction to the world of real estate finance.

"Lender Liability" by Michael R. Pfeifer (*Mortgage Banking*, September 2000, vol. 60, issue 12, p. 56).

Real Estate Finance, 8th ed. by John P. Wiedemer and J. Keith Baker (OnCourse Learning, 2013). Focuses on the development of land; places primary emphasis on residential real estate.

Residential Mortgage Lending: Principles & Practices 6th ed. by Thomas J. Pinkowish (OnCourse Learning, 2012). Written for students and professionals; includes mortgage lending techniques, procedures, law, history, and case studies of actual mortgage transactions.

Deed of Trust

CHAPTER **10**

LEARNING OBJECTIVES

After reading this chapter, you should be able to:

❮ Define the parties to a deed of trust.

❮ Discuss the various standard provisions for a deed of trust.

❮ Understand the purpose of the trustee in the deed of trust.

❮ Discuss the advantages and disadvantages of the use of a deed of trust.

KEY TERMS

Assignment of rents • Beneficiary • Deed of trust • Naked title • Reconveyance or release deed • Trustee • Trustor

In the last chapter we talked about mortgages in general terms. In this chapter we will discuss the deed of trust as a mortgage instrument, how it differs from traditional mortgage theories, and an analysis of the parties and the roles they play, both in creating the mortgage and during the foreclosure process.

The basic purpose of a *deed of trust*, also referred to as a *trust deed*, is the same as a mortgage. Real property is used as security for a debt; if the debt is not repaid, the property is sold and the proceeds are applied to the balance owed. The main legal difference between a deed of trust and a mortgage is diagrammed in Figure 10.1.

Parties to a Deed of Trust

Figure 10.1A shows that when a debt is secured by a mortgage, the borrower delivers his promissory note and mortgage to the lender, who keeps them until the debt is paid. But when a note is secured by a deed of trust, three parties are involved: the borrower (the **trustor** or **grantor**), the lender (the **beneficiary**), and a neutral third party (the **trustee**). The lender makes a loan to the borrower, and the borrower gives the lender a promissory note (like the one shown in Chapter 9) and a deed of trust. In the deed of trust document, the borrower conveys title to the trustee, to be held in trust until the note is paid in full. (This is one of the distinguishing features of a deed of trust.)

The deed of trust is recorded in the county where the property is located, and is then given to either the lender or the trustee for safekeeping. Anyone searching the title records would find the deed of trust conveying title to the trustee. This would alert the title searcher to the existence of a debt against the property.

trustor

One who creates a trust; the borrower in a deed of trust arrangement.

beneficiary

One for whose benefit a trust is created; the lender in a deed of trust arrangement.

trustee

One who holds property in trust for another.

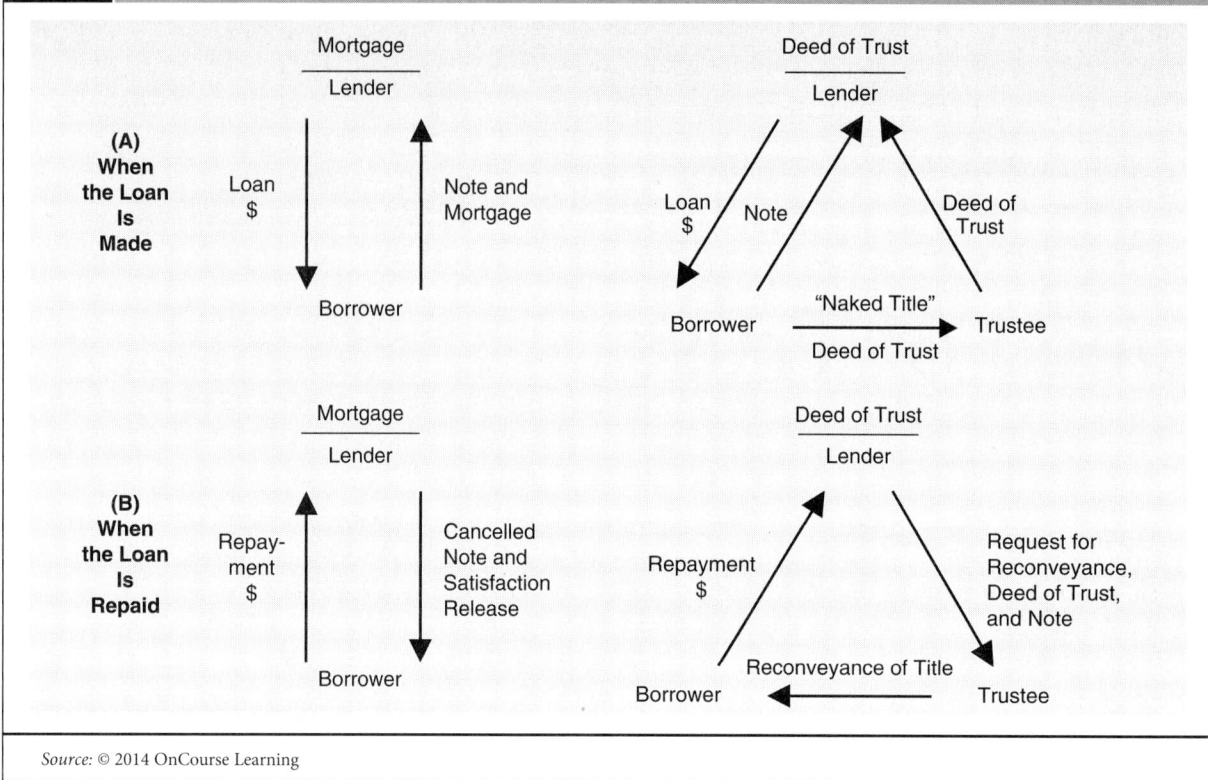

FIGURE 10.1 Comparison of a Mortgage with Deed of Trust

Source: © 2014 OnCourse Learning

naked title

Title that lacks the rights and privileges usually associated with ownership.

The title that the borrower grants to the trustee is sometimes referred to as a **naked title** or **bare title**. This is because the borrower still retains the usual rights of an owner, such as the right to occupy and use the property, and the right to sell it. The title held by the trustee is limited only to what is necessary to carry out the terms of the trust. In fact, as long as the note is not in default, the trustee's title lies dormant. The lender does not receive title, but only a right that allows the lender to request the trustee to act in the event of a default.

Reconveyance

Referring to Figure 10.1B, we see that when the note is repaid in full under a regular mortgage, the lender cancels the note and returns it to the borrower together with a mortgage satisfaction or release. Upon recordation, the mortgage satisfaction or release informs the world at large that the mortgage is nullified and no longer encumbers the property. Under the deed of trust arrangement, the lender sends to the trustee the note, the deed of trust, and a **request for reconveyance**. The trustee cancels the note and issues to the borrower a **reconveyance** or a **release deed** that releases the item and/or reconveys title back to the borrower. The borrower records this document to inform the world that the trustee no longer has title. At the recorder's office, a marginal note may be made on the record copy of the original deed of trust to show that it has been discharged.

reconveyance or release deed

A document used to reconvey title from the trustee back to the property owner once the debt has been paid.

DEFAULT

If a borrower defaults under a deed of trust, the lender delivers the deed of trust to the trustee with instructions to sell the property and pay the balance due on the note. The trustee can do this because of two important features found in the deed of trust. First, by virtue of signing the deed of trust, the borrower has already conveyed title to the trustee. Second, the power of sale clause found in a deed of trust is designed to give the trustee the authority to sell the property without having to go through a court-ordered foreclosure proceeding.

TRUSTEE

In nearly all states, a title, trust, escrow company, or the trust department of a bank may act as a *trustee*. An individual can be named as a trustee in most jurisdictions. However, this can present a problem if the person dies before reconveyance is made. Therefore, a corporate trustee is preferred because its life span is not limited by the human life span. In a few jurisdictions, Colorado for example, the role of trustee is performed by a government official known as a **public trustee**. Whether public or private, the trustee is expected to be neutral and fair to both the borrower and the lender. To accomplish this, the trustee carefully abides by the agreements found in the deed of trust.

Deed of Trust Document

Figure 10.2 reflects the pertinent provisions of a Federal National Mortgage Association (FNMA) form deed of trust that shows the agreements between the borrower and lender, and states the responsibilities of the trustee. Beginning at [1], the document is identified as a deed of trust. This is followed by the date of its execution and the names of the trustor, beneficiary, and trustee. For discussion purposes, this chapter will continue to refer to them as the borrower, lender, and trustee, respectively.

At [2], the promissory note that accompanies this deed of trust is identified, and it is clearly stated that the purpose of this deed is to provide security for that note. In other words, although this deed grants and conveys title to the trustee at [3], it is understood that the quantity of title the trustee receives is only that which is necessary to protect the note. This permits the borrower to continue to possess and enjoy the use of the property as long as the promissory note is not in default.

POWER OF SALE

Under the *power of sale* clause at [4], if the borrower defaults, the trustee has the right to foreclose and sell the property and convey ownership to the purchaser. If the borrower does not default, this power lies dormant. The presence of a power of sale right does not prohibit the trustee from using a court-ordered foreclosure. If the rights of the parties involved, including junior debt holders and other claimants, are not clear, the trustee can request a court-ordered foreclosure.

At [5], the property being conveyed to the trustee is described, and at [6], the borrower states that he has title to the property, and he will defend that title against the claims of others. At [7], the procedure that must be followed to reconvey the title is described or provide a release of lien. State laws require that when the note is paid, the lender must deliver a request for reconveyance to the trustee. The lender must also deliver the promissory note and deed of trust to the trustee. Upon receiving these three items, the trustee reconveys title to the borrower, and the trust arrangement is terminated. (A simplified request for reconveyance is illustrated in Figure 10.3 on page 175 and a simplified full reconveyance in Figure 10.4 on page 175).

Continuing in Figure 10.2, the sections identified at [8], [9], and [10] (paragraphs 1 through 7) are similar to those found in a regular mortgage, as discussed in Chapter 9.

FIGURE
10.2   Deed of Trust

After Recording Return To:

_____

_____

_____

_____

_____[Space Above This Line For Recording Data]_____

DEED OF TRUST [1]

DEFINITIONS

Words used in multiple sections of this document are defined below and other words are defined in Sections 3, 11, 13, 18, 20 and 21. Certain rules regarding the usage of words used in this document are also provided in Section 16.

(A) "Security Instrument" means this document, which is dated _____,
_____, together with all Riders to this document.
(B) "Borrower" is _____. Borrower
is the grantor under this Security Instrument.
(C) "Lender" is _____. Lender is a
_____ organized and existing under the laws of _____.
Lender's address is _____. Lender is the beneficiary under this Security Instrument.
[12] **(D) "Trustee"** is _____. Trustee's
address is _____.
[2] **(E) "Note"** means the promissory note signed by Borrower and dated _____,
_____. The Note states that Borrower owes Lender _____
Dollars (U.S. $_____) plus interest. Borrower has promised to pay this debt in regular Periodic
Payments and to pay the debt in full not later than _____.
(F) "Property" means the property that is described below under the heading "Transfer of Rights in the Property."
(G) "Loan" means the debt evidenced by the Note, plus interest, any prepayment charges and late charges
due under the Note, and all sums due under this Security Instrument, plus interest.

TRANSFER OF RIGHTS IN THE PROPERTY

This Security Instrument secures to Lender: (i) the repayment of the Loan, and all renewals, extensions and modifications of the Note; and (ii) the performance of Borrower's covenants and agreements under this Security Instrument and the Note. For this purpose, Borrower irrevocably grants and conveys to Trustee, in trust, with power of sale, the following described property located in the _____ of _____:

[3]

          [Type of Recording Jurisdiction]   [Name of Recording Jurisdiction]

(continued)

FIGURE
10.2   Deed of Trust (continued)

[5]

which currently has the address of _____

[Street]

_____, Texas _____ ("Property Address"):

[City]   [Zip Code]

    TOGETHER WITH all the improvements now or hereafter erected on the property, and all easements, appurtenances, and fixtures now or hereafter a part of the property. All replacements and additions shall also be covered by this Security Instrument. All of the foregoing is referred to in this Security Instrument as the "Property."

[6]   BORROWER COVENANTS that Borrower is lawfully seised of the estate hereby conveyed and has the right to grant and convey the Property and that the Property is unencumbered, except for encumbrances of record. Borrower warrants and will defend generally the title to the Property against all claims and demands, subject to any encumbrances of record.

    THIS SECURITY INSTRUMENT combines uniform covenants for national use and non-uniform covenants with limited variations by jurisdiction to constitute a uniform security instrument covering real property.

    UNIFORM COVENANTS. Borrower and Lender covenant and agree as follows:

[8]   **1. Payment of Principal, Interest, Escrow Items, Prepayment Charges, and Late Charges.** Borrower shall pay when due the principal of, and interest on, the debt evidenced by the Note and any prepayment charges and late charges due under the Note. Borrower shall also pay funds for Escrow Items pursuant to Section 3. Payments due under the Note and this Security Instrument shall be made in U.S. currency. However, if any check or other instrument received by Lender as payment under the Note or this Security Instrument is returned to Lender unpaid, Lender may require that any or all subsequent payments due under the Note and this Security Instrument be made in one or more of the following forms, as selected by Lender: (a) cash; (b) money order; (c) certified check, bank check, treasurer's check or cashier's check, provided any such check is drawn upon an institution whose deposits are insured by a federal agency, instrumentality, or entity; or (d) Electronic Funds Transfer.

[10]   **7. Preservation, Maintenance and Protection of the Property; Inspections.** Borrower shall not destroy, damage or impair the Property, allow the Property to deteriorate or commit waste on the Property. Whether or not Borrower is residing in the Property, Borrower shall maintain the Property in order to prevent the Property from deteriorating or decreasing in value due to its condition. Unless it is determined pursuant to Section 5 that repair or restoration is not economically feasible, Borrower shall promptly repair the Property if damaged to avoid further deterioration or damage. If insurance or condemnation proceeds are paid in connection with damage to, or the taking of, the Property, Borrower shall be responsible for repairing or restoring the Property only if Lender has released proceeds for such purposes. Lender may disburse proceeds for the repairs and restoration in a single payment or in a series of progress payments as the work is completed. If the insurance or condemnation proceeds are not sufficient to repair or restore the Property, Borrower is not relieved of Borrower's obligation for the completion of such repair or restoration.

    Lender or its agent may make reasonable entries upon and inspections of the Property. If it has reasonable cause, Lender may inspect the interior of the improvements on the Property. Lender shall give Borrower notice at the time of or prior to such an interior inspection specifying such reasonable cause.

(continued)

FIGURE
10.2   Deed of Trust (continued)

[10]   9. Protection of Lender's Interest in the Property and Rights Under this Security Instrument. If (a) Borrower fails to perform the covenants and agreements contained in this Security Instrument, (b) there is a legal proceeding that might significantly affect Lender's interest in the Property and/or rights under this Security Instrument (such as a proceeding in bankruptcy, probate, for condemnation or forfeiture, for enforcement of a lien which may attain priority over this Security Instrument or to enforce laws or regulations), or (c) Borrower has abandoned the Property, then Lender may do and pay for whatever is reasonable or appropriate to protect Lender's interest in the Property and rights under this Security Instrument, including protecting and/or assessing the value of the Property, and securing and/or repairing the Property. Lender's actions can include, but are not limited to: (a) paying any sums secured by a lien which has priority over this Security Instrument; (b) appearing in court; and (c) paying reasonable attorneys' fees to protect its interest in the Property and/or rights under this Security Instrument, including its secured position in a bankruptcy proceeding. Securing the Property includes, but is not limited to, entering the Property to make repairs, change locks, replace or board up doors and windows, drain water from pipes, eliminate building or other code violations or dangerous conditions, and have utilities turned on or off. Although Lender may take action under this Section 9, Lender does not have to do so and is not under any duty or obligation to do so. It is agreed that Lender incurs no liability for not taking any or all actions authorized under this Section 9.

Any amounts disbursed by Lender under this Section 9 shall become additional debt of Borrower secured by this Security Instrument. These amounts shall bear interest at the Note rate from the date of disbursement and shall be payable, with such interest, upon notice from Lender to Borrower requesting payment.

If this Security Instrument is on a leasehold, Borrower shall comply with all the provisions of the lease. If Borrower acquires fee title to the Property, the leasehold and the fee title shall not merge unless Lender agrees to the merger in writing.

NON-UNIFORM COVENANTS. Borrower and Lender further covenant and agree as follows:

[4]   22. Acceleration; Remedies. Lender shall give notice to Borrower prior to acceleration following Borrower's breach of any covenant or agreement in this Security Instrument (but not prior to acceleration under Section 18 unless Applicable Law provides otherwise). The notice shall specify: (a) the default; (b) the action required to cure the default; (c) a date, not less than 30 days from the date the notice is given to Borrower, by which the default must be cured; and (d) that failure to cure the default on or before the date specified in the notice will result in acceleration of the sums secured by this Security Instrument and sale of the Property. The notice shall further inform Borrower of the right to reinstate after acceleration and the right to bring a court action to assert the non-existence of a default or any other defense of Borrower to acceleration and sale. If the default is not cured on or before the date specified in the notice, Lender at its option may require immediate payment in full of all sums secured by this Security Instrument without further demand and may invoke the power of sale and any other remedies permitted by Applicable Law. Lender shall be entitled to collect all expenses incurred in pursuing the remedies provided in this Section 22, including, but not limited to, reasonable attorneys' fees and costs of title evidence. For the purposes of this Section 22, the term "Lender" includes any holder of the Note who is entitled to receive payments under the Note.

[11]   If Lender invokes the power of sale, Lender or Trustee shall give notice of the time, place and terms of sale by posting and filing the notice at least 21 days prior to sale as provided by Applicable Law. Lender shall mail a copy of the notice to Borrower in the manner prescribed by Applicable Law. Sale shall be made at public vendue. The sale must begin at the time stated in the notice of sale or not later than three hours after that time and between the hours of 10 a.m. and 4 p.m. on

(continued)

FIGURE
10.2   Deed of Trust (continued)

the first Tuesday of the month. Borrower authorizes Trustee to sell the Property to the highest bidder for cash in one or more parcels and in any order Trustee determines. Lender or its designee may purchase the Property at any sale.

Trustee shall deliver to the purchaser Trustee's deed conveying indefeasible title to the Property with covenants of general warranty from Borrower. Borrower covenants and agrees to defend generally the purchaser's title to the Property against all claims and demands. The recitals in the Trustee's deed shall be prima facie evidence of the truth of the statements made therein. Trustee shall apply the proceeds of the sale in the following order: (a) to all expenses of the sale, including, but not limited to, reasonable Trustee's and attorneys' fees; (b) to all sums secured by this Security Instrument; and (c) any excess to the person or persons legally entitled to it.

If the Property is sold pursuant to this Section 22, Borrower or any person holding possession of the Property through Borrower shall immediately surrender possession of the Property to the purchaser at that sale. If possession is not surrendered, Borrower or such person shall be a tenant at sufferance and may be removed by writ of possession or other court proceeding.

[7]   **23. Release.** Upon payment of all sums secured by this Security Instrument, Lender shall provide a release of this Security Instrument to Borrower or Borrower's designated agent in accordance with Applicable Law. Borrower shall pay any recordation costs. Lender may charge Borrower a fee for releasing this Security Instrument, but only if the fee is paid to a third party for services rendered and the charging of the fee is permitted under Applicable Law.

[13]   **24. Substitute Trustee; Trustee Liability.** All rights, remedies and duties of Trustee under this Security Instrument may be exercised or performed by one or more trustees acting alone or together. Lender, at its option and with or without cause, may from time to time, by power of attorney or otherwise, remove or substitute any trustee, add one or more trustees, or appoint a successor trustee to any Trustee without the necessity of any formality other than a designation by Lender in writing. Without any further act or conveyance of the Property the substitute, additional or successor trustee shall become vested with the title, rights, remedies, powers and duties conferred upon Trustee herein and by Applicable Law.

Trustee shall not be liable if acting upon any notice, request, consent, demand, statement or other document believed by Trustee to be correct. Trustee shall not be liable for any act or omission unless such act or omission is willful.

(continued)

FIGURE
10.2   Deed of Trust (continued)

BY SIGNING BELOW, Borrower accepts and agrees to the terms and covenants contained in this Security Instrument and in any Rider executed by Borrower and recorded with it.

Witnesses:

_____   _____(Seal) [14]
                                                                                          -Borrower

_____   _____(Seal)
                                                                                          -Borrower

_____[Space Below This Line For Acknowledgment]_____

[15]

FIGURE
10.3
FIGURE
10.3 A Simplified Reconveyance Request

REQUEST FOR FULL RECONVEYANCE

To: <u>Safety Title and Trust Company, Inc.</u>, trustee.

The undersigned is the owner of the debt secured by the above Deed of Trust. This debt has been fully paid and you are requested to reconvey to the parties designated in the Deed of Trust, the estate now held by you under same.

Date _____   <u>District Mortgage</u>
                                    Beneficiary

[As a matter of convenience, this form is often printed at the bottom or on the reverse of the trust deed itself.]

Source: © 2014 OnCourse Learning

ASSIGNMENT OF RENTS

At **[10]**, the lender reserves the right to take physical possession of the pledged property, operate it, and collect any rents or income generated by it. The right to collect rents in the event of default is called an **assignment of rents** clause. The lender would only exercise this right if the borrower continued to collect rental income from the property without paying on the note. The right to take physical possession in the event of default is important because it gives the lender the opportunity to preserve the value of the property until the

assignment of rents
Establishes the lender's right to take possession and collect rents in the event of loan default.

FIGURE
10.4 A Simplified Reconveyance

FULL RECONVEYANCE

<u>Safety Title and Trust Company, Inc.</u>, the Trustee under a deed of trust executed by <u>Victor Raffaelli and Mary Raffaelli, husband and wife</u>, Trustors, dated <u>April 15, 20xx</u>, and recorded as instrument number <u>12345</u> in Book <u>876</u>, Page <u>345</u>, in the Official Records of <u>Graham</u> County, State of _____, having been requested in writing by the holder of the obligation secured by said deed of trust DOES HEREBY RECONVEY WITHOUT WARRANTY to the person(s) legally entitled thereto the estate held by it under said deed of trust.

(Brief property description)

[acknowledgment of   <u>*Safety Title*</u>
trustee's signature is   Trustee
placed here.]

[This document must be recorded to give public notice that the debt has been paid.]

Source: © 2014 OnCourse Learning

foreclosure sale takes place. Very likely, if the borrower has defaulted on the note, his financial condition is such that he is no longer maintaining the property. If this continues, the property will be less valuable by the time the foreclosure sale occurs.

FORECLOSURE

At [11] is the lender's right to instruct the trustee to sell the property in the event of the borrower's default on the note or nonperformance of the agreements in the deed of trust. This section also sets forth the rules the trustee is to follow if there is a foreclosure sale. Either appropriate state laws are referred to or each step of the process is listed in the deed of trust. Generally, state laws regarding power of sale foreclosure require that: (1) the lender demonstrate to the trustee that there is reason to cut off the borrower's interest in the property, (2) a notice of default be filed with the public recorder, (3) the notice of default be followed by a 90- to 120-day waiting period before sale advertising begins, (4) advertising of the proposed foreclosure sale occur for at least three weeks in public places and in a local newspaper, (5) the sale itself be a public auction held in the county where the property is located, and (6) the purchaser at the sale be given a **trustee's deed** conveying all title held by the trustee. This is all the right, title, and interest the borrower had at the time he deeded the property to the trustee.

PROCEEDS. Proceeds from the sale are used to pay: (1) the expenses of the sale, (2) the lender, (3) any junior claims, and (4) the borrower, in that order. Once the sale is held, the borrower's equitable right of redemption ends. In some states, statutory redemption may still exist. Anyone can bid at the sale, including the borrower. However, junior claims that would normally be cut off by the sale are not extinguished if the borrower is the successful bidder.

TRUSTEE APPOINTMENT

The wording at [12] reflects what is called the **automatic form of trusteeship**. The *trustee* is named in the deed of trust but is not personally notified of the appointment. In fact, the trustee is not usually aware of the appointment until called upon to either reconvey or proceed under the power of sale provision. The alternative method is called the **accepted form**: The trustee is notified in advance and either accepts or rejects the appointment. Its primary advantage is that it provides positive acceptance of appointment. The main advantage of the automatic form is that it is faster and easier. In the event the trustee cannot or will not perform when called upon by the lender, the wording at [13] permits the lender to name a substitute trustee. This would be necessary if an individual appointed as a trustee had died, or a corporate trustee was dissolved, or an appointed trustee refused to perform. Finally, the borrowers sign at [14], their signatures are acknowledged at [15], and the deed of trust is recorded in the county where the property is located. Figure 10.5 is a summary comparison of a deed of trust, regular mortgage, and land contract at creation, foreclosure, and repayment.

Jurisdictions Using Deeds of Trust

The deed of trust is the customary security instrument in Alaska, Arizona, California, Colorado, the District of Columbia, Idaho, Maryland, Mississippi, Missouri, North Carolina, Oregon, Tennessee, Texas, Virginia, and West Virginia. The deed of trust is also used to a certain extent in Alabama, Delaware, Hawaii, Illinois, Montana, Nevada, New

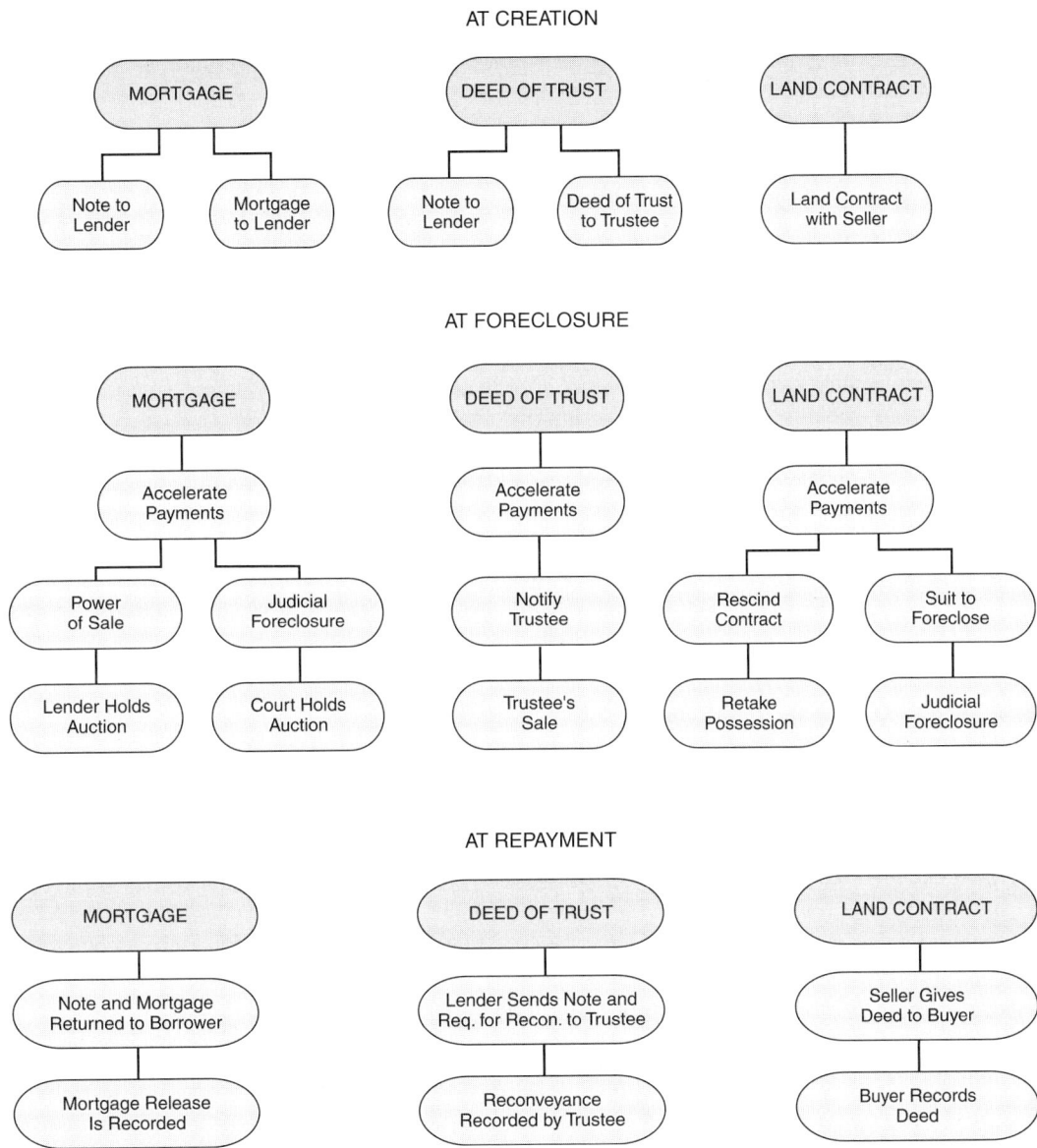

FIGURE 10.5 Comparison of a Mortgage, Deed of Trust, and Land Contract

AT CREATION

MORTGAGE — Note to Lender — Mortgage to Lender

DEED OF TRUST — Note to Lender — Deed of Trust to Trustee

LAND CONTRACT — Land Contract with Seller

AT FORECLOSURE

MORTGAGE — Accelerate Payments — Power of Sale — Lender Holds Auction / Judicial Foreclosure — Court Holds Auction

DEED OF TRUST — Accelerate Payments — Notify Trustee — Trustee's Sale

LAND CONTRACT — Accelerate Payments — Rescind Contract — Retake Possession / Suit to Foreclose — Judicial Foreclosure

AT REPAYMENT

MORTGAGE — Note and Mortgage Returned to Borrower — Mortgage Release Is Recorded

DEED OF TRUST — Lender Sends Note and Req. for Recon. to Trustee — Reconveyance Recorded by Trustee

LAND CONTRACT — Seller Gives Deed to Buyer — Buyer Records Deed

Source: © 2014 OnCourse Learning

Mexico, Utah, Washington, and a few other states. The extent of use in a state is governed by the state's attitude toward conveyance of title to the trustee, power of sale, assignment of rents, and statutory redemption privileges. Many states not listed here allow the use of a deed of trust but require that it be foreclosed just like a regular mortgage.

The deed of trust may be the customary security instrument because state law recognizes a power of sale clause in a deed of trust, but not in a regular mortgage. Or, state law may require a statutory redemption period for mortgages but not for deeds of trust.

In those states that allow all the provisions of a deed of trust to function without hindrance, the deed of trust has flourished. In California, for example, where it is legally well established that a trust deed does convey title to the trustee, that the trustee has the power of sale, and that there is no statutory redemption on trust deeds, trust deed recordings outnumber regular mortgages by a ratio of more than 500 to 1.

Advantages of the Deed of Trust

deed of trust

A document that conveys legal title to a neutral third party (a trustee) as security for a debt.

The popularity of the **deed of trust** can be traced to the following attributes: (1) if a borrower defaults, the lender can take possession of the property to protect it and collect the rents; (2) the time between default and foreclosure is relatively short, on the order of 90 to 180 days; (3) the foreclosure process under the power of sale provision is far less expensive and complex than a court-ordered foreclosure; (4) title is already in the name of the trustee, thus permitting the trustee to grant title to the purchaser after the foreclosure sale; and (5) once the foreclosure sale takes place, there is usually no statutory redemption. These are primarily advantages to the lender, but such advantages have attracted lenders and made real estate loans easier and less expensive for borrowers to obtain. Some states prohibit or restrict the use of deficiency judgments when a deed of trust is used.

Property can be purchased "subject to" an existing deed of trust or it can be "assumed," just as with a regular mortgage. Debt priorities are established as for mortgages: There are first and second, senior and junior trust deeds. Deeds of trust can be subordinated, and partial releases are possible.

Vocabulary Review

Match terms a–l with statements 1–12.

a. Assignment of rents
b. Automatic form
c. Beneficiary
d. Deed of trust
e. Naked title
f. Power of sale
g. Public trustee
h. Reconveyance deed
i. Request for reconveyance
j. Trustee
k. Trustee's deed
l. Trustor

_____ 1. A document that conveys legal title to a neutral third party as security for a debt.

_____ 2. One who creates a trust; the borrower under a deed of trust.

_____ 3. The lender.

_____ 4. One who holds property in trust for another.

_____ 5. Transfers title from the trustee to the trustor.

_____ 6. A publicly appointed official who acts as a trustee in some states.

_____ 7. The trustee is named in the deed of trust but is not personally notified of the appointment.

_____ 8. Title in a legal sense only and without the usual rights of ownership.

_____ 9. The beneficiary's request to the trustee to deed the secured property to the trustor.

_____ 10. A clause in a deed of trust that gives the trustee the right to conduct a foreclosure sale without first going to court.

_____ 11. The lender's right to take possession and collect rents in the event of loan default.

_____ 12. Conveys to the purchaser at foreclosure the right, title, and interest held by the trustee.

Questions and Problems

1. Does possession of a deed of trust give the trustee any rights of entry or use of the property as long as the promissory note is not in default? Explain.

2. How does a deed of trust differ from a mortgage?

3. What is the purpose of a request for reconveyance?

4. What is the purpose of a power of sale clause in a deed of trust?

5. Explain the purpose of an assignment of rents clause.

6. How does the automatic form of trusteeship differ from the accepted form?

7. What is your state's attitude toward trust deeds, power of sale, statutory redemption, and deficiency judgments?

Additional Readings

"Contract or Closing: When Does the Sale Occur? [Tax Implications for Real Estate Sales]" by Ronald A. Morris and Elliot Pisem (*National Real Estate Investor*, July 1, 1995, vol. 37, pp. 28–30).

Real Estate Investment, 7th ed. by John P. Wiedemer, Joseph E. Goeters and J. Edward Graham (OnCourse Learning, 2011). Concise introduction to making investments wisely.

Real Estate Investment Trusts: Structure, Performance, and Investment Opportunities by Su Han Chan, John Erickson, and Ko Wang (Oxford University Press, Inc., 2002).

"There's More Than One Path to Early Payoff" by Benny L. Kass (*The Washington Post*, March 30, 2002, p. H9).

CHAPTER 11

Lending Practices

LEARNING OBJECTIVES

After reading this chapter, you should be able to:

❮ Determine the distinction between term loans and amortized loans.

❮ Calculate monthly payments on loans.

❮ Discuss the purpose of a budget mortgage.

❮ Discuss the benefits of early payoff on loans.

❮ Understand the term *loan-to-value ratio*.

❮ Identify the various FHA insurance programs.

❮ Determine the importance of the up front mortgage insurance premium.

❮ Discuss the benefits of a VA loan.

❮ Discuss the purpose of private mortgage insurance.

KEY TERMS

VA Amortized loan • Balloon loan • Conventional loans • Equity • FHA • Impound or reserve account • Loan origination fee • Loan-to-value ratio • Maturity • PITI payment • PMI • Point • Principal • UFMIP

Whereas Chapter 10 dealt with the legal aspects of notes, mortgages, and trust deeds, Chapters 11 and 12 deal with the money aspects of these instruments. We begin in this chapter with term loans, amortized loans, balloon loans, partially amortized loans, loan-to-value ratio, equity, and points. These topics are followed by the functions and importance of the Federal Housing Administration (FHA), Veterans Affairs (VA), and private mortgage insurance. Chapter 12 discusses Truth in Lending and provides a helpful and informative description of the loan application and approval process you (or your buyer) will experience when applying for a real estate loan. In Chapters 13 and 14, we look at sources and types of financing, including where to find mortgage loan money, where mortgage lenders obtain their money, and various types of financing instruments, such as the adjustable rate mortgage, equity mortgage, wraparound mortgage, seller financing, and so forth. Note that from here on, whatever is said about mortgages applies equally to deeds of trust.

One more thought before we start. The United States has had a long-standing commitment to individual home ownership. We have long had governmental assistance in the form of tax-deductible interest on mortgages and government-insured or guaranteed loans. Other countries require significant down payments and have short-term loans. We have standardized appraisal systems, standardized secondary mortgage markets, and a proliferation of loan originators. For the next few chapters, we'll discuss how all these factors interrelate to produce this very profitable system and a unique way of life.

Term Loans

A loan that requires only interest payments until the last day of its life, at which time the full amount borrowed is due, is called a **term loan** (or straight loan). Until 1930, the term loan was the standard method of financing real estate in the United States. These loans were typically made for a period of three to five years. The borrower signed a note or bond agreeing: (1) to pay the lender interest on the loan every six months, and (2) to repay the entire amount of the loan upon **maturity**—that is, at the end of the life of the loan. As security, the borrower mortgaged the property to the lender.

maturity

The end of the life of a loan.

LOAN RENEWAL

In practice, most real estate term loans were not paid off when they matured. Instead, the borrower asked the lender, typically a bank, to renew the loan for another three to five years. The major flaw in this approach to lending was that the borrower might never own the property free and clear of debt. It also left the borrower continuously at the mercy of the lender for renewals. As long as the lender was not pressed for funds, the borrower's renewal request was granted. However, if the lender was short of funds, no renewal was granted, and the borrower was expected to pay in full.

The inability to renew term loans caused hardship to hundreds of thousands of property owners during the Great Depression that began in 1930, and lasted most of the decade. Banks were unable to accommodate requests for loan renewals and, at the same time, satisfy unemployed depositors who needed to withdraw their savings to live. As a result, owners of homes, farms, office buildings, factories, and vacant land lost their property as foreclosures reached into the millions. The market was so glutted with properties being offered for sale to satisfy unpaid mortgage loans that real estate prices fell at a sickening pace.

Amortized Loans

In 1933, a congressionally legislated Home Owner's Loan Corporation (HOLC) was created to assist financially distressed homeowners by acquiring mortgages that were about to be foreclosed. The HOLC then offered monthly repayment plans tailored to fit the homeowner's budget that would repay the loan in full by its maturity date without the need for a balloon payment. The HOLC was terminated in 1951 after rescuing over a million mortgages in its 18-year life. However, the use of this stretched-out payment plan, known as an **amortized loan**, took hold in American real estate, and today it is the accepted method of loan repayment. In the United States, 66% of all mortgages are 30-year, fixed-rate, long-term loans, which is a rarity in most other countries.

amortized loan

A loan requiring periodic payments that include both interest and partial repayment of principal.

As a practical matter, there are a number of handheld computers that can help a student analyze loans in a variety of ways. Real estate agents are continually trained in the variety of types of loans to meet their clients' needs. As more loan products become available, it is always a new learning experience. Our purpose here is to discuss the fundamentals of how the amortization system works. As one becomes more experienced, the high-tech approach to loan analysis changes from market to market, but the basics remain the same.

REPAYMENT METHODS

The amortized loan requires regular, equal payments during the life of the loan, of sufficient size and number to pay all interest due on the loan, and to reduce the amount owed to zero by the loan's maturity date. Figure 11.1 illustrates the contrast between

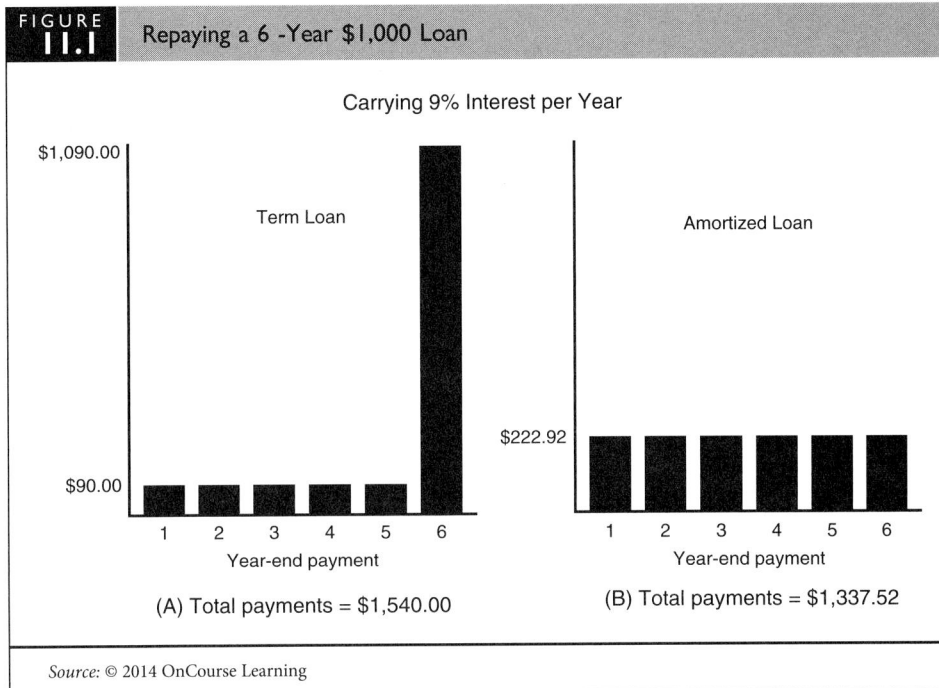

FIGURE 11.1 Repaying a 6-Year $1,000 Loan

Carrying 9% Interest per Year

Term Loan

Amortized Loan

$1,090.00

$90.00

$222.92

Year-end payment

Year-end payment

(A) Total payments = $1,540.00

(B) Total payments = $1,337.52

amortized and term loans. Figure 11.1A shows a six-year, $1,000 term loan with interest of $90 due each year of its life. At the end of the sixth year, the entire **principal** (the amount owed) is due in one lump sum payment, along with the final interest payment. In Figure 11.1B, the same $1,000 loan is fully amortized by making six equal annual payments of $222.92. From the borrower's standpoint, $222.92 once each year is easier to budget than $90 for five years and $1,090 in the sixth year.

principal
The balance owing on a loan.

Furthermore, the amortized loan shown in Figure 11.1 actually costs the borrower less than the term loan. The total payments made under the term loan are $90 + $90 + $90 + $90 + $90 + $1,090 = $1,540. Amortizing the same loan requires total payments of 6 × $222.92 = $1,337.52. The difference is due to the fact that under the amortized loan the borrower begins to pay back part of the $1,000 principal with the first payment. In the first year, $90 of the $222.92 payment goes to interest and the remaining $132.92 reduces the principal owed. Thus, the borrower starts the second year owing only $867.08. At 9% interest per year, the interest on $867.08 is $78.04; therefore, when the borrower makes the second payment of $222.92, only $78.04 goes to interest. The remaining $144.88 is applied to reduce the loan balance, and the borrower starts the third year owing $722.20. Figure 11.2 charts this repayment program. Notice that the balance owed drops faster as the loan becomes older, that is, as it matures.

MONTHLY PAYMENTS

As you have just seen, calculating the payments on a term loan is relatively simple compared with calculating amortized loan payments. The widespread use of computers has greatly simplified the calculations, however. To illustrate how the amortization works, though, we should note that *amortization tables* are published and used throughout the real estate industry. Table 11.1 on page 185 shows the monthly payments per $1,000 of loan for interest rates from 5% to 15% for periods ranging from 5 to 40 years. (Amortization tables are also published for quarterly, semiannual, and annual payments.) When you use an amortization table, notice that there are five variables: (1) frequency of payment, (2) interest rate, (3) maturity, (4) amount of the loan, and (5) amount of the periodic

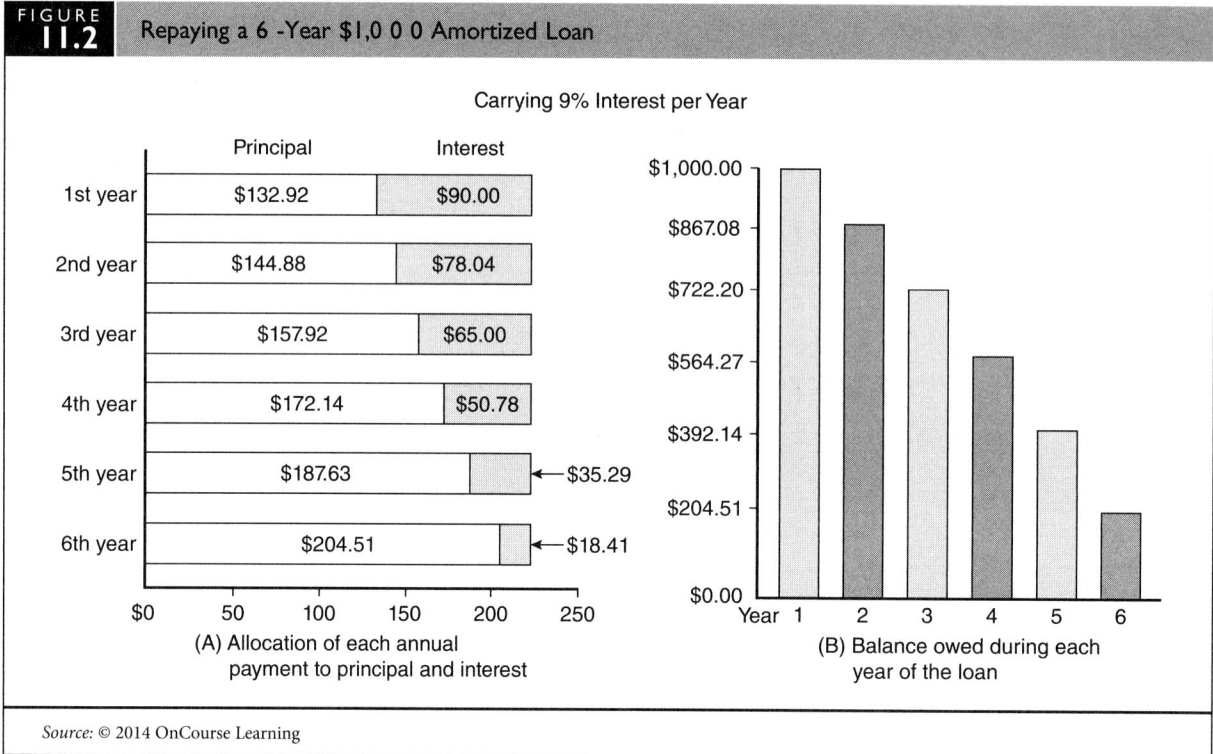

FIGURE 11.2 Repaying a 6 -Year $1,0 0 0 Amortized Loan

Carrying 9% Interest per Year

(A) Allocation of each annual payment to principal and interest

	Principal	Interest
1st year	$132.92	$90.00
2nd year	$144.88	$78.04
3rd year	$157.92	$65.00
4th year	$172.14	$50.78
5th year	$187.63	$35.29
6th year	$204.51	$18.41

(B) Balance owed during each year of the loan

Source: © 2014 OnCourse Learning

payment. If you know any four of these, you can obtain the fifth variable from the tables. For example, suppose that you want to know the monthly payment necessary to amortize a $260,000 loan over 30 years at 8.5% interest. The first step is to look at Table 11.1 for the 8.5% line. Then locate the 30-year column. Where they cross, you will find the necessary monthly payment per $1,000: $7.69. Next, multiply $7.69 by 260 to get the monthly payment for a $260,000 loan: $1,999.40. If the loan is to be $270,500, then multiply $7.69 by 270 to get the monthly payment: $2,076.30.

Continuing the foregoing example, suppose we reduce the repayment period to 15 years. First look for the 8.5% line, then go over to the 15-year column. The number there is $9.85. Next, multiply $9.85 by 260 to get the monthly payment for a $260,000 loan: $2,561.00. If the loan is to be $270,000, then multiply $9.85 by 270 to get the monthly payment: $2,659.50.

LOAN SIZE

Amortization tables are also used to determine the amount of loan a borrower can support if you know how much the borrower has available to spend each month on loan payments. Suppose that a prospective home buyer can afford monthly principal and interest payments of $1,250 and lenders are making 30-year loans at 7%. How large a loan can this buyer afford? In Table 11.1, find where the 7% line and the 30-year column meet. You will see 6.66 there. This means that every $6.66 of monthly payment will support $1,000 of loan. To find how many thousands of dollars $1,250 per month will support, just divide $1,250 by $6.66. The answer is 187.687 thousands or $187,687. By adding the buyer's down payment, you know what property price the buyer can afford to purchase. If interest rates are 7.5%, the number from the table is 7.00, and the loan amount is $178,571. (You can begin to see why the level of interest rate is so important to real estate prices.)

TABLE 11.1	Amortization Table Monthly Payment Per $1,000 of Loan							
Interest Rate per Year	**Life of the Loan**							
	5 Years	**10 Years**	**15 Years**	**20 Years**	**25 Years**	**30 Years**	**35 Years**	**40 Years**
5 %	$18.88	$10.61	$ 7.91	$ 6.60	$ 5.85	$ 5.37	$ 5.05	$ 4.83
5.5	19.11	10.86	8.18	6.88	6.15	5.68	5.38	5.16
6	19.34	11.11	8.44	7.17	6.45	ʼ6.00	5.71	5.51
6.5	19.57	11.36	8.72	7.46	6.76	6.32	6.05	5.86
7	19.81	11.62	8.99	7.76	7.07	6.66	6.39	6.22
7.5	20.04	11.88	9.28	8.06	7.39	7.00	6.75	6.59
8	20.28	12.14	9.56	8.37	7.72	7.34	7.11	6.96
8.5	20.52	12.40	9.85	8.68	8.06	7.69	7.47	7.34
9	20.76	12.67	10.15	9.00	8.40	8.05	7.84	7.72
9.5	21.01	12.94	10.45	9.33	8.74	8.41	8.22	8.11
10	21.25	13.22	10.75	9.66	9.09	8.78	8.60	8.50
10.5	21.50	13.50	11.06	9.99	9.45	9.15	8.99	8.89
11	21.75	13.78	11.37	10.33	9.81	9.53	9.37	9.29
11.5	22.00	14.06	11.69	10.67	10.17	9.91	9.77	9.69
12	22.25	14.35	12.01	11.02	10.54	10.29	10.16	10.09
12.5	22.50	14.64	12.33	11.37	10.91	10.68	10.56	10.49
13	22.76	14.94	12.66	11.72	11.28	11.07	10.96	10.90
13.5	23.01	15.23	12.99	12.08	11.66	11.46	11.36	11.31
14	23.27	15.53	13.32	12.44	12.04	11.85	11.76	11.72
14.5	23.53	15.83	13.66	12.80	12.43	12.25	12.17	12.13
15	23.79	16.14	14.00	13.17	12.81	12.65	12.57	12.54

Source: © 2014 OnCourse Learning

As you have noticed, everything in Table 11.1 is on a monthly payment per thousand basis. With a full book of amortization tables rather than one page, it is possible to look up monthly payments for loans from $100 to $100,000 to determine loan maturities for each year from 1 to 40 years, and to calculate many more interest rates. Amortization books are available at most local bookstores.

CHANGE IN MATURITY DATE

An amortization table also shows the impact on the size of the monthly payment when the life of a loan is extended. For example, at 11% interest, a 10-year loan requires a monthly payment of $13.78 per thousand of loan. Increasing the life of the loan to 20 years drops the monthly payment to $10.33 per $1,000. Extending the loan payback to 30 years reduces the monthly payment to $9.53 per thousand. The smaller monthly payment is the reason why 30 years is a popular loan term with borrowers. Note, however, that going beyond 30 years does not significantly reduce the monthly payment. Going from 30 to 35 years reduces the monthly payment by only 16¢ per thousand but adds 5 years of monthly payments. Extending the payback period from 35 to 40 years reduces the monthly payment by just 8¢ per $1,000 ($4 per month on a $50,000 loan) and adds another 60 months of payments at $464.50 per month. As a practical matter, amortized real estate loans are seldom made for more than 30 years.

Budget Mortgage

The **budget mortgage** takes the amortized loan one step further. In addition to collecting the monthly principal and interest payment (often called $P + I$), the lender collects one-twelfth of the estimated cost of the annual property taxes and hazard insurance on the mortgaged property. The money for tax and insurance payments is placed in an **impound account** (also called an **escrow** or **reserve account**). When taxes and insurance payments are due, the lender pays them. Thus, the lender makes certain that the value of the mortgaged property will not be undermined by unpaid property taxes or by uninsured fire or weather damage. This form of mortgage also helps the borrower to budget for property taxes and insurance on a monthly basis. To illustrate, if insurance is $240 per year and property taxes are $1,800 per year, the lender collects an additional $20 and $150 each month along with the regular principal and interest payment. This combined principal, interest, taxes, and insurance payment is often referred to as a **PITI payment**.

impound or reserve account

An account into which the lender places monthly tax and insurance payments.

PITI payment

A loan payment that combines principal, interest, taxes, and insurance.

balloon loan

Any loan in which the final payment is larger than the preceding payments.

Balloon Loan

A **balloon loan** is any loan that has a final payment larger than any of the previous payments on the loan. The final payment is called a **balloon payment**. The term loan described at the beginning of this chapter is a type of balloon loan. Partially amortized loans, discussed next, are another type of balloon loan. In tight money markets, the use of balloon loans increased considerably. Balloon loans with maturities as short as three to five years were commonplace. This arrangement gives the buyer (borrower) three to five years to find cheaper and longer-term financing elsewhere. If such financing does not materialize, and the loan is not repaid on time, the lender has the right to foreclose. The alternative is for the lender and borrower to agree to an extension of the loan, usually at prevailing interest rates.

Partially Amortized Loan

When the repayment schedule of a loan calls for a series of amortized payments followed by a balloon payment at maturity, it is called a **partially amortized loan**. For example, a lender might agree to a 30-year amortization schedule with a provision that at the end of the tenth year all the remaining principal be paid in a single balloon payment. The advantage to the borrower is that for 10 years the monthly payments will be smaller than if the loan was completely amortized in 10 years. (You can verify this in Table 11.1.) However, the disadvantage is that the balloon payment due at the end of the tenth year might be the borrower's financial downfall. Just how large that balloon payment will be can be determined in advance by using a **loan balance table** (also called a *remaining balance table*). Presuming an interest rate of 11.5% and a 30-year loan, at the end of 10 years the loan balance table in Table 11.2 shows that for each $1,000 originally loaned, $929 would still be owed. If the original loan was for $100,000, at the end of 10 years 100 × $929 = $92,900 would be due as one payment. This qualifies it as a balloon loan.

As you can see from this example, when an amortized loan has a long maturity, relatively little of the debt is paid off during the initial years of the loan's life. Nearly all the early payments go for interest, so little remains for principal reduction. For example, Table 11.2 shows that even after 16 years of payments on a 30-year, 11.5% loan, 82.5%

TABLE 11.2	Balance Owing on a $1,000 Amortized Loan											

	9.5% Annual Interest							11.5% Annual Interest					
Age of Loan (yrs.)	Original Life (years)						Age of Loan (yrs.)	Original Life (years)					
	10	**15**	**20**	**25**	**30**	**35**		**10**	**15**	**20**	**25**	**30**	**35**
2	$868	$934	$963	$978	$987	$992	2	$880	$944	$971	$984	$991	$995
4	708	853	918	952	971	983	4	729	873	935	965	981	989
6	515	756	864	921	953	971	6	539	784	889	940	967	982
8	282	639	799	883	930	957	8	300	672	831	909	950	972
10		497	720	837	902	940	10		531	759	870	929	960
12		326	625	781	869	920	12		354	667	821	902	945
14		119	510	714	828	896	14		132	553	759	868	926
16			371	633	780	866	16			409	682	825	903
18			203	535	721	830	18			228	585	772	873
20				416	650	787	20				462	704	836
22				273	564	735	22				308	620	789
24				100	460	671	24				115	513	729
26					335	595	26					380	655
28					183	503	28					211	561
30						391	30						444
32						256	32						296
34						94	34						110

Source: © 2014 OnCourse Learning

of the loan is still unpaid. Not until this loan is about six years from maturity will half of it have been repaid.

Earlier Payoff

During the late 1970s, when inflation rates exceeded interest rates, the popular philosophy was to borrow as much as possible for as long as possible. Then in the early 1980s, inflation rates dropped below interest rates and the opposite philosophy became attractive to many borrowers. This was especially true for those who had borrowed (or were contemplating borrowing) at double-digit interest rates. Let us use as an example an $80,000 loan at 11.5% interest. If the loan has a maturity of 30 years, from Table 11.1 we can determine the monthly payments to be $792.80. (Follow this example on your own.)

15-YEAR LOAN

Suppose the maturity of the aforementioned loan is changed from 30 to 15 years. Looking at Table 11.1, the monthly payments would now be $935.20. This is $142.40 more per month, but the loan is fully paid in 15 years, not 30 years. The total amount of interest paid on the 15-year loan is $(15 \times 12 \times \$935.20) - \$80,000 = \$88,336$. The total amount of interest paid on the 30-year loan is $(30 \times 12 \times \$792.80) - \$80,000 = \$205,408$. Thus, for an extra $142.40 per month for 180 months (which amounts to $25,632), the borrower saves the difference between $205,408 and $88,336 (which is $117,072). Many borrowers consider this a very good return on their money. (It is, in fact, an 11.5% compounded rate of return.) Lenders are also more receptive to making fixed-rate loans for 15 years than for 30 years. This is because the lender is locked into the loan for 15 years, not 30 years. As a result, a lender is usually willing to offer a 15-year loan at a lower rate of interest than that of a 30-year loan. In view of these benefits to borrower and lender alike, the 15-year loan is becoming a popular home financing tool.

BIWEEKLY PAYMENTS

A growing number of lenders offer a biweekly repayment plan. The loan is amortized as if it were going to last 30 years. But instead of paying once a month, the borrower makes one-half the monthly payment every two weeks. This may not sound like much of a difference but the results are eye-opening. Assume you borrow $100,000 at 7% interest, paying (see Table 11.1) $666.00 per month. You will retire the loan in 30 years at a cost of $139,509 in interest. If you decide to pay half of $666.00 every two weeks, the loan will be fully paid in just 18 years and will have cost you $105,046 in interest. This happens because biweekly compounding works in your favor, and because you make 26 half-size payments a year, not 24.

EXISTING LOANS

Borrowers with existing loans who want to celebrate with an early mortgage burning can simply add a few dollars each month to the required monthly payment. This can be particularly beneficial for people who borrowed at rates of 11% or more. In effect, whatever extra amount is added to the monthly payment will "earn" interest at the loan's interest rate. Thus, if a loan has a 14% rate, early payments "earn" at 14%. If the borrower has no alternative places to invest that will yield 14%, then a few additional dollars each month will work miracles. For example, a 30-year, $100,000 loan at 14% interest requires monthly payments (see Table 11.1) of $1,185. Voluntarily adding an extra $19 per month reduces the maturity (payoff) date from 30 years to 25 years (see Table 11.1 again). If an extra $40 is added to the $19, the maturity date shrinks to 20 years. In other words, an extra $59 per month eliminates 10 years of payments.

You may be wondering why this has not been a popular idea with borrowers. When interest rates are around 6% and 7%, the mathematics of early payoff are not nearly as impressive.

Loan-to-Value Ratio

loan-to-value ratio
A percentage reflecting what a lender will lend divided by the sale price or market value of the property, whichever is less.

The relationship between the amount of money a lender is willing to loan and the lender's estimate of the market value of the property that will serve as security is called the **loan-to-value ratio** (often abbreviated L/V or LTV ratio). For example, a prospective home buyer wants to purchase a house priced at $200,000. A local lender appraises the house, finds it has a market value of $200,000 and agrees to make an 80% L/V loan. This means that the lender will loan up to 80% of the $200,000, and the buyer must provide at least 20% in cash. In dollars, the lender will loan up to $160,000, and the buyer must make a cash down payment of at least $40,000. If the lender appraises the home for more than $200,000, the loan will still be $160,000. If the appraisal is for less than $200,000, the loan will be 80% of the appraised value, and the buyer must pay the balance in cash. The rule is that price or value, whichever is lower, is applied to the L/V ratio. This rule exists to prevent the lender from over lending on a property just because the borrower overpaid for it.

Equity

The difference between the market value of a property and the debt owed against it is called the owner's **equity**. On a newly purchased $150,000 home with a $30,000 cash down payment, the buyer's equity is $30,000. As the value of the property rises or falls, and as the mortgage loan is paid down, the equity changes. For example, if the value of the home rises to $180,000 and the loan is paid down to $115,000, the owner's equity will be $65,000. If the owner completely repays the loan so that there is no debt against the home, the owner's equity is equal to the market value of the property.

equity
The market value of a property less the debt against it.

Loan Points

Probably no single term in real estate finance causes as much confusion and consternation as the word *points*. In finance, the word **point** means 1% of the loan amount. Thus, on a $100,000 loan, one point is $1,000. On an $80,000 loan, three points is $2,400.

The use of points in real estate mortgage finance can be split into two categories: (1) loan origination fees expressed in terms of points, and (2) the use of points to change the effective yield of a mortgage loan to a lender. Let us look at these two uses in more detail.

point
One percent of the loan amount.

ORIGINATION FEE

When a borrower asks for a mortgage loan, the lender incurs a number of expenses, including such things as the time its loan officer spends interviewing the borrower, office overhead, the purchase and review of credit reports on the borrower, an on-site appraisal of the property to be mortgaged, title searches and review, legal and recording fees, and so on. For these, some lenders make an itemized billing, charging so many dollars for the appraisal, credit report, title search, and so on. The total becomes the **loan origination fee**, which the borrower pays to get the loan. Other lenders do not make an itemized bill, but instead simply state the origination fee in terms of a percentage of the loan amount, for example, one point. Thus, a lender quoting a loan origination fee of one point is saying that for a $95,000 loan, its fee to originate the loan will be $950.

loan origination fee
The expenses a lender incurs in processing a mortgage loan.

DISCOUNT POINTS

Points charged to raise the lender's monetary return on a loan are known as **discount points**. A simplified example illustrates their use and effect. If you are a lender and agree to make a term loan of $100 to a borrower for one year at 10% interest, you would normally expect to give the borrower $100 now (disregard loan origination fees for a moment) and, one year later, the borrower would give you $110. In percentage terms, the **effective yield** on your loan is 10% per annum (year) because you received $10 for your one-year, $100 loan. Now suppose that instead of handing the borrower $100, you handed him $99 but still required him to repay $100 plus $10 in interest at the end of the year. This is a discount of one point ($1 in this case), and the borrower would pay it out of the loan funds. The effect of this financial maneuver is to raise the effective yield (yield to maturity) to you without raising the interest rate itself. Therefore, if you loan out $99 and receive $110 at the end of the year, you effectively have a return of $11 for a $99 loan. This gives you an effective yield of $11/$99 or 11.1%, rather than 10%.

Calculating the effective yield on a discounted 20- or 30-year mortgage loan is more difficult because the amount owed drops over the life of the loan and because the majority are paid in full ahead of schedule due to refinancing. Computers and calculators usually make these calculations; however, a useful rule of thumb states that on the typical home loan, each point of discount raises the effective yield by one-eighth of 1%. Thus, four discount points would raise the effective yield by approximately one-half of 1% and eight points would raise it by 1%. Discount points are most often charged during periods of **tight money**, that is, when mortgage money is in short supply. During periods of **loose money**, when lenders have adequate funds to lend and are actively seeking borrowers, discount points disappear.

conventional loans

Real estate loans that are not insured by the FHA or guaranteed by the VA.

Real estate loans that are not insured by the FHA or guaranteed by the VA are termed **conventional loans**. The conventional loan market has a growing presence in the marketplace, as conventional lenders are very competitive with rates and loan processing procedures. FHA and VA loans are now only a small fraction of the single-family loan origination market. FHA handles a little over 12%; VA about 2%. Let's discuss the impact of the FHA and VA.

FHA Insurance Programs

The Great Depression caused a major change in the attitude of the federal government toward home financing in the United States. In 1934, one year after the Home Owners Loan Corporation was established, Congress passed the National Housing Act. The Act's most far-reaching provision was to establish the **Federal Housing Administration (FHA)** for the purpose of encouraging new construction as a means of creating jobs. To accomplish this goal, the FHA offered to insure lenders against losses due to nonrepayment when they made loans on both new and existing homes. In turn, the lender had to grant 20-year fully amortized loans with loan-to-value ratios of 80% rather than the 3- to 5-year, 50% to 60% term loans common up to that time.

FHA

Federal Housing Administration.

The FHA did its best to keep from becoming a burden to the U.S. taxpayer. When a prospective borrower approached a lender for an FHA-secured home loan, the FHA reviewed the borrower's income, expenses, assets, and debts. The objective was to determine whether there was adequate room in the borrower's budget for the proposed loan payments. The FHA also sent inspectors to the property to make certain that it was of acceptable construction quality and to determine its fair market value. To offset losses that would still inevitably occur, the FHA charged the borrower an annual insurance fee of approximately one-half of 1% of the balance owed to the loan. The FHA was immensely successful in its task. Not only did it create construction jobs, but it raised the level of housing quality in the nation, and, in a pleasant surprise to taxpayers, actually returned annual profits to the U.S. Treasury. In 1946, in response to its success, Congress changed its status from temporary to permanent.

CURRENT FHA COVERAGE

The FHA has had a marked influence on lending policies in the real estate industry. Foremost among these is the widespread acceptance of the high loan-to-value, fully amortized loan. In the 1930s, lenders required FHA insurance before making 80 percent L/V loans. By the 1960s, lenders were readily making 80 percent L/V loans without FHA insurance. Meanwhile, the FHA insurance program was working so well that the FHA raised the portion it was willing to insure. Down payment programs historically have been very complex. Effective January 1, 2009, the borrower must make a contribution (down payment) of at least 3.5 %, making the maximum loan-to-value ratio for a purchase transaction 96.5%. The maximum amount the FHA will insure has varied from city to city and changes from time to time. As of 2011, the maximum loan amount in high-cost areas was $729,750.

Private investors are banned from the FHA single-family program. In addition, no single-family loans can be assumed by investors. Any loan made before December 15, 1989, may be assumed by an investor, but additional restrictions have to be met: (1) the balance due must be no more than 75% of the cost of the property, and (2) if the monthly mortgage payment exceeds the net rental income, the mortgage amount must be reduced so that its payment does not exceed the amount amortized by the net rental income.

ASSUMABILITY

Traditionally, FHA loans were popular because the 30-year, fixed-rate loans could be assumed without any increase in interest. This is still true for loans that were originated prior to December 1, 1986. The assumption procedure can be one of two types: a simple assumption or a formal assumption. In the **simple assumption** procedure, the property is sold and the loan is assumed by the buyer without notification to the FHA or its agent. The seller remains fully liable to the FHA for full repayment. In the **formal assumption**, the property is not conveyed to a new buyer until the new buyer's creditworthiness has been approved by the FHA or its agent. When the creditworthy buyer assumes the loan, the seller may obtain a full release of liability from the FHA.

If the FHA loan was originated between December 1, 1986, and December 15, 1989, the owner-occupant cannot sell the property with a loan assumption during the first 12 months after execution of the mortgage without creditworthiness approval for each person who assumes the loan. If the seller is an investor, the assumption cannot be made without prior approval during the first 24 months after execution of the mortgage. Failure to comply with either requirement results in an acceleration of the loan balance. After the one- or two-year loan period, the loan can be assumed without approval. If the assumption is a simple assumption, the seller remains fully liable for five years after the new mortgage is executed. If the loan is not in default after the five years, the seller is automatically released from liability.

If the loan was originated after December 15, 1989, the FHA requires the creditworthiness approval prior to the conveyance of title on all assumption loans. If the borrower assumes a mortgage loan, the lender cannot refuse to release the original borrower from liability on the loan.

MORTGAGE INSURANCE

The FHA charges a one-time **up-front mortgage insurance premium (UFMIP)** that is paid when the loan is made. Effective October 4, 2010, premiums were dropped to 1% of the loan amount.

The FHA now also charges an annual premium. The annual premium is calculated based on the term of the loan and the amount of the down payment. For loans greater than 15 year term, the amount paid depends on the down payment. If the down payment is equal to or greater than 5%, the premium is 1.1% per annum. If the down payment is less than 5%, the new annual premium is 1.15% per annum. On the loans equal to or less than 15 years, the premium is much lower. If the down payment is equal to or greater than 10%, the new annual premium is 0.25% per annum. If the down payment is less than 10%, the new annual premium is 0.5%.

The monthly mortgage insurance payment will be automatically terminated when:

1. the mortgage with terms of 15 years and less with loan-to-value ratios 90% and greater, the annual premiums will be cancelled when the loan-to-value ratio reaches 78%; or

UFMIP

Up-front mortgage insurance premium—a one-time charge by the FHA for insuring a loan.

2. the mortgage with terms of more than 15 years, the annual insurance premiums will be canceled when the loan-to-value ratio reaches 78% provided the borrower has paid the annual premium for at least 5 years.

The mortgage with terms of 15 years and less and with loan-to-value ratios of 89.99% and less will not be charged annual mortgage insurance premiums.

FLOATING INTEREST RATES

At one time, FHA set interest rate ceilings. Fixed-rate FHA loans are now negotiable and float with the market, and the seller also has a choice in how many points to contribute toward the borrower's loan. This can be none, some, or all of the points, and the seller can even pay the borrower's mortgage insurance premium (MIP). Typical purchase contract language is, "The seller will pay X points, and the buyer will pay not more than Y points, and the agreed-on interest rate is Z%." Thus, X is the contribution the seller will make, and the seller is protected from having to pay more. The buyer will pay any additional points, but not more than Y points. Beyond that, the buyer can cancel the purchase contract. That would happen if the market rates rose quickly while the rate at Z is fixed.

LOAN QUALIFICATION

Before leaving the topic of the FHA, it is interesting to note that much of what we take for granted as standard loan practice today was the result of FHA innovation years ago. As already noted, before 1934, standard real estate loan practice called for short-term renewable loans. Then the FHA boldly offered 20-year amortized loans. Once these were shown to be successful investments for lenders, loans without FHA insurance were made for 20 years. Later, when the FHA successfully went to 30 years, non–FHA-insured loans followed. The FHA also established loan application review techniques that have been widely accepted and copied throughout the real estate industry. The biggest step in this direction was to analyze a borrower's loan application in terms of earning power.

FHA loans are the easiest type of real estate mortgage loan to qualify for. The loan requirement guidelines for loan qualification are the most flexible of all mortgage loans. They require less than a 5% down payment. The basic FHA loan requirements are: (1) two years of steady employment, preferably with the same employer; (2) the last two years income should be the same or increasing; (3) the borrower's credit report should typically have less than two 30-day lates in the last two years with a minimum credit score of 620; (4) if the borrower has declared bankruptcy, it must be at least two years old, with perfect credit since the bankruptcy discharge; (5) if borrower has been through a foreclosure proceeding it must be at least three years old with perfect credit since the foreclosure; and (6) the new mortgage payment should be approximately 30% of the gross income before taxes.

CONSTRUCTION REGULATIONS

Since its inception, the FHA has imposed its own minimum construction requirements. Often, this was essential where local building codes did not exist or were weaker than what the FHA wanted. Before issuing a loan, particularly on new construction, the FHA would impose minimum requirements as to the quantity and quality of building materials to be used. Lot size, street access, landscaping, siting, and general house design were also required to fit within broad FHA guidelines. During construction, an FHA inspector would come to the property several times to check on whether work was being done correctly.

The reason for such care in building standards was that the FHA recognized that if a building is defective either from a design or construction standpoint, the borrower is more likely to default on the loan and create an insurance claim against the FHA. Furthermore, the same defects will lower the price the property will bring at its foreclosure sale, thus increasing losses to the FHA.

Since building codes are much stricter and more standardized than most cities, HUD has had less emphasis on the construction inspections on FHA loans, relying mostly on their appraisers. HUD has published Handbook 4910.1 that has an Appendix K, which deals with minimum property standards for housing and contains the summary of the basic requirements for a newly constructed single-family home insured by FHA. The appraiser must have a complete set of plans and specifications and the builder certification in order to the appraisal. After January 1, 2010, the validity period for all appraisals on existing and proposed or under construction properties will be 120 days. This is a change from the prior current validity periods of 6 months for an appraisal of an existing property that is completed, and 12 months for proposed and under construction properties. If the property is under construction and less than 90% complete at the time of the appraisal, the appraisal must call for a final inspection to be completed by an FHA Fee Inspector, or, if applicable, the local authority or equivalent. When the final inspection is completed by a Fee Inspector, the inspection must include photographs.

As we leave our discussion of the FHA and go to the Department of Veterans Affairs, keep in mind that the FHA is not a lender. The FHA is an insurance agency. The loan itself is obtained from a savings and loan, bank, mortgage company, or similar lender. In addition to principal and interest payments, the lender collects an insurance premium from the borrower that is forwarded to the FHA. The FHA, in turn, guarantees repayment of the loan to the lender. This arrangement makes lenders much more willing to loan to buyers who are putting only 3% to 5% cash down. Thus, when you hear the phrase "FHA loan" in real estate circles, know that it is an FHA-*insured* loan, not a loan from the FHA.

Department of Veterans Affairs

In 1944, to show its appreciation to servicemen returning from World War II, Congress passed far-reaching legislation to aid veterans in education, hospitalization, employment training, and housing. In housing, the popularly named GI Bill of Rights empowered the comptroller general of the United States to guarantee the repayment of a portion of first mortgage real estate loans made to veterans. For this guarantee, no fee would be charged to the veteran. Rather, the government itself would stand the losses. The Veterans Administration was elevated to cabinet level and is now officially called the **Department of Veterans Affairs**, but still uses its old initials, the **VA**.

VA

Department of Veterans Affairs.

NO DOWN PAYMENT

The original 1944 law provided that lenders would be guaranteed against losses up to 50% of the amount of the loan, but in no case for more than $2,000. The objective was to make it possible for a veteran to buy a home with no cash down payment. Thus, on a house offered for sale at $5,000 (houses were much cheaper in 1944), this guarantee enabled a veteran to borrow the entire $5,000. From the lender's standpoint, having the top $2,000 of the loan guaranteed by the U.S. government offered the same asset protection as a $2,000 cash down payment. If the veteran defaulted and the property went into foreclosure, the lender had to net less than $3,000 before suffering a loss.

TABLE 11.3	VA Loan Guarantee Amounts
Loan Amount	**Guarantee**
Up to $45,000	50% of the loan amount
$45,001 to $56,250	$22,500
$56,251 to $144,000	40% of the loan amount, with a maximum of $36,000
$144,001 and higher	25% of the loan amount, with a maximum of $104,250 for 2008
Some lenders will go higher if the borrower makes a down payment.	

Source: © 2014 OnCourse Learning

To keep up with the increased cost of homes, the guarantee has been increased several times. The VA now uses the sliding-scale system for calculating the applicable guarantee amounts. The guarantee increases with the amount of the loan using fixed dollar amounts and percentages of loan amounts. The current limits are shown in Table 11.3.

In the original GI Bill of 1944, eligibility was limited to World War II veterans. However, subsequent legislation has broadened eligibility to include any veteran who served for a period of at least 90 days in the armed forces of the United States or an ally between September 16, 1940, and July 25, 1947, or between June 27, 1950, and January 31, 1955. If service was during the Vietnam conflict period (August 5, 1964, to May 7, 1975) or the Gulf War, 90 days is sufficient to qualify. Any veteran of the United States who has served at least 181 days of continuous active duty during peacetime is also eligible.

The VA requires a length of service of at least two years for a veteran who enlisted after September 7, 1980, or was an officer and began service after October 16, 1981. These veterans must have completed either: (1) at least 24 months, or (2) the full period ordered active duty (not less than 90 days during wartime or 181 days during peacetime). The benefit is also available to those who serve in the Select Reserves or National Guard at least six years with an honorable discharge.

The veteran's discharge must be on conditions other than dishonorable, and the guarantee entitlement is good until used. If not remarried, the spouse of a veteran who died as a result of service can also obtain a housing guarantee. Active duty personnel can also qualify. Shorter active duty periods are allowed for service-connected disabilities.

VA CERTIFICATES

To determine benefits, a veteran should apply to the Department of Veterans Affairs for a *certificate of eligibility*, which shows whether the veteran is qualified and the amount of guarantee available. This document (Form 26-1880), along with a copy of the veteran's discharge papers, is necessary to obtain a VA-guaranteed loan.

The VA works diligently to protect veterans and reduce foreclosure losses. When a veteran applies for a VA guarantee, the property is appraised and the VA issues a *certificate of reasonable value*. Often abbreviated **CRV**, it reflects the estimated value of the property as determined by the VA staff appraiser. Similarly, the VA establishes income guidelines to make certain that the veteran can comfortably meet the proposed loan payments. Also, the veteran must agree to occupy the property. Pursuant to the newly enacted Safe Drinking Water Act, if the building was constructed after June 19, 1988, the CRV must now reflect a certification that any solders or fluxes used in construction did not contain more than 0.2% lead in any pipes or that the pipe fittings used did not contain more than 8% lead.

The VA guarantees fixed-rate loans for as long as 30 years on homes, and no prepayment penalty is charged if the borrower wishes to pay sooner. Moreover, there is no due-on-sale clause that requires the loan to be repaid if the property is sold. The VA guarantees loans for the purchase of townhouses and condominiums, to build or improve a home, and to buy a mobile home as a residence. A veteran wishing to refinance an existing home or farm can obtain a VA-guaranteed loan provided that there is existing debt that will be repaid. The VA also makes direct loans to veterans if there are no private lending institutions nearby.

FINANCIAL LIABILITY

No matter what loan guarantee program is selected, the veteran should know that in the event of default and subsequent foreclosure, he or she is required eventually to make good any losses suffered by the VA on the loan. (This is not the case with FHA-insured loans, in which the borrower pays for protection against foreclosure losses that may result from the loan.) Even if the veteran sells the property and the buyer assumes the VA loan, the veteran is still financially responsible if the buyer later defaults. To avoid this, the veteran must arrange with the VA to be released from liability. For VA loans underwritten after March 1, 1988, Congress created a new Guarantee and Indemnity Fund that allows a release from liability to the VA in the event of foreclosure, provided that the following requirements are met:

1. The loan payments must be current.
2. The prospective purchasers must meet creditworthiness standards as required by the VA.
3. The prospective purchaser must assume full liability for repayment of the loan, including indemnity liability to the VA.

In the event borrowers are unable to make their mortgage payments, the VA offers an assistance procedure that may be helpful in declining markets. If the borrower can obtain a purchase offer that is insufficient to pay off the existing loan balance, a *compromise agreement* may allow the VA to pay the difference between the sales proceeds and the mortgage balance. To effect the compromise agreement, the borrower must be willing to find a purchaser who will pay the fair market value of the house, and the original borrower must agree to remain liable to the government for the amount that the VA pays to the note holder.

A veteran is permitted a full new guarantee entitlement if complete repayment of a previous VA-guaranteed loan has been made. If a veteran has sold and let the buyer assume the VA loan, the balance of the entitlement is still available. For example, if a veteran has used $15,000 of his or her entitlement to date, the difference between $15,000 and the current VA guarantee amount is still available for use.

FUNDING FEE

From its inception until October 1, 1982, the VA made loan guarantees on behalf of veterans without a charge. Congress initially enacted a funding fee in 1982, increased it in 1991, and in 1993 established a funding fee that includes three categories of veterans, each with different fees depending on the veteran status and down payment. Note the new rates set out in Table 11.4. Funding fees for interest-rate-reduction refinancing loans were reduced to one-half of 1%. Funding fees on manufactured homes remain at 1% for all veterans and reservists. The fee still remains at one-half of 1% for assumptions by veterans or reservists. Funding fees can be added to the loan amount for calculating the loan-to-value ratio.

TABLE 11.4	VA Funding Fees

Purchase and Construction Loans

Loan Type	Required Down Payment	Active Duty Personnel and Veterans	National Guard and Reservists
First Time Use of VA Loan Guarantee Benefits			
Purchase/Construction	0% down	2.15%	2.40%
	5% down	1.50%	1.75%
	10% down	1.25%	2.40%
Second or Subsequent Use of VA Loan Guarantee Benefits			
Purchase/Construction	0%	3.35%	3.35%
	5%	1.50%	1.75%
	10%	1.25%	1.50%

Other Loans

Loan Type	Active Duty Personnel and Veterans	National Guard and Reservists
All Interest Rate Reduction Refinance Loans	0.50%	0.50%
Native American Direct Loans	1.25%	1.25%
Manufactured (Mobile) Home Loans	1.00%	1.00%
Assumptions*	0.50%	0.50%

*This pertains to loans originally closed on or after March 1, 1988. There is no funding fee required for assumption of loans closed prior to March 1, 1988.

Source: © 2014 OnCourse Learning

INTEREST RATES

In 1992, Congress eliminated the interest rate ceilings on VA loans. The program allows an interest rate and discount points agreed on by the veteran and the lender. Discount points may not be financed on any loan except interest-rate-reduction refinancing loans (IRRRLs). IRRRLs are limited to two discount points. The two-point limit does not include origination fees, which are limited to one point.

ASSUMPTION REQUIREMENTS

On VA loans assumed prior to March 1, 1988, approval was not required prior to loan assumption. Therefore, sellers could sell their property on assumption without obtaining any approval from the VA, but sellers remained fully liable for repayment. As stated previously, they could be released from liability if the VA approved the creditworthiness of the new purchaser. After March 1, 1988, the VA required prior approval for transfer of the property. Federal law now requires that the mortgage or deed of trust and note for loans carry, on the first page, in type 2½ times larger than the regular type, the following statement:

THIS LOAN IS NOT ASSUMABLE WITHOUT THE PRIOR APPROVAL OF THE DEPARTMENT OF VETERANS AFFAIRS OR AUTHORIZED AGENT.

Because Congress frequently changes eligibility and benefits, a person contemplating a VA or FHA loan should make inquiry to the field offices of these two agencies and to mortgage lenders to ascertain the current status and details of the law, as well as the availability of loan money. Field offices also have information on foreclosed properties that are for sale. Additionally, one should query lenders as to the availability of state veteran benefits. A number of states offer special advantages, including mortgage loan assistance, to residents who have served in the armed forces.

ADJUSTABLE-RATE MORTGAGES

The VA can also issue its guarantee for an adjustable-rate mortgage. The approved plan is structured the same as the FHA adjustable-rate mortgages, underwritten at an interest rate 1% above the initial rate agreed on by the veteran and the lender. Increases in the interest rate are limited to an annual adjustment of 1% and are capped at 5% over the life of the loan. The index for calculating interest-rate adjustments is the weekly average yield on treasury securities to a constant maturity of one year as reported by the Federal Reserve Board. Additional information on the VA can be obtained from the Web site, **www.homeloans.va.gov**.

Private Mortgage Insurance

In 1957, the Mortgage Guaranty Insurance Corporation (MGIC) was formed in Milwaukee, Wisconsin, as a privately owned business venture to insure home mortgage loans. Demand was slow but steady for the first 10 years and then grew rapidly, until today when there are over a dozen private mortgage insurance companies. Like FHA insurance, the object of **private mortgage insurance (PMI)** is to insure lenders against foreclosure losses. But, unlike the FHA, PMI insures only the top 20% to 25% of a loan, not the whole loan. This allows a lender to make 90% and 95% L/V loans with about the same exposure to foreclosure losses as a 70% to 75% L/V loan. The borrower, meanwhile, can purchase a home with a cash down payment of either 10% or 5% rather than the 20% to 30% down required by lenders when mortgage insurance is not purchased. For this privilege, the borrower pays a PMI fee of 1% or less when the loan is made, plus an annual fee of a fraction of 1%. When the loan is partially repaid (e.g., to a 70% L/V), the premiums and coverage can be terminated. PMI is also available on apartment buildings, offices, stores, warehouses, and leaseholds, but at higher rates than on homes.

> **PMI**
> Private mortgage insurance—a private mortgage insurance source to insure lenders against foreclosure loss.

Under a 1997 Texas statute, a lender must now provide an annual promulgated notice to each borrower who is required to purchase mortgage guaranty insurance. The notice informs the borrower that if the principal of their loan is 80% or less of the current fair market value of their home, the borrower may have the right to cancel the insurance.

In 1999, Congress passed the Homeowner's Protection Act (HPA), which became effective in 2000. The Act requires services to automatically cancel PMI once a loan reaches 78% of the property's original value. The Act also requires notification to the borrower that they can request PMI cancellation when their equity reaches 80% of the property value. Lenders are allowed to require an appraisal to prove the value at that time, so some owners may choose to wait until the automatic cancellation is triggered. The Act also allows lenders to refuse to cancel the insurance if the borrower does not have a good payment record. FHA and VA loans are exempted from this new legislation.

APPROVAL PROCEDURE

Private mortgage insurers work to keep their losses to a minimum by first approving the lenders with whom they do business. Particular emphasis is placed on the lender's operating policy, appraisal procedure, and degree of government regulation. Once approved, a lender simply sends the borrower's loan application, credit report, and property appraisal to the insurer. Based on these documents, the insurer either agrees or refuses to issue a policy. Although the insurer relies on the appraisal prepared by the lender, the insurer sends, on a random basis, its own appraiser to verify the quality of the information being submitted. When an insured loan goes into default, the insurer has the option of either buying the property from the lender for the balance due or letting the lender foreclose and then paying the lender's losses up to the amount of the insurance. As a rule, insurers take the first option because it is more popular with lenders and it leaves the lender with immediate cash to relend. The insurer is then responsible for foreclosing.

Rural Housing Services Administration

The *Rural Housing Services Administration* (RHSA) is a federal agency under the U.S. Department of Agriculture. Like the FHA, it came into existence due to the financial crises of the 1930s. The RHSA offers programs to help purchase or operate farms. The RHSA will either guarantee a portion of a loan made by a private lender or it will make the loan itself. RHSA loans can also be used to help finance the purchase of homes in rural areas.

Vocabulary Review

Match terms a–k with statements 1–11.

a. Amortized loan

b. Balloon payment

c. RHSA

d. Impound account

e. Loan balance table

f. Maturity

g. Partially amortized loan

h. PITI payment

i. Point

j. Principal

k. Term loan

_____ 1. Balance owing on a loan.

_____ 2. A loan that requires the borrower to pay interest only until maturity, at which time the full amount of the loan must be repaid.

_____ 3. Refers to a monthly loan payment that includes principal, interest, property taxes, and property insurance.

_____ 4. An escrow or reserve account into which the lender places the borrower's monthly tax and insurance payments.

_____ 5. One-hundredth of the total amount; 1% of a loan.

_____ 6. A loan requiring periodic payments that include both interest and principal.

_____ 7. A payment that is larger than any of the previous payments.

_____ 8. The end of the life of a loan.

_____ 9. A loan with a series of amortized payments followed by a balloon payment at maturity.

_____ 10. Shows the principal still owing during the life of a loan.

_____ 11. A federal agency under the U.S. Department of Agriculture that will help purchase and operate farms and finance homes in rural areas.

Questions and Problems

1. What is the major risk a borrower takes when she agrees to a loan with a balloon payment?

2. Explain how an amortized loan works.

3. Using Table 11.1, calculate the monthly payment necessary to completely amortize a $65,000, 30-year loan at 11½ percent interest.

4. A prospective home buyer has a $10,000 down payment, and can afford $800 per month for principal and interest payments. If 30-year, 11 percent amortized loans are available, what price home can the buyer afford?

5. Same problem as in number 4 except that the interest rate has dropped to 9%. What price home can the buyer afford now?

6. Using Table 11.2, calculate the balance still owed on a $90,000, 9½ percent interest, 30-year amortized loan that is 10 years old.

7. What advantage does the Department of Veterans Affairs offer veterans who wish to purchase a home?

8. Explain "points" and their application to real estate lending.

Additional Readings

Closing and Funding Standards of Practices by the Professional Resource Group Staff (School of Mortgage Lending, 1997).

Residential Mortgage Lending: From Application to Servicing by The Institute of Financial Education (1998).

Residential Mortgage Lending Origination by Abby Kamadia, (Kamrock Publishing, 2004).

The Loan and the Consumer

The previous chapter discussed lending practices applied to the types of payment arrangements that can be made in retiring debt. Consumer protection was enabled through the Federal Consumer Credit Protection Act, and additional protections have been created through standardized loan procedures. This chapter will discuss the federal Truth-in-Lending Act and standard loan procedures that consumers need to use in order to apply for a loan.

Truth-in-Lending Act

The *Federal Consumer Credit Protection Act*, popularly known as the **Truth-in-Lending Act**, went into effect in 1969. The act, implemented by Federal Reserve Board **Regulation Z**, requires that a borrower be clearly shown, before committing to a loan, how much is being paid for credit in both dollar terms and percentage terms. The borrower is also given the right to rescind (cancel) the transaction in certain instances. The act came into being because it was not uncommon to see loans advertised for rates lower than the borrower actually wound up paying. Today, some of this has been replaced by the new Loan Estimate form published under the new TIL-RESPA Integrated Disclosure (TRID) Rules, discussed later in this chapter. It incorporates the RESPA Good Faith Estimate Form and the REG Z form to create this new Loan Estimate form, shown as Figure 12.1.

ADVERTISING

Whether you are a real estate practitioner or a property owner acting on your own behalf, TIL rules affect you when you advertise just about anything (including real estate) and include financing terms in the ad.

LEARNING OBJECTIVES

After reading this chapter, you should be able to:

- Discuss the significance of the Federal Truth-in-Lending Act and the use of trigger terms.
- Define "annual percentage rate" and "finance charge."
- Review the various provisions of the Uniform Residential Loan Application.
- Define the apply the concepts of "credit scoring."
- Define the "subprime loans."
- Understand and explain simple concepts of mortgage fraud and determine the "red flags" of various types of a mortgage fraud.

KEY TERMS

APR • Credit report • Fair Credit Reporting Act • Liquid assets • Redlining • Regulation Z • Truth-in-Lending Act

truth-in-lending act
A federal law that requires certain disclosures when extending or advertising credit.

regulation Z
Federal regulations that implement the enforcement of the Truth-in-Lending Act.

FIGURE
12.1   Loan Estimate Form-Completed

FICUS BANK
4321 Random Boulevard • Somecity, ST 12340

Save this Loan Estimate to compare with your Closing Disclosure.

Loan Estimate

DATE ISSUED	2/15/2013
APPLICANTS	Michael Jones and Mary Stone
	123 Anywhere Street
	Anytown, ST 12345
PROPERTY	456 Somewhere Avenue
	Anytown, ST 12345
SALE PRICE	$180,000

LOAN TERM	30 years
PURPOSE	Purchase
PRODUCT	Fixed Rate
LOAN TYPE	☒ Conventional ☐ FHA ☐ VA ☐ _____
LOAN ID #	123456789
RATE LOCK	☐ NO ☒ YES, until 4/16/2013 at 5:00 p.m. EDT

*Before closing, your interest rate, points, and lender credits can change unless you lock the interest rate. All other estimated closing costs expire on **3/4/2013** at 5:00 p.m. EDT*

Loan Terms

		Can this amount increase after closing?
Loan Amount	$162,000	NO
Interest Rate	3.875%	NO
Monthly Principal & Interest *See Projected Payments below for your Estimated Total Monthly Payment*	$761.78	NO

	Does the loan have these features?
Prepayment Penalty	YES • As high as **$3,240** if you pay off the loan during the first 2 years
Balloon Payment	NO

Projected Payments

Payment Calculation	Years 1-7	Years 8-30
Principal & Interest	$761.78	$761.78
Mortgage Insurance	+ 82	+ —
Estimated Escrow *Amount can increase over time*	+ 206	+ 206
Estimated Total Monthly Payment	$1,050	$968

		This estimate includes	In escrow?
Estimated Taxes, Insurance & Assessments *Amount can increase over time*	$206 a month	☒ Property Taxes	YES
		☒ Homeowner's Insurance	YES
		☐ Other:	

See Section G on page 2 for escrowed property costs. You must pay for other property costs separately.

Costs at Closing

Estimated Closing Costs	$8,054	Includes $5,672 in Loan Costs + $2,382 in Other Costs – $0 in Lender Credits. *See page 2 for details.*
Estimated Cash to Close	$16,054	Includes Closing Costs. *See Calculating Cash to Close on page 2 for details.*

Visit **www.consumerfinance.gov/mortgage-estimate** for general information and tools.

FIGURE 12.1   Loan Estimate Form-Completed (continued)

Closing Cost Details

Loan Costs

A. Origination Charges	$1,802
.25 % of Loan Amount (Points)	$405
Application Fee	$300
Underwriting Fee	$1,097

B. Services You Cannot Shop For	$672
Appraisal Fee	$405
Credit Report Fee	$30
Flood Determination Fee	$20
Flood Monitoring Fee	$32
Tax Monitoring Fee	$75
Tax Status Research Fee	$110

C. Services You Can Shop For	$3,198
Pest Inspection Fee	$135
Survey Fee	$65
Title – Insurance Binder	$700
Title – Lender's Title Policy	$535
Title – Settlement Agent Fee	$502
Title – Title Search	$1,261

D. TOTAL LOAN COSTS (A + B + C)	$5,672

Other Costs

E. Taxes and Other Government Fees	$85
Recording Fees and Other Taxes	$85
Transfer Taxes	

F. Prepaids	$867
Homeowner's Insurance Premium (6 months)	$605
Mortgage Insurance Premium (months)	
Prepaid Interest ($17.44 per day for 15 days @ 3.875%)	$262
Property Taxes (months)	

G. Initial Escrow Payment at Closing		$413
Homeowner's Insurance	$100.83 per month for 2 mo.	$202
Mortgage Insurance	per month for mo.	
Property Taxes	$105.30 per month for 2 mo.	$211

H. Other	$1,017
Title – Owner's Title Policy (optional)	$1,017

I. TOTAL OTHER COSTS (E + F + G + H)	$2,382

J. TOTAL CLOSING COSTS	$8,054
D + I	$8,054
Lender Credits	

Calculating Cash to Close

Total Closing Costs (J)	$8,054
Closing Costs Financed (Paid from your Loan Amount)	$0
Down Payment/Funds from Borrower	$18,000
Deposit	– $10,000
Funds for Borrower	$0
Seller Credits	$0
Adjustments and Other Credits	$0
Estimated Cash to Close	$16,054

FIGURE 12.1 Loan Estimate Form-Completed (continued)

Additional Information About This Loan

LENDER	Ficus Bank	**MORTGAGE BROKER**	
NMLS/__ LICENSE ID		**NMLS/__ LICENSE ID**	
LOAN OFFICER	Joe Smith	**LOAN OFFICER**	
NMLS/__ LICENSE ID	12345	**NMLS/__ LICENSE ID**	
EMAIL	joesmith@ficusbank.com	**EMAIL**	
PHONE	123-456-7890	**PHONE**	

Comparisons

Use these measures to compare this loan with other loans.

In 5 Years	$56,582	Total you will have paid in principal, interest, mortgage insurance, and loan costs.
	$15,773	Principal you will have paid off.
Annual Percentage Rate (APR)	4.274%	Your costs over the loan term expressed as a rate. This is not your interest rate.
Total Interest Percentage (TIP)	69.45%	The total amount of interest that you will pay over the loan term as a percentage of your loan amount.

Other Considerations

Appraisal	We may order an appraisal to determine the property's value and charge you for this appraisal. We will promptly give you a copy of any appraisal, even if your loan does not close. You can pay for an additional appraisal for your own use at your own cost.
Assumption	If you sell or transfer this property to another person, we ☐ will allow, under certain conditions, this person to assume this loan on the original terms. ☒ will not allow assumption of this loan on the original terms.
Homeowner's Insurance	This loan requires homeowner's insurance on the property, which you may obtain from a company of your choice that we find acceptable.
Late Payment	If your payment is more than *15* days late, we will charge a late fee of *5% of the monthly principal and interest payment.*
Refinance	Refinancing this loan will depend on your future financial situation, the property value, and market conditions. You may not be able to refinance this loan.
Servicing	We intend ☐ to service your loan. If so, you will make your payments to us. ☒ to transfer servicing of your loan.

Confirm Receipt

By signing, you are only confirming that you have received this form. You do not have to accept this loan because you have signed or received this form.

_____   _____   _____   _____
Applicant Signature   Date   Co-Applicant Signature   Date

TRIGGER TERMS

Five specific disclosures must be included in any ad that contains even one of the following trigger terms: (1) the amount of down payment (for example, only 5% down, 10% down, $4,995 down, 95% financing); (2) the amount of any payment (for example, monthly payments only $499, buy for less than $650 a month, payments only 1% per month); (3) the number of payments (for example, only 36 monthly payments and you own it, all paid up in 10 annual payments); (4) the period of repayment (for example, 30-year financing, owner will carry for 5 years, 10-year second available); and (5) the dollar amount of any finance charge (finance this for only $999), or the statement that there is no charge for credit (pay no interest for 3 years).

If any of the aforementioned trigger terms are used, then the following five disclosures must appear in the ad: (1) the amount financed; (2) the finance charge; (3) the number, amount, and frequency of repayments; (4) the annual percentage rate; and (5) a statement that a security interest has been taken in the property purchased. If the loan has a required Good Faith Estimate disclosure under the Real Estate Settlement Procedures Act (see Chapter 16), the disclosure must contain the statement: "You are not required to complete this agreement merely because you have received this disclosure or signed a loan application."

As previously stated, the TIL disclosed costs of a loan. The Real Estate Settlement Procedures Act discloses costs of closing. These federal statutes overlap quite a bit, and the term used in both statutes often conflict while trying to disclose the same information that is part of the Mortgage Reform and Anti-Predatory Lending Act, passed in 2010, along with the Dodd-Frank Wall Street Reform and Consumer Protection Act of 2010, created a Bureau for Consumer Financial Protection as another (another!) federal consumer watchdog agency. One of its charges is to reconcile the disclosure requirements of both statutes so we will have one disclosure form in the future that will serve the purposes of both federal statutes.

ANNUAL PERCENTAGE RATE

The **annual percentage rate (APR)** combines the interest rate with the other costs of the loan into a single figure that shows the true annual cost of borrowing. This is one of the most helpful features of the law as it gives the prospective borrower a standardized yardstick by which to compare financing from different sources.

APR

The annual percentage rate as calculated under the federal Truth-in-Lending Act by combining the interest rate with other costs of the loan.

If the annual percentage rate being offered is subject to increase after the transaction takes place (such as with an adjustable rate mortgage), that fact must be stated, for example, "9% annual percentage rate subject to increase after settlement." If the loan has interest rate changes that follow a predetermined schedule, those terms must be stated, for example, "7% first year, 9% second year, 11% third year, 13% remainder of loan, 12.5% annual percentage rate."

If you wish to say something about financing and avoid triggering full disclosure, you may use general statements. The following would be acceptable: "assumable loan," "financing available," "owner will carry," "terms to fit your budget," "easy monthly payments," or "FHA and VA financing available."

LOAN ESTIMATE DISCLOSURES

If you are in the business of making loans, you are making loan estimate disclosures to your borrower in the Loan Estimate form. Of these, the four that must be most prominently displayed on the papers the borrower signs are: (1) the loan terms, (2) the projected payments, (3) the annual percentage rate, and (4) the costs at closing.

The **loan amount** is the amount of credit provided to the borrower. These disclosures must be delivered or mailed to the credit applicant within three business days after the creditor receives the applicant's written request for credit.

WHO MUST COMPLY?

Any person or firm that regularly extends consumer credit subject to a finance charge (such as interest), or payable by written agreement in more than four installments, must comply with the lending disclosures. This includes banks, savings and loans, credit unions, finance companies, and so on, as well as private individuals who extend credit more than five times a year.

Whoever is named on the note as the creditor must make the lending disclosures even if the note is to be resold. A key difference between the old and the new TIL acts is that the new TIL act does not include mortgage brokers or real estate practitioners as creditors just because they brokered a deal containing financing. This is because they do not appear as creditors on the note. But if a broker takes back a note for part of the commission on a deal, that is an extension of credit, and the lending disclosures must be made.

EXEMPT TRANSACTIONS

Certain transactions are exempt from the lending disclosure requirement. The first exemption is for credit extended primarily for business, commercial, or agricultural purposes. This exemption includes dwelling units purchased for rental purposes (unless the property contains four or fewer units and the owner occupies one of them, in which case special rules apply).

The second exemption applies to credit over $25,000 secured by personal property, unless the property is the principal residence of the borrower. For example, a mobile home that secures a loan over $25,000 qualifies under this exemption if it is used as a vacation home, but is not exempt if it is used as a principal residence.

RIGHT TO CANCEL

A borrower has a limited *right to rescission* (right to cancel) in a credit transaction. The borrower has three business days (which includes Saturdays) to back out after signing the loan papers. This aspect of the law was inserted primarily to protect a homeowner from unscrupulous sellers of home improvements and appliances when the credit to purchase is secured by a lien on the home. Vacant lots for sale on credit to buyers who expect to use them for principal residences are also subject to cancellation privileges.

The right to rescind does not apply to credit used for the acquisition or initial construction of one's principal dwelling.

Loan Application and Approval

When a mortgage lender reviews a real estate loan application, the primary concern for both applicant and lender is to approve loan requests that show a high probability of being repaid in full and on time, and to disapprove requests that are likely to result in default and eventual foreclosure. How is this decision made? Loan analysis varies. However, the five major federal agencies have recently combined their requirements for credit reports. All loans intended for underwriting by Fannie Mae, Freddie Mac, HUD, FHA, or VA must comply with the new standards. Figure 12.2 shows the new Uniform Residential Loan Application (a requirement for standardized loan applications), and summarizes the key terms that a loan officer considers when making a decision regarding a loan request. Let's review these items and observe how they affect the acceptance of a loan by a lender.

FIGURE
12.2   Uniform Residential Loan Application

Uniform Residential Loan Application

This application is designed to be completed by the applicant(s) with the Lender's assistance. Applicants should complete this form as "Borrower" or "Co-Borrower," as applicable. Co-Borrower information must also be provided (and the appropriate box checked) when ☐ the income or assets of a person other than the Borrower (including the Borrower's spouse) will be used as a basis for loan qualification or ☐ the income or assets of the Borrower's spouse or other person who has community property or similar rights pursuant to applicable state law will not be used as a basis for loan qualification, but his or her liabilities must be considered because the spouse or other person who has community property or similar rights and the Borrower resides in a community property state, the security property is located in a community property state, or the Borrower is relying on other property located in a community property state as a basis for repayment of the loan.

If this is an application for joint credit, Borrower and Co-Borrower each agree that we intend to apply for joint credit (sign below):

Borrower _____   Co-Borrower _____

I. TYPE OF MORTGAGE AND TERMS OF LOAN			
Mortgage Applied for:	☐ VA ☐ USDA/Rural Housing Service ☐ FHA ☐ Conventional ☐ Other (explain):	Agency Case Number	Lender Case Number

Amount $	Interest Rate %	No. of Months	Amortization Type:	☐ Fixed Rate ☐ Other (explain): ☐ GPM ☐ ARM (type):

II. PROPERTY INFORMATION AND PURPOSE OF LOAN

Subject Property Address (street, city, state & ZIP)	No. of Units

Legal Description of Subject Property (attach description if necessary)	Year Built

Purpose of Loan ☐ Purchase ☐ Refinance ☐ Construction ☐ Construction-Permanent ☐ Other (explain):	Property will be: ☐ Primary Residence ☐ Secondary Residence ☐ Investment

Complete this line if construction or construction-permanent loan.

Year Lot Acquired	Original Cost	Amount Existing Liens	(a) Present Value of Lot	(b) Cost of Improvements	Total (a + b)
	$	$	$	$	$

Complete this line if this is a refinance loan.

Year Acquired	Original Cost	Amount Existing Liens	Purpose of Refinance	Describe Improvements	☐ made ☐ to be made
	$	$			

Title will be held in what Name(s)	Manner in which Title will be held	Estate will be held in: ☐ Fee Simple ☐ Leasehold (show expiration date)

Source of Down Payment, Settlement Charges, and/or Subordinate Financing (explain)

FIGURE 12.2 Uniform Residential Loan Application (continued)

Borrower	III. BORROWER INFORMATION	Co-Borrower

Borrower's Name (include Jr. or Sr. if applicable)

Co-Borrower's Name (include Jr. or Sr. if applicable)

Social Security Number	Home Phone (incl. Area code)	DOB (mm/dd/yyyy)	Yrs. School	Social Security Number	Home Phone (incl. Area code)	DOB (mm/dd/yyyy)	Yrs. School

☐ Married   ☐ Separated
☐ Unmarried
(include single, divorced, widowed)

Dependents (not listed by Co-Borrower)
no.   ages

☐ Married   ☐ Separated
☐ Unmarried
(include single, divorced, widowed)

Dependents (not listed by Borrower)
no.   ages

Present Address (street, city, state, ZIP)   ☐ Own ☐ Rent __No. Yrs.

Present Address (street, city, state, ZIP)   ☐ Own ☐ Rent __No. Yrs.

Mailing Address, if different from Present Address

Mailing Address, if different from Present Address

If residing at present address for less than two years, complete the following:

Former Address (street, city, state, ZIP)   ☐ Own ☐ Rent __No. Yrs.

Former Address (street, city, state, ZIP)   ☐ Own ☐ Rent __No. Yrs.

Borrower	IV. EMPLOYMENT INFORMATION	Co-Borrower

Name & Address of Employer   ☐ Self Employed

Yrs. on this job

Yrs. employed in this line of work/profession

Name & Address of Employer   ☐ Self Employed

Yrs. on this job

Yrs. employed in this line of work/profession

Position/Title/Type of Business

Business Phone (incl. area code)

Position/Title/Type of Business

Business Phone (incl. area code)

If employed in current position for less than two years or if currently employed in more than one position, complete the following:

Name & Address of Employer   ☐ Self Employed

Dates (from - to)

Monthly Income
$

Name & Address of Employer   ☐ Self Employed

Dates (from - to)

Monthly Income
$

Position/Title/Type of Business

Business Phone (incl. area code)

Position/Title/Type of Business

Business Phone (incl. area code)

Name & Address of Employer   ☐ Self Employed

Dates (from - to)

Monthly Income
$

Name & Address of Employer   ☐ Self Employed

Dates (from - to)

Monthly Income
$

Position/Title/Type of Business

Business Phone (incl. area code)

Position/Title/Type of Business

Business Phone (incl. area code)

FIGURE
12.2 Uniform Residential Loan Application (continued)

V. MONTHLY INCOME AND COMBINED HOUSING EXPENSE INFORMATION

Gross Monthly Income	Borrower	Co-Borrower	Total	Combined Monthly Housing Expense	Present	Proposed
Base Empl. Income*	$	$	$	Rent	$	
Overtime				First Mortgage (P&I)		$
Bonuses				Other Financing (P&I)		
Commissions				Hazard Insurance		
Dividends/ Interest				Real Estate Taxes		
Net Rental Income				Mortgage Insurance		
Other (before completing, see the notice in "describe other income," below)				Homeowner Assn. Dues		
				Other:		
Total	$	$	$	Total	$	$

* Self Employed Borrower(s) may be required to provide additional documentation such as tax returns and financial statements.

Describe Other Income   *Notice:* Alimony, child support, or separate maintenance income need not be revealed if the Borrower (B) or Co-Borrower (C) does not choose to have it considered for repaying this loan.

B/C		Monthly Amount
		$

VI. ASSETS AND LIABILITIES

This Statement and any applicable supporting schedules may be completed jointly by both married and unmarried Co-Borrowers if their assets and liabilities are sufficiently joined so that the Statement can be meaningfully and fairly presented on a combined basis; otherwise, separate Statements and Schedules are required. If the Co-Borrower section was completed about a non-applicant spouse or other person, this Statement and supporting schedules must be completed about that spouse or other person also.

Completed ☐ Jointly ☐ Not Jointly

ASSETS Description	Cash or Market Value	Liabilities and Pledged Assets. List the creditor's name, address, and account number for all outstanding debts, including automobile loans, revolving charge accounts, real estate loans, alimony, child support, stock pledges, etc. Use continuation sheet, if necessary. Indicate by (*) those liabilities, which will be satisfied upon sale of real estate owned or upon refinancing of the subject property.		
Cash deposit toward purchase held by:	$	LIABILITIES	Monthly Payment & Months Left to Pay	Unpaid Balance
List checking and savings accounts below		Name and address of Company	$ Payment/Months	$
Name and address of Bank, S&L, or Credit Union				
		Acct. no.		
Acct. no.	$	Name and address of Company	$ Payment/Months	$

FIGURE 12.2   Uniform Residential Loan Application (continued)

VI. ASSETS AND LIABILITIES (cont'd)

Name and address of Bank, S&L, or Credit Union		Acct. no.		
Acct. no.	$	Name and address of Company	$ Payment/Months	$
Name and address of Bank, S&L, or Credit Union				
		Acct. no.		
Acct. no.	$	Name and address of Company	$ Payment/Months	$
Name and address of Bank, S&L, or Credit Union				
		Acct. no.		
Acct. no.	$	Name and address of Company	$ Payment/Months	$
Stocks & Bonds (Company name/number & description)	$			
		Acct. no.		
Life insurance net cash value Face amount: $	$	Name and address of Company	$ Payment/Months	$
Subtotal Liquid Assets	$	Acct. no.		
Real estate owned (enter market value from schedule of real estate owned)	$	Alimony/Child Support/Separate Maintenance Payments Owned to:	$	$
Vested interest in retirement fund	$			
Net worth of business(es) owned (attach financial statement)	$	Job-Related Expense (child care, union dues, etc.)	$	
Automobiles owned (make and year)	$			
Other Assets (itemize)	$			
		Total Monthly Payments	$	
Total Assets a.	$	Net Worth (a minus b) $	Total Liabilities b.	$

| FIGURE 12.2 | Uniform Residential Loan Application (continued) |

Schedule of Real Estate Owned (If additional properties are owned, use continuation sheet.)

Property Address (enter S if sold, PS if pending sale or R if rental being held for income)	Type of Property	Present Market Value	Amount of Mortgages & Liens	Gross Rental Income	Mortgage Payments	Insurance, Maintenance, Taxes & Misc.	Net Rental Income
		$	$	$	$	$	$
	Totals	$	$	$	$	$	$

List any additional names under which credit has previously been received and indicate appropriate creditor name(s) and account number(s):

Alternate Name	Creditor Name	Account Number

VII. DETAILS OF TRANSACTION		VIII. DECLARATIONS				
			Borrower		Co-Borrower	
a. Purchase price	$	If you answer "Yes" to any questions a through i, please use continuation sheet for explanation.				
			Yes	No	Yes	No
b. Alterations, improvements, repairs						
c. Land (if acquired separately)		a. Are there any outstanding judgments against you?	☐	☐	☐	☐
d. Refinance (incl. debts to be paid off)		b. Have you been declared bankrupt within the past 7 years?	☐	☐	☐	☐
e. Estimated prepaid items		c. Have you had property foreclosed upon or given title or deed in lieu thereof in the last 7 years?	☐	☐	☐	☐
f. Estimated closing costs		d. Are you a party to a lawsuit?	☐	☐	☐	☐
g. PMI, MIP, Funding Fee		e. Have you directly or indirectly been obligated on any loan of which resulted in foreclosure, transfer of title in lieu of foreclosure, or judgment? (This would include such loans as home mortgage loans, SBA loans, home improvement loans, educational loans, manufactured (mobile) home loans, any mortgage, financial obligation, bond, or loan guarantee. If "Yes," provide details, including date, name, and address of Lender, FHA or VA case number, if any, and reasons for the action.)	☐	☐	☐	☐
h. Discount (if Borrower will pay)		f. Are you presently delinquent or in default on any Federal debt or any other loan, mortgage, financial obligation, bond, or loan guarantee? If "Yes," give details as described in the preceding question.	☐	☐	☐	☐
i. Total costs (add items a through h)		g. Are you obligated to pay alimony, child support, or separate maintenance?	☐	☐	☐	☐
j. Subordinate financing		h. Is any part of the down payment borrowed?	☐	☐	☐	☐

FIGURE 12.2 Uniform Residential Loan Application (continued)

VII. DETAILS OF TRANSACTION (cont'd)		VIII. DECLARATIONS (cont'd)				
k.	Borrower's closing costs paid by Seller	i. Are you a co-maker or endorser on a note?	☐	☐	☐	☐
l.	Other Credits (explain)	--				
		j. Are you a U.S. citizen?	☐	☐	☐	☐
		k. Are you a permanent resident alien?	☐	☐	☐	☐
m.	Loan amount (exclude PMI, MIP, Funding Fee financed)	l. Do you intend to occupy the property as your primary residence? If "Yes," complete question m below.	☐	☐	☐	☐
n.	PMI, MIP, Funding Fee financed	m. Have you had an ownership interest in a property in the last three years?	☐	☐	☐	☐
o.	Loan amount (add m & n)	(1) What type of property did you own—principal residence (PR), second home (SH), or investment property (IP)?	___	___	___	___
p.	Cash from/to Borrower (subtract j, k, l & o from i)	(2) How did you hold title to the home— by yourself (S), jointly with your spouse or jointly with another person (O)?	___	___	___	___

ACKNOWLEDGMENT AND AGREEMENT

Each of the undersigned specifically represents to Lender and to Lender's actual or potential agents, brokers, processors, attorneys, insurers, servicers, successors and assigns and agrees and acknowledges that: (1) the information provided in this application is true and correct as of the date set forth opposite my signature and that any intentional or negligent misrepresentation of this information contained in this application may result in civil liability, including monetary damages, to any person who may suffer any loss due to reliance upon any misrepresentation that I have made on this application, and/or in criminal penalties including, but not limited to, fine or imprisonment or both under the provisions of Title 18, United States Code, Sec. 1001, et seq.; (2) the loan requested pursuant to this application (the "Loan") will be secured by a mortgage or deed of trust on the property described in this application; (3) the property will not be used for any illegal or prohibited purpose or use; (4) all statements made in this application are made for the purpose of obtaining a residential mortgage loan; (5) the property will be occupied as indicated in this application; (6) the Lender, its servicers, successors or assigns may retain the original and/or an electronic record of this application, whether or not the Loan is approved; (7) the Lender and its agents, brokers, insurers, servicers, successors, and assigns may continuously rely on the information contained in the application, and I am obligated to amend and/or supplement the information provided in this application if any of the material facts that I have represented should change prior to closing of the Loan; (8) in the event that my payments on the Loan become delinquent, the Lender, its servicers, successors or assigns may, in addition to any other rights and remedies that it may have relating to such delinquency, report my name and account information to one or more consumer reporting agencies; (9) ownership of the Loan and/or administration of the Loan account may be transferred with such notice as may be required by law; (10) neither Lender nor its agents, brokers, insurers, servicers, successors or assigns has made any representation or warranty, express or implied, to me regarding the property or the condition or value of the property; and (11) my transmission of this application as an "electronic record" containing my "electronic signature," as those terms are defined in applicable federal and/or state laws (excluding audio and video recordings), or my facsimile transmission of this application containing a facsimile of my signature, shall be as effective, enforceable and valid as if a paper version of this application were delivered containing my original written signature.

Acknowledgement. Each of the undersigned hereby acknowledges that any owner of the Loan, its servicers, successors and assigns, may verify or reverify any information contained in this application or obtain any information or data relating to the Loan, for any legitimate business purpose through any source, including a source named in this application or a consumer reporting agency.

Borrower's Signature X	Date	Co-Borrower's Signature X	Date

X. INFORMATION FOR GOVERNMENT MONITORING PURPOSES

FIGURE 12.2	Uniform Residential Loan Application (continued)

The following information is requested by the Federal Government for certain types of loans related to a dwelling in order to monitor the lender's compliance with equal credit opportunity, fair housing and home mortgage disclosure laws. You are not required to furnish this information, but are encouraged to do so. The law provides that a lender may not discriminate either on the basis of this information, or on whether you choose to furnish it. If you furnish the information, please provide both ethnicity and race. For race, you may check more than one designation. If you do not furnish ethnicity, race, or sex, under Federal regulations, this lender is required to note the information on the basis of visual observation and surname if you have made this application in person. If you do not wish to furnish the information, please check the box below. (Lender must review the above material to assure that the disclosures satisfy all requirements to which the lender is subject under applicable state law for the particular type of loan applied for.) _____

BORROWER	CO-BORROWER
☐ I do not wish to furnish this information	☐ I do not wish to furnish this information
Ethnicity: ☐ Hispanic or Latino ☐ Not Hispanic or Latino	Ethnicity: ☐ Hispanic or Latino ☐ Not Hispanic or Latino
Race: ☐ American Indian or Alaska Native ☐ Asian ☐ Black or African American ☐ Native Hawaiian or Other Pacific Islander ☐ White	Race: ☐ American Indian or Alaska Native ☐ Asian ☐ Black or African American ☐ Native Hawaiian or Other Pacific Islander ☐ White
Sex: ☐ Female ☐ Male	Sex: ☐ Female ☐ Male

To be Completed by Loan Originator
This information was provided:
☐ In a face-to-face interview
☐ In a telephone interview
☐ By the applicant and submitted by fax or mail
☐ By the applicant and submitted via e-mail or the Internet

Loan Originator's Signature	Date
Loan Originator's Name (print or type)	Loan Originator Identifier	Loan Originator's Phone Number (including area code)
Loan Origination Company's Name	Loan Origination Company Identifier	Loan Origination Company's Address

FIGURE 12.2   Uniform Residential Loan Application (continued)

CONTINUATION SHEET/RESIDENTIAL LOAN APPLICATION

Use this continuation sheet if you need more space to complete the Residential Loan Application. Mark **B** for Borrower or **C** for Co-Borrower.	Borrower:	Agency Case Number:
	Co-Borrower:	Lender Case Number:

I/We fully understand that it is a Federal crime punishable by fine or imprisonment, or both, to knowingly make any false statements concerning any of the above facts as applicable under the provisions of Title 18, United States Code, Section 1001, et seq.

Borrower's Signature	Date	Co-Borrower's Signature	Date
X		X	

Uniform Residential Loan Application
Freddie Mac Form 65   7/05 (rev.6 /09)   Page 8 of 8   Fannie Mae Form 1003   7/05 (rev.6/09)

Source: https://www.fanniemae.com/content/guide_form/1003irev.pdf

Note that at [1] the borrower is requested to specify the type of mortgage and terms of the loan being sought. This greatly facilitates the lender's ability to determine the availability of the loan that the borrower may be seeking.

In [2] the lender begins the loan analysis procedure by looking at the property and the proposed financing. Using the property address and legal description, an appraiser is assigned to prepare an appraisal of the property and a title search is ordered. These steps are taken to determine the fair market value of the property and the condition of title. In the event of default, the property is the collateral the lender must fall back on to recover the loan. If the loan request is in connection with a purchase rather than the refinancing of an existing property, the lender will know the purchase price. As a rule, loans are made on the basis of the appraised value or purchase price, whichever is lower. If the appraised value is lower than the purchase price, the usual procedure is to require the buyer to make a larger cash down payment. The lender does not want to over loan simply because the buyer overpaid for the property.

SETTLEMENT FUNDS

Next, also at [2], the lender wants to know whether the borrower has adequate funds for settlement. Are these funds presently in a checking or savings account, or are they coming from the sale of the borrower's present property? In the latter case, the lender knows that the present loan is contingent on closing that escrow. If the down payment and settlement funds are to be borrowed, then the lender needs to be extra cautious, as experience has shown that the less money a borrower personally puts into a purchase, the higher is the probability of default and foreclosure.

PURPOSE OF LOAN

The lender is also interested in the proposed use of the property. Lenders feel most comfortable when a loan is for the purchase or improvement of a property the loan applicant will actually occupy. This is because owner-occupants usually have pride of ownership in maintaining their property, and, even during bad economic conditions, will continue to make the monthly payments.

An owner-occupant also realizes that losing the home still means paying for shelter elsewhere. It is standard practice for lenders to ask loan applicants to sign a statement declaring whether they intend to occupy the property.

If the loan applicant intends to purchase a dwelling to rent out as an investment, the lender will be more cautious because, during periods of high vacancy, the property may not generate enough income to meet the loan payments. At that point, a strapped-for-cash borrower is likely to default. Note, too, that lenders generally avoid loans secured by purely speculative real estate. If the value of the property drops below the amount owed, the borrower may see no further logic in making the loan payments.

Finally, the lender assesses the borrower's attitude toward the proposed loan. Someone with a casual attitude, such as "I'm buying because real estate always goes up," or an applicant who does not appear to understand the obligation being undertaken, would bring a low rating here. Much more welcome is the applicant who shows a mature attitude and understanding of the loan obligation, and who exhibits a strong and logical desire for ownership.

BORROWER ANALYSIS

In [3] and [4] the lender begins an analysis of the borrower and, if there is one, the co-borrower. At one time age, sex, and marital status played an important role in the lender's decision to lend or not to lend. Often the young and the old had trouble getting loans, as did women and persons who were single, divorced, or widowed. Today, the federal Equal Credit Opportunity Act prohibits discrimination based on age, sex, race, and marital status. Lenders are no longer permitted to discount income earned by women because a job is part-time or the woman is of childbearing age. If the applicant chooses to disclose it, alimony, separate maintenance, and child support must be counted in full. Young adults and single persons cannot be turned down because the lender feels they have not "put down roots." Seniors cannot be turned down as long as life expectancy exceeds the early risk period of the loan and collateral is adequate. In other words, the emphasis in borrower analysis is now focused on job stability, income adequacy, net worth, and credit rating.

Thus, at [5] and [6] we see questions directed at how long the applicants have held their present jobs and the stability of the jobs themselves. An applicant who possesses marketable job skills and has been regularly employed with a stable employer is considered the ideal risk. Persons whose income can rise and fall erratically, such as commissioned salespersons, present greater risks. Persons whose skills (or lack of skills) or lack of job seniority result in frequent unemployment are more likely to have difficulty repaying a loan. In these sections the lender also inquires as to the number of dependents the applicant must support from his or her income. This information provides some insight as to how much will be left for monthly house payments.

MONTHLY INCOME

In section [7] the lender looks at the amount and sources of the applicants' income. Quantity alone is not enough for loan approval because the income sources must be stable too. Thus, a lender will look carefully at overtime, bonus, and commission income in order to estimate the levels at which these may be expected to continue. Interest, dividend, and rental income is considered in light of the stability of their sources also. Income from Social Security and retirement pensions is entered and added to the totals for the applicants. Alimony, child support, and separate maintenance payments received need not be revealed. However, such sums must be listed in order to be considered as a basis for repaying the loan.

In section [8] the lender compares what the applicants have been paying for housing with what they will be paying if the loan is approved. Included in the proposed housing expense total are principal, interest, taxes, and insurance, along with any assessments or homeowner association dues (such as for a condominium). Some lenders add the monthly cost of utilities to this list.

At [9] the proposed monthly housing expense is compared with gross monthly income (your debt-to-income ratio). A general rule of thumb (sometimes referred to as the front end ratio) is that the monthly housing expense (PITI) should not exceed 28% to 30% of gross monthly income. A second guideline (sometimes referred to as the back end ratio) is that total fixed monthly expenses should not exceed 36% of income. This includes housing payments plus automobile payments, installment loan payments, alimony, child support, and investments with negative cash flows. These are general guidelines, but lenders recognize that food, health care, clothing, transportation, entertainment, and income taxes must also come from the applicants' income. For instance, a location efficient mortgage (LEM) now being offered allows homeowners in urban areas to qualify for larger mortgages when they have significantly reduced transportation costs.

For FHA loans the recommended debt-to-income limit is 31% for the front end ratio and 43% for the back end ratio.

ASSETS AND LIABILITIES

In section **[10]** the lender is interested in the applicants' sources of funds for closing, and whether, once the loan is granted, the applicants have assets to fall back on in the event of an income decrease (a job layoff) or unexpected expenses (hospital bills). Of particular interest is the portion of those assets that are in cash or are readily convertible into cash in a few days. These are called **liquid assets**. If income drops, they are much more useful in meeting living expenses and loan payments than assets that may require months to sell and convert to cash—that is, assets that are *illiquid*.

liquid asset
Asset that is in cash or is readily convertible to cash.

Note in section **[10]** that two values are shown for life insurance. **Cash value** is the amount of money the policyholder would receive if the policy were surrendered to the insurance company or, alternatively, the amount the policyholder could borrow against the policy. **Face amount** is the amount that would be paid in the event of the insured's death. Lenders feel most comfortable if the face amount of the policy equals or exceeds the amount of the proposed loan. Obviously, a borrower's death is not anticipated before the loan is repaid, but lenders recognize that its possibility increases the probability of default. The likelihood of foreclosure is lessened considerably if the survivors receive life insurance benefits.

In section **[11]** the lender is interested in the applicants' existing debts and liabilities for two reasons. First, each month these items compete against housing expenses for available monthly income. Thus, high monthly payments in this section may lower the lender's estimate of what the applicants will be able to repay and, consequently, may influence the lender to reduce the size of the loan. The presence of monthly liabilities is not all negative, it can also show the lender that the applicants are capable of repaying their debts. Second, the applicants' total debts are subtracted from their total assets to obtain their *net worth*, reported at **[12]**. If the result is negative (more owed than owned), the loan request will probably be turned down as too risky. In contrast, a substantial net worth can often offset weaknesses elsewhere in the application, such as too little monthly income in relation to monthly housing expense, or an income that can rise and fall erratically.

REFERENCES

At number **[13]** lenders ask for credit references as an indicator of the future. Applicants with no previous credit experience will have more weight placed on income and employment history. Applicants with a history of collections, adverse judgments, foreclosure, or bankruptcy will have to convince the lender that this loan will be repaid on time. Additionally, the applicants may be considered poorer risks if they have guaranteed the repayment of someone else's debt by acting as a co-maker or endorser.

REDLINING

In the past, it was not uncommon for lenders to refuse to make loans in certain neighborhoods regardless of the quality of the structure or the ability of the borrower to repay. This practice was known as **redlining**, and it effectively shut off mortgage loans in many older or so-called bad risk neighborhoods across the country. Today, a lender cannot refuse to make a loan simply because of the age or location of a property; the neighborhood income level; or the racial, ethnic, or religious composition of the neighborhood.

redlining
A lender's refusal to make loans in certain neighborhoods.

A lender can refuse to lend on a structure intended for demolition; a property in a known geological hazard area; a single-family dwelling in an area devoted to industrial or commercial use; or a property that is in violation of zoning laws, deed covenants, conditions or restrictions, or significant health, safety, or building codes.

LOAN-TO-VALUE RATIOS

The lender next looks at the amount of down payment the borrower proposes to make, the size of the loan being requested, and the amount of other financing the borrower plans to use. This information is then converted into loan-to-value ratios. As a rule, the larger the down payment is, the safer the loan is for the lender. On an uninsured loan, the ideal loan-to-value (L/V) ratio for a lender on owner-occupied residential property is 70% or less. This means the value of the property would have to fall more than 30% before the debt owed would exceed the property's value, thus encouraging the borrower to stop making loan payments.

Loan-to-value ratios from 70% through 80% are considered acceptable but do expose the lender to more risk. Lenders sometimes compensate by charging slightly higher interest rates. Loan-to-value ratios above 80% present even more risk of default to the lender, and the lender will either increase the interest rate charged on these loans or require insurance coverage from an outside insurer, such as the FHA or a private mortgage insurer.

CREDIT REPORT

credit report

A report reflecting the creditworthiness of a borrower by showing past credit history.

fair credit reporting act

Federal law giving an individual the right to inspect his or her file with the credit bureau and correct any errors.

As part of the loan application, the lender will order a **credit report** on the applicant(s). The applicant is asked to authorize this and to pay for the report. This provides the lender with an independent means of checking the applicant's credit history. A credit report that shows active use of credit with a good repayment record and no derogatory information is most desirable. The applicant will be asked by the lender to explain any negative information. Congress passed the **Fair Credit Reporting Act** because in a credit report it is possible for inaccurate or untrue information to unfairly damage a person's credit reputation. This act gives individuals the right to inspect their file at a credit bureau, correct any errors, and make explanatory statements to supplement the file. You can access your credit report by going online to www.AnnualCreditReport.com, or you can call 1-877-322-8228.

As previously discussed, the major federal agencies have combined their requirements for credit reports, and loans intended for underwriting by federal government agencies must comply with the new credit standards. Under these newly adopted rules, the name of the consumer reporting agency must be clearly identified, as well as who ordered the report and who is paying for it. The information must be obtained from at least two national repositories for each area in which the borrower resided in the past two years, and must be verified for the previous two years. An explanation must be provided if the information is unavailable, and all questions must be responded to, even if the answer must be "unable to verify." A history must be furnished and all missing information must be verified by the lender. The history must have been checked within 90 days of the credit report, and the age of information that is not considered obsolete by the Fair Credit Reporting Act (7 years general credit date or 10 years for bankruptcy) must be indicated. If any credit information is incomplete or if undisclosed information is discovered, the lender must have a personal interview with the borrower. The lender is additionally required to warrant that the credit report complies with all of the new standards.

Real estate practitioners should be particularly aware of this law. If an applicant for rental of a property is rejected on the basis of a credit report, there are special disclosures (set out by federal law) the owner, or the owner's agent, must make. If the applicant is rejected for reasons other than a credit report, the reasons must be disclosed. All disclosures must be made even if no request is made by the applicant.

CREDIT SCORING. A relatively new innovation, *credit scoring* is being used as a method of evaluating credit risk. The scoring system is applied to a list of subjective factors that are considered relevant in evaluating credit risks. Credit scores often are shown on the credit report as additional information. It should be pointed out, however, that no standards exist for credit scoring. Most producers of credit scores are privately owned, and they maintain confidentiality regarding how the credit scores are calculated, stating "contractual arrangements between the producer and the credit reporting agencies prohibit disclosure of the factors that generated the score."

Both Fannie Mae and Freddie Mac announced recently that they will make information about their credit scoring more available to the public. These agencies explain that they are committed to working with lenders to help borrowers understand the lending process, and thus improve their ability to qualify for an affordable mortgage. Many states, too, are requiring credit scoring processes to be more open.

More than 75% of mortgage lenders and 80% of the largest financial institutions use scores developed by Fair, Isaac & Company (called FICO) in their evaluations in approvals and processing credit applications. Lenders maintain that these scores provide a better assessment of how customers will perform on loan payments, and allow them to better balance the credit risk they take into their loan portfolios. The scores generally run from about 500 to 850. A score of 720 or higher will get the borrower the most favorable interest rate on a mortgage. As the interest rate charged by the lender may vary depending on the applicant's credit score, bad credit can result in paying significantly higher interest rates, which, with the term of the loan, can be a huge differential in payments.

How does one improve their credit score? Fair, Isaac & Company determines five different factors, each of which is weighted differently. They include type of credit use (10%), application for new credit (10%), length of credit history (15%), payment history (35%), and amounts owed (30%). The most important factors in evaluating credit are payment history and amounts owed. Most creditors suggest that you check your credit score frequently and correct any blatant errors that may show up (identify theft is a major problem in this area). Other factors considered in creating the credit score include paying your bills on time, consistently reducing your credit card balances (and keeping them below 25% of your credit card limit), and not "moving debt around," for example, transferring debts to different credit cards or other sources of debt. What a surprise! Making your payments on time and keeping your debt within a manageable range gives you a better credit score. The simplest rules are often overlooked by consumers. Lots of information is available on how to improve your credit score through the FICO Web site, **http://www.myfico.com**.

FHA recently released a credit scoring procedure that is open to the mortgage industry. It is called "TOTAL," an acronym for "Technology Open To All Lenders." The program assesses creditworthiness for FHA borrowers by evaluating certain mortgage applications and credit information to accurately predict the likelihood of a borrower default. It is intended to be used along with FHA's automated underwriting system.

There is a new, private credit scoring company called VantageScore, created by the three major credit reporting companies. They maintain that they will provide consumers and businesses with a highly predictive, consistent score that is easy to understand and apply. VantageScore uses score ranges from 501 to 990.

SUBPRIME LOANS. There is another market for what are called *subprime loans*. Subprime loans have risk-based pricing and rates are not quoted. Usually a rate is found, or negotiated, if it fits the risk profile. Interest rates are typically one to five percentage points higher than for good credit risks. With these loans, appraisals are critical and the risk profiles tend to be variable from lender to lender. The lowest risk borrowers are considered prime borrowers and are rated an "A" classification. Higher risk loans fall into lower categories from "A–" to "F." Although exact criteria vary, the "A" to "F" credit scoring has become somewhat standard in the last few years.

There is a new, private credit scoring company called VantageScore, created by the three major credit reporting companies. They maintain that they will provide consumers and businesses with a highly predictive, consistent score that is easy to understand and apply. VantageScore uses score ranges from 501 to 990.

This is a lucrative market for lenders. They can charge much higher interest rates and produce bigger returns for their investors. With the higher return, however, comes much higher risk. A lot of investors saw huge defaults in home mortgages in late 2007 through the early part of 2008. Those companies that invested large amounts in the subprime market had devastating losses, and some even closed their doors. These losses have been mostly focused on the private secondary market (not the government, discussed in Chapter 13). Many of the losses were not only due to risky investing, but also due to predatory lending and mortgage fraud, discussed next.

The Consumer Finance Protection Bureau

The nature of the mortgage lending industry is undergoing dramatic changes. The Dodd Frank Wall Street Reform and Consumer Protection Act of 2010 established the Consumer Finance Protection Bureau (CFPB) whose stated mission is to make markets for consumer financial products and services work for Americans, whether they are applying for a mortgage, choosing among credit cards, or using a number of other consumer financial purposes. Congress established the CFPB to protect the consumer by carrying out Federal Consumer Financial loss including writing rules, supervising companies, taking consumer complaints, and monitoring financial markets for new risks to consumers.

On January 10, 2013, the Consumer Finance Protection Bureau (CFPB) issued three "final" rules sending out significant new standards for mortgage underwriting and escrow requirements. The final rules address:

1. the standards on "ability-to-repay" ("ATR") and "qualified mortgages" ("QM Rule");
2. changes in Home Ownership and Equity Protection Act ("HOEPA"); and
3. the escrow account requirements for higher-priced mortgage loans.

THE QUALIFIED RULES

The QM Rules sets standards for mortgage terms and apply to consumer credit transactions secured by a dwelling *other than* home equity lines of credit, mortgages secured by time-share plan interests, reverse mortgages, or temporary or bridge loans with terms of 12 months or less.

The standard mortgages must have terms of less than 30 years, a fixed-rate interest rate for at least 5 years after consummation, points and fees are generally kept at 3%. They must also have periodic payments that do not result in an increase to the principle balance, deferral of principal repayments, or billing payments. Borrowers may have no more than one payment that is 30 days delinquent in the 12 months before applying for the standard loan (and none in the 6 months before applying).

THE ATR RULES

A residential mortgage lender is prohibited from making mortgage loans unless it has made a reasonable good faith determination at or before consummation of the transaction that the borrower has a reasonable ability to repay (ATR). The mortgage lender must take into account the borrowers income and assets, current employment status, monthly payments on loan, and monthly payments on any simultaneous loans, monthly payments for mortgage-related obligations (insurance, tax, etc.) and other debt obligations, alimony and child support and monthly debt-to-income ratio or residual income and the applicant's credit history. If the lenders don't comply with all these rules, they are subject to fines.

The borrower's income, assets, debt obligations, alimony and child support must be verified and the borrower's debt-to-income ratio cannot exceed 43% at the time of consummation of the mortgage. One can only conclude that these strict standards will deny many low-income and moderate-income borrowers, affordable mortgages.

Another issue is compliance. Who, at your bank, would undertake the burden of making all these decisions and assuring compliance with these new federal rules? There is a very good chance the smaller banks and smaller lending institutions, simply can't afford the compliance requirements and they could very well be out of the home mortgage business altogether. The Bureau has effectively barred FANNIE MAE and FREDDIE MAC from purchasing non-qualified mortgages, and this will undoubtedly increase the cost of mortgages over the long term.

NEW APPRAISAL REQUIREMENTS

Six federal financial regulatory agencies issued their final rule that establishes new appraisal requirements for "higher-priced mortgage loans". They include amendments to the Truth and Lending Act made by the Dodd-Frank Wall Street Reform and the Consumer Protection Act of 2010. Mortgage loans are "higher-priced" if they are secured by a consumer's home and have interest rates above certain thresholds. For these high-priced loans, the rule requires creditors to use a licensed or certified appraiser who prepares a written appraisal report based on a physical inspection of the interior of the property. The rule also requires the creditor to disclose to applicants information and the purpose of the appraisal and provide consumers with a free copy of the appraisal report.

Another new rules applies if the seller acquired the property at a lower price during the prior 6 months. In those situations, creditors have to obtain a second appraisal at no cost to the consumer. It is intended to address flipping property.

NEW FORECLOSURE REQUIREMENTS

Lenders are now also required to wait until borrowers are 120 days or more delinquent prior to sending an acceleration notice or actually filing for foreclosure.

THE TIL-RESPA INTEGRATED DISCLOSURE RULE

Last year we discussed the impact of the Consumer Finance Protection Bureau, which was enabled through the Dodd-Frank Wall Street Reformed Consumer Protection Act, and its impact on the mortgage lending business. This year, they have passed voluminous new regulations on closing disclosures and good faith estimate disclosures for lenders.

New Forms

There were two big changes. First, the good faith estimate and the initial truth-in-lending disclosure statement have been combined into one new form, the **Loan Estimate** form.

Second, the **HUD-1** and final **Truth-In-Lending Disclosure** (Final TIL) have been combined into another new form, the **Closing Disclosure** form, which is designed to provide disclosures that will be helpful to consumers in understanding all of the costs of the transaction. These new forms become effective October 3, 2015, and apply to all closed in consumer credit transactions, but does not apply to HELOC, reverse mortgages, or mobile home loans.

THE LOAN ESTIMATE FORM – TIMING REQUIREMENTS

1. The Loan Estimate Form must be provided no later than the **3rd business day** after receiving the consumer's loan application.

2. It must also be delivered or placed in the mail no later than the **7th business day** before consummation of the transaction.

3. The creditor must also ensure that the consumer receive any revised Loan Estimates (if any) no later than 4 business days prior to consummation.

Consummation occurs when the consumer becomes contractually obligated to the creditor on the loan (i.e. when he signs the real estate lien note). A business day is defined in two ways: (1) as a day on which the creditor's offices are open to the public for carrying out substantially all its business functions; and (2) means all calendar days except Sundays, and legal public holidays specified under federal law, such as New Year's Day, the birthday of Martin Luther King, Jr., Washington's birthday, Memorial Day, Independence Day, Labor Day, Columbus Day, Veterans' Day, Thanksgiving Day and Christmas Day.

HUD has also published a new Special Information Booklet which must be provided to the consumer not later than 3 business days after the loan application.

CLOSING DISCLOSURE FORM – TIMING REQUIREMENTS

1. The creditor is required to ensure that the consumer/borrower receives the Closing Disclosure no later than **3 days before consummation** of the loan.

2. Settlement Agents are also required to provide the seller with the Closing Disclosure reflecting the actual terms of the seller's transaction. The settlement agent must provide the **seller** its copy of the Closing Disclosure no later than **the day** of consummation.

Creditors may contract with settlement agents to have the settlement agent provide the closing disclosure to consumers on the creditor's behalf. Creditors and settlement agents can also agree to divide responsibility with regard to completing the Closing Disclosure, with the settlement agent assuming the responsibility to complete some or all of the Closing Disclosure.

Predatory Lending and Mortgage Fraud

In the next chapter we are going to discuss sources of financing. There are many sources of financing readily available to most consumers, but a lot of consumers lack the knowledge to evaluate lending practices, and are often preyed upon by unscrupulous lenders who are taking advantage of that lack of knowledge. In general terms, the industry refers to this as **predatory lending**. The Mortgage Bankers Association has identified 12 practices considered to be predatory. These are: (1) steering borrowers and buyers to high-rate lenders; (2) engaging in the practice of intentionally structuring high-cost loans with payments the borrower cannot afford; (3) falsifying loan documents; (4) making loans to mentally incapacitated homeowners; (5) forging signatures on loan documents; (6) changing the loan terms at closing; (7) requiring credit insurance; (8) falsely identifying loans as lines of credit or open-end mortgages; (9) increasing interest charges for loan payments when loan payments are late; (10) charging excessive prepayment penalties or excessive charges for preparing releases; (11) failing to report good payment on borrowers' credit reports; and (12) failing to provide accurate loan balance and payoff amounts, which includes not responding in a timely manner to credit inquiries for payoff information.

Coupled with the lending practices are shoddy appraisals made by unscrupulous appraisers to falsely inflate the value of the house. This allows a borrower to: (1) make no down payment, or (2) resell property shortly after closing for large profits to a "straw man" who will not make any payments on the loans. This practice is merely duping their lender into making too large a loan on the property because of these false appraisal practices. Most states are dealing with curbing this practice through state legislation against predatory lending and mortgage fraud. This is part of the mortgage fraud and credit crisis we are now experiencing. The FBI has stepped up its investigation of these practices.

Mortgage fraud almost always involves a conspiracy between a loan originator and an appraiser. Additional conspirators can include a buyer's broker (it can also be the mortgage broker), a title company, and the seller's real estate agent. An additional conspirator could be the purchaser of the loan in the secondary market who is encouraging loan originators to make loans as fast as possible so they can be sold to investors in the secondary market (discussed in Chapter 13). Many of these loans are sold with very little due diligence as to the quality of the borrower or credit scores. Let's talk about the potential fact situations.

THE FACT SITUATIONS

While not illegal on their face, "flip" closings have been blamed for a number of mortgage fraud transactions in which the title company was allegedly complicit, resulting in fines in the millions of dollars against various underwriters throughout the United States levied both by the Department of Housing and Urban Development and the State Department of Insurance. One cannot be too careful to note the "red flags," which can turn a seemingly simple transaction into active mortgage fraud against a lender.

THE "FLIP." In a "flip" transaction, the red flag uses a straw man established in the middle of the transaction. For instance, in an A to B to C transaction, B would be a mere nominee (phony company) who is buying at a low price from a legitimate seller, but selling at a much higher price to a buyer, either legitimate or another straw man. The fraud involved is a phony appraisal which reflects a property value much higher than its real sales price, and a loan application to a lender loaning far more than what the property is worth. The problem is that the sale from B to C has to close before the sale from A to B, so that funds are available to pay A. For instance, if there is a $400,000 initial sales price, and a $600,000 conveyance from B to C, the lender has to fund the $600,000 in order to get the $400,000 to pay A. The straw man (B) nets the $200,000. Under most computer programs the transaction is caught because you can't close the second transaction until the first transaction is closed (B is not in title yet). In an effort to appease the greed, however, the escrow officer may override the program or use no program at all (filling out the closing documents by hand). In this case, it's difficult to defend if a lender discovers the fraud. The escrow officer has to step out of standard office procedure in order to complete the transactions. If the A to B transaction closes at one title company, and the B to C transaction closes at another, it may be easier to juggle the timing, but the "conspiracy" net grows!

THE OLD SWITCH. In this mortgage fraud, the buyer and seller agree to change the sales price in the contract, and the seller kicks money back to the buyer at the closing. In this scenario, the house sells for $400,000, it appraises for $600,000, and the buyer then returns to the seller to ask that they increase the sales price to $600,000 so he can get the higher loan and pocket the difference. The seller then has to agree to kick back the excess proceeds to the buyer, either in cash or through a "soft second lien," which will never be repaid. Once again, we have a lender making a loan for more than the property is worth, putting money in the buyer's pocket, and destroying the loan-to-value ratio that the lender had anticipated. The problem with this scenario is that the seller is happy to do it, and the real estate broker is happy to do it, because the seller ultimately gets his agreed sales price and doesn't care that the buyer profits in the transaction. In addition to this, the seller and the broker make their sale! The buyer never makes one mortgage payment, and moves on to his next transaction.

THE CONTRACTOR'S SCHEME. In this scenario, the buyer, who is supposedly going to do a substantial amount of improvements to the property, gets a bid from a contractor (a straw company), and then pays that contractor at closing... who turns out to be the buyer. Using the previous example, there is a $400,000 purchase, a $200,000 home improvement, and a loan is based on the inflated $600,000 appraisal. There is no construction loan! The deal is closed and funded, the contractor turns out to be a front for the buyer, and no improvements are ever made. Again, the buyer never makes one mortgage payment, puts the money in his pocket, and moves on to the next transaction.

THE ULTIMATE LIE. In this scenario, there is a borrower who simply lies to the lender. At the closing, the lender provides his loan application which may include income tax returns, W-2s, paycheck stubs, and a number of other backup documents from the borrower's application. The problem is that the loan application information (submitted by the borrower earlier in the loan application process) turns out to be completely false. If the title company doesn't properly check picture identifications, or confirm signatures of the applicant and their spouse, it could be liable for aiding and abetting the fraudulent loan application process.

THE INNOCENT "INVESTOR." A smart mortgage broker encourages uninformed, first-time investors to invest in a home. He will set up the mortgage plan; he will get them a good price (often buying homes in bulk from a builder with a low sales volume); and he will help the new investor "get rich quick" by investing in real estate. Many of these investors are foreign and easily duped by a glib-tongued mortgage broker who is licensed by the state, and can apparently be trusted. The broker even pays the buyer $1,000.00, then sets up a "flip" transaction where the broker takes the money out of the middle and sets up a loan for the new investor who can't really afford to make the monthly payments. He often promises to lease the property and manage it for the investor, in order to make it an easy closing. After closing, when no tenants are obtained, the buyer determines that the loan broker made a significant amount of money on the transaction, and the investor can't afford to the make the monthly payments when no tenant can be found. The investor has been duped, but is personally liable for a significant mortgage loan.

"TRUST ME." In this scam, elderly or uninformed homeowners may be facing a foreclosure and, once again, are desperate for relief. In this fraud, the investor requests that the homeowners place the land in a trust with the investor (or investor's lackey) as a trustee, which gives the investor complete control over the ownership of the property. The owners may maintain a "beneficial" interest, or they may assign their beneficial interest to another investor in the trust. In almost every case, a third investor then takes complete control of the property, and the homeowner is unaware of the impact of signing these odd-looking documents. In the homeowners' minds, it has not triggered the "due on transfer" clause of their mortgage, and they trust the smooth-talking investor. After the homeowners can no longer pay the investor, keep up their lease payments, or whatever their relationship happens to be, the investor simply informs the homeowners that they no longer own the property and he is free to resell it at a profit, although he is happy to inform them that he has "saved their credit."

Believe it or not, there are seminars that teach people how to do this scam. Similar to the "Flip" scam, the entire transaction may be technically legal, with paperwork in apple-pie order, but the homeowner is duped with a wink and a nod.

IDENTITY THEFT. Another scheme has recently surfaced wherein the fraud perpetrator will search the real property records and find the name of somebody who is deceased, the name of a corporation or limited liability company (LLC), and they will assume the identity of the individual, the manager in charge of the LLC, or an officer of the corporation. During most closings, a simple check of identify is all that is required. It's amazing how far a fake driver's license can get you, particularly when closings are handled by mail or the perpetrator (always in a hurry) signs documents and leaves in a very short period of time. In one recent case, the perpetrator listed property, had their Realtor put a sign on it, sold it at a bargain sale price, and had a very quick closing. As it turned out, the real owner had no idea that the property was on the market, and certainly did not know that it was sold. When construction began, the real owner got upset and discovered that the perpetrator had assumed their identity, sold the property, took all of the money, and was now nowhere to be found. Title companies and escrow agents can be duped, just like anybody else.

FAKE CHECK/FAST CLOSING. Another new fraud issue which is becoming more common is the buyer who is usually out of state and often out of the country. They have immediate cash and want to close as fast as possible. He will frequently call an attorney or real estate broker indicating that because of his absence and frequent business travels, must close quickly. He forwards a cashier's check from an out of state bank to aid in the quick closing process. The buyer's representative (attorney or broker) proudly tenders the check to the title company as "certified funds" or a "cashier's check" to prove availability of funds to confirm the closing. The title company deposits the funds, closes the next day, and funds the sales price to the seller who promptly disappears with his cash.

The next day or so, the title company is informed that the cashier's check, in fact, was a fake cashier's check. There are no funds available and the title company has to cover the losses. This is a new "red flag." All cashier's checks, certified checks, and teller's checks, should be tendered to the drawee bank and confirmed the funds in the title company's account before completing the closing.

WHO'S LIABLE?

The fraud is typically uncovered when the buyer refuses to make any payments (or doesn't make one payment!) and the lender pursues foreclosure. If the lender is an investor, he may look to the loan originator as the fraudulent party for selling him a loan that the loan originator knew was for a bad (or maybe nonexistent) applicant. There is usually a pattern to these fraudulent transactions, and they can almost always be tied to a loan originator working in concert with an appraiser. The appraiser, however, only gives an opinion of value, and, therefore, it is hard to find liability with the appraiser, provided his opinion can be justified.

The real estate brokers may have some potential liability, particularly if the buyer's representative is also the loan broker. This tends to lead to conflicts of interest wherein a real estate broker loses a sale (and his share of the commission) if the buyer does not qualify for the loan. In situations where there is excess money being funded back to the buyer at the closing, there is a concern that both the buyer's broker and the seller's broker may have some liability if they "turn a blind eye" to an obvious fraud being committed on the lender because of over-inflated appraisals, suggested contract prices, or false debtor information. By the way, these issues are being criminally prosecuted as well as civilly prosecuted in the courts today.

The title company seems to be in the middle of everything! While the title company tends to be a disinterested third party, they are present when the closing takes place, when the instructions from the lender are tendered, and when the parties sign the documents. Remember though, that as a disinterested third party, they cannot take sides in representing one party against another, and courts have held that the traditionally fiduciary escrow duties are somewhat limited to the instructions of the parties, because the title company necessarily serves two conflicting parties. One bad case has arisen, however, wherein the court held that the title company was a fiduciary to all parties of the transaction and had a 100% duty of disclosure to all parties of the transaction.

Note the following list of "Red Flags":

- Investors making offers significantly above asking price, particularly on property which has been on the market for a long time

- Investor, buyer, or mortgage officers telling buyers that they can acquire appraisals in excess of the sales price

- Investors claiming property as their primary principal residence, which is to be owner occupied

---

CREATE YOUR OWN MARKET?

Mortgage fraud surfaced in Houston, Texas, involving several large condominium projects. One project had less than half the units sold. All of a sudden, two buyers started buying condominiums at above market prices, creating a "market" that raised the appraised values of those in several nearby projects. The conspirators recruited a 23-year-old single woman and supplied fraudulent employment and rental history documents enabling her to qualify for loans totaling $434,100 per unit. The title company (now defunct) transferred money to various accounts controlled by the two real estate investors. Surprisingly, they were all handled by the same mortgage company. How many red flags can you see? Two people engineered foreclosures for 60 properties. These foreclosures were not the result of a bad economy, nor people losing their jobs; it was mortgage fraud, pure and simple.

- Investors and/or sellers receiving excess sales proceeds after acquiring the property
- Use of for-sale-by-owner transactions to circumvent the use of real estate professionals
- Use of inexperienced or unsupervised licensees
- Undisclosed concessions at the closing table
- Not knowing the source or actual amount of the buyer's down payment, inflated appraisals, false information about the borrower's credit, and undisclosed rebates to an unknown third party
- Secret second mortgages, earnest money deposits paid outside of closing
- "Double contracting," closing the sale on one tract while closing the loan on the second, higher priced contract

When any of the foregoing become apparent, the advice is easy: Get out of the transaction. If you are an escrow officer, don't close the transaction. While one may forego a commission or a title insurance premium, it is a lot cheaper than what may be a cost of defense at a later date. If it doesn't "smell" right, or if information is being withheld from a lender during the closing, don't do it.

Vocabulary Review

Match terms a–f with statements 1–6.

a. Equity

b. Illiquid assets

c. Liquid assets

d. Redlining

e. Truth-in-Lending Act

f. Trigger term

_____ 1. The market value of a property less the debt against it.

_____ 2. A federal law that requires certain disclosures when extending or advertising credit.

_____ 3. Assets that may require months to sell and convert to cash.

_____ 4. Credit information used in advertising that requires additional credit disclosures.

_____ 5. Refusal to make a real estate loan based solely on the location of the property.

_____ 6. Assets that are in cash or are readily convertible to cash in a few days.

Questions and Problems

1. Why is the monthly income of a loan applicant more important to a lender than the sheer size of the applicant's assets?

2. What is the basic purpose of the Truth-in-Lending Act?

3. Will the annual percentage rate (APR) and interest rate reflected in the note be the same?

4. How does the Fair Credit Reporting Act help a borrower?

5. Why is a right of rescission important?

Additional Readings

"Creative Financing Can Facilitate Transaction Closings" by Jeff Wilder (*Hotel & Motel Management*, November 6, 1995, vol. 210, p. 30).

Fair Credit Reporting Act: Cumulative Supplement with Disk Update by the National Consumer Law Center (2000).

Getting and Keeping Credit: Your Guide to Credit Cards and Credit Reports by the American Bar Association (1996).

Real Estate Finance: Theory and Practice, 7th ed. by Terrence M. Clauretie and G. Stacy Sirmans (OnCourse Learning, 2014).

Residential Mortgage Lending, 6th ed. by Thomas Pinkowish (OnCourse Learning, 2012).

Sources of Financing

After reading this chapter, you will be able to: (1) identify various mortgage lenders (the primary market), (2) describe where these lenders get much of their money (the secondary market), and (3) explain provisions of mortgage loan instruments that have an impact on the cost of funds. Many people feel that understanding the financing market is the most important of all real estate topics because, without financing, real estate profits and commissions would be difficult to achieve.

Primary Market

The **primary market** (also called the *primary mortgage market*) is where lenders originate loans—that is, where lenders make funds available to borrowers. The primary market is what the borrower sees as the source of mortgage loan money, the institution with which the borrower has direct and personal contact. It's the place where the loan application is taken, where the loan officer interviews the loan applicant, where the loan check comes from, and the place where loan payments are sent by the borrower.

These sources of funds can generally be divided into two markets: (1) those markets regulated by the federal government, and (2) those markets that are not regulated by the government. The regulated lenders are commercial banks, savings and loan (S&L) associations, and savings banks. The nonregulated lenders are commercial finance companies, investment bankers, life insurance companies, and finance companies. Nonregulated sources of funds are not subject to the same restrictive regulations that are designed to protect the lender with deposits insured by the federal government. The regulated lenders are subject to

primary market
The market in which lenders originate loans and make funds available to borrowers.

examinations by federal regulators, pay risk-based premiums on their deposit insurance, and are restricted to certain loan-to-value ratios. In today's markets, a purchaser is wise to contact both regulated and nonregulated lenders to make an adequate comparison of available loan money. Markets differ widely within states and even within certain urban areas.

Most borrowers assume that the loan they receive comes from depositors who visit the same bank or S&L to leave their excess funds. This is partly true. But this, by itself, is an inadequate source of loan funds in today's market. Thus, primary lenders often sell their loans in what is called the secondary market. Insurance companies, pension funds, and individual investors, as well as other primary lenders with excess deposits, buy these loans for cash. This makes more money available to a primary lender who, in turn, can loan these additional funds to borrowers. The secondary market is so huge that it rivals the entire U.S. corporate bond market in size of annual offerings. We discuss the secondary market later in this chapter. Meanwhile, let's discuss the various lenders a borrower will encounter when looking for a real estate loan.

Savings and Loan Associations

Historically, the origin of *savings and loan associations* can be traced to early building societies in England and Germany, and to the first American building society, the Oxford Provident Building Association, started in 1831 in Pennsylvania. These early building societies were cooperatives whose savers were also borrowers. As times progressed, savings and loan associations became a primary source of residential real estate loans. To encourage residential lending, the federally chartered savings and loans were required by federal regulation to hold at least 80% of their assets in residential loans. In addition, they were subjected to special tax laws that permitted a savings and loan association to defer payment of income taxes on profits, so long as those profits were held in surplus accounts and not distributed to the savings and loan association's owners. During this same period, there were also limits on the interest rate that could be paid on savings accounts. This provided the savings and loan associations with a dependable source of funds at a fixed interest rate, which gave them the potential for making long-term loans at reasonable rates. For instance, if the passbook savings account was limited to 5.25% per annum, home loans in the vicinity of 7.5% to 8.5% would still allow for reasonable profit margins. Unfortunately, the nature of the finance markets began to change in the late 1970s when an inflationary economy caused interest rates to skyrocket. This created problems that were unforeseen by the savings and loan industry.

DISINTERMEDIATION

disintermediation

The result created when lenders are required to pay high rates of interest for deposits while receiving long-term income from low-interest rate mortgage loans.

In order to attract depositors, savings and loans offer, in addition to passbook accounts, **certificates of deposit (CDs)** at rates higher than passbook rates. These are necessary to compete with higher yields offered by U.S. Treasury bills, notes, and bonds and to prevent disintermediation. **Disintermediation** results when depositors take money out of their savings accounts and invest directly in government securities, corporate bonds, and money market funds. A major problem, and one that nearly brought the S&L industry to its knees in the late 1970s and early 1980s, was that S&Ls traditionally relied heavily on short-term deposits from savers, and then loaned that money on long-term (often 30-year) loans to borrowers. When interest rates rose sharply in the 1970s, S&Ls either had to raise the interest paid to their depositors or watch depositors withdraw their savings and take the money elsewhere for higher returns. Meanwhile, the S&Ls were holding long-term, fixed-rate mortgage loans, and, with interest rates rising, borrowers were not anxious to repay those loans early.

RESTRUCTURING THE SYSTEM

Disintermediation was only the beginning of the problems. Loan demand at S&Ls was declining. In 1976, 57% of the residential mortgage loans were held by savings and loan institutions. By 2000, the percentage fell to 13%. There are many reasons for this flow of funds out of the S&L industry. One of the primary reasons, however, appears to be the deregulation of the lending industry. This, coupled with bad investments, inadequately trained executives, and loose government controls on S&L risks and investments, resulted in an industry that could not remain solvent.

In August 1989, President George H. W. Bush signed into law a sweeping revision of the regulatory authorities governing savings and loans. This law is referred to as the *Financial Institutions Reform, Recovery, and Enforcement Act of 1989*, commonly called *FIRREA*. The law redefined or created seven new regulatory authorities and initiated a system of federally designated real property appraisers, discussed in greater detail in Chapter 18. Because federal regulations of commercial banks and savings and loans are virtually the same, the difference between savings and loans and commercial banks as a primary source of funds is indistinguishable to the average borrower.

Commercial Banks

The nation's *commercial banks* store far more of the country's money than the S&Ls. However, only one bank dollar in six goes to real estate lending. Of the loans made by banks for real estate, the tendency is to emphasize short-term maturities and adjustable rate mortgages because the bulk of a bank's deposit money comes from demand deposits (checking accounts), and a much smaller portion comes from savings and time deposits.

Oddly enough, the same factors that have plagued the S&Ls helped the commercial banks. During the Deregulation Acts of 1980 and 1982, banks began making more home loans, but they were short-term, with adjustable rates. These types of loans prevent the problem of disintermediation, as the loan rates can rise with the rates that are required by the source of funds. Commercial banks, too, have realized that first-lien residential loans are very secure, low-risk loans. Banks have also determined that maintaining all of a customer's loan accounts, including a home loan, in the bank's portfolio provides a market advantage. "One-stop banking" has become a very successful marketing tool. The merger of many banks into large multistate national banks has created a larger source of funds to lend. To accommodate higher demand and facilitate the organization of sources of funds for the bank's lending purposes, many banks have organized their own mortgage departments to assist customers in making home loans, even through sources other than bank deposits.

In 1999, Congress passed the Financial Services Modernization (FSM) bill, which lifted banking restrictions imposed by legislation dating back to 1933. The new legislation allows banks to become one-stop financial conglomerates marketing a range of financial products such as annuities, certificates of deposits, stocks, and bonds, creating a tremendous potential for cross-marketing in very large banks. This diversification may have a far-reaching impact on future banking practices, including the availability of mortgage money and other financial services to homeowners.

Life Insurance Companies

As a group, the nation's *life insurance companies* have long been active investors in real estate as developers, owners, and long-term lenders. Although not federally regulated, life insurance companies are subject to state regulations. Their source of money is the premiums paid by policyholders. These premiums are invested and ultimately returned to the policyholders. Because premiums are collected in regular amounts on regular dates and because policy payoffs can be calculated from actuarial tables, life insurers are in ideal positions to commit money to long-term investments. Life insurance companies channel their funds primarily into government and corporate bonds and real estate. The dollars allocated to real estate go to buy land and buildings, which are leased to users, and to make loans on commercial, industrial, and residential property. Generally, life insurers specialize in large-scale investments, such as shopping centers, office and apartment buildings, and million-dollar blocks of home loans purchased in the **secondary mortgage market**, which is discussed later in this chapter.

secondary mortgage market

A market in which mortgage loans can be sold to investors.

Repayment terms on loans made by insurance companies for shopping centers, office buildings, and apartment complexes sometimes call for interest and a percentage of any profits from rentals over a certain level. These **participation loans**, which provide a "piece of the action" for the insurance company, also provide the insurance company with more inflation protection than a fixed rate of interest.

Mortgage Companies

mortgage company

A firm that makes mortgage loans and then sells them to investors.

A **mortgage company** makes a mortgage loan and then sells it to a long-term investor. The process begins with locating borrowers, qualifying them, preparing the necessary loan papers, and, finally, making the loans. Once a loan is made, it is sold for cash on the secondary market. The mortgage company will usually continue to *service the loan*— that is, collect the monthly payments and handle such matters as insurance and property tax impounds, delinquencies, early payoffs, and mortgage releases.

Mortgage companies, also known as **mortgage bankers**, vary in size from one or two persons to several dozen. As a rule, they close loans in their own names and are locally oriented, finding and making loans within 25 or 50 miles of their offices. This gives them a feel for their market, greatly aids in identifying sound loans, and makes loan servicing much easier. For their efforts, mortgage bankers typically receive 1% to 3% of the amount of the loan when it is originated, and from one-fourth to one-half of 1% of the outstanding balance each year thereafter for servicing. Mortgage banking, as this business is called, is not limited to mortgage companies. Commercial banks, savings and loan associations, and mutual savings banks in active real estate areas often originate more real estate loans than they can hold themselves, and these are sold on the secondary market.

Mortgage Brokers

mortgage broker

One who brings together borrowers and lenders.

Mortgage brokers, in contrast to mortgage bankers, specialize in bringing together borrowers and lenders, just as real estate brokers bring together buyers and sellers. The mortgage broker does not lend money, and usually does not service loans. The mortgage broker's fee is expressed in points, and is usually paid by the borrower. Mortgage brokers are locally oriented, often small firms of 1 to 10 persons. They seldom make loans in their own names as lender.

The mortgage brokering businesses actually felt an explosion during the late 1980s and early 1990s. The secondary market (discussed later in this chapter) has made investors' funds more readily available, and virtually anyone with some expertise in loan qualifications can originate loans and sell to secondary market purchasers. As a result, the field became crowded with new loan originators, such as home builders, finance companies, commercial credit companies, insurance agents, attorneys, and real estate brokers. These have generally been considered nontraditional lenders, but they can originate mortgage loans with their own resources or, through various networks, have the loan funded directly to the secondary market purchaser. These new loan originators have offered substantial competition to regulated lenders. The proliferation of mortgage brokers has led to a number of cases of abuses, fraud, and predatory lending practices. Congress responded to these abuses by passing the federal Secure and Fair Enforcement (SAFE) for Mortgage Licensing Act of 2008. Under SAFE, a residential mortgage loan originator who is an employee or subsidiary of a depository institution must be registered with a federal banking agency having jurisdiction over that institution, and will be included in the Nationwide Mortgage Licensing System. A residential loan originator is defined as an individual who, for compensation or gain or any expectation of compensation or gain, takes a residential mortgage loan application or offers to negotiate the terms of a residential mortgage loan. All states have passed very similar state laws to assure compliance with the federal SAFE Act.

Municipal Bonds

In some cities, **municipal bonds** provide a source of mortgage money for home buyers. The special advantage to borrowers is that municipal bonds pay interest that is tax free from federal income taxes. Knowing this, bond investors will accept a lower rate of interest than they would if the interest were taxable—as it normally is on mortgage loans. This saving is passed on to the home buyer. Those who qualify will typically pay about 2% less than if they had borrowed through conventional channels.

The objective of such programs is to make home ownership more affordable for low- and middle-income households. Also, a city may stipulate that loans be used in neighborhoods the city wants to revitalize. The loans are made by local lenders who are paid a fee for originating and servicing these loans. Although popular with the real estate industry, the U.S. Treasury has been less than enthusiastic about the concept because it bears the cost in lost tax revenues. As a result, federal legislation has been passed to limit the future use of this source of money.

Other Lenders

Pension funds and *trust funds* traditionally have channeled their money to high-grade government and corporate bonds and stocks. However, the trend now is to place more money into real estate loans. Already active buyers on the secondary market, pension and trust funds will likely become a still larger source of real estate financing in the future. In some localities, pension fund members can tap their own pension funds for home mortgages at very reasonable rates. Pension funds are often an overlooked source of primary market financing.

Finance companies that specialize in making business and consumer loans also provide limited financing for real estate. As a rule, finance companies seek second mortgages at interest rates of 2% to 5% higher than the rates prevailing on first mortgages. First mortgages are also taken as collateral; however, the lenders already discussed usually charge lower interest rates for these loans and thus are more competitive.

Credit unions normally specialize in consumer loans. However, real estate loans are becoming more and more important as many of the country's credit unions have branched out into first and second mortgage loans. Credit unions are an often overlooked but excellent source of home loan money.

Commercial finance companies also have entered the mortgage lending fields. These are private companies, such as General Electric Capital Mortgage Corporation, General Motors Acceptance Corporation, and Ford Motor Company, which are subject to neither banking restrictions nor deposit insurance regulations. They are becoming a more widely used source of finance money, particularly in affordable housing loans, discussed in the next chapter.

Individuals are sometimes a source of cash loans for real estate, with the bulk of these loans made between relatives or friends, often as investments with their IRAs or private pension plans that require a low-risk investment with attractive rates. Generally, loan maturities are shorter than those obtainable from the institutional lenders already described. In some cities, persons can be found who specialize in making or buying second and third mortgage loans of up to 10-year maturities. Individuals are also beginning to invest substantial amounts of money in secondary mortgage market securities. Ironically, these investments are often made with money that would have otherwise been deposited in a savings and loan.

Computerized Loan Origination

computerized loan origination

Originating loans through the use of a networked computer system.

The growth of computer networks has also enabled many independent loan processors to work under the guidance of large lending institutions and mortgage companies. Using a **computerized loan origination (CLO)**, real estate brokers, attorneys, insurance agents, or mortgage companies can arrange to have a computer link installed in their offices, connected to lenders' mainframe computers. By utilizing a series of questions, borrowers can obtain preliminary loan approval immediately from the loan originator, with a firm acceptance or rejection from the lending institution within a few days.

A full-featured CLO has three basic functions: (1) It provides information on current mortgage loan terms and loan types available on the market, (2) it conveys loan application information electronically, and (3) it monitors the loan approval process so that the practitioner can check on the progress of the loan application at any time. From the home buyer's perspective, the CLO provides the convenience of seeking home financing alternatives without calling and visiting a large number of local lenders, and in many cases it can increase the number of choices available. However, a broker should exercise caution, as conflicts can exist.

Secondary Market

The *secondary market* (also called the *secondary mortgage market*) provides a way for a lender to sell a loan. It also permits investment in real estate loans without the need for loan origination and servicing facilities. Although not directly encountered by real estate buyers, sellers, and agents, the secondary market plays an important role in getting money from those who want to lend to those who want to borrow. In other words, think of the secondary market as a pipeline for loan money. Visualize that pipeline running via the Wall Street financial district in New York City, as Wall Street is now a major participant in residential mortgage lending. Figure 13.1 illustrates this pipeline, and diagrams key differences between the traditional mortgage delivery system and the secondary market system.

TRADITIONAL DELIVERY SYSTEM

Notice in Figure 13.1 that, in the traditional system, the lender is a local institution gathering deposits from the community and then lending that money as real estate loans in the same community. Traditionally, each lender (S&L bank, commercial bank, credit

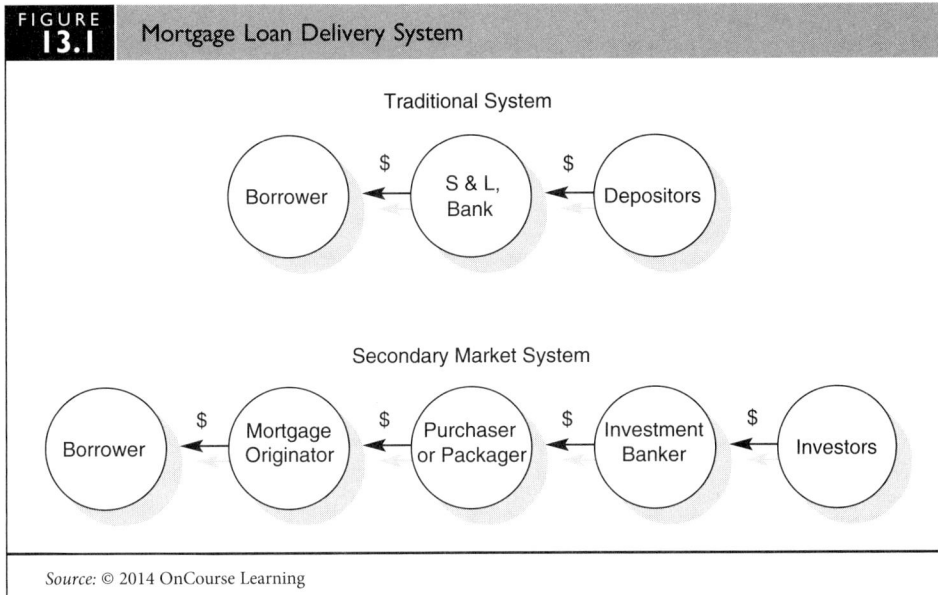

FIGURE 13.1 Mortgage Loan Delivery System

Traditional System

Borrower ← \$ ← S & L, Bank ← \$ ← Depositors

Secondary Market System

Borrower ← \$ ← Mortgage Originator ← \$ ← Purchaser or Packager ← \$ ← Investment Banker ← \$ ← Investors

Source: © 2014 OnCourse Learning

union) was an independent unit that developed its own appraisal technique, loan application form, loan approval criteria, note and mortgage forms, servicing method, and foreclosure policy. Nonetheless, three major problems needed solving. The first occurred when an institution had an imbalance of depositors and borrowers. Rapidly growing areas of the United States often needed more loan money than their savers were capable of depositing. Stable regions had more depositors than loan opportunities. Thus, it was common to see correspondent relationships between lenders; for example, a lender in Los Angeles would sell some of its mortgage loans to a savings bank in Brooklyn. This provided loans for borrowers and interest for savers. The system worked well, but required individual correspondent relationships.

The second problem occurred when depositors wanted to withdraw money from their accounts and invest it in other sources. Lenders, seeking to attract these depositors, raised the interest rates, which resulted in increase in loan rates. The third problem was timing. Lenders borrowed "short" (from their deposit relationships) and lent "long" (30-year mortgages). Savers, then, were encouraged to leave their money on deposit for longer periods of time.

The answer to these three problems is relatively simple: Find a market to sell your loans to investors who will pay cash for them and reimburse the primary lender. The result, then, is that there is an investor who is willing to hold the loan long term for its guaranteed rate of return. The primary lender continues to make loans, gambling that he will find another investor in the secondary market to buy that loan for a long term. In effect, the primary lenders can make loans from the secondary market funds instead of their own deposits.

SECONDARY MARKET DELIVERY SYSTEMS

As shown in Figure 13.1, with the secondary market system the borrower obtains a loan from a mortgage originator in the primary market. The mortgage originator packages the loan with other loans, and then either sells the package as a whole or keeps the package and sells securities that are backed by the loans in the package. If the originator is not large enough to package its own mortgages, it will sell the loans to someone who can.

There are now two sources for this secondary market. The first is private investors such as commercial banks, savings and loans, pension plans, trust funds, and other investors who are looking for low-risk, long-term returns on their investments. The second group of investors, relatively new in the investment business, is the investment "pools" or "poolers" who are looking for more security in their investments. This results in two primary investors in the secondary market: (1) the pure portfolio purchasers, who are looking for the initial investments with an attractive return, and (2) the "poolers," who are looking for the longer term, more stable return.

STANDARDIZED LOAN PROCEDURES

A major stumbling block to a highly organized and efficient secondary market has been the uniqueness of both lenders and loans. Traditionally, each primary lender developed its own special loan forms and procedures. Moreover, each loan is a unique combination of real estate and borrower. No two are exactly alike. How do you package such diversity into an attractive package for investors? A large part of the answer has come through standardized loan application forms; standardized appraisal forms; standardized credit report forms; standardized closing statements; standardized loan approval criteria; and standardized promissory notes, mortgages, and trust deeds. Loan terms have been standardized into categories, for example, fixed-rate, 30-year loans; fixed-rate, 15-year loans; and various adjustable rate combinations. Nearly all loans must be insured. This can take the form of Federal Housing Administration (FHA) or private mortgage insurance, or a Veterans Affairs (VA) guarantee on each loan in the package. Additionally, there must be some form of assurance of timely repayment of the mortgage package as a whole. The net result is a mortgage security that is attractive to investors who in the past have not been interested in investing in mortgages.

Let's now look at some of the key secondary market participants including the giants of the industry: the Federal National Mortgage Association, the Government National Mortgage Association, the Federal Home Loan Mortgage Corporation, and Farmer Mac, and their oversight agencies.

OFHEO

In the early 1990s, there was a growing concern about the liquidity and self-regulation of the government-sponsored entities in the secondary market. The **Office of Federal Housing Enterprise Oversight (OFHEO)** was established as an independent entity within the Department of Housing and Urban Development. Its purpose is to ensure the capital adequacy and financial soundness of Fannie Mae and Freddie Mac, to ensure that both comply with the public purposes set forth in their charters, and to exercise regulatory authority over them. It examines them using a risk-based capital standard and makes quarterly findings of capital adequacy. In exchange for carrying out these public purposes, Fannie Mae and Freddie Mac are given various privileges that provide them with some benefits not available to other private corporations. These benefits include an exemption from state and local taxes (except property taxes) and conditional access to a $2.2 billion line of credit from the U.S. Treasury Department. With these benefits, they are able to fund their operations at lower costs than other private firms with similar financial characteristics. OFHEO also requires Fannie Mae and Freddie Mac to meet certain affordable housing goals set annually by the secretary of HUD to purchase low-income, moderate-income, and central-city homes.

The credit profile of FNMA and FHLMC fell in 2006 and 2007. In the first half of 2007, roughly one-third of their new loans were composed of mortgages that had less than standard documentation, interest-only, or Option ARM products, and mortgages with multiple risk characteristics.

As a result of the perceived increase in risk for investors in FNMA and FHLMC, the Federal Housing Financing Agency (FHFA) was created by merging the Federal Housing Finance Board (FHFB) with OFHEO. This created an expanded legal and regulatory authority as part of the Federal Housing Finance Regulatory Reform Act of 2008.

Investors who had traditionally bought FNMA and FHLMC certificates ceased doing so. On September 7, 2008, the FHFA director put FNMA and FHLMC under the conservatorship of the FHFA, and FHFA is now managing both FNMA and FHLMC until they are stabilized. Congress has appropriated funds up to $700 billion to purchase these securities to prop up the liquidity of both Fannie Mae and Freddie Mac. What follows is a discussion of Fannie Mae and Freddie Mac's traditional roles in the secondary and investment markets. However, there may be big changes ahead.

FNMA

The **Federal National Mortgage Association (FNMA)** was organized by the federal government in 1938 to buy FHA mortgage loans from lenders. This made it possible for lenders to grant more loans to consumers. Ten years later it began purchasing VA loans. FNMA (fondly known in the real estate business and to itself as **Fannie Mae**) was successful in its mission.

In 1968, Congress divided the FNMA into two organizations: the Government National Mortgage Association (to be discussed in the next section) and the FNMA, as we know it today. As part of that division, the FNMA changed from a government agency to a private profit-making corporation, chartered by Congress but owned by its shareholders and managed independently of the government. Some 60 million shares of Fannie Mae stock are in existence, and it is one of the most actively traded issues on the New York Stock Exchange. Fannie Mae buys FHA, VA, and conventional whole loans from lenders across the United States. Money to buy these loans comes from the sale of FNMA stock plus the sale of FNMA bonds and notes. FNMA bond and note holders look to Fannie Mae for timely payment of principal and interest on these bonds and notes, and Fannie Mae looks to its mortgagors for principal and interest payments on the loans it owns. Thus, Fannie Mae stands in the middle and, although it is very careful to match interest rates and maturities between the loans it buys and the bonds and notes it sells, it still takes the risk of the middleman. In this respect, it is like a giant thrift institution.

fannie mae
A real estate industry nickname for the Federal National Mortgage Association.

COMMITMENTS. Fannie Mae's method of operation is to sell commitments to lenders pledging to buy specified dollar amounts of mortgage loans within a fixed period of time and usually at a specified yield. Lenders are not obligated to sell loans to Fannie Mae if they can find better terms elsewhere. However, Fannie Mae must purchase all loans delivered to it under the terms of the commitments. Loans must be made using FNMA-approved forms and loan approval criteria. The largest loan Fannie Mae bought in 2011 was $729,750 for a single-family unit. In 2013, the largest loan amount was $625,500. This limit is adjusted each year as housing prices change. Fannie Mae also buys loans on duplexes, triplexes, and fourplexes all at larger loan limits. Although the FNMA loan limit may seem inadequate for some houses and neighborhoods, the intention of Congress is that Fannie Mae cater to the mid-range of housing prices and leave the upper end of the market to others.

In addition to purchasing first mortgages, Fannie Mae also purchases second mortgages from lenders. The loan limit for second mortgages as of 2012 was $208,500. FNMA forms and criteria must be followed and the loan-to-value ratio of the combined first and second mortgages cannot exceed 80% if owner-occupied and 70% if not owner-occupied. This is a very helpful program for those who have watched the value of their homes increase and want to borrow against that increase without first having to repay the existing mortgage loan. Updates on these loan limits are available on their Web site, **www.fanniemae.com**.

FNMA POOLING. The demand for loans in the primary market could not match the demand that investors required in the secondary market, so Fannie Mae began purchasing large blocks of mortgage loans, and then assigned them to specified pools with an "agency guarantee" certificate that guaranteed long-term return to the pool investors. Fannie Mae guarantees to pass through to the certificate holders whatever principal, interest, and prepayments of principal are generated by the loans into the underlying pool of mortgage investors. Fannie Mae's pooling arrangements undertook the issuance of **mortgage-backed securities (MBS)**. Utilizing this system of issuing securities that are backed by mortgages, the securities markets could then be used as a source for investment funds. In the third quarter of 2007, Fannie Mae held $2,081 billion of loans in portfolio investments. At the same time, however, Fannie Mae had underwritten $2,094 billion in mortgage pools, totaling 21% of all single-family residential loans. This is also a strong indication that the government-guaranteed loan pools provide a much better procedure for making funds available in the secondary market. This, in turn, assures funds are available for the primary market's long-term mortgage loans to individual home purchasers.

HOME SELLER PROGRAM. Another innovation of Fannie Mae to help real estate is the **home seller program**. This is a secondary market for sellers who carry back mortgages. To qualify, the note and mortgage must be prepared by a FNMA-approved lender using standard FNMA loan-qualification procedures. The note and mortgage may be kept by the home seller as an investment or sold to a FNMA-approved lender for possible resale to the FNMA.

In other developments, Fannie Mae has standardized the terms of adjustable rate mortgages it will purchase. This is a major step forward in reducing the proliferation of variety in these loans. Fannie Mae is also test marketing mortgage-backed securities in $1,000 increments to appeal to individual investors, particularly for Individual Retirement Accounts. Additionally, Fannie Mae has started a collateralized mortgage obligation program and begun a mortgage pass-through program, both of which will be defined momentarily.

REVISED LENDING PRACTICES. In 1992, as pressure increased from both Congress and the U.S. Department of Housing and Urban Development to become more socially responsible in lending practices, Congress passed legislation requiring stricter supervision of Fannie Mae by a HUD-appointed oversight committee. In March 1994, Fannie Mae announced a plan to provide one trillion dollars in financing over the rest of the decade to poor families, rural communities, and disabled people. Fannie Mae now cooperates with others to facilitate loans for low- to moderate-income borrowers in the purchase of 97% conventional loans and flexible mortgages, working with local housing authorities, nonprofit associations, nonprofit housing groups, and private mortgage insurance, to spread the risk of some of these loans. Fannie Mae has also very aggressively adopted practices to provide affordable housing and prevent fraud in real estate loan transactions, discussed in the next chapter under Affordable Housing Loans.

This oversight, being Congressional, became political. The pressure to help the poor created a much higher risk loan portfolio that contributed heavily to predatory lending practices, resulting in foreclosures, and the mortgage crisis.

FHLMC

The **Federal Home Loan Mortgage Corporation** (**FHLMC**, also known to the industry and to itself as **Freddie Mac** or the "Mortgage Corporation") was created by Congress in 1970. Its goal, like that of the FNMA and GNMA, is Freddie Mac was initially established to serve as a secondary market for S&L members of the Federal Home Loan Bank System. The ownership of Freddie Mac was originally held by more than 3,000 savings associations. In 1988, the shares were released and sold publicly by the savings associations. Unlike Ginnie Mae, which guarantees securities issued by others, Freddie Mac issues its own securities against its own mortgage pools. These securities are its participation certificates and collateralized mortgage obligations. By the third quarter of 2007, Freddie Mac held nearly $1,637 billion in its own loan portfolio, accounting for almost 15% (including FHLMC pools) of all outstanding loans in residential lending.

freddie mac

A real estate industry nickname for the Federal Home Loan Mortgage Corporation to increase the availability of financing for residential mortgages. Where FHLMC differs is that Freddie Mac deals primarily in conventional mortgages.

PARTICIPATION CERTIFICATES. Participation certificates (PCs) allow a mortgage originator to deliver to Freddie Mac either whole mortgages or part interest in a pool of whole mortgages. In return, Freddie Mac gives the mortgage originator a PC representing an undivided interest in a pool of investment-quality conventional mortgages created from mortgages and mortgage interests purchased by Freddie Mac. Freddie Mac guarantees that the interest and principal on these PCs will be repaid in full and on time, even if the underlying mortgages are in default. (Freddie Mac reduces its losses by setting strict loan qualification criteria and requiring mortgage insurance on high loan-to-value loans.) The PCs can be kept as investments, sold for cash, or used as collateral for loans. PCs are popular investments for S&Ls, pension funds, and other institutional investors looking for high-yield investments. Individuals who can meet the $25,000 minimum also find PCs attractive. Freddie Mac also has a collateralized mortgage obligation program and plans to offer a trust for investments in mortgages. Both of these programs are designed to deal with the unpredictability of mortgage maturities caused by early repayment by dividing the cash flows from a mortgage pool into separate securities with separate maturities, which are then sold to investors.

participation certificate

A certificate representing an undivided interest in a Freddie Mac pool.

As with Fannie Mae, Congress and HUD provide the oversight committee to Freddie Mac. New guidelines provided by HUD call for both Freddie Mac and Fannie Mae to purchase about 30% of their mortgages in inner-city areas and from lower-income home buyers. Is it wise to make loans to those who can't repay them?

GNMA

The **Government National Mortgage Association** (**GNMA**, popularly known to the industry and to itself as **Ginnie Mae**) was created in 1968 when the FNMA was partitioned into two separate corporations. Ginnie Mae is a federal agency entirely within the HUD. Although Ginnie Mae has some low-income housing functions, it is best known for its mortgage-backed securities (MBS) program. Previously discussed, the MBS program attracts additional sources of credit to FHA, VA, and certain Rural Housing Service mortgages. Ginnie Mae does this by guaranteeing timely repayment of privately issued securities backed by pools of these mortgages. Remember that the FNMA

MBS program offers "agency guarantees" for their investors. GNMA offers a government guarantee of repayment, backed by the full faith and credit of the U.S. government.

GINNIE MAE PROCEDURES. Ginnie Mae is limited to underwriting only HUD/ FHA, VA, and certain other loans. It is not possible to purchase loans as both FNMA and FHLMC (discussed next). Ginnie Mae sets its own requirements for loans that can be accepted into their mortgage pool, then it subsequently approves loan poolers who are committed to comply with those requirements. Ginnie Mae must examine the loans and the loan poolers before it can determine its ability to guarantee those loans into the loan pooler source of funds.

The result is that Ginnie Mae issues guarantee certificates, popularly known as "Ginnie Maes." By the fourth quarter of 2012, Ginnie Maes accounted for 12.7% of all residential loans. A Ginnie Mae certificate carries the equivalent of a U.S. government bond guarantee and pays the holder of those certificates, the loan pooler, an interest rate of 1% to 1.5% higher than that of a government bond.

FARMER MAC

The newest agency created by Congress to underwrite loan pools is the Federal Agricultural Mortgage Corporation, known as "Farmer Mac." The Agricultural Credit Act of 1987 established Farmer Mac as a separate agency within the Farm Credit System to establish the secondary market needed for farm real estate loans. Farmer Mac started actual operations in 1989.

Originally, Farmer Mac functioned similarly to Ginnie Mae in that it certified loan poolers rather than purchase loans. Farmer Mac guaranteed timely repayment of principal and interest in the loan pool, but did not guarantee any individual loans within that pool.

In 1996, Congress passed the *Farm Credit System Reform Act* allowing Farmer Mac to act as a pooler for qualified loans. Farmer Mac is now permitted to purchase loans directly from originators and to issue its own 100% guaranteed securities backed by the loans. For the first time, Farmer Mac became a true secondary market. By the fourth quarter of 2012, Farmer Mac held $12 billion in its portfolio, a huge increase since 2007.

LOAN QUALIFICATION

To qualify for a Farmer Mac pool, a loan must be collateralized by agricultural real estate located in the United States. The real estate can include a home, which can cost no more than $100,000, and must be located in a rural community with a population of 2,500 or less. The maximum loan is $2.5 million or the amount secured by no more than 1,000 acres, whichever is larger. The loan-to-value ratio must be less than 80%, and the borrower must be a U.S. citizen engaged in agriculture and must demonstrate a capability to repay the loan.

PRIVATE CONDUITS

The financial success of the three giants of the secondary mortgage market (FNMA, GNMA, and FHLMC) has brought private mortgage packagers into the marketplace. The 1990s saw substantial growth in commercial loan fundings for the sale of mortgage bank securities, called **Commercial Mortgage-Backed Securities (CMBS)**.

Organizations that handle CMBS are called **conduits**, which originate commercial and multifamily housing loans for purposes of pooling them as collateral for the issuance of Commercial Mortgage Backed Securities, rather than holding them in the lender's own portfolio. Conduits are often subsidiaries of commercial banks and security firms that participate loans out to other banks or private investment sources. It is effectively a commercial secondary market without government support, and has been very successful in generating fund availability for commercial projects.

These are organizations such as MGIC Investment Corporation (a subsidiary of Mortgage Guaranty Investment Corporation); Residential Funding Corporation (a subsidiary of Norwest Mortgage Corp.); financial subsidiaries of such household-name companies as General Electric, Lockheed Aircraft, Bear Sterns, Lehman Brothers, and Sears, Roebuck; and mortgage packaging subsidiaries of state REALTOR® associations. These organizations both compete with the big three and specialize in markets not served by them, including commercial lending markets. For example, Residential Funding Corp. will package mortgage loans as large as $500,000, well above the limits imposed by FNMA and FHLMC and on FHA and VA loans. All of these organizations will buy from loan originators who are not large enough to create their own pools.

The entry of these private investment sources into the single-family residential market was initially met with great success as it created an entirely new secondary market for first lien purchase money home loans and a tremendous source of new investment funds. It encouraged substantial growth in the housing market with easy to obtain attractive loans for homeowners, particularly first-time homeowners. The new source of funds enabled more funds to be available at lower cost, and enabled many homeowners to move into a home with mortgage payments cheaper than the rent they were paying in their existing apartment. By the third quarter of 2007, the private mortgage conduits held $2,179 billion, or 19.76% of the one- to four-family loans. This is an increase of 192% from 2003. The credit crisis has adjusted this significantly, with conduits totalling only $1,523 billion, or 15.35% of the one- to four-family loans.

There is a downside to the market, however. Many loans were made to borrowers who couldn't really qualify for the loans. In many cases, encouraging new home loans also led to predatory lending practices and mortgage fraud, as a lot of these private conduits didn't properly monitor the quality of the loans that were being made in the primary market and didn't exercise proper due diligence in managing the loan portfolio. This is a major factor in our "credit crisis" or "mortgage crisis" that the government is now dealing with.

COMPUTERIZATION

Before leaving the topic of the secondary market, it is important to note that, without electronic data transmission and computers, the programs just described would be severely handicapped. There are currently thousands of mortgage pools, each containing from $1 million to $500 million (and more) in mortgage loans. Each loan in a pool has its own monthly payment schedule, and each payment must be broken down into its principal and interest components, and any property tax and insurance impounds. Computers do this work, as well as issue receipts and late notices. The pool, in turn, will be owned by several dozen to a hundred or more investors, each with a different fractional interest in the pool. Once a month, incoming mortgage payments are tallied, a small fee is deducted for the operation of the pool, and the balance is allotted among the investors—all by computer. A computer also prints and mails checks to investors and provides them with an accounting of the pool's asset level.

MORTGAGE CRISIS

We have all read about the mortgage crisis and credit crunch in the nation's economy. At least one scholar[*] has noted a pattern to these crises. The crises always occur after a booming economic climate. This climate creates a "rush to invest" mentality. The lending system responds with easy loan requirements to support the growth. While optimism prevails, old restraints (such as the appraisal requirements imposed during the last crisis in the 1980s) are overlooked or ignored as inconvenient obstacles for those who point out the historical reality of the boom-to-crisis cycle. In every case, existing safeguards do not prevent the problem. In the most recent market crisis, the secondary market investment vehicles became major players with virtually no regulation. This also moved beyond national borders to credit markets in Europe and South America. Safeguards in American markets cannot be effective, and historically the cycle again returns. Civil and criminal lawsuits follow, and new regulations (RESPA and new Truth-in-Lending requirements) are put in place by both federal and state legislatures to create new stability in the marketplace. When the stability returns, the economy booms,... and it may start all over again!

[*]Charles E. Gilliland, Research Economist for the Texas Real Estate Center

---

Automated Underwriting Systems

The computer age has introduced a whole new system in underwriting procedures as they apply to the relationship between the loan originator and the investor (secondary market). In the "old days," underwriting guidelines would be published and circulated to the primary lenders weekly. As interest rates began to fluctuate wildly in the 1970s, the sheet was updated and circulated more often. In some real estate offices, one person was given the job of calling lenders daily for quotes on loan availability and interest rates.

The entire process is being overhauled by a computerized mortgage loan underwriting system with the introduction of Freddie Mac's Loan Prospector program, which was made available on the Internet in 1999. At this time, the program is limited to Freddie Mac's approved sellers and servicers. This process is very streamlined. The regular uniform residential loan application is submitted to the lender and the lender then verifies the applicant's employment, income, and assets. This information is fed into the computer and is promptly analyzed by the computer program. If the borrower is accepted and if the loan-to-value ratio is greater than 80%, the application is then forwarded to a private mortgage insurer. Those that are not accepted are considered as "refer" or "caution." Those classified as "refer" are sent to the underwriting department with at least four reasons stating why the loan is referred. The "caution" category indicates that there are serious issues preventing the loan's purchase. The real estate can be appraised and a loan completely processed in as little as two hours if the lender requests an "expedited" appraisal. A nonexpedited appraisal can take less than 72 hours. Freddie Mac reports that about 60% of all applicants can be accepted in four minutes. It is anticipated that by using this streamlined program, the cost of processing the loan is cut in half.

FNMA now has its own software programs, also available on the Internet, called Desktop Originator/Desktop Underwriter (DO/DU) Government Underwriting Service (used by a broker or practitioner to submit information to a lender) and DO/DU (used by a lender to submit the application directly to FNMA). As with the Freddie Mac program, responses can be confirmed in seconds. In mid-2001, the mortgage banking industry agreed to adopt automated underwriting standards set by the mortgage bankers association known as MISMO (Mortgage Industry Standards Maintenance

Organization). It is expected that the use of a common automated underwriting standard will simplify the electronic mortgage application process and reduce the cost. Both Fannie Mae and Freddie Mac have agreed to adopt the standard.

The **automated underwriting system** specifications consist of a data dictionary and a document type definition, plus a set of rules used to build an extensible markup language (EML) file for the underwriting request. This will enable all lenders to send the same "base" data file to both Fannie Mae and Freddie Mac for an underwriting decision.

In October 2004, Fannie Mae introduced several enhancements to the DO/DU service to help lenders identify and stop fraud in mortgage transactions before the loan is closed. The new program includes a standardized property address implementation to determine if there are matches to addresses or similar addresses for potential loan applicants, which helps develop a potential "red flag." Red flags consist of inconsistent or contradictory loan data (usually fraudulent appraisals) in a given neighborhood. This new program, in an attempt to prevent identity theft, also determines matches for Social Security numbers.

> **automated underwriting system**
> Computerized system for loan approval communication between a loan originator and the investor.

Availability and Price of Mortgage Money

Thus far we have been concerned with the money pipelines between lenders and borrowers. Ultimately, though, money must have a source. These sources are savings generated by individuals and businesses, as a result of their spending less than they earn (**real savings**), and government-created money, called **fiat money** or "printing press money." This second source does not represent unconsumed labor and materials; instead, it competes for available goods and services alongside the savings of individuals and businesses.

In the arena of money and capital, real estate borrowers must compete with the needs of government, business, and consumers. Governments, particularly the federal government, compete the hardest when they borrow to finance a deficit. Not to borrow would mean bankruptcy, and the inability to pay government employees and provide government programs and services. Strong competition also comes from business and consumer credit sectors. In the face of such strong competition for loan funds, home buyers must either pay higher interest or be outbid.

One "solution" to this problem is for the federal government to create more money, thus making competition for funds easier and interest rates lower. Unfortunately, the net result is often too much money chasing too few goods, and prices are pulled upward by the demand caused by the newly created money. This is followed by rising interest rates as savers demand higher returns to compensate for losses in purchasing power. Many economists feel that the higher price levels and interest rates of the 1970s resulted from applying too much of this "solution" to the economy since 1965. In recent years, we started the fiat money idea again. The government has pumped over $800 billion into the economy by borrowing it. Inflation is sure to follow.

The alternative solution, from the standpoint of residential loans, is to increase real savings or decrease competing demands for available money. A number of plans and ideas have been put forth by civic, business, and political leaders. They include proposals to simplify income taxes and balance the federal budget, incentives to increase productive output, and incentives to save money in retirement accounts. These ideas are not inflationary. The resolution to these conflicts, unfortunately are now mired in politics, not education, or sound fiscal policy.

Usury

An old idea that has been tried, but is of dubious value for holding down interest rates, is legislation to impose interest rate ceilings. Known as **usury** laws and found in nearly all states, these laws were originally enacted to prohibit lenders from overcharging interest on loans to individuals. Most states raised usury limits in response to higher interest rates. Additionally, the U.S. Congress passed legislation in 1980 that exempts from state usury limits most first-lien home loans made by institutional lenders. Low interest rates and the availability of funds have made loans so competitive that usury is not much of an issue anymore.

Price to the Borrower

Ultimately, the rate of interest the borrower must pay to obtain a loan is dependent on the cost of money to the lender, reserves for default, loan servicing costs, and available investment alternatives. For example, go to a savings institution and see what they are paying depositors on various accounts. To this add 2% for the cost of maintaining cash in the tills, office space, personnel, advertising, free gifts for depositors, deposit insurance, loan servicing, loan reserves for defaults, and a ½% profit margin. This gives you an idea of how much borrowers must be charged.

Life insurance companies, pension funds, and trust funds do not have to "pay" for their money as do thrift institutions. Nonetheless, they do want to earn the highest possible yields, with safety, on the money in their custody. Thus, if a real estate buyer wants to borrow in order to buy a home, the buyer must compete successfully with the other investment opportunities available on the open market. To determine the rate for yourself, look at the yields on newly issued corporate bonds as shown in the financial section of your daily newspaper. Add one-half of 1% to this for the extra work in packaging and servicing mortgage loans, and you will have the interest rate home borrowers must pay to attract lenders.

Due-on-Sale

From an investment risk standpoint, when a lender makes a loan with a fixed interest rate, the lender recognizes that during the life of the loan interest rates may rise or fall. When they rise, the lender remains locked into a lower rate. Most loans contain a *due-on-sale clause* (also called an **alienation clause** or a *call clause*). In the past, these were inserted by lenders so that if the borrower sold the property to someone considered uncreditworthy by the lender, the lender could call the loan balance due. When interest rates increase, though, lenders can use these clauses to increase the rate of interest on the loan when the property changes hands by threatening to accelerate the balance of the loan unless the new owner accepts a higher rate of interest.

Prepayment

If loan rates drop, it becomes worthwhile for a borrower to shop for a new loan and repay the existing one in full. To compensate, loan contracts sometimes call for a **prepayment penalty** in return for giving the borrower the right to repay the loan early. A typical prepayment penalty amounts to the equivalent of six months interest on the amount that is being paid early. However, the penalty varies from loan to loan and from state to state. Some loan contracts permit up to 20% of the unpaid balance to be paid in any one year without penalty. Other contracts make the penalty stiffest when the loan is young. In certain states, laws do not permit prepayment penalties on loans more than five years old. By federal law, prepayment penalties are not allowed on FHA and VA loans.

Vocabulary Review

Match terms a–j with statements 1–10.

a. Automated underwriting systems

b. Computerized loan origination

c. Due-on-sale clause

d. Fannie Mae

e. Mortgage company

f. Mortgage-backed securities

g. Participation certificates

h. Prepayment penalty

i. Secondary mortgage market

j. Usury

_____ 1. Securities issued, backed by the mortgages securing the loans and the full faith of the federal government.

_____ 2. Requires immediate repayment of the loan if ownership transfers; also called an alienation clause.

_____ 3. A market where mortgage loans can be sold to investors.

_____ 4. A firm that makes mortgage loans and then sells them to investors.

_____ 5. A lending industry name for the Federal National Mortgage Association.

_____ 6. A certificate representing an undivided interest in a Freddie Mac pool.

_____ 7. Charging a rate of interest higher than that permitted by law.

_____ 8. Penalty charged for paying a loan off prior to maturity.

_____ 9. Computerized communication systems for loan approval between a loan originator and the investor.

_____ 10. Originating loans through the use of a networked computer system.

Questions and Problems

1. What is the most significant difference between a mortgage broker and a mortgage banker?

2. In the secondary mortgage market, who provides the loan money?

3. What is meant by the term *loan servicing*?

4. By what financing methods do FNMA and GNMA provide money for real estate loans?

5. If a dollar is a dollar no matter where it comes from, what difference does it make if the source of a real estate loan was real savings or fiat money?

6. Why are the secondary market pooling arrangements successful?

Additional Readings

Keys to Mortgage Financing and Refinancing by Jack P. Friedman and Jack C. Harris (Barron's Educational Series, 4th ed., 2006).

"Meet Fannie and Freddie" by Mike Fickes (*National Real Estate Investor*, June 2001).

Real Estate Finance, 9th ed. by John Wiedemer and J. Keith Baker (OnCourse Learning, 2013).

"Structural Change in the Mortgage Market and the Propensity to Refinance" by Paul Bennett, et al. (*Journal of Money, Credit & Banking*, November 2001, p. 955).

CHAPTER 14

Types of Financing

LEARNING OBJECTIVES

After reading this chapter, you should be able to:

❮ Understand and explain adjustable rate mortgages.

❮ Understand and explain graduated payment mortgages.

❮ Discuss the market for reverse mortgages.

❮ Discuss portable loan issues including the Nehemiah Program.

❮ Define and discuss a wraparound mortgage.

❮ Understand the reason for investing in mortgages and the significance of a long-term land lease.

KEY TERMS

Adjustable rate mortgage (ARM) • Blanket mortgage • Construction loan • Equity sharing • Graduated payment mortgage • Negative amortization • Option • Package mortgage • RAM • Seller financing • Wraparound mortgage

An "alphabet soup" of mortgaging alternatives is now available to a borrower. With computerized loan origination, the expanded secondary market, and the availability of mortgage funds from nonregulated lending sources, a vast array of available mortgaging techniques and types of financing have been created. Loan brokers are now using computer programs to customize mortgages for individual home buyers, usually on the Internet. "Customized mortgages" are now part of an individualized pricing trend sweeping through the U.S. economy. What was once a "prime" or "subprime" generalized loan is now replaced by an almost endless array of mortgage rates and accompanying fees. The documents (discussed in Chapter 9) and the sources of funds (discussed in Chapter 13) still remain the same, but the number of alternative types of financing continues to expand. Only the most fundamental concepts will be discussed in this chapter, including types of financing, adjustable rate mortgages, other generally accepted types of loans often encountered by a broker in real estate lending, and the newest concepts of the affordable housing programs.

Adjustable Rate Mortgages

As we have already seen, a major problem for savings institutions is that they are locked into long-term loans while being dependent on short-term savings deposits. As a result, savings institutions now prefer to make mortgage loans that allow the interest rate to rise and fall during the life of the loan. To make this arrangement more attractive to borrowers, these loans are offered at a lower rate of interest than a fixed-rate loan of similar maturity.

The first step toward mortgage loans with adjustable interest rates came in the late 1970s. The loan was called a **variable rate**

mortgage and the interest rate could be adjusted up or down by the lender during the 30-year life of the loan to reflect the rise and fall in interest rates paid to savers by the lender.

CURRENT FORMAT

adjustable rate mortgage (ARM)

A mortgage on which the interest rate rises and falls with changes in prevailing interest rates.

The Office of Thrift Supervision (OTS) authorizes institutions to make the type of adjustable mortgage loan you are most likely to encounter in today's loan marketplace. This loan format is called an **adjustable rate mortgage (ARM)**. Other federal agencies followed, but used different guidelines. The main ARM requirement is that the interest rate on these loans be tied to some publicly available index that is mutually acceptable to the lender and the borrower. As interest rates rise and fall in the open market, the interest rate the lender is entitled to receive from the borrower rises and falls (Figure 14.1). The purpose is to match more closely what the savings institution receives from borrowers to what it must pay savers to attract funds. The benefit of an ARM to a borrower is that ARMs carry an initial interest rate that is lower than the rate on a fixed-rate mortgage of similar maturity. This often makes the difference between being able to qualify for a desired home loan and not qualifying for it. Other advantages to the borrower are that if market interest rates fall, the borrower's monthly payments fall. (This happens without incurring prepayment penalties or new loan origination costs, which could be the case with a fixed-rate loan.) Most ARMs allow assumption by a new buyer at the terms in the ARM, and most allow total prepayment without penalty, particularly if there has been an upward adjustment in the interest rate.

For the borrower, the disadvantage of an ARM is that if interest rates rise, the borrower is going to pay more. During periods of rising interest rates, property values and wages presumably will also rise. But the possibility of progressively larger monthly payments for the family home is still not attractive. As a result, various compromises have been worked out between lenders and borrowers whereby rates can rise on loans, but not by too much. In view of the fact that about one-half of all mortgage loans being originated by thrifts, banks, and mortgage companies are now adjustable, let's take a closer look at what a borrower gets with this loan format.

FIGURE **14.1** Adjustable Rate Mortgage

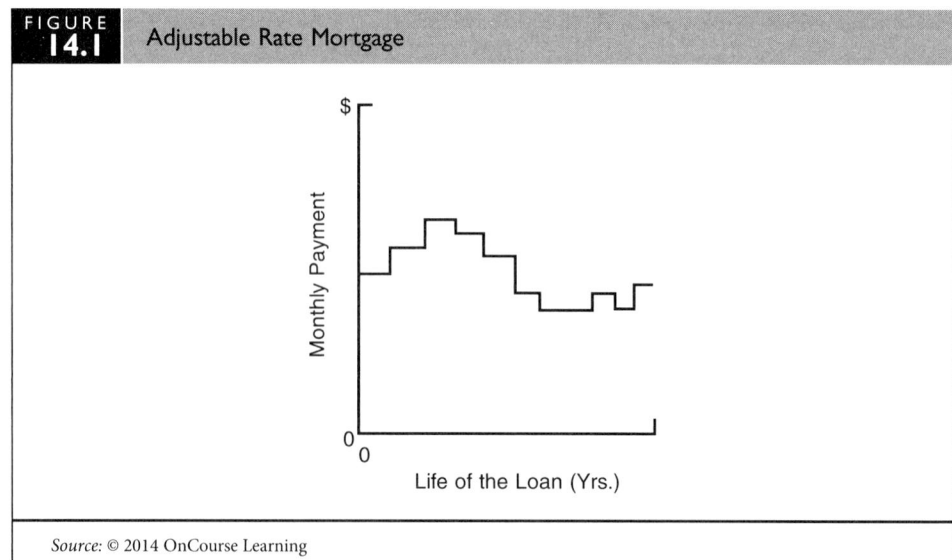

Source: © 2014 OnCourse Learning

INTEREST RATE

The interest rate on an ARM is tied to an index rate. As the index rate moves up or down, so do the borrower's payments when adjustment time arrives. Lenders and borrowers alike want a rate that genuinely reflects current market conditions for interest rates and that can be easily verified. The most popular index is based on an index that includes interest rates of all treasuries and securities, from 3-month bills to 30-year bonds. This index, called a one-year constant maturity treasury, is published by the Federal Reserve based on daily calculations.

MARGIN

To the index rate is added the margin. The **margin** is for the lender's cost of doing business, risk of loss on the loan, and profit. Currently this runs from 2% to 3%, depending on the characteristics of the loan. The margin is a useful comparison device because if two lenders are offering the same loan terms and the same index, but one loan has a margin of 2% and the other 3%, then the one with the 2% margin will have lower loan payments. As a rule, the margin stays constant during the life of the loan. At each adjustment point in the loan's life, the lender takes the index rate and adds the margin. The total becomes the interest rate the borrower will pay until the next adjustment occurs.

ADJUSTMENT PERIOD

The amount of time that elapses between adjustments is called the **adjustment period**. By far the most common adjustment period is one year. Less commonly used are six-month, three-year, and five-year adjustment periods. When market rates are rising, the longer adjustment periods benefit the borrower. When market rates are falling, the shorter periods benefit the borrower because index decreases will show up sooner in their monthly payments.

INTEREST RATE CAP

Lenders are now required by federal law to disclose an **interest rate cap** or ceiling on how much the interest rate can increase for any one adjustment period during the life of the loan. If the cap is very low, say 0.5% per year, the lender does not have much more flexibility than if holding a fixed-rate loan. Thus, there would be little reduction of initial rate on the loan compared with a fixed-rate loan. Compromises have prevailed, and the two most popular caps are 1% and 2% per year. In other words, the index rate may rise by 3%, but the cap limits the borrower's rate increase to 1% or 2%. Any unused difference may be added the next year, assuming the index rate has not fallen in the meantime. Because federal law now requires the ceiling, many lenders simply impose a very high ceiling (e.g., 18%) if they choose not to negotiate with the borrower.

PAYMENT CAP

What if a loan's index rate rises so fast that the annual rate cap is reached each year and the lifetime cap is reached soon in the life of the loan? A borrower might be able to handle a modest increase in payments each year, but not big jumps in quick succession. To counteract this possibility, a **payment cap** sets a limit on how much the borrower's monthly payment can increase in any one year. A popular figure now in use is 7.5%. In other words, no matter how high a payment is called for by the index rate, the borrower's monthly payment can rise, at the most, 7.5% per year. For example, given an initial rate of 10% on a 30-year ARM for $100,000, the monthly payment of interest and principal is $878 (see Table 11.1). If the index rate calls for a 2% upward adjustment at the end of one year, the payment on the loan would be $1,029. This is an increase of $151 or 17.2%. A 7.5% payment cap would limit the increase to 107.5% × $878 = $943.85.

NEGATIVE AMORTIZATION

negative amortization

Accrual of interest on a loan balance so that, as loan payments are made, the loan balance rises.

Although the 7.5% payment cap in the foregoing example protects the borrower against a monthly payment that rises too fast, it does not make the difference between what's called for ($1,029) and what's paid ($943.85) go away. The difference ($85.15) is added to the balance owed on the loan and earns interest just like the original amount borrowed. This is called **negative amortization**: Instead of the loan balance dropping each month as loan payments are made, the balance owed rises. This can bring concern to the lender who can visualize the day the loan balance exceeds the value of the property. A popular arrangement is to set a limit of 125% of the original loan balance. At that point, either the lender accrues no more negative amortization or the loan is reamortized depending on the wording of the loan contract. *Reamortized* in this situation means the monthly payments will be adjusted upward by enough to stop the negative amortization.

DISCLOSURES

In response to consumers' concern over adjustable rate mortgages, Regulation Z requires creditors to provide consumers with more extensive information about the variable rate feature of ARMs. The amendments apply only to closed-end credit transactions secured by the consumer's principal dwelling. Transactions secured by the consumer's principal dwelling with a term of one year or less are exempt from the new disclosure. To comply with the amendment, lenders must provide consumers with a historical example that shows how actual changes in index values would have affected payments on a $10,000 loan, as well as provide a statement of initial and maximum interest rates. Lenders must also provide prospective borrowers with an educational brochure about ARMs called "The Consumer Handbook on Adjustable Rate and Mortgages" or a suitable substitute. All the information must be given to the consumer at the time the loan application form is provided or before a nonrefundable fee is paid, whichever is earlier. The maximum interest rate must be stated as a specified amount or stated in a manner in which the consumer may easily ascertain the maximum interest rate at the time of entering the obligation.

CHOOSING WISELY

When a lender makes an ARM loan, the lender must explain to the borrower, in writing, the *worst-case scenario*. In other words, the lender must explain what will happen to the borrower's payments if the index rises the maximum amount each period up to the lifetime interest cap. If there is a payment cap, that and any possibility of negative amortization must also be explained. If the borrower is uneasy with these possibilities, then a fixed-rate loan should be considered. Most lenders offer fixed-rate loans as well as adjustable rate loans. VA loans are fixed-rate loans, but FHA now provides an adjustable rate loan program.

"**Teaser rate**" adjustables have been offered from time to time by a few lenders and are best avoided. This type of loan is an ARM with an enticingly attractive, below-market initial rate. For example, the teaser rate may be offered at 2% below market. A borrower who cannot qualify at the market rate might be able to do so at the teaser rate. However, in a year the loan contract calls for a 2% jump followed by additional annual increases. This overwhelms the borrower who, unable to pay, allows foreclosure to take place.

Graduated Payment Mortgage

The objective of a **graduated payment mortgage** is to help borrowers qualify for loans by basing repayment schedules on salary expectations. With this type of mortgage, the interest rate and maturity are fixed but the monthly payment gradually rises. For example, a 10%, $60,000, 30-year loan normally requires monthly payments of $527 for complete amortization. Under the graduated payment mortgage, payments could start out as low as $437 per month the first year, then gradually increase to $590 in the eleventh year, and remain at that level until the thirtieth year. Because the interest alone on this $60,000 loan is $500 per month, the amount owed on the loan actually increases during its early years. Only when the monthly payment exceeds the monthly interest does the balance owed on the loan decrease. These loans were very common during periods of high inflation. They are seldom used now that inflation and interest rates remain moderate.

graduated payment mortgage

A mortgage with an interest rate and maturity that are fixed, but the monthly payment gradually rises, because the initial monthly payments are insufficient to fully amortize the loan.

Equity Sharing

Giving the party that provides the financing a "piece of the action in the deal" is not an innovation. Insurance companies financing shopping centers and office buildings have long used the idea of requiring part of the rental income and/or part of the profits plus interest on the loan itself. In other words, in return for providing financing, the lender wants to share in some of the benefits normally reserved for the equity holder, called **equity sharing**. The equity holder would agree to this either to get a lower rate of interest or to get financing when financing was scarce or where the equity holder was not big enough to handle the deal alone. For example, on a $5 million project, the lender might agree to make a loan of $4 million at a very attractive rate if it can buy a half-interest in the equity for $500,000.

equity sharing

An arrangement whereby a party providing financing gets a portion of the ownership.

A variation of equity sharing that is becoming popular once again is a **shared appreciation mortgage (SAM)**. While the format of SAMs varies considerably, the typical SAM offers an interest rate of 1% to 2% below market rates, which makes buyer qualification easier. The lender earns about half the increase in appreciation over the term of the loan. At loan termination, the borrower is obligated to pay the loan balance plus the lender's share of the appreciated value of the home. For older homeowners this may have more of an appeal than the reverse mortgage (discussed later) in that it preserves some equity in the home for the benefit of their heirs.

"Rich Uncle" Financing

A second variation of equity sharing is often called *rich uncle financing*. The investor may be a parent helping a son or daughter buy a home, or a son or daughter buying a parent's present home while giving the parent(s) the right to occupy it. A third variation is for an investor to provide most of the down payment for a home buyer, collect rent from the home buyer, pay the mortgage payments and property taxes, and claim depreciation. Each party has a right to a portion of any appreciation and the right to buy out the other. The FHLMC will buy mortgage loans on shared-equity properties. The Federal Home Loan Mortgage Corporation (FHLMC) requires that the owner-occupant contribute at least 5% of the equity, that the owner-occupant and the owner-investor sign the mortgage and note, that both be individuals, and that there be no agreement requiring sale or buy out within seven years of the loan date. Equity sharing can provide attractive tax benefits; however, you must seek competent tax advice before involving yourself or someone else in such a plan.

Package Mortgage

package mortgage
A mortgage that secures personal property in addition to real property.

Normally, we think of real estate mortgage loans as being secured solely by real estate. However, it is possible to include items classed as personal property in a real estate mortgage, thus creating a **package mortgage**. In residential loans (particularly in new construction or remodeling), such items as the refrigerator, clothes washer, and dryer can be pledged along with the house and land in a single mortgage. The purpose is to raise the value of the collateral in order to raise the amount a lender is willing to loan. For the borrower, it offers the opportunity of financing major appliances at the same rate of interest as the real estate itself. This rate is usually lower than if the borrower finances the appliances separately. Once an item of personal property is included in a package mortgage, selling it without the prior consent of the lender is a violation of the mortgage.

Blanket Mortgage

blanket mortgage
A mortgage secured by two or more properties.

A mortgage secured by two or more properties is called a **blanket mortgage**. Suppose you want to buy a house plus the vacant lot next door, financing the purchase with a single mortgage that covers both properties. The cost of preparing one mortgage instead of two is a savings. Also, by combining the house and the lot, the lot can be financed on better terms than if it were financed separately, as lenders more readily loan on a house and land than on land alone. Note, however, that if the vacant lot is later sold separately from the house before the mortgage loan is fully repaid, it will be necessary to have it released from the blanket mortgage. This is usually accomplished by including in the original mortgage agreement a partial release clause that specifies how much of the loan must be repaid before the lot can be released.

Reverse Mortgage

RAM
Reverse-annuity mortgage.

With a regular mortgage, the lender makes a lump-sum payment to the borrower, who, in turn, repays it through monthly payments to the lender. With a **reverse mortgage**, the lender has two alternatives: (1) payment to the homeowner in a lump sum (sometimes referred to as a "line of credit" **RAM**), or (2) monthly payments to the homeowner as an annuity for the reverse term of the loan. The reverse mortgage can be particularly valuable for an elderly homeowner who does not want to sell, but whose retirement income is not quite enough for comfortable living. The homeowner receives a monthly check, has full use of the property, and is not required to repay until he or she sells or dies. If the home is sold, money from the sale is taken to repay the loan. If the borrower dies first, the property is sold through the estate and the loan repaid.

In 1997, Fannie Mae introduced another type of reverse annuity mortgage aimed at senior citizens, which is activated at the time the house is purchased. It allows senior citizens (who must be 62 years or older) to obtain a mortgage against the equity in a house if a substantial down payment is made. Repayment of the mortgage is deferred until the borrower no longer occupies the principal residence. If the loan balance exceeds the value of the property, the borrower, or the estate, will never owe more than the value of the property. For instance, if a homeowner sells an existing home for $100,000 and chooses to purchase a retirement home, also costing $100,000, the homeowner would immediately qualify for a $52,000 loan, with a $48,000 down payment. There would be no monthly payments, and the homeowner would have $52,000 in cash!

What happens at the end of the loan? It depends on the loan documents, but the lender ultimately gets title to the house. If the children choose to do so, they can pay off the loan and the title to the house will pass by terms of the will or by intestacy. If the loan has a term (15 or 30 years) you can outlive the loan and may lose title to the house unless it is refinanced.

Another alternative is a "loan for life" wherein the lender anticipates the life expectancy of the homeowner, makes an amortization monthly payment to the owner based on the life expectancy so "outliving the loan" cannot be a result. Understandably, if you're only 62 years old and have a healthy lifestyle, your amortization may be based on a 40-year amortization, and your monthly income payments will be relatively low.

Because of the complications of these loans, many states require that before an owner can sign a reverse mortgage, they have to go to counseling or take classes that advise them as to the risks and alternatives of the reverse mortgage.

Construction Loan

Under a **construction loan**, also called an **interim loan**, money is advanced as construction takes place. For example, a vacant lot owner arranges to borrow $60,000 to build a house. The lender does not advance all $60,000 at once because the value of the collateral is insufficient to warrant that amount until the house is finished. Instead, the lender will parcel out the loan as the building is being constructed, always holding a portion until the property is ready for occupancy or, in some cases, actually occupied. Some lenders specialize only in construction loans and do not want to wait 20 or 30 years to be repaid. In this case, the buyer will have to obtain a permanent long-term mortgage from another source for the purpose of repaying the construction loan. This is known as a *permanent commitment* or a *take-out loan* because it takes the construction lender out of the financial picture when construction is completed and allows the lender to recycle its money into new construction projects.

construction loan
Short-term loan for new construction or remodeling of an existing structure.

Blended-Rate Loan

Many real estate lenders still hold long-term loans that were made at interest rates below the current market. One way of raising the return on these loans is to offer borrowers who have them a **blended-rate loan**. Suppose you owe $50,000 on your home loan and the interest rate on it is 7%. Suppose further that the current rate on home loans is 12%. Your lender might offer to refinance your home for $70,000 at 9%, presuming the property will appraise high enough and you have the income to qualify. The $70,000 refinance offer would put $20,000 in your pocket (less loan fees), but would increase the interest you pay from 7% to 9% on the original $50,000. This makes the cost of the $20,000, 14% per year. The arithmetic is as follows: You will now be paying 9% × $70,000 = $6,300 in interest. Before, you paid 7% × $50,000 = $3,500 in interest. The difference, $2,800, is what you pay to borrow the additional $20,000. This equates to $2,800/$20,000 = 14% interest. This is the figure you should use in comparing other sources of financing (such as a second mortgage) or deciding whether you even want to borrow.

A blended-rate loan can be very attractive in a situation in which you want to sell your home and you do not want to help finance the buyer. Suppose your home is worth $87,500 and you have the aforementioned $50,000, 7% loan. A buyer would normally expect to make a down payment of $17,500 and pay 12% interest on a new $70,000 loan. But, with a blended loan, your lender could offer the buyer the needed $70,000 financing at 9%, a far more attractive rate and one that requires less income in order to qualify. Blended loans are available on FHA, VA, and conventional loans held by the FNMA. Other lenders also offer them on fixed-rate assumable loans they hold.

Equity Mortgage

An **equity mortgage** is a loan arrangement wherein the lender agrees to make a loan based on the amount of equity in a borrower's home. The maximum amount of the loan is generally 70% or 80% of the home's value (although some lenders advertise 125%) minus any first mortgage or other liens against the property.

It is typically a second mortgage that is used to tap the increase in equity resulting from rising home prices and first loan principal reductions. It's all done without having to refinance the first loan and uses the home as an asset against which the homeowner can borrow and repay as needed. Equity mortgages are very popular as a source of home improvement loans, money for college expenses, money to start a business, money for a major vacation, and money to buy more real estate.

Because the Internal Revenue Code of 1986 limited personal interest deductions to home mortgages, these loans have become one of the fastest growing areas of real estate lending.

Affordable Housing Loans

An **affordable housing loan** is an umbrella term that covers many slightly different loans that target first-time home buyers and low- to moderate-income borrowers. Although there are no fixed standards for measurement, the generally accepted definition of a *low-income borrower* is a person or family with an income of not more than 80% of the median income for the local area. *Moderate income* is 115% of the median income for the area. *Median* means an equal number of people have incomes above or below the number. Funding for the programs is obtained through a commitment from an investor to buy the loans. Freddie Mac and Fannie Mae cooperate with local community, labor union, or trade associations by committing to buy a large block of mortgage loans provided they meet the agreed-on standards. Affordable housing loans can be privately insured through the Mortgage Guaranty Insurance Company or GE Capital Mortgage Insurance Corporation.

Freddie Mac now offers two programs supporting construction of affordable single-family homes in urban centers. One allows builders to cover up to 3% of a borrower's down payment, and borrowers are allowed to pay for closing costs with cash in combination with gifts, grants, affordable second loans, or other flexible options. The second mortgage product benefits builders by reducing some of the economic risks associated with building homes in urban centers. The program extends flexible underwriting and low down payments to buyers and provides builders with access to a cash reserve fund as a financial safety net. The reserve fund covers principal, interest, taxes, and insurance payments during construction for a period of up to six months. The program was tested in five cities, including San Antonio, Texas.

Fannie Mae has also introduced its "Home Style Construction-to-Permanent Mortgage," which enables a borrower to cover the construction loan and a permanent mortgage with one loan. One interest rate can be locked in for both phases of the loan, which is sold to Fannie Mae as soon as it is closed.

The Department of Housing and Urban Development is also encouraging affordable housing loans. It is currently promoting the "Officer Next Door" (OND) housing program, which allows police officers to buy FHA-foreclosed properties at half price if the officers live in the cities in which they work. The program has been highly successful. HUD plans to offer a "Teacher Next Door" program patterned after the OND program. HUD also has a program to sell foreclosed single-family homes to local governments for $1 each. The houses are FHA foreclosures that have remained unsold for six months. The program is designed to create housing for families in need and to revitalize neighborhoods. HUD also sets goals for Fannie Mae and Freddie Mac for the purchase of mortgages made to low- and moderate-income persons, African Americans, Hispanics, and other minorities in under-served areas.

Fannie Mae also promotes their **Community Solutions Program** of flexible mortgages for school employees, police officers, firefighters, and health-care workers. It provides greater flexibility with credit scores and their credit histories, allows for a greater portion of income to go towards mortgage payments, and gives credit for overtime or part-time income. It offers 97% and 100% loan programs.

Fannie Mae also produces the **MyCommunityMortgage Program**, which provides mortgage options for borrowers of one to four family homes. It includes extra flexibilities for rural residents and may offer additional incentives for buyers of energy-efficient homes. It has a $417,000 loan limit on single-family homes and allows for a $500 or 1% down payment on single-unit properties, greater flexibility on credit histories, and income limits up to 115% in rural areas. A 3% contribution is required on two to four family homes.

As a part of the MyCommunityMortgage Program, **Fannie Neighbors** is a nationwide, neighborhood-based mortgage program designed to increase home ownership and revitalization in areas underserved by HUD, in low- to moderate-income minorities census tracts, or in central cities. Lenders and other urban area professionals can use the Fannie Mae Property GeoCoder, a free, online application, to determine whether a property qualifies for the Fannie Neighbors option.

CREDIT CRITERIA

Underwriting standards for affordable housing loans are modified to recognize different forms of credit responsibility. Many low- and moderate-income families do not have checking accounts. Recognizing the lack of payment records, most affordable housing programs accept timely payment of rent and utility bills as credit criteria. Initial cash down payments can be reduced by allowing borrowing or acceptance of grants from housing agencies or local communities, which sometimes offer cash assistance. Studies indicate that lower-income families pay a higher percentage of their income for housing than others, so an affordable housing program allows a higher ratio of income to be applied to housing (33% of gross income instead of 28% found in similar loans; you may recall that the FHA housing guideline is 29%).

CONSUMER EDUCATION

One of the requirements to qualify for an affordable housing loan is for the borrower to take a prepurchase home buyer education course. Many of these first-time home buyers are unaware of real estate brokers, title insurance, or appraisals. These subjects, plus the care and maintenance of a home, are included in the variety of courses now available through community colleges, banks, and mortgage companies. The four major supporting entities of these programs are Fannie Mae, Freddie Mac, MGIC, and GE Capital Mortgage Insurance Corporation. All of these entities provide videotapes and course outlines that are available for these educational purposes.

Licensees should be aware that these programs are most effective if presented to a group of applicants. If there is no program in your area, one could be started. An agent may want to contact local lenders, as many are still not fully aware of the opportunities available, and some tend to overlook the lower income market for economic reasons. Participation in the program, however, greatly benefits their Community Reinvestment Act rating. Effectively marketing these programs can be very profitable and provide a great amount of personal satisfaction.

97% CONVENTIONAL LOAN

One of the most significant developments in mortgage lending has been the introduction of a **3%-down-payment conventional loan**. FIRREA and the Community Reinvestment Act (discussed in Chapter 19) provided strong incentives for private lenders to engage in affordable housing loans to help lower- to middle-income homeowners. To encourage homeownership among lower- and middle-income people, General Electric Capital Mortgage Insurance Corporation experimented with affordable housing loans, which it calls "community home buyer's program" loans. Results show that the rates of default among their borrowers prove to be as good or better than those of its regular loan portfolio. GE introduced a 97% conventional loan in February 1994. Fannie Mae agreed to purchase 97% loans as long as the applicant met Fannie Mae guidelines, which include an income limit not to exceed 100% of the local area median income. Another conduit has been established by the investment banker Goldman Sachs to purchase these loans for buyers with up to 115% of area median income.

THE NEHEMIAH PROGRAM

The Nehemiah Corporation was founded with a $5,000 grant from a local Baptist church in 1994, with the intention of rebuilding parts of Sacramento, California. It has now grown into a national program handling over $150,000,000 a year.

The inspiration for the program was Reverend Don Harris, following the teachings of the Old Testament in which Nehemiah rebuilt Jerusalem after it had been destroyed. It has become the largest down payment assistance program in the United States and now operates in 4,900 cities and every state except Hawaii. The down payment assistance is usually 1% to 6% percent of the loan amount, and the candidates must meet Nehemiah's qualifying criteria, which may include taking a free home ownership education course. After closing, the builder, lender, or real estate agent may agree to make a "like" contribution, called a "service fee," to the Nehemiah pool. This has resulted in a much larger volume of eligible buyers. The housing inventory moves quicker—a benefit to builders, agents, and lenders.

Seller Financing

seller financing

A note accepted by a seller instead of cash.

When a seller is willing to accept part of the property's purchase price in the form of the buyer's promissory note accompanied by a mortgage or deed of trust, it is called **seller financing**. This allows the buyer to substitute a promissory note for cash, and the seller is said to be "taking back paper." Seller financing is popular for land sales (where lenders rarely loan), on property where an existing mortgage is being assumed by the buyer, and on property where the seller prefers to receive the money spread out over a period of time with interest instead of lump-sum cash. For example, a retired couple sells a rental home they own. The home is worth $120,000, and they owe $20,000. If they need only $60,000 in cash, they might be more than happy to take $60,000 down, let the buyer assume the existing mortgage, and accept the remaining $40,000 in monthly payments at current interest rates. Alternatively, the buyer and seller can agree to structure the $40,000 as an adjustable, graduated, partially amortized, or interest-only loan.

If the seller receives the sales price spread out over two or more years, income taxes are calculated using the installment reporting method discussed in Chapter 15. Being able to spread out the taxes on a gain may be an incentive to use seller financing. The seller should be aware, however, that the "paper" may not be convertible to cash without a long wait or without having to sell it at a substantial discount to an investor (although this can be remedied by a "balloon" provision). Additionally, the seller is responsible for servicing the loan and is subject to losses due to default and foreclosure.

Note that some real estate agents and lenders refer to a loan that is carried back by a seller as a **purchase money loan**. Others define a purchase money loan as any loan, carryback, or institutional that is used to finance the purchase of real property.

Wraparound Mortgage

An alternative method of financing a real estate sale such as the one just reviewed is to use a **wraparound mortgage** or **wraparound deed of trust**. A wraparound encompasses existing mortgages and is subordinate (junior) to them. The existing mortgages stay on the property and the new mortgage wraps around them. Note Figure 14.2.

wraparound mortgage

A mortgage that encompasses any existing mortgages and is subordinate to them.

To illustrate, presume the existing $20,000 loan in the previous example carries an interest rate of 7% and that there are 10 years remaining on the loan. Presume further that current interest rates are 12%, and the current seller chooses to sell for $100,000. This is done by taking the buyer's $40,000 down payment, and then creating a new junior mortgage (for $60,000) that includes not only the $20,000 owed on the existing first mortgage but also the $40,000 the buyer owes the seller. The seller continues to remain liable for payment of the first mortgage. If the interest rate on the wraparound is set at 10%, the buyer saves by not having to pay 12% as he would on an entirely new loan. The advantage to the seller is that she is earning 10%, not only on her $40,000 equity, but also on the $20,000 loan for which she is paying 7% interest. This gives the seller an actual yield of 11.5% on her $40,000. (The calculation is as follows. The seller receives 10% on $60,000, which amounts to $6,000. She pays 7% on $20,000, which is $1,400. The difference, $4,600, is divided by $40,000 to get the seller's actual yield of 11.5%.) There is an additional point of concern. If the monthly payment on the underlying $20,000 debt includes taxes and insurance (PITI payment), the wraparound mortgage payment amount should also include taxes and insurance so that the monthly payment is sufficient to meet *all* of the underlying debt.

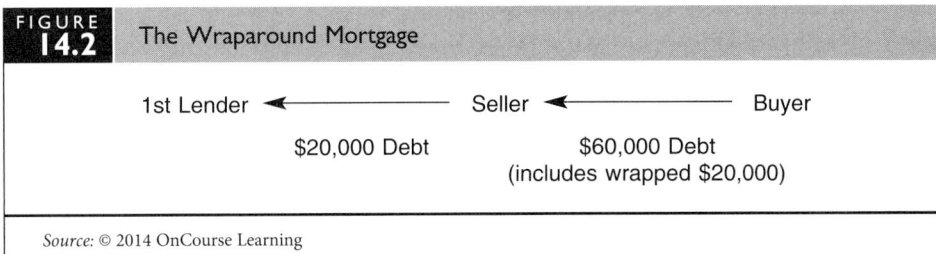

FIGURE 14.2 The Wraparound Mortgage

1st Lender ← Seller ← Buyer

$20,000 Debt $60,000 Debt
(includes wrapped $20,000)

Source: © 2014 OnCourse Learning

Wraparounds are not limited to seller financing. If the seller in the foregoing example did not want to finance the sale, a third-party lender could provide the needed $40,000 and take a wraparound mortgage. The wraparound concept does not work when the underlying mortgage debt to be "wrapped" contains a due-on-sale clause. One other word of caution: If the seller defaults (and doesn't tell the buyer), the buyer may have an unwelcome surprise.

Subordination

Another financing technique is **subordination**. For example, a person owns a $200,000 vacant lot suitable for building, and a builder wants to build an $800,000 building on the lot. The builder has only $100,000 cash and the largest construction loan available is $800,000. If the builder can convince the lot owner to take $100,000 in cash and $100,000 later, the buyer would have the $1 million total. However, the lender making the $800,000 loan will want to be the first mortgagee to protect its position in the event of foreclosure. The lot owner must be willing to take a subordinate position, in this case a second mortgage. If the project is successful, the lot owner will receive $100,000, plus interest, either in cash after the building is built and sold, or as monthly payments. If the project goes into foreclosure, the lot owner can be paid only if the $800,000 first mortgage claim is satisfied in full from the sale proceeds. As you can surmise here, the lot owner must be very careful that the money loaned by the lender actually goes into construction and that whatever is built is worth at least $800,000 in addition to the land.

Contract for Deed

A **contract for deed**, also called an **installment contract** or **land contract**, enables the seller to finance a buyer by permitting him to make a down payment followed by monthly payments. However, title remains in the name of the seller. In addition to its wide use in financing land sales, it has also been a very effective financing tool in several states as a means of selling homes. For example, a homeowner owes $25,000 on his home and wants to sell it for $85,000. A buyer is found but does not have the $60,000 down payment necessary to assume the existing loan. The buyer does have $8,000, but for one reason or another cannot or chooses not to borrow from an institutional lender. If the seller is agreeable, the buyer can pay the seller $8,000 and enter into an installment contract with the seller for the remaining $77,000. The contract calls for monthly payments by the buyer to the seller that are large enough to allow the seller to meet the payments on the $25,000 loan plus repay the $52,000 owed to the seller, with interest. Unless property taxes and insurance are billed to the buyer, the seller will also collect for these and pay them. When the final payment is made to the seller (or the property is refinanced through an institutional lender), title is conveyed to the buyer. Meanwhile, the seller continues to hold title and is responsible for paying the mortgage. In addition to wrapping around a mortgage, an installment contract can also be used to wrap around another installment contract, provided it does not contain an enforceable due-on-sale clause. (See Chapter 9 for more about the contractual side of installment contracts.)

Option

option

A right, for a given period of time, to buy, sell, or lease property at a specified price and terms.

When viewed as a financing tool, an **option** provides a method by which the need to finance the full price of a property immediately can be postponed. For example, a developer is offered 100 acres of land for a house subdivision but is not sure that the market will absorb that many houses. The solution is to buy 25 acres outright and take three 25-acre options at present prices on the remainder. If the houses on the first 25 acres sell promptly, the builder can exercise the options to buy the remaining land. If sales are not good, the builder can let the remaining options expire and avoid being stuck with unwanted acreage.

A popular variation on the option idea is the **lease with option to buy** combination. Under it, an owner leases to a tenant who, in addition to paying rent and using the property, also obtains the right to purchase it at a present price for a fixed period of time. Homes are often sold this way, particularly when the resale market is sluggish. (See Chapter 8 for more about these topics.)

Options can provide speculative opportunities to persons with limited amounts of capital. If prices do not rise, the optionee loses only the cost of the option; if prices do rise, the optionee exercises the option and realizes a profit.

Overly Creative Financing?

Some financing arrangements deserve special attention because of its traps for the unwary that results in **overencumbered property**. Institutional lenders are supposed to be closely regulated regarding the amount of money they can loan against the appraised value of the property. However, it is not always the case. In competition for making loans to borrowers, lenders often become more flexible and take exceptions to traditional policies. ARMs, which we have discussed, run a very high risk of increasing payments dramatically at the end of the initial loan period. People's payments can even double in some circumstances and interest rates can be increased. However, the lender may encourage somebody to take a loan like this so that they can afford to buy more home, utilizing the teaser rate as a monthly payment, when, in fact, the teaser rate actually gets the borrower in trouble in subsequent years. The same is true of graduated payment mortgages.

Sellers are not regulated by the federal government, and often come up with schemes to sell homes at high prices with no down payment, low initial monthly payments, and with no appraisal, no loan qualification for the borrower.

In all three of these scenarios, we end up with overencumbered property. Once the payments go up, the interest rates go up, or the seller needs to sell the property. He finds the property is overencumbered and is unable to sell the property at fair market value.

The obvious conclusion of this issue is that there is no free lunch. If you don't see an ability to pay fair market value for property, have it properly appraised, make an appropriate down payment, you run a high risk of foreclosure in the future. There was a time when we encouraged people to make small down payments and take out huge mortgages (there is a tax deduction for the interest payment!), so this type of leverage was considered to be a smart thing to do. In today's economy, however, people are getting to see the benefit of high down payments, small mortgages and very low risk of foreclosure in the future.

Investing in Mortgages

Individuals can invest in mortgages in two ways. One is to invest in mortgage loan pools through certificates guaranteed by Ginnie Mae and Freddie Mac and available from stockbrokers. These yield about 0.5 of 1% below what FHA and VA borrowers are paying. In 2008, for example, this was approximately 5%, and the certificates are readily convertible to cash at current market prices on the open market if the investor does not want to hold them through maturity.

Individuals can also buy junior mortgages at yields above Ginnie Mae and Freddie Mac certificates. These junior mortgages are seconds, thirds, and fourths offered by mortgage brokers. They yield more because they are riskier as to repayment and much more difficult to convert to cash before maturity. "There is," as the wise old adage says, "no such thing as a free lunch." Thus, it is important to recognize that when an investment of any kind promises above-market returns, there is some kind of added risk attached. With junior mortgages, it is important to realize that when a borrower offers to pay a premium above the best loan rates available from banks and thrift institutions, it is because the borrower and/or the property do not qualify for the best rates.

Before buying a mortgage as an investment, one should have the title to the property searched. This is the only way to know for certain what priority the mortgage will have in the event of foreclosure. There have been cases where investors have purchased what they were told to be first and second mortgages, only to find in foreclosure that they were actually holding third and fourth mortgages, and the amount of debt exceeded the value of the property.

And how does one find the value of a property? By having it appraised by a professional appraiser who is independent of the party making or selling the mortgage investment. This value is compared to the existing and proposed debt against the property. The investor should also run a credit check on the borrower. The investor's final protection is, however, in making certain that the market value of the property is well in excess of the loans against it and that the property is well constructed, well located, and functional.

Rental

Even though tenants do not acquire fee ownership, **rentals** and **leases** are means of financing real estate. Whether the tenant is a bachelor receiving the use of a $30,000 apartment for which he pays $350 rent per month or a large corporation leasing a warehouse for 20 years, leasing is an ideal method of financing when the tenant does not want to buy, cannot raise the funds to buy, or prefers to invest available funds elsewhere. Similarly, *farming leases* provide for the use of land without the need to purchase it. Some farm leases call for fixed rental payment. Other leases require the farmer to pay the landowner a share of the value of the crop that is actually produced—say 25%—and the landowner shares with the farmer the risks of weather, crop output, and prices.

Under a **sale and leaseback** arrangement, an owner-occupant sells the property and then remains as a tenant. Thus, the buyer acquires an investment and the seller obtains capital for other purposes while retaining the use of the property. A variation is for the tenant to construct a building, sell it to a prearranged buyer, and immediately lease it back.

Land Leases

Although *leased land* arrangements are common throughout the United States for both commercial and industrial users and for farmers, anything other than fee ownership of residential land is unthinkable in many areas. Yet in some parts of the United States (e.g., Baltimore, Maryland; Orange County, California; throughout Hawaii; and parts of Florida), homes built on leased land are commonplace. Typically, these leases are at least 55 years in length and, barring an agreement to the contrary, the improvements to the land become the property of the fee owner at the end of the lease. Rents may be fixed in advance for the life of the lease, renegotiated at present points during the life of the lease, or a combination of both.

To hedge against inflation, when fixed rents are used in a long-term lease, it is common practice to use **step-up rentals**. For example, under a 55-year house-lot lease, the rent may be set at $400 per year for the first 15 years, $600 per year for the next 10 years, $800 for the next 10 years, and so forth. An alternative is to renegotiate the rent at various points during the life of a lease so that the effects of land value changes are more closely equalized between the lessor and the lessee. For example, a 60-year lease may contain renegotiation points at the fifteenth, thirtieth, and forty-fifth years. At those points, the property would be reappraised and the lease rent adjusted to reflect any changes in the value of the property. Property taxes and any increases in property taxes are paid by the lessee.

Financing Overview

If people always paid cash for real estate, the last several chapters would not have been necessary. But 95% of the time they don't; thus, means have been devised to finance their purchases. This has been true since the beginning of recorded history and will continue into the future. The financing methods that evolve will depend on the problems to be solved. For example, long-term, fixed-rate, amortized loans were the solution to foreclosures in the 1930s, and they worked well as long as interest rates did not fluctuate greatly. Graduated payment loans were devised when housing prices rose faster than buyers' incomes. Adjustable rate loans were developed so that lenders could more closely align the interest they receive from borrowers with the interest they pay their savers. Extensive use of loan assumptions, wraparounds, and seller financing became necessary in the early 1980s because borrowers could not qualify for 16% and 18% loans and sellers were unwilling to drop prices.

With regard to the future, if mortgage money is expensive or in short supply, seller financing will play a large role. With the experience of rapidly fluctuating interest rates fresh in people's minds, loans with adjustable rates will continue to be widely offered. Fixed-rate loans will either have short maturities or carry a premium to compensate the lender for being locked into a fixed rate for a long period. When interest rates are low, borrowers with adjustable loans will benefit from lower monthly payments. If rates stay down long enough, fixed-rate loans will become more popular again.

Vocabulary Review

Match terms a–s with statements 1–19.

a. Adjustment period

b. Adjustable rate mortgage (ARM)

c. Blanket mortgage

d. Blended-rate loan

e. Carryback financing

f. Contract for deed

g. Equity mortgage

h. Equity sharing

i. Graduated payment mortgage

j. Interest rate cap

_____ 1. The amount of time that elapses between interest rate changes on a loan.

_____ 2. A mortgage secured by two or more properties.

_____ 3. A mortgage secured by real and personal property.

_____ 4. To voluntarily give up a higher mortgage priority for a lower one.

_____ 5. A situation where the loans against a property exceed the value of the property.

_____ 6. A financing arrangement whereby an owner-occupant sells the property and then remains as a tenant.

_____ 7. Results when monthly interest exceeds monthly payment and the difference is added to the principal.

_____ 8. A refinanced loan wherein the lender combines the interest rate of the existing loan with a current rate.

k. Negative amortization
l. Option
m. Overencumbered property
n. Package mortgage
o. Payment cap
p. Reverse mortgage
q. Sale and leaseback
r. Subordination
s. Wraparound mortgage

_____ 9. A mortgage wherein the lender extends a line of credit based on the amount of equity in a person's home.

_____ 10. A loan wherein the lender makes monthly payments to the property owner who later repays in a lump sum.

_____ 11. The ceiling to which the interest rate on a loan can rise.

_____ 12. A limit on how much a borrower's payment can increase in any one year.

_____ 13. A note is accepted by a seller instead of cash.

_____ 14. An arrangement whereby a party providing financing gets a portion of the ownership.

_____ 15. A right, for a given period of time, to buy, sell, or lease property at a preset price and terms.

_____ 16. A method of selling and financing property whereby the buyer obtains possession but the seller retains the title.

_____ 17. A mortgage loan on which the rate of interest can rise and fall with changes in prevailing interest rates.

_____ 18. A mortgage repayment plan that allows the borrower to make smaller monthly payments at first and larger ones later.

_____ 19. A debt instrument that encompasses existing mortgages and is subordinate to them.

Questions and Problems

1. Regarding adjustable rate mortgage loans, what are the advantages and disadvantages to the borrower and lender?

2. What is an adjustable rate mortgage?

3. Explain why rentals and leases are considered forms of real estate financing.

4. What is the single most important precaution an investor can make before buying a junior mortgage?

Additional Readings

"The Consumer Handbook on Adjustable Rate and Mortgages." An educational brochure published by the federal government explaining ARM mortgages, it is available from most brokers who have an ARM loan program.

Creating Your Own Wealth: Your Housing Expense Can Be the Key to Unlocking Financial Security by Alan Schein (American Financial Publishing, 2001).

"HUD's Hybrid ARM Program Moves Ahead" by Brian Collins (*Origination News*, December 2001, p. 2).

"Jumbo Hybrid ARM Securities: A Comprehensive Introduction" by Sharad Chaudhary and Laurent Gauthier (*Journal of Fixed Income*, March 2002).

Real Estate Finance, 9th ed. by John Wiedemer and J. Keith Baker (OnCourse Learning, 2013). Includes sources of long-term mortgage money, financing instruments, loan procedures, FNMA, FHLMC, GNMA, FHA, and VA. Also includes loan analysis, carryback financing, and settlement procedures.

Real Estate Finance: Theory and Practice, 7th ed. by Terrence M. Clauretie and G. Stacy Sirmans (OnCourse Learning, 2014).

Residential Mortgage Lending, 6th ed. by Thomas J. Pinkowish (OnCourse Learning, 2012). Explains residential mortgage lending, assuming no prior knowledge.

Securitizations: Legal and Regulatory Issues by Patrick D. Dolan and C. VanLeer Davis III (American Lawyer Media, 2000).

The following periodicals may also be of interest to you: *Freddie Mac Reports, Federal Reserve Bulletin, FHLBB News, Housing Finance, Housing Finance Review, National Savings and Loan League Journal, Real Estate Finance,* and *Real Estate Lenders Report.*

CHAPTER 15

Taxes and Assessments

Property Taxes

The largest single source of income in America for local government programs and services is the property tax. Schools (from kindergarten through two-year colleges), fire and police departments, local welfare programs, public libraries, street maintenance, parks, and public hospital facilities are mainly supported by property taxes. Some state governments also obtain a portion of their revenues from this source.

Property taxes are **ad valorem taxes**. This means that they are levied according to the value of one's property; the more valuable the property, the higher the tax, and vice versa. The underlying theory of ad valorem taxation is that those owning the more valuable properties are wealthier and, hence, able to pay more taxes.

How does a local government determine the amount of tax to collect each year from each property owner? Step 1 is local budget preparation and appropriation. Step 2 is the appraisal of all taxable property within the taxation district. Step 3 is to allocate the amount to be collected among the taxable properties in the district. Let's look more closely at this process.

BUDGET AND APPROPRIATION

Each taxing body with the authority to tax prepares its *budget* for the coming year. Taxing bodies include counties, cities, boroughs, towns, and villages, and, in some states, school boards, sanitation districts, and county road departments. Each budget, along with a list of sources from which the money will be derived, is enacted into law. This is the **appropriation process**. Then estimated sales taxes, state and federal revenue sharing,

LEARNING OBJECTIVES

After reading this chapter, you should be able to:

❮ Discuss the purpose of real property taxes.

❮ Discuss how property taxes are determined.

❮ Utilize the concept of fair market value and tax rates.

❮ Understand the significance of assessment appeals.

❮ Discuss certain properties which are tax-exempt.

❮ Define and discuss "special assessments" made by a governmental body.

❮ Determine income taxes on the sale of a residence.

❮ Know the exclusions on gains on the sale of a principal residence.

KEY TERMS

Ad valorem taxes • Adjusted basis • Assessed value • Assessment appeal board • Basis • Documentary tax • Installment method • Mill rate • Tax certificate • Tax lien

ad valorem taxes
Taxes charged according to the value of a property.

business licenses, and city income taxes are subtracted from the budget. The balance must come from property taxes.

APPRAISAL AND ASSESSMENT

Next, the valuation of the taxable property within each taxing body's district must be determined. A county or state assessor's office **appraises** each taxable parcel of land and the improvements thereon. In some states, this job is contracted out to private appraisal companies. Appraisal procedures vary from state to state. In some, the appraised value is the estimated fair market cash value of the property. This is the cash price one would expect a buyer and a seller to agree upon in a normal open market transaction. Other states start with the fair market value of the land and add to it the cost of replacing the buildings and other improvements on it, minus an allowance for depreciation due to wear and tear and obsolescence. Since there is such a large volume of property to appraise, most tax assessors utilize a **mass appraisal** technique, discussed in Chapter 18.

assessed value

A value placed on a property for the purpose of taxation.

The appraised value is converted into an assessed value upon which taxes are based. In some states, the **assessed value** is set equal to the appraised value; in others, it is a percentage of the appraised value. Mathematically, the percentage selected makes no difference as long as each property in a taxing district is treated equally. Consider two houses with appraised values of $120,000 and $240,000, respectively. Whether the assessed values are set equal to appraised values or at a percentage of appraised values, the second house will still bear twice the property tax burden of the first.

TAX RATE CALCULATION

The assessed values of all properties subject to property taxation are added together in order to calculate the tax rate. To explain this process, suppose that a building lies within the taxation districts of the Westside School District, the city of Rostin, and the county of Pearl River. The school district's budget for the coming year requires $8 million from property taxes, and the assessed value of taxable property within the district is $200 million. By dividing $8 million by $200 million, we see that the school district must collect a tax of 4¢ for every dollar of assessed valuation. This levy can be expressed three ways: (1) as a mill rate, (2) as dollars per hundred, or (3) as dollars per thousand. All three rating methods are found in the United States.

mill rate

Property tax rate expressed in tenths of a cent per dollar of assessed valuation.

As a **mill rate**, this tax rate is expressed as mills per dollar of assessed valuation. Since 1 mill equals one-tenth of a cent, a 4¢ tax rate is the same as 40 mills. Expressed as *dollars per hundred*, the same rate would be $4 per hundred of assessed valuation. As *dollars per thousand*, it would be $40 per thousand.

The city of Rostin also calculates its tax rate by dividing its property tax requirements by the assessed value of the property within its boundaries. Suppose that its needs are $3 million and the city limits enclose property totaling $100 million in assessed valuation. (In this example, the city covers a smaller geographical area than the school district.) Thus, the city must collect 3¢ for each dollar of assessed valuation in order to balance its budget.

The county government's budget requires $20 million from property taxes and the county contains $2 billion in assessed valuation. This makes the county tax rate 1¢ per dollar of assessed valuation. Table 15.1 shows the school district, city, and county tax rates expressed as mills, dollars per hundred, and dollars per thousand.

TABLE 15.1 Expressing Property Tax Rates	Mill Rate	Dollars per Hundred	Dollars per Thousand
School District	40 mills	$4.00	$40.00
City	30	3.00	30.00
County	10	1.00	10.00
Total	80 mills	$8.00	$80.00

Source: © 2014 OnCourse Learning

APPLYING THE RATE

The final step is to apply the tax rate to each property. Applying the mill rate to a home with an assessed value of $200,000 is simply a matter of multiplying the 80 mills (the equivalent of 8¢) by the assessed valuation to arrive at property taxes of $16,000 per year. On a dollars per hundred basis, divide the $200,000 assessed valuation by $100 and multiply by $8. The result is $16,000. To ensure collection, a lien for this amount is placed against the property. It is removed when the tax is paid. Property **tax liens** are superior to other types of liens. A mortgage foreclosure does not clear property tax liens; they still must be paid.

tax lien

A charge or hold by the government against property to ensure the payment of taxes.

To avoid duplicate tax bill mailings, it is a common practice for all taxing bodies in a given county to have the county collect for them at the same time that the county collects on its own behalf. Property tax years generally fall into two categories: January 1 through December 31, and July 1 through the following June 30. Some states require one payment per year; others collect in two installments. A few allow a small discount for early payment, and all charge penalties for late payments.

Because of the monumental volume of numbers and calculations necessary to budget, appropriate, appraise, assess, and calculate property taxes, computers are widely used in property tax offices. Computers also prepare property tax bills, account for property tax receipts, and mail computer-generated notices to those who have not paid.

Unpaid Property Taxes

If you own real estate and fail to pay the property taxes, you will lose the property. In some states, title to delinquent property is transferred to the county or state. A redemption period follows during which the owner or any lienholder can redeem the property by paying back taxes and penalties. If redemption does not occur, the property is sold at a publicly announced auction and the highest bidder receives a *tax deed*. In other states, the sale is held soon after the delinquency occurs and the redemption period follows. At the sale, a **tax certificate** or *certificate of sale* in the amount of the unpaid taxes is sold. The purchaser is entitled to a deed to the property provided the delinquent taxpayer or anyone holding a lien on the property does not step forward and redeem it during the redemption period that follows. If it is redeemed, the purchaser receives his money back plus interest. The reason that a lienholder (such as a mortgage lender) is allowed to redeem a property is that if the property taxes are not paid, the lienholder's creditor rights in the property are cut off due to the superiority of the tax lien.

tax certificate

A document issued at a tax sale that entitles the purchaser to a deed at a later date if the property is not redeemed.

The right of government to divorce a property owner from his land for nonpayment of property taxes is well established by law. However, if the sale procedure is not properly followed, the purchaser may later find the property's title successfully challenged in court. Thus, it behooves the purchaser to obtain a title search and title insurance and, if necessary, to conduct a quiet title suit.

Assessment Appeal

By law, assessment procedures must be uniformly applied to all properties within a taxing jurisdiction. To this end, the assessed values of all lands and buildings are made available for public inspection. These are the **assessment rolls**. They permit a property owner to compare the assessed valuation on his property with assessed valuations on similar properties. If an owner feels over assessed, he can then file an appeal before an **assessment appeal board** or before a board of review, board of equalization, or tribunal. Some states also provide further appeal channels or permit appeal to a court of law if the property owner remains dissatisfied with the assessment. Note that the appeal process deals only with the methods of assessment and taxation, not with the tax rate or the amount of tax.

In some states, the **board of equalization** performs another assessment-related task, that of equalizing assessment procedures between counties. This is particularly important where county-collected property taxes are shared with the state or other counties. Without equalization, it would be to a county's financial advantage to under assess so as to lessen its contribution. At present, two equalization methods are in common usage: One requires that all counties use the same appraisal procedure and assessed valuation ratio, and the other allows each county to choose its own method and then applies a correction as determined by the board. For example, a state may contain counties that assess at 20%, 24%, and 30% of fair market value. These could be equalized by multiplying assessed values in the 20% counties by 1.50, in the 24% counties by 1.25, and in the 30% counties by 1.

Property Tax Exemptions

More than half the land in many cities and counties is exempt from real property taxation. This is because governments and their agencies do not tax themselves or each other. Thus, government-owned offices of all types, public roads and parks, schools, military bases, and government-owned utilities are exempt from property taxes. Also exempted are most properties owned by religious and charitable organizations (so long as they are used for religious or charitable purposes), hospitals, and cemeteries. In rural areas of many states, large tracts of land are owned by federal and state governments, and these too are exempt from taxation.

Property tax exemptions are used to attract industries. For example, a local government agency buys industrial land and buildings, and leases them to industries at a price lower than would be possible if they were privately owned and, hence, taxed. Alternatively, outright property tax reductions can be granted for a certain length of time to newly established or relocating firms. The rationale is that the cost to the public is outweighed by the economic boost that the new industry brings to the community. A number of states grant assessment reductions (often called **homestead exemption**) to homeowners for their primary residence. This increases the tax burden for households that rent and for commercial properties.

California and several other states have enacted laws that allow elderly homeowners to postpone payment of their property taxes. The state delays collection of the taxes and puts a lien on the property. Interest is charged each year on the postponed taxes and postponement can continue indefinitely. The amount due is not payable until the home is sold, or the owners die (in which case the estate or heirs would pay), or the property, for some other reason, ceases to qualify. To qualify, all owners must live in the home and have reached a certain age—62 years, for example. Additionally, there may be a limitation on household income in order to qualify.

Property Tax Variations

Property taxes on similarly priced homes within a city or county can vary widely when prices change faster than the assessor's office can reappraise. As a result, a home worth $90,000 in one neighborhood may receive a tax bill of $1,800 per year, while a $90,000 home in another neighborhood will be billed $2,400. When the assessor's office conducts a reappraisal, taxes in the first neighborhood will suddenly rise to 33%, undoubtedly provoking complaints from property owners who were unaware that previously they were under assessed. In times of slow-changing real estate prices, reappraisals were made only once every 10 years. Today, many assessors have computerized appraisal systems that can make adjustments annually.

As an aid to keeping current on property value changes, states are enacting laws that require a real estate buyer to advise the assessor's office of the price and terms of his purchase within 90 days after taking title. This information, coupled with building permit records and on-site visits by assessor's office employees, provides the data necessary to regularly update assessments.

The amount of property taxes a property owner may expect to pay varies from one city to the next and one state to the next. Why is this? The answer is found by looking at the level of services offered, other sources of revenue, taxable property, and government efficiency. Generally, cities with low property taxes offer fewer services to their residents. This may be by choice, such as smaller welfare payments, lower school expenditures per student, no subsidized public transportation, fewer parks and libraries, or because the city does not include the cost of some services in the property tax. For example, sewer fees may be added to the water bill and trash may be hauled by private firms. Lower rates can also be due to location. Wage rates are lower in some regions of the country, and a city not subject to ice and snow will have lower street maintenance expenses. Finally, a city may have other sources of revenue, such as oil royalties from wells on city property.

Property tax levels are also influenced by the ability of local tax districts to obtain federal funds and state revenues (especially for schools), and to share in collections from sales taxes, license fees, liquor and tobacco taxes, and fines.

The amount and type of taxable property in a community greatly affect local tax rates. Taxable property must bear the burden avoided by tax-exempt property, whereas privately owned vacant land, stores, factories, and high-priced homes generally produce more taxes than they consume in local government services and help to keep rates lower. Finally, one must look at the efficiency of the city. Has it managed its affairs in prior years so that the current budget is not burdened with large interest payments on debts caused by deficits in previous years? Is the city or county itself laid out in a compact and efficient manner, or does its sheer size make administration expensive? How many employees are required to perform a given service?

Special Assessments

Often, the need arises to make local municipal improvements that will benefit property owners within a limited area. Improvements may include paving a street; installing street lights, curbs, storm drains, and sanitary sewer lines; or constructing irrigation and drainage ditches. Such improvements can be provided through **special assessments** (sometimes referred to as **impact fees**) on property.

The theory underlying special assessments is that the improvements must benefit the land against which the cost will be charged, and the value of the benefits must exceed the cost. The area receiving the benefit of an improvement is the **improvement district** or **assessment district**, and the property within that district bears the cost of the improvement. This is different from a **public improvement**. A public improvement, such as reconstruction of the city's sewage plant, benefits the general public and is financed through the general (ad valorem) property tax. A local improvement, such as extending a sewer line into a street of homes presently using septic tanks or cesspools, does not benefit the public at large and should properly be charged only to those who directly benefit. Similarly, when streets are widened, owners of homes lining a 20-foot-wide street in a strictly residential neighborhood would be expected to bear the cost of widening it to 30 or 40 feet and to donate the needed land from their front yards. But a street widening from two lanes to four to accommodate traffic not generated by the homes on the street is a different situation because the widening benefits the public at large. In this case, the street widening is funded from public monies, and the homeowners are paid for any land taken from them.

FORMING AN IMPROVEMENT DISTRICT

An improvement district can be formed by the action of a group of concerned citizens who want and are willing to pay for an improvement. Property owners desiring the improvement take their proposal to the local board of assessors or similar public body in charge of levying assessments. A public notice showing the proposed improvements, the extent of the improvement district, and the anticipated costs is prepared by the board. This notice is mailed to landowners in the proposed improvement district, posted conspicuously in the district, and published in a local newspaper. The notice also contains the date and place of public hearings on the matter at which property owners within the proposed district are invited to voice their comments and objections.

CONFIRMATION

If the hearings result in a decision to proceed, then under the authority granted by state laws regarding special improvements, a local government ordinance is passed that describes the project and its costs and the improvement district boundaries. An assessment roll is also prepared that shows the cost to each parcel in the district. Hearings are held regarding the assessment roll. When everything is in order, the roll is **confirmed** (approved). Then the contract to construct the improvements is awarded and work is started.

The proposal to create an improvement district can also come from a city council, board of trustees, or board of supervisors. When this happens, notices are distributed and hearings held to hear objections from affected parties. Objections are ruled upon by a court of law, and if found to have merit, the assessment plans must be revised or dropped. Once approved, assessment rolls are prepared, more hearings are held, the roll is confirmed, and the contract is awarded.

BOND ISSUES

Upon completion of the improvement, each landowner receives a bill for his portion of the cost. If the cost to a landowner is less than $100, the landowner either pays the amount in full to the contractor directly or to a designated public official who, in turn, pays the contractor. If the assessment is larger, the landowner can immediately pay it in full or let it go to bond. If he lets it **go to bond**, local government officials prepare a bond issue that totals all the unpaid assessments in the improvement district. These bonds are either given to the contractor as payment for his work or sold to the public through a securities dealer, and the proceeds are used to pay the contractor. The collateral for the bonds is the land in the district upon which assessments have not been paid.

The bonds spread the cost of the improvements over a period of 5 to 10 years and are payable in equal annual (or semiannual) installments plus accumulated interest. Thus, a $2,000 sewer and street-widening assessment on a 10-year bond would be charged to a property owner at the rate of $200 per year (or $100 each six months) plus interest. As the bond is gradually retired, the amount of interest added to the regular principal payment declines.

Like property taxes, special assessments are a lien against the property. Consequently, if a property owner fails to pay his assessment, the assessed property can be sold in the same manner as when property taxes are delinquent.

APPORTIONMENT

Special assessments are apportioned according to benefits received rather than by the value of the land and buildings being assessed. In fact, the presence of buildings in an improvement district is not usually considered in preparing the assessment roll; the theory is that the land receives all the benefit of the improvement. Several illustrations can best explain how assessments are apportioned. In a residential neighborhood, the assessment for installation of storm drains, curbs, and gutters is made on a **front-foot basis**. A property owner is charged for each foot of his lot that abuts the street being improved.

In the case of a sanitary sewer line assessment, the charge per lot can either be based on front footage or on a simple count of the lots in the district. In the latter case, if there are 100 lots on the new sewer line, each would pay 1% of the cost. In the case of a park or playground, lots nearest the new facility are deemed to benefit more and, are assessed more than lots located farther away. This form of allocation is very subjective, and usually results in spirited objections at public hearings from those who do not feel they will use the facility in proportion to the assessment that their lots will bear.

Income Taxes on the Sale of One's Residence

We now turn to the income taxes that are due if you sell your personal residence for more than you paid. Income taxes are levied by the federal government, by 41 states (the exceptions are Florida, Nevada, South Dakota, Texas, Washington, and Wyoming), and by 48 cities, including New York City, Baltimore, Pittsburgh, Philadelphia, Cincinnati, Cleveland, and Detroit. The discussion here centers on the federal income tax and includes key provisions of the **Internal Revenue Code** as it applies to owner-occupied residences. Aspects of this act that apply to real estate investments are located in Chapter 27. State and city income tax laws generally follow the pattern of federal tax laws.

CALCULATING A HOME'S BASIS

The first step in determining the amount of taxable gain upon the sale of an owner-occupied residence is to calculate the home's **basis**. This is the price originally paid for the home plus any fees paid for closing services and legal counsel and any fee or commission paid to help find the property. If the home was built rather than purchased, the basis is the cost of the land plus the cost of construction, such as the cost of materials and construction labor, architect's fees, building permit fees, planning and zoning commission approval costs, utility connection charges, and legal fees. The value of labor contributed by the homeowner and free labor from friends and relatives cannot be added. If the home was received as compensation, a gift, an inheritance, or in a trade, or if a portion of the home was depreciated for business purposes, special rules apply

basis

The price paid for property; used in calculating income taxes.

that will not be covered here, and the seller should consult the Internal Revenue Service (IRS), or an experienced CPA, or tax attorney.

Assessments for local improvements and any improvements made by the seller are added to the original cost of the home. An improvement is a permanent betterment that materially adds to the value of a home, prolongs its life, or changes its use. For example, finishing an unfinished basement or upper floor, building a swimming pool, adding a bedroom or bathroom, installing new plumbing or wiring, installing a new roof, erecting a new fence, and paving a new driveway are classed as improvements and are added to the home's basis. Maintenance and repairs are not added as they merely maintain the property in ordinary operating condition. Fixing gutters, mending leaks in plumbing, replacing broken windowpanes, and painting the inside or outside of the home are considered maintenance and repair items. However, repairs made as part of an extensive remodeling or restoration job may be added to the basis.

CALCULATING THE AMOUNT REALIZED

The next step in determining taxable gain is to calculate the **amount realized** from the sale. This is the selling price of the home, less selling expenses. Selling expenses include brokerage commissions, advertising, legal fees, title services, escrow or closing fees, and mortgage points paid by the seller. If the sale includes furnishings, the value of those furnishings is deducted from the selling price and reported separately as personal property. If the seller takes back a note and mortgage which are immediately sold at a discount, the discounted value of the note, not its face amount, is used.

CALCULATING GAIN ON THE SALE

The **gain on the sale** is the difference between the amount realized and the basis. Table 15.2 illustrates this with an example. Unless the seller qualifies for tax postponement or tax exclusion (discussed next), this is the amount to be reported as gain on the seller's annual income tax forms. To increase compliance with this rule, effective January 1, 1987, reporting of real estate transactions on IRS Form1099 is required of persons in the following order: (1) the person responsible for the closing, (2) the mortgage lender, (3) the seller's broker, (4) the buyer's broker, and (5) any person designated by the IRS.

INCOME TAX EXCLUSION

A special rule applies to the sale or exchange of a taxpayer's principal residence. Under the rule, a taxpayer can exclude $250,000 of gain from the sale of the taxpayer's principal

TABLE 15.2	Calculation of Gain		
Buy home for $200,000; closing costs are $1,500		Basis is	$201,500
Add landscaping and fencing for $10,000		Basis is	211,500
Add bedroom and bathroom for $45,000		Basis is	256,500
Sell home for $325,000; sales commissions and closing costs are $26,000		Amount realized	$299,000
Calculation of gain		Amount realized	$299,000
		Less basis	256,500
		Equals gain	$42,500

Source: © 2014 OnCourse Learning

residence. If the taxpayer is married, there is a $500,000 exclusion for married individuals filing jointly, if: (1) either spouse meets the ownership test, (2) both spouses meet the use test (the taxpayer has resided there for two of the last five years), (3) a husband and wife file a joint return in the year of sale or exchange, and (4) neither spouse is ineligible for exclusion by virtue of sale or exchange of residence within the last two years. There is a new rule for surviving spouses (surviving spouses are unmarried and therefore would be subject to the $250,000 limitation rather than the $500,000 limitation). A new 2008 amendment to the Internal Revenue Code allows the taxpayer to extend the $500,000 benefit so long as the property is sold within two years after the date of the death of the spouse and the other requirements for tax exclusion are met. This eliminates taxable gain on the sale of a residence up to these limits. This exclusion is allowable each time the homeowner meets the eligibility requirement, but generally no more frequently than once every two years.

The IRS no longer receives notification of any home sales of $250,000, or under $500,000 for married taxpayers, provided that the homebuyer provides to the escrow agent assurances that: (1) the home was a principal residence, (2) there was no federally subsidized mortgage financing assistance, and (3) the final gain is excludable from gross income.

There are a few exceptions to the two-year use rule: If a uniformed or foreign service personnel is called away to active duty, there's a change in the taxpayer's place of employment, the taxpayer is forced to move for health reasons, or other unforeseen circumstances recognized by the IRS, the taxpayer can prorate their tax exclusion.

One thing we have learned is that in the expensive housing market, a profit in excess of $500,000 is relatively common. For instance, buying a $2 million house, holding it for five or six years, and reselling it for $2.6 million, yields a tax on the extra $100,000 after the $500,000 exclusion. So, what looks like a big tax benefit results on a higher tax for more expensive housing.

There is still a need to keep records for home improvements, however. The gain is calculated as the sales price, less the home's basis, or **adjusted basis**, whichever is applicable. If you are in a house that will never exceed the allowable gain, then there is no need to keep a record of requirements.

adjusted basis
The sales price of a property less commissions, fix-up, and closing costs.

Capital Gains

The **Jobs and Growth Tax Relief Reconciliation Act of 2003** reduced the 10% on the adjusted net capital gain to 5% for individuals in the 10% or 15% tax bracket, and reduced the 20% rates on the adjusted net capital gain to 15% for individuals in the 25% to 35% tax brackets. This created lower rates for capital assets sold or exchanged (and installment payments received) on or after May 6, 2003, that were held for more than 12 months. In addition, the 5% tax rate is reduced to 0% (as in "tax-free") for taxable years beginning after December 31, 2007, and before January 1, 2009. This favorable tax treatment expired in 2012. Two big changes became effective in 2013. The first is the increase of capital gains tax from 15% to 20% for those in the top tax bracket. The second is an additional 3.8% Medicare contribution tax which is defined as a tax on higher income individuals, estates, and trusts on the taxpayer's net investment income (NII). Upper income individuals are defined as people who earn more than $400,000 ($450,000 if filing jointly) per year and it applies only to the profit earned by the taxpayer after deducting the exclusions from the sales price. See Table 15.3.

There are interesting economic philosophies about capital gains tax. It is supposed to stimulate capital investments (good for a growing economy) by providing tax breaks on

TABLE 15.3	Long-Term Capital Gains Rates				
Tax Bracket	**1/1/01–5/5/03**	**5/6/03–12/31/07**	**2008–2010**	**2011–2012**	**2013**
10% and 15%	8%/10%	5%	0%	10%	15%
25%	20%	15%	15%	15%	20%*

*upper income only

Source: © 2014 OnCourse Learning

the profit when the capital asset is resold. Capital gains have a secondary effect, however. When the asset is sold, brokers, lawyers, title companies, and various service providers all make their fees. These fees are taxed at normal income rates. The result: more total tax income to the government. If there are no tax incentives, and the capital asset is not sold (because the investor prefers to keep the income), no fees are generated. History has shown us that when capital gains tax is reduced, the economy tends to strengthen. The latest capital gains tax cuts have shown that history has repeated itself. Because tax rules continue to change, creating many "window periods" involving sales dates and rate fluctuations, tax counsel should be consulted to determine the exact date and rate applicable for any given transaction.

Installment Method

installment method

Sale of real estate in which the proceeds of the sale are deferred beyond the year of sale.

When a gain cannot be postponed or excluded, a popular method of deferring income taxes is to use the **installment method** of reporting the gain. This can be applied to homeowner gains that do not qualify for postponement or exclusion.

Suppose that your property, which is free and clear of debt, is sold for $100,000. The real estate commission and closing costs are $7,500 and your basis is $40,000. As a result, the gain on this sale is $52,500. If you sell for all cash, you are required to pay all the income taxes due on that gain in the year of sale, a situation that may force you into a higher tax bracket. A solution is to sell to the buyer on terms rather than to send him to a lender to obtain a loan.

For example, if the buyer pays you $20,000 down and gives you a promissory note calling for a principal payment of $5,000, plus interest this year, and a principal payment of $25,000 plus interest in each of the next three years, your gain is calculated and reported as follows: Of each dollar of sales price received, 52.5¢ is reported as gain. Thus, $13,125 is reported this year and in each of the next three years. The interest you earn on the promissory note is reported and taxed separately as interest income.

If there is a $30,000 mortgage on the property that the buyer agrees to assume, the $100,000 sales price is reduced by $30,000 to $70,000 for tax-calculating purposes. The portion of each dollar paid to you by the buyer that must be reported as gain is $52,500 divided by $70,000, or 75%. If the down payment is $20,000 followed by $10,000 per year for five years, you would report 75% of $20,000, or $15,000 this year, and $7,500 in each of the next five years. The gain is taxed at the income tax rates in effect at the time the installment is received.

If you sell by the installment method, that is, you sell property at a gain in one taxable year and receive one or more payments in later taxable years, the installment method of reporting is automatically applied. If this is not suitable, you can elect to pay all the taxes in the year of sale. The installment method is only available to those who are not "dealers" in real property. All dealers in real property are required to pay all the taxes in the year of sale.

Property Tax and Interest Deductions

The Internal Revenue Code provides for the deductibility of state and local real estate taxes. A homeowner can deduct real property taxes and personal property taxes from other income when calculating income taxes. This applies to single-family residences, condominiums, and cooperatives. The deduction does not extend to special assessment taxes for improvement districts.

The Internal Revenue Code also provides for the deductibility of interest (subject to two limitations that will be discussed separately). However, the basic rule is that interest paid to finance the purchase of a home is deductible against a homeowner's other income. Also deductible are interest paid on improvement district bonds, loan prepayment penalties, and the deduction of points on new loans that are clearly distinguishable as interest and not service fees for making the loan. Loan points paid by a seller to help a buyer obtain an FHA or VA loan are not deductible as interest (it is not the seller's debt), but can be deducted from the home's selling price in computing a gain or loss on the sale. FHA mortgage insurance premiums are not deductible, nor are those paid to private mortgage insurers.

Interest Deduction Limitations

The Internal Revenue Code limits the interest deduction to the taxpayer's principal residence plus one other residence.

All of the interest is deductible on a loan to purchase a first or second home, although the aggregate amount of acquisition indebtedness may not exceed $1 million. However, if a home is refinanced, and the amount borrowed exceeds the home's basis (original cost plus improvements, etc.), the interest on the excess amount is not deductible. The aggregate amount of home equity indebtedness may not exceed $100,000. Thus, a homeowner will want to keep records of his or her home's basis for sale purposes but also as information for refinancing. Also, if refinancing above basis is for medical or educational purposes, then careful records of those expenses must be kept in order to justify the deduction.

From an individual taxpayer's standpoint, the ability to deduct property taxes and mortgage interest on one's residence becomes more valuable in higher tax brackets. As viewed from a national standpoint, the deductibility of interest and property taxes encourages widespread ownership of the country's land and buildings.

Impact on Real Estate

Because tax rules for real estate are continually changing, only the major rules have been reported and discussed here and in Chapter 27. As a real estate owner or agent, you need a source of more frequent and more detailed information, such as the annual income tax guide published by the Internal Revenue Service (free) or the privately published guides available in most bookstores. Additionally, you may wish to subscribe to a tax newsletter for up-to-the-minute tax information.

Please be aware that tax law changes have an impact on real estate values. In the past, tax laws have been very generous to real estate—particularly deductions for depreciation and interest, as well as credits for there habilitation of old buildings. Many otherwise uneconomic real estate projects have become economically feasible because of tax laws. As tax laws have changed to reduce the incentive to buy real estate, they have had a dramatic effect on real estate investors and, predictably, the sales price of parcels of real estate.

Agent's Liability for Tax Advice

The real estate industry's desire for professional recognition, coupled with the results of several key court cases, strongly suggests that a real estate agent be reasonably knowledgeable about taxes. This does not mean the agent must have knowledge of tax laws at the level of an accountant or tax attorney. Neither does it mean an agent can plead ignorance of tax laws. Rather it means a real estate agent is now liable for tax advice (or lack of it) if the advice is material to the transaction, and to give such advice is common in the brokerage business. What this means is that an agent should have enough general knowledge of real estate tax laws to be able to answer basic questions accurately, and to warn clients and recommend tax counsel if the questions posed by the transaction are beyond the agent's knowledge. Note that the obligation to inform exists even when a client fails to ask about tax consequences. This is to avoid situations in which, after the deed is recorded, the client says, "Gee, I didn't know I'd have to pay all these taxes, my agent should have warned me," and then sues the agent. Lastly, if the agent tries to fill the role of an accountant or a tax attorney for the client, then the agent will be held liable to the standards of an accountant or a tax attorney.

To summarize, an agent must be aware of tax laws that affect the properties the agent is handling. An agent has a responsibility to alert clients to potential tax consequences, liabilities, and advantages whether they ask for it or not. Lastly, an agent is responsible for the quality and accuracy of tax information given out by the agent.

Conveyance Taxes

documentary tax

A fee or tax on deeds and other documents payable at the time of recordation.

Before 1968, the federal government required the purchase and placement of federal **documentary tax** stamps on deeds. The rate was 55¢ for each $500 or fraction thereof computed on the "new money" in the transaction. Thus, if a person bought a home for $75,000 and either paid cash or arranged for a new mortgage, the tax was based on the full $75,000. If the buyer assumed or took title subject to an existing $50,000 loan, then the tax was based on $25,000. Examples of federal documentary tax stamps, which look much like postage stamps, can still be seen on deeds recorded prior to 1968.

Effective January 1, 1968, the federal deed tax program ended, and many states took the opportunity to begin charging a deed tax or **conveyance tax** of their own. Some adopted fee schedules that are substantially the same as the federal government previously charged. Others base their fee on the purchase price without regard to any existing indebtedness left on the property by the seller. Forty-one states, the District of Columbia, and some counties and cities charge a transfer tax. The amount ranges from just a few dollars to as much as $4,500 on the sale of a $100,000 property. These fees are paid to the county recorder prior to recording and are in addition to the charge for recording the document itself. Some states also charge a separate tax on the value of any mortgage debt created by a transaction.

Vocabulary Review

Match terms a–p with statements 1–16.

a. Adjusted basis
b. Ad valorem tax
c. Appropriation process
d. Assessed value
e. Assessment appeal board
f. Assessment roll
g. Conveyance tax
h. Front-foot basis
i. Improvement district
j. Installment method
k. Long-term capital gain
l. Mill rate
m. Public improvement
n. Special assessments
o. Tax certificate
p. Tax deed

_____ 1. A tax rate expressed in tenths of a cent per dollar of assessed valuation.

_____ 2. According to value.

_____ 3. A document issued at a tax sale that entitles the purchaser to a deed at a later date if the property is not redeemed.

_____ 4. The enactment of a taxing body's budget and sources of money into law.

_____ 5. A book that contains the assessed value of each property in the county or taxing district.

_____ 6. A document conveying title to property purchased at a tax sale.

_____ 7. A value placed on a property for the purpose of taxation.

_____ 8. Assessments levied to provide publicly built improvements that will primarily benefit property owners within a small geographical area.

_____ 9. A charge or levy based directly on the measured distance that a parcel of land abuts a street.

_____ 10. Sales price of a property less fix-up costs and sales commissions, closing costs, and other selling costs.

_____ 11. A preferential income tax treatment on the sale of an appreciated asset.

_____ 12. Sale of an appreciated property structured to spread out the payment of income taxes on the gain.

_____ 13. Hears complaints from property owners regarding their assessments.

_____ 14. A state or local tax charged on deeds at the time of recording.

_____ 15. The geographical area which will be assessed for a local improvement.

_____ 16. An improvement that benefits the public at large and is therefore financed by general property taxes.

Questions and Problems

1. Explain the process of calculating the property tax rate for a taxation district.

2. The Southside School District contains property totaling $120 million in assessed valuation. If the district's budget is $960,000, what will the mill rate be?

3. Continuing with Problem 2 above, if a home situated in the Southside School District carries an assessed valuation of $40,000, how much will the homeowner be required to pay to support the district this year?

4. The Lakeview Mosquito Abatement District levies an annual tax of $0.05 per $100 of assessed valuation to pay for a mosquito control program. How much does that amount to for a property in the district with an assessed valuation of $10,000?

5. In your county, if a property owner wishes to appeal an assessment, what procedure must be followed?

6. If the property taxes on your home were to rise 90% in one year, where would you go to protest the increase: to the assessment appeal board, to the city council, or to the county government? Explain.

7. How does the amount of tax-exempt real estate in a community affect nonexempt property owners?

8. What methods and techniques are used by your local assessor's office to keep up to date with the changing real estate prices?

9. The Smiths bought a house in 1993 for $210,000, including closing costs. Five years later they made improvements costing $12,000 and five years after that more improvements that cost $15,000. Today they sell the house; the sales price is $268,000, and commissions and closing costs total $15,000. For income tax purposes, what is their gain?

10. What is the conveyance tax rate in your state? What would the conveyance tax be on a $100,000 home?

Additional Readings

"Financing New Home Construction Can Be 'Taxing' the Loan Closer" by John McDermott (*Origination News*, April 2001, p. 8).

Glossary for Property Appraisal and Assessment (International Association of Assessing Officers, 1997).

"Low Income Housing Contracts Considered in Real Estate Taxes" (*Appraisal Journal*, January 2002, p. 2).

Price It Right For Profit: Tax Assessment Approach to Real Estate Values by John R. Hough (Hough Company, Incorporated, 1997).

Property Assessment Valuation (International Association of Assessing Officers, 1996).

Real Estate Investment, 7th ed. by John P. Wiedemer, Joseph E. Goeters and J. Edward Graham (OnCourse Learning, 2011). Analyzes and compares the relative benefits of real estate investment opportunities.

Tax Considerations for the Residential Real Estate Professional, Updated for 1997 Laws, by Randall S. van Reken (OnCourse Learning, 1998). A concise overview of relevant tax issues for practicing agents.

Tax Information on Selling Your Home (Internal Revenue Service, Publication 523). This publication is free and is offered annually from the IRS.

CHAPTER 16

Title Closing and Escrow

N umerous details must be handled between the time a buyer and seller sign a sales contract and the day title is conveyed to the buyer. Title must be searched (Chapter 6), a decision made as to how to take title (Chapter 4), a deed prepared (Chapter 5), loan arrangements made (Chapters 9 through 14), property tax records checked (Chapter 15), and so forth. In this chapter we will look at the final steps in the process, in particular, the buyer's walk-through, the closing meeting or escrow, prorations, and the settlement statement.

Buyers' Walk-Through

To protect both the buyer and the seller, it is good practice for a buyer to make a **walk-through**. This is a final inspection of the property just prior to the settlement date. It is quite possible the buyer has not been on the parcel or inside the structure since the initial offer and acceptance. Now, several weeks later, the buyer wants to make certain that the premises have been vacated, that no damage has occurred, that the seller has left behind personal property agreed upon, and that the seller has not removed and taken any real property. If the sales contract requires all mechanical items to be in normal working order, then the buyer will want to test the heating and air-conditioning systems, dishwasher, disposer, stove, garage door opener, and so on, and the refrigerator, washer, and dryer, if included. The buyer will also want to test all of the plumbing to be certain the hot water heater works, faucets and showers run, toilets flush, and sinks drain. A final inspection of the structure is made, including walls, roof, gutters, driveway, decks, patios, and so on, as well as the land and landscaping.

LEARNING OBJECTIVES

After reading this chapter, you should be able to:

❬ Describe the benefits of a buyer's walk-through.

❬ Define and understand the meaning of a closing or settlement meeting.

❬ Describe the purposes of an escrow and the duties of an escrow agent.

❬ Describe and calculate how to prorate taxes, insurance, and rents on a closing statement.

❬ Understand the requirements for the Closing Disclosure

❬ Understand the requirements of the Real Estate Settlement Procedures Act and its application to a residential transaction.

❬ Understand the application of the most recent changes to RESPA.

KEY TERMS

Closing meeting • Escrow agent • Escrow closing • Prorating • Real Estate Settlement • Real Estate Settlement Procedures Act (RESPA) • Settlement statement • Title closing • Walk-through

walk-through
A final inspection of the property just prior to settlement.

Note that a walk-through is not the time for the buyer to make the initial inspection of the property. That is done before the contract is signed, and if there are questions in the buyer's mind regarding the structural soundness of the property, a thorough inspection (possibly with the aid of a professional house inspector) should be conducted after signing the purchase contract, making the satisfactory inspection a condition to the buyer's obligation to purchase.

The walk-through is for the purpose of giving the buyer the opportunity to make certain that agreements regarding the condition of the premises have been kept. If during the walk-through the buyer notes the walls were damaged when the seller moved out, or the furnace does not function, the buyer (or the buyer's agent) notes these items and asks that funds be withheld at the closing to pay for repairs.

Title Closing

title closing

The process of completing a real estate transaction.

Title closing refers to the completion of a real estate transaction. This is when the buyer pays for the property and the seller delivers the deed. The day on which this occurs is called the **closing date**. Depending on where one resides in the United States, the title closing process is referred to as a **closing**, **settlement**, or **escrow**. All accomplish the same basic goal, but the method of reaching that goal can follow one of two paths.

In some parts of the United States, particularly in the East, and to a certain extent in the mountain states, the Midwest, and the South, the title closing process is concluded at a meeting of all parties to the transaction or their representatives. Elsewhere, title closing is conducted by an escrow agent who is a neutral third party mutually selected by the buyer and seller to carry out the closing. With an escrow, there is no closing meeting; in fact, most of the closing process is conducted by mail. Let's look at the operation of each method.

Closing or Settlement Meeting

When a meeting is used to close a real estate transaction, the seller meets in person with the buyer and delivers the deed. At the same time, the buyer pays the seller for the property. To ascertain that everything promised in the sales contract has been properly carried out, it is customary for the buyer and seller each to have an attorney present. The real estate agents who brought the buyer and seller together are also present, along with a representative of the firm that conducted the title search. If a new loan is being made or an existing one is being paid off at the closing, a representative of each lender may be present.

closing meeting

A meeting at which the buyer pays for the property and receives a deed to it, and all other matters pertaining to the sale are concluded.

The location of the meeting and the selection of the person responsible for conducting the closing will depend on local custom and the nature of the closing. It is the custom in some states to conduct the closing at the real estate agent's office. In other localities it is conducted in the office of the seller's attorney. An alternative is to have the title company responsible for the title search and title policy conduct the closing at its office. If a new loan is involved, the lender may want to conduct the closing. If the seller is unable to attend the **closing meeting**, the seller appoints someone, such as his lawyer or real estate agent, to represent him at the meeting. Similarly, a buyer who is unable to attend can appoint a representative to be present at the meeting. Appointment of a representative is accomplished by preparing and signing a power of attorney.

SELLER'S RESPONSIBILITIES AT CLOSING

To assure a smooth closing, each person attending is responsible for bringing certain documents. The seller and his attorney are responsible for preparing and bringing the deed together with the most recent property tax bill (and receipt if it has been paid). If required by the sales contract, they also bring the insurance policy for the property, the termite and wood-rot inspection report, deeds or documents showing the removal of unacceptable liens and encumbrances, a title insurance policy, a bill of sale for personal property, a survey map, and any needed offset statements or beneficiary statements. An **offset statement** is a statement by an owner or lienholder as to the balance due on an existing lien against the property. A **beneficiary statement** is a statement of the unpaid balance on a note secured by a trust deed. The loan payment booklet, keys to the property, the garage door opener, and the like are also brought to the meeting. If the property is a condominium, cooperative, or planned unit development, the seller will bring to the closing items such as the articles of incorporation; bylaws; conditions, covenants, and restrictions (CC&Rs); annual budget; reserve fund status report; and management company's name. If the property produces income, existing leases, rent schedules, current expenditures, and letters advising the tenants of the new owner must also be furnished.

BUYER'S RESPONSIBILITIES AT CLOSING

The buyer's responsibilities include having adequate settlement funds ready, having an attorney present if desired, and, if borrowing, obtaining the loan commitment, and advising the lender of the meeting time and place. The real estate agent is present because it is the custom in some localities that the agent be in charge of the closing and prepare the proration calculations. The agent also receives a commission check at that time and, as a matter of good business, will make certain that all goes well.

If a new loan is involved, the lender usually wires the funds to the escrow agent in the amount of the loan along with a note and mortgage for the borrower to sign. If an existing loan is to be paid off as part of the transaction, the lender will forward the balance due to the escrow agent in order to receive a check and release the mortgage held on the property. A title insurance representative is also present to provide the latest status of title and the title insurance policy. If title insurance is not used, the seller is responsible for bringing an abstract or asking the abstracter to be present.

REAL ESTATE AGENT'S DUTIES

The seller and the seller's attorney may be unaware of all the things expected of them at the closing. Therefore, it is the duty of the agent who listed the property to make certain that they are prepared for the meeting. Similarly, it is the duty of the agent who found the buyer to make certain that the buyer and the buyer's attorney are prepared for the closing. If the agent both lists and sells the property, the agent assists both the buyer and the seller. If more than one agent is involved in the transaction, each should keep the other(s) fully informed so the transaction will go as well as possible. At all times the buyer and seller are to be kept informed as to the status of the closing. An agent should give them a preview of what will take place, explain each payment or receipt, and in general prepare the parties for informed participation at the closing.

THE TRANSACTION

When everyone concerned has arrived at the meeting place, the closing begins. Those present record each other's names as witnesses to the meeting. The various documents called for by the sales contract are exchanged for inspection. The buyer and his attorney inspect the deed the seller is offering, the title search, and/or title policy, the mortgage papers, survey, leases, removals of encumbrances, and proration calculations. The lender also inspects the deed, survey, title search, and title policy. This continues until each party has a chance to inspect each document of interest.

settlement statement

An accounting of funds to the buyer and the seller at the completion of a real estate transaction.

A **settlement statement** (also called a closing statement) is given to the buyer and seller to summarize the financial aspects of their transaction. It is prepared by the person in charge of the closing either just prior to or at the meeting. It provides a clear picture of where the buyer's and seller's money is going at the closing by identifying each party to whom money is being paid. (See Figure 16.2.)

If everyone involved in the closing has done his or her homework and comes prepared to the meeting, the closing usually goes smoothly. When everything is in order, the seller hands a completed deed to the buyer. Simultaneously, the buyer gives the seller a check that combines the down payment and net result of the prorations. The lender has the buyer sign the mortgage and note and hands checks to the seller and the existing lender, if one is involved. The seller writes a check to his real estate broker, attorney, and the abstracter. The buyer writes a check to his attorney. These items may also be simply shown on the settlement statement, and credited or debited so only a "net" check needs to be issued to the party at the closing. At the end, everyone stands, shakes hands, and departs. The deed, new mortgage, and release of the old mortgage are recorded and the transaction is complete.

DRY CLOSING

Occasionally, an unavoidable circumstance can cause delays in a closing. Perhaps an important document, known to be in the mail, has not arrived. Yet it will be difficult to reschedule the meeting. In such a situation, the parties concerned may agree to a **dry closing** or **close into escrow**. In a dry closing, all parties sign their documents and entrust them to the person in charge of the closing for safekeeping. No money is disbursed and the deed is not delivered until the missing paperwork arrives. When it does, the transaction is completed and the money and documents are delivered by mail or messenger.

Escrow

escrow agent

The person placed in charge of an escrow.

The use of an **escrow** to close a real estate transaction involves a neutral third party called an **escrow agent**, escrow holder, or escrowee who acts as a trusted stakeholder for all the parties to the transaction. Instead of delivering a deed directly to the buyer at the closing meeting, the seller gives the deed to the escrow agent with instructions that it be delivered only after the buyer has completed all of the buyer's promises in the sales contract. Similarly, the buyer hands the escrow agent the money for the purchase price plus instructions that it be given to the seller only after fulfillment of the seller's promises. Let's look more closely at this arrangement.

escrow closing

The deposit of documents and funds with a neutral third party along with instructions as to how to conduct the closing.

A typical real estate **escrow closing** starts when a sales contract is signed by the buyer and seller. They select a neutral escrow agent to handle the closing. This may be the escrow department of a bank or savings and loan or other lending agency, an independent escrow company, an attorney, or the escrow department of a title insurance company. Sometimes real estate brokers offer escrow services. However, if the broker is earning a sales commission in the transaction, the broker cannot be classed as neutral and disinterested. Because escrow agents are entrusted with valuable documents and large sums of money, most states have licensing and bonding requirements that escrow agents must meet.

ESCROW AGENT'S DUTIES

The escrow agent's task begins with the deposit of the buyer's earnest money in a special bank trust account and the preparation of a set of escrow instructions based on the signed sales contract. These must be promptly signed by the buyer and seller. The instructions establish an agency relationship between the escrow agent and the buyer and between the escrow agent and the seller. The instructions also detail in writing everything that each party to the sale must do before the deed is delivered to the buyer. In a typical transaction, the escrow instructions will tell the escrow agent to order a title search and obtain title insurance.

If an existing loan against the property is to be repaid as part of the sale, the escrow agent is asked to contact the seller's lender to request a statement of the amount of money necessary to repay the loan and to request a mortgage release. The lender then enters into an agreement with the escrow agent wherein the lender is to give the completed release papers to the escrow agent; but the agent may not deliver them to the seller until the agent has remitted the amount demanded by the lender. If the existing loan is to be assumed, the escrow agent asks the lender for the current balance and any documents that the buyer must sign.

When the title search is completed, the escrow agent forwards it to the buyer or his attorney for approval. The property insurance and tax papers, the seller would otherwise bring to the closing meeting, are sent to the escrow agent for proration. Leases, service contracts, and notices to tenants are also sent to the escrow agent for proration and delivery to the buyer. The deed conveying title to the buyer is prepared by the seller's attorney (in some states by the escrow agent), signed by the seller, and given to the escrow agent. Once delivered into escrow, even if the seller dies, marries, or is declared legally incompetent before the close of escrow, the deed will still pass title to the buyer.

THE CLOSING

As the closing date draws near, and provided all the instructions are otherwise complete, the escrow agent requests any additional money the buyer and lender must deposit in order to close. The day before closing, the escrow agent calls the title company and orders a last-minute check on the title. If no changes have occurred since the first (preliminary) title search, the deed, mortgage, mortgage release, and other documents to be recorded as part of the transaction are recorded first thing the following morning. As soon as the recording is confirmed, the escrow agent hands or mails a check to every party to whom funds are due from the escrow (usually the seller, real estate broker, and previous lender), along with any papers or documents that must be delivered through escrow (such as the fire insurance policy, a copy of the property tax bill, and tenant leases). Several days later, the buyer and lender will receive a title insurance policy in the mail from the title company. The public recorder's office also mails the documents it recorded to each party. The deed is sent to the buyer, the mortgage release to the seller, and the new mortgage to the lender.

DEED DELIVERY

In the escrow closing method, the closing, delivery of title, and recordation usually take place all at the same moment. Technically, the seller does not physically hand a deed to the buyer on the closing day. However, once all the conditions of the escrow are met, the escrow agent becomes both an agent of the seller, in regard to the money in the transaction, and an agent of the buyer, in regard to the deed. Thus, the buyer, through an agent, receives the deed, and the law regarding **deed delivery** is fulfilled.

In an escrow closing, it is not necessary for the buyer and seller to meet face to face during the escrow period or at the closing. This can eliminate personality conflicts that might be detrimental to an otherwise sound transaction. The escrow agent, having accumulated all the documents, approvals, deeds, and monies prior to the closing date, does the closing alone.

In transactions involving real estate agents, the agent may be the only person who actually meets the escrow agent. All communication can be handled through the broker, by mail, or by telephone. If a real estate agent is not involved, the buyer and/or seller can open the escrow, either in person or by mail. The use of an escrow agent does not eliminate the need for an attorney. Although there is no closing meeting for the attorneys to attend, they play a vital role in advising the buyer and seller on each document sent by the escrow agent for approval and signature.

Delays and Failure to Close

When a real estate purchase contract is written, a closing date is also negotiated and placed in the contract. The choice of closing date will depend on when the buyer wants possession, when the seller wants to move out, and how long it will take to obtain a loan, title search, and termite report, and otherwise fulfill the contract requirements. In a typical residential sale, this is 30 to 60 days, with 45 days being a popular choice when new financing is involved.

Delays along the way are sometimes encountered and may cause a delay in the closing. This is usually not a problem as long as the buyer still intends to buy, the seller still intends to sell, and the delay is for a reasonable cause and a justifiable length of time. Many pre-printed real estate purchase contracts include a statement that the broker may extend the time for performance including the closing date. Even if the contract contains a "time is of the essence" clause, unless there is supporting evidence in the contract that time really is of the essence, reasonable delays for reasonable causes are usually permitted by law.

Suppose the delay will be quite lengthy. For example, there may be a previously undisclosed title defect that will take months to clear, or perhaps there are unusual problems in financing, or there has been major damage to the premises. In such cases, relieving all parties from further obligations may be the wisest choice for all involved. If so, it is essential that the buyer and seller sign mutual release papers. These are necessary to rescind the purchase contract and cancel the escrow if one has been opened. The buyer's deposit is also returned. Without release papers, the buyer still has a vaguely defined liability to buy and the seller can still be required to convey the property. A mutual release gives the buyer the freedom to choose another property and the seller the chance to fix the problem and remarket the property later.

A stickier problem occurs when one party wants out of the contract and attempts to use any delay in closing as grounds for contract termination. The buyer may have found a preferable property for less money and better terms, or the seller may have received a higher offer since signing the purchase contract. Although the party wishing to cancel may threaten with a lawsuit, courts will rarely enforce cancellation of valuable contract rights because of reasonable delays that are not the fault of the other party. Moreover, courts will not go along with a reluctant buyer or seller who manufactures delays so as to delay the closing and then claim default and cancellation of the contract. If the reluctance continues and negotiations to end it fail, the performing party may choose to complete its requirements and then ask the courts to force the reluctant party to the closing table.

Loan Escrows

Escrows can be used for purposes other than real estate sales transactions. For example, a homeowner who is refinancing his property could enter into a **loan escrow** with the lender. The conditions of the escrow would be that the homeowner deliver a properly executed note and mortgage to the escrow agent and that the lender deposit the loan money.

Upon closing, the escrow agent delivers the documents to the lender and the money to the homeowner. Or, in reverse, an escrow could be used to pay off the balance of a loan. The conditions would be the borrower's deposit of the balance due and the lender's deposit of the mortgage release and note. Even the weekly office sports pool is an escrow—with the person holding the pool money acting as escrow agent for the participants.

Reporting Requirements

The Internal Revenue Code now requires that the seller's proceeds from all sales of real estate be reported to the Internal Revenue Service on their Form 1099-S. The responsibility for filing Form 1099-S goes in the following order: the person responsible for the closing, the mortgage lender, the seller's broker, the buyer's broker, and any person designated by the U.S. Treasury. It is important to determine at the closing who needs to file the Form 1099-S. These forms must be filed at no charge to the taxpayer.

The Taxpayer Relief Act of 1997 provides that real estate reporting persons generally do not need to file Form 1099-S for sales or exchanges of a principal residence with a sales price at or below $250,000 for a single individual or $500,000 for a married couple, so long as the reporting person obtains a certification from the seller in a form that is satisfactory to the Secretary of the Treasury. The form must be in writing and signed by the seller, and it must confirm that:

1. the seller has owned and used the principal residence for two of the last five years;
2. the seller has not owned or exchanged another principal residence during this two-year period;
3. no portion of the residence has been used for business or rental purposes; and
4. the sales price, capital gains, and marital status filing requirements are met.

The form must be sworn to, under penalty of perjury. It must be obtained on or before January 31 of the year following the sale or exchange, and retained in the title company's files for four years.

Prorating at the Closing

Ongoing expenses and income items must be **prorated** between the seller and buyer when property ownership changes hands. Items subject to proration include property insurance premiums, property taxes, accrued interest on assumed loans, and rents and operating expenses if the property produces income. If heating is done by oil and the oil tank is partially filled when title transfers, that oil can be prorated, as can utility bills when service is not shut off between owners. Several sample prorations common to most closings will help clarify the process.

prorating
The division of ongoing expenses and income items between the buyer and the seller.

HAZARD INSURANCE

Hazard insurance policies for such things as fire, wind, storm, and flood damage are paid for in advance. At the beginning of each year of the policy's life, the premium for that year's coverage must be paid. When real estate is sold, the buyer may ask the seller to transfer the remaining coverage. The seller usually agrees if the buyer pays for the value of the remaining coverage on a prorated basis.

The first step in prorating hazard insurance is to find out how often the premium is paid, how much it is, and what period of time it covers. Suppose that the seller has a one-year policy that cost $180 and started on January 1 of the current year. If the property is sold and the closing date is July 1, the policy is half-used. Therefore, if the buyer wants the policy transferred, the buyer pays the seller $90 for the remaining six months of coverage.

Because closing dates do not always occur on neat, evenly divided portions of the year, nor do most items that need prorating, it is usually necessary to break the year into months and the months into days to make proration calculations. Suppose in the previous hazard insurance example that prorations are to be made on June 30 instead of July 1. This would give the buyer six months and one day of coverage. How much does the buyer owe the seller? The first step is to calculate the monthly and daily rates for the policy: $180 divided by 12 is $15 per month. Dividing the monthly rate of $15 by 30 days gives a daily rate of 50¢. The second step is to add six months at $15 and one day at 50¢. Thus, the buyer owes the seller $90.50 for the unused portion of the policy.

LOAN INTEREST

When a buyer agrees to assume an existing loan from the seller, an interest proration is necessary. For example, a sales contract calls for the buyer to assume a 9% mortgage loan with a principal balance of $80,505 at the time of closing. Loan payments are due the tenth of each month, and the sales contract calls for a July 3 closing date, with interest on the loan to be prorated through July 2. How much is to be prorated and to whom?

First, we must recognize that interest is normally paid in arrears. On a loan that is payable monthly, the borrower pays interest for the use of the loan at the end of each month he has had the loan. Thus, the July 10 monthly loan payment includes the interest due for the use of $80,505 from June 10 through July 9. However, the seller owned the property through July 2, and from June 10 through July 2 is 23 days. At the closing the seller must give the buyer enough money to pay for 23 days' interest on the $80,505. If the annual interest rate is 9%, one month's interest is $80,505 times 9% divided by 12, which is $603.79. Divide this by 30 days to get a daily interest rate of $20.126. Multiply the daily rate by 23 to obtain the interest for 23 days: $462.90.

30-DAY MONTH

In many parts of the country, it is the custom to use a 30-day month when prorating interest, property taxes, water bills, and insurance because it simplifies proration calculations. Naturally, using a 30-day month produces some inaccuracy when dealing with months that do not have 30 days. If this inaccuracy is significant to the buyer and seller, they can agree to prorate either by using the exact number of days in the closing month or by dividing the year rate by 365 to find a daily rate. Some states avoid this question altogether by requiring that the exact number of days be used in prorating.

RENTS

It is the custom throughout the country to prorate rents on the basis of the actual number of days in the month. Using the July 3 closing date again, if the property is currently rented for $450 per month, paid in advance on the first of each month, what would the proration be? If the seller has already collected the rent for the month of July, he is obligated to hand over to the buyer that portion of the rent earned between July 3 and July 31, inclusive, a period of 29 days. To determine how many dollars this is, divide $450 by the number of days in July. This gives $14.516 as the rent per day. Then multiply the daily rate by 29 days to get $420.96, the portion of the July rent that the seller must hand over to the buyer. If the renter has not paid the July rent by the July 3 closing date, no proration is made. If the buyer later collects the July rent, he must return two days' rent to the seller.

PROPERTY TAXES

Prorated property taxes are common to nearly all real estate transactions. The amount of proration depends on when the property taxes are due, what portion has already been paid, and what period of time they cover. Property taxes are levied on an annual basis, but, depending on the locality, they may be due at the beginning, middle, or end of the tax year. In some parts of the country, property owners are permitted to pay in two or more installments.

Suppose you live in a state where the property tax year runs from January 1 through December 31, property tax bills are mailed to property owners in late February, and taxes for the full year are due April 10. If a transaction calls for property taxes to be prorated through January 31, how is the calculation made? Since the new bill is not yet available, the old bill is often used as a guide. Suppose it was $1,200 for the year. The proration is from January 1 through January 31, a period of one month. One month's taxes are calculated as one-twelfth of $1,200, or $100. The seller owes the buyer $100 because the seller owned the property through January 31, yet the buyer will later receive and pay the property tax bill for the full year. If it is likely the new tax bill will be substantially different from the previous year's, the buyer and seller can agree to make another adjustment between themselves when the new bill is available. If property tax bills had been issued in January and taxes for the full year paid by the seller, the seller would be credited with 11 months × $100/month = $1,100, and the buyer charged $1,100.

HOMEOWNERS' ASSOCIATION

If the property being sold is a condominium unit or in a cooperative or a planned unit development, there will be a monthly homeowners' association payment to be prorated. Suppose the monthly fee is $120 and is paid in advance on the first of the month. If the closing takes place on the 20th, then the buyer owes the seller $40 for the unused portion of the month.

PRORATION DATE

Prorations need not be calculated as of the closing date. In the sales contract, the buyer and seller can mutually agree to a different proration date if they wish. If nothing is said, local law and custom will prevail. In some states it is customary to prorate as of the day before closing, the theory being that the buyer is the new owner beginning on the day the transaction closes. Other states prorate as of the day of closing. If the difference of one day is important to the buyer or seller, they should not rely on local custom, but agree in writing on a proration day of their own choosing.

Special assessments for such things as street improvements, water mains, and sewer lines are not usually prorated. As a rule, the selling price of the property reflects the added value of the improvements, and the seller pays any assessments in full before closing. This is not an ironclad rule; the buyer and seller in their sales contract can agree to do whatever they want about the assessment.

PRORATION SUMMARY

Figure 16.1 summarizes the most common proration situations found in real estate closings. The figure also shows who is to be charged, and who is to be credited, whether the proration is to be worked forward or backward from the closing date. As a rule, items

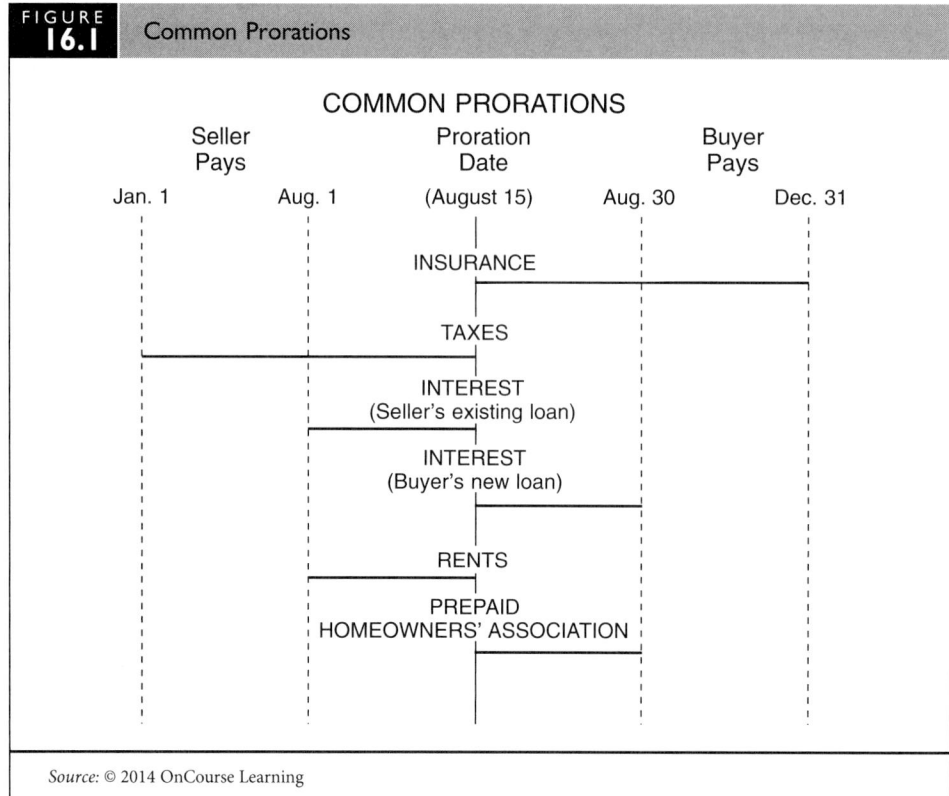

FIGURE **16.1**   Common Prorations

COMMON PRORATIONS

Source: © 2014 OnCourse Learning

that are paid in advance are prorated forward from the closing date—for example, prepaid fire insurance. Items that are paid in arrears, such as interest on an existing loan, are prorated backward from the closing date.

Sample Closing

To illustrate the arithmetic involved, let us work through a residential closing situation. Note that this example is not particular to any region of the United States, but is rather a composite that shows you how the most commonly encountered residential closing items are handled.

Homer Leavitt has listed his home for sale with List-Rite Realty for $125,000, and the sales commission is to be 6% of the selling price. A salesperson from Quick-Sale Realty learns about the property through the multiple listing service and produces a buyer willing to pay $123,000 with $33,000 down payment. The offer is conditional on the seller paying off the existing $48,000, 12% interest mortgage loan, and the buyer obtaining a new loan for $90,000. Property taxes, hazard insurance, and heating oil in the home's oil tank are to be prorated as of the closing date. The buyer also asks the seller to pay for a termite inspection and repairs if necessary, a title search, an owner's title insurance policy, conveyance taxes, and one-half of the closing fee. The seller accepts this offer on July 15, and they agree to close on August 15.

The property tax year for this home runs from January 1 through December 31. Mr. Leavitt has paid the taxes for last year, but not for the current year as yet. Newly issued tax bills show that $1,680 will be due on October 15 for the current year.

The hazard insurance policy (fire, windstorm, etc.) that the buyer wishes to assume was purchased by the seller for $240, and covers the period August 15 through the following May 14. The Safety Title Insurance Company will charge the seller $400 for a combined title search, title examination, and owner's title policy package.

The buyer obtains a loan commitment from the Ajax National Bank for $90,000. To make this loan, the bank will charge a $900 loan origination fee, $100 for an appraisal, and $25 for a credit report on the buyer. The bank also requires a lender's title policy in the amount of $90,000 (added cost $90), 12 months of property tax reserves, and 4 months of hazard insurance reserves. The loan is to be repaid in equal monthly installments beginning October 1. The termite inspection by Dead-Bug Pest Company costs $39, and recording fees are $5 for deeds and mortgage releases and $10 for mortgages. The bank charges the buyer and the seller $110 each to conduct the closing plus $10 to prepare a deed for the seller and $2 to notarize it. The state levies a transfer tax on deeds of 50¢ per $500 of sales price, and the seller is leaving $130 worth of heating oil for the buyer.

The buyer and seller have each hired an attorney to advise them on legal matters in connection with the sales contract and closing. They are to be paid $150 and $120, respectively, out of the settlement. List-Rite Realty and Quick-Sale Realty have advised the closing agent that they are splitting the $7,380 sales commission equally.

Finally, the $3,000 earnest money deposit that the buyer made with the offer is to be credited toward the down payment. Using this information, which is summarized in Table 16.1 for your convenience, let's see how a settlement statement is prepared.

Closing Disclosure

Figure 16.2 is the current Closing Disclosure Form, and it is filled out to reflect the transaction outlined in Table 16.1. Let's work through this sample transaction in order to see where each item is placed on the Closing Disclosure. Note that the buyer is referred to "Borrower" in Figure 16.2.

The sales price is set out at the top of the Closing Disclosure, along with the settlement agent, date, and street address of the property. Along with this information is the transaction information identifying each of the parties and the loan information to reflect the loan type that will be executed at the closing.

The next section of the Closing Disclosure discloses the loan terms including the loan amount, interest rate, and monthly principal and interest. Under "Projected Payments" we see the amount of principal and interest and the amount of escrow which gives us the estimated total monthly payment. The total costs of the closing are at the bottom of the first page which includes the total closing costs by the buyer and the cash needed to close after prorations.

On page 2, the first section gives all the origination charges and the loan costs and breaks down the services that the borrower did shop for and those the borrower did not shop for (required by the new RESPA Rules). Other costs, including recording fees, prepaid interests (generally prorated during the month of closing). Paragraph G specifies the initial escrow payment to the lender and other fees are shown in Paragraph H. This includes the Realtor's fees (paid by the seller), attorney's fees, and title insurance premium. Total costs, shown on page 1 are totaled in Paragraph J for both the buyer and the seller.

Page 3 begins discussing calculating the cash to close which includes total closing costs, less prorations which are a credit to the buyer's side, which yields us a cash to close of $2,772.00.

TABLE 16.1	Transaction Summary	
Sale price	$123,000	
Down payment	33,000	
Deposit (Earnest money)	3,000	Credit to buyer's down payment.
Existing loan	48,000	Seller to pay off through settlement. Interest rate is 12%.
New loan	90,000	Monthly payments begin October 1. Interest rate is 9.6%.
Loan origination fee	900	
Appraisal fee	100	Paid by buyer in connection with obtaining $90,000 loan.
Credit report	25	
Owner's title policy	400	Seller pays Safety Title Insurance Co.
Lender's title policy	90	Buyer pays Safety Title Insurance Co.
County property taxes	1,680/yr	Due October 15 for the period January 1 through December 31. Not yet paid.
Hazard insurance	$240/yr	Existing policy with nine months to run. Transfer to buyer.
Heating oil	130	Oil in tank. Transfer to buyer.
Pest inspection	39	Seller pays Dead-Bug Pest Co.
Property tax reserves	1,680	12 months at $140 for lender.
Hazard insurance reserves	80	Four months at $20 for lender.
Buyer's attorney	150	
Seller's attorney	120	
Closing fee	220	Ajax National Bank charge; buyer & seller each pay $110.
Deed preparation	10	Seller pays bank.
Notary	4	Seller pays $2 for deed. Buyer pays $2 for mortgage.
Conveyance tax	123	Seller pays.
Record deed	5	Buyer pays.
Record mortgage release	5	Seller pays.
Record mortgage	10	Buyer pays.
Brokerage commission	7,380	Seller pays; to be split equally between List-Rite Realty And Quick-Sale Realty.

Source: Settlement and proration date is August 15. All prorations are to be based on a 30-day banker's month.

In the next section, it discloses the summaries of transactions for both buyers and sellers, which reflects amount due from borrower at closing (down payment and loan amount, total closing cost and tax prorations). The "bottom line" on amounts due from borrower and amounts to be disbursed from seller, are shown under the Calculation Paragraph at the bottom of page 3.

Page 4 shows the new loan disclosure information, which shows the amounts calculated for the escrow account. Page 5 reflects the total of the amount financed.

Is this more confusing than the prior forms? Well, all of them look confusing to somebody who is not used to reviewing them. These new rules were created to: (1) encourage the borrowers to think through their mortgage choices; (2) encourage borrowers to apply for loan estimates to multiple lenders;

FIGURE 16.2   Sample Completed Closing Disclosure

Closing Disclosure

This form is a statement of final loan terms and closing costs. Compare this document with your Loan Estimate.

Closing Information

Date Issued	8/8/2016
Closing Date	8/15/2016
Disbursement Date	8/15/2016
Settlement Agent	Charter Title Company
File #	02150000
Property	1654 West 12th Street
	City , TX 00000
Sale Price	$123,000.00

Transaction Information

Borrower	Neidi Delone
	2424 Newpage Lane
	City, TX 00000
Seller	Homer Leavitt
	1654 West 12th Street
	City, TX 00000
Lender	Acme National Bank

Loan Information

Loan Term	
Purpose	Purchase
Product	Fixed Rate
Loan Type	☒ Conventional ☐ FHA
	☐ VA ☐ _____
Loan ID #	
MIC #	

Loan Terms

		Can this amount increase after closing?
Loan Amount	$90,000	NO
Interest Rate	4.5%	NO
Monthly Principal & Interest *See Projected payments below for your Estimated Total Monthly Payment*	$456.02	NO
		Does the loan have these features?
Prepayment Penalty		NO
Balloon Payment		NO

Projected Payments

Payment Calculation	Years 1-30	Years -
Principal & Interest	$456.02	_____
Mortgage Insurance	+	+ _____
Estimated Escrow *Amount can increase over time*	+ $160.00	+ _____
Estimated Total Monthly Payment	**$616.02**	

Estimated Taxes, Insurance & Assessments *Amount can increase over time* *See page 4 for details*	$160.00 monthly	This estimate includes ☒ Property Taxes ☒ Homeowner's Insurance ☐ Other: *See Escrow Account on page 4 for details. You must pay for other property costs separately.*	In escrow? YES YES NO

Costs at Closing

Closing Costs	$3,512.00	Includes $1,227.00 in Loan Costs + $2,285.00 in Other Costs - $0.00 in Lender Credits. *See page 2 for details.*
Cash to Close	$2,772.00	Includes Closing Costs. *See Calculating Cash to Close on page 3 for details.*

FIGURE 16.2   Sample Completed Closing Disclosure (continued)

Closing Cost Details

Loan Costs			Borrower-Paid		Seller-Paid		Paid by
			At Closing	Before Closing	At Closing	Before Closing	Others
A. Origination Charges			**$900.00**				
01 1% of Loan Amount (Points)	to	Acme National Bank	$900.00				
B. Services Borrower Did Not Shop For			**$125.00**				
01 Appraisal Fee	to		$100.00				
02 Credit Report	to		$25.00				
C. Services Borrower Did Shop For			**$202.00**				
01 Doc Prep Fee	to	Acme National Bank			$10.00		
02 Title - Closing Fee	to	Charter Title Company	$110.00		$110.00		
03 Title - Lender Title's Insurance	to	Charter Title Company	$90.00				
04 Title - Notary Fee	to	Charter Title Company	$2.00		$2.00		
D. TOTAL LOAN COSTS (Borrower-Paid)			**$1,227.00**				
Loan Costs Subtotals (A + B + C)			$1,227.00				

Other Costs							
E. Taxes and Other Government Fees			**$15.00**				
01 Recording Fees Deed: $5.00 Mortgage: $10.00 to Harris County Clerk			$15.00		$5.00		
02 Transfer Tax	to						
03 State Tax/Stamp Deed	to				$123.00		
F. Prepaids			**$360.00**				
01 Homeowner's Insurance Premium (mo.)	to						
02 Mortgage Insurance Premium (mo.)	to						
03 Prepaid Interest ($24 per day from 8/15/2016 to Acme National Bank to 8/30/2016)			$360.00				
04 Property Taxes (mo.)	to						
G. Initial Escrow Payment at Closing to Acme National Bank			**$1,760.00**				
01 Homeowner's Insurance	$20.00 per month for 4 mo.		$80.00				
02 Mortgage Insurance	per month for mo.						
03 Property Taxes	per month for mo.						
04 City Property Taxes	per month for mo.						
05 County Property Taxes	$140.00 per month for 12 mo.		$1,680.00				
06 Annual Assessments	per month for mo.						
07 School Property Taxes	per month for mo.						
08 MUD Taxes	per month for mo.						
09 Other	per month for mo.						
10 Aggregate Adjustment							
H. Other			**$150.00**				
01 Buyer's Attorney Fee	to		$150.00				
02 Pest Inspection	to	Dead-Bug Pest Control			$39.00		
03 Real Estate Commission - Listing	to	List-Rite Realty			$3,690.00		
04 Real Estate Commission - Selling	to	Quick-Sale Realty			$3,690.00		
05 Seller's Attorney Fee	to				$120.00		
06 Title - Owner's Title Insurance	to	Charter Title Company			$400.00		
I. TOTAL OTHER COSTS (Borrower-Paid)			**$2,285.00**				
Other Costs Subtotals (E + F + G + H)			$2,285.00				
J. TOTAL CLOSING COSTS (Borrower-Paid)			**$3,512.00**				
Closing Costs Subtotals (D + I)			$3,512.00		$8,189.00		
Lender Credits							

FIGURE 16.2 Sample Completed Closing Disclosure (continued)

Calculating Cash to Close

Use this table to see what has changed from your Loan Estimate.

	Loan Estimate	Final	Did this change?
Total Closing Costs (J)	$3,512.00	$3,512.00	NO
Closing Costs Paid Before Closing	$0.00	$0.00	NO
Closing Costs Financed (Paid from your Loan Amount)	$0.00	$0.00	NO
Down Payment/Funds from Borrower	$0.00	$0.00	NO
Deposit	$0.00	$0.00	NO
Funds for Borrower	$0.00	$0.00	NO
Seller Credits	$0.00	$0.00	NO
Adjustments and Other Credits	$0.00	-$740.00	YES · See details in **Sections K and L**
Cash to Close	$3,512.00	$2,772.00	

Summaries of Transactions

Use this table to see a summary of your transaction.

BORROWER'S TRANSACTION

K. Due from Borrower at Closing	$126,822.00
01 Sale Price of Property	$123,000.00
02 Sale Price of Any Personal Property Included in Sale	
03 Closing Costs Paid at Closing (J)	$3,512.00
04	
Adjustments	
05	
06	
07	
Adjustments for Items Paid by Seller in Advance	
08 City Property Taxes	
09 County Property Taxes	
10 Annual Assessments	
11 School Property Taxes	
12 MUD Taxes	
13 Other	
14 Hazard Insurance 8/15-5/14	$180.00
15 Heating Oil	$130.00

L. Paid Already by or on Behalf of Borrower at Closing	$91,050.00
01 Deposit	
02 Loan Amount	$90,000.00
03 Existing Loan(s) Assumed or Taken Subject to	
04	
05	
Other Credits	
06	
07	
Adjustments	
08	
09	
10	
11	
Adjustments for Items Unpaid by Seller	
12 City Property Taxes	
13 County Property Taxes 1/1/2016 thru 8/15/2016	$1,050.00
14 Annual Assessments	
15 School Property Taxes	
16 MUD Taxes	
17 Other	

CALCULATION	
Total Due from Borrower at Closing (K)	$126,822.00
Total Paid Already by or on Behalf of Borrower at Closing (L)	-$91,050.00
Cash to Close ☒ From ☐ To Borrower	**$35,772.00**

SELLER'S TRANSACTION

M. Due to Seller at Closing	$123,310.00
01 Sale Price of Property	$123,000.00
02 Sale Price of Any Personal Property Included in Sale	
03	
04	
05	
06	
07	
08	
Adjustments for Items Paid by Seller in Advance	
09 City Property Taxes	
10 County Property Taxes	
11 Annual Assessments	
12 School Property Taxes	
13 MUD Taxes	
14 Other	
15 Hazard Insurance 8/15-5/14	$180.00
16 Heating Oil	$130.00

N. Due from Seller at Closing	$57,479.00
01 Excess Deposit	
02 Closing Costs Paid at Closing (J)	$8,189.00
03 Existing Loan(s) Assumed or Taken Subject to	
04 Payoff of First Mortgage to Payoff 1st lien Loan	$48,000.00
05 Payoff of Second Mortgage Loan	
06 Accrued Interst 9/1 to 9/15	$240.00
07	
08	
09	
10	
11	
12	
13	
Adjustments for Items Unpaid by Seller	
14 City Property Taxes	
15 County Property Taxes 1/1/2016 thru 8/15/2016	$1,050.00
16 Annual Assessments	
17 School Property Taxes	
18 MUD Taxes	
19 Other	

CALCULATION	
Total Due to Seller at Closing (M)	$123,310.00
Total Due from Seller at Closing (N)	-$57,479.00
Cash ☐ From ☒ To Seller	**$65,831.00**

FIGURE 16.2 Sample Completed Closing Disclosure (continued)

Additional Information About This Loan

Loan Disclosures

Assumption
If you sell or transfer this property to another person, your lender
- ☐ will allow, under certain conditions, this person to assume this loan on the original terms.
- ☒ will not allow assumption of this loan on the original terms.

Demand Feature
Your loan
- ☐ has a demand feature, which permits your lender to require early repayment of the loan. You should review your note for details.
- ☒ does not have a demand feature.

Late Payment
If your payment is more than ___ days late, your lender will charge a late fee of ___ .

Negative Amortization (Increase in Loan Amount)
Under your loan terms, you
- ☐ are scheduled to make monthly payments that do not pay all of the interest due that month. As a result, your loan amount will increase (negatively amortize), and your loan amount will likely become larger than your original loan amount. Increases in your loan amount lower the equity you have in this property.
- ☐ may have monthly payments that do not pay all of the interest due that month. If you do, your loan amount will increase (negatively amortize), and, as a result, your loan amount may become larger than your original loan amount. Increases in your loan amount lower the equity you have in this property.
- ☒ do not have a negative amortization feature.

Partial Payments
Your lender
- ☐ may accept payments that are less than the full amount due (partial payments) and apply them to your loan.
- ☐ may hold them in a separate account until you pay the rest of the payment, and then apply the full payment to your loan.
- ☒ does not accept any partial payments.

If this loan is sold, your new lender may have a different policy.

Security Interest
You are granting a security interest in
1654 West 12th Street
City , TX 00000

You may lose this property if you do not make your payments or satisfy other obligations for this loan.

Escrow Account
For now, your loan
- ☒ will have an escrow account (also called an "impound" or "trust" account) to pay the property costs listed below. Without an escrow account, you would pay them directly, possibly in one or two large payments a year. Your lender may be liable for penalties and interest for failing to make a payment.

Escrow		
Escrowed Property Costs over Year 1	$1,920.00	Estimated total amount over year 1 for your escrowed property costs: *Homeowner's Insurance Property Taxes*
Non-Escrowed Property Costs over Year 1		Estimated total amount over year 1 for your non-escrowed property costs: You may have other property costs.
Initial Escrow Payment	$1,760.00	A cushion for the escrow account you pay at closing. See Section G on Page 2.
Monthly Escrow Payment	$160.00	The amount included in your total monthly payment.

- ☐ will not have an escrow account because ☐ you declined it ☐ your lender does not offer one. You must directly pay your property costs, such as taxes and homeowner's insurance. Contact your lender to ask if your loan can have an escrow account.

No Escrow		
Estimated Property Costs over Year 1		Estimated total amount over year 1. You must pay these costs directly, possibly in one or two large payments a year.
Escrow Waiver Fee		

In the future,
Your property costs may change and, as a result, your escrow payment may change. You may be able to cancel your escrow account, but if you do, you must pay your property costs directly. If you fail to pay your property taxes, your state or local government may (1) impose fines and penalties or (2) place a tax lien on this property. If you fail to pay any of your property costs, your lender may (1) add the amounts to your loan balance, (2) add an escrow account to your loan, or (3) require you to pay for property insurance that the lender buys on your behalf, which likely would cost more and provide fewer benefits than what you could buy on your own.

FIGURE 16.2 Sample Completed Closing Disclosure (continued)

Loan Calculations

Total of Payments. Total you will have paid after you make all payments of principal, interest, mortgage insurance, and loan costs, as scheduled	
Finance Charge. The dollar amount the loan will cost you.	
Amount Financed. The loan amount available after paying your upfront finance charge.	$90,000
Annual Percentage Rate (APR). Your costs over the loan term expressed as a rate. This is not your interest rate.	0%
Total Interest Percentage (TIP). The total amount of interest that you will pay over the loan term as a percentage of your loan amount.	0%

? Questions? If you have questions about the loan terms or costs on this form, use the contact information below. To get more information or make a complaint, contact the Consumer Financial Protection Bureau at **www.consumerfinance.gov/mortgage-closing**

Other Disclosures

Appraisal
If the property was appraised for your loan, your lender is required to give you a copy at no additional cost at least 3 days before closing. If you have not yet received it, please contact you lender at the information listed below.

Contract Details
See your note and security instrument for information about
- what happens if you fail to make your payments,
- what is a default on the loan,
- situations in which your lender can require early repayment of the loan, and
- the rules for making payments before they are due

Liability after Foreclosure
If you lender forecloses on this property and the foreclosure does not cover the amount of unpaid balance on this loan,
- [x] state law may protect you from liability for the unpaid balance. If you refinance or take on any additional debt on this property, you may lose this protection and have to pay any debt remaining even after foreclosure. You may want to consult a lawyer for more information.
- [ ] state law does not protect you from liability for the unpaid balance.

Refinance
Refinancing this loan will depend on your future financial situation, the property value, and market conditions. You may not be able to refinance this loan.

Tax Deductions
If you borrow more than this property is worth, the interest on the loan amount above this property's fair market value is not deductible from your federal income taxes. You should consult a tax advisor for more information.

Contact Information

	Lender	Real Estate Broker(B)	Settlement Agent
Name	Acme National Bank	Quick-Sale Realty	Charter Title Company
Address	1111 West 1st Street City, TX 00000		4265 San Felipe, Ste 350 Houston, TX 77027
NMLSID			
TX License ID			
Contact			
Contact NMLS ID			
Contact TX License ID			
Email			
Phone			713-871-9700

Confirm Receipt

By signing, you are only confirming that you have received this form. You do not have to accept this loan because you have signed or received this form.

_____   _____
Applicant Signature   Date

_____   _____
Co-Applicant Signature   Date

Source: © 2014 OnCourse Learning

(3) make sure the borrowers indicate their intent to proceed with the loan; (4) be the source of accurate and timely information about the property and transaction; and (5) find out who provides the closing disclosures. This is all done to create smooth and on-time closings, according to the CFPB.

Real Estate Settlement Procedures Act

In response to consumer complaints regarding real estate closing costs and procedures, Congress passed the **Real Estate Settlement Procedures Act (RESPA)** effective June 20, 1975. The purpose of RESPA, which is administered by the U.S. Department of Housing and Urban Development (HUD), is to regulate and standardize real estate settlement practices when *federally related* first mortgage loans are made on one- to four-family residences, condominiums, and cooperatives. *Federally related* is defined to include Federal Housing Administration (FHA), or Veterans Affairs (VA), or other government-backed or assisted loans, loans from lenders with federally insured deposits, loans that are to be purchased by Federal National Mortgage Association (FNMA), Government National Mortgage Association (GNMA), Federal Home Loan Mortgage Corporation (FHLMC), or other federally controlled secondary mortgage market institutions, and loans made by lenders who make or invest more than $1 million per year in residential loans. As the bulk of all home loans now fall into one of these categories, the impact of this law is far-reaching.

RESTRICTIONS

RESPA prohibits kickbacks and fees for services not performed during the closing process. For example, in some regions of the United States prior to this act, it was common practice for attorneys and closing agents to channel title business to certain title companies in return for a fee. This increased settlement costs without adding services. Now there must be a justifiable service rendered for each closing fee charge. The act also prohibits the seller from requiring that the buyer purchase title insurance from a particular title company. Recall the discussion in Chapter 12 regarding disclosures, which are now required for business referrals and origination fees.

RESPA also contains restrictions on the amount of advance property tax and insurance payments a lender can collect and place in an impound or reserve account. The amount is limited to the property owner's share of taxes and insurance accrued prior to settlement, plus one-sixth of the estimated amount that will come due for these items in the 12-month period beginning at settlement. This requirement assures that the lender has an adequate but not excessive amount of money impounded when taxes and insurance payments fall due. If the amount in the reserve account is not sufficient to pay an item when it comes due, the lender must temporarily use its own funds to make up the difference. Then the lender bills the borrower or increases the monthly reserve payment. If there is a drop in the amount the lender must pay out, then the monthly reserve requirement can be reduced.

The law also allows a voluntary increased payment into escrow for newly constructed homes. The homes are often taxed at the vacant lot rate, then increased dramatically after construction. This results in escrow shortages and huge increases in monthly payments to cover those shortages. The new rule intended to prevent "payment shock" because it increases the initial monthly payment.

Considerable criticism and debate have raged over the topic of reserves. Traditionally, lenders have not paid interest to borrowers on money held as reserves, effectively creating an interest-free loan to themselves. This has tempted many lenders to require overly adequate reserves. RESPA sets a reasonable limit on reserve requirements and some states now require that interest be paid on reserves. Although not always required to do so, some lenders now voluntarily pay interest on reserves.

BENEFITS

Anyone applying for a RESPA-regulated loan will receive several benefits. First is a CFPB information booklet explaining RESPA. Second is a good faith estimate of closing costs from the lender. Third, the lender will use the CFPB Settlement Statement shown in Figure 16.2. Fourth, the borrower has the right to inspect the CFPB Settlement Statement three business day before the day of closing.

The primary reason lenders are required to promptly give loan applicants an estimate of closing costs is to allow the loan applicant an opportunity to compare prices for the various services his transaction will require. Additionally, these estimates help the borrower estimate closing costs. Figure 16.3 illustrates a sample loan estimate form.

RESPA does not require the lender to disclose estimates of escrow impounds for property taxes and insurance, although the lender can voluntarily add these items to the form. A new RESPA regulation does, however, require servicers of loans to disclose their calculation of escrow estimates for taxes and insurance. Note also that RESPA allows lenders to make estimates in terms of ranges. For example, escrow fees may be stated as $150 to $175 to reflect the range of rates being charged by local escrow companies for that service.

New RESPA Regulations

New RESPA rules were adopted in 2008 by HUD. Effective since January 16, 2009, all third parties charges paid by title agents must be separately itemized and cannot exceed the amount actually paid to the service provider. The new rule does permit any provider to use an average charge calculation to collect the amount due for a service billed by a third party provider that is paid for by the borrower or the seller provided this "average charge calculation" meets the criteria of the new rule (it's easier just to pass their actual cost if you know them). Another amendment to the rules affects affiliated businesses. The rule still prohibits participants in affiliated business to require the use of an affiliated business. However, under the new rule, a settlement service provider may offer combined services at a price lower than the sum of individuals' service without triggering "required use" concerns if: (1) the use is optional to the consumer; and (2) the lower price is not made up of higher costs elsewhere in the transaction. This allows a settlement service provider to provide economic incentives. The rule does not apply to homebuilders, as they are not settlement service providers.

Lenders and mortgage brokers are now required to provide a new Loan Estimate Form to a potential borrower within three days after loan application. As shown in Figure 16.3, the new form must state dates and terms of the loan and charges for the loan. The quoted terms and prices in the form must be available for at least 10 business days after the estimate is issued. The cost quoted in the form is subject to "tolerances" lender charges for taking, underwriting, and processing the application. The points for origination fees and the real property transfer tax must be exact and fall under the category of "zero tolerance." When the lender requires the settlement service provider or provides settlement services from a list of providers for title services and title insurance, the tolerances are allowed to increase as much as 10% over the original Loan Estimate disclosure. If the borrower chooses providers (including title insurance) the escrow amounts, per diem interest and homeowner's insurance, there is unlimited tolerance, as the provider has no control over the costs.

FIGURE
16.3   Loan Estimate Form-Blank

Save this Loan Estimate to compare with your Closing Disclosure.

Loan Estimate

DATE ISSUED
APPLICANTS

PROPERTY
SALE PRICE

LOAN TERM
PURPOSE
PRODUCT
LOAN TYPE   □ Conventional □ FHA □ VA □ _____
LOAN ID #
RATE LOCK   □ NO □ YES, until
Before closing, your interest rate, points, and lender credits can change unless you lock the interest rate. All other estimated closing costs expire on

Loan Terms

Can this amount increase after closing?

Loan Amount

Interest Rate

Monthly Principal & Interest
See Projected Payments below for your Estimated Total Monthly Payment

Does the loan have these features?

Prepayment Penalty

Balloon Payment

Projected Payments

Payment Calculation

Principal & Interest

Mortgage Insurance

Estimated Escrow
Amount can increase over time

Estimated Total Monthly Payment

Estimated Taxes, Insurance & Assessments
Amount can increase over time

This estimate includes   **In escrow?**
□ Property Taxes
□ Homeowner's Insurance
□ Other:
See Section G on page 2 for escrowed property costs. You must pay for other property costs separately.

Costs at Closing

Estimated Closing Costs

Includes   in Loan Costs +   in Other Costs –
in Lender Credits. *See page 2 for details.*

Estimated Cash to Close

Includes Closing Costs. *See Calculating Cash to Close on page 2 for details.*

Visit **www.consumerfinance.gov/mortgage-estimate** for general information and tools.

FIGURE
16.3   Loan Estimate Form-Blank (continued)

Closing Cost Details

Loan Costs

A. Origination Charges

% of Loan Amount (Points)

B. Services You Cannot Shop For

C. Services You Can Shop For

D. TOTAL LOAN COSTS (A + B + C)

Other Costs

E. Taxes and Other Government Fees

Recording Fees and Other Taxes
Transfer Taxes

F. Prepaids

Homeowner's Insurance Premium (months)
Mortgage Insurance Premium (months)
Prepaid Interest (per day for   days @   )
Property Taxes (months)

G. Initial Escrow Payment at Closing

Homeowner's Insurance	per month for	mo.
Mortgage Insurance	per month for	mo.
Property Taxes	per month for	mo.

H. Other

I. TOTAL OTHER COSTS (E + F + G + H)

J. TOTAL CLOSING COSTS

D + I
Lender Credits

Calculating Cash to Close

Total Closing Costs (J)

Closing Costs Financed (Paid from your Loan Amount)

Down Payment/Funds from Borrower

Deposit

Funds for Borrower

Seller Credits

Adjustments and Other Credits

Estimated Cash to Close

FIGURE 16.3 Loan Estimate Form-Blank (continued)

Additional Information About This Loan

LENDER	**MORTGAGE BROKER**
NMLS/___ LICENSE ID	**NMLS/___ LICENSE ID**
LOAN OFFICER	**LOAN OFFICER**
NMLS/___ LICENSE ID	**NMLS/___ LICENSE ID**
EMAIL	**EMAIL**
PHONE	**PHONE**

Comparisons

Use these measures to compare this loan with other loans.

In 5 Years	Total you will have paid in principal, interest, mortgage insurance, and loan costs.
	Principal you will have paid off.
Annual Percentage Rate (APR)	Your costs over the loan term expressed as a rate. This is not your interest rate.
Total Interest Percentage (TIP)	The total amount of interest that you will pay over the loan term as a percentage of your loan amount.

Other Considerations

Appraisal
We may order an appraisal to determine the property's value and charge you for this appraisal. We will promptly give you a copy of any appraisal, even if your loan does not close. You can pay for an additional appraisal for your own use at your own cost.

Assumption
If you sell or transfer this property to another person, we
☐ will allow, under certain conditions, this person to assume this loan on the original terms.
☐ will not allow assumption of this loan on the original terms.

Homeowner's Insurance
This loan requires homeowner's insurance on the property, which you may obtain from a company of your choice that we find acceptable.

Late Payment
If your payment is more than ___ days late, we will charge a late fee of _____

Refinance
Refinancing this loan will depend on your future financial situation, the property value, and market conditions. You may not be able to refinance this loan.

Servicing
We intend
☐ to service your loan. If so, you will make your payments to us.
☐ to transfer servicing of your loan.

Confirm Receipt

By signing, you are only confirming that you have received this form. You do not have to accept this loan because you have signed or received this form.

_____   _____
Applicant Signature   Date

_____   _____
Co-Applicant Signature   Date

LOAN ESTIMATE   PAGE 3 OF 3 · LOAN ID #

Source: www.consumerfinance.gov/mortgage-estimate

FIGURE
16.4   Closing Disclosure Form-Blank

Closing Disclosure

This form is a statement of final loan terms and closing costs. Compare this document with your Loan Estimate.

Closing Information	Transaction Information	Loan Information
Date Issued	**Borrower**	**Loan Term**
Closing Date		**Purpose**
Disbursement Date		**Product**
Settlement Agent	**Seller**	
File #		**Loan Type** ☐ Conventional ☐ FHA
Property		☐ VA ☐ _____
	Lender	**Loan ID #**
Sale Price		**MIC #**

Loan Terms

Can this amount increase after closing?

Loan Amount

Interest Rate

Monthly Principal & Interest
See Projected Payments below for your Estimated Total Monthly Payment

Does the loan have these features?

Prepayment Penalty

Balloon Payment

Projected Payments

Payment Calculation

Principal & Interest

Mortgage Insurance

Estimated Escrow
Amount can increase over time

**Estimated Total
Monthly Payment**

**Estimated Taxes, Insurance
& Assessments**
Amount can increase over time
See page 4 for details

This estimate includes   **In escrow?**
☐ Property Taxes
☐ Homeowner's Insurance
☐ Other:
See Escrow Account on page 4 for details. You must pay for other property costs separately.

Costs at Closing

Closing Costs

Includes   in Loan Costs +   in Other Costs –
in Lender Credits. *See page 2 for details.*

Cash to Close

Includes Closing Costs. *See Calculating Cash to Close on page 3 for details.*

FIGURE 16.4	Closing Disclosure Form-Blank (continued)

Closing Cost Details

Loan Costs	Borrower-Paid		Seller-Paid		Paid by Others
	At Closing	Before Closing	At Closing	Before Closing	
A. Origination Charges					
01 % of Loan Amount (Points)					
02					
03					
04					
05					
06					
07					
08					
B. Services Borrower Did Not Shop For					
01					
02					
03					
04					
05					
06					
07					
08					
09					
10					
C. Services Borrower Did Shop For					
01					
02					
03					
04					
05					
06					
07					
08					
D. TOTAL LOAN COSTS (Borrower-Paid)					
Loan Costs Subtotals (A + B + C)					

Other Costs					
E. Taxes and Other Government Fees					
01 Recording Fees Deed: Mortgage:					
02					
F. Prepaids					
01 Homeowner's Insurance Premium (mo.)					
02 Mortgage Insurance Premium (mo.)					
03 Prepaid Interest (per day from to)					
04 Property Taxes (mo.)					
05					
G. Initial Escrow Payment at Closing					
01 Homeowner's Insurance per month for mo.					
02 Mortgage Insurance per month for mo.					
03 Property Taxes per month for mo.					
04					
05					
06					
07					
08 Aggregate Adjustment					
H. Other					
01					
02					
03					
04					
05					
06					
07					
08					
I. TOTAL OTHER COSTS (Borrower-Paid)					
Other Costs Subtotals (E + F + G + H)					
J. TOTAL CLOSING COSTS (Borrower-Paid)					
Closing Costs Subtotals (D + I)					
Lender Credits					

FIGURE 16.4 Closing Disclosure Form-Blank (continued)

Calculating Cash to Close

Use this table to see what has changed from your Loan Estimate.

	Loan Estimate	Final	Did this change?
Total Closing Costs (J)			
Closing Costs Paid Before Closing			
Closing Costs Financed (Paid from your Loan Amount)			
Down Payment/Funds from Borrower			
Deposit			
Funds for Borrower			
Seller Credits			
Adjustments and Other Credits			
Cash to Close			

Summaries of Transactions

Use this table to see a summary of your transaction.

BORROWER'S TRANSACTION

K. Due from Borrower at Closing
01 Sale Price of Property
02 Sale Price of Any Personal Property Included in Sale
03 Closing Costs Paid at Closing (J)
04

Adjustments
05
06
07

Adjustments for Items Paid by Seller in Advance
08 City/Town Taxes   to
09 County Taxes   to
10 Assessments   to
11
12
13
14
15

L. Paid Already by or on Behalf of Borrower at Closing
01 Deposit
02 Loan Amount
03 Existing Loan(s) Assumed or Taken Subject to
04
05 Seller Credit

Other Credits
06
07

Adjustments
08
09
10
11

Adjustments for Items Unpaid by Seller
12 City/Town Taxes   to
13 County Taxes   to
14 Assessments   to
15
16
17

CALCULATION
Total Due from Borrower at Closing (K)
Total Paid Already by or on Behalf of Borrower at Closing (L)

Cash to Close ☐ From ☐ To Borrower

SELLER'S TRANSACTION

M. Due to Seller at Closing
01 Sale Price of Property
02 Sale Price of Any Personal Property Included in Sale
03
04
05
06
07
08

Adjustments for Items Paid by Seller in Advance
09 City/Town Taxes   to
10 County Taxes   to
11 Assessments   to
12
13
14
15
16

N. Due from Seller at Closing
01 Excess Deposit
02 Closing Costs Paid at Closing (J)
03 Existing Loan(s) Assumed or Taken Subject to
04 Payoff of First Mortgage Loan
05 Payoff of Second Mortgage Loan
06
07
08 Seller Credit
09
10
11
12
13

Adjustments for Items Unpaid by Seller
14 City/Town Taxes   to
15 County Taxes   to
16 Assessments   to
17
18
19

CALCULATION
Total Due to Seller at Closing (M)
Total Due from Seller at Closing (N)

Cash ☐ From ☐ To Seller

FIGURE
16.4   Closing Disclosure Form-Blank (continued)

Additional Information About This Loan

Loan Disclosures

Assumption

If you sell or transfer this property to another person, your lender

☐ will allow, under certain conditions, this person to assume this loan on the original terms.

☐ will not allow assumption of this loan on the original terms.

Demand Feature

Your loan

☐ has a demand feature, which permits your lender to require early repayment of the loan. You should review your note for details.

☐ does not have a demand feature.

Late Payment

If your payment is more than ___ days late, your lender will charge a late fee of _____

Negative Amortization (Increase in Loan Amount)

Under your loan terms, you

☐ are scheduled to make monthly payments that do not pay all of the interest due that month. As a result, your loan amount will increase (negatively amortize), and your loan amount will likely become larger than your original loan amount. Increases in your loan amount lower the equity you have in this property.

☐ may have monthly payments that do not pay all of the interest due that month. If you do, your loan amount will increase (negatively amortize), and, as a result, your loan amount may become larger than your original loan amount. Increases in your loan amount lower the equity you have in this property.

☐ do not have a negative amortization feature.

Partial Payments

Your lender

☐ may accept payments that are less than the full amount due (partial payments) and apply them to your loan.

☐ may hold them in a separate account until you pay the rest of the payment, and then apply the full payment to your loan.

☐ does not accept any partial payments.

If this loan is sold, your new lender may have a different policy.

Security Interest

You are granting a security interest in _____

_____

_____

You may lose this property if you do not make your payments or satisfy other obligations for this loan.

Escrow Account

For now, your loan

☐ will have an escrow account (also called an "impound" or "trust" account) to pay the property costs listed below. Without an escrow account, you would pay them directly, possibly in one or two large payments a year. Your lender may be liable for penalties and interest for failing to make a payment.

Escrow		
Escrowed Property Costs over Year 1		Estimated total amount over year 1 for your escrowed property costs:
Non-Escrowed Property Costs over Year 1		Estimated total amount over year 1 for your non-escrowed property costs:
		You may have other property costs.
Initial Escrow Payment		A cushion for the escrow account you pay at closing. See Section G on page 2.
Monthly Escrow Payment		The amount included in your total monthly payment.

☐ will not have an escrow account because ☐ you declined it ☐ your lender does not offer one. You must directly pay your property costs, such as taxes and homeowner's insurance. Contact your lender to ask if your loan can have an escrow account.

No Escrow		
Estimated Property Costs over Year 1		Estimated total amount over year 1. You must pay these costs directly, possibly in one or two large payments a year.
Escrow Waiver Fee		

In the future,

Your property costs may change and, as a result, your escrow payment may change. You may be able to cancel your escrow account, but if you do, you must pay your property costs directly. If you fail to pay your property taxes, your state or local government may (1) impose fines and penalties or (2) place a tax lien on this property. If you fail to pay any of your property costs, your lender may (1) add the amounts to your loan balance, (2) add an escrow account to your loan, or (3) require you to pay for property insurance that the lender buys on your behalf, which likely would cost more and provide fewer benefits than what you could buy on your own.

FIGURE
16.4   Closing Disclosure Form-Blank (continued)

Loan Calculations

Total of Payments. Total you will have paid after you make all payments of principal, interest, mortgage insurance, and loan costs, as scheduled.	
Finance Charge. The dollar amount the loan will cost you.	
Amount Financed. The loan amount available after paying your upfront finance charge.	
Annual Percentage Rate (APR). Your costs over the loan term expressed as a rate. This is not your interest rate.	
Total Interest Percentage (TIP). The total amount of interest that you will pay over the loan term as a percentage of your loan amount.	

Questions? If you have questions about the loan terms or costs on this form, use the contact information below. To get more information or make a complaint, contact the Consumer Financial Protection Bureau at **www.consumerfinance.gov/mortgage-closing**

Other Disclosures

Appraisal
If the property was appraised for your loan, your lender is required to give you a copy at no additional cost at least 3 days before closing. If you have not yet received it, please contact your lender at the information listed below.

Contract Details
See your note and security instrument for information about
- what happens if you fail to make your payments,
- what is a default on the loan,
- situations in which your lender can require early repayment of the loan, and
- the rules for making payments before they are due.

Liability after Foreclosure
If your lender forecloses on this property and the foreclosure does not cover the amount of unpaid balance on this loan,
- ☐ state law may protect you from liability for the unpaid balance. If you refinance or take on any additional debt on this property, you may lose this protection and have to pay any debt remaining even after foreclosure. You may want to consult a lawyer for more information.
- ☐ state law does not protect you from liability for the unpaid balance.

Refinance
Refinancing this loan will depend on your future financial situation, the property value, and market conditions. You may not be able to refinance this loan.

Tax Deductions
If you borrow more than this property is worth, the interest on the loan amount above this property's fair market value is not deductible from your federal income taxes. You should consult a tax advisor for more information.

Contact Information

	Lender	Mortgage Broker	Real Estate Broker (B)	Real Estate Broker (S)	Settlement Agent
Name					
Address					
NMLS ID					
__ License ID					
Contact					
Contact NMLS ID					
Contact __ License ID					
Email					
Phone					

Confirm Receipt

By signing, you are only confirming that you have received this form. You do not have to accept this loan because you have signed or received this form.

_____   Date _____   _____   Date _____
Applicant Signature   Co-Applicant Signature

CLOSING DISCLOSURE   PAGE 5 OF 5 • LOAN ID #

Source: www.consumerfinance.gov/mortgage-estimate

RIGHT TO CURE

The rules give the loan originator the opportunity to cure any violation by reimbursing the borrower in any amount in which the tolerance has over exceeded. This reimbursement may be made at settlement or within 30 calendar days after settlement.

Vocabulary Review

Match terms a–p with statements 1–16.

a. Beneficiary statement
b. Closing date
c. Closing meeting
d. Deed delivery
e. Dry closing
f. Escrow agent
g. Escrow closing
h. Good faith estimate
i. HUD Settlement Statement (HUD-1)
j. Loan escrow
k. Outside of the closing
l. Prorate
m. RESPA
n. Settlement statement
o. Title closing
p. Walk-through

_____ 1. An accounting of funds to the buyer and seller at the completion of a real estate transaction.

_____ 2. Deposit of documents and funds with a neutral third party plus instructions as to how to conduct the closing.

_____ 3. The moment at which title passes from the seller to the buyer.

_____ 4. To divide the ongoing income and expenses of a property between the buyer and the seller.

_____ 5. A federal law that deals with procedures to be followed in certain types of real estate closings.

_____ 6. The person or firm in charge of an escrow.

_____ 7. An escrow for the purpose of financing a property not in connection with a sale.

_____ 8. Refers to closing costs paid by the buyer or seller that did not go through the closing agent.

_____ 9. A list of anticipated closing costs given to the borrower by the lender as required by RESPA.

_____ 10. Federally related lenders are required to use this particular closing statement format.

_____ 11. The day on which the closing is finalized; also called the settlement date.

_____ 12. The process of completing a real estate transaction.

_____ 13. A final inspection of the property just prior to the settlement date.

_____ 14. A meeting at which the buyer pays for the property and receives a deed for it; also called a settlement meeting.

_____ 15. Shows the unpaid balance on a loan and is provided by the lender.

_____ 16. A method to avoid rescheduling a closing meeting when a document, known to be on its way, has not yet arrived.

Questions and Problems

1. As a means of closing a real estate transaction, how does an escrow closing differ from a settlement meeting?

2. What are the duties of an escrow agent?

3. Is an escrow agent the agent of the buyer or the seller? Explain.

4. The buyer agrees to accept the seller's fire insurance policy as part of the purchase agreement. The policy costs $180 and covers the period from January 16 through the following January 15, and the settlement date is March 12. How much does the buyer owe the seller (closest whole dollar)?

5. A buyer agrees to assume an existing 8% mortgage on which $45,000 is still owed; the last monthly payment was made on March 1 and the next payment is due April 1. The settlement date is March 12. The local custom is to use a 30-day month and charge the buyer interest beginning with the settlement day. Calculate the interest proration. To whom is it credited? To whom is it charged?

6. In real estate closing, does the buyer or seller normally pay for the following items: conveyance tax, deed preparation, lender's title policy, loan appraisal fee, mortgage recording, and mortgage release?

7. Why is it important to have the buyer and seller sign mutual release papers if a transaction does not close?

Additional Readings

"The Future of the Residential Real Estate Brokerage Industry" by G. Donald Jud and Stephen Roulac (*Real Estate Issues*, Summer 2001, p. 22).

The Mortgage Industry Guide to RESPA: Compliance, Disclosures, and Procedures by James H. Pannabecker and David McF. Stemler (Sheshunoff & Company, 1999).

Reform of the Real Estate Settlement Procedures Act (RESPA) and the Truth in Lending Act (TILA): Joint Hearings Before the Subcommittee on Financial Institutions and Consumer Credit and the Subcommittee on Housing and Community Opportunity of the Committee on Banking and Financial Services, U.S. House of Representatives, One Hundred Fifth Congress, Second Session, July 22, September 16, 1998 (United States Government Printing Office, 1998).

RESPA News Monthly Edition, February, 2013.

Real Estate Leases

Earlier chapters of this book discussed leases as estates in land (Chapter 3) and as a means of financing (Chapter 14). This chapter will look at leases from the standpoint of the tenant, the property owner, and the property manager. (During your lifetime you will be in one of these roles, and perhaps all three.) Our discussion will begin with some important terminology. Then comes a sample lease document with explanation, plus information on locating, qualifying, and keeping tenants. The chapter concludes with information on job opportunities available in professional property management. Emphasis will be on residential property, although a number of key points regarding commercial property leases will also be included.

The Leasehold Estate

A lease conveys to the **lessee** (tenant) the right to possess and use another's property for a period of time. During this time the **lessor** (the landlord or fee owner) possesses a **reversion** that entitles him to retake possession at the end of the lease period. Notice that a lease separates the right to use property from the property's ownership. The tenant gets the use of the property during the lease period and pays rent. The property owner is denied use of the property but receives rent in return. At the end of the lease, the property owner gets the use of the property back but no more rent. The tenant no longer has the use of the property and no longer pays rent. This chapter describes how this very simple idea is carried out in practice.

A tenant's right to occupy land and/or buildings thereon is called a *lease hold estate*. The two most commonly found

lessee
The tenant.

lessor
The landlord.

reversion
The right to retake possession at a future date.

leasehold estates are the periodic estate and the estate for years. The periodic estate is one that continually renews itself for like periods of time until the tenant or landlord acts to terminate it. A **month-to-month lease** is an example of this. An *estate for years* is a lease with a specific starting date and a specific ending date. It can be for any length of time, and it does not automatically renew itself. A lease for one year is an example. There are two other leasehold categories: estate at will and tenancy at sufferance. An *estate at will*, rather seldom found, can be terminated by either the tenant or the landlord at any time. For example, when the owner of a rental house decides to sell it upon expiration of the current lease, the owner and tenant may agree that the tenant will be able to continue to rent until the house is sold. A **tenancy at sufferance** occurs when a tenant stays beyond his legal tenancy without the consent of the landlord. The tenant is commonly called a *holdover tenant*, and no advance notice is required for eviction. He differs from a trespasser only in that his original entry onto the property was legal.

Creating a Valid Lease

A lease is both a conveyance and a contract. As a conveyance, it conveys rights of possession to the tenant in the form of a leasehold estate. As a contract, it contains provisions for the payment of rent and any other obligations the landlord and tenant have to each other.

For a valid lease to exist, it must meet the usual requirements of a contract as described in Chapter 7. That is to say, the parties involved must be legally competent, and there must be mutual agreement, lawful objective, and sufficient consideration. The main elements of a lease are: (1) the names of the lessee and lessor, (2) a description of the premises, (3) an agreement to convey (let) the premises by the lessor and to accept possession by the lessee, (4) provisions for the payment of rent, (5) the starting date and duration of the lease, and (6) signatures of the parties to the lease.

In most states, a lease for a term longer than one year must be in writing to be enforceable in court. A lease for one year or less or a month-to-month lease could be oral and still be valid, but as a matter of good business practice, any lease should be put in writing and signed. This gives all parties involved a written reminder of their obligations under the lease and reduces chances for dispute.

The Lease Document

Figure 17.1 illustrates a lease document that contains provisions typically found in a residential lease. These provisions are presented in simplified language to help you easily grasp the rights and responsibilities created by a lease.

CONVEYANCE

The first paragraph is the conveyance portion of the lease. At [1] and [2], the lessor and lessee are identified. At [3], the lessor conveys to the lessee and the lessee accepts the property. A description of the property follows at [4] and the *term* of the conveyance at [5]. The property must be described so that there is no question as to the extent of the premises the lessee is renting. While a tenant, the lessee is entitled to **quiet enjoyment** of the property. This means uninterrupted use of the property without interference from the owner, the property manager, or any third party.

Quiet enjoyment

The right of possession and use of property without undue disturbance by others.

LEASE

This lease agreement is entered into the __10th__ day of __April__ , 20 xx between __John and Sally Landlord__ (hereinafter called the Lessor) and __Lou and Barbara Tenant__ [1] [2] (hereinafter called the Lessee). The Lessor hereby leases to the Lessee [3] and the Lessee hereby leases from the Lessor the premises known as __Apartment 24, 1234 Maple St., City, State__ [4] for the term of __one__ [5] year beginning 12:00 noon on __April 15, 20xx__ and ending 12:00 noon on __April 15, 20xx__ unless sooner terminated as herein set forth.

The rent for the term of this lease is __$ 6,000.00__ [6] payable in equal monthly installments of __$ 500.00__ [7] on the __15th__ day of each month beginning on __April 15, 20xx__ . Receipt of the first monthly installment and __$ 500.00__ [8] as a security, damage, and clean-up deposit is hereby acknowledged. It is furthermore agreed that:

[9]   The use of the premises shall be as a residential dwelling for the above named Lessee only.

[10]   The Lessee may not assign this lease or sublet any portion of the premises without written permission from the Lessor.

[11]   The Lessee agrees to abide by the house rules as posted. A current copy is attached to this lease.

[12]   The Lessor shall furnish water, sewer, and heat as part of the rent. Electricity and telephone shall be paid for by the Lessee.

[13]   The Lessor agrees to keep the premises structure maintained and in habitable condition.

[14]   The Lessee agrees to maintain the interior of said premises and at the termination of this lease to return said premises to the Lessor in as good condition as it is now except for ordinary wear and tear.

[15]   The Lessee shall not make any alterations or improvements to the premises without the Lessor's prior written consent. Any alterations or improvements become the property of the Lessor at the end of this lease.

[16]   If the premises are not ready for occupancy on the date herein provided, the Lessee may cancel this agreement and the Lessor shall return in full all money paid by the Lessee.

[17]   If the Lessee defaults on this lease agreement, the Lessor may give the Lessee three days notice of intention to terminate the lease. At the end of those three days the lease shall terminate and the Lessee shall vacate and surrender the premises to the Lessor.

[18]   If the Lessee holds over after the expiration of this lease without the Lessor's consent, the tenancy shall be month to month at twice the monthly rate indicated herein.

[19]   If the premises are destroyed or rendered uninhabitable by fire or other cause, this lease shall terminate as of the date of the casualty.

[20]   The Lessor shall have access to the premises for the purpose of inspecting for damage, making repairs, and showing to prospective tenants or buyers.

[21]   _John Landlord_
     Lessor

     Sally Landlord
     Lessor

[22]   _Lou Tenant_
     Lessee

     Barbara Tenant
     Lessee

If the lease illustrated here was a month-to-month lease, the wording at [5] would be changed to read, "commencing April 15, 20xx and continuing on a month-to-month basis until terminated by either the lessee or the lessor." A month-to-month rental is a very flexible arrangement. It allows the owner to recover possession of the property on one-month notice and the tenant to leave on one-month notice with no further obligation to the owner. In rental agreements for longer periods of time, each party gives up some flexibility to gain commitment from the other. Under a one-year lease the owner commits the property to the tenant for a year. In return, the tenant is committed to paying rent for a full year. In a like manner, the owner has the tenant's commitment to pay rent for a year but loses the flexibility of being able to regain possession of the property until the year is over.

CONTRACT

The balance of the lease document is concerned with contract aspects of the lease. At [6], the amount of rent that the lessee will pay for the use of the property is set forth. In an estate for years, the usual practice is to state the total rent for the entire lease period. This is the total number of dollars the lessee is obligated to pay to the lessor. The lessee can vacate the premises before the lease period expires, but is still liable for the full amount of the contract. The method of payment of the obligation is shown at [7]. Unless the contract calls for rent to be paid in advance, under common law it is not due until the end of the rental period. At [8], the lessor has taken a deposit in the form of the first monthly installment and acknowledges receipt of it. The lessor has also taken additional money as security against the possibility of uncollected rent or damage to the premises and for cleanup expenses. (The tenant is supposed to leave the premises clean.) The deposit is refunded, less legitimate charges, when the tenant leaves.

Items [9] through [20] summarize commonly found lease clauses. At [9] and [10], the lessor wants to maintain control over the use and occupancy of the premises. Without this, he might find the premises used for an entirely different purpose or by people he did not rent to. At [11], the tenant agrees to abide by the house rules. These normally cover such things as use of laundry and trash facilities, swimming pool rules, noise rules, and so on. Number [12] states the responsibility of the lessee and lessor with regard to the payment of utilities.

A strict legal interpretation of a lease as a conveyance means the tenant is responsible for upkeep and repairs unless the lessor promises to do so in the lease contract. The paragraph at [13] is that promise. Consumerism has had a profound influence on this matter. As a result, courts and legislatures now take the position that the landlord is obligated to keep a residential property repaired and habitable even though this is not specifically stated in the contract. (Commercial property still goes by the strict interpretation—that is, the landlord has to promise upkeep and repairs or the tenant doesn't get them.)

Number [14] is the tenant's promise to maintain the interior of the dwelling. If the tenant damages the property, the tenant must repair or pay for it. Normal wear and tear are considered to be part of the rent. At paragraph [15], the landlord protects himself against unauthorized alterations and improvements, and then goes on to point out that anything the tenant affixes to the building becomes realty. As realty, it remains a part of the building when the tenant leaves.

Paragraphs [16] through [19] deal with the rights of both parties if the premises are not ready for occupancy, if the lessee defaults after moving in, if the lessee holds over, or if the premises are destroyed. The lessor also retains the right (paragraph [20]) to enter the leased premises from time to time for business purposes.

Finally, at [21] and [22], the lessor and lessee sign. It is not necessary to have these signatures notarized. That is done only if the lease is to be recorded, and then only the lessor's signature is notarized. The purpose of recording is to give constructive notice that the lessee has an estate in the property. Recording is usually done only when the lessee's rights are not apparent from inspection of the property or where the lease is to run for more than three years. From the property owner's standpoint, the lease is an encumbrance on the property. If the owner should subsequently sell the property or mortgage it, the lessee's tenancy remains undisturbed. The buyer or lender must accept the property subject to the lease.

If one of the lessors dies, the lease is still binding on the remaining lessor(s) and upon the estate of the deceased lessor. Similarly, if one of the lessees dies, the lease is still binding on the remaining lessee(s) and upon the estate of the deceased lessee. This is based on common law doctrine that applies to contracts in general (see Chapter 7, "Deceased Party"). The lessee and lessor can, however, agree to do otherwise. The lessee could ask the lessor to **waive** (give up) the right to hold the lessee's estate to the lease in the event of the lessee's death. For example, an elderly tenant about to sign a lease might want to add wording to the lease, whereby the tenant's death would allow his estate to terminate the lease early.

Landlord-Tenant Laws

Traditionally, courts have been strict interpreters of lease agreements. This philosophy still prevails for leases on commercial property. However, with regard to residential rental property, the trend today is for state legislatures to establish special landlord-tenant laws. The intent is to strike a reasonable balance between the responsibilities of landlords to tenants and vice versa. Typically, these laws limit the amount of security deposit a landlord can require, tell the tenant how many days notice he has to give before vacating a periodic tenancy, and require the landlord to deliver possession on the date agreed. The landlord must maintain the premises in a fit condition for living, and the tenant is to keep his unit clean and not damage it. The tenant is to obey the house rules, and the landlord must give advance notice before entering an apartment except in legitimate emergencies. Additionally, the laws set forth such things as the procedure for accounting for any deposit money not returned, the right of the tenant to make needed repairs and bill the landlord, the right of the landlord to file court actions for unpaid rent, and the proper procedure for evicting a tenant.

Setting Rents

There are several methods for setting rents. The most common is the **gross lease**. Under a gross lease, the tenant pays a fixed rent, and the landlord pays all the operating expenses of the property. A tenant paying $600 per month on a month-to-month apartment lease or a person paying $13,000 per year for a one-year house lease are both examples of fixed rents.

A landlord will usually agree to a level rent for one year, but what if the tenant wants a longer lease term such as 2 years, 5 years, 10 years, 25 years, or 99 years? For these situations the following rent-setting methods are used in the real estate industry. The simplest is to have a *step-up* or **graduated rent**. For example, a five-year office lease might call for monthly rents of $0.90 per square foot of floor space the first year, $0.95 the second year, $1 the third year, $1.05 the fourth year, and $1.10 the fifth year.

gross lease

Tenant pays a fixed rent and the landlord pays all property expenses.

A residential tenant wanting a two-year lease might find the landlord more receptive if the monthly rent is stepped up the second year.

Office and industrial leases of five or more years often include an **escalator** or **participation clause**. This allows the landlord to pass along to the tenant increases in such items as property taxes, utility charges, and maintenance. A variation is to have the tenant pay for all property taxes, insurance, repairs, utilities, and so on, in addition to the base rent. This arrangement is called a **net lease** or a **triple net lease**. It is commonly used when an entire building is being leased and for long-term ground leases.

net lease

Tenant pays a base rent plus maintenance, property taxes, and insurance.

Another system for setting rents is the **percentage lease**, wherein the owner receives a percentage of the tenant's gross receipts as rent. For example, a farmer who leases land may give the landowner 20% of the value of the crop when it is sold. The monthly rent for a small hardware store might be $600 plus 6% of gross sales above $10,000. A gasoline station may pay $1,000 plus 2¢ per gallon pumped. A supermarket may pay $7,500 plus 1½% of gross receipts above $50,000 per month.

Still another way of setting rents on long-term leases is to create an **index lease** to index the rent to some economic indicator, such as an inflation index. If there is inflation, rents increase; if there is deflation, rents decrease. Arrangements such as step-ups, escalators, percentages, indexes, and net leases are all efforts by landlords to protect against rising costs of property operation and declining purchasing power, yet meet tenants' needs to have property committed to them for more than a year.

Option Clauses

option clause

Gives the right at some future time to purchase or lease a property at a predetermined price.

Option clauses give the tenant the right at some future time to purchase or lease the property at a predetermined price. This gives a tenant flexibility. For example, suppose that a prospective tenant is starting a new business and is not certain how successful it will be. Therefore, in looking for space to rent, he will want a lease that allows an "out" if the new venture does not succeed, but will permit him to stay if the venture is successful. The solution is a lease with options. The landlord could offer a one-year lease, plus an option to stay for two more years at a higher rent plus a second option for an additional five years at a still higher rent. If the venture is not successful, the tenant is obligated for only one year. But if successful, he has the option of staying two more years, and if still successful, for five years after that.

Another option possibility is to offer the tenant a lease that also contains an option to buy the property for a fixed period of time at a preset price. This is called a *lease with option to buy* and is discussed in Chapter 8.

Assignment and Subletting

assignment

The total transfer of the lessee's rights to another party.

Unless otherwise provided in the lease contract, a lessee may assign the lease or sublet. An **assignment** is the total transfer of the lessee's rights to another person. These parties are referred to as the **assignor** and the **assignee**, respectively. The assignee acquires all the rights, title, and interest of the assignor, no more and no less. However, the assignor remains liable for the performance of the contract unless released in writing by the landlord.

sublet

To transfer only a portion of one's lease rights.

sublessee

A lessee who rents from another lessee.

sublessor

A lessee who rents to another lessee.

To **sublet** means to transfer only a portion of the rights held under a lease. The **sublease** thereby created may be for a portion of the premises, or for a part of the lease term. The party acquiring those rights is called the **sublessee**. The original lessee is the **sublessor** with respect to the sublessee. The sublessee pays rent to the lessee, who in turn remains liable to the landlord for rent on the entire premises.

Ground Lease

A **ground lease** is a lease of land alone. The lessor is the fee simple owner of the land and conveys to the lessee an estate for years, typically lasting from 25 to 99 years. The lessee pays for and owns the improvements. Thus, a ground lease separates the ownership of land from the ownership of buildings on that land. The lease rent, called the **ground rent**, is on a net lease basis. As a hedge against inflation, the rent is usually increased every 10 to 25 years. This is done either by a graduated lease, or by requiring a reappraisal of the land and then charging a new rent based on that valuation. Ground leases for residential properties can be found in Baltimore, Maryland; Orange County, California; and the state of Hawaii. Mostly, however, they are used for commercial and industrial properties such as office buildings, shopping centers, motels, and warehouses.

Vertical Lease

A lease need not be restricted to the use of the earth's surface. In Chapter 2, it was shown that land extends from the center of the earth skyward. Consequently it is possible for one person to own the mineral rights, another the surface rights, and a third the air rights. This can also be done with leases. A landowner can lease to an oil company the right to find and extract oil and gas below the land, and at the same time lease the surface rights to a farmer. In Chicago and New York City, railroads have leased surface and air rights above their downtown tracks for the purpose of constructing high-rise office buildings.

Contract Rent, Economic Rent

The amount of rent that the tenant must pay the landlord for the use of the premises is called the **contract rent**. The rent that a property can command in the competitive open market is called the **economic rent**. When a lease contract is negotiated, the contract rent and economic rent are nearly always the same. However, as time passes, the market value of the right to use the premises may rise above the contract rent. When this occurs, the lease itself becomes valuable. That value is determined by the difference between the contract rent and the economic rent, and how long the lease has to run. An example would be a five-year lease with three years left at a contract rent of $600 per month where the current rental value of the premises is now $800 per month. If the lease is assignable, the fact that it offers a $200 per month savings for three years makes it valuable. Similarly, an oil lease obtained for $50 per acre before oil was discovered might be worth millions after its discovery. Conversely, when contract rent exceeds economic rent, the lease takes on a negative value.

Lease Termination

Most leases terminate because of the expiration of the term of the lease. The tenant has received the use of the premises and the landlord has received rent in return. However, a lease can be terminated if the landlord and the tenant mutually agree. The tenant surrenders the premises and the landlord releases him from the contract. This should, of course, be done in writing.

EVICTION

If a tenant fails to live up to the terms of the lease agreement, the landlord has grounds for eviction. Usually this is for nonpayment of rent, but it can also be for violation of some other aspect of the agreement such as holding over past the term of the lease, bringing animals into a "no pets" apartment, occupancy by more than the number of persons specified in the agreement, or operating in an illegal manner on the premises. Called **actual eviction**, the process usually begins with the landlord having a notice served on the tenant requiring the tenant to comply with the lease agreement or move out. If the tenant neither complies nor vacates, the landlord takes the matter to court. If the landlord wins the case, either by a preponderance of evidence or because the tenant does not appear to contest the eviction, then the court will terminate the tenant's lease rights and authorize a marshal or sheriff to go on the premises and force the tenant out.

A lease agreement may also be terminated through **constructive eviction**. This occurs when the landlord does not keep the premises fit for occupancy and the tenant is forced to move. For example, the landlord may be continually failing to repair broken plumbing lines or a leaking roof. The tenant's legal remedies are to claim wrongful eviction, move out, stop paying rent, or sue the landlord for breach of contract, either forcing the landlord to make repairs or to terminate the lease, possibly with money damages.

A **retaliatory eviction** is one whereby a landlord evicts a tenant because of a complaint made by the tenant. For example, a tenant may have complained to public health officials or building and safety authorities about conditions on the premises that are in violation of health laws or building codes. The landlord may retaliate or threaten to retaliate with an eviction (or a rent increase or a decrease in services); however, this is illegal.

EMINENT DOMAIN

The government, under its right of *eminent domain*, can also terminate a lease, but must provide just compensation. An example of this would be the construction of a new highway that requires the demolition of a building rented to tenants. Both the property owner and the tenants would be entitled to compensation.

A mortgage foreclosure can also bring about lease termination; it all depends on priority. If the mortgage was recorded before the lease was signed, then foreclosure of the mortgage also forecloses the lease. If the lease was recorded first, then the lease still stands. Because a lease can cloud a lender's title, wording is sometimes inserted in leases that makes them subordinate to any future financing of the property. This is highly technical, but nonetheless a very significant matter in long-term shopping center, office building, and industrial leases.

Rent Control

For the most part, until 1970 the concept of residential **rent control** was reserved for wartime use in the United States. During World War I, six states and several major cities imposed limits on how much rent an owner could charge for the use of his real property. During World War II, the federal government also imposed limits. The purpose was twofold: (1) to discourage the construction of new housing so that the resources could be channeled to war needs, and (2) to set ceilings so that American households would not drive up prices by bidding against each other for available rental housing. With limits on rents, but no price controls on the cost of construction materials and labor, the construction of new housing was slowed without the need for a direct government order to stop building.

Within a few years after World War I, and again after World War II, rent controls disappeared in nearly all parts of the country. The notable exception was New York City, where they have survived since the end of World War II and are still in use. However, beginning in the 1970s, a number of other cities enacted rent control laws. This time the major attraction was inflation protection.

Although it is true that since 1956 residential rents in the United States have not risen as rapidly as the general level of consumer prices, any relief from rent increases would nonetheless be welcomed by the 36% of American households that rent. Most tenants recognize that newly constructed properties must command higher rents to meet higher construction, land, and interest costs. However, in existing buildings, tenants resent rent increases that have nothing to do with the original cost of the building or the cost of operating it. The argument of rent control supporters is that only increases in such things as property taxes, utilities, and maintenance should be passed on to tenants. The tenant's assumption in this argument is that rent alone is enough to attract dollars into housing investments. In reality, rents would have to be even higher if the investor could not look forward to price appreciation of his property.

RENT CONTROL EXPERIENCE

Experience to date strongly suggests that rent control creates more problems than it solves. In New York City and Washington, DC, for example, it is generally agreed that controlled rents have taken existing dwelling units out of circulation. Despite relatively low vacancy rates, thousands of dwelling units are abandoned each year by their owners at a cost of millions of dollars in lost property taxes. With controls on rents but no controls on expenses, property owners are often better off abandoning their properties than operating them.

Another problem with controlled rents is that a vacating tenant may demand a substantial cash payment from a tenant who wants to move in. Although this is illegal, the vacating tenant may attempt to circumvent the law by requiring the incoming tenant to purchase his furniture for several times its actual worth. Sometimes this payment is called a "key fee," suggesting that the new tenant is purchasing the key. This places the actual cost of the controlled apartment much closer to the value of the unit on the open market, and the advantage of low, controlled rents is lost to the incoming tenant.

A side effect of rent control has been conversions of existing rental apartments to condominiums since there are no controls on sales prices of dwelling units. Some cities have responded by restricting conversions. Owners began to demolish buildings to build new condominiums; however, laws were then enacted to restrict demolition permits.

Other side effects of rent control in the United States are that lenders prefer not to lend on rent-controlled buildings. This is because lenders do not like to loan unless the investor is assured of reasonable returns. Developers find it hard to attract tenants to new rental units from rent-controlled buildings where they are enjoying below-market rents. Owner-occupied properties and noncontrolled properties are charged higher property taxes to make up for the falling values of controlled properties. Also there is a significant cost to the public to operate the government offices that administer the controls.

One of the ironies of rent control is that although controlled rents are very attractive to the tenant, he soon finds that the number of people like himself who want to buy at controlled prices exceeds the number who want to sell. Consequently, a shortage develops. A better solution is to pursue public policies that encourage, rather than discourage, the construction of housing.

Property Management

As real estate becomes a more and more popular investment vehicle, more individuals are buying houses, apartment buildings, offices, and stores to rent out. Many choose to operate these themselves, thus entering the field of property management. Others hire professional managers, as do partnerships and corporations that own real estate. The balance of this chapter will give you a sampling of some of the things you can expect as a manager of residential property, as well as an overview of the employment opportunities in this important aspect of real estate.

BEFORE BUYING

Successful operation of rental property begins with building or selecting existing buildings that meet the needs of tenants. Although this sounds simple enough, in reality it requires considerable reading, legwork, and telephoning. There is no sense in building or buying one-bedroom apartment units when the local demand is for two-bedroom units. A wise investor will conduct an informal survey of existing rents and vacancy rates, plus gather information on the age, household status, and numbers of renters in the local rental market. Market rents are then compared with operating costs and the balance capitalized to determine how much to pay for the building. (This process is explained in Chapter 18 under "Income Approach.")

ADVERTISING

The usual search pattern of a prospective residential tenant is to drive through neighborhoods of interest and to read newspaper classified ads. Thus, advertising money is most effectively spent on signs and arrows on and near the property plus newspaper advertising. Ads should tell enough about the property to motivate the prospect to call for an inspection. Signs should be well placed so prospects do not get lost trying to locate the property.

Tenant Selection

Just as a prospective tenant qualifies each house or apartment from the standpoint of suitability, the property manager must also qualify the tenant. If it appears that a prospect, once moved in, will not pay the rent or will be destructive to the premises or will be obnoxious to the neighbors, the time to avoid the problem is before the tenant moves in.

A thorough application form, a personal interview with a seasoned manager, and a substantial security deposit are valuable screening tools. A thorough application form acts to discourage prospects who themselves feel only marginally qualified or who prefer not to divulge the information requested. It also provides a basis for checking the tenant's references. This includes talking with former landlords to ask why she left, checking with the local credit bureau to learn if she pays her bills on time, and, in some cities, checking with a landlord's reference bureau to find out if she left a previous apartment without paying rent.

The purpose of the interview is to determine whether the prospect has the income to support the rental and will be compatible with the other tenants. For example, if the project does not allow pets or disassembled automobiles on the premises, the manager will want to make certain the prospect understands this.

Security Deposit

The requirement of a **security deposit** (against which the manager can deduct for unpaid rent or damage to the building) also serves as a screening device. If, for example, a prospect wants to rent a $400 per month apartment but does not have the money for a $200 security deposit, it is doubtful that he will be able to pay $400 rent each month.

Most states allow a damage deposit equal to one month's rent. In addition, many states also allow the landlord to collect the last month's rent in advance. A prospective tenant who, before moving in, can deposit the first and last month's rent plus a damage deposit not only provides an impressive financial picture but a solid cushion against future unpaid rent and damage.

Federal laws require owners and managers to disregard matters of race, color, religion, sex, national origin, disability, and familial status. State and local laws may extend this to age, marital status, presence of children, physical handicaps, sexual orientation, and welfare status. These laws cover not only the obvious discrimination of refusing to rent, but also discrimination in such matters as the size of the security deposit, choice of apartment unit, length of lease offered, and any number of more subtle discouragements. These laws are designed to give equal access to housing to anyone who can meet the financial requirements and is willing to abide by the lease contract and the house rules.

RENT CONCESSIONS

Two methods by which a building owner can attract tenants in an otherwise soft rental market are: (1) reduce the monthly rent, and (2) offer a rent concession. With a **rent concession**, the property owner keeps the rents at the same level, but offers a premium to entice a prospective tenant to move in. Often this is a free month's rent for prospects who will sign a one-year lease. Alternatives are to offer the tenant a cash moving allowance or a free weekend vacation at a nearby resort. The philosophy behind using concessions rather than outright rent reductions is that when the rental market firms up, it is easier to stop offering concessions than it is to raise rents.

Tenant Retention

Tenant retention begins with finding tenants who will pay the rent and respect their contract agreements. Having once found good tenants, the next task is to keep them as long as possible. Besides the rent lost while the apartment is empty, the costs of apartment cleanup and finding a new tenant are high.

Statistically, about one-third of the units in a typical apartment project must be rerented each year. Certainly, many moves are as a result of job relocation or the need for larger or smaller quarters. But some moves occur because tenants find something they dislike about the way their apartments are managed. For example, if a building is poorly kept up or the manager gives the impression that he does not care about the tenants or the owner increases the rent with no apparent justification, people will move out. To retain tenants, the property owner and manager should think of them as permanent residents, even though turnover is expected. This begins with using a rental contract that an average tenant can read and understand. A complicated and legalistic contract may be seen by the tenant as the first step in a sparring match with management that will last as long as he resides there. The tenant also expects the property to be clean and properly maintained and repairs to his unit to be made promptly.

COMMUNICATIONS

Good communication between management and tenants is also crucial to tenant retention. If the swimming pool is closed or utilities are shut off with no announcement or for no apparent reason, tenants become disgusted and add it to their private lists of reasons for ultimately leaving. Tenants expect management to keep them informed through bulletin board announcements or notices placed under their doors. In many larger apartment projects, managers publish newsletters to keep tenants informed and to provide a means by which tenants can communicate with one another. For example, one page can explain why rents must go up because of rising property taxes, maintenance, and utility costs, while another page can announce the formation of a bowling league among apartment dwellers.

LEASES

A very straightforward approach to improving tenant retention is to use leases. Once signed to a one-year lease, a tenant is much less likely to leave after a few months than if on a month-to-month agreement. Similarly, leases for longer than one year will reduce tenant turnover even more, although residential tenants are often wary about committing themselves that far into the future. A tenant can also be encouraged to stay by offering a renewal lease at a slightly lower rate than that being offered to new tenants. Another inducement is to offer long-time tenants free carpet shampooing, drapery cleaning, and wall painting, all things normally done if the tenant leaves and the apartment must be rented.

Collecting Rents

Ultimately, the success of a rental building depends on the ability of management to collect the rents due from tenants. In accomplishing this, it is generally agreed among property managers that a firm and consistent collection policy handled in a businesslike manner is the best approach. Monthly rent statements can be mailed to each tenant. More often, though, tenants are told in the rental contract when the rent is due each month and they are expected to pay it on time. Rents can also be collected door to door, but most managers prefer that rent checks be mailed or brought to their office when due. For security reasons, some managers do not accept cash.

LATE RENTS

When a tenant's rent is not received on time, the manager must decide what action to take. Is the lateness simply a matter of delayed mail or temporary but honest forgetfulness, or is the delay an early sign of a deeper problem, one that may cost the property owner lost rent and ultimately lead to eviction? The accepted procedure is to wait five days before sending the tenant a reminder. This avoids generating a negative feeling when the problem was due to a minor delay, for it is a fact that the vast majority of tenants do pay their rent on time. However, if payment is not received by the tenth day after it was due, a second reminder goes out requesting that the tenant personally call on the manager. By meeting with the tenant, the manager may obtain an indication as to what the underlying problem is. If the tenant is suffering from a temporary financial setback, the manager can weigh the humanitarian side, and the possibility that payment will never be received, against the cost of rerenting the apartment.

EVICTION PROBLEMS

When it is apparent that a delinquent tenant will never bring his rent up to date, it is time to ask the tenant to leave and for the manager to rerent the space. What happens if the tenant will neither leave nor pay the rent? Years ago it was not uncommon for an owner to enter a tenant's unit, remove all the tenant's belongings, and lock them up. The key to the apartment door was changed and the apartment rerented; if the delinquent tenant wanted his belongings back, he had to pay the back rent. Today, a landlord must obtain a court order to move a tenant out. Meanwhile, a nonpaying tenant who is well versed in the law can remain for several rent-free weeks. This is possible because of the time required to go through the legal procedures of eviction. When the delinquent tenant finally leaves a month or two later, he may owe several hundred dollars in back rent. The legal cost of forcing payment may be more than what is owed. The tenant knows this and hopes he will not be pursued.

MANAGER REMEDIES

More and more tenants are learning that if they are brash enough, they can use the method just described to live rent-free and then move on. Others stop just short of the sheriff knocking on their door and leave on their own. The delinquent tenant hopes the manager or owner will not go to the trouble of pursuing the issue. Tenants are also learning to use the courts to pursue all sorts of real and fancied complaints against management, and managers are learning that judges often favor the tenant in these cases. What can owners and managers do about this? The best defense is careful tenant selection, substantial security deposits, good service, and a businesslike policy on rent collection. In other words, the old idea of filling up a building as fast as possible and later weeding out the problem tenants is no longer practical. Beyond that, the presence of a full-time manager means tenants are likely to take better care of the premises and are less likely to leave without paying the rent.

Managers can also make more effective use of the law by using the courts to obtain judgments against those who won't pay, those who move out without paying, and those who write bad checks for rent payments. Although a tenant may have left the area and it may not be worth the effort of locating him, the fact that a manager does take a firm stand serves as a deterrent to those planning the same tactics. For the nonpaying tenant, the judgment against him becomes part of his credit record and a warning to the next manager he approaches for an apartment.

On-Site Management

On-site management is a term that refers to property management duties that are performed on the premises. Showing apartment units to prospective tenants, taking applications, conducting interviews, signing leases, maintaining good tenant relations, collecting rents, and handling vacancies and evictions are usually handled by a property manager at the rent site. The on-site manager, also called a **resident manager** or **superintendent**, is also responsible for the repair, maintenance, and security of the building and grounds. This includes ordering supplies, as well as hiring trades people, gardeners, and a swimming pool maintenance firm. It involves walking through the entire premises at least once a day for security purposes and to make certain everything, such as lights in the hallways, security doors, elevators, swimming pool pumps, and recreation equipment, is working.

The resident manager is also responsible for keeping the premises clean and the trash collected and for supervising hired help. The resident manager is on call in the event of emergencies, such as when a tenant or guest becomes boisterous, there are shutdowns in heat or utilities, or the fire alarm goes off. The resident manager is the eyes and ears of the property management company and the owner, and makes suggestions as to needed repairs and improvements, needed changes in landlord-tenant policies, and ways to better look after the building and its tenants. The resident manager and management company are fiduciaries of the property owner, as they hold a position of trust, responsibility, confidence, and fidelity toward the owner.

MANAGEMENT-UNIT RATIOS

A rule of thumb in apartment management is that one on-site manager can handle 50 or 60 units alone. With 60 to 100 units, the manager needs an assistant to help with management chores and to make it possible to have someone on the property at all times. In projects of over 100 units, a popular approach is to hire husband–wife teams, placing both on the payroll and adding assistants in proportion to project size. For example, a 150-unit apartment building would be managed by a husband–wife team and one assistant (usually a full-time custodian). A 200-unit building would have a husband–wife team plus two full-time assistants, and so on, adding an additional employee for each additional 50 to 60 apartment units. Larger projects also mean that assistants can specialize. For example, in a 625-unit complex with a husband–wife team and nine assistants, two assistants might run the leasing office, two might specialize in cleaning apartments when tenants leave, and one might act as a gardener, one as a repairman, one as a custodian, one as a rent collector and bookkeeper, and one as a recreational facilities director.

Off-Site Management

Off-site management consists of duties that can be accomplished without being on the premises. Examples of off-site management are accounting for rents collected, handling payrolls, and paying bills. All of these are well suited for computerized data processing, and property management programs are available. These programs not only computerize bookkeeping chores, but pinpoint late rental payments, ensure that lease renewals are mailed promptly, identify upcoming vacancies, and make any contract-required rent adjustments. These systems will also keep track of every item that affects income and outgo, help manage cash flow so there is always enough money available to pay bills and the mortgage payment, and even type the checks. Moreover, available programs will generate reports such as tenant directories, rent rolls, tenant ledgers, upcoming lease expirations, and unit vacancies. To further assist management, these programs will generate operating statements for each property managed, construct budgets, make projections, and even analyze the financial health of the management firm.

Although a large part of off-site management is centered on accounting services, off-site managers have other responsibilities. For example, hazard and liability insurance must be purchased in the right coverages and for the best rates possible, resident managers must be hired and trained, and bids for contracted services must be taken and contracts awarded. Decisions as to rent policies, rent levels, advertising, major repairs, and capital improvements are made off-site. The off-site manager may even be asked to recommend when to refinance or sell the property and buy another.

Job Opportunities

In reading this chapter, you may have become interested in a career in real property management. The most successful apartment managers seem to be those who have had previous experience in managing people and money, and who are handy with tools. Those with prior military experience or experience as owners or managers of small businesses are eagerly sought after. Least successful as on-site property managers are those who see it as a quiet, peaceful retirement job, those who are unable to work with and understand people, those who can't organize or make decisions, those without a few handyman skills, and those strictly looking for an 8:00 a.m. to 5:00 p.m., Monday-to-Friday job. Commercial and industrial property management positions tend to be filled by persons who have had prior property management experience and who have a good understanding of how business and industry make use of real estate.

In a medium-to-large property management firm, there will be job opportunities for building service personnel, purchasing agents, bookkeepers, clerks, secretaries, office managers, field supervisors, and executive managers. In a small office, one person plus a secretary will be responsible for all the off-site duties.

TRAINING PROGRAMS

Finding experienced and capable property managers is not an easy task. Formal education in property management is not widely available in the United States. Instead, most managers learn their profession almost entirely by experience. An individual property owner can place an advertisement in a newspaper and attract a manager from another project, but most professional management firms have found it necessary to develop their own internal training programs. With such a program, a management firm can start a person with no previous property management experience as an assistant manager on a large project. If a person learns the job and enjoys the work, there is a promotion to manager of a 50- or 60-unit building and an increase in salary. If this works well, there is a move to a larger complex with an assistant and another increase in salary. Each step brings more responsibility and more pay. This system provides a steady stream of qualified managers for the management firm. It is also a source of executive-level personnel for the off-site management office. In larger cities, executive-level positions pay upward of $100,000 per year.

The dominant professional organization in the property management field is the **Institute of Real Estate Management (IREM)**. Established in 1933, the Institute is a division within the National Association of REALTORS®. Its primary purposes are to serve as an exchange medium for management ideas and to recognize specialists in the field. The Institute awards the designation **Certified Property Manager (CPM)** to members who successfully complete required educational courses in property management. The Institute also offers an educational program for resident managers of apartment buildings. The designation **Accredited Resident Manager (ARM)** is awarded upon successful completion. Forty-five percent of all property to be managed in the United States is managed by IREM members, and there are in excess of 10,000 CPMs.

Second in size to IREM is the **Building Owners and Managers Institute (BOMI)**. Incorporated in 1970, BOMI provides educational programs aimed primarily at the commercial property management industry. Seven courses are offered ranging from design, operation, and maintenance of buildings, to accounting, insurance, law, investments, and administration. Successful completion of the seven courses leads to the designation of **Real Property Administrator (RPA)**. BOMI also offers eight courses in heating, plumbing, refrigeration, air handling, electrical systems, control systems maintenance, energy management, and supervision, as they apply to commercial buildings. Those who complete these courses receive the **Systems Maintenance Administrator (SMA)** designation.

CPM, RPA
Professional designations for property managers.

Vocabulary Review

Match terms a–z with statements 1–26.

a. Actual eviction

b. Assignment

c. Assignor

d. Constructive eviction

e. Contract rent

f. CPM, RPA

g. Gross lease

h. Ground rent

i. Holdover tenant

j. Landlord-tenant laws

k. Lessee

l. Lessor

m. Month-to-month lease

n. Net lease

o. On-site management

p. Option clause

q. Participation clause

r. Percentage lease

s. Quiet enjoyment

t. Rent concession

u. Rent control

v. Reversion

w. Security deposit

x. Step-up rent

y. Sublessee

z. Sublet

_____ 1. The landlord.

_____ 2. The tenant.

_____ 3. Partial transfer of rights held under a lease.

_____ 4. Complete transfer of rights held under a lease.

_____ 5. One who holds a tenancy at sufferance.

_____ 6. Example of a periodic estate.

_____ 7. Entitles the landowner to retake possession at the end of the lease.

_____ 8. Rent charged for the use of land.

_____ 9. Specified rent increases at various points in time during the life of the lease.

_____ 10. A lease clause that allows the landlord to add to the tenant's rent any increases in property taxes, maintenance, and utilities during the life of the lease.

_____ 11. Gives a tenant the opportunity of renewing his lease at a predetermined rental without obligating him to do so.

_____ 12. A lease where the amount of rent paid is related to the income the lessee obtains from the use of the premises.

_____ 13. Describes leases wherein the tenant pays a fixed rent.

_____ 14. Entitles the tenant to uninterrupted use of the property without interference from the owner or third parties.

_____ 15. Statutes that set forth the responsibilities and rights of landlords and tenants.

_____ 16. A lease wherein a tenant pays a base rent plus maintenance, property taxes, and insurance.

_____ 17. The party acquiring possession under a sublet agreement.

_____ 18. The party who assigns her lease rights to another.

_____ 19. Nonpayment of rent would be grounds for this.

_____ 20. The amount of rent the tenant must pay the landlord as stated in the lease agreement.

_____ 21. An unfit premises would be grounds for this.

_____ 22. Government-imposed limits on how much a landlord can charge for space.

_____ 23. An advance deposit given by a tenant to a landlord against which the landlord can deduct for unpaid rent or damage.

_____ 24. A premium, such as a free month's rent, given to entice a prospective tenant to sign a lease.

_____ 25. A resident manager would be in this management category.

_____ 26. Professional designations for property managers.

Questions and Problems

1. From the standpoint of the tenant, what are the advantages and disadvantages of a lease versus a month-to-month rental?

2. What remedies does a property manager in your state have when a tenant does not pay his rent and/or refuses to move out?

3. Does your state have a landlord-tenant code? What are its major provisions? If no specific code or act currently exists in your state, where does one look for laws pertaining to landlords and tenants?

4. What is the difference between contract rent and economic rent?

5. On what basis could a tenant claim constructive eviction? What would the tenant's purpose be in doing this?

6. Is an option to renew a lease to the advantage of the lessor or the lessee?

7. Is rent control currently in effect in your community? If so, what effects have these controls had on the sales of investment properties and on the construction of new rental buildings in your community?

8. If you were an apartment building manager interviewing prospective tenants, what questions would you ask?

Additional Readings

ALI-ALA's Practice Checklist Manual for Drafting Leases III: Checklists, Forms and Drafting Advice from the Practical Real Estate (American Law Institute, 2001).

Commercial Real Estate Leases: Preparation and Negotiation by Mark A. Senn (Aspen Publishers, 2012). Discusses negotiating leases of all different types of commercial property and contains forms for office leases, shopping centers, and so on.

Essential Guide to Real Estate Leases by Mark Warda (Sourcebooks, Incorporated, 2001).

How to Negotiate Real Estate Leases: For Landlords and Tenants by Mark Warda (Sourcebooks, Incorporated, 1998; E-Book: net Library, Incorporated, 1998).

Leasing and Marketing for Property Managers by Doug Rossi (BOMI Institute, 1999).

Property Management by Walt Huber (South-Western Educational Pub, 2010). Covers leases, residential management, shopping centers, office buildings, maintenance, and landlord-tenant law. Case studies are included.

Real Estate Brokerage: A Management Guide, 17th ed. by Laurel Mcadams, John E Cyr, and Joan Sobeck (Kaplan Publishing, 2008). Applies management techniques and organization for small- to medium-sized businesses.

CHAPTER 18

Real Estate Appraisal

Purpose and Use of Appraisals

An **appraisal** is a necessary part of most real estate transactions. Often, the decision to buy, sell, or grant a loan on real estate hinges on a real estate appraiser's estimate of property value. Appraisals are also used to set prices on property listed for sale and to set premiums on fire insurance policies; they are used by government to acquire and manage public property and to establish property tax levels for taxpayers.

To *appraise* real estate means to estimate its value. Thus, an **informal appraisal** can be defined simply as an estimate of value. But a **formal appraisal** is more accurately defined as "an independently and impartially prepared written statement expressing an opinion of a defined value of an adequately described property as of a specific date, that is supported by the presentation and analysis of relevant market information."

The Real Property Valuation Process

The **valuation process** is the step-by-step procedure that appraisers use to conduct their work. The conventions for this process have been developed over a period of many years. However, this system has been refined and modified in recent years by the **Uniform Standards of Professional Appraisal Practice (USPAP)**.

Following the guidelines of USPAP, the valuation process involves the following steps: (1) define the appraisal problem; (2) conduct a preliminary analysis, formulate an appraisal plan, and collect the data; (3) estimate the highest and best use of the

LEARNING OBJECTIVES

After reading this chapter, you should be able to:

‹ Describe the purpose and use of appraisals.

‹ Recognize the different value approaches to appraisals.

‹ Understand and describe the sales comparison approach to evaluation.

‹ Understand and describe the income approach to evaluation.

‹ Understand and describe the cost approach to appraisal.

‹ Understand the difference between various formats for appraisal reports and understand the qualifications for appraisers.

‹ Be able to define the multiple meanings of the word *value*.

KEY TERMS

Appraisal • Capitalize • Comparables • Cost approach • Depreciation • FIRREA • Gross rent multiplier (GRM) • Highest and best use • Income approach • Market approach • Market value • Operating expenses • Scheduled gross (projected gross) • USPAP

appraisal
The estimate of the value of something.

land as if vacant, and the property as improved; (4) estimate land value; (5) estimate the improved property value through the appropriate value approaches; (6) reconcile the results to arrive at a defined value estimate; and (7) report the conclusion of value.

Value Approaches

There are three approaches to making this estimate. The first is to locate similar properties that have sold recently, and use them as benchmarks in estimating the value of the property you are appraising. This is the **sales comparison approach**, also called the **market data approach** or **market comparison approach**. The second approach is to add together the cost of the individual components that make up the property being appraised. This is the **cost approach**; it starts with the cost of a similar parcel of vacant land and adds the cost of the lumber, concrete, plumbing, wiring, labor, and so on, necessary to build a similar building. Depreciation is then subtracted. The third approach is to consider only the amount of net income that the property can reasonably be expected to produce for its owner plus any anticipated price increase or decrease. This is the **income approach**. For the person who owns or plans to own real estate, knowing how much a property is worth is a crucial part of the buying or selling decision. For the real estate agent, being able to estimate the value of a property is an essential part of taking a listing and conducting negotiations.

cost approach

Land value plus current construction costs minus depreciation.

income approach

A method of valuing a property based on the monetary returns it can be expected to produce.

Market Value Defined

In this chapter you will see demonstrations of the market, cost, and income approaches and how they are used in determining market value. **Market value**, also called **fair market value**, is the most probable price that a property should bring in a competitive and open market under all conditions requisite to a fair sale, the buyer and seller each acting prudently, knowledgeably, and assuming the price is not affected by undue stimulus.

This definition implies the consummation of a sale at a specified date and the passing of title from seller to buyer under conditions whereby: (1) buyer and seller are typically motivated; (2) both parties are well-informed or well-advised and each is acting in what he or she considers his or her own best interest; (3) a reasonable time is allowed for exposure in the open market; (4) payment is made in terms of cash in U.S. dollars or in terms of financial arrangements comparable thereto; and (5) the price represents the normal consideration for the property sold, unaffected by special or creative financing or sales concessions granted by anyone associated with the sale. Market value is at the heart of nearly all real estate transactions.

market value

The cash price that a willing buyer and a willing seller would agree upon, given reasonable exposure of the property to the marketplace, full information as to the potential uses of the property, and no undue compulsion to act.

Sales Comparison Approach

Let's begin by demonstrating the application of the **sales comparison approach** to a single-family residence. The residence to be appraised is called the **subject property** and is described as follows:

The subject property is a one-story, wood-frame house of 1,520 square feet containing three bedrooms, two bathrooms, a living room, dining room, kitchen, and utility room. There is a two-car garage with concrete driveway to the street, a 300-square-foot concrete patio in the backyard, and an average amount of landscaping. The house is located on a 10,200-square-foot, level lot that measures 85 by 120 feet. The house is 12 years old, in good repair, and located in a well-maintained neighborhood of houses of similar construction and age.

LOT FEATURES AND LOCATION

Line 9 in Table 18.1, deals with any differences in lot size, slope, view, and neighborhood. In this example, all comparables are in the same neighborhood as the subject property, thus eliminating the need to judge, in dollar terms, the relative merit of one neighborhood over another. However, comparable A has a slightly larger lot and a better view than the subject property. Based on recent lot sales in the area, the difference is judged to be $890 for the larger lot and $3,000 for the better view. Comparable B has a slightly smaller lot judged to be worth $900 less, and comparable C is similar in all respects.

COMPARABLES

After becoming familiar with the location, physical features and amenities of the subject property, the next step in the **market approach** is to locate houses with similar physical features and amenities that have sold recently under market value conditions. These are known as **comparables** or "comps." The more similar they are to the subject property, the fewer and smaller the adjustments that must be made in the comparison process, and hence the less room for error. As a rule, it is best to use comparable sales no more than six months old. During periods of relatively stable prices, this can be extended to one year. However, during periods of rapidly changing prices, even a sale of six months old may be out of date.

market approach
A method of valuing property based on recent sales of similar properties.

comparables
Properties similar to the subject property that have sold recently.

TABLE 18.1 Valuing a House by the Sales Comparison Approach

Line	Item	Comparable Sale A		Comparable Sale B		Comparable Sale C	
1	Address	1702 Brookside Ave.		1912 Brookside Ave.		1501 18th Street	
2	Sales price		$191,800		$188,000		$188,300
3	Time adjustment	sold 6 mos. ago, add 5%	+4,590	sold 3 mos. ago, add 2.5%	+2,200	just sold	0
4	House size	160 sq ft larger at $60 per sq ft	−9,600	20 sq ft smaller at $60 per sq ft	+1,200	same size	0
5	Garage/carport	carport	+4,000	3-car garage	−2,000	2-car garage	0
6	Other	larger patio	−300	no patio	+900		
7	Age, upkeep, & overall quality of house	superior	−3,000	inferior	+800	equal	0
8	Landscaping	inferior	+2,000	equal	0	superior	−900
9	Lot size, features, & location	superior	−3,890	inferior	+900	equal	0
10	Terms & conditions of sale	equal	0	special financing	−1,500	equal	0
11	Total adjustments		−6,200		+2,500		−900
12	ADJUSTED MARKET PRICE		$185,600		$190,500		$187,400
13	Correlation process:						
	Comparable A $185,600 × 20% =		$ 37,120				
	Comparable B $190,500 × 30% =		57,150				
	Comparable C $187,400 × 50% =		93,700				
14	INDICATED VALUE		$187,970				
	Round to		$188,000				

Source: © 2014 OnCourse Learning

SALES RECORDS

To apply the sales comparison approach, the following information must be collected for each comparable sale: date of sale, sales price, financing terms, location of the property, and a description of its physical characteristics and amenities. Recorded deeds at public records offices can provide dates and locations of recent sales. Although a deed seldom states the purchase price, nearly all states levy a deed transfer fee or conveyance tax, the amount of which is shown on the recorded deed. This tax can sometimes provide a clue as to the purchase price.

Records of past sales can often be obtained from title and abstract companies. Property tax assessors keep records on changes in ownership, as well as property values. Where these records are kept up to date and are available to the public, they can provide information on what has sold recently and for how much. Assessors also keep detailed records of improvements made to land. This can be quite helpful in making adjustments between the subject property and the comparables. For real estate salespeople, locally operated multiple listing services provide asking prices and descriptions of properties currently offered for sale by member brokers along with descriptions, sales prices, and dates for properties that have been sold. In some cities, commercially operated financial services such as CoStar, publish information on local real estate transactions and sell it on a subscription basis. Their Web site is accessible and extremely helpful for gathering data: http://www.costar.com.

VERIFICATION

To produce the most accurate appraisal possible, each sale used as a comparable should be inspected and the price and terms verified. An agent who specializes in a given neighborhood will have already visited the comparables when they were still for sale. The agent can verify price and terms with the selling broker or from multiple listing service sales records.

NUMBER OF COMPARABLES

Three to five comparables usually provide enough basis for reliable comparison. To use more than five, the additional accuracy must be weighed against the extra effort involved. When the supply of comparable sales is more than adequate, one should choose the sales that require the fewest adjustments.

It is also important that the comparables selected represent current market conditions. Sales between relatives or close friends may result in an advantageous price to the buyer or seller, and sales prices that for some other reason appear to be out of line with the general market should not be used. Listings and offers to buy should not be used in place of actual sales. They do not represent a meeting of minds between a buyer and a seller. Listing prices do indicate the upper limit of prices, whereas offers to buy indicate lower limits. Thus, if a property is listed for sale at $180,000 and there have been offers as high as $170,000, it is reasonable to presume the market price lies somewhere between $170,000 and $180,000. Some lenders require a few listings to be reported, particularly if the property is in a declining neighborhood.

ADJUSTMENT PROCESS

Let's now work through the example shown in Table 18.1 to demonstrate the application of the market comparison approach to a house. We begin at lines 1 and 2 by entering the address and sale price of each comparable property. For convenience, we shall refer to these as comparables A, B, and C. On lines 3 through 10, we make time adjustments to the sale price of each comparable to make it equivalent to the subject property today. **Adjustments** are made for price changes since each comparable was sold, as well as for differences in physical features, amenities, and financial terms. The result indicates the market value of the subject property.

TIME ADJUSTMENTS

Returning to line 3 in Table 18.1, let us assume that house prices in the neighborhood where the subject property and comparables are located have risen 5% during the six months that have elapsed since comparable A was sold. If it were for sale today, comparable A would bring 5% or $4,590 more. Therefore, we must add $4,590 to bring it up to the present. Comparable B was sold three months ago, and to bring it up to the present we need to add 2.5% or $2,200 to its sales price. Comparable C was just sold and needs no time correction as its price reflects today's market.

When using the market comparison approach, all adjustments are made to the comparable properties, not to the subject property. This is because we cannot adjust the value of something for which we do not yet know the value.

HOUSE SIZE

Because house A is 160 square feet larger than the subject house, it is logical to expect that the subject property would sell for less money. Hence, a deduction is made from the sales price of comparable A on line 4. The amount of this deduction is based on the difference in floor area and the current cost of similar construction, minus an allowance for depreciation. If we value the extra 160 square feet at $60 per square foot, we must subtract $9,600. For comparable B, the house is 20 square feet smaller than the subject house. At $60 per square foot, we add $1,200 to comparable B, as it is reasonable to expect that the subject property would sell for that much more because it is that much larger. Comparable C is the same-sized house as the subject property, so no adjustment is needed.

GARAGE AND PATIO ADJUSTMENTS

Next, the parking facilities (line 5) are adjusted. We first look at the current cost of garage and carport construction and the condition of these structures. Assume that the value of a carport is $3,000; a one-car garage, $5,000; a two-car garage, $7,000; and a three-car garage, $9,000. Adjustments would be made as follows. The subject property has a two-car garage worth $7,000 and comparable A has a carport worth $3,000. Therefore, based on the difference in garage facilities, we can reasonably expect the subject property to command $4,000 more than comparable A. By adding $4,000 to comparable A, we effectively equalize this difference. Comparable B has a garage worth $2,000 more than the subject property's garage. Therefore, $2,000 must be subtracted from comparable B to equalize it with the subject property. For comparable C, no adjustment is required, as comparable C and the subject property have similar garage facilities.

At line 6, the subject property has a 300-square-foot patio in the backyard worth $900. Comparable A has a patio worth $1,200; therefore, $300 is deducted from comparable A's selling price. Comparable B has no patio. As it would have sold for $900 more if it had one, a +$900 adjustment is required. The patio at comparable C is the same as the subject property's. Any other differences between the comparables and the subject property such as swimming pools, fireplaces, carpeting, drapes, roofing materials, and kitchen appliances would be adjusted in a similar manner.

BUILDING AGE, CONDITION, AND QUALITY

On line 7, we recognize differences in building age, wear and tear, construction quality, and design usefulness. Where the difference between the subject property and a comparable can be measured in terms of material and labor, the adjustment is the cost of that material and labor. For example, the $800 adjustment for comparable B reflects the cost of roof repair needed at the time B was sold. The adjustment of $3,000 for comparable A reflects that it has better-quality plumbing and electrical fixtures than the subject property. Differences that cannot be quantified in terms of labor and materials are usually dealt with as lump-sum judgments. Thus, one might allow $1,500 for each year of age difference between the subject and a comparable, or make a lump-sum adjustment of $3,000 for an inconvenient kitchen design.

Keep in mind that adjustments are made on the basis of what each comparable property was like on the day it was sold. Thus, if an extra bedroom was added or the house was painted after its sale date, these items are not included in the adjustment process.

LANDSCAPING

Line 8 shows the landscaping at comparable A to be inferior to the subject property. A positive correction is necessary here to equalize it with the subject. The landscaping at comparable B is similar and requires no correction; that at comparable C is better, and thus, requires a negative adjustment. The dollar amount of each adjustment is based on the market value of lawn, bushes, trees, and the like.

TERMS AND CONDITIONS OF SALE

Line 10 in Table 18.1 accounts for differences in financing. As a rule, the more accommodating the terms of the sale to the buyer, the higher the sales price, and vice versa. We are looking for the highest cash price the subject property may reasonably be expected to bring, given adequate exposure to the marketplace and a knowledgeable buyer and seller not under undue pressure. If the comparables were sold under these conditions, no corrections would be needed in this category. However, if it can be determined that a comparable was sold under different conditions, an adjustment is necessary. For example, if the going rate of interest on home mortgages is 12% per year, and the seller offers to finance the buyer at 9% interest, it is reasonable to expect that the seller can charge a higher selling price. Similarly, the seller can get a higher price if he has a low-interest loan that can be assumed by the buyer. Favorable financing terms (such as expensive seller concessions) offered by the seller of comparable B enabled him to obtain an extra $1,500 in selling price. Therefore, we must subtract $1,500 from comparable B. Another situation that requires an adjustment on line 10 is if a comparable was sold on a rush basis. If a seller is in a hurry to sell, a lower selling price usually must be accepted than if the property can be given more time in the marketplace.

ADJUSTED MARKET PRICE

Adjustments for each comparable are totaled and either added or subtracted from its sale price. The result is the **adjusted market price** shown at line 12. This is the dollar value of each comparable sale after it has gone through an adjustment process to make it the same as the subject property. If it were possible to precisely evaluate every adjustment, and if the buyers of comparables A, B, and C had paid exactly what their properties were worth at the time they purchased them, the three prices shown on line 12 would be the same. However, buyers are not that precise, particularly in purchasing a home where amenity value influences price and varies considerably from one person to the next.

CORRELATION PROCESS

While comparing the properties, it will usually become apparent that some comparables are more like the subject property than others. The **correlation process** gives the appraiser the opportunity to assign more weight to the more similar comparables and less to the others. A mathematical weighting is one available technique. At line 13, comparable C is given a weight of 50% since it is more like the subject and required fewer adjustments. Moreover, this sameness is in areas where adjustments tend to be the hardest to estimate accurately: time, age, quality, location, view, and financial conditions. Of the remaining two comparables, comparable B is weighted slightly higher than comparable A because it is a more recent sale and required fewer adjustments overall.

In the correlation process, the adjusted market price of each comparable is multiplied by its weighting factor and totaled at line 14. The result is the **indicated value** of the subject property. It is customary to round off to the nearest $50 or $100 for properties under $10,000; to the nearest $250 or $500 for properties between $10,000 and $100,000; to the nearest $1,000 or $2,500 for properties between $100,000 and $250,000; and to the nearest $2,500 or $5,000 above that.

The correlation process is probably the most difficult factor in the appraisal. Whether or not to increase the value or decrease the value of a house, and for what reason, can vary widely. For instance, does an elevator increase or decrease the value of the house? It depends heavily on the location, size and, occupants of the house. The same is true for swimming pools, sculptures, and fountains. It is the experience and judgment of an appraiser that makes the appraisal accurate in these kinds of situations.

UNIQUE ISSUES

CONDOMINIUM, TOWNHOUSE, AND COOPERATIVE APPRAISAL.

The process for estimating the market value of a condominium, townhouse, or cooperative living unit by the market approach is similar to the process for houses except that fewer steps are involved. For example, in a condominium complex with a large number of two-bedroom units of identical floor plan, data on a sufficient number of comparable sales may be available within the building. This would eliminate adjustments for differences in unit floor plan, neighborhood, lot size and features, age and upkeep of the building, and landscaping. The only corrections needed would be those that make one unit different from another. This would include the location of the individual unit within the building (end units and units with better views sell for more), the upkeep and interior decoration of the unit, a time adjustment, and an adjustment for terms and conditions of the sale.

When there are not enough comparable sales of the same floor plan within the same building and it is necessary to use different-sized units, an adjustment must be made for floor area. If the number of comparables is still inadequate and units in different condominium buildings must be used, adjustments will be necessary for neighborhood, lot features, management, upkeep, age, and overall condition of the building.

VACANT LAND VALUATION. Subdivided lots zoned for commercial, industrial, or apartment buildings are usually appraised and sold on a square-foot basis. Thus, if apartment land is currently selling for $30 per square foot, a 100,000-square-foot parcel of comparable zoning and usefulness would be appraised at $3,000,000. Another method is to value on a front-foot basis. For example, if a lot has 70 feet of street frontage and if similar lots are selling for $1,000 per front foot, that lot would be appraised at $70,000. Storefront land is often sold this way. House lots can be valued either by the square foot, front foot, or lot method. The lot method is useful when one is comparing lots of similar size and zoning in the same neighborhood. For example, recent sales of 100-foot by 100-foot house lots in the $180,000 to $200,000 range would establish the value of similar lots in the same neighborhood.

Rural land and large parcels that have not been subdivided are usually valued and sold by the acre. For example, how would you value 21 acres of vacant land when the only comparables available are 16-acre and 25-acre sales? The method is to establish a per acre value from comparables and apply it to the subject land. Thus, if 16- and 25-acre parcels sold for $32,000 and $50,000 respectively, and are similar in all other respects to the 21-acre subject property, it would be reasonable to conclude that land is selling for $2,000 per acre. Therefore, the subject property is worth $42,000.

COMPETITIVE MARKET ANALYSIS

A variation of the market comparison approach, and one that is very popular with agents who list and sell residential property, is the **competitive market analysis (CMA).** This method is based on the principle that value can be estimated not only by looking at similar homes that have sold recently, but also by taking into account homes presently on the market plus homes that were listed for sale but did not sell. The CMA is a listing tool that a sales agent prepares in order to show a seller what the home is likely to sell for, and the CMA helps the agent decide whether to accept the listing.

Figure 18.1 shows a competitive market analysis form previously published by the National Association of REALTORS˚. There are many similar forms utilized by relocation companies today, so we will discuss this one as an example. The procedure in preparing a CMA is to select homes that are comparable to the subject property. The greater the similarity, the more accurate the appraisal will be and the more likely it is that the client will accept the agent's estimate of value and counsel. It is usually best to use only properties in the same neighborhood; this is easier for the seller to relate to and removes the need to compensate for neighborhood differences. The comparables should also be similar in size, age, and quality. Although a CMA does not require that individual adjustments be shown as in Table 18.1, it does depend on the agent's understanding of the process that takes place in that table. That is why Table 18.1 and its explanation are important. A residential agent may not be called upon to make a presentation as is done in Table 18.1; nonetheless, all those steps are considered and consolidated in the agent's mind before entering a probable final sales price on the CMA.

HOMES FOR SALE. In section [1] of the CMA shown in Figure 18.1, similar homes presently offered for sale are listed. This information is usually taken directly from the agent's multiple listing service (MLS) book, and ideally the agent will already have toured these properties and have first-hand knowledge of their condition. These are the homes the seller's property will compete against in the marketplace.

In section [2], the agent lists similar properties that have sold in the past several months. Ideally, the agent will have toured the properties when they were for sale. Sale

FIGURE
18.1 Competitive Market Analysis

Property Address _____ Date _____

For Sale Now: [1]

	Bed-rms.	Baths	Den	Sq. Ft.	1st Loan	List Price	Days on Market	Terms

Sold Past 12 Mos. [2]

	Bed-rms.	Baths	Den	Sq. Ft.	1st Loan	List Price	Days on Market	Date Sold	Sale Price	Terms

Expired Past 12 Mos. [3]

	Bed-rms.	Baths	Den	Sq. Ft.	1st Loan	List Price	Days on Market	Terms

[4] F.H.A. – V.A. Appraisals

Address	Appraisal	Address	Appraisal

[5] Buyer Appeal **[6] Marketing Position**

(Grade each item 0 to 20% on the basis of desirability or urgency)

1. Fine Location _____ %
2. Exciting Extras _____ %
3. Extra Special Financing _____ %
4. Exceptional Appeal _____ %
5. Under Market Price _____ Yes _____ No ____ %

Rating Total _____ %

1. Why Are They Selling _____ %
2. How Soon Must They Sell _____ %
3. Will They Help Finance .... Yes _____ No_____ %
4. Will They List at Competitive Market Value .... Yes _____ No_____ %
5. Will They Pay for Appraisal .... Yes _____ No_____ %

Rating Total _____ %

[7]
Assets _____
Drawbacks _____
Area Market Conditions _____
_____

Recommended Terms _____

[8] Selling Costs

Brokerage	$
Loan Payoff	$
Prepayment Penalty	$
FHA – VA Points	$
Title and Escrow Fees: IRS Stamps Recons Recording	$
Termite Clearance	$
Misc. Payoffs: 2nd T.D., Pool, Patio, Water Softener, Fence, Improvement Bond.	$
	$
	$
Total	$

Top Competitive Market Value $ _____

[9]
Probable Final Sales Price $ _____

Total Selling Costs $ _____

Net Proceeds $ _____   Plus or Minus $ _____

The statements and figures presented herein, while not guaranteed, are secured from sources we believe authoritative

Prepared by_____

Source: Reprinted with permission by the Council of Real Estate Brokerage Managers.

prices are usually available through MLS sales records. Section [3] is for listing homes that were offered for sale but did not sell. In other words, buyers were unwilling to take these homes at the prices offered.

In section [4], recent Federal Housing Administration (FHA) and Veterans Affairs (VA) appraisals of comparable homes can be included if it is felt that they will be useful in determining the price at which to list. Two words of caution are in order here. First, using someone else's opinion of value is risky. It is better to determine your own opinion based on actual facts. Second, FHA and VA appraisals often tend to lag behind the market. This means in a rising market they will be too low; in a declining market they will be too high.

BUYER APPEAL. In section [5], buyer appeal, and in section [6], market position, the agent evaluates the subject property from the standpoint of whether it will sell if placed on the market. It is important to make the right decision to take or not to take a listing. Once taken, the agent knows that valuable time and money must be committed to get a property sold. Factors that make a property more appealing to a buyer include good location, extra features, small down payment, low interest, meticulous maintenance, and a price below market. Similarly, a property is more saleable if the sellers are motivated to sell, want to sell soon, will help with financing, and will list at or below market. A busy agent will want to avoid spending time on overpriced listings, listings for which no financing is available, and listings where the sellers have no motivation to sell. Under the rating systems in sections [5] and [6], the closer the total is to zero, the less desirable the listing; the closer to 100%, the more desirable the listing.

Section [7] provides space to list the property's high and low points, current market conditions, and recommended terms of sale. Section [8] shows the seller how much to expect in selling costs. Section [9] shows the seller what to expect in the way of a sales price and the amount of cash that can be expected from the sale.

The emphasis in CMA is on a visual inspection of the data on the form in order to arrive at market value directly. No pencil-and-paper adjustments are made. Instead, adjustments are made in a generalized fashion in the minds of the agent and the seller. In addition to its application to single-family houses, CMA can also be used on condominiums, cooperative apartments, townhouses, and vacant lots—provided sufficient comparables are available.

GROSS RENT MULTIPLIERS

gross rent multiplier (GRM)

A number that is multiplied by a property's gross rents to produce an estimate of the property's worth.

A popular market comparison method that is used when a property produces income is the **gross rent multiplier**, or **GRM**. The GRM is an economic comparison factor that relates the gross rent a property can produce to its purchase price. For apartment buildings and commercial and industrial properties, the GRM is computed by dividing the sales price of the property by its gross annual rent. For example, if an apartment building grosses $100,000 per year in rents and has just sold for $700,000, it is said to have a GRM of 7. The use of a GRM to value single-family houses is questionable since they are usually sold as owner-occupied residences rather than as income properties. Note that if you do work a GRM for a house, it is customary to use the monthly (not yearly) rent.

Where comparable properties have been sold at fairly consistent gross rent multiples, the GRM technique presumes the subject property can be valued by multiplying its gross rent by that multiplier. To illustrate, suppose that apartment buildings were recently sold in your community as shown in Table 18.2. These sales indicate that the market is

TABLE 18.2	Calculating Gross Rent Multipliers				
Building	**Sales Price**		**Gross Annual Rents**		**Gross Rent Multiplier**
No. 1	$245,000	÷	$ 34,900	=	7.02
No. 2	160,000	÷	22,988	=	6.96
No. 3	204,000	÷	29,352	=	6.95
No. 4	196,000	÷	27,762	=	7.06
As a group:	$805,000	÷	$115,002	=	7.00

Source: © 2014 OnCourse Learning

currently paying seven times gross. Therefore, to find the value of a similar apartment building grossing $24,000 per year, multiply by 7 to get an indicated value of $168,000.

The GRM method is popular because it is simple to apply. Having once established what multiplier the market is paying, one need only know the gross rents of a building to set a value. However, this simplicity is also the weakness of the GRM method because the GRM takes into account only the gross rent a property produces. Gross rent does not allow for variations in vacancies, uncollectible rents, property taxes, maintenance, management, insurance, utilities, or reserves for replacements.

WEAKNESS OF GRM. To illustrate the problem, suppose that two apartment buildings each gross $100,000 per year. However, the first has expenses amounting to $40,000 per year and the second has expenses of $50,000 per year. Using the same GRM, the buildings would be valued the same, yet the first produces $10,000 more in net income for its owner. The GRM also overlooks the expected economic life span of a property. For example, a building with an expected remaining life span of 30 years would be valued exactly the same as one expected to last 20 years, if both currently produce the same rents. One method of partially offsetting these errors is to use different GRMs under different circumstances. Thus, a property with low operating expenses and a long expected economic life span might call for a GRM of 7 or more, whereas a property with high operating expenses or a shorter expected life span would be valued using a GRM of 6 or 5 or even less.

Cost Approach

There are times when the market approach is an inappropriate valuation tool. For example, the market approach is of limited usefulness in valuing a fire station, school building, courthouse, or highway bridge. These properties are rarely placed on the market, and comparables are rarely found. Even with properties that are well-suited to the market approach, there may be times when it is valuable to apply another valuation approach. For example, a real estate agent may find that comparables indicate that a certain style and size of house is selling in a particular neighborhood for $150,000. Yet the astute agent discovers through the cost approach that the same house can be built from scratch, including land, for $125,000. The agent builds and sells 10 of these and concludes that, yes, there really is money to be made in real estate. Let's take a closer look at the cost approach.

Table 18.3 demonstrates the **cost approach**. Step 1 is to estimate the value of the land upon which the building is located. The land is valued as though vacant using the market

TABLE 18.3	Cost Approach to Value		
Step 1:	Estimate land as vacant		$ 30,000
Step 2:	Estimate new construction cost of similar building	$120,000	
Step 3:	Less estimated depreciation	−12,000	108,000
Step 4:	Indicated value of building		
Step 5:	Appraised property value by the cost approach		$138,000

Source: © 2014 OnCourse Learning

comparison approach described earlier. In Step 2, the cost of constructing a similar building at today's costs is estimated. These costs include the current prices of building materials, construction wages, architect's fees, contractor's services, building permits, utility hookups, and so on, plus the cost of financing during the construction stage and the cost of construction equipment used at the project site. Step 3 is the calculation of the amount of money that represents the subject building's wear and tear, lack of usefulness, and obsolescence when compared to the new building of Step 2. In Step 4, depreciation is subtracted from today's construction cost to give the current value of the subject building on a used basis. Step 5 is to add this amount to the land value. Let us work through these steps.

ESTIMATING NEW CONSTRUCTION COSTS

In order to choose a method of estimating construction costs, one must decide whether cost will be approached on a reproduction basis or on a replacement basis. **Reproduction cost** is the cost at today's prices of constructing an *exact replica* of the subject improvements using the same or very similar materials.

Replacement cost is the cost, at today's prices and using today's methods of construction, for an improvement having the same or *equivalent usefulness* as the subject property. Replacement cost is the more practical choice of the two as it eliminates nonessential or obsolete features and takes full advantage of current construction materials and techniques. It is the approach that will be described next.

COMPARATIVE UNIT METHOD

The most widely used approach for estimating construction costs is the **square-foot method**. It provides reasonably accurate estimates that are fast and simple to prepare.

The square-foot method is based on finding a newly constructed building that is similar to the subject building in size, type of occupancy, design, materials, and construction quality. The cost of this building is converted to cost per square foot by dividing its current construction cost by the number of square feet in the building.

COST HANDBOOKS

Cost information is also available from construction cost handbooks. Using a **cost handbook** starts with selecting a handbook appropriate to the type of building being appraised, such as the Marshall Valuation Service. From photographs of houses included in the handbook along with brief descriptions of the buildings' features, the appraiser finds a house that most nearly fits the description of the subject house. Next to pictures of the house is the current cost per square foot to construct it. If the subject house has a better quality roof, floor covering, or heating system; more or fewer built-in appliances, or plumbing fixtures; or a garage, basement, porch, or swimming pool, the handbook provides costs for each of these. Figure 18.2 illustrates the calculations involved in the square-foot method.

FIGURE 18.2   Square-Foot Method of Cost Estimating

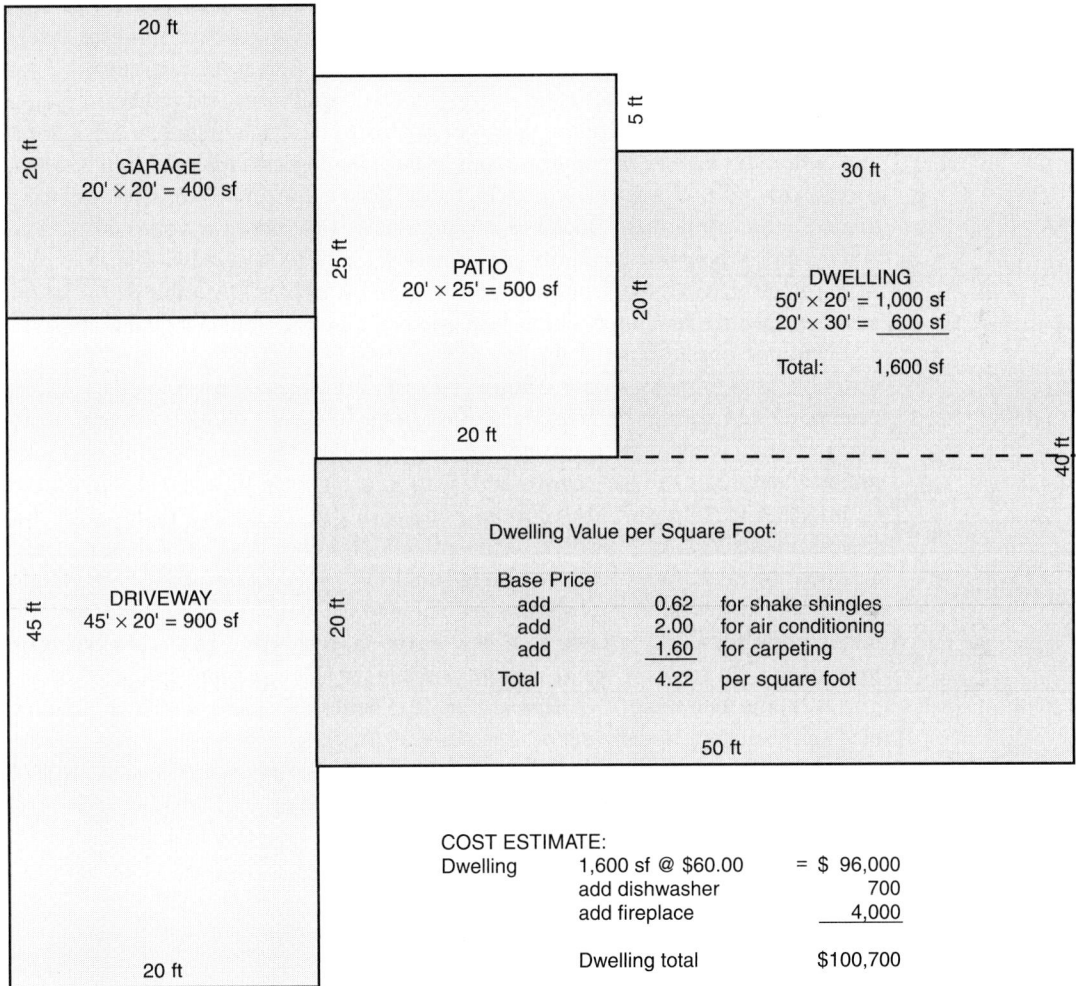

GARAGE
20' × 20' = 400 sf

PATIO
20' × 25' = 500 sf

DWELLING
50' × 20' = 1,000 sf
20' × 30' =   600 sf

Total: 1,600 sf

DRIVEWAY
45' × 20' = 900 sf

Dwelling Value per Square Foot:

Base Price		
add	0.62	for shake shingles
add	2.00	for air conditioning
add	1.60	for carpeting
Total	4.22	per square foot

COST ESTIMATE:

Dwelling	1,600 sf @ $60.00	=	$ 96,000
	add dishwasher		700
	add fireplace		4,000
	Dwelling total		$100,700
Garage	400 sf @ $15.00	=	12,000
Driveway	900 sf @ $ 2.00		1,800
Patio	500 sf @ $ 6.00		3,000
Landscaping			2,000
	Subtotal		$119,500
Construction financing, real estate taxes, and title policy, add 10%			10,331
	GRAND TOTAL		$129,831

ESTIMATING DEPRECIATION

depreciation

Loss in value due to deterioration and obsolescence.

Having estimated the current cost of constructing the subject improvements, the next step in the cost approach is to estimate the loss in value due to depreciation since they were built. In making this estimate, we look for three kinds of **depreciation**: physical deterioration, functional obsolescence, and economic obsolescence.

Physical deterioration results from wear and tear through use, such as wall-to-wall carpet that has been worn thin or a dishwasher, garbage disposal, or water heater that must be replaced. Physical deterioration also results from the action of nature in the form of sun, rain, heat, cold, and wind, and from damage due to plants and animal life, such as tree roots breaking sidewalks and termites eating wood. Physical deterioration can also result from neglect (an overflowing bathtub) and from vandalism.

Functional obsolescence results from outmoded equipment (old-fashioned plumbing fixtures in the bathrooms and kitchen), faulty or outdated design (a single bathroom in a three- or four-bedroom house or an illogical room layout), inadequate structural facilities (inadequate wiring to handle today's household appliance loads), and overadequate structural facilities (high ceilings in a home). Functional and physical obsolescence can be separated into curable and incurable components. **Curable depreciation** can be fixed at reasonable cost; for example, worn carpeting, a leaky roof, or outdated faucets in bathrooms. **Incurable depreciation** cannot be reasonably fixed and must simply be lived with; for example, an illogical room layout.

Economic obsolescence is the loss of value due to external forces or events. It is always incurable as a property owner cannot "cure" this problem. For example, a once-popular neighborhood becomes undesirable because of air or noise pollution or because surrounding property owners fail to maintain their properties. Or, a city that is dependent on a military base finds the base closed and, with it, a big drop in demand for real estate. Or, the motel district in town loses customers because a new interstate highway has been built several miles away. An estimate of economic obsolescence is an important part of the cost approach to value. However, in the long run, most properties experience economic appreciation and not economic obsolescence. The appreciation can come from new industries moving into town, city growth in a new direction, a shortage of land in beach or waterfront areas, and so on. Thus, it is quite possible for the economic appreciation of a property to more than offset the depreciation it experiences. The result is a building that is physically and functionally depreciating and at the same time appreciating in value. Consequently, while the chronological age of a building is important to value, what is more important is the remaining economic life of the building and whether it is functionally adequate for use in the future. This is what real estate investors look for.

FINAL STEPS IN THE COST APPROACH

After calculating the current construction cost of the subject improvements and estimating the amount of depreciation, the next step is to subtract the amount of depreciation from the current construction cost to get the depreciated value of the improvements. This is added to the value of the land upon which the subject improvements rest. The total is the value of the property by the cost approach.

Income Approach

capitalize

To convert future income to current value.

The **income approach** considers the monetary returns a property can be expected to produce and converts that into a value the property should sell for if placed on the market today. This is called capitalizing the income stream. To **capitalize** means to convert future income to current value. To illustrate, suppose that an available apartment building is expected to return, after expenses, $18,000 per year. How much would you, as an investor, pay for the building? The answer depends on the return you require on each dollar you invest. Suppose you will accept a return of 9% per year. In that case you will pay $200,000 for this building. The calculation is as follows:

$$\frac{\text{Income}}{\text{Rate}} = \text{Value} \quad\text{quad}\quad \frac{\$18,000}{0.09} = \$200,000$$

This is the basic principle of capitalization. The appraisal work comes in estimating the net income a property will produce and looking at recent sales of similar properties to see what capitalization rates are currently acceptable to investors. Let's look at the techniques one would use in estimating a property's income. Pay close attention, because each $1 error in projected annual income or expenses can make a difference of $8 to $15 in the market value of the property.

INCOME AND EXPENSE FORECASTING

The best starting point is to look at the actual record of income and expenses for the subject property over the past three to five years. Although the future will not be an exact repetition of the past, the past record of a property is usually the best guide to future performance. These historical data are blended with the current operating experience of similar buildings in order to estimate what the future will bring. The result is a projected operating statement, such as the one shown in Table 18.4, which begins with the estimated rents that the property can be expected to produce on an annual basis. This is the **projected gross**, or **scheduled gross**, and represents expected rentals from the subject property on a fully occupied basis. From this, vacancy and collection losses are subtracted. These are based partly on the building's past experience and partly on the operating experience of similar buildings.

scheduled gross (projected gross)
The estimated rent a fully occupied property can be expected to produce on an annual basis.

OPERATING EXPENSES

The next step is to itemize anticipated **operating expenses** for the subject property. These are expenses necessary to maintain the production of income. For an apartment building without recreational facilities or an elevator, the list in Table 18.4 is typical. Again, we must consider both the property's past operating expenses and what we expect those expenses to be in the future. For example, even though a property is currently being managed by its owner and no management fee is being paid, a typical management fee, say 5% of the gross rent, is included.

operating expenses
Expenditures necessary to maintain the production of income.

Not included as operating expenses are outlays for capital improvements, such as the construction of a new swimming pool, the expansion of parking facilities, and assessments for street improvements. Improvements are not classified as expenses because they increase the usefulness of the property, which increases the rent the property will generate, and therefore, the property value.

RESERVES

Reserves for replacement are established for items that do not require an expenditure of cash each year. To illustrate, lobby furniture (and furniture in apartments rented as "furnished") wears out a little each year, eventually requiring replacement. Suppose that these items cost $7,200 and are expected to last six years, at which time they must be replaced. An annual $1,200 reserve for replacement not only reflects wear and tear of the furniture during the

TABLE 18.4	Projected Annual Operating Statement (Also Called a Pro Forma Statement)		
Scheduled gross annual income		$84,000	
Vacancy allowance and collection losses		4,200	
Effective gross income			$79,800
Operating expenses			
Property taxes		$7,000	
Hazard and liability insurance		2,100	
Property management		4,200	
Janitorial services		1,500	
Gardener		1,200	
Utilities		3,940	
Trash pickup		850	
Repairs and maintenance		4,000	
Other		1,330	
Reserves for replacement			
Furniture and furnishings		1,200	
Stoves and refrigerators		600	
Furnace and/or air conditioning		700	
Plumbing and electrical		800	
Roof		750	
Exterior painting		900	
Total operating expenses			31,070
Net operating income			$48,730
Operating expense ratio: $31,070 ÷ $79,800 = 38.9%			

Source: © 2014 OnCourse Learning

year, but also reminds us that to avoid having to meet the entire furniture and furnishings replacement cost out of one year's income, money should be set aside for this purpose each year. In a similar manner, reserves are established for other items that must be replaced or repaired more than once during the life of the building, but not yearly.

NET OPERATING INCOME

The operating expense total is then subtracted from the effective gross income. The balance that remains is the **net operating income (NOI)**. From the net operating income, the property owner receives both a return *on* and a return *of* investment. The return *on* investment is the interest received for investing money in the property. The return *of* investment is compensation for the fact that the building is wearing out.

OPERATING EXPENSE RATIO

At this point, the **operating expense ratio** can be calculated. It is obtained by dividing the total operating expenses by the effective gross income. The resulting ratio provides a handy yardstick against which similar properties can be compared. If the operating expense ratio is out of step compared to similar properties, it signals the need for further investigation. A range of 25% to 45% is typical for apartment buildings. The Institute of Real Estate Management of the National Association of REALTORS® publishes books and articles that give typical operating ratios for various types of income properties across the United States. Local inquiry to appraisers and brokers who specialize in income properties will also provide typical ratios for buildings in a community.

CAPITALIZING INCOME

The final step in the income approach is to capitalize the net operating income. In other words, what price should an investor offer to pay for a property that produces a given net income per year? The solution is as follows: income ÷ rate = value. If the annual net operating income is $45,400 and if the investor intends to pay all cash, expects to receive a 10% return on his investment, and anticipates no change in the value of the property while he owns it, the solution is to divide $45,400 by 10%. However, most investors today borrow much of the purchase price and usually expect an increase in property value. Under these conditions, how much should the investor pay?

The best known method for solving this type of investment question involves using the Ellwood Tables, published in 1959 by L. W. Ellwood, MAI. However, for the person who does not use these tables regularly, the arithmetic involved can prove confusing. As a result, **mortgage-equity tables** are now available from bookstores. These allow the user to look up a single number, called an **overall rate**, and divide it into the net operating income to find a value for the property.

For example, suppose an investor who is interested in buying the property can obtain a 9%, fully amortized, 25-year mortgage loan for 75% of the purchase price. He wants an 18% return on his equity in the property, plans to hold it 10 years, and expects it will increase 50% in value (after selling costs) during that time. How much should he offer to pay the seller? In Table 18.5,

TABLE 18.5	Overall Rates—10-Year Holding Period, 25-Year Loan for 75% of the Purchase Price, 18% Investor Return			
	Loan Interest Rate			
Appreciation, Depreciation	**9%**	**10%**	**11%**	**12%**
+100%	0.07251	0.07935	0.08631	0.09338
+50%	**0.09376**	0.10060	0.10756	0.11463
+25%	0.10439	0.11123	0.11819	0.12526
+15%	0.10864	0.11548	0.12244	0.12951
+10%	0.11077	0.11761	0.12457	0.13164
+5%	0.11289	0.11973	0.12669	0.13376
0	0.11502	0.12186	0.12882	0.13589
−5%	0.11715	0.12399	0.13095	0.13802
−10%	0.11927	0.12611	0.13307	0.14014
−15%	0.12140	0.12824	0.13520	0.14227
−25%	0.12565	0.13249	0.13945	0.14652
−50%	0.13628	0.14312	0.15008	0.15715
−100%	0.15753	0.16437	0.17133	0.17840

Data from *Financial Capitalization Rate Tables*

Source: © 2014 OnCourse Learning

we look for an interest rate of 9% and for appreciation of 50%. This gives an overall rate of 0.09376, and the solution is:

$$\frac{\text{Income}}{\text{Overall Rate}} = \text{Value} \qquad \frac{\$45,400}{0.09376} = \$484,215$$

Further exploration of the numbers in Table 18.5 shows that as loan money becomes more costly, the overall rate rises, and as interest rates fall, so does the overall rate. If the investor can anticipate appreciation in value, the overall rate drops; if he can't, the overall rate climbs. You can experiment by dividing some of the other overall rates in this table into $45,400 to see how the value of this property changes under different circumstances.

DEPRECIATION

The pro forma in Table 18.4 provides reserves for replacement of such items as the roof, furnace, air conditioning, plumbing, electrical, exterior paint, and so forth. Nonetheless, as the building ages, the style of the building will become dated, the neighborhood will change, and the structure will experience physical deterioration. Allowance for this is usually accounted for in the selection of the capitalization rate. The less functional, economic, and physical obsolescence that is expected to take place, the lower the acceptable "cap" rate, and vice versa.

FICTIONAL DEPRECIATION. In contrast to actual depreciation, there is the **fictional depreciation** that the U.S. Treasury allows income property owners to deduct as an expense when calculating income taxes. The Internal Revenue Service allows a purchaser of an apartment building to completely depreciate the structure over a period of 27½ years, regardless of the age or condition of the structure. This figure may be an understatement of the remaining life of the structure, but it was chosen by Congress to create an incentive to invest in real estate, not as an accurate gauge of a property's life. Thus, it is quite common to see depreciation claimed on buildings that are, in reality, appreciating because of rising income from rents and/or falling capitalization rates.

Choice of Approaches

Whenever possible, all three appraisal methods discussed in this chapter should be used to provide an indication, as well as a cross-check, of a property's value. If the marketplace is acting rationally and is not restricted in any way, all three approaches will produce the same value. If one approach is out of line with the others, it may indicate an error in the appraiser's work or a problem in the market itself. It is not unusual to find individual sales that seem out of line with prevailing market prices. Similarly, there are times when buyers will temporarily bid the market price of a property above its replacement cost.

For certain types of real property, some approaches are more suitable than others. This is especially true for single-family residences. Here you must rely almost entirely on the market and cost approaches, as very few houses are sold on their ability to generate cash rent. Unless you can develop a measure of the "psychic income" in home ownership, relying heavily on rental value will lead to a property value below the market and cost approaches. Applying all three approaches to special-purpose buildings may also prove to be impractical. For example, in valuing a college or university campus or a state capitol building, the income and market approaches have only limited applicability.

When appraising a property that is bought for investment purposes, such as an apartment building, shopping center, office building, or warehouse, the income approach is the primary method of valuation. As a cross-check on the income approach, an apartment building should be compared to other apartment buildings on a price per apartment unit basis or price per square foot basis. Similarly, an office, store, or warehouse can be compared to other recent office, store, or warehouse sales on a price per square foot basis. Additionally, the cost approach can be used to determine whether it would be cheaper to buy land and build rather than to buy an existing building.

Reconciliation

After applying the market, cost, and income approaches to the subject property, the appraiser must reconcile the differences found in the results. One method is to assign each approach a weighting factor based on a judgment of its relevance and reliability in the appraisal of this property. To demonstrate, the results of a 20-year-old, single-family house appraisal might be reconciled as follows:

Market approach	$180,000 × 75%	=	$135,000
Cost approach	$200,000 × 20%	=	40,000
Income approach	$160,000 × 5%	=	8,000
Final indicated value			$183,000

What the appraiser is suggesting here is that recent sales of comparable properties have the most influence on current sales prices. Thus, the market approach is given the most weight. The cost approach is given much less weight because it required a difficult judgment of accrued depreciation for the subject improvements. By weighting the income approach at only 5%, the appraiser is recognizing that houses in this neighborhood are mostly owner-occupied, and rarely bought for rental purposes.

Appraiser's Best Estimate

It is important to realize that the appraised value is the appraiser's best *estimate* of the subject property's worth. Thus, no matter how painstakingly it is done, property valuation requires the appraiser to make many subjective judgments. Because of this, it is not unusual for three highly qualified appraisers to look at the same property and produce three different appraised values. It is also important to recognize that an appraisal is made as of a specific date. It is not a certificate of value, good forever until used. If a property was valued at $115,000 on January 5 of this year, the more time that has elapsed since that date, the less accurate that value is as an indication of the property's current worth.

An appraisal does not take into consideration the financial condition of the owner, the owner's health, sentimental attachment, or any other personal matter. An appraisal does not guarantee that the property will sell for the appraised market value. (The buyer and the seller determine the actual selling price.) Nor does buying at the appraised market value guarantee a future profit for the purchaser. (The real estate market can change.) An appraisal is not a guarantee that the roof will not leak, that there are no termites, or that everything in the building works. An appraisal is not an offer to buy, although a buyer can order one made so as to know how much to offer. An appraisal is not a loan commitment, although a lender can order one made so as to apply a loan-to-value ratio when making a loan.

Appraisal Regulation
THE APPRAISAL FOUNDATION

When the country was suffering from harsh economic times, standards of appraisals came under extremely close scrutiny by many lenders. For instance, two appraisers may appraise the same property for significantly different values while using the same data, both acting in good faith. It is hard to draw a distinction, however, between an error in judgment and a fraudulent appraisal. The more difficult question is: How can a lender, in reviewing an appraisal, distinguish between good and bad appraisals? At least part of the answer is being addressed by an organization called **The Appraisal Foundation**. It is a private organization whose purpose is to establish and approve: (1) uniform appraisal standards, (2) appropriate criteria for the certification and recertification of qualified appraisers, and (3) appropriate systems for the certification and recertification of qualified appraisers.

To put into effect this result, The Appraisal Foundation has established two sub-committees: the Appraiser Qualifications Board and the Appraisal Standards Board. The first establishes criteria for appraisers. The second sets standards for the appraisal to be performed. The Foundation's aim is to disseminate such qualification criteria to the various states, governmental entities, and others to assist them in establishing and maintaining an appropriate system for the certification and recertification of qualified appraisers.

FEDERAL REGULATION

FIRREA

The Financial Institution's Reform, Recovery, and Enforcement Act of 1989.

Congress addressed the appraisal issue by enacting Title XI of the Financial Institution's Reform, Recovery, and Enforcement Act (**FIRREA**) of 1989. The act, for the first time in history, establishes standards that will have a far-reaching impact on the appraisal industry.

Congress also created the Appraisal Subcommittee of the Federal Financial Institution's Examination Council to establish standards. The Subcommittee looks exclusively to the Appraisal Foundation for establishing standards under FIRREA for both appraiser qualifications, as well as appraisal standards. This has proven to be an excellent effort by leaders in the appraisal industry, coupled with the governmental enforcement powers, to establish standards that ultimately benefit lenders and the public in general.

DEVELOPING THE APPRAISAL

USPAP

The Uniform Standards of Professional Appraisal Practice.

FIRREA created mandatory requirements for certain federally related real estate appraisals. These requirements are known as the Uniform Standards of Professional Appraisal Practice, commonly referred to as **USPAP**.

In developing an appraisal, USPAP requires that the appraiser must be aware of, understand, and correctly employ those recognized methods and techniques that are necessary to produce a credible appraisal. There are specific requirements for an appraiser's analysis, requiring consideration of current sales, options, or listings within certain time periods prior to the date of the appraisal. Specifically, this analysis of market data must consider all sales, options, or listings: (1) within one year for a one- to four-family residential property, and (2) within three years for all other property types. The act further requires that the appraiser must consider and reconcile the quality and quantity of data available and analyze, within the approaches used, the applicability or suitability of the approaches used as they pertain to the subject parcel of real estate.

DEPARTURE PROVISIONS

There were significant changes to the USPAP in 1994. The Uniform Standards now provide for a Departure Provision that permits limited departures from the standards that are classified as specific guidelines rather than binding requirements.

Before entering into an agreement to perform an appraisal that contains a departure: (1) the appraiser must have determined that the appraisal or consulting process to be performed is not so limited that the resulting assignment would tend to mislead or confuse the client or the intended users of the report; (2) the appraiser has advised the client that the assignment calls for something less than, or different from, the work required by the specific guidelines, and that the report will clearly identify and explain the departure(s); and (3) the client has agreed that the performance of a limited appraisal or consulting service would be appropriate.

The Definition Section of the USPAP defines "appraisal" as "the act or process of estimating value; an estimate of value," and then defines two types of appraisals:

1. A **complete appraisal**, which is defined as the act or process of estimating value without invoking the Departure Provision. A complete appraisal report may not depart from Specific USPAP Guidelines; and

2. A **limited appraisal**, defined as the act or process of estimating value performed under and resulting from invoking the Departure Provision.

REPORTING OPTIONS

In addition, the revised USPAP now defines three optional levels of reporting:

1. The **self-contained appraisal report**, which is the most detailed and encompassing of the report options. The length and descriptive detail in such a report should fully support (in a self-contained format) the conclusions of the appraiser;

2. The **summary report**, which is less detailed than a self-contained report. The information contained and the appraisal procedures that were followed may be summarized in this report rather than describing the information in detail; and

3. The **restricted report**, which is the least detailed of the reporting options. There is only a minimal presentation of information and it is intended for use only by the client. This level of report must contain a prominent use restriction that limits the reliance on the report to the client and warns that the report cannot be properly understood without additional information from the work file of the appraiser.

REPORTING STANDARDS

USPAP also sets forth required standards for the appraisal report. Each self-contained appraisal report must: (1) identify and describe the real estate being appraised; (2) state the real property interest being appraised; (3) state the purpose and intended use of the appraisal; (4) define the value to be estimated; (5) state the effective date of the appraisal and the date of the report; (6) state the extent of the process of collecting, confirming, and reporting data; (7) state all assumptions and limiting conditions that affect the analyses, opinions, and conclusions; (8) describe the information considered, the appraisal procedures followed, and the reasoning that supports the analyses, opinions, and conclusions; (9) describe the appraiser's opinion of the highest and best use of the real estate, when such an opinion is necessary and appropriate; (10) explain and support the exclusion of any of the usual valuation approaches; (11) describe any additional information that may be appropriate to show compliance with, or clearly identify and explain permitted departures from the specific guidelines of Standard 1 (on developing an appraisal); and (12) include a signed certification.

Each appraisal report must also: (1) clearly and accurately set forth the appraisal in a manner that will not be misleading; (2) contain sufficient information to enable person(s) who are expected to receive or rely on the report to understand it properly; and (3) clearly and accurately disclose any extraordinary assumption or limiting condition that directly affects the appraisal and indicate its impact on value.

USPAP requires that each written real property appraisal report include a signed certification similar in content to the following form:

I certify that, to the best of my knowledge and belief:

- The statements of fact contained in this report are true and correct.

- The reported analyses, opinions, and conclusions are limited only by the reported assumptions and limiting conditions, and are my personal, unbiased, professional analyses, opinions, and conclusions.

- I have no (or the specified) present or prospective interest in the property that is the subject of this report, and I have no (or the specified) personal interest or bias with respect to the parties involved.

- My compensation is not contingent upon the reporting of a predetermined value or direction in value that favors the cause of the client, the amount of the value estimate, the attainment of a stipulated result, or the occurrence of a subsequent event.

- My analyses, opinions, and conclusions were developed, and this report has been prepared, in conformity with the Uniform Standards of Professional Appraisal Practice.

- I have (or have not) made a personal inspection of the property that is the subject of this report. (If more than one person signs the report, this certification must clearly specify which individuals did and which individuals did not make a personal inspection of the appraised property.)

- No one provided significant professional assistance to the person signing this report. (If there are exceptions, the name of each individual providing significant professional assistance must be stated.)

NEW APPRAISAL REGULATIONS

As a result of the wide-spread mortgage fraud, we went back to more regulation of the appraisal process. Some appraisers were merely incompetent, others were outright fraudulent. They packaged their appraisal products so that the collateral would support the sales price of the property. Starting in 2009, the federal government, once again, found it important to impose new regulations. Fannie Mae and Freddie Mac adopted the Home Valuation Code of Conduct (HVCC), which attempts to insulate appraisers from any undue influence arising from potential conflicts of interests between lenders, brokers and appraisers. It applies only to one- to four-family loans.

As a result of this, a number of banks have turned to appraisal management companies for their appraisal work. At least in theory, this separates the appraisal process from any undue influence by third parties, as the lender and appraiser do not communicate except through the management company. This has complicated the appraisal process such that Fannie Mae, Freddie Mac, and the Federal Housing Finance Agency devised Appraiser Independence Requirements (AIR) to replace HVCC. More regulations! AIR retained most of the original plans imposed by HVCC. AIR imposed a few new rules designed to comply with Regulation Z of the Truth-in-Lending Act, but lenders continue to employ AMCs to comply with the requirements.

In 2010, the Dodd-Frank Act specifically adopted the appraisal requirements imposed by AIR. The Act codified and expanded on the existing AIR rules and as a provision requiring the lenders to pay customary and reasonable fees to appraisers without specifying any amounts. It also created the Consumer Financial Protection Bureau, which took over rule-making authority for appraisal fees that started in July 2011. Will all of these new regulations help? It certainly makes the appraisal process more burdensome for all of the parties. Those who commit fraud don't follow the regulations, anyway, do they?

Formats of Appraisal Reports

There are three traditional formats for written reports. The choice depends on the amount of detail required by the client, the intended use of the report, and the appraisal standards to be met. The format to be used also depends on the reporting option (self-contained, summary, or restricted). A brief description of reporting formats follows.

THE LETTER REPORT

The least formal report option, a **letter report**, is usually only one to five pages long. It contains the conditions of the assignment, a summary of the nature and scope of the appraiser's investigation, and an opinion of value. While brief, the letter report must describe the extent of the appraisal process performed, and clearly state its detail. Whether reporting a complete or limited appraisal, the letter format is most suited to the restricted appraisal report. It is used most often when the client is familiar with the property and when appraisal details are not needed.

THE FORM REPORT

The form report is an appraisal made on a preprinted form. A checklist is often used for describing and rating property characteristics. This makes the appraisal form a logical choice for the summary report option.

Institutions and government agencies use forms designed to suit their special needs. Standard forms are usually available for single-family residential, multifamily residential, commercial, and industrial properties. This is the most common type of report used for real estate loan appraisals.

THE NARRATIVE REPORT

The narrative appraisal is the longest and most formal of the appraisal reports. It is a step-by-step presentation of the facts used by the appraiser to arrive at a value. This report also contains a detailed discussion of the methods used to interpret the data presented. Narrative appraisal reports are used when the client needs to review each logical step taken by the appraiser. They are the preferred format for self-contained appraisal reports.

REVIEW APPRAISALS

FIRREA also developed standards for reviewing appraisals and reporting their adequacy and appropriateness. In reviewing the appraisal, the appraiser must observe specific guidelines that identify the report being reviewed and the real property being appraised, the effective date of the report, and the date of the review. The review appraiser must also identify the scope of the review process to be conducted and form an opinion as to the adequacy and relevance of the data and propriety of any adjustments to the data. The opinion must also reflect the appropriateness of the appraisal and the methods and techniques used to develop the reasons for any disagreement with the appraiser.

REAL ESTATE ANALYSIS

An **analysis** is the act or process of providing information, recommendations, and/or conclusions on diversified problems in real estate other than estimating the value, and can include a number of different forms of analysis, such as cash flow analysis, feasibility analysis, investment analysis, or market analysis. This differs from an *appraisal*, which, under USPAP standards, is defined as the act or process of estimating value.

In developing the real estate analysis, the analyst must be aware of, understand, and correctly employ those recognized methods and techniques that are necessary to produce a credible analysis. The analyst must not commit a substantial error of omission or commission that significantly affects the analysis and must not render services in a careless or negligent manner, which, when considering the results of the analysis, could be considered to be misleading. The analyst must also observe the following specific guidelines: (1) clearly identify the client's objective; (2) define the problem to be considered and the purpose and intended use of the analysis, consider the scope of the assignment, adequately identify the real estate under consideration and describe any special limiting condition; (3) collect, verify, and reconcile such data as may be required to complete the assignment and withhold no pertinent information; (4) apply the appropriate tools and techniques of analysis to data collected; and (5) base all projections of the analysis on reasonably clear and appropriate evidence. There are additional requirements established and separate criteria for each type of analysis being utilized by the analyst.

In reporting the results of the real estate analysis, the analyst must communicate each analysis, opinion, and conclusion in a manner that is not misleading, and the report must contain sufficient information to enable the persons who receive it to understand it properly, and must clearly and accurately disclose any extraordinary assumptions that would indicate an impact on the final conclusions or recommendation of the analysis.

The analysis report must contain a certification that is similar in content to that of the appraisal certification.

APPRAISER QUALIFICATIONS

To comply with new federal regulations established by the Appraisal Subcommittee, the Appraiser Qualifications Board of the Appraisal Foundation has established federal standards for certification and licensing of appraisers. Appraisers must be either licensed or certified as general or residential appraisers to be qualified to appraise for federal related institutions and regulated loans. The appraisers are certified or licensed by their respective states, based on their examination, education, and experience requirements. Examinations are administered by a state board in accordance with the Appraisal Foundation guidelines. Effective since January 1, 2008, applicants for general real estate appraiser certification must have successfully completed:

1. a bachelor's degree, or higher, from an accredited college; or

2. 30 semester hours in collegiate level courses from an accredited college, junior college, or university in English composition, microeconomics, macroeconomics, finance, algebra (or geometry or higher mathematics), statistics, computer science, and business (or real estate) law, and two elective courses in accounting, geography, agricultural economics, business management, or real estate.

Applicants for residential real estate appraiser certification must have successfully completed:

1. an associate degree, or higher, from an accredited college, junior college, community college, or university; or

2. 21 semester credit hours in collegiate courses from an accredited college, junior college, community college, or university in English composition, principles of economics, finance, algebra (or geometry or higher mathematics), statistics, computer science, and business (or real estate) law.

In either category of certification, the course work submitted must have included a minimum of 15 hours of coverage of the Uniform Standards of Professional Appraisal Practice. Applicants for a real estate appraiser license must have successfully completed 150 classroom hours in classes approved by the board, including the 15 hours of USPAP coverage.

In addition to the educational requirements, an applicant for general real estate appraiser certification must provide evidence satisfactory to the state licensing board that the applicant possesses the equivalent of 3,000 hours of appraisal experience over a minimum of 30 months. At least 1,500 hours of experience must be in nonresidential work. An applicant for a residential appraiser certification must provide evidence satisfactory to the board that the applicant possesses the equivalent of 2,500 hours of appraisal experience over a minimum of two calendar years. There is no requirement for nonresidential work. An applicant for a state real estate appraiser license must provide evidence satisfactory to the state licensing board that the applicant possesses the equivalent of 2,000 hours of appraisal experience. There is no minimum time requirement.

APPRAISAL LICENSE. Several states require that any person who appraises real estate for a fee must hold a license to do so. Depending on the state, this may be a regular real estate sales or broker license or a special appraiser's license. If you plan to make appraisals for a fee (apart from appraisal in connection with listing or selling a property as a licensed real estate salesperson or broker), make inquiry to your state's real estate licensing department as to appraisal licensing requirements.

The federal regulations outlined here present some interesting questions in appraisal practice. At present, no license or certification is required for federally related appraisals when the transaction value falls below $250,000. This seems to exempt most residential appraisals from regulation. It should be noted, however, that a number of federal underwriters (FNMA, GNMA, etc.) still have internal controls that require the use of a licensed or certified appraiser.

Characteristics of Value

Up to this point we have been concerned primarily with value based on evidence found in the marketplace and how to report it. Before concluding this chapter, let us briefly touch on what creates value, the principles of real property valuation, and appraisal for purposes other than market value.

For a good or service to have value in the marketplace, it must possess four characteristics: demand, utility, scarcity, and transferability. **Demand** is a need or desire coupled with the purchasing power to fill it, whereas **utility** is the ability of a good or service to fill that need. **Scarcity** means there must be a short supply relative to demand. Air, for example, has utility and is in demand, but it is not scarce. Finally, a good or service must be **transferable** to have value to anyone other than the person possessing it.

Principles of Value

The **principle of anticipation** reflects the fact that what a person will pay for a property depends on the expected benefits from the property in the future. Thus, the buyer of a home anticipates receiving shelter, plus the investment and psychic benefits of home ownership. The investor buys property in anticipation of future income.

The **principle of substitution** states that the maximum value of a property in the marketplace tends to be set by the cost of purchasing an equally desirable substitute property, provided no costly delay is encountered in making the substitution. In other words, substitution sets an upper limit on price. Thus, if there are two similar houses for sale, or two similar apartments for rent, the lower priced one will generally be purchased or rented first. In the same manner, the cost of buying land and constructing a new building sets a limit on the value of existing buildings.

The **highest and best use** of a property is the use that will give the property its greatest current value. This means you must be alert to the possibility that the present use of a parcel of land may not be the one that makes the land the most valuable. Consider a 30-year-old house located at a busy intersection in a shopping area. To place a value on that property based on its continued use as a residence would be misleading if the property would be worth more with the house removed and shopping or commercial facilities built on the land instead.

The **principle of competition** recognizes that where substantial profits are being made, competition will be encouraged. For example, if apartment rents increase to the point where owners of existing apartment buildings are making substantial profits, builders and investors will be encouraged to build more apartment buildings.

Applied to real estate, the **principle of supply and demand** refers to the ability of people to pay for land coupled with the relative scarcity of land. This means that attention must be given on the demand side to such matters as population growth, personal income, and preferences of people. On the supply side, you must look at the available supply of land and its relative scarcity. When the supply of land is limited and demand is great, the result is rising land prices. Conversely, where land is abundant and there are relatively few buyers, supply and demand will be in balance at only a few cents per square foot.

The **principle of change** reminds us that real property uses are always in a state of change. Although it may be imperceptible on a day-to-day basis, change can easily be seen over longer periods of time. Because the present value of a property is related to its future uses, the more potential changes that can be identified, the more accurate the estimate of its present worth will be.

The **principle of conformity** holds that maximum value is realized when there is a reasonable degree of homogeneity in a neighborhood. This is the basis for zoning laws across the country; certain tracts in a community are zoned for single-family houses, others for apartment buildings, stores, and industry. Within a tract, there should also be a reasonable amount of homogeneity. For example, a $200,000 house would be out of place in a neighborhood of $90,000 houses.

The **principle of diminishing marginal returns**, also called the **principle of contribution**, refers to the relationship between added cost and the value it returns. It tells us that we should invest dollars whenever they will return to us more than $1 of value for each $1 invested, and we should stop when each dollar invested returns less than $1 in value.

Multiple Meanings of the Word *Value*

When we hear the word *value*, we tend to think of market value. However, at any given moment in time, a single property can have other values too. This is because value or worth is very much affected by the purpose for which the valuation was performed. For example, **assessed value** is the value given to a property by the county tax assessor for purposes of property taxation. It utilizes a **mass appraisal** technique to determine value, and is recognized by USPAP as an acceptable method of appraisal for tax assessors. Estate **tax value** is the value that federal and state taxation authorities establish for a deceased person's property; it is used to calculate the amount of estate taxes that must be paid. **Insurance value** is concerned with the cost of replacing damaged property. It differs from market value in two major respects: (1) the value of the land is not included, as it is presumed only the structures are destructible, and (2) the amount of coverage is based on the replacement cost of the structures. **Loan value** is the value set on a property for the purpose of making a loan.

PLOTTAGE VALUE

When two or more adjoining parcels are combined into a single large parcel, it is called **assemblage**. The increased value of the large parcel over and above the sum of the smaller parcels is called **plottage value**. For example, local zoning laws may permit a six-unit apartment building on a single 10,000-square-foot lot. However, if two of these lots can be combined, zoning laws could permit as many as 15 units. This makes the lots more valuable if sold together.

INVESTMENT VALUE

Investment value is the value of a property expressed in terms of the right to its use for a specific period of time. The fee simple interest in a house may have a market value of $80,000, whereas the market value of one month's occupancy might be $600.

REPLACEMENT VALUE

Replacement value is value as measured by the current cost of building a structure of equivalent utility. **Salvage value** is what a structure is worth if it has to be removed and taken elsewhere, either whole or dismantled for parts. Because salvage operations require much labor, the salvage value of most buildings is usually very low.

This list of values is not exhaustive, but it points out that the word *value* has many meanings. When reading an appraisal report, always read the first paragraph to see why the appraisal was prepared. Before preparing an appraisal, make certain you know its purpose, and then state it at the beginning of your report.

Buyer's and Seller's Markets

Whenever supply and demand are unbalanced because of excess supply, a **buyer's market** exists. This means buyers can negotiate prices and terms more to their liking, and sellers who want to sell must accept them. When the imbalance occurs because demand exceeds supply, it is a **seller's market**; sellers are able to negotiate prices and terms more to their liking as buyers compete for the available merchandise.

A **broad market** means that many buyers and sellers are in the market at the same time. This makes it relatively easy to establish the price of a property and for a seller to find a buyer quickly, and vice versa. A **thin market** is said to exist when there are only a few buyers and a few sellers in the market at the same time. It is often difficult to appraise a property in a thin market because there are so few sales to use as comparables.

Professional Appraisal Societies

During the 1930s, two well-known professional appraisal societies were organized: **The American Institute of Real Estate Appraisers (AIREA)** and the **Society of Real Estate Appraisers**. Although a person offering services as a real estate appraiser didn't need to be associated with either of these groups, there were advantages to membership. Both organizations developed designation systems to recognize appraisal education, experience, and competence. The Society and AIREA were unified in 1991, named The Appraisal Institute, and now provide the most highly respected designations in the industry. Within the Appraisal Institute, the highest-level designation is the MAI (member of the Appraisal Institute). To become an MAI requires a four-year college degree or equivalent education, various Appraisal Institute courses, examinations, an income property demonstration appraisal, and at least 4,500 hours (with a maximum of 1,500 hours allowed in a 12-month period) of appraisal experience. There are about 6,000 MAIs in the United States. Also available is the SRA designation for residential appraisers, which requires a four-year college degree or acceptable alternative, appraisal course work, a passing appraisal examination score, a residential demonstration appraisal, and 3,000 hours of experience in residential real estate, with a maximum of 1,500 hours allowed in any 12-month period.

In addition to the institute and the society, there are several other professional appraisal organizations in the United States. They are the National Association of Independent Fee Appraisers, the Farm Managers and Rural Appraisers, the National Society of Real Estate Appraisers, and the American Society of Appraisers. All exist to promote and maintain high standards of appraisal services and all offer a variety of appraisal education and designation programs.

Vocabulary Review

Match terms a–z with statements 1–26.

a. Adjustments
b. Appraisal
c. Buyer's market
d. Capitalize
e. Comparables
f. Competitive market analysis (CMA)
g. Cost approach
h. Curable depreciation
i. Depreciation
j. Functional obsolescence
k. Gross rent multiplier (GRM)
l. Highest and best use
m. Income approach
n. Incurable depreciation
o. Market approach
p. Market value
q. Net operating income (NOI)
r. Operating expenses
s. Physical deterioration
t. Principle of substitution
u. Replacement cost
v. Reproduction cost
w. Scheduled gross income
x. Square-foot method
y. Subject property
z. The Appraisal Foundation

_____ 1. Properties similar to the subject property that have sold recently.

_____ 2. Cost, at today's prices and using today's methods of construction, to build an improvement having the same usefulness as the subject property.

_____ 3. Cost at today's prices of constructing an exact replica of the subject improvements using the same or similar methods.

_____ 4. A method of valuing property based on the prices of recent sales of similar properties.

_____ 5. Land value plus current construction costs less depreciation.

_____ 6. The property that is being appraised.

_____ 7. Corrections made to comparable properties to account for differences between them and the subject property.

_____ 8. A property valuation and listing technique that looks at properties currently for sale, recent sales, and properties that did not sell, and which does not make specific dollar adjustments for differences.

_____ 9. Depreciation resulting from wear and tear of the improvements.

_____ 10. Depreciation resulting from improvements that are inadequate, overly adequate, or improperly designed for today's needs.

_____ 11. The estimated rent a fully occupied property can be expected to produce on an annual basis.

_____ 12. To convert future income to current value.

_____ 13. Gross income less operating expenses, vacancies, and collection losses.

_____ 14. Expenditures necessary to maintain the production of income.

_____ 15. Acts as an upper limit on prices; the lower priced of two similar properties will usually sell first.

_____ 16. To estimate the value of something.

_____ 17. A method of valuing property based on the monetary return it is expected to produce.

_____ 18. A number that is multiplied by a property's gross rents to produce an estimate of its worth.

_____ 19. A method for estimating construction costs that is based on the cost per square foot to build a structure.

_____ 20. Depreciation that can be fixed at a reasonable cost.

_____ 21. Depreciation that cannot be fixed at a reasonable cost.

_____ 22. Organization whose purpose is to establish appraisal standards.

_____ 23. A market where there are few buyers and many sellers.

_____ 24. Use of a parcel of land that will produce the greatest current value for the parcel.

_____25. Loss in value due to deterioration and obsolescence.
_____26. The cash price that a willing buyer and a willing seller would agree upon, given reasonable exposure of the property to the marketplace, full information as to the potential uses of the property, and no undue compulsion to act.

Questions and Problems

1. When making a market comparison appraisal, how many comparable properties should be used?

2. How useful are asking prices and offers to buy when making a market comparison appraisal?

3. In the market approach, are the adjustments made to the subject property or to the comparables? Why?

4. Why is it important when valuing vacant land that comparable properties have similar zoning, neighborhoods, size, and usefulness?

5. Explain the use of gross rent multipliers in valuing real properties. What are the strengths and the weaknesses of this method?

6. What are the five steps used in valuing an improved property by the cost approach?

7. Briefly explain the concept of the income approach to valuing real property.

8. Explain how the competitive market analysis method differs from the standard market approach method. Which method is better? Why?

9. What precaution does the principle of diminishing marginal returns suggest to a real estate owner?

10. With regard to appraising a single-family house, what type of appraisal format would most likely be requested by a lender? A prospective buyer? An executor of an estate? A highway department?

11. Why was The Appraisal Foundation formed? What should its impact be on the appraisal industry?

Additional Readings

The Appraisal of Real Estate by Appraisal Institute Staff (Appraisal Institute, 2008).

"Appraisal or Valuation: An Art or a Science?" by Barry G. Gilbertson (*Real Estate Issues*, Fall 2001).

Basic Real Estate Appraisal: Principles and Procedures, 8th ed. by Richard M. Betts (OnCourse Learning, 2013). Provides a practical guide to real estate appraisal for students, real estate professionals, and consumers. This text continuously references and explains the Uniform Standards of Professional Appraisal Practice and their impact on the appraisal process.

The Concepts of Residential Real Estate Appraisal by Michael K. Grady (National Appraisal & Consulting Services, 1997).

Glossary for Property Appraisal and Assessment (International Association of Assessing Officers, 1997).

The Valuation of Apartment Properties by Arlen C. Mills and Anthony Reynolds (Appraisal Institute, 1999).

CHAPTER 19

Licensing Laws and Professional Affiliation

For most owners of real estate, the decision to sell means hiring a broker to find a buyer. Although some owners choose to market their properties themselves, most find it advantageous to turn the job over to a real estate broker and pay a commission for the service of finding a buyer and carrying the deal through closing. The next three chapters are for the owners who plan to use a broker and for the persons who plan to be real estate salespersons or brokers. This chapter discusses examination and licensing requirements and gives an overview of how states regulate the real estate profession, including a section on how to choose a broker with whom to affiliate and a section about professional real estate associations, in particular the National Association of REALTORS®. In Chapter 20, we begin with a simplified real estate listing contract. Next, we take a close look at the agency responsibilities a broker has toward a seller together with the seller's obligations toward the broker. Then we discuss seller and broker responsibilities toward persons who are interested in purchasing the listed property.

Rationale for Licensing

Does the public have a vested interest in seeing that real estate salespersons and brokers have the qualifications of honesty, truthfulness, good reputation, and real estate knowledge before they are allowed to negotiate real estate transactions on behalf of others? It was this concern that brought about real estate licensing laws as we know them today. Until 1917, no state required real estate agents to be licensed. Anyone who wanted to be an agent could simply hang up a sign stating that he was an agent. In larger cities, there were persons and firms who specialized in bringing buyers and sellers together. In smaller towns, a local banker, attorney, or barber would know who had what for sale and be the person a buyer would ask for property information.

The first attempt to require that persons acting as real estate agents be licensed was made by the California legislature in 1917. That law was declared unconstitutional, with the main opposition being that the state was unreasonably interfering with the right of every citizen to engage in a useful and legitimate occupation. Two years later, in 1919, the California legislature passed a second real estate licensing act. This time it was upheld by the Supreme Court. That same year, Michigan, Oregon, and Tennessee also passed real estate licensing acts. Today, all 50 states and the District of Columbia require that persons who offer their services as real estate agents be licensed.

LOYALTY, HONESTY, AND TRUTHFULNESS

The first licensing laws did not require examinations for competency, nor did they require real estate education. They were aimed at weeding out persons who placed loyalty to themselves above loyalty to those whom they were representing. By requiring persons to be licensed, the state had the power to refuse to issue a license to someone with a past record of dishonesty and untruthfulness. Additionally, the state could temporarily or permanently take away a license once it had been issued. To help make licensing laws work, the state refused to allow its courts to enforce claims for commissions by unlicensed persons.

In the 1930s and 1940s, states began adding the requirement of a license examination in an attempt to determine whether the license applicant also had some level of technical ability in real estate. Then, beginning in the 1950s, states began adding the requirement that a person take a certain number of hours of real estate education before being licensed. Thus, what we see today is that a person who plans to be a real estate agent must qualify both ethically and technically before being issued a license.

That a real estate license applicant have a good reputation for honesty and truthfulness is still a very important part of real estate licensing today. If you apply for a license, you may be asked to provide a photograph, credit report, fingerprints, and/or personal character references. The state licensing agency will check for links to any past criminal convictions or other significant infractions of the law. Inquiry may be made of your character references to learn more about your reputation.

Persons Required to Be Licensed

In what situations does a person need a real estate license? A person who, for another, and for compensation or the promise of compensation, lists or offers to list, sells or offers to sell, buys or offers to buy, negotiates or offers to negotiate, either directly or indirectly, for the purpose of bringing about a sale, purchase or option to purchase, exchange, auction, lease, or rental of real estate, or any interest in real estate, is required to hold a valid real estate license. Some states also require persons offering their services as real estate appraisers, property managers, mortgage bankers, apartment locators, or rent collectors to hold real estate licenses.

Property owners dealing with their own property, and licensed attorneys conducting a real estate transaction as an incidental part of their duties as an attorney for a client are exempt from holding a license. Also exempt are trustees and receivers in bankruptcy, legal guardians, administrators and executors handling a deceased's estate, officers and employees of a government agency dealing in real estate, and persons holding power of attorney from an owner. However, the law does not permit a person to use the exemptions as a means of conducting a brokerage business without the proper license. That is, an unlicensed person cannot take a listing under the guise of a power of attorney and then act as a real estate broker.

Broker

Before the advent of licensing laws, there was no differentiation between real estate brokers and real estate salespersons. People who brought about transactions were simply called real estate agents, or whatever else they wanted to be called. With licensing laws came two classes of **licensee**: real estate broker and real estate salesperson. A **real estate broker** is a person licensed to act independently in conducting a real estate brokerage business. A **broker** brings together those with real estate to be marketed and those seeking to buy real estate and negotiates a transaction. For those services, the broker receives a fee, usually in the form of a commission based on the selling price or lease rent. The broker may represent the buyer or the seller, or, upon full disclosure, both at the same time. The role is more than that of a middleman who puts two interested parties in contact with each other, for the broker usually takes an active role in negotiating price and terms acceptable to both the buyer and the seller. A broker can be an actual person or a legal entity—that is, a business firm. If it is a business firm, the person in charge must be a broker. The laws of all states permit a real estate broker to hire others for the purpose of bringing about real estate transactions. These persons may be other licensed real estate brokers or they may be licensed real estate salespersons.

licensee
One who holds a license.

broker
A person or legal entity licensed to act independently in conducting a real estate brokerage business.

Salesperson

A **real estate salesperson**, within the meaning of the license laws, is a person working for a real estate broker to list and negotiate the sale, exchange, lease, or rental of real property for others for compensation, under the direction, guidance, and responsibility of the employing broker. In some states, only an actual person can be licensed as a salesperson (a business firm cannot be licensed as a salesperson). A **salesperson** must be employed by a broker; a salesperson cannot operate independently. Thus, a salesperson who takes a listing on a property does so in the name of his broker, and in some states, the broker must sign along with the salesperson for the listing to be valid. In the event of a legal dispute caused by a salesperson, the dispute would be between the principal and the broker. Therefore, some brokers take considerable care to oversee the documents that their salespeople prepare and sign. Other brokers do not, relying instead on the knowledge and sensibility of their salespeople—and accepting a certain amount of risk in the process.

The salesperson is a means by which brokers can expand their sales force. Presumably, the more salespeople a broker employs, the more listings and sales generated, and thus the more commissions earned by the broker. Against this, the broker must pay enough to keep the sales force from leaving, provide sales facilities and personnel management, and take ultimate responsibility for any mistakes the salespersons make.

salesperson
A person employed by a broker to list, negotiate, sell, or lease real property for others.

Sales Associate

sales associate

A salesperson or broker employed by a broker.

The term **sales associate** is not a license category. It refers to anyone with a real estate license who works under a sponsoring broker. Most often this will be a real estate salesperson. However, a person who holds a broker license can work for another broker. Such a person is a regular member of the employing broker's sales force just like someone with a salesperson license. The salespersons and brokers who work for a broker are known collectively as the broker's sales associates or sales force or sales staff. You will also hear the term *real estate agent* used in a general sense. Correctly speaking, the broker is a special agent of the property owner and the sales associate is a general agent of the broker. In common language, real estate agent refers to anyone, broker or salesperson, who negotiates real estate transactions for others.

A number of States only have one level of licensure, being a broker. They still provide for different levels of broker licensure (for instance, one could be a supervising broker, another merely a broker). The same responsibility applies as a broker sales associate.

Qualifications for Licensing

Of the two license levels, the salesperson's license is regarded as the entry-level license and, as such, requires no previous real estate sales experience. The minimum age is 18 years. By comparison, the broker's license, in nearly all states, requires one to five years of experience (two or three years is most common) as a real estate salesperson. Related real estate experience and education in real estate can sometimes shorten the experience requirement. As a practical matter, however, a person is wise to gain plenty of experience as a salesperson before becoming a broker for the purpose of operating independently.

EXAMINATION

Examination of the license applicant's knowledge of real estate law and practices, mathematics, valuation, finance, and the like is required for license granting in all states. Salesperson exams and broker exams typically contain 100 to 140 multiple-choice questions. Usually, three to four hours are allowed to complete the exam. Salesperson exams cover the basic aspects of state license law, contracts and agency, real property ownership, transfer and use, subdivision map reading, fair housing laws, real estate mathematics, and the ability to follow written instructions. Broker exams cover the same topics in more depth and test the applicant's ability to prepare listings, offer and acceptance contracts, leasing contracts, and closing statements. The applicant's knowledge of real estate finance, appraisal, and office management is also tested.

EDUCATION REQUIREMENTS

Nearly all states require that license applicants take real estate education courses at private real estate schools, colleges, or through adult education programs at high schools. Table 19.1 shows education and experience requirements in the United States at the time this book was written. The table is included to give you an overview of the emphasis currently being placed on education and experience by the various states. For up-to-the-minute information on education and experience requirements, you should contact the real estate licensing department at your state capital.

CONTINUING EDUCATION

Licensing authorities require additional course work each time a license is renewed. This is called **continuing education**, and its purpose is to force licensees to stay up-to-date in their

TABLE 19.1	Real Estate Education and Experience Requirements				
	SALESPERSON LICENSE		**BROKER LICENSE (ADDITIONAL HOURS)**		
State	**Education Requirement**	**Education**	**Education Requirement**	**Experience Requirement**	**Continuing Education**
Alabama	60 hours		60 hours	2 years	Yes
Alaska	40 hours		15 hours	2 years	Yes
Arizona	90 hours		90 hours	3 years	Yes
Arkansas	60 hours		60 hours	2 years	Yes
California	135 hours		360 hours	2 years	Yes
Colorado	N/A		168 hours	N/A	No
Connecticut	60 hours		60 hours	2 years	Yes
Delaware	99 hours		99 hours	5 years	Yes
Dist. of Col.	60 hours		135 hours	2 years	Yes
Florida	63 hours		117 hours	2 years	Yes
Georgia	75 hours		60 hours	3 years	Yes
Hawaii	60 hours		80 hours	3 years	Yes
Idaho	90 hours		90 hours	2 years	Yes
Illinois	45 hours		120 hours	N/A	Yes
Indiana	54 hours		2 hours	N/A	Yes
Iowa	96 hours		72 hours	2 years	Yes
Kansas	60 hours		24 hours	2 years	Yes
Kentucky	96 hours		48 hours	N/A	Yes
Louisiana	90 hours		150 hours	4 years	Yes
Maine	60 hours		105 hours	3 years	Yes
Maryland	60 hours		135 hours	3 years	Yes
Massachusetts	24 hours		30 hours	1 year	Yes
Michigan	40 hours		N/A	3 years	Yes
Minnesota	90 hours		120 hours	2 years	Yes
Mississippi	60 hours		60 hours	1 year	Yes
Missouri	72 hours		48 hours	2 years	Yes
Montana	60 hours		60 hours	2 years	Yes
Nebraska	60 hours		120 hours	2 years	Yes
Nevada	90 hours		64 college credit hours	8 years	
New Hampshire	40 hours		60 hours or 2,000 hours part time	1 year/5 years	
New Jersey	75 hours		150 hours	3 years	No
New Mexico	90 hours		120 hours	2 years	Yes
New York	45 hours		45 hours	1 year	Yes
North Carolina	N/A		75 hours	N/A	Yes
North Dakota	45 hours		60 hours	2 years	Yes
Ohio	120 hours		240 hours	2 years	Yes

(continued)

TABLE 19.1	Real Estate Education and Experience Requirements (continued)				
	SALESPERSON LICENSE		**BROKER LICENSE (ADDITIONAL HOURS)**		
State	**Education Requirement**	**Education**	**Education Requirement**	**Experience Requirement**	**Continuing Education**
Oklahoma	90 hours		90 hours	2 years	Yes
Oregon	N/A		150 hours	3 years	Yes
Pennsylvania	60 hours		240 hours	3 years	Yes
Rhode Island	18 hours		90 hours	1 year	Yes
South Carolina	60 hours		60 hours	3 years	Yes
South Dakota	N/A		116 hours	2 years	No
Tennessee	90 hours		30 hours	3 years	Yes
Texas	210 hours		630 hours	4 years	Yes
Utah	90 hours		120 hours	3 years	Yes
Vermont	40 hours		40 hours	2 years	Yes
Virginia	60 hours		180 hours	3 years	Yes
Washington	60 hours		120 hours	2 years	Yes
West Virginia	90 hours		90 hours	2 years	Yes
Wisconsin	72 hours		108 hours	N/A	Yes
Wyoming	54 hours		54 hours	2 years	Yes

Explanation: Hours are clock-hours in the classroom; experience requirement is experience as a licensed real estate salesperson; continuing education refers to education required for license renewal. Some states credit completed salesperson education toward the broker education requirement.

Source: Association of Real Estate License Law Officials, 125 S. Wacker Drive, Suite 300, Chicago, Illinois, 60606, ARELLO *Digest*, 2012. Check with your state for any subsequent changes.

field as a prerequisite to license renewal. All states have continuing education requirements. The courses vary, but average about 15 hours of classroom hours every two years.

Licensing Procedure

An application for a real estate salesperson or broker license can be obtained either in person or by mail from a state's real estate licensing department. The application is completed and returned to the department with the required fee. The character aspects of the applicant are checked, and, if approved, an examination date is scheduled. (Some states reverse this and give the exam first and check the references second.) Most states offer their real estate exams monthly. A few offer testing bimonthly or quarterly. Five states offer exams at least once a week.

The applicant is notified of the results within a few weeks. If passed, the fee for the license itself is now paid. Also, a salesperson applicant must name the broker he will be working for. This information is usually provided on a form signed by the employing broker. A broker applicant must give the address where he plans to operate his brokerage business. These forms are processed by the department, and a license is mailed to the applicant (in the case of a broker, or to the employing broker in the case of a salesperson). Upon receipt, the licensee can operate as a real estate salesperson or broker, as the case may be.

If the applicant fails the written examination, the usual procedure is to allow the applicant to repeat it until passed. A fee is charged to retake the exam, and the applicant must wait until the next testing date.

RENEWAL

Once licensed, as long as a person remains active in real estate and meets any continuing education requirements, the license can be renewed by paying the required renewal fee. If a license is not renewed before it expires, most states allow a grace period and charge a late renewal fee. Once the grace period expires, all license rights lapse, and the individual must meet current application requirements and take the current written exam. If a licensee wishes to be temporarily inactive from the business but does not wish to let the license lapse, some states permit the license to be placed on inactive status. When the licensee wishes to reactivate the license, he pays a fee to the department. Then the license is moved from inactive to active status, and the licensee can start selling again.

Examination Services

Real estate license examinations are administered by Applied Measurement Professionals (AMP), Pearson Vue (Pearson), and Psychological Services, Inc. (PSI). The remaining states write and grade their own exams, some being administered by an examination service.

At the time of this publication, Pearson examinations are used in the following states: Alaska, Arkansas, Delaware, Idaho, Indiana, Kansas, Maine, Massachusetts, Rhode Island, Utah, and Wisconsin. AMP exams are being used in Alabama, Georgia, Illinois, Missouri, Montana, Nebraska, New Hampshire, North Carolina, North Dakota, South Dakota, Washington, and Wyoming. The PSI examinations are used in Colorado, Connecticut, Hawaii, Iowa, Kentucky, Louisiana, Maryland, Michigan, Minnesota, Mississippi, Nevada, New Jersey, New Mexico, Ohio, Oklahoma, Oregon, Pennsylvania, South Carolina, Tennessee, Texas, and Virginia. The following states use their own exams, in some cases purchasing questions from one of the national services: California, Florida, New York, Oklahoma, and West Virginia.

Exams written by the national testing services are divided into two parts. Part 1, called the **uniform test**, contains 80 to 100 questions that are relevant to the general principles and practices of real estate that are common or uniform across the country. Part 2, called the **state test**, contains 20 to 50 questions regarding the laws, rules, regulations, and practices of the jurisdiction where the examination is being given.

In general, the tests are composed entirely of objective, multiple-choice questions that are constantly being revised and updated to keep them current with the changing practices and laws of real estate. There are many different versions of the tests, but all are equal in difficulty. AMP is developing "case study" models covering work related problems; an innovative approach, to be sure. Sample exams are available from all examination services. Like the national exam services, states that write their own tests have question banks of several thousand questions from which approximately 100 are chosen each time a test is given.

Nonresident Licensing

The general rule regarding license requirements is that a person must be licensed in the state within which he negotiates. Thus, if a broker or one of the broker's sales associates sells an out-of-state property but conducts the negotiations entirely within the borders of his own state, a license is not needed in the state where the land is located. State laws also permit a broker in one state to split a commission with a broker in another state provided each conducts negotiations only within the state where the broker is licensed. Therefore, if Broker B, licensed in State B, takes a listing at his office on a parcel of land located in State B, and Broker C in State C sells it, conducting the sale negotiations within State C, then Brokers B and C can split the commission. If, however, Broker C comes to State B to negotiate a contract, then a license in State B is necessary.

Many states will issue a **nonresident license** to out-of-state brokers. This is particularly helpful where a broker is located near a state border. In issuing a nonresident license, a state will usually require substantially the same examination and experience requirements as demanded of resident brokers. Some states will give the out-of-state broker credit for the uniform part of a license test already taken, requiring only passage of a test on local law, custom, and practice. Others require a complete examination. Many states have reciprocal licensing agreements with other states (especially bordering states) that allow resident licensees of one state to obtain a nonresident license in another state without taking an examination.

LICENSE RECIPROCITY

In recent years, there has been considerable effort to design real estate licensing systems that permit a broker and the broker's sales staff to conduct negotiations in other states without having to obtain a nonresident license. The result is **license reciprocity**, and it applies when one state honors another's license. In permitting reciprocity, state officials are primarily concerned with a nonresident's knowledge of real estate law and practice as it applies to the state in which the applicant wishes to operate.

Eighteen states accepted real estate licenses issued by other states. This is called **full reciprocity**. It means that a licensee can operate in another state without having to take that state's examination and meet its education and experience requirements. More commonly, states have **partial reciprocity** that gives credit to the licensees of another state for experience, education, and examination. An in-depth comparison of license reciprocity among the various states is set out in the *Digest of Real Estate License Laws*, 2012 edition, published by the Association of Real Estate License Law Officials (ARELLO).

NOTICE OF CONSENT

When brokers operate outside of their home state, they may be required to file a *notice of consent* in each state in which they intend to operate, usually with the secretary of state. This permits the secretary of state to receive legal summonses on behalf of nonresident brokers, and provides a state resident an avenue by which to sue a broker who is a resident of another state.

MOVING TO ANOTHER STATE

When a broker or salesperson moves her place of business from one state to another, a license is required in the new state. Many states will give credit for experience and part or all of the examination that was passed in the previous state. This can be particularly helpful for two-income families when one spouse is transferred to another state. Details of what a state will allow as credit are too complex and too changeable to include here. If negotiating across state lines or moving to another state as a real estate agent is of interest to you, you should contact that state's real estate licensing authority.

Licensing the Business Firm

When a real estate broker wishes to establish a brokerage, the simplest method is a sole proprietorship under the broker's own name, such as David Lee, Real Estate Broker. Some states permit a broker to operate out of his residence. However, operating a business in a residential neighborhood can be bothersome to neighbors, and most states require brokers to maintain a place of business in a location that is zoned for businesses.

FICTITIOUS BUSINESS NAME

When brokers operate under a name other than their own, they must register that name by filing a **fictitious business name statement** (sometimes called an **assumed name certificate**) with the county clerk and the state real estate licensing authority. This statement must also be published in a local newspaper. Thus, if David Lee wishes to call his brokerage business Great Lakes Realty, his business certificate would show "David Lee, doing business as Great Lakes Realty." (Sometimes *doing business as* is shortened to dba or d/b/a.)

A real estate broker can operate as a sole proprietorship either under the broker's own name or under a fictitious name. A broker can also operate in partnership with other brokers or as a corporation. Since a corporation is an artificial being (not an actual person), it cannot take a real estate examination. Therefore, its chief executive officer (usually the president), or some designated officer, must be a licensed real estate broker and be responsible for the management of the firm. Other officers and stockholders may include brokers and salespersons and nonlicensed persons. However, only those actually licensed can represent the corporation in activities requiring a real estate license.

BRANCH OFFICES

If a broker expands by establishing branch offices that are geographically separate from the main or home office, each branch must have a branch office license and a licensed broker in charge. Often referred to as a **principal broker**, this person can be a partner, a corporate owner who is a broker, or a sales associate who has a broker's license. A few states allow a salesperson licensee to be in charge.

principal broker
The broker in charge of a real estate office.

Real Estate Regulation

Thus far we have discussed why and when a real estate license is required and how to obtain one. The next question is, "Who makes these rules and how are they enforced?" The starting point is the state legislature. The legislature of each state has the authority to enact laws to promote the safety, health, morals, order, and general welfare of its population. This includes the licensing and regulation of real estate brokers and salespersons. The legislature establishes general requirements. For example, the legislature enacts laws requiring that real estate agents be licensed, that there will be two classes of licenses, that there will be a prelicense education requirement, that there will be a license examination, and that continuing education will be required. The legislature also establishes two bodies to carry out the requirements. One body deals primarily with adopting rules and regulations to implement the license law as established by the legislature. This body or group is called a **real estate commission** in most states and has five to nine members. Some members are licensees from the real estate community while others are

real estate commission
A state board that advises and sets policies regarding real estate licensees and transaction procedures.

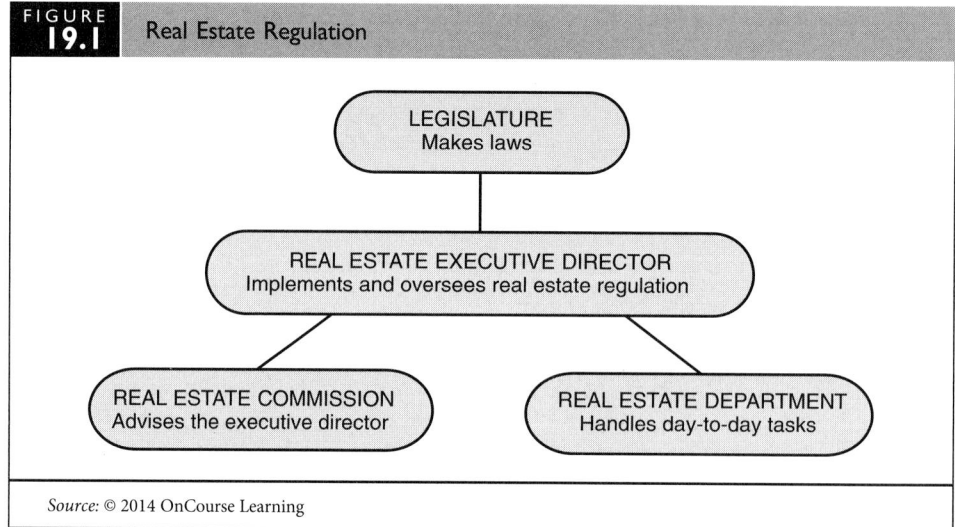

FIGURE 19.1 Real Estate Regulation

Source: © 2014 OnCourse Learning

nonlicensed members of the general public. Commission members are volunteers selected by the governor to represent all geographical parts of the state. Meetings are usually held monthly at which time members provide input to the state on such matters as the needs of real estate licensees, state policies regarding real estate, and the welfare of the general public in dealing with licensees.

The state's real estate **executive director**, or similar title, is appointed by the state to oversee real estate regulation. This person's responsibility is to carry out the wishes of the legislature and the real estate commission on a day-to-day basis. To assist in this, the legislature establishes a second body called a real estate department or real estate division.

REAL ESTATE DEPARTMENT

Staffed by full-time civil service employees, the **real estate department** or **real estate division** answers correspondence, sends out application forms, arranges for examinations, collects fees, issues licenses, approves subdivision reports, and so forth. Staff is also available for the investigation of alleged malpractices and for audits of broker trust fund accounts. Additionally, the department publishes a periodic newsletter or magazine to keep licensees informed about changes in real estate law and prints books or leaflets describing the state's license and subdivision laws. In short, it is the real estate department with which licensees have the most contact, but it is the commission, the executive director, and the legislature that set license requirements and tell licensees what they can and cannot do in real estate transactions. Figure 19.1 provides a visual summary of what has just been discussed.

license revocation

To recall and make void a license.

license suspension

To temporarily make a license ineffective.

License Suspension and Revocation

The most important control mechanism a state has over its real estate salespersons and brokers is that it can **suspend** (temporarily make ineffective) or **revoke** (recall and make void) a real estate license. Without one, it is unlawful for a person to engage in real estate activities for the purpose of earning a commission or fee. Unless an agent has a valid license, a court of law will not uphold his claim for a commission from a client.

Reasons for license suspension and revocation include any violation of the state's real estate act, misrepresentation or false promises, undisclosed dual agency, commingling, and acting as an undisclosed principal. Licenses can also be revoked or suspended for false advertising, obtaining a license by fraud, negligence, incompetence, failure to supervise salespersons, failure to properly account for clients' funds, practicing law without a license, paying commissions to unlicensed persons, conviction of a felony or certain types of misdemeanors, dishonest conduct in general, and, in many states, failure to have a fixed termination date on an exclusive listing.

When the real estate commissioner or department receives a complaint from someone who feels wronged by a licensee, an investigation is conducted by the real estate department staff. Statements are received from witnesses. Title company records, public records, and the licensee's bank records are checked as necessary. The commissioner or director may call an informal conference and invite all parties involved to attend. If it appears that the complaint is serious enough and that a violation of the law has occurred, a formal hearing is held in the presence of the full commission. The licensee, the party bringing the complaint, and any necessary witnesses appear. Testimony is taken under oath, and a written record is made of the proceedings. If the commissioner or director decides to suspend or revoke the respondent's license, the respondent has the right of appeal to the courts.

Bonds, Recovery Funds, and E&O Insurance

The potential of license loss for a wrongdoing strongly encourages licensees to operate within the law. However, suspension or revocation of a license does nothing to provide financial compensation for any losses suffered by a wronged party. This must be recovered from the broker either through a mutually agreed upon monetary settlement or a court judgment resulting from a civil lawsuit brought by the wronged party. But all too often court judgments turn out to be uncollectible because the defendant has no money.

There are three common solutions to the uncollectible judgment problem. Some states require that a person post a bond with the state before a license is issued. In the event of an otherwise uncollectible court judgment against a licensee, the bond money is used to provide payment. Bond requirements vary from $1,000 to $100,000, with $5,000 to $10,000 being the most popular range. Licensees can obtain these bonds from bonding companies for an annual fee or post the required amount of cash or securities with the state.

The second method of protecting the public is through a state-sponsored **recovery fund**. A portion of the money that each licensee pays for a real estate license is set aside in a fund to pay otherwise uncollectible judgments. Recovery funds offer coverage ranging from $50,000 to $400,000 per licensee, with most states in the $100,000 to $1,000,000 range. The District of Columbia and 33 states use recovery funds. The states are Alabama, Alaska, Arizona, Arkansas, California, Connecticut, Delaware, Florida, Georgia, Hawaii, Idaho, Illinois, Indiana, Kansas, Kentucky, Louisiana, Maryland, Minnesota, Montana, Nevada, New Jersey, New Mexico, North Carolina, North Dakota, Ohio, Oklahoma, Pennsylvania, Rhode Island, South Dakota, Tennessee, Texas, Utah, Virginia, and Wyoming.

The requirement for bonds and the establishment of recovery funds are not perfect solutions to the problem of uncollectible judgments because the wronged party must expend considerable effort to recover the loss, and it is quite possible that the maximum amount available per transaction or licensee will not fully compensate for the losses suffered. However, either system is better than none at all.

recovery fund
A state-operated fund that can be tapped to pay for uncollectible judgments against real estate licensees.

How is a consumer protected in states that have no fund at all? More and more states are now requiring errors and omissions insurance (discussed in Chapter 21). Colorado, Idaho, Kentucky, Louisiana, Mississippi, Nebraska, New Mexico, North Dakota, Rhode Island, South Dakota, Tennessee, and Wyoming all require that licensees carry errors and omissions (E&O) insurance. Minimum plans can range from $100,000 to as much as $1,000,000, depending upon the state. This may solve the limitation issues that are provided by bonds and recovery funds. It also indirectly regulates licensees. Those who have had a history of problems, can't get E&O coverage (there is no right to it).

How Much Can the Regulators Regulate?

A new issue has arisen recently concerning regulating authorities. How much can they regulate? Can they set standards that require a minimum level of services? Can they require that licensees perform certain functions as a part of a licensee's real estate brokerage activity? There are brokers who prefer to provide few services (except perhaps placing the listing in MLS or placing a sign in the yard) for a reduced commission. Alternatively, the broker may kickback a portion of their half of the commission to a principal if the broker provides less than the full amount of services.

This can produce different results. First, the consumer may not be getting services that they really need but don't know about since they are not provided. The second issue concerns the liability and extra work provided by the "other broker." The other broker may have the listing, but when the buyer requests additional help in applying for loans, getting inspections, and evaluating market conditions, it can result in more work and liability on that listing broker. The broker who provides the traditional full range of services does more work, but for the same compensation, and the discount broker still expects a full one-half of the fee.

In light of this, several states have provided regulations and amendments to their license acts, which provide that a broker must provide a minimum level of services. This minimum level of services generally provides that all licensees must be available for questions, be available to deliver offers and counteroffers, help negotiate contract terms, and keep parties informed of material information related to their transaction. At least nine states require a minimum level of services (Alabama, Idaho, Illinois, Indiana, Iowa, Missouri, Texas, Utah, and Washington). An additional eight states have minimum service requirements, but allow consumers to waive those extra services (Delaware, Florida, Nevada, New Mexico, Ohio, Pennsylvania, Tennessee, and Wisconsin). The general theory is that if a state agency can set minimum standards of performance for plumbers and cosmetologists, then it should also be able to set minimum standards for real estate licensees.

The Department of Justice takes the position that the real estate regulators who require the minimum level of services are forcing consumers to purchase more services than they want, that it is anticompetitive, and that it forces up the price of real estate services. They strongly suggest that fee-for-service real estate brokers will dramatically lower the cost of real estate sales and break down barriers, creating a more competitive market for real estate licensees. There will be more to come on this issue, for sure.

Securities License

Be aware that there may be times when a real estate salesperson or broker also needs a **securities license**. This occurs when the property being sold is an investment contract in real estate rather than real estate itself. This investment contract is classified as a

security. Examples of securities include real estate limited partnerships, rental pools where condominium owners put their units into a pool for a percentage of the pool's income, and some time-shares. Securities licenses are issued by the National Association of Securities Dealers based on successful completion of their examination. Legal counsel is advised if there is the possibility you may be selling securities. Counsel will also advise on state and federal laws requiring the registration of real estate securities before they are sold.

Affiliating with a Broker

If you plan to enter real estate sales, selecting a broker to work for is one of the most important decisions you must make. The best way to approach it is to carefully consider what you have to offer the real estate business and what you expect in return. And look at it in that order! It is easy to become captivated by the big commission income you visualize coming your way. But if that is your only perspective, you will meet with disappointment. The reason people will pay you money is to receive some product or service in return. Your clients are not concerned with your income goal; it is only incidental to their goals. If you help them attain their goals, you will reach yours.

Before applying for a real estate license, ask yourself whether the working hours and conditions of a real estate agent are suitable to you. Specifically, are you prepared to work on a commission-only basis? Evenings and weekends? On your own? With people you've never met before? If you can comfortably answer yes to these questions, then start looking for a broker to sponsor you. (Salesperson license educational requirements can be completed and the examination taken without broker sponsorship, but a salesperson must have a broker to work for before the actual license is issued.)

TRAINING

Your next step is to look for those features and qualities in a broker that will complement, enhance, and encourage your personal development in real estate. If you are new to the industry, training and education will most likely be at the top of your list. Therefore, in looking for a broker, you will want to find one who will offer you some on-the-job training. (What you have learned to date from books, classes, and license examination preparation will be helpful, but you will need additional specific training.) Real estate franchise operations and large brokerage offices usually offer extensive training. In smaller offices, the broker in charge is usually responsible for seeing that newcomers receive training. An office that offers no training to a newcomer should be avoided.

COMPENSATION

Another question high on your list will be compensation. Very few offices provide a newcomer with a guaranteed minimum wage or even a draw against future commissions. Most brokers feel that one must produce to be paid, and the hungrier the salesperson, the quicker the production. A broker who pays salespersons regardless of sales produced simply must siphon the money from those who are producing. The old saying, "There's no such thing as a free lunch" applies to sales commissions.

Compensation for salespersons is usually a percentage of the commissions they earn for the broker. How much each receives is open to negotiation between the broker and each salesperson working for him. A broker who provides office space, extensive secretarial help, a large advertising budget, a mailing program, and generous long-distance telephone privileges might take 40% to 50% of each incoming commission dollar for office overhead. A broker who provides fewer services might take 25% or 30%.

Salespersons with proven sales records can usually reduce the portion of each commission dollar that must go to the broker. This is because the broker knows that with an outstanding sales performer, a high volume of sales will offset a smaller percentage for overhead. Conversely, a new and untried salesperson, or one with a mediocre past sales record, may have to give up a larger portion of each dollar for the broker's overhead.

When one brokerage agency lists a property and another locates the buyer, the commission is split according to any agreement the two brokers wish to make. The most common arrangement is a 50–50 split. After splitting, each broker pays a portion of the money he receives to the salesperson involved in accordance with their commission agreement.

While investigating commission arrangements, one should also inquire about incentive and bonus plans, automobile expense reimbursement, health insurance, life insurance, E&O insurance, and retirement plans.

An alternative commission arrangement is the **100% commission** wherein the salesperson does not share his commission with the broker. Instead, the salesperson is charged a fee for office space, advertising, telephone, multiple listing, and any other expenses the broker incurs on behalf of the salesperson. Generally speaking, 100% arrangements are more popular with proven performers than with newcomers.

100% commission

Compensation arrangement where the agent does not share any commission with the sponsoring broker.

BROKER SUPPORT

Broker support will have an impact on success. Specifically: Does each salesperson have a desk to work from? Are office facilities efficient and modern? Does the broker provide secretarial services? What is the broker's advertising policy and who pays for ads? Who pays for signs, business cards, franchise fees, and realty board dues? Does the broker have sources of financing for clients? Does the broker allow her salespersons to invest in real estate? Does the broker have a good reputation in the community?

FINDING A BROKER

Many licensees associate with a particular broker as a result of friendship or word-of-mouth information. However, there are other ways to find a suitable position. An excellent way to start your search is to decide what geographical area you want to work in. If you choose the same community or neighborhood in which you live, you will already possess a valuable sense and feel for that area.

Having selected a geographical area, look at Web sites, the Sunday newspaper real estate advertisements section, and the telephone book *yellow pages* for names of brokers. Hold interviews with several brokers, and as you do, remember that you are interviewing them just as intensively as they are interviewing you. At your visits with brokers, be particularly alert to your feelings. Intuition can be as valuable a guide to a sound working relationship as a list of questions and answers regarding the job.

As you narrow your choices, revisit the offices of brokers who particularly impressed you. Talk with some of the salespersons who have worked or are working there. They can be very candid and valuable sources of information. Be wary of individuals who are extreme in their opinions: rely instead on the consensus of opinion. Locate clients who have used the firm's services and ask them their opinions of the firm. You might also talk to local appraisers, lenders, and escrow agents for candid opinions. If you do all this advance work, the benefits to you will be greater enjoyment of your work, more money in your pocket, and less likelihood of wanting to quit or move to another office.

EMPLOYMENT CONTRACT

Having selected a broker with whom to associate, your next step is to make an employment contract. An **employment contract** formalizes the working arrangement between the broker and his salespersons. An oral contract may be satisfactory, but a written one is preferred because it sets forth the relationship with a higher degree of precision and is a written record of the agreement. This greatly reduces the potential for future controversy and litigation.

The employment contract will cover such matters as compensation (how much and under what circumstances), training (how often and if required), hours of work (including assigned office hours and open houses), company identification (distinctive articles of clothing and name tags), fees and dues (license and realty board), expenses (automobile, advertising, telephone), fringe benefits (health and life insurance, pension, and profit-sharing plans), withholding (income taxes and Social Security), territory (assigned area of the community), termination of employment (quitting and firing), and general office policies and procedures (office manual).

Independent Contractor Status

Is the real estate sales associate an employee of the broker or an independent contractor? The answer is both. On one hand, the sales associate acts like an employee because the associate works for the broker, usually at the broker's place of business, prepares listings and sales documents on forms specified by the broker, and upon closing, receives payment from the broker. On the other hand, the sales associate acts like an **independent contractor** because the associate is paid only if the associate brings about a sale that produces a commission. An important distinction between the two is whether the broker must withhold income taxes and Social Security from the associate's commission checks. If the sales associate is considered by the Internal Revenue Service (IRS) to be an employee for tax purposes, the broker must withhold. If classed as an independent contractor for tax purposes, the sales associate is responsible for his own income taxes and Social Security. The IRS prefers employee status because it is easier to collect taxes from an employer than from an employee.

independent contractor

One who contracts to do work according to one's own methods and is responsible to his employer for the results of only that work.

The IRS will treat real estate sales associates as independent contractors if they meet all of the following three requirements. First, the associate must be a licensed real estate agent. Second, a large percentage of the associate's payment for services as a real estate agent must be directly related to sales and not to hours worked. Third, a written agreement must exist between the associate and the broker stating that the associate will be treated as an independent contractor for tax purposes. If an agent and his sponsoring broker do not comply with this statute, they run the risk of losing their independent contractor status.

If this occurs, the sponsoring broker becomes subject to the same filing requirements as any other employer in the normal course of business.

These are highlights of the issue. If you plan to work for a broker, you may find it valuable to have this matter, as well as your entire employment contract, reviewed by an attorney before you sign it.

Franchised Offices

Prior to the early 1970s, real estate brokerage was a small business industry. Most brokerages were one-office firms. A large brokerage was one having four or five offices and selling 200 properties a year. Then real estate franchise organizations entered the real estate business in a big way. **Franchisers** such as Century 21, Prudential, RE/MAX, and ERA offered brokerage firms national identification, large-scale advertising, sales staff training programs, management advice, customer referrals, financing help for buyers, and guaranteed sales plans. In return, the brokerage firm (the franchisee) paid a fee of 3% to 8% of gross commission income. The idea became popular, and by the mid-1990s, approximately half of the real estate licensees affiliated with the National Association of REALTORS® were working in franchised offices, and their numbers are continuing to grow. Meanwhile, the number of franchisers grew to over 60, and new franchisers seem to be created often, offering attractive franchise opportunities to small firms.

Statistics show that franchising appeals mostly to firms with 10 to 50 sales associates. Larger firms are more capable of providing the advantages of a franchise for themselves. Smaller firms tend to occupy market niches and often consist of one or two licensees who do not bring in additional sales associates. For a newly licensed salesperson wishing to affiliate with a firm, a franchised firm offers immediate public recognition, extensive training opportunities, established office routines, regular sales meetings, and access to a nationwide referral system. Franchise affiliation is not magic, however; success still depends on the individual to make sales calls, value property, get listings, advertise, show property, qualify, negotiate, and close transactions.

NATIONAL REAL ESTATE FIRMS

During the late 1970s, a large real estate firm in California—Coldwell Banker—began an expansion program by purchasing multibranched real estate firms in other states. Today, a number of national firms have offices across the United States. Cendant Corp. (formerly HFS, Inc.) has acquired three major franchises to create a huge network of firms that may offer a number of other services to complement their brokerage services—some refer to it as "full service." The additional services can include access to auto dealers, interior decorators, contractors, and other services commonly used by home buyers. Other large national and regional firms include Cushman & Wakefield, RE/MAX, Grubb & Ellis, Long & Foster, Shannon & Luchs, Marcus & Millichap, and Rubloff.

For a newcomer, affiliating with a national or regional real estate firm offers benefits like those of a franchised firm (recognition, training, routines, etc.). The main difference is who owns the firm. A franchised firm will be locally owned and managed (i.e., an independent firm). Regional and national firms are locally managed, but the sales associate will only occasionally, if ever, meet the owner(s).

Professional Real Estate Associations

Even before laws required real estate agents to have licenses, there were professional real estate organizations. Called real estate boards, they joined together agents within a city or county on a voluntary basis. The push to organize came from real estate people who saw the need for some sort of controlling organization that could supervise the activities of individual agents and elevate the profession's status in the minds of the public. Next came the gradual grouping of local boards into state associations, and finally, in 1908, the National Association of Real Estate Boards (NAREB) was formed. In 1914, NAREB developed a model license law that became the basis for real estate license laws in many states.

Today the local boards and associations are still the fundamental units of the National Association of REALTORS® (NAR; the name was changed from NAREB in 1974). Local board membership is open to anyone holding a real estate license. Called boards of REALTORS®, real estate boards, realty boards, or Associations of REALTORS®, they promote fair dealing among their members and with the public, and protect members from dishonest and irresponsible licensees. They also promote legislation that protects property rights, offer short seminars to keep members up to date with current laws and practices, and in general, do whatever is necessary to build the dignity, stability, and professionalism of the industry. Local boards often operate the local multiple listing service, although in some communities, a privately owned and operated business does so.

State associations are composed of the members of local boards plus sales associates and brokers who live in areas where no local board exists. The purposes of the state associations are to unite members statewide, to encourage legislation that benefits and protects the real estate industry and safeguards the public in their real estate transactions, and to promote economic growth and development in the state. Also, state associations hold conventions to educate members and foster contacts among them.

REALTOR®

The NAR is made up of local boards and state associations in the United States. The term **REALTOR®** is a registered trade name that belongs to NAR. The designation *REALTOR®* is not synonymous with real estate agent. It is reserved for the exclusive use of members of the National Association of REALTORS®, who as part of their membership pledge themselves to abide by the association's Code of Ethics. The term *REALTOR®* cannot be used by nonmembers, and in some states the unauthorized use of the term is a violation of the real estate law. Before 1974, the use of the term *REALTOR®* was primarily reserved for principal brokers. Then, by a national membership vote, the decision was made to create an additional membership class, the **REALTOR®-Associate**, for salespersons and broker licensees working for members.

REALTOR®
A registered trademark owned by the National Association of REALTORS® for use by its members.

Code of Ethics

One of the most important features of the National Association of REALTORS® is its **Code of Ethics**. First adopted in 1913, the REALTOR® Code of Ethics has been revised several times since then and now contains 17 articles that pertain to the REALTOR's® relation to his clients, to other real estate agents, and to the public as a whole. The full code is reproduced in Figure 19.2.

Although a complete review of each article is beyond the scope of this chapter, it can be seen that some articles parallel existing laws. For example, Article 10 speaks against racial discrimination and Article 12 speaks for full disclosure. However, the code addresses itself to the aspirations and obligations of a REALTOR® that may be beyond the written law. In other words, to be recognized as a REALTOR®, one must not only comply with the letter of the law, but also observe the ethical standards by which the industry operates.

FIGURE
19.2 NAR Code of Ethics

Code of Ethics and Standards of Practice of the NATIONAL ASSOCIATION OF REALTORS®
Effective January 1, 2013

Where the word REALTORS® is used in this Code and Preamble, it shall be deemed to include REALTOR-ASSOCIATE®s.

While the Code of Ethics establishes obligations that may be higher than those mandated by law, in any instance where the Code of Ethics and the law conflict, the obligations of the law must take precedence.

Preamble

Under all is the land. Upon its wise utilization and widely allocated ownership depend the survival and growth of free institutions and of our civilization. REALTORS® should recognize that the interests of the nation and its citizens require the highest and best use of the land and the widest distribution of land ownership. They require the creation of adequate housing, the building of functioning cities, the development of productive industries and farms, and the preservation of a healthful environment.

Such interests impose obligations beyond those of ordinary commerce. They impose grave social responsibility and a patriotic duty to which REALTORS® should dedicate themselves, and for which they should be diligent in preparing themselves. REALTORS®, therefore, are zealous to maintain and improve the standards of their calling and share with their fellow REALTORS® a common responsibility for its integrity and honor.

In recognition and appreciation of their obligations to clients, customers, the public, and each other, REALTORS® continuously strive to become and remain informed on issues affecting real estate and, as knowledgeable professionals, they willingly share the fruit of their experience and study with others. They identify and take steps, through enforcement of this Code of Ethics and by assisting appropriate regulatory bodies, to eliminate practices which may damage the public or which might discredit or bring dishonor to the real estate profession. REALTORS® having direct personal knowledge of conduct that may violate the Code of Ethics involving misappropriation of client or customer funds or property, willful discrimination, or fraud resulting in substantial economic harm, bring such matters to the attention of the appropriate Board or Association of REALTORS®. (*Amended 1/00*)

Realizing that cooperation with other real estate professionals promotes the best interests of those who utilize their services, REALTORS® urge exclusive representation of clients; do not attempt to gain any unfair advantage over their competitors; and they refrain from making unsolicited comments about other practitioners. In instances where their opinion is sought, or where REALTORS® believe that comment is necessary, their opinion is offered in an objective, professional manner, uninfluenced by any personal motivation or potential advantage or gain.

The term REALTOR® has come to connote competency, fairness, and high integrity resulting from adherence to a lofty ideal of moral conduct in business relations. No inducement of profit and no instruction from clients ever can justify departure from this ideal.

In the interpretation of this obligation, REALTORS® can take no safer guide than that which has been handed down through the centuries, embodied in the Golden Rule, "Whatsoever ye would that others should do to you, do ye even so to them."

Accepting this standard as their own, REALTORS® pledge to observe its spirit in all of their activities whether conducted personally, through associates or others, or via technological means, and to conduct their business in accordance with the tenets set forth below. (*Amended 1/07*)

Duties to Clients and Customers

Article 1

When representing a buyer, seller, landlord, tenant, or other client as an agent, REALTORS® pledge themselves to protect and promote the interests of their client. This obligation to the client is primary, but it does not relieve REALTORS® of their obligation to treat all parties honestly. When serving a buyer, seller, landlord, tenant or other party in a nonagency capacity, REALTORS® remain obligated to treat all parties honestly. (*Amended 1/01*)

- **Standard of Practice 1-1**
  REALTORS®, when acting as principals in a real estate transaction, remain obligated by the duties imposed by the Code of Ethics. (*Amended 1/93*)

(*continued*)

FIGURE 19.2 NAR Code of Ethics (continued)

- **Standard of Practice 1-2**

  The duties imposed by the Code of Ethics encompass all real estate-related activities and transactions whether conducted in person, electronically, or through any other means.

  The duties the Code of Ethics imposes are applicable whether REALTORS® are acting as agents or in legally recognized non-agency capacities except that any duty imposed exclusively on agents by law or regulation shall not be imposed by this Code of Ethics on REALTORS® acting in non-agency capacities.

  As used in this Code of Ethics, "client" means the person(s) or entity(ies) with whom a REALTOR® or a REALTOR®'s firm has an agency or legally recognized non-agency relationship; "customer" means a party to a real estate transaction who receives information, services, or benefits but has no contractual relationship with the REALTOR® or the REALTOR®'s firm; "prospect" means a purchaser, seller, tenant, or landlord who is not subject to a representation relationship with the REALTOR® or REALTOR®'s firm; "agent" means a real estate licensee (including brokers and sales associates) acting in an agency relationship as defined by state law or regulation; and "broker" means a real estate licensee (including brokers and sales associates) acting as an agent or in a legally recognized non-agency capacity. (*Adopted 1/95, Amended 1/07*)

- **Standard of Practice 1-3**

  REALTORS®, in attempting to secure a listing, shall not deliberately mislead the owner as to market value.

- **Standard of Practice 1-4**

  REALTORS®, when seeking to become a buyer/tenant representative, shall not mislead buyers or tenants as to savings or other benefits that might be realized through use of the REALTOR®'s services. (*Amended 1/93*)

- **Standard of Practice 1-5**

  REALTORS® may represent the seller/landlord and buyer/tenant in the same transaction only after full disclosure to and with informed consent of both parties. (*Adopted 1/93*)

- **Standard of Practice 1-6**

  REALTORS® shall submit offers and counter-offers objectively and as quickly as possible. (*Adopted 1/93, Amended 1/95*)

- **Standard of Practice 1-7**

  When acting as listing brokers, REALTORS® shall continue to submit to the seller/landlord all offers and counter-offers until closing or execution of a lease unless the seller/landlord has waived this obligation in writing. REALTORS® shall not be obligated to continue to market the property after an offer has been accepted by the seller/landlord. REALTORS® shall recommend that sellers/landlords obtain the advice of legal counsel prior to acceptance of a subsequent offer except where the acceptance is contingent on the termination of the pre-existing purchase contract or lease. (*Amended 1/93*)

- **Standard of Practice 1-8**

  REALTORS®, acting as agents or brokers of buyers/tenants, shall submit to buyers/tenants all offers and counter-offers until acceptance but have no obligation to continue to show properties to their clients after an offer has been accepted unless otherwise agreed in writing. REALTORS®, acting as agents or brokers of buyers/tenants, shall recommend that buyers/tenants obtain the advice of legal counsel if there is a question as to whether a pre-existing contract has been terminated. (*Adopted 1/93, Amended 1/99*)

- **Standard of Practice 1-9**

  The obligation of REALTORS® to preserve confidential information (as defined by state law) provided by their clients in the course of any agency relationship or non-agency relationship recognized by law continues after termination of agency relationships or any non-agency relationships recognized by law. REALTORS® shall not knowingly, during or following the termination of professional relationships with their clients:

  1) reveal confidential information of clients; or
  2) use confidential information of clients to the disadvantage of clients; or
  3) use confidential information of clients for the REALTOR®'s advantage or the advantage of third parties unless:
     a) clients consent after full disclosure; or
     b) REALTORS® are required by court order; or
     c) it is the intention of a client to commit a crime and the information is necessary to prevent the crime; or

(continued)

FIGURE 19.2   NAR Code of Ethics (continued)

d) it is necessary to defend a REALTOR® or the REALTOR®'s employees or associates against an accusation of wrongful conduct.

Information concerning latent material defects is not considered confidential information under this Code of Ethics. *(Adopted 1/93, Amended 1/01)*

- **Standard of Practice 1-10**
REALTORS® shall, consistent with the terms and conditions of their real estate licensure and their property management agreement, competently manage the property of clients with due regard for the rights, safety and health of tenants and others lawfully on the premises. *(Adopted 1/95, Amended 1/00)*

- **Standard of Practice 1-11**
REALTORS® who are employed to maintain or manage a client's property shall exercise due diligence and make reasonable efforts to protect it against reasonably foreseeable contingencies and losses. *(Adopted 1/95)*

- **Standard of Practice 1-12**
When entering into listing contracts, REALTORS® must advise sellers/ landlords of:
1) the REALTOR*'s company policies regarding cooperation and the amount(s) of any compensation that will be offered to subagents, buyer/tenant agents, and/or brokers acting in legally recognized non-agency capacities;
2) the fact that buyer/tenant agents or brokers, even if compensated by listing brokers, or by sellers/ landlords may represent the interests of buyers/ tenants; and
3) any potential for listing brokers to act as disclosed dual agents, e.g., buyer/tenant agents. *(Adopted 1/93, Renumbered 1/98, Amended 1/03)*

- **Standard of Practice 1-13**
When entering into buyer/tenant agreements, REALTORS® must advise potential clients of:
1) the REALTOR*'s company policies regarding cooperation;
2) the amount of compensation to be paid by the client;

3) the potential for additional or offsetting compensation from other brokers, from the seller or landlord, or from other parties;
4) any potential for the buyer/tenant representative to act as a disclosed dual agent, e.g., listing broker, subagent, landlord's agent, etc., and
5) the possibility that sellers or sellers' representatives may not treat the existence, terms, or conditions of offers as confidential unless confidentiality is required by law, regulation, or by any confidentiality agreement between the parties. *(Adopted 1/93, Renumbered 1/98, Amended 1/06)*

- **Standard of Practice 1-14**
Fees for preparing appraisals or other valuations shall not be contingent upon the amount of the appraisal or valuation. *(Adopted 1/02)*

- **Standard of Practice 1-15**
REALTORS®, in response to inquiries from buyers or cooperating brokers shall, with the sellers' approval, disclose the existence of offers on the property. Where disclosure is authorized, REALTORS® shall also disclose, if asked, whether offers were obtained by the listing licensee, another licensee in the listing firm, or by a cooperating broker. *(Adopted 1/03, Amended 1/09)*

- **Standard of Practice 1-16**
REALTORS® shall not access or use, or permit or enable others to access or use, listed or managed property on terms or conditions other than those authorized by the owner or seller. *(Adopted 1/12)*

Article 2

REALTORS® shall avoid exaggeration, misrepresentation, or concealment of pertinent facts relating to the property or the transaction. REALTORS® shall not, however, be obligated to discover latent defects in the property, to advise on matters outside the scope of their real estate license, or to disclose facts which are confidential under the scope of agency or non-agency relationships as defined by state law. *(Amended 1/00)*

(continued)

FIGURE 19.2   NAR Code of Ethics (continued)

- **Standard of Practice 2-1**
REALTORS® shall only be obligated to discover and disclose adverse factors reasonably apparent to someone with expertise in those areas required by their real estate licensing authority. Article 2 does not impose upon the REALTOR® the obligation of expertise in other professional or technical disciplines. *(Amended 1/96)*

- **Standard of Practice 2-2**
(Renumbered as Standard of Practice 1-12 1/98)

- **Standard of Practice 2-3**
(Renumbered as Standard of Practice 1-13 1/98)

- **Standard of Practice 2-4**
REALTORS® shall not be parties to the naming of a false consideration in any document, unless it be the naming of an obviously nominal consideration.

- **Standard of Practice 2-5**
Factors defined as "non-material" by law or regulation or which are expressly referenced in law or regulation as not being subject to disclosure are considered not "pertinent" for purposes of Article 2. *(Adopted 1/93)*

Article 3

REALTORS® shall cooperate with other brokers except when cooperation is not in the client's best interest. The obligation to cooperate does not include the obligation to share commissions, fees, or to otherwise compensate another broker. *(Amended 1/95)*

- **Standard of Practice 3-1**
REALTORS®, acting as exclusive agents or brokers of sellers/landlords, establish the terms and conditions of offers to cooperate. Unless expressly indicated in offers to cooperate, cooperating brokers may not assume that the offer of cooperation includes an offer of compensation. Terms of compensation, if any, shall be ascertained by cooperating brokers before beginning efforts to accept the offer of cooperation. *(Amended 1/99)*

- **Standard of Practice 3-2**
To be effective, any change in compensation offered for cooperative services must be communicated to the other REALTOR® prior to the time that REALTOR® submits an offer to purchase/lease the property. *(Amended 1/10)*

- **Standard of Practice 3-3**
Standard of Practice 3-2 does not preclude the listing broker and cooperating broker from entering into an agreement to change cooperative compensation. *(Adopted 1/94)*

- **Standard of Practice 3-4**
REALTORS®, acting as listing brokers, have an affirmative obligation to disclose the existence of dual or variable rate commission arrangements (i.e., listings where one amount of commission is payable if the listing broker's firm is the procuring cause of sale/lease and a different amount of commission is payable if the sale/lease results through the efforts of the seller/landlord or a cooperating broker). The listing broker shall, as soon as practical, disclose the existence of such arrangements to potential cooperating brokers and shall, in response to inquiries from cooperating brokers, disclose the differential that would result in a cooperative transaction or in a sale/lease that results through the efforts of the seller/landlord. If the cooperating broker is a buyer/tenant representative, the buyer/tenant representative must disclose such information to their client before the client makes an offer to purchase or lease. *(Amended 1/02)*

- **Standard of Practice 3-5**
It is the obligation of subagents to promptly disclose all pertinent facts to the principal's agent prior to as well as after a purchase or lease agreement is executed. *(Amended 1/93)*

- **Standard of Practice 3-6**
REALTORS® shall disclose the existence of accepted offers, including offers with unresolved contingencies, to any broker seeking cooperation. *(Adopted 5/86, Amended 1/04)*

- **Standard of Practice 3-7**
When seeking information from another REALTOR® concerning property under a management or listing agreement, REALTORS® shall disclose their REALTOR® status and whether their interest is personal or on behalf of a client and, if on behalf of a client, their relationship with the client. *(Amended 1/11)*

- **Standard of Practice 3-8**
REALTORS® shall not misrepresent the availability of access to show or inspect a listed property. *(Amended 11/87)*

(continued)

FIGURE
19.2 NAR Code of Ethics (continued)

- **Standard of Practice 3-9**
  REALTORS® shall not provide access to listed property on terms other than those established by the owner or the listing broker. *(Adopted 1/10)*

- **Standard of Practice 3-10**
  The duty to cooperate established in Article 3 relates to the obligation to share information on listed property, and to make property available to other brokers for showing to prospective purchasers/tenants when it is in the best interests of the seller/landlords. *(Adopted 1/11)*

Article 4

REALTORS® shall not acquire an interest in or buy or present offers from themselves, any member of their immediate families, their firms or any member thereof, or any entities in which they have any ownership interest, any real property without making their true position known to the owner or the owner's agent or broker. In selling property they own, or in which they have any interest, REALTORS® shall reveal their ownership or interest in writing to the purchaser or the purchaser's representative. *(Amended 1/00)*

- **Standard of Practice 4-1**
  For the protection of all parties, the disclosures required by Article 4 shall be in writing and provided by REALTORS® prior to the signing of any contract. *(Adopted 2/86)*

Article 5

REALTORS® shall not undertake to provide professional services concerning a property or its value where they have a present or contemplated interest unless such interest is specifically disclosed to all affected parties.

Article 6

REALTORS® shall not accept any commission, rebate, or profit on expenditures made for their client, without the client's knowledge and consent.

When recommending real estate products or services (e.g., homeowner's insurance, warranty programs, mortgage financing, title insurance, etc.), REALTORS® shall disclose to the client or customer to whom the recommendation is made any financial benefits or fees, other than real estate referral fees, the REALTOR® or REALTOR®'s firm may receive as a direct result of such recommendation. *(Amended 1/99)*

- **Standard of Practice 6-1**
  REALTORS® shall not recommend or suggest to a client or a customer the use of services of another organization or business entity in which they have a direct interest without disclosing such interest at the time of the recommendation or suggestion. *(Amended 5/88)*

Article 7

In a transaction, REALTORS® shall not accept compensation from more than one party, even if permitted by law, without disclosure to all parties and the informed consent of the REALTOR®'s client or clients. *(Amended 1/93)*

Article 8

REALTORS® shall keep in a special account in an appropriate financial institution, separated from their own funds, monies coming into their possession in trust for other persons, such as escrows, trust funds, clients' monies, and other like items.

Article 9

REALTORS®, for the protection of all parties, shall assure whenever possible that all agreements related to real estate transactions including, but not limited to, listing and representation agreements, purchase contracts, and leases are in writing in clear and understandable language expressing the specific terms, conditions, obligations and commitments of the parties. A copy of each agreement shall be furnished to each party to such agreements upon their signing or initialing. *(Amended 1/04)*

- **Standard of Practice 9-1**
  For the protection of all parties, REALTORS® shall use reasonable care to ensure that documents pertaining to the purchase, sale, or lease of real estate are kept current through the use of written extensions or amendments. *(Amended 1/93)*

- **Standard of Practice 9-2**
  When assisting or enabling a client or customer in establishing a contractual relationship (e.g., listing and representation agreements, purchase agreements, leases, etc.) electronically, REALTORS® shall make reasonable efforts to explain the nature and disclose the specific terms of the contractual relationship being established prior to it being agreed to by a contracting party. *(Adopted 1/07)*

(continued)

FIGURE 19.2   NAR Code of Ethics (continued)

Duties to the Public

Article 10

REALTORS® shall not deny equal professional services to any person for reasons of race, color, religion, sex, handicap, familial status, national origin, or sexual orientation. REALTORS® shall not be parties to any plan or agreement to discriminate against a person or persons on the basis of race, color, religion, sex, handicap, familial status, national origin, or sexual orientation. (*Amended 1/11*)

REALTORS®, in their real estate employment practices, shall not discriminate against any person or persons on the basis of race, color, religion, sex, handicap, familial status, national origin, or sexual orientation. (*Amended 1/11*)

- **Standard of Practice 10-1**
  When involved in the sale or lease of a residence, REALTORS® shall not volunteer information regarding the racial, religious or ethnic composition of any neighborhood nor shall they engage in any activity which may result in panic selling, however, REALTORS® may provide other demographic information. (*Adopted 1/94, Amended 1/06*)

- **Standard of Practice 10-2**
  When not involved in the sale or lease of a residence, REALTORS® may provide demographic information related to a property, transaction or professional assignment to a party if such demographic information is (a) deemed by the REALTOR® to be needed to assist with or complete, in a manner consistent with Article 10, a real estate transaction or professional assignment and (b) is obtained or derived from a recognized, reliable, independent, and impartial source. The source of such information and any additions, deletions, modifications, interpretations, or other changes shall be disclosed in reasonable detail. (*Adopted 1/05, Renumbered 1/06*)

- **Standard of Practice 10-3**
  REALTORS® shall not print, display or circulate any statement or advertisement with respect to selling or renting of a property that indicates any preference, limitations or discrimination based on race, color, religion, sex, handicap, familial status,

national origin, or sexual orientation. (*Adopted 1/94, Renumbered 1/05 and 1/06, Amended 1/11*)

- **Standard of Practice 10-4**
  As used in Article 10 "real estate employment practices" relates to employees and independent contractors providing real estate-related services and the administrative and clerical staff directly supporting those individuals. (*Adopted 1/00, Renumbered 1/05 and 1/06*)

Article 11

The services which REALTORS® provide to their clients and customers shall conform to the standards of practice and competence which are reasonably expected in the specific real estate disciplines in which they engage; specifically, residential real estate brokerage, real property management, commercial and industrial real estate brokerage, land brokerage, real estate appraisal, real estate counseling, real estate syndication, real estate auction, and international real estate.

REALTORS® shall not undertake to provide specialized professional services concerning a type of property or service that is outside their field of competence unless they engage the assistance of one who is competent on such types of property or service, or unless the facts are fully disclosed to the client. Any persons engaged to provide such assistance shall be so identified to the client and their contribution to the assignment should be set forth. (*Amended 1/10*)

- **Standard of Practice 11-1**
  When REALTORS® prepare opinions of real property value or price, other than in pursuit of a listing or to assist a potential purchaser in formulating a purchase offer, such opinions shall include the following unless the party requesting the opinion requires a specific type of report or different data set:
  1) identification of the subject property
  2) date prepared
  3) defined value or price
  4) limiting conditions, including statements of purpose(s) and intended user(s)
  5) any present or contemplated interest, including the possibility of representing the seller/landlord or buyers/tenants
  6) basis for the opinion, including applicable market data

(continued)

FIGURE 19.2   NAR Code of Ethics (continued)

7) if the opinion is not an appraisal, a statement to that effect *(Amended 1/10)*

- **Standard of Practice 11-2**

  The obligations of the Code of Ethics in respect of real estate disciplines other than appraisal shall be interpreted and applied in accordance with the standards of competence and practice which clients and the public reasonably require to protect their rights and interests considering the complexity of the transaction, the availability of expert assistance, and, where the REALTOR® is an agent or subagent, the obligations of a fiduciary. *(Adopted 1/95)*

- **Standard of Practice 11-3**

  When REALTORS® provide consultive services to clients which involve advice or counsel for a fee (not a commission), such advice shall be rendered in an objective manner and the fee shall not be contingent on the substance of the advice or counsel given. If brokerage or transaction services are to be provided in addition to consultive services, a separate compensation may be paid with prior agreement between the client and REALTOR®. *(Adopted 1/96)*

- **Standard of Practice 11-4**

  The competency required by Article 11 relates to services contracted for between REALTORS® and their clients or customers; the duties expressly imposed by the Code of Ethics; and the duties imposed by law or regulation. *(Adopted 1/02)*

Article 12

REALTORS® shall be honest and truthful in their real estate communications and shall present a true picture in their advertising, marketing, and other representations. REALTORS® shall ensure that their status as real estate professionals is readily apparent in their advertising, marketing, and other representations, and that the recipients of all real estate communications are, or have been, notified that those communications are from a real estate professional. *(Amended 1/08)*

- **Standard of Practice 12-1**

  REALTORS® may use the term "free" and similar terms in their advertising and in other representations provided that all terms governing availability of the offered product or service are clearly disclosed at the same time. *(Amended 1/97)*

- **Standard of Practice 12-2**

  REALTORS® may represent their services as "free" or without cost even if they expect to receive compensation from a source other than their client provided that the potential for the REALTOR® to obtain a benefit from a third party is clearly disclosed at the same time. *(Amended 1/97)*

- **Standard of Practice 12-3**

  The offering of premiums, prizes, merchandise discounts or other inducements to list, sell, purchase, or lease is not, in itself, unethical even if receipt of the benefit is contingent on listing, selling, purchasing, or leasing through the REALTOR® making the offer. However, REALTORS® must exercise care and candor in any such advertising or other public or private representations so that any party interested in receiving or otherwise benefiting from the REALTOR®'s offer will have clear, thorough, advance understanding of all the terms and conditions of the offer. The offering of any inducements to do business is subject to the limitations and restrictions of state law and the ethical obligations established by any applicable Standard of Practice. *(Amended 1/95)*

- **Standard of Practice 12-4**

  REALTORS® shall not offer for sale/lease or advertise property without authority. When acting as listing brokers or as subagents, REALTORS® shall not quote a price different from that agreed upon with the seller/landlord. *(Amended 1/93)*

- **Standard of Practice 12-5**

  REALTORS® shall not advertise nor permit any person employed by or affiliated with them to advertise real estate services or listed property in any medium (e.g., electronically, print, radio, television, etc.) without disclosing the name of that REALTOR®'s firm in a reasonable and readily apparent manner. This Standard of Practice acknowledges that disclosing the name of the firm may not be practical in electronic displays of limited information (e.g. "thumbnails", text messages, "tweets", etc.). Such displays are exempt from the disclosure requirement established in the Standard of Practice, but only when linked to a display that includes all required disclosures. *(Adopted 11/86, Amended 1/11)*

(continued)

FIGURE 19.2 NAR Code of Ethics (continued)

- **Standard of Practice 12-6**
  REALTORS®, when advertising unlisted real property for sale/lease in which they have an ownership interest, shall disclose their status as both owners/landlords and as REALTORS® or real estate licensees. *(Amended 1/93)*

- **Standard of Practice 12-7**
  Only REALTORS® who participated in the transaction as the listing broker or cooperating broker (selling broker) may claim to have "sold" the property. Prior to closing, a cooperating broker may post a "sold" sign only with the consent of the listing broker. *(Amended 1/96)*

- **Standard of Practice 12-8**
  The obligation to present a true picture in representations to the public includes information presented, provided, or displayed on REALTORS®' websites. REALTORS® shall use reasonable efforts to ensure that information on their websites is current. When it becomes apparent that information on a REALTOR®'s website is no longer current or accurate, REALTORS® shall promptly take corrective action. *(Adopted 1/07)*

- **Standard of Practice 12-9**
  REALTOR® firm websites shall disclose the firm's name and statc(s) of licensure in a reasonable and readily apparent manner.

  Websites of REALTORS® and non-member licensees affiliated with a REALTOR® firm shall disclose the firm's name and that REALTOR®'s or non-member licensee's state(s) of licensure in a reasonable and readily apparent manner. *(Adopted 1/07)*

- **Standard of Practice 12-10**
  REALTORS®' obligation to present a true picture in their advertising and representations to the public includes Internet content posted, and the URLs and domain names they use, and prohibits REALTORS® from:
  1) engaging in deceptive or unauthorized framing of real estate brokerage websites;
  2) manipulating (e.g., presenting content developed by others) listing and other content in any way that produces a deceptive or misleading result;
  3) deceptively using metatags, keywords or other devices/methods to direct, drive, or divert Internet traffic; or
  4) presenting content developed by others without either attribution or without permission, or
  5) to otherwise mislead consumers. *(Adopted 1/07, Amended 1/13)*

- **Standard of Practice 12-11**
  REALTORS® intending to share or sell consumer information gathered via the Internet shall disclose that possibility in a reasonable and readily apparent manner. *(Adopted 1/07)*

- **Standard of Practice 12-12**
  REALTORS® shall not:
  1) use URLs or domain names that present less than a true picture, or
  2) register URLs or domain names which, if used, would present less than a true picture. *(Adopted 1/08)*

- **Standard of Practice 12-13**
  The obligation to present a true picture in advertising, marketing, and representations allows REALTORS® to use and display only professional designations, certifications, and other credentials to which they are legitimately entitled. *(Adopted 1/08)*

Article 13

REALTORS® shall not engage in activities that constitute the unauthorized practice of law and shall recommend that legal counsel be obtained when the interest of any party to the transaction requires it.

Article 14

If charged with unethical practice or asked to present evidence or to cooperate in any other way, in any professional standards proceeding or investigation, REALTORS® shall place all pertinent facts before the proper tribunals of the Member Board or affiliated institute, society, or council in which membership is held and shall take no action to disrupt or obstruct such processes. *(Amended 1/99)*

- **Standard of Practice 14-1**
  REALTORS® shall not be subject to disciplinary proceedings in more than one Board of REALTORS® or affiliated institute, society, or council in which they hold membership with respect to alleged violations of the Code of Ethics relating to the same transaction or event. *(Amended 1/95)*

- **Standard of Practice 14-2**
  REALTORS® shall not make any unauthorized disclosure or dissemination of the allegations, findings, or decision developed in connection with an ethics hearing or appeal or in connection with an arbitration hearing or procedural review. *(Amended 1/92)*

(continued)

FIGURE 19.2   NAR Code of Ethics (continued)

- **Standard of Practice 14-3**

  REALTORS® shall not obstruct the Board's investigative or professional standards proceedings by instituting or threatening to institute actions for libel, slander, or defamation against any party to a professional standards proceeding or their witnesses based on the filing of an arbitration request, an ethics complaint, or testimony given before any tribunal. *(Adopted 11/87, Amended 1/99)*

- **Standard of Practice 14-4**

  REALTORS® shall not intentionally impede the Board's investigative or disciplinary proceedings by filing multiple ethics complaints based on the same event or transaction. *(Adopted 11/88)*

Duties to REALTORS®

Article 15

REALTORS® shall not knowingly or recklessly make false or misleading statements about other real estate professionals, their businesses, or their business practices. *(Amended 1/12)*

- **Standard of Practice 15-1**

  REALTORS® shall not knowingly or recklessly file false or unfounded ethics complaints. *(Adopted 1/00)*

- **Standard of Practice 15-2**

  The obligation to refrain from making false or misleading statements about other real estate professionals, their businesses, and their business practices includes the duty to not knowingly or recklessly publish, repeat, retransmit, or republish false or misleading statements made by others. This duty applies whether false or misleading statements are repeated in person, in writing, by technological means (e.g., the Internet), or by any other means. *(Adopted 1/07, Amended 1/12)*

- **Standard of Practice 15-3**

  The obligation to refrain from making false or misleading statements about other real estate professionals, their businesses, and their business practices includes the duty to publish a clarification about or to remove statements made by others on electronic media the REALTOR® controls once the REALTOR® knows the statement is false or misleading. *(Adopted 1/10, Amended 1/12)*

Article 16

REALTORS® shall not engage in any practice or take any action inconsistent with exclusive representation or exclusive brokerage relationship agreements that other REALTORS® have with clients. *(Amended 1/04)*

- **Standard of Practice 16-1**

  Article 16 is not intended to prohibit aggressive or innovative business practices which are otherwise ethical and does not prohibit disagreements with other REALTORS® involving commission, fees, compensation or other forms of payment or expenses. *(Adopted 1/93, Amended 1/95)*

- **Standard of Practice 16-2**

  Article 16 does not preclude REALTORS® from making general announcements to prospects describing their services and the terms of their availability even though some recipients may have entered into agency agreements or other exclusive relationships with another REALTOR®. A general telephone canvass, general mailing or distribution addressed to all prospects in a given geographical area or in a given profession, business, club, or organization, or other classification or group is deemed "general" for purposes of this standard. *(Amended 1/04)*

Article 16 is intended to recognize as unethical two basic types of solicitations:

First, telephone or personal solicitations of property owners who have been identified by a real estate sign, multiple listing compilation, or other information service as having exclusively listed their property with another REALTOR® and

Second, mail or other forms of written solicitations of prospects whose properties are exclusively listed with another REALTOR® when such solicitations are not part of a general mailing but are directed specifically to property owners identified through compilations of current listings, "for sale" or "for rent" signs, or other sources of information required by Article 3 and Multiple Listing Service rules to be made available to other REALTORS® under offers of subagency or cooperation. *(Amended 1/04)*

- **Standard of Practice 16-3**

  Article 16 does not preclude REALTORS® from contacting the client of another broker for the purpose of offering to provide, or entering into a contract to provide, a different type of real estate service unrelated to the type of service currently being provided (e.g., property management as opposed to brokerage) or from offering the same type of service for property not subject to other brokers' exclusive agreements. However, information received through a Multiple Listing Service or any other offer of cooperation may not be used to target clients of other REALTORS® to whom such offers to provide services may be made. *(Amended 1/04)*

(continued)

FIGURE
19.2   NAR Code of Ethics (continued)

- **Standard of Practice 16-4**

  REALTORS® shall not solicit a listing which is currently listed exclusively with another broker. However, if the listing broker, when asked by the REALTOR®, refuses to disclose the expiration date and nature of such listing, i.e., an exclusive right to sell, an exclusive agency, open listing, or other form of contractual agreement between the listing broker and the client, the REALTOR® may contact the owner to secure such information and may discuss the terms upon which the REALTOR® might take a future listing or, alternatively, may take a listing to become effective upon expiration of any existing exclusive listing. *(Amended 1/94)*

- **Standard of Practice 16-5**

  REALTORS® shall not solicit buyer/tenant agreements from buyers/ tenants who are subject to exclusive buyer/tenant agreements. However, if asked by a REALTOR®, the broker refuses to disclose the expiration date of the exclusive buyer/tenant agreement, the REALTOR® may contact the buyer/tenant to secure such information and may discuss the terms upon which the REALTOR® might enter into a future buyer/tenant agreement or, alternatively, may enter into a buyer/tenant agreement to become effective upon the expiration of any existing exclusive buyer/tenant agreement. *(Adopted 1/94, Amended 1/98)*

- **Standard of Practice 16-6**

  When REALTORS® are contacted by the client of another REALTOR® regarding the creation of an exclusive relationship to provide the same type of service, and REALTORS® have not directly or indirectly initiated such discussions, they may discuss the terms upon which they might enter into a future agreement or, alternatively, may enter into an agreement which becomes effective upon expiration of any existing exclusive agreement. *(Amended 1/98)*

- **Standard of Practice 16-7**

  The fact that a prospect has retained a REALTOR® as an exclusive representative or exclusive broker in one or more past transactions does not preclude other REALTORS® from seeking such prospect's future business. *(Amended 1/04)*

- **Standard of Practice 16-8**

  The fact that an exclusive agreement has been entered into with a REALTOR® shall not preclude or inhibit any other REALTOR® from entering into a similar agreement after the expiration of the prior agreement. *(Amended 1/98)*

- **Standard of Practice 16-9**

  REALTORS®, prior to entering into a representation agreement, have an affirmative obligation to make reasonable efforts to determine whether the prospect is subject to a current, valid exclusive agreement to provide the same type of real estate service. *(Amended 1/04)*

- **Standard of Practice 16-10**

  REALTORS®, acting as buyer or tenant representatives or brokers, shall disclose that relationship to the seller/landlord's representative or broker at first contact and shall provide written confirmation of that disclosure to the seller/landlord's representative or broker not later than execution of a purchase agreement or lease. *(Amended 1/04)*

- **Standard of Practice 16-11**

  On unlisted property, REALTORS® acting as buyer/tenant representatives or brokers shall disclose that relationship to the seller/landlord at first contact for that buyer/tenant and shall provide written confirmation of such disclosure to the seller/landlord not later than execution of any purchase or lease agreement. *(Amended 1/04)*

  REALTORS® shall make any request for anticipated compensation from the seller/landlord at first contact. *(Amended 1/98)*

- **Standard of Practice 16-12**

  REALTORS®, acting as representatives or brokers of sellers/landlords or as subagents of listing brokers, shall disclose that relationship to buyers/tenants as soon as practicable and shall provide written confirmation of such disclosure to buyers/tenants not later than execution of any purchase or lease agreement. *(Amended 1/04)*

- **Standard of Practice 16-13**

  All dealings concerning property exclusively listed, or with buyer/tenants who are subject to an exclusive agreement shall be carried on with the client's representative or broker, and not with the client, except with the consent of the client's representative or broker or except where such dealings are initiated by the client.

  Before providing substantive services (such as writing a purchase offer or presenting a CMA) to prospects, REALTORS® shall ask prospects whether they are a party to any exclusive representation agreement.

(continued)

FIGURE 19.2 NAR Code of Ethics (continued)

REALTORS® shall not knowingly provide substantive services concerning a prospective transaction to prospects who are parties to exclusive representation agreements, except with the consent of the prospects' exclusive representatives or at the direction of prospects. *(Adopted 1/93, Amended 1/04)*

- **Standard of Practice 16-14**

  REALTORS® are free to enter into contractual relationships or to negotiate with sellers/landlords, buyers/tenants or others who are not subject to an exclusive agreement but shall not knowingly obligate them to pay more than one commission except with their informed consent. *(Amended 1/98)*

- **Standard of Practice 16-15**

  In cooperative transactions REALTORS® shall compensate cooperating REALTORS® (principal brokers) and shall not compensate nor offer to compensate, directly or indirectly, any of the sales licensees employed by or affiliated with other REALTORS® without the prior express knowledge and consent of the cooperating broker.

- **Standard of Practice 16-16**

  REALTORS®, acting as subagents or buyer/tenant representatives or brokers, shall not use the terms of an offer to purchase/lease to attempt to modify the listing broker's offer of compensation to subagents or buyer/tenant representatives or brokers nor make the submission of an executed offer to purchase/lease contingent on the listing broker's agreement to modify the offer of compensation. *(Amended 1/04)*

- **Standard of Practice 16-17**

  REALTORS®, acting as subagents or as buyer/tenant representatives or brokers, shall not attempt to extend a listing broker's offer of cooperation and/or compensation to other brokers without the consent of the listing broker. *(Amended 1/04)*

- **Standard of Practice 16-18**

  REALTORS® shall not use information obtained from listing brokers through offers to cooperate made through multiple listing services or through other offers of cooperation to refer listing brokers' clients to other brokers or to create buyer/tenant relationships with listing brokers' clients, unless such use is authorized by listing brokers. *(Amended 1/02)*

- **Standard of Practice 16-19**

  Signs giving notice of property for sale, rent, lease, or exchange shall not be placed on property without consent of the seller/landlord. *(Amended 1/93)*

- **Standard of Practice 16-20**

  REALTORS®, prior to or after their relationship with their current firm is terminated, shall not induce clients of their current firm to cancel exclusive contractual agreements between the client and that firm. This does not preclude REALTORS® (principals) from establishing agreements with their associated licensees governing assignability of exclusive agreements. *(Adopted 1/98, Amended 1/10)*

Article 17

In the event of contractual disputes or specific noncontractual disputes as defined in Standard of Practice 17-4 between REALTORS® (principals) associated with different firms, arising out of their relationship as REALTORS®, the REALTORS® shall mediate the dispute if the Board requires its members to mediate. If the dispute is not resolved through mediation, or if mediation is not required, REALTORS® shall submit the dispute to arbitration in accordance with the policies of the Board rather than litigate the matter.

In the event clients of REALTORS® wish to mediate or arbitrate contractual disputes arising out of real estate transactions, REALTORS® shall mediate or arbitrate those disputes in accordance with the policies of the Board, provided the clients agree to be bound by any resulting agreement or award.

The obligation to participate in mediation and arbitration contemplated by this Article includes the obligation of REALTORS® (principals) to cause their firms to mediate and arbitrate and be bound by the resulting agreement or award. *(Amended 1/12)*

- **Standard of Practice 17-1**

  The filing of litigation and refusal to withdraw from it by REALTORS® in an arbitrable matter constitutes a refusal to arbitrate. *(Adopted 2/86)*

- **Standard of Practice 17-2**

  Article 17 does not require REALTORS® to mediate in those circumstances when all parties to the dispute advise the Board in writing that they choose not to mediate through the Board's facilities. The fact that all parties decline to participate in mediation does not relieve REALTORS® of the duty to arbitrate.

  Article 17 does not require REALTORS® to arbitrate in those circumstances when all parties to the dispute advise the Board in writing that they choose not to arbitrate before the Board. *(Amended 1/12)*

(continued)

FIGURE 19.2	NAR Code of Ethics (continued)

- **Standard of Practice 17-3**

  REALTORS®, when acting solely as principals in a real estate transaction, are not obligated to arbitrate disputes with other REALTORS® absent a specific written agreement to the contrary. *(Adopted 1/96)*

- **Standard of Practice 17-4**

  Specific non-contractual disputes that are subject to arbitration pursuant to Article 17 are:

  1) Where a listing broker has compensated a cooperating broker and another cooperating broker subsequently claims to be the procuring cause of the sale or lease. In such cases the complainant may name the first cooperating broker as respondent and arbitration may proceed without the listing broker being named as a respondent. When arbitration occurs between two (or more) cooperating brokers and where the listing broker is not a party, the amount in dispute and the amount of any potential resulting award is limited to the amount paid to the respondent by the listing broker and any amount credited or paid to a party to the transaction at the direction of the respondent. Alternatively, if the complaint is brought against the listing broker, the listing broker may name the first cooperating broker as a third-party respondent. In either instance the decision of the hearing panel as to procuring cause shall be conclusive with respect to all current or subsequent claims of the parties for compensation arising out of the underlying cooperative transaction. *(Adopted 1/97, Amended 1/07)*

  2) Where a buyer or tenant representative is compensated by the seller or landlord, and not by the listing broker, and the listing broker, as a result, reduces the commission owed by the seller or landlord and, subsequent to such actions, another cooperating broker claims to be the procuring cause of sale or lease. In such cases the complainant may name the first cooperating broker as respondent and arbitration may proceed without the listing broker being named as a respondent. When arbitration occurs between two (or more) cooperating brokers and where the listing broker is not a party, the amount in dispute and the amount of any potential resulting award is limited to the amount paid to the respondent by the seller or landlord and any amount credited or paid to a party to the transaction at the direction of the

  respondent. Alternatively, if the complaint is brought against the listing broker, the listing broker may name the first cooperating broker as a third-party respondent. In either instance the decision of the hearing panel as to procuring cause shall be conclusive with respect to all current or subsequent claims of the parties for compensation arising out of the underlying cooperative transaction. *(Adopted 1/97, Amended 1/07)*

  3) Where a buyer or tenant representative is compensated by the buyer or tenant and, as a result, the listing broker reduces the commission owed by the seller or landlord and, subsequent to such actions, another cooperating broker claims to be the procuring cause of sale or lease. In such cases the complainant may name the first cooperating broker as respondent and arbitration may proceed without the listing broker being named as a respondent. Alternatively, if the complaint is brought against the listing broker, the listing broker may name the first cooperating broker as a third-party respondent. In either instance the decision of the hearing panel as to procuring cause shall be conclusive with respect to all current or subsequent claims of the parties for compensation arising out of the underlying cooperative transaction. *(Adopted 1/97)*

  4) Where two or more listing brokers claim entitlement to compensation pursuant to open listings with a seller or landlord who agrees to participate in arbitration (or who requests arbitration) and who agrees to be bound by the decision. In cases where one of the listing brokers has been compensated by the seller or landlord, the other listing broker, as complainant, may name the first listing broker as respondent and arbitration may proceed between the brokers. *(Adopted 1/97)*

  5) Where a buyer or tenant representative is compensated by the seller or landlord, and not by the listing broker, and the listing broker, as a result, reduces the commission owed by the seller or landlord and, subsequent to such actions, claims to be the procuring cause of sale or lease. In such cases arbitration shall be between the listing broker and the buyer or tenant representative and the amount in dispute is limited to the amount of the reduction of commission to which the listing broker agreed. *(Adopted 1/05)*

(continued)

FIGURE 19.2 NAR Code of Ethics (continued)

- **Standard of Practice 17-5**

  The obligation to arbitrate established in Article 17 includes disputes between REALTORS® (principals) in different states in instances where, absent an established inter-association arbitration agreement, the REALTOR® (principal) requesting arbitration agrees to submit to the jurisdiction of, travel to, participate in, and be bound by any resulting award rendered in arbitration conducted by the respondent(s) REALTOR®'s association, in instances where the respondent(s) REALTOR®'s association determines that an arbitrable issue exists. *(Adopted 1/07)*

*The **Code of Ethics** was adopted in 1913. Amended at the Annual Convention in 1914, 1915, 1924, 1928, 1950, 1952, 1955, 1956, 1961, 1962, 1974, 1975, 1982, 1986, 1987, 1989, 1990, 1991, 1992, 1993, 1994, 1995, 1996, 1997, 1998, 1999, 2000, 2001, 2002, 2003, 2004, 2005, 2006, 2007, 2008, 2009, 2010, 2011, and 2012.*

Explanatory Notes

The reader should be aware of the following policies which have been approved by the Board of Directors of the National Association:

In filing a charge of an alleged violation of the Code of Ethics by a REALTOR®, the charge must read as an alleged violation of one or more Articles of the Code. Standards of Practice may be cited in support of the charge.

The Standards of Practice serve to clarify the ethical obligations imposed by the various Articles and supplement, and do not substitute for, the Case Interpretations in *Interpretations of the Code of Ethics*.

Modifications to existing Standards of Practice and additional new Standards of Practice are approved from time to time. Readers are cautioned to ensure that the most recent publications are utilized.

© 2013, NATIONAL ASSOCIATION OF REALTORS®, All Rights Reserved Form No. 166-2887-13 (1/13) BFC

In some states, ethical standards such as those in the NAR Code of Ethics have been legislated into law. Called **canons** or **standards of conduct**, their intent is to promote ethical practices by all real estate licensees, not just by those who join the National Association of REALTORS®. Additionally, the National Association of REALTORS® publishes 34 **Standards of Practice**. These interpret various articles in the Code of Ethics.

The NATIONAL ASSOCIATION OF REALTORS® reserves exclusively unto itself the right to officially comment on and interpret the CODE and particular provisions thereof. For the NATIONAL ASSOCIATION's official interpretations of the CODE, see INTERPRETATIONS OF THE CODE OF ETHICS; NATIONAL ASSOCIATION OFREALTORS®.

In addition to its emphasis on real estate brokerage, the National Association of REALTORS® also contains a number of specialized professional groups within itself. These include the American Institute of Real Estate Appraisers, the Farm and Land Institute, the Institute of Real Estate Management, the REALTORS® National Marketing Institute, the Society of Industrial REALTORS®, the Real Estate Securities and Syndication Institute, the American Society of Real Estate Counselors, the American Chapter of the International Real Estate Federation, and the Women's Council of REALTORS®. Membership is open to REALTORS® interested in these specialties.

REALTOR® DESIGNATIONS

NAR, in promoting professionalism, has created a number of designations, which advertise to the public areas of expertise that REALTORS® have in designated areas.

GRI DESIGNATIONS

To help encourage and recognize professionalism in the real estate industry, state Boards of REALTORS® sponsor education courses leading to the **GRI** designation. Course offerings typically include real estate law, finance, appraisal, investments, office management, and salesmanship. Upon completion of the prescribed curriculum, the designation Graduate REALTOR's® Institute is awarded.

If the buyer is looking for a buyer representative, they have traded the Accredited Buyer's Representative (ABR) designation, which they consider to be the mark of excellence in comprehensive buyer representation services and expertise.

For commercial investment real estate expertise and financial analysis skills, the Certified Commercial Investment Member (CCIM) designation is available. Agents who want to earn the highest professional designated award available to residential agents, can obtain the Certified Residential Specialist (CRS) designation.

NAR also recognizes a Green designation which is designed for residential, commercial, and property management professionals that is offered through the Green Resource Council and counsels agents about green materials, energy efficient technology, green ratings, green design, green incentives, green living, and more.

REALTIST

The National Association of Real Estate Brokers (NAREB) is a national trade association representing minority real estate professionals actively engaged in the industry. Founded in 1947, its 5,000 members use the trade name **Realtist**. The organization extends through 14 regions across the country with more than 60 active local boards. NAREB education and certification programs include the Real Estate Management Brokers Institute, National Society of Real Estate Appraisers, Real Estate Brokerage Institute, and United Developers Council. The organization's purposes are to promote high standards of service and conduct and to protect the public against unethical, improper, or fraudulent real estate practices.

Vocabulary Review

Match terms a–x with statements 1–24.

a. Broker

b. Code of Ethics

c. Continuing education

d. Employment contract

e. Fictitious business name

f. Franchisee

g. GRI

h. Independent contractor

i. Licensee

j. Nonresident license

k. Notice of consent

l. Principal broker

m. Real estate commission

n. Real estate salesperson

o. Realtist

p. REALTOR®

q. REALTOR®-Associate

_____ 1. One who holds a license.

_____ 2. A person who is licensed to bring about real estate transactions for a fee, but who must do so only in the employment of a real estate broker.

_____ 3. A registered trademark owned by the National Association of REALTORS® for exclusive use by its members.

_____ 4. Broker in charge of an office.

_____ 5. A business operated under any name other than the owner's name.

_____ 6. An independent agent who negotiates transactions for a fee.

_____ 7. To temporarily make ineffective.

_____ 8. To recall and make void.

_____ 9. A local trade organization for real estate licensees and other persons allied with the real estate industry.

_____ 10. A state-operated fund that can be tapped to pay for uncollectible judgments against real estate licensees.

_____ 11. A salesperson or broker employed by a broker.

_____ 12. A state board that advises and sets policies regarding real estate licensees and real estate transaction procedures.

r. Realty board
s. Recovery fund
t. Revoke
u. Sales associate
v. Securities license
w. Standards of Practice
x. Suspend

_____13. One who uses his own methods and is responsible only as to the results.

_____14. A requirement for license renewal in many states, its purpose is to help licensees keep up to date in real estate.

_____15. Required of a real estate broker in order to conduct negotiations within another state.

_____16. Permits the secretary of state to receive legal summonses on behalf of a nonresident broker.

_____17. Required when selling an investment contract.

_____18. Formalizes the working arrangement between the broker and his salespersons.

_____19. The party holding a franchise such as a franchised brokerage office.

_____20. Membership designation for salespersons and broker licensees working for Realtors®.

_____21. Standards by which members of the National Association of REALTORS® agree to abide.

_____22. Interpretations of various articles of the REALTORS® Code of Ethics.

_____23. A registered trademark for use by members of the National Association of Real Estate Brokers.

_____24. A designation awarded for completion of real estate courses sponsored by Boards of REALTORS®.

Questions and Problems

1. What factors do brokers consider when deciding what percentage of commissions should be paid to the salespersons in their office?

2. When is a person required to hold a real estate license?

3. What was the purpose of early real estate license law?

4. Does your state subscribe to an examination service? How often are the exams conducted?

5. What trends are apparent in your state with regard to real estate education requirements?

6. What is the name of the person currently in charge of real estate regulation for your state? What are his or her duties and responsibilities?

7. How is the real estate commission selected in your state? What are its duties and responsibilities?

8. Under what circumstances are real estate licenses suspended or revoked in your state?

9. What is the purpose of a bond requirement or recovery fund? What does your state require?

10. What is the purpose of the National Association of REALTORS®?

11. Which items are covered in an employment contract between a broker and a salesperson?

12. If you were seeking employment as a salesperson for a brokerage firm, how would you decide which firm to be associated with?

Additional Readings

Digest of Real Estate License Laws (ARELLO—Association of Real Estate License Law Officials, 2005). Contains summaries of real estate license laws for each of the states and the Canadian provinces.

Ethics for the Real Estate Professional, 3rd Ed. by Deborah H. Long (OnCourse Learning, 2008).

Interpretations of the Code of Ethics (National Association of REALTORS®).

Preparing for the ASI Real Estate Exam: A Guide to Successful Test Taking by Randall S. van Reken (OnCourse Learning, 1996). Includes two 80-question practice exams.

Preparing for the PSI Real Estate Exam: A Guide to Successful Test Taking, 2d ed. by Randall S. van Reken (OnCourse Learning, 1997). Includes over 600 sample questions.

"Real Estate: It's About Competition" by Jim Smith (*ABA Banking Journal*, February 2002, p. 81).

CHAPTER 20

The Principal– Broker Relationship: Employment

Chapter 19 discussed licensure requirements and professional affiliations. This chapter will discuss the principal–broker relationship as it relates to employment, listing agreements, and compensation of real estate brokers. Chapter 21 will then expand into theories of agency relationships and duties of care that result from the laws of agency. Note that the formalities of employment are not necessarily required to establish an agency relationship, so the licensee may be responsible as an agent without the benefits of formal employment! In addition, a broker may be hired by the seller or landlord, a buyer or tenant, or both. Let's discuss how this occurs.

LEARNING OBJECTIVES

After reading this chapter, you should be able to:

❮ Discuss, understand, and complete a listing agreement.

❮ Understand the different types of listing agreements.

❮ Understand the purpose and reason for multiple listing services.

❮ Understand the difference between commissions being earned and commissions being paid.

❮ Define ways to terminate the brokerage contract.

❮ Recognize different types of compensation agreements with real estate licensees.

KEY TERMS

Advance fee listing • Exclusive authority to purchase • Exclusive right to sell • Multiple listing service (MLS) • Net listing • Ready, willing, and able buyer • Real estate listing

Listing Agreement

A **real estate listing** is an *employment contract* between a property owner and a real estate broker. Through it, the property owner appoints the broker as the owner's agent for the specific purpose of finding a buyer or tenant who is willing to meet the conditions set forth in the listing. It does not authorize the broker to sell or convey title to the property or to sign contracts.

Although persons licensed as real estate salespersons perform listing and sales functions, they are actually extensions of the broker. A seller may conduct all aspects of a listing and sale through

real estate listing

A contract wherein a broker is employed to find a buyer or tenant.

385

a salesperson licensee, but it is the broker behind the salesperson with whom the seller has the listing contract and who is legally liable for its proper execution. If you plan to be a salesperson for a broker, be aware of what is legally and ethically required of a broker because you are the broker's eyes, ears, hands, and mouth. If your interest is in listing the property with a broker, know that it is the broker with whom you have the listing contract even though your day-to-day contact is with the broker's sales associates. Sales associates are the licensed salespersons or brokers who work for a broker.

When a property owner signs a listing, all the essential elements of a valid contract must be present. The owner and broker must be legally capable of contracting, there must be mutual assent, and the agreement must be for a lawful purpose. Nearly all states require that a listing be in writing and signed to be valid and thereby enforceable in a court of law.

exclusive right to sell

A listing that gives the broker the right to collect a commission no matter who sells the property during the listing period.

Figure 20.1 illustrates a simplified **exclusive right to sell** listing agreement. Actual listing contracts tend to be longer and more complex and vary in detail from one contract to the next. The listing in Figure 20.1 is an educational introduction to listings that provides, in plain English, commonly found listing contract provisions. Beginning at [1], there is a description of the property plus the price and terms at which the broker is instructed to find a buyer. At [2], the broker promises to make a reasonable effort to find a buyer. The period of time that the listing is to be in effect is shown at [3]. It is usually to the broker's advantage to make the listing period for as long as possible, as this provides more time to find a buyer. Sometimes, even an overpriced property will become saleable if the listing period is long enough and prices rise fast enough. However, most owners want a balance between their flexibility and the amount of time necessary for a broker to conduct a sales campaign. In residential sales, three to four months is a popular compromise; farm, ranch, commercial, and industrial listings are usually made for six months to one year.

At [4], the owner agrees not to list the property with any other brokers, permit other brokers to have a sign on the property, or advertise it during the listing period. Also, the owner agrees not to revoke the broker's exclusive right to find a buyer as set forth by this contract.

The broker recognizes that the owner may later accept a price and terms that are different from those in the listing. The wording at [5] states that the broker will earn a commission no matter what price and terms the owner ultimately accepts.

BROKERAGE COMMISSION

At [6], the amount of compensation the owner agrees to pay the broker is established. The usual arrangement is to express the amount as a percentage of the sale or exchange price, although a stated dollar amount could be used if the owner and broker agreed. In any event, the amount of the fee is negotiable between the owner and the broker. An owner who feels the fee is too high can list with someone who charges less or sell the property without a broker. The broker recognizes that if the fee is too low, it will not be worthwhile spending time and effort finding a buyer. The typical commission fee in the United States at present is 5% to 7% of the selling price for houses, condominiums, and small apartment buildings, and 6% to 10% for farms, ranches, and vacant land. On multimillion-dollar improved properties, commissions usually drop to the 1% to 4% range. Brokerage commissions are not set by a state regulatory agency or by local real estate associations. In fact, any effort by brokers to set commission rates among themselves is a violation of federal and state antitrust laws. The penalty can be as much as triple damages and criminal liability.

The conditions under which a commission must be paid by the owner to the broker appear next. At [7], a commission is deemed to be earned if the owner agrees to a sale or exchange of the property no matter who finds the buyer. (Recall that this is an "exclusive right to sell" listing agreement.) In other words, even if the owner finds a buyer, or a friend of the owner finds a buyer, the broker is entitled to a full commission fee. If the

| FIGURE 20.1 | Sample of Exclusive Right to Sell Listing Contract |

EXCLUSIVE RIGHT TO SELL LISTING CONTRACT

[1] Property Description: A single-family house at 2424 E. Main Street, City, State. Legally described as Lot 17, Tract 191, County, State.

Price: $105,000

Terms: Cash

[2] In consideration of the services of ABC Realty Company (herein called the "Broker"), to be rendered to Roger Leeving and Mary Leeving (herein called the "Owner"), and the promise of said Broker to make reasonable efforts to obtain a purchaser; therefore, the Owner hereby grants to the Broker [3] for the period of time from noon on April 1, 20xx to noon on July 1, 20xx (herein called the "listing period") [4] the exclusive and irrevocable right to advertise and find a purchaser for the above described property at the price and terms shown [5] or for such sum and terms or exchange as the owner later agrees to accept.

[6] The Owner hereby agrees to pay Broker a cash fee of 6% of the selling or exchange price:

[7] A) in case of any sale or exchange of the above property within the listing period either by the Broker, the Owner, or any other person, or

[8] B) upon the Broker finding a purchaser who is ready, willing, and able to complete the purchase as proposed by the owner, or

[9] C) in the event of a sale or exchange within 60 days of the expiration of the listing period to any party shown the above property during the listing period by the Broker or his representative and where the name was disclosed to the Owner.

[10] The Owner agrees to give the Broker access to the buildings on the property for the purposes of showing them at reasonable hours, and allows the Broker to post a "For Sale" sign on the premises.

[11] The Owner agrees to allow the Broker to place this listing information in any multiple listing organization of which he is a member and to engage the cooperation of other brokers as subagents to bring about a sale.

[12] The Owner agrees to refer to the Broker all inquiries regarding this property during the listing period.

[13] Accepted:

ABC Realty Company

By: *Kurt Kwiklister*

Date: *April 1, 20xx*

Owner: *Roger Leeving*
Owner: *Mary Leeving*

Source: © 2014 OnCourse Learning

owner disregards the promise at [4] and lists with another broker who then sells the property, the owner is liable for two full commissions.

PROTECTING THE BROKER

The wording at [8] is included to protect the broker against the possibility that the owner may refuse to sell after the broker has expended time and effort to find a buyer at the price and terms of the listing contract. The listing itself is not an offer to sell property. It is strictly a contract whereby the owner employs the broker to find a buyer. Thus, even though a buyer offers to pay the exact price and terms shown in the listing, the buyer does not have a binding sales contract until the offer is accepted in writing by the owner. However, if the owner refuses to sell at the listed price and terms, the broker is still entitled to a commission. If the owner does not pay the broker voluntarily, the broker can file a lawsuit against the owner to collect.

PROTECTING THE OWNER

At [9], the broker is protected against the possibility that the listing period will expire while still working with a prospective purchaser. In fairness to the owner, however, two limitations are placed on the broker. First, a sales contract must be concluded within a reasonable time after the listing expires, and second, the name of the purchaser must have been given to the owner before the listing period expires.

Continuing at [10], the owner agrees to let the broker enter the property at reasonable hours to show it and put a "For Sale" sign on the property. At [11], the property owner gives the broker specific permission to enter the property into a multiple listing service and to engage the cooperation of other brokers as subagents to bring about a sale.

At [12], the owner agrees to refer all inquiries regarding the availability of the property to the broker. The purpose is to discourage the owner from thinking that he might be able to save a commission by personally selling it during the listing period, and to provide sales leads for the broker. Finally, at [13], the owner and the broker (or the broker's sales associate if authorized to do so) sign and date the agreement.

Exclusive Right to Sell Listing

The listing illustrated in Figure 20.1 is called an **exclusive right to sell** or **exclusive authorization to sell** listing. Its distinguishing characteristic is that no matter who sells the property during the listing period, the listing broker is entitled to a commission. This is the most widely used type of listing in the United States. Once signed by the owner and accepted by the broker, the primary advantage to the broker is that the money and effort the broker expends on advertising and showing the property will be to the broker's benefit. The advantage to the owner is that the broker will usually put more effort into selling a property if the broker holds an exclusive right to sell than if the broker has an exclusive agency or an open listing.

Exclusive Agency Listing

The **exclusive agency listing** is similar to the listing shown in Figure 20.1, except that the owner may sell the property himself during the listing period and not owe a commission to the broker. The broker, however, is the only broker who can act as an agent during the listing period; hence the term *exclusive agency*. For an owner, this type of listing may seem like the best of two worlds: The owner has a broker looking for a buyer, but if the owner finds a buyer first, the owner can save a commission fee. The broker is less enthusiastic because the broker's efforts can too easily be undermined by the owner. Consequently, the broker may not expend as much effort on advertising and showing the property as with an exclusive right to sell.

Open Listing

Open listings carry no exclusive rights. An owner can give an open listing to any number of brokers at the same time, and the owner can still find a buyer and avoid a commission. This gives the owner the greatest freedom of any listing form, but there is little incentive for the broker to expend time and money showing the property, as the broker has little control over who will be compensated if the property is sold. The broker's only protection is that if the broker does find a buyer at the listing price and terms, the broker is entitled to a commission. This reluctance to develop a sales effort usually means that few, if any, offers will be received, and the result may be no sale or a sale below market price. Yet, if a broker does find a buyer, the commission earned may be the same as with an exclusive right to sell.

Net Listing

A **net listing** is created when an owner states the price he wants for his property and then agrees to pay the broker anything above that price as the commission. It can be written in the form of an exclusive right to sell, an exclusive agency, or an open listing. If a homeowner asks for a "net $60,000" and the broker sells the home for $65,000, the commission would be $5,000. By using the net listing method, many owners feel that they are forcing the broker to look to the buyer for the commission by marking up the price of the property. In reality though, would a buyer pay $65,000 for a home that is worth $60,000? Because of widespread misunderstanding regarding net listings, some states prohibit them outright, and most brokers strenuously avoid them even when requested by property owners. There is no law that says a broker must accept a listing; a broker is free to accept only those listings for which the broker can perform a valuable service and earn an honest profit.

net listing
A listing agreement that pays the broker an uncertain amount of commission, generating the principal net proceeds from the sale.

Advance Fee Listing

Traditionally, real estate brokers charge a fee for their services based on a percentage of the sales price. Out of this percentage, the broker: (1) pays all out-of-pocket costs of marketing the property such as advertising and office overhead, (2) pays those who negotiate the transaction, and (3) earns a profit for the firm. If a buyer is not found, the broker receives no money. This means commissions earned from sold properties must also pay for costs incurred by non sales. Sellers who have marketable property that is priced to sell subsidize sellers whose property is either unattractive or overpriced. As a solution to this inequity, attention is now being given by the real estate industry to the concept of advance fee listings and advance cost listings.

An **advance fee listing** is a listing wherein a broker charges a seller much like an attorney charges a client. In other words, the broker asks for an advance deposit from the seller. Against this, the broker charges an hourly fee for time spent selling the property plus out-of-pocket expenses. With the seller paying for services as consumed, the seller becomes much more realistic about marketability and listed price. There is less inclination to price above market in hopes that if the broker works long enough, a buyer might be found who will pay above market or that the market will eventually rise to the asking price.

advance fee listing
Listing in which a broker gets paid in advance and charges an hourly rate.

ADVANCE COST LISTING

An **advance cost listing** covers only out-of-pocket costs incurred by the broker, such as advertising, multiple listing fees, flyers, mailings, toll calls, survey, soil report, title report, travel expenses, and food served during open houses. With either the advance fee or advance cost arrangement, the broker can still charge a commission based on sales price. In this case, costs and hourly fees are deducted from the commission at the closing. With the broker receiving payment for costs (and effort) up front, the sales commission can be lowered.

The mechanics of advance fee and advance cost listings must be very clearly explained to the seller before the listing is signed. There must be an accurate accounting of where the seller's money is being spent. (This is an ideal task for a computer.) Moreover, state real estate regulators may have specific rules and prohibitions that must be followed.

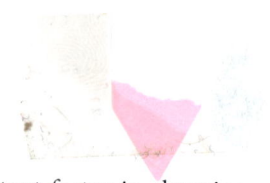

Watch the advance fee trend. If it takes hold, it will be an important factor in changing real estate agents from commissioned salespeople to professionals who can command an hourly fee for their time.

Exclusive Authority to Purchase

Previous portions of this chapter have presumed the general rule that the real estate broker represents the seller. Historically, it has been the seller who has hired a broker to assist in marketing property. Consumers, though, are far more sophisticated and informed today. They are aware of the complexities of the market, property condition, and consumer protection laws. They want, and often need, advice from a real estate professional. The Real Estate Buyers Agents Counsel (REBAC), a division of the National Association of REALTORS, has increased its membership dramatically, reflecting expanded interest in buyer representation. Buyers employ real estate practitioners to help them locate property or to assist them in negotiating the acquisition of a specified property.

In such cases, the broker's primary responsibility is to the purchaser rather than to the seller. In this circumstance, the purchaser can reveal confidential information to the broker and rely on the broker's expertise and competence. This may be particularly helpful in situations where a real estate transaction is complex or where there are peculiar concerns unique to certain regions of the country (termites in Houston, radon in Maine, soil conditions in California) about which a buyer wants to be adequately advised before buying real estate in that area.

In these situations, the principal (now the buyer) needs to be assured as to the scope of employment of the broker (i.e., locating the property), and, similar to a listing contract, the broker needs to be assured that he is protected and that the buyer does not "go around" the broker and cut the broker out of a commission once the property has been identified. This is a major concern for buyer's brokers. An agent may educate, then have the buyer cut out the broker in the hope of a better sales price (with a lower or no commission paid). Buyers, then, need to be committed to their agent, and building that level of trust and confidence is not easy. A good employment contract, coupled with good service, develops this trust.

exclusive authority to purchase

Listing utilized by buyer's brokers.

Figure 20.2 shows a simplified version of an **exclusive authority to purchase** contract. Note at **[1]** the parties are named. The real difference in this contract, versus the Listing

---

FIGURE 20.2   Exclusive Authority to Purchase Contract

This Agreement is made in _____ [1] _____ on this _____ day of _____ , 20 _____ , whereby _____ (hereinafter referred to as "Buyer") hereby appoints Buyer's Broker (hereinafter referred to as "Broker") as Buyer's exclusive agent for the purposes set forth in Section 2 hereof and under the terms specified herein.

Section 1. Buyer agrees to conduct all negotiations for property of the type described in Section 2 hereof through Broker, and to refer to Broker all inquiries received in any form from real estate brokers, salespersons, prospective sellers, or any other source, during the time this Agreement is in effect.

Section 2. Buyer desires to purchase or lease real property (which may include items of personal property) described as follows:

[2] Type: (__) Residential   (__) Residential Income   (__) Other
              (__) Commercial   (__) Industrial   (__) Vacant Land

(continued)

FIGURE 20.2	Exclusive Authority to Purchase Contract (continued)

General Description: _____

Approximate price range: $ _____ to $_____ , or any other amount which Buyer ultimately decides to spend.

Preferred Terms: _____

[3] Section 3. Broker's authority as Buyer's exclusive agent shall begin upon Buyer's signing this Agreement, and shall continue until _____ , 20 _____ , unless sooner terminated or by completion of the purpose(s) of the agency as set forth in Section 2 hereof.

[4] Section 4. Broker represents that Broker is duly licensed as a real estate broker, and agrees that Broker will use Broker's best efforts as Buyer's agent to locate property as described in Section 2 hereof, and to negotiate acceptance of any offer to purchase or lease such property. Broker shall submit to Buyer for the Buyer's consideration, properties appearing to Broker to substantially meet the criteria set forth in Section 2.

Section 5. In consideration of the services to be performed by Broker, Buyer agrees to pay Broker an amount equal to the greater of:

[5] (a) (__) Retainer Fee. Buyer will pay Broker a nonrefundable retainer fee of $ ___*1500*___ due and payable upon signing of this Agreement. (__) Retainer Fee shall be credited against commission, IF ANY, as set forth in Subsection 5(c) herein or Retainer Fee shall be retained by Broker in addition to commission; or

(b) (__) Hourly Fee. Buyer will pay Broker at the rate of $ ___*150 00*___ per hour for the time spent by Broker pursuant to this Agreement, to be paid to Broker when billed to Buyer. (__) Fee shall be credited against commission, IF ANY, or (__) Fee shall be considered full payment of Broker's compensation; or

(c) (__) Commission. Parties hereby agree that Broker shall first seek compensation out of the transaction. Should the fee so obtained be greater than that listed in Subsection (c) (1) or (2) below, Broker shall pay Buyer the difference at closing. Should the fee so obtained be less than that listed in Subsection (1) or (2) hereof, Buyer shall pay Broker the difference at closing.

Section 6. If a seller in an agreement made on behalf of Buyer fails to close such agreement, with no fault on the part of Buyer, the commission provided in Section 5, Subsection (c), shall be waived. If such transaction fails to close because of any fault on the part of Buyer, such commission will not be waived, but will be due and payable immediately in an amount no less than that referred to in Paragraph 6, said amount to be agreed upon by the parties to be liquidated damages. In no case shall Broker be obligated to advance funds for the benefit of Buyer in order to complete a closing.

Section 7. (__) Broker does (__) does not have Buyer's permission to disclose Buyer's identity to third parties without prior written consent of Buyer.

Section 8. Buyer understands that other potential buyers may consider, make offers on, or purchase through, Broker the same or similar properties as Buyer is seeking to acquire. Buyer consents to Broker's representation of such other potential buyers before, during, and after the expiration of this Agreement.

Section 9. The parties agree not to discriminate against any prospective seller or lessor because of the race, creed, color, sex, marital status, national origin, familial, or handicapped status of such person.

[6] Accepted:

_____   _____
(Buyer's Broker)   (Buyer)

By:

_____   _____
(Title)   (Buyer)

Agreement, occurs at [2], designating the property to be acquired in general terms, so that the broker has guidance as to what type of property to be looking for. Compensation is also different. Most buyers' brokers would anticipate being able to access commission splits through the traditional MLS system. Note at [3] that there is an expiration date for the term of the agreement; at [4], a requirement that the broker should submit suitable properties to the buyer. If, however, a seller or listing broker refuses to split a commission, there must be an alternative for compensation at [5] for that buyer's broker; and at [6], there is a signature provision for both the buyer's broker and the purchaser.

Multiple Listing Service

multiple listing service (MLS)

Organization of member brokers agreeing to share listing information and share commissions.

Multiple listing service (MLS) organizations enable a broker with a listing to make a blanket offering of subagency and/or compensation to other member brokers, thus broadening the market exposure for a given property. Member brokers are authorized to show each other's properties to their prospects. If a sale results, the commission is divided between the broker who found the buyer and the broker who obtained the listing.

MARKET EXPOSURE

A property listed with a broker who is a multiple listing service member receives the advantage of greater sales exposure, which, in turn, means a better price and a quicker sale. For the buyer it means learning about what is for sale at many offices without having to visit each office individually. For a broker or salesperson with a prospect but not a suitable property listed in that office, the opportunity to make a sale is not lost because the prospect can be shown the listings of other brokers.

To give a property the widest possible market exposure and to maintain fairness among its members, most multiple listing organizations obligate each member broker to provide information to the organization on each new listing within three to seven days after the listing is taken. To facilitate the exchange of information, multiple listing organizations have developed customized listing forms. These forms are a combination of an exclusive right to sell listing agreement (with authority to place the listing into MLS). The latest MLS systems are extremely "hi-tech." The information on the property is entered into a computer at the local broker's office. A photograph of the home is included in the data, and the listing is officially on MLS. Then, if Broker B has a prospect interested in a property listed by Broker A, Broker B telephones or e-mails Broker A and arranges to show the property. If Broker B's prospect makes an offer on the property, Broker B contacts Broker A, and together they can present the offer.

In looking for a new property on behalf of the buyer, Broker B can scan the MLS computer and sort elements to locate homes by zone area, square footage, number of bedrooms and bathrooms, price range, and any number of other input data items that the buyer may be looking for. Obviously, this eliminates combing through the old MLS books of the past. Since the MLS computer data is updated as the information is posted, the system stays current all the time.

MLS organizations have been taken to court for being open only to members of local real estate associations. Another idea that has been tested in courts is that an MLS be open to anyone who wants to list a property, broker or owner. It is generally held, though, that the MLS membership criterion is valid and important to the system's function. Owners lacking real estate sophistication would place inaccurate information in the MLS, and this would do considerable harm to MLS members who must rely on that information when describing and showing properties. It is important to note that the sharing of MLS information with nonmembers may violate federal copyright and/or trademark laws.

COMPUTERIZED MLS

A salesperson with a laptop computer can access the MLS system, and request up-to-the-minute information for any property in the computer. This is a popular system with salespeople who are constantly in the field showing property or in their cars (as they can linkup by cellular telephone or handheld computer). It is also quicker than waiting for updated printed MLS information.

LISTING BROKERS

A prospective buyer can now, via video or the Web, take a visual tour through a neighborhood without leaving the broker's office. Using computerized access to MLS files, the salesperson can show a prospect a color picture of each property for sale along with pictures of the street and neighborhood plus nearby schools and shopping facilities. Most MLS systems allow several photographs to be loaded into its data bank so that the buyer can see several pictures of the property prior to a personal inspection. There are also "virtual tours" or "visual tours" available on most MLS data systems. It is up to the listing broker whether these additional marketing tools will be utilized. Both the multiple photographs and the virtual tour system are very effective marketing devices.

The Web now dominates the market for both practitioners and individual buyers and sellers. Not only can an individual seller post on many Internet services (alternative sources are available for buyers and buyer's brokers), but the MLS is also on the Internet in all locations. In addition, real estate offices have their own Web sites (both buyer's and seller's brokers) and a few real estate companies have been developed to market solely to the Internet customer and client. Some of these companies offer fewer services, and as a result, offer lower fees, or rebates, to their principals. These two companies frequently take the position that they are providing fewer man hours for their services, so they can charge lower fees. Free enterprise and competition are wonderful things! In just a few short years, the Web and the Internet have made a huge impact on the way real estate agents handle their business.

Broker Compensation

The broker earns a commission at whatever point in the transaction the broker and owner agree upon. In nearly all listing contracts, this point occurs when the broker produces a **ready, willing, and able buyer** at a price and terms acceptable to the owner. (See [8] in Figure 20.1.) "Ready and willing" means a buyer who is ready to buy at the seller's price and terms. "Able" means financially capable of completing the transaction. An alternative arrangement is for the broker and owner to agree to a "no sale, no commission" arrangement whereby the broker is not entitled to a commission until the transaction is closed.

The difference between the two arrangements becomes important when a buyer is found at a price and terms acceptable to the owner, but no sale results. The "ready, willing, and able" contract provides more protection for the broker since the commission does not depend on the deal reaching settlement. The "no sale, no commission" approach is to the owner's advantage, for commission payment is not required unless there is a completed sale. Court decisions have tended to blur the clear-cut distinction

ready, willing, and able buyer

A buyer who is ready to buy at the seller's price and terms and who has the financial capability to do so.

between the two. For example, if the owner has a "no sale, no commission" agreement, it would appear that if the broker found a ready, willing, and able buyer at the listing price and terms and the owner refused to sell, the owner would owe no commission for there was no sale. However, a court of law would find in favor of the broker for the full amount of the commission if the refusal to sell was arbitrary and without reasonable cause or in bad faith.

In today's marketplace, buyers are usually prequalified for financial ability. Increased competition among lenders has made this process quick, inexpensive, and easy. Licensees should be careful to only pass on information, though, and not make representations about a buyer's financial ability.

BUYERS' BROKERS

Buyer's broker issues are a little more complicated. As previously stated, buyers might have an incentive to "go around" the broker to achieve a lower sales price. In addition, the buyer's brokers agreement cannot specify the property to be purchased, as it hasn't been identified yet. Most agreements provide that the buyer's broker will be compensated by the seller's broker, but should contain provisions that if the seller or seller's broker refuses to pay the buyer's agent, the buyer is obligated to pay.

Procuring Cause

A broker who possesses an employment agreement (either with the seller or the buyer) is entitled to a commission if the broker can prove that the resulting sale was primarily due to his efforts. That is, the broker has been the **procuring cause**, the one whose efforts originated procurement of the sale. Suppose the broker shows an open listed property to a prospect and, during the listing period or an extension, that prospect goes directly to the owner and concludes a deal. Even though the owner negotiated the transaction and prepared the sales contract, the broker is entitled to full commission for finding the buyer. This would also be true if the owner and the buyer used a "straw man" to purchase the property to avoid paying the commission. In general, the law protects a broker who has, in good faith, produced a buyer at the request of an owner.

When an open listing is given to two or more brokers, the first one who produces a buyer is entitled to the commission. For example, Broker 1 shows a property to Prospect B but no sale is made. Later, Prospect B goes to Broker 2 and makes an offer, which is accepted by the owner. Although two brokers have attempted to sell the property, only one has succeeded, and that one is entitled to the commission. The fact that Broker 1 receives nothing, and may have expended considerable effort, is an important reason why brokers dislike open listings.

Buyer's brokers create a more complicated issue involving procuring cause; one that has caused considerable unrest in the real estate brokerage community. At times, the prospect may visit a property one or more times and spend a great deal of the listing broker's time asking questions and getting information. Before submitting an offer, however, the prospect may request the assistance and advice of a buyer's broker in preparing a contract for presentation to the owner's agent. Who was the procuring cause? While the listing agent may feel that he was the procuring cause, the buyer is likely to support the buyer's broker's position since the seller chose to retain the services of that agent in presenting the offer. In the age of e-mail, the Internet, and highly informed consumers, there is an argument that buyers want and need representation. Once a consumer has sought and obtained a buyer's broker's advice, technically the buyer's broker may become the procuring cause when the contract is signed and presented to the listing broker.

Terminating the Employment Contract

The usual situation in an employment contract is that the broker produces a buyer acceptable to the owner. Thus, in most employment contracts the agency terminates because the objective of the employment contract has been completed. In the bulk of the transactions for which a buyer is not produced, the agency is terminated because the employment period expires. If no employment period is specified, the employment is considered to be effective for a "reasonable" length of time. A court might consider three to six months reasonable. Employment contracts without termination dates are revocable by the principal at any time, provided the purpose of the revocation is not to deprive the broker of an earned commission. A major disadvantage of employment contracts without termination dates is that, all too often, they evolve into expensive and time-consuming legal hassles.

Even when an employment contract has a specific termination date, it is still possible for the owner to tell the broker to stop working. The theory is that no one can force their services on a consumer who does not want them. However, liability for breach of the employment aspect of the contract remains, and the broker can demand compensation for effort expended on behalf of the owner to that point. This can be as much as a full commission if the listing broker has already found a ready, willing, and able buyer at the owner's price and terms. Similarly, if a buyer's broker finds the product that meets the buyer's criteria, and the buyer refuses to purchase, the broker is entitled to be compensated. In these situations, however, there is very little legal precedent for pursuing compensation through the courts.

MUTUAL AGREEMENT

An employment agreement can be terminated by mutual agreement of both the principal and broker without money damages. Because these agreements are the stock in trade of the brokerage business, brokers do not like to lose them, but sometimes this is the only logical alternative open, since the time and effort in setting and collecting damages can be very expensive. Suppose, however, that a broker has an employment agreement and suspects that the owner or buyer wants to cancel in order to avoid paying a commission. The broker can stop working, but the principal is still obligated to pay a commission if the property is sold or acquired before the employment period expires. Whatever the broker and principal decide, they should put it in writing and sign it.

ABANDONMENT

A listing can be terminated by improper performance or abandonment by the broker. Thus, if a broker acts counter to the principal's best financial interests, the employment is terminated, no commission is payable, and the broker may be subject to a lawsuit for any damages suffered by the principal. If a broker accepts an employment opportunity and then does nothing to promote it, the principal can assume that the broker abandoned it and, thereby, has grounds for revocation. The principal should keep written documentation in the event the matter ever goes to court.

The agency is automatically terminated by the death of either the principal or the broker, or if either is judged legally incompetent by virtue of insanity, and might also be terminated if the principal becomes bankrupt.

Bargain Brokers

The full-service real estate broker who takes a listing and places it in the multiple listing service, places and pays for advertising, holds open houses, qualifies prospects, shows property, obtains offers, negotiates, opens escrow, and follows through until closing is the mainstay of the real estate selling industry. The vast majority of open-market sales are handled that way. The remainder are sold by owners, some handling everything themselves and some using brokers who oversee the transaction but do not do the actual showing and selling. Some homeowners don't want these additional services. Some may think they are getting a better bargain by not utilizing extra services when they want to do some of the work themselves and save money. This proves that there is competition in the marketplace and there is no "standard" real estate commission that is paid in the industry. Commissions are always negotiable.

FLAT-FEE BROKERS

For a fee that typically ranges from $400 to $1,500, a **flat-fee broker** will list a property, suggest a market price, write advertising, assist with negotiations, draw up a sales contract, and turn the signed papers over to an escrow company for closing. The homeowner is responsible for paying for advertising, answering inquiries, setting appointments with prospects, showing the property, and applying whatever salesmanship is necessary to induce the prospect to make an offer. Under the flat-fee arrangement, also called self-help brokerage, the homeowner is effectively buying real estate services on an à la carte basis. Some brokerage firms have been very successful offering sellers a choice between à la carte and full service.

DISCOUNT BROKER

A **discount broker** is a full-service broker who charges less than the prevailing commission rates in his community. The discount broker attracts sellers by offering to do the job for less money, for example, 3% or 4% instead of 5% to 7%. Charging less means a discount broker must sell more properties to be successful. Consequently, most discount brokers are careful to take listings only on properties that will sell quickly.

VARIABLE RATE COMMISSIONS

Another variation bargain brokers have utilized is the **variable rate commission**. This commission structure retains the lower commission for the bargain broker but allows the commission to increase (i.e., to a full 3%) to the other broker in order to give other brokers an incentive to help market their properties. It still gives the seller a lower commission structure. It can create conflict, however, when a seller doesn't want to pay the increased commission and chooses to favor contracts without cooperating brokers. The buyer's broker can do a significant amount of work and be cut out at the last minute because of the seller's preference to pay a lower commission rate.

Perceived Value

Before leaving the topic of listings, it will be valuable to spend a moment on the perceived value of real estate sales services. Several studies have been conducted that show home-sellers feel the fee charged by brokers is too high in relation to time spent selling the property. Those in the real estate business know that the amount of time and effort to market a property is extensive and that often it is all for nothing if the property does not sell. However, the public does not see this, and believes that very little effort is involved, especially if the home sells at market value in two or three weeks after being shown only a handful of times. Ironically, a market value sale within a month and without the inconvenience of dozens of showings is what the seller is actually seeking. Once it is achieved, however, the fee seems too expensive for the time involved. This leads some sellers to think in terms of selling their property themselves, perhaps with the aid of a self-help brokerage service. For example, if a person is selling a $100,000 house with an $80,000 loan against it, there is but $20,000 in equity to work with. If the broker's commission is 6% of the sales price ($6,000), the seller is actually paying 30% of his equity to the broker.

What stops more people from do-it-yourself selling is that they need a broker to evaluate the property, describe current market and financing conditions, estimate the most probable selling price, write the sales contract, and handle the closing. To a considerable degree, a real estate licensee's success will come from providing the services homeowners feel they need, listing property at or near market, emphasizing the value of services rendered, and operating in a professional manner to bring about a smooth and speedy sale.

Vocabulary Review

Match terms a–i with statements 1–9.

a. Advance fee listing
b. Agent
c. Exclusive agency listing
d. Exclusive right to sell
e. Flat-fee broker
f. Multiple listing service (MLS)
g. Net listing
h. Open listing
i. Procuring cause

_H_ 1. A listing that gives a broker a nonexclusive right to find a purchaser.

_D_ 2. A listing that gives the broker the right to collect a commission no matter who sells the property during the listing period.

_C_ 3. A listing wherein the owner reserves the right to sell the property himself, but agrees to list with no other broker during the listing period.

_B_ 4. Person empowered to act by and on behalf of the principal.

_G_ 5. A listing for which the commission is the difference between the sales price and a minimum price set by the seller.

_F_ 6. An organization of real estate brokers that exists for the purpose of exchanging listing information.

_I_ 7. The broker who is the primary cause of a transaction.

_A_ 8. A listing where the broker charges for time by the hour and for out-of-pocket expenses to market a property.

_E_ 9. A broker who charges a preset brokerage fee that is collected whether the property sells or not.

Questions and Problems

1. Why do brokers strongly prefer to take exclusive right to sell listings rather than exclusive agency or open listings?

2. What does the phrase *ready, willing, and able buyer* mean in a real estate contract?

3. How are listings terminated?

4. What are the primary differences between a broker employed by a seller and a broker employed by a buyer?

Additional Readings

Coping with Broker-Dealer Regulation and Enforcement by Robert M. Romano (Practicing Law Institute, 1998).

"Multiple Listing Service, Q & A" (*Real Estate News*, January 1994, pp. 7–8). Written by the National Association of REALTORS®, this article discusses the MLS and its operation.

Real Estate Brokerage Law by Arthur Gaudio (West Publishing, updated annually). This current book is one of the most complete studies of agency law available.

Real Estate Brokerage: A Guide to Success, 1st ed. by Dan Hamilton (OnCourse Learning, 2007).

Real Estate Law, 10th ed. by Marianne M. Jennings (OnCourse Learning, 2014).

The Real Estate Pro's Internet Edgeö Broker's Edition: Maximizing Your Business on the World Wide Web by Barbara Ling (Lingstar, 1999).

"Speed of Home Sale Affected by Type of Listing, Researchers Say" by Robyn A. Friedman (*Knight-Ridder/Tribune Business News*, March 26, 2001).

CHAPTER 21

The Principal–Broker Relationship: Agency

LEARNING OBJECTIVES

After reading this chapter, you should be able to:

❮ Understand the principle concepts of agency.

❮ Define broker's obligations to principals.

❮ Define broker's obligations to third parties.

❮ Recognize a principal's obligations to real estate licensees.

❮ Understand and define "buyer brokerage," "dual agency," and "transactional brokers."

❮ Recognize the need and requirements for agency disclosures.

❮ Recognize the application of antitrust laws as it relates to real estate brokerage.

KEY TERMS

Agent • Boycotting • Commingling • Dual agency • Middleman • Ostensible authority • Price fixing • Principal • Puffing • Third parties

The previous chapter stressed the mechanics of real estate employment agreements. Let's now take a close look at the agency aspects of the principal–broker relationship—that is, the legal responsibilities of the broker toward the principal and vice versa. The concept of agency is changing dramatically and is being addressed on a state-by-state basis, so a working knowledge of any individual state license law is going to be of primary importance in determining the scope of a real estate agency. The more complex aspects of agency will then be expanded in the later part of the chapter.

Agency

An **agency** is created when one person (called the **principal**) delegates to another person (called the **agent**) the right to act on the principal's behalf. There are three levels of agency: universal, general, and specific. In a **universal agency**, the principal gives the agent legal power to transact matters of all types on the principal's behalf. An example is an unlimited power of attorney. Universal agencies are rarely encountered in practice, and courts generally frown on them because they are so broad. In a **general agency**, the agent is given the power to bind the principal in a particular trade or business. For example, a salesperson is a

principal
A person who authorizes another to act.

agent
The person empowered to act by and on behalf of the principal.

general agent of the sponsoring broker. Another example is that of a property manager for a property owner. A **special agency** empowers the agent to perform a particular act or transaction. One example is a real estate listing. Another is a power of attorney to sign a deed on behalf of someone who will be out of the country.

The principal in an agency relationship can either be a natural or a legal person such as a corporation. Likewise, an agent can either be a natural person or a corporation such as a real estate brokerage company. The persons and firms with whom the principal and agent negotiate are called **third parties**.

third parties

Persons who are not parties to a contract but who may be affected by it.

When a broker represents a seller, the buyers are third parties, often referred to as **customers**. The seller is often referred to as the **client**. When a broker represents a buyer, the sellers become the third parties, and the buyer is the client.

Sometimes you will see the phrase "principals only" in real estate advertisements. This means the owner wants to be contacted by persons who want to buy and not by real estate agents who want to list the property.

ESTABLISHING THE AGENT'S AUTHORITY

An agency relationship can be established through a contractual agreement or by acts of the parties. In a contract, the written listing agreement outlines the agent's (broker's) authority to act on behalf of the principal (owner) and the principal's obligations to the agent. This is agency by **actual authority**. A written agreement is the preferred method of creating an agency because it provides a document to evidence the existence of the agency relationship.

Agency authority may also arise from custom in the industry, common usage, and conduct of the parties involved. For example, the right of an agent to post a "For Sale" sign on the listed property may not be expressly stated in the listing. However, if it is the custom in the industry to do so, and presuming there are no deed restrictions or city ordinances to the contrary, the agent has **implied authority** (a part of the actual authority given to the agent) to post the sign. A similar situation exists with regard to showing a listed property to prospects. The seller of a home can expect to have it shown on weekends and evenings, whereas a commercial property owner may expect showings during only business hours.

Ostensible authority

An agency relationship created by the conduct of the principal.

Ostensible authority or **apparent authority** is conferred when a principal gives a third party reason to believe that another person is his agent even though that person is unaware of the appointment. If the third party accepts this as true, the principal may well be bound by the acts of his agent. For example, you give your house key to a plumber with instructions that when he has finished unstopping the waste line, he is to lock the house and give the key to your next-door neighbor. Even though you do not call and appoint your neighbor as the agent to receive the key, once the plumber gives the key to your neighbor, the neighbor becomes your agent with regard to that key. Since you told the plumber to leave the key there, he has every reason to believe that you appointed your neighbor as the agent to receive the key.

An **agency by ratification** is one established after the fact. For example, if an agent secures a contract on behalf of a principal and the principal subsequently ratifies or agrees to it, a court may hold that an agency was created at the time the initial negotiations started.

An **agency by estoppel** can result when a principal fails to maintain due diligence over her agent and the agent exercises powers not granted to him. If the principal's conduct causes a third party to believe the agent has these powers, an agency by estoppel has been created.

An **agency coupled with an interest** is said to exist when an agent holds an interest in the property he is representing. For example, a broker is a part-owner in a property he has listed for sale.

Remember, all these methods of establishing agency apply to buyers' brokers as well as to sellers' brokers. A licensee must be always vigilant to assure that agency is not created without proper contracts and/or required agency disclosures.

Broker's Obligations to the Principal

Anytime an agency is created, such as an attorney for a client, a property manager for an owner, or a broker for a principal, a **fiduciary relationship** is created. The agent (called the **fiduciary**) must be faithful to the principal, exhibit trust and honesty, and exercise good business judgment. For a real estate broker, this means the broker must faithfully perform the agency agreement, be loyal to the principal, exercise competence, and account for all funds handled in performing the agency. Due to the rapidly growing number of buyers' agents, you must keep in mind that the principal–agent relationship includes buyers' agents as well as sellers' agents. Let's look at the various requirements more closely.

FAITHFUL PERFORMANCE

Faithful performance (also referred to as **obedience**) means that the agent is to obey all legal instructions given by the principal, and to apply best efforts and diligence to carry out the objectives of the agency. For a real estate broker, this means performance as promised in the listing contract. A broker who promises to make a "reasonable effort" or apply "diligence" in finding a buyer and then does nothing to promote the listing gives the owner legal grounds for terminating the listing. Faithful performance also means not departing from the principal's instructions. If the agent does so (except in extreme emergencies not foreseen by the principal), it is at the agent's own risk. If the principal thereby suffers a loss, the agent is responsible for that loss. For example, a broker accepts a personal note from a buyer as an earnest money deposit, but fails to tell the seller that the deposit is not in cash. If the seller accepts the offer and the note is later found to be worthless, the broker is liable for the amount of the note.

Another aspect of faithful performance is that the agent must personally perform the tasks delegated to him. This protects the principal, who has selected an agent on the basis of trust and confidence, from finding that the agent has delegated that responsibility to another person. However, a major question arises on this point in real estate brokerage, as a large part of the success in finding a buyer for a property results from the cooperative efforts of other brokers and their salespeople. Therefore, listing agreements usually include a statement that the listing broker is authorized to secure the cooperation of other brokers and pay them part of the commission from the sale.

A genuine concern arises over how much information a real estate broker is free to disclose to other brokers or other industry members who rely on this information in determining statistical data, market values, and other pertinent real estate related information. For instance, can a real estate agent maintain a confidential relationship with a principal, yet disclose pertinent details of sales prices and financial terms related to the principal's business? Most state license laws specifically relieve a broker from liability for providing information about real property sales prices or terms for the purposes of facilitating the listing, selling, leasing, financing, or appraising of real property unless this disclosure is specifically prohibited by a state statute or written agreement. Any licensee would be well advised to make this provision to the principals so that the principal can make an informed decision of whether to disclose certain information.

LOYALTY TO THE PRINCIPAL

Once an agency is created, the agent must be loyal to the principal. The law is clear in all states that in an employment agreement, the broker (and the broker's sales staff) occupy a position of trust, confidence, and responsibility. As such, the broker is legally bound to keep the principal fully informed of all matters that might affect the sale of the listed property, and to promote and protect the principal's interests.

Unfortunately, greed and expediency sometimes get in the way. As a result, numerous laws have been enacted for the purpose of protecting the principal and threatening the agent with court action for misplaced loyalty. For example, an out-of-town landowner who is not fully up-to-date on the value of his land visits a local broker and wants to list it for $230,000. The broker is much more knowledgeable of local land prices and is aware of a recent city council decision to extend roads and utilities to the area of this property. As a result, the broker knows the land is now worth $300,000. The broker remains silent on the matter, and the property is listed for sale at $230,000. At this price, the broker can find a buyer before the day is over and have a commission on the sale. However, the opportunity for a quick $70,000 is too tempting to let pass. He buys the property (or to cover up, buys in the name of his wife or a friend) and shortly thereafter resells it for $300,000. Whether he sold the property to a buyer for $230,000 or bought it and resold it for $300,000, the broker did not exhibit loyalty to the principal. Laws and penalties for breach of loyalty are stiff: The broker can be sued for recovery of the price difference and the commission paid, his real estate license can be suspended or revoked, and he may be required to pay additional fines and money damages pursuant to various consumer protection statutes.

If a licensee intends to purchase a property listed for sale by his agency or through a cooperating broker, he is under both a moral and a legal obligation to make certain that the price paid is the fair market value and that the seller knows who the buyer is and that the buyer is a licensee.

PROTECTING THE PRINCIPAL'S INTEREST

Loyalty to the principal also means that when seeking a buyer or negotiating a sale, the broker must continue to protect the owner's financial interests. Suppose that an owner lists her home at $182,000 but confides in the broker, "If I cannot get $182,000, anything over $179,000 will be fine." The broker shows the home to a prospect who says, "$182,000 is too much. What will the owner really take?" or "Will she take $179,000?" Loyalty to the principal requires the broker to say that the owner will take $182,000— that is, the price in the listing agreement. If the buyer balks, the broker can suggest that the buyer submit an offer for the seller's consideration. State laws require that all offers be submitted to the owner, no matter what the offering price and terms. This prevents the agent from rejecting an offer that the owner might have accepted if she had known about it. If the seller really intends for the broker to quote $179,000 as an acceptable price, the listing price should be changed; then the broker can say, "The property was previously listed for $182,000, but is now priced at $179,000."

Similarly, if a broker represents a buyer who is willing to pay $182,000, and that would be the highest price paid in the market, the buyer's agent should inform the buyer of that fact.

A broker's loyalty to his principal includes keeping the principal informed of changes in market conditions during the listing period. If, after a listing is taken, an adjacent landowner is successful in rezoning his land to a higher use and the listed property becomes more valuable, the broker's responsibility is to inform the seller. Similarly, if a buyer is looking at a property priced at $130,000 and tells the listing broker, "I'll offer $127,000 and come up if need be," it is the duty of the broker to report this to the owner. The owner can then decide if she wants to accept the $127,000 offer or try for more. A broker who does not keep the principal fully informed is not properly fulfilling the duties of an agent.

REASONABLE CARE

The duty of **reasonable care** implies competence and expertise on the part of the broker. It is the broker's responsibility to disclose all knowledge and material facts concerning a property to his principal. Also, the broker must not become a party to any fraud or misrepresentation likely to affect the sound judgment of the principal.

Although the broker has a duty to disclose all material facts of a transaction, legal interpretations must be avoided. Giving legal interpretations of documents involved in a transaction can be construed as practicing law without a license, an act specifically prohibited by real estate licensing acts. Moreover, brokers can be held financially responsible for any wrong legal information they give to clients.

The duty of reasonable care also requires an agent to take proper care of property entrusted to him by a principal. For example, if a broker is entrusted with a key to an owner's building to show it to prospects, it is the broker's responsibility to see that it is used for only that purpose and that the building is locked upon leaving. Similarly, if a broker receives a check as an earnest money deposit, he must properly deposit it in a bank and not carry it around for several weeks.

ACCOUNTING FOR FUNDS RECEIVED

The earnest money that accompanies an offer on a property does not belong to the broker, even though the broker's name is on the check. For the purpose of holding clients' and customers' money, laws in nearly all states require a broker to maintain a **trust account**. All monies received by a broker as agent for a principal are to be promptly deposited in this account or in the trust account of the attorney, escrow, or title company handling the transaction. Most states require that a trust account be a demand deposit (checking account) at a bank or a trust account at a trust company. Some states allow brokers to deposit trust funds in bank accounts that earn interest. The broker's trust account must be separate from his personal bank account, and the broker is required by law to accurately account for all funds received into and paid out of the trust account. As a rule, a broker will have one trust account for properties listed for sale and another trust account for rental properties managed by the broker. State-conducted surprise audits are made on brokers' trust accounts to ensure compliance with the law. Failure to comply with trust fund requirements can result in the loss of one's real estate license.

COMMINGLING

If a broker places money belonging to a client or customer in a personal account, it is called **commingling** and is grounds for suspension or revocation of the broker's real estate license. The reason for such severe action is that from commingling, it is a very short step to **conversion**—that is, the agent's personal use of money belonging to others.

commingling
The mixing of clients' or customers' funds with an agent's personal funds.

Also, clients' and customers' money placed in a personal bank account can be attached by a court of law to pay personal claims against the broker.

If a broker receives a check as an earnest money deposit, along with instructions from the buyer that it remain uncashed, the broker may comply with the buyer's request as long as the seller is informed of this fact when the offer is presented. (Some state regulations may prohibit this—check your state's guidelines.) The earnest money can take any form. The broker can accept a promissory note if the seller is informed. The objective is to disclose all material facts to the seller that might influence the decision to accept or reject the offer. The fact that the deposit accompanying the offer is not cash is a material fact. If the broker withholds this information, there is a violation of agency.

Broker's Obligations to Third Parties

A broker's fiduciary obligations are to the principal who has employed the broker. State laws nonetheless make certain demands on the broker in relation to the third parties the broker deals with on behalf of the principal. Foremost among these are honesty, integrity, and fair business dealing. This includes the proper care of deposit money and offers, as well as responsibility for written or verbal statements. Misrepresenting a property by omitting vital information is as wrong as giving false information. Disclosure of such misconduct usually results in a broker losing the right to a commission. Also possible are loss of the broker's real estate license and a lawsuit by any party to the transaction who suffered a financial loss because of the misrepresentation.

In guarding against misrepresentation, a broker must be careful not to make statements not known to be true. For example, a prospect looks at a house listed for sale and asks if it is connected to the city sewer system. The broker does not know the answer, but sensing it is important to making a sale, says yes. If the prospect relies on this statement, purchases the house, and finds out that there is no sewer connection, the broker may be at the center of litigation regarding sale cancellation, commission loss, money damages, and state license discipline. The answer should be, "I don't know, but I will find out for you," then do it!

Suppose the seller has told the broker that the house is connected to the city sewer system, and the broker, having no reason to doubt the statement, accepts it in good faith and gives that information to prospective buyers. If this statement is not true, the owner is at fault, owes the broker a commission, and both the owner *and* the broker may be subject to legal action for sale cancellation and money damages. When a broker must rely on information supplied by the seller, it is best to have it in writing and verify its accuracy. However, relying on the seller for information does not completely relieve the broker's responsibility to third parties. If a seller says his house is connected to the city sewer system and the broker knows that is impossible because there is no sewer line on that street, the broker should make an effort to correct the erroneous statement.

Most people have a good sense of what constitutes intentional fraud and vigorously avoid it. Not quite so obvious, and yet equally dangerous from the standpoint of dissatisfaction and legal liability, is the area of ignorance. Ignorance results from not knowing all the pertinent facts about a property. This may result from the broker not taking time to check the facts or from not knowing what to look for in the first place. The theory is called "what the agent should have known," and there has been some far-reaching litigation that is forcing real estate brokers and their salespeople to know more about the product they are selling. In addition to the traditional common law theory of disclosures to third parties, there is now at least one additional obligation imposed by the federal government involving lead-based paint.

LEAD-BASED PAINT

The United States Department of Housing and Urban Development (HUD) requires FHA buyers to be notified and advised about the possibility of lead-based paint in homes built prior to the 1978 ban on such paint. The two-page notice must be given to the buyers and signed before the execution of the sales contract, which would seem to make it the duty of the real estate salesperson. HUD will not permit FHA financing without a signed form delivered to the lender. If a loan is to be refinanced on a home built before 1978, the notice must be signed before the refinancing is finalized, even if the refinancing is conventional and not HUD/FHA insured.

RED FLAGS

For the real estate agent, this means a careful inspection of the property must be performed to determine obvious defects or red flags. A **red flag** is something that would warn a reasonably observant agent that there may be an underlying problem. The agent is then responsible for disclosing this to the seller and any prospective buyers. The agent is not responsible for knowing the underlying problem that produces the red flag. It is strongly suggested that a broker recommend to the seller and/or buyer that a specialist be hired to determine whether there is an underlying problem causing the red flag. The careful agent will also want to inspect such things as kitchen appliances, water heater, water supply, swimming pool, sewer hookup, heating and air-conditioning systems, electrical capacity, plumbing, roof, walls, ceiling, fireplace, foundation, garage, fences, sidewalks, sprinklers, and so on. The broker may also want to have the seller purchase a home warranty for the buyer as a means of reducing legal liability for all involved. What we see in the courts today is that the legal system is pushing the real estate industry further toward professionalism. When instructing the jury in one case the judge said, "A real estate broker is a licensed person or entity who holds himself out to the public as having particular skills and knowledge in the real estate field." In the future, you may expect to see more court cases on this issue as well as legislation that defines the standard of care owed by a broker to a prospective purchaser.

[handwritten margin note: Start a warranty company]

"AS IS"

After reading broker liability cases, you may begin to think that selling a property "as is" is a safe way to avoid the liability to disclose. This is not necessarily so. In another case that found its way to the courts, a property had been condemned by local government authorities for building code violations. The broker listed and sold it, making it very clear and in writing to the buyer that the property was being sold "as is." Although "as is" means the seller is not going to make repairs, courts here found this statement did not excuse the broker from failing to disclose material information.

In general terms, an agreed "as is" provision can shift a burden from the seller to the buyer, provided that the buyer is given ample opportunity to inspect the premises and agrees to assume the liability as part of his contractual agreement. Most of these "as is" provisions, however, will not protect the seller if the seller has engaged in fraud, misrepresentation, or similar deception.

PUFFING

Puffing refers to nonfactual or extravagant statements that a reasonable person would recognize as exaggeration. Thus, a buyer may have no legal complaint against a broker who told him that a certain hillside lot had the most beautiful view in the world or that a listed property had the finest landscaping in the county. Usually a reasonable buyer can

puffing
Statements a reasonable person would recognize as nonfactual or extravagant.

see these things and make up his own mind. However, if a broker, in showing a rural property, says it has the world's purest well water, there had better be plenty of good water when the buyer moves in. If a consumer believes the broker and relies on the representation, the broker may have a potential liability. The line between puffing and misrepresentation is subjective. It is best to simply avoid puffing.

Buyer Agency

It has long been recognized that a real estate agent can represent the purchaser. Buyer's brokerage is a common topic in real estate seminars and it is often touted as the solution to the dual agency/intermediary conflict of interest (discussed next). It gives the buyer representation, which some people feel the buyer is entitled to, or needs, in any circumstance. Buyer brokerage may even ease the duty of a listing broker because some duties to the buyer may be performed by the buyer's broker. In cases of office building leasing and more sophisticated commercial property acquisitions, parties frequently seek the assistance of a real estate broker to represent them in making prudent purchases when they lack the expertise to do their own investigations. This has now become more common in residential real estate.

Buyer representation shifts the entire agency theory in the opposite direction of traditional seller representation. When representing a seller, a real estate agent (and the resulting fiduciary duty) focuses on the marketing of the project for the benefit of the owner. This involves "getting the highest price in the marketplace," maintaining the confidentiality of information, and trying to effect a sale within the shortest period of time for the benefit of the seller. Traditional multiple listing service (MLS) subagency focuses on the same concept for cooperating brokers. Historically, the MLS system and most state laws on agency encourage agents to be trained as seller's brokers or cooperating brokers, so few agents had training as a buyer's broker. Today, however, buyer's brokerage courses are available in virtually every real estate market. The courses are well attended, reflecting a need for this type of expanded education. Let's talk about buyers' brokers in more detail.

FOCUS

The buyer's broker has a different focus. The emphasis in buyer's brokerage is to help the buyer make informed decisions and obtain the desired product at a fair price, giving the buyer's interests the highest priority. This emphasis would apparently include getting the lowest price in the marketplace, or at least a "good deal" for the buyer, to facilitate resale or investment potential (a main reason why relocation companies use buyer's brokers), and finding a "safe" purchase of a product without latent defects. There is also a shift of focus away from effecting the sale of the property, because the buyer's broker is more concerned with a satisfactory purchase of the buyer, and not just making a sale. Simply searching the MLS may not be enough. Buyer's brokers should also search newspaper advertisements, Web sites, and other information sources for potential sellers.

DUTIES

What are the duties of a buyer's broker? There is little law to guide us at this point. It is presumed that the same care of agency duties that apply to sellers as principals also apply to buyers as principals. However, the situations differ. The buyer may request assistance in finding out certain information, or the buyer may need help in pursuing certain issues (homeowners' associations, deed restrictions, financing, and final walk-through) in which the buyer's agent may take on additional duties (remember, the buyer's agent isn't trying to market the property, but is trying to obtain the desired product). If this is the case, most state license acts impose a duty of diligence and competency in undertaking those additional duties. Most buyers who hire a buyer's broker want advice, or they wouldn't hire them.

This situation may create a conflict between the seller's and buyer's brokers. The result may end up being the same (the sale is made), but the means to achieve the sale may vary from the "typical" transaction in the past. The buyer's broker is expected to be more protective of the buyer (the primary focus) than focused on effecting the sale (the focus of the listing broker). Buyer brokerage is gaining wide acceptance. A growing niche in the agency marketplace has been created by consumers moving into a new area and by relocation companies that may want to utilize the services of a buyer's broker. Brokers may perceive buyer representation and/or cooperation with buyer's brokers as both beneficial and cost-effective given that a homebuyer may be a home seller in a few years.

Principal's Obligations

The principal also has certain obligations to the agent. Although these do not receive much statutory attention in most states, they are important when the principal fails to live up to those obligations. The principal's primary obligation is **compensation**. Additionally, the agent is eligible for **reimbursement** for expenses not related to the sale itself. For example, if an agent had to pay a plumber to fix a broken pipe for the owner, the agent could expect reimbursement from the owner over and above the sales commission.

The other two obligations of the principal are indemnification and performance. An agent is entitled to **indemnification** upon suffering a loss through no fault of his own, such as when a misrepresentation by the principal to the agent was passed on in good faith to the buyer. The duty of **performance** means the principal is expected to do whatever he reasonably can to accomplish the purpose of the agency, such as referring inquiries by prospective buyers to the broker.

Broker's Sales Staff

A broker's sales associates are general agents of the broker. A sales associate owes the broker the duties of competence, obedience, accounting, loyalty, and full disclosure. The broker's obligations to the sales associate are compensation, reimbursement, indemnification, and performance. In addition, the broker will authorize the extent to which the sales associate can bind the broker. For example, is the sales associate's signature by itself sufficient to bind the broker to a listing, or must the broker also sign it? With regard to third parties, the sales associate owes them honesty, integrity, and fair business dealings. Because a sales associate is an agent of the broker and the broker is an agent of the principal, the sales associate is called a **subagent** of the principal.

Cooperating Broker

The fiduciary obligation of the cooperating broker is one of the most difficult legal problems of real estate brokerage. In approximately 70% of all sales made through multiple listing services, the broker who locates the buyer is not the same broker that listed the property. This results in a dilemma: Is the broker who located the buyer (the **cooperating broker**) an agent of the buyer or the seller?

The traditional view (Theory 1) is that everyone is an agent (or subagent) of the seller because the seller has an employment contract with the listing broker and the cooperating broker has his rights through that employment contract. Theory 2 is that, since the cooperating broker has no contract with the seller (only an agreement to share with the listing broker) and none with the buyer, he is the agent of neither.

THE COMPLICATING ISSUES

You will recall that the real estate broker has a fiduciary duty to the seller in the traditional listing relationship. Part of that duty is that he must make full disclosure of every item he knows concerning the real estate and his agency relationship. What then is an agent to do if a buyer gives him confidential information? If the agent attempts to be a dual agent, can he represent both parties and disclose all information to both without violating confidential relationships? In many cases, it is not what the agent intends, but what the consumer perceives as the agent's duty of care. That is, does the buyer think that the cooperating broker represents him?

A Federal Trade Commission study found that 71% of buyers surveyed believe this to be the case. And buyers come to believe this because it is the cooperating broker who is spending time with them *and* is taking them to see properties *and* will write and present the offer *and*, if needed, will come back with a counteroffer. Moreover, the cooperating broker hopes to make a good enough impression that a sale will be made and the buyer in the future will return to that broker for more real estate dealings.

middleman

A person who brings two or more parties together but does not represent either party.

MIDDLEMAN PRINCIPLE. Under this legal theory, the broker operates as a middleman who represents neither party. He simply brings the parties together and neither party expects the middleman's loyalty. This **middleman** principle can work in some sophisticated real estate transactions. The problem with this theory is that if either party thinks that the broker represents him, an agency relationship could be created and fiduciary duties established, resulting in potential liability for the broker. It is very difficult, in most situations, to represent neither party, yet still be an effective agent.

Many states are now dealing with the concept of an **intermediary**, **transactional broker**, **designated broker**, or a **facilitator**, who is, in effect, a statutorily created middleman. These state laws are attempting to exempt brokers from liability. In some states (21 to date), the statute specifically recites that a broker is not the agent of either party (but can give advice!?), supercedes the common law of agency, and attempts to redefine the agent's obligations to the principal. While a number of states have enacted this type of legislation, these statutes are new, and the courts have not had the time to interpret them. One may wonder, however, that if a principal (seller or buyer) wants to hire an agent for expertise and advise, wouldn't they want an agent to represent their interests? If the agent does not provide the expertise, advice, or a fiduciary relationship with one of the parties, should their commission be lowered? It is safe to say that this is a developing area of agency law.

dual agency

Representation of two or more principals in a transaction by the same agent.

DUAL AGENCY. If a broker represents a seller, it is the broker's duty to obtain the highest price and the best terms possible for the seller. If a broker represents a buyer, the broker's duty is to obtain the lowest price and best terms for the buyer. When the same broker represents two or more principals in the same transaction, it is a **dual**, or divided, **agency** and a conflict of interest results. If the broker represents both principals in the same transaction, to whom is the broker loyal? Does he work equally hard for each principal? This is an unanswerable question; therefore, the law requires that each principal be told not to expect the broker's full allegiance, and thus each principal is responsible for looking after his own interest. If a broker represents more than one principal and does not obtain their informed consent, the broker cannot claim a commission and the defrauded principal(s) may be able to rescind the transaction. Moreover, the broker's real estate license may be suspended or revoked. This is true even though the broker does his best to be equally fair to each principal.

A dual agency also develops when a buyer agrees to pay a broker a fee for finding a property and the broker finds one, lists it, and earns a fee from the seller as well as the buyer. Again, both the buyer and the seller must be informed of the dual agency in advance of negotiations. If either principal does not approve of the dual agency, they can refuse to participate.

IS NONAGENCY THE ANSWER?

You may recall from Chapter 19, the theory here is that the departments of real estate and real estate commissions' purpose is to protect the public from unscrupulous licensees. Some states have established a statutory "nonagency" where the state's real estate license act does not presume agency in real estate transactions. Alabama, Colorado, Connecticut, Florida, Georgia, Idaho, Illinois, Kansas, Kentucky, Maine, Massachusetts, Michigan, Missouri, New Hampshire, New Jersey, New Mexico, Oklahoma, South Dakota, Tennessee, Utah, West Virginia, and Wyoming, provide for nonagency positions in the owner-broker relationship. But several of these states do provide for an agency relationship should they be chosen by the parties. There have been very few cases on these issues.

In one case, an owner agreed to pay a real estate brokerage firm a commission if the broker "procured a purchaser for [defendant's] property... which results in the sale of the property." The parties agree that the broker would be a "transaction-broker," as defined by state law. When the broker procured a buyer for the property, the owner refused to pay the commission, alleging that deficiencies in the broker's performance warranted forfeiture of the commission. The trial court found in favor of the broker and awarded the commission.

The appeal centered on the statutory duties imposed on transaction brokers as defined by state law, but it has wide implications on whether similar legislation has been enacted by other states. The court noted that the statute was a significant departure from the traditional common law view of agency relationships in real estate transactions and that the States License Act recognized a nonagent real estate professional (the transaction broker). The court noted that the transaction broker is not an agent for either party "absent a written agency agreement or a subagency relationship." The court noted that while a real estate broker acting as agent owes a fiduciary duty to his or her principal, a transaction broker is not in a fiduciary relationship with either party to a real estate transaction. Under Colorado law, the duties of a transaction broker include (1) presenting offers and counteroffers in a timely manner, (2) advising the parties and keeping them informed, (3) accounting for money and property received, (4) assisting the parties in complying with contractual terms and conditions, and (5) disclosing certain information. In what may be a key issue, the court noted that the State Real Estate License Act does not prescribe a remedy for nonperformance of these obligations. Therefore, even it was violated and the duties were not performed. Forfeiture of the commission was not a remedy for nonperformance based on the fact that the agent was not a fiduciary. The court further noted, however, that the defendant would have a remedy for any out-of-pocket expenses accrued as a result of the broker's inaction, but found that the seller never asserted such a claim.

This case may support the theory that a transaction broker can be legally upheld, but it creates confusion over what happens if the broker breaches his or her "duty" as outlined in the State's License Act. If a real estate license act does not regulate the industry for violations of statutory duties, what is it regulating?

Agency Disclosure

One can easily see that the problem of agency representation, particularly with the complication of the cooperating broker, can be a difficult subject. Agency relationships can be created without written agreements (ostensible authority), consumers can misunderstand the broker's role in a transaction, and there are very few rules under the traditional laws of agency that give the agent or the consumer an easy understanding of how the agency relationships work in the real world.

The simplest solution to this complicated problem is education, both for the real estate licensees and for the consumers. In many cases, the brokers do not really understand which party they represent. For instance, if a broker's best friend requests some help in acquiring property and wants to buy one of the broker's listings, it is easy to see the problem of divided loyalty a broker can encounter. The buyer, on the other hand, has requested the broker's help, and, as previously discussed, often thinks the broker represents him in these situations. The solutions have been developed through the National Association of REALTORS®, the Association of Real Estate License Law Officials, and various state real estate commissions. That solution is merely disclosure to the extent that all parties to the transaction understand who the real estate licensee represents. Many states now have required disclosure forms that every licensee is required to use. A sample of a simplified version of these forms is shown in Figure 21.1. This form discloses to the buyer that the broker represents the seller in all transactions unless the buyer chooses to hire that broker to represent him. One should also note that the disclosure must be made very early in the transaction, usually at the point of first significant contact with the buyer(i.e., obtaining specific information from the buyer as to her financial capacity, the property she wants to purchase, or regarding other information that may be deemed to be confidential).

Another situation develops when the buyer decides that he wants the broker to represent him. Many states now provide that if you are going to be a buyer's broker, you must give a similar disclosure to the seller early in the transaction. A simplified version of this form is shown in Figure 21.2 on page 412. Most state regulations provide that this form be given to the seller before submitting any written offers or prior to any personal contact with the seller. In both of these situations, the purpose is to inform the opposing principal not to confide in the other party's agent.

Perhaps the most difficult problem is when you represent the buyer and the buyer requests that you, as buyer's agent, submit an offer on one of your own listings. This clearly establishes a dual agency, where the licensee represents the buyer and also represents the seller. There is simply no way you can disclose to both parties all the confidences that a broker knows without breaching your fiduciary duty. Six states have outlawed dual agency, and this theory is still difficult to deal with in everyday practice. A licensee is better advised to disclose any conflict of interest to both parties or to offer to withdraw from the transaction if either party complains of the conflict.

There are two key factors in this disclosure of dual agency. The first is that it is the principal's decision to make, not the broker's. It is the principal who stands to lose on a breach of confidential information and has the most at risk. The second key factor in the disclosure is that the principals must understand how serious the conflict of interest is. Most states allow dual agency when written consent by all parties has been obtained.

FIGURE
21.1

Agency Disclosure to Buyer

INFORMATION FOR A PROSPECTIVE REAL ESTATE BUYER OR TENANT

When working with a real estate broker in buying or leasing real estate, Texas law requires that you be informed of whom the broker is representing in the transaction.

As a prospective buyer or tenant, you should know that:

- Both the broker who lists property for sale or lease (the listing broker) and the broker who deals with a buyer or tenant (the "co-broker" or "selling" broker) are usually paid by the owner and are the owner's agents.

- Their duties, loyalties, and faithfulness are owed to the owner, and they must inform the owner of all important information they know which might affect the owner's decision concerning the sale or lease of the property.

- While neither broker is your agent, the brokers can provide you with information about available properties and sources of financing and aid you in analyzing and comparing the physical and economic features of different properties, as well as showing you the properties and assisting you in making an offer to purchase or lease.

Both brokers are obligated by law to treat you honestly and fairly. They must:

- Present all written offers to the owner promptly.

- Disclose material facts about the property known to the broker.

- Offer the property without regard to race, creed, sex, religion, or national origin.

If you choose to have a real estate broker represent you as your agent, you should enter into a written contract that:

- Clearly establishes the obligations of both parties; and,

- Sets out how your agent will be paid and by whom.

If you have any questions regarding the roles and responsibilties of real estate brokers, please ask.

I certify that I have provided _____ the Prospective Buyer or Tenant with a copy of this information.

_____
Broker or Sales Associate

_____
Date

I have received, read, and understand this information.

_____
Prospective Buyer/Tenant or its representative

_____
Prospective Buyer/Tenant or its representative

FIGURE
21.2   Agency Disclosure to Seller

INFORMATION FOR A PROSPECTIVE REAL ESTATE SELLER OR LANDLORD

When working with a real estate broker in selling or leasing real estate, Texas law requires that you be informed of whom the broker is representing in the transaction.

As a prospective seller or landlord, you should know that:

- Broker is the agent of buyer or tenant.

- The duties, loyalties, and faithfulness of a broker representing a buyer or tenant are owed to the buyer or tenant, and he must inform the buyer or tenant of all important information he knows which might affect the buyer or tenant's decision concerning the purchase or lease of the property.

Brokers are obligated by law to treat you honestly and fairly. They must:

- Present all written offers to the owner promptly.

- Disclose to the buyer or tenant material facts about the property known to the broker.

- Present or show property without regard to race, creed, sex, religion, or national origin.

If you currently do not have a real estate broker representing you, and want to have one, you should enter into a written contract that:

- Clearly establishes the obligations of both parties; and,

- Sets out how your agent will be paid and by whom.

If you have any questions regarding the roles and responsibilities of real estate brokers, please ask.

I certify that I have provided

the Prospective Seller or Landlord or its representative with a copy of this information.

_____
Brokerage Company Name

_____
Broker or Sales Associate

_____
Date

I have received, read, and understand this information.

_____
Prospective Seller/Landlord or its representative

_____
Prospective Seller/Landlord or its representative

The more important emphasis is **informed consent**. An agent should make sure that the principals understand the ramifications of the dual agency. A broker who says "here is a disclosure you have to sign—it's a required standard form" may not be making an effective disclosure. The broker must be sure that the parties understand who that broker represents and the nature of that confidential relationship. This should eliminate misplaced confidences.

Seller Disclosure Statement

Seller disclosure statements are a detailed disclosure of property defects (or lack thereof) on a form often produced by a real estate trade association. As a general rule, the seller needs to fill out the forms, which are then presented to the buyer as a representation of the seller's statement of condition of the property. The seller is the most likely person to fill out the disclosure because the seller simply knows more about the property than anybody else. A few states have mandated seller disclosure statements. They have had excellent results and very few consumer complaints. More than two-thirds of the states now require owner disclosures about property defects and health hazards. The risks of using the form are nominal, and the benefits are great.

In the last 10 years, there has been extensive litigation on the sales of real property based on misrepresentations and material omissions. When the buyer sues, the broker is often a defendant because the seller is gone and the broker marketed the property. This creates an unfair burden on a broker who may have neither knowledge of the defect nor the expertise to investigate the potential for defects.

For the seller's benefit, the seller disclosure form gives the opportunity for the seller to reinvestigate the house. Very few of us have perfect homes. Many sellers simply overlook the defects (we all learn to live with them or forget about them, particularly when it's our house). This failure to disclose, however, results in misrepresentation on the part of seller (not the broker), either because of negligence, or perhaps because he innocently overlooked it. In the worst-case scenario, he may intentionally misrepresent, or intentionally fail to mention, a defect in order to induce the buyer to purchase. In all circumstances, the seller's disclosure form yields these benefits: (1) the seller (not the broker) informs the buyer as to which defects exist, (2) it provides a basis from which the buyer can conduct further investigation on the property, (3) it allows the buyer to make an informed decision as to whether to purchase, and (4) it may provide a more concrete basis for litigation if the buyer can determine that the seller filled out the disclosure statement incorrectly or failed to disclose a defect that the seller knew was material.

Similarly, brokers can find the disclosure statement beneficial because they now have written proof as to what disclosures were made (which should be compared with their listing agreement and the MLS disclosures) to assure consistency in marketing their product. In addition, knowing that there is a defect allows the broker to effectively market the property "as is," disclosing the defects and therefore limiting liability for both the seller (they sometimes overlook potential liability in their eagerness to sell) and the broker.

Interstate Land Sales Disclosure Statements

The federal government, through the Department of HUD, has enacted legislation aimed at protecting purchasers of property in new subdivisions from misrepresentation, fraud, and deceit. The HUD requirements, administered by the Office of Interstate Land Sales Registration, apply primarily to subdivision lots located in one state and sold to residents of another state. The purpose of this law, which took effect in 1969 and was amended in 1979, is to require that developers give prospective purchasers extensive disclosures regarding the lots in the form of a **property report**.

The requirement that a property report be prepared according to HUD specifications was the response of Congress to the concern that all too often buyers were receiving inaccurate or inadequate information. A color brochure might be handed to prospects picturing an artificial lake and boat marina within the subdivision, yet the developer has not obtained the necessary permits to build either and may never do so. Or, a developer implies that the lots being offered for sale are ready for building, when in fact there is no sewer system and the soil cannot handle septic tanks. Or prospects are not told that many roads in the subdivision will not be built for several years, and when they are, lot owners will face a hefty paving assessment followed by annual maintenance fees because the county has no intention of maintaining them as public roads.

PROPERTY REPORT

In addition to addressing these issues, the property report also discloses payment terms, what happens if there is a default, any soil problems, distance to school and stores, any additional costs to expect, availability of utilities, restrictive covenants, oil and mineral rights, and so on. The property report must be given to each purchaser before a contract to purchase is signed. Failure to do so gives the purchaser the right to cancel any contract or agreement.

NOT AN APPROVAL

The property report is *not* a government approval of the subdivision. It is strictly a disclosure of pertinent facts that the prospective purchaser is strongly encouraged to read before buying. A number of states also have enacted their own disclosure laws. Typically, these apply to developers of housing subdivisions, condominiums, cooperatives, and vacant lots. In these reports, the developer is required to make a number of pertinent disclosures about the lot, structure, owners' association, neighborhood, financing terms, and so on, and this must be given to the prospective purchaser before a purchase contract can be signed. Once signed, HUD and most states allow the buyer a "cooling-off" period of from three to seven days during which the buyer can cancel the contract and receive all his money back. Like the HUD property report, a state-required property report does not mean the state has approved or disapproved the subdivision. The property report is strictly a disclosure statement designed to help the prospective purchaser make an informed decision about buying.

Antitrust Laws

Federal antitrust laws, particularly the Sherman Antitrust Act, have had a major impact on the real estate brokerage industry. The purpose of federal antitrust laws is to promote competition in an open marketplace. To some people not familiar with the real estate business, it could appear that all real estate brokers charge the same fee (i.e., 6%). In fact and in practice, nothing is further from the truth. Real estate brokers establish their fees from a complex integration of market factors, and all real estate brokerage fees are a result of a negotiated agreement between the owner and the broker. In tougher markets, a broker may charge a much higher fee (10% to 12% of the gross sales price). Very expensive property, in a good market, may be listed by a broker for an amount that is substantially less (2% to 5% of the gross sales price).

PRICE FIXING

Price fixing in any industry is so grossly anticompetitive and contrary to the free enterprise form of government that it is construed to be *per se illegal*. This means that the conduct of price fixing is, in itself, so illegal that no series of mitigating circumstances can correct it. While a brokerage company can establish a policy on fees, they should be acutely aware that any hint, or any perceived hint, of price fixing between brokers can result in both civil and criminal penalties. That is, if the court determines that a broker has engaged in price fixing with another broker or group of brokers, the licensee could serve time in the federal penitentiary in addition to paying a substantial fine. Consequently, brokers are well advised *never* to discuss their fees, under *any* circumstances, except with the owner of the property.

price fixing
Two or more people conspiring to charge a fixed fee, having an anticompetitive effect.

BOYCOTTING

Another aspect of antitrust laws that has affected brokers has been **boycotting** of other brokers in the marketplace. This, too, is a violation of the Sherman Antitrust Act. In some circumstances, realtor trade associations have established rules for membership that have resulted in some brokers being unfairly excluded (unreasonably high fees, part-time employment, "discount" brokers, etc.). Standards for membership are usually an attempt to upgrade the professionalism of the industry and maintain high standards. The difficulty that is encountered, however, is that high-quality real estate brokers are excluded from competing with members of broker trade associations, and this results in an unfair market advantage. However, antitrust cases involving boycotting have tended to recognize the procompetitive efforts of Associations of REALTORS®, MLS systems, and other similar trade associations. Therefore, Associations of REALTORS® and other trade associations can establish reasonable fees, residency requirements, and other pertinent requirements for membership. However, no membership requirements can be established that may arbitrarily exclude licensed real estate brokers from participation.

boycotting
Two or more people conspiring to restrain competition.

Most boards or Associations of REALTORS® have opened up their membership to eliminate arbitrary exclusion of licensees from other boards who may wish to access pertinent information. This area of law is constantly changing as REALTORS® are concerned about protecting their rights, but also want to accommodate the needs of consumers. Real estate is still a service business!

Errors and Omission Insurance

Because of the trend in recent years to a more consumer-oriented and more litigious society, the possibility of a broker being sued has risen to the point that **errors and omission insurance (E&O)** has become very popular. The broker pays an annual fee to an insurance company that, in turn, will defend the broker and pay legal costs and judgments. E&O, as it is sometimes called, does not cover intentional acts of a broker to deceive, punitive damages, and negligence or misrepresentation when buying or selling for one's own account. Other than that, E&O offers quite a broad coverage. This includes defending so-called nuisance cases in which the broker may not beat fault but must defend anyway. Moreover, E&O covers not only courtroom costs and judgments but pretrial conferences, negotiations, and out-of-court settlements. Today E&O is simply a cost of the real estate business just like rent, telephone, and automobile expenses.

Vocabulary Review

Match terms a–o with statements 1–15.

a. Boycotting
b. Buyer's broker
c. Commingling
d. Dual agency
e. Fiduciary relationship
f. Implied authority
g. Middleman
h. Price fixing
i. Principal
j. Property report
k. Sales associate
l. Special agency
m. Subagent
n. Third parties
o. Trust account

_____ 1. A person who authorizes another to act.

_____ 2. Persons who are not parties to a contract but who may be affected by it.

_____ 3. An agency created for the performance of specific acts only.

_____ 4. A person who brings two or more parties together but does not assist in conducting negotiations.

_____ 5. One broker representing two or more parties in a transaction.

_____ 6. Mixing of clients' or customers' funds with an agent's personal funds.

_____ 7. Two or more listing brokers agreeing to charge a 7% commission.

_____ 8. A licensed salesperson or broker who works for a broker.

_____ 9. Agency authority arising from industry custom, common usage, and conduct of the parties involved.

_____ 10. A relationship that requires trust, honesty, and exercise of good business judgment.

_____ 11. A separate account for holding clients' and customers' money.

_____ 12. Refusing to work with another broker because of an arbitrary set of rules.

_____ 13. Refers to the agency relationship of a broker's sales associate to the seller.

_____ 14. A broker employed by and therefore loyal to the buyer.

_____ 15. Government-required information that must be given to purchasers in subdivisions.

Questions and Problems

1. The laws of agency require that the agent be faithful and loyal to the principal. What does this mean to a real estate broker who has just taken a listing? What does it mean when a real estate broker represents the buyer?

2. What does *broker cooperation* refer to? How is it achieved?

3. What are we referring to when we speak of the laws of agency?

4. What is an agency coupled with an interest?

5. What is the purpose of a property disclosure statement? Has your state adopted one?

6. What is the purpose of errors and omissions insurance?

7. A buyer employs you, acknowledging that you may be a dual agent. He requests that his identity be kept secret. He likes one of your listings. When you present the offer, the seller informs you for the first time that he will sell to anyone "except that buyer." How do you handle this situation?

Additional Readings

Doing the Right Thing: A Real Estate Practitioner's Guide to Ethical Decision Making, 4th ed. by Deborah H. Long (OnCourse Learning, 2008).

Real Estate Office Management: A Guide to Success by Robert Herd (OnCourse Learning, 2003). A concise look at contemporary real estate office management covering the essential day-to-day knowledge needed to successfully operate the office.

CHAPTER 22

Fair Housing, ADA, Equal Credit, and Community Reinvestment

LEARNING OBJECTIVES

After reading this chapter, you should be able to:

❮ Understand the fundamentals and reasons for fair housing legislation.

❮ Define "steering," "block busting," and housing covered by the "1968 Fair Housing Act."

❮ Discuss the most recent amendments to the Fair Housing Act.

❮ Understand the scope of the Americans with Disabilities Act.

❮ Understand the scope and application of the Equal Credit Opportunity Act.

❮ Understand the scope and application of the Community Reinvestment Act.

KEY TERMS

Americans with Disabilities Act (ADA) • Block busting • Community Reinvestment Act • Equal Credit Opportunity Act • Familial status • Handicapped • Protected class • Steering • Tester

This chapter concentrates on federal and state legislation that has had a strong impact on expanding the ability of individuals to own real estate. The concept of fair housing prohibits discrimination in the purchase of real property. Equal credit has made lending sources available for thousands who could not previously qualify for loans, and the Community Reinvestment Act encourages lenders to make loans in disadvantaged areas. It is almost impossible to fully explain the effects of federal legislation on real estate over the last 40 years. The scope and effect of the changes resulting from federal legislation are felt daily and have touched virtually every aspect of the real estate business. The federal government's emphasis on protection of individual rights was imposed because many states found this goal politically difficult to pursue, and in many cases a long history of prejudice was an overwhelming obstacle.

Fair Housing

This federal legislation has been liberally applied to virtually all areas of discrimination—race, color, creed, national origin, alienage, sex, marital status, age, familial status, and handicapped status. The theories supporting these federal laws are applied differently though, depending on the source of the law and enforcement of the applicable statute. Let's review these theories in greater detail.

CONSTITUTIONAL IMPACT ON OWNERSHIP OF REAL PROPERTY

The most fundamental rights in real property are obtained in the U.S. Constitution. These rights are so firmly established and they so broadly affect real estate that they deserve discussion at the outset. The Declaration of Independence declared that all men are created equal and set the stage for an attitude of the government that we enjoy in the United States. It was with this forethought that our founders wrote the Constitution that vested in all citizens certain inalienable rights of which they can never be deprived. As far as real property ownership is concerned, the most significant of these rights are stated in the Fifth, Fourteenth, and Thirteenth Amendments to the Constitution.

The **Fifth Amendment** clearly states that no person shall "… be deprived of life, liberty, or property without due process of law…." It was from this fundamental statement that we have developed the inherent right that nobody can have their property taken from them without court proceedings. This concept has been expanded over the last 25 years or so to include the prohibition of certain types of discrimination, creating certain "protected classes" of people who may not be discriminated against.

To date, the types of discrimination that have been deemed "suspect" by the U.S. Supreme Court have included discrimination on the basis of race, color, religion, national origin, and alienage. This is logical in that a citizen of the United States cannot alter his race, color, national origin, or alienage and is entitled to practice the religion of his choice. Therefore, very strict constitutional prohibitions have been established by the courts to eliminate this type of discrimination for any citizen in the United States. It should be emphasized that there is no *constitutional* prohibition of discrimination on the basis of sex, age, or marital status.

One of the most significant areas of litigation has been based on racial discrimination. This has been applied to all federal activity through the Fifth Amendment, and to state and individual actions through the Thirteenth and Fourteenth Amendments to the Constitution.

The **Thirteenth Amendment** to the Constitution prohibits slavery and involuntary servitude. This amendment formed the basis for the most significant landmark case on discrimination, *Jones v. Alfred H. Mayer Company*. That case basically held that any form of discrimination, even by individuals, creates a "badge of slavery," which, in turn, results in the violation of the Thirteenth Amendment. The Supreme Court stated that in enforcing the Civil Rights Act of 1866, Congress is empowered under the Thirteenth Amendment to secure to all citizens the right to buy whatever a white man can buy and the right to live wherever a white man can live. The court further stated, "If Congress cannot say that being a free man means at least this much, then the Thirteenth Amendment has a promise the Nation cannot keep." This case effectively prohibits discrimination of all types and is applicable to real estate transactions.

The **Fourteenth Amendment** prohibits any state (as distinguished from the federal government) from depriving a person of life, liberty, or property without due process of law and prohibits any state from denying any person within its jurisdiction the equal protection of the laws. The significant case in interpreting the Fourteenth Amendment as it applies to the states was *Shelley v. Kraemer*. In this Supreme Court case, some white property owners were attempting to enforce a deed restriction that required that all property owners must be Caucasian. The state courts granted the relief sought. The Supreme Court, however, reversed the case, stating that the action of state courts in imposing penalties deprived parties of their substantive right, without due process of law, to have access to housing. The opportunity to defend against discrimination has long been regarded as a denial of due process of law as guaranteed by the Fourteenth Amendment. The court stated that equality and the enjoyment of property rights were regarded by the framers of the Fourteenth Amendment as an essential precondition to realization of other basic civil rights and liberties, which the Fourteenth Amendment was intended to guarantee. Therefore, it was concluded that the "equal protection" clause of the Fourteenth Amendment should prohibit the judicial enforcement by state courts of restrictive covenants based on race or color.

FAIR HOUSING LAWS

In addition to the constitutional issues, two major federal laws prohibit discrimination in housing. The first is the **Civil Rights Act of 1866**. It states that, "All citizens of the United States shall have the same right in every State and Territory, as is enjoyed by the white citizens thereof to inherit, purchase, lease, sell, hold, and convey real and personal property." In 1968, the Supreme Court affirmed that the 1866 act prohibits "all racial discrimination, private as well as public, in the sale of real property." The second is the **Fair Housing Act**, officially known as **Title VIII** of the Civil Rights Act of 1968, as amended. This law creates **protected classes** of people, making it illegal to discriminate, or show a preference, on the basis of race, color, religion, sex (gender), national origin, handicap, or familial status in connection with the sale or rental of housing and any vacant land offered for residential construction or use.

protected class
A class of people that by law are protected from discrimination.

There are three ways that a Fair Housing Act violation can be proven. The first is obvious, an intentional discrimination against someone in a protected class, such as: "I refuse to sell to the Irish." The second requires that a regulation, while appearing neutral, results in a discriminatory impact. For instance, a "one person per bedroom" restriction that effectively eliminates occupancy by families or children has a discriminatory impact, even though it isn't specifically set out in the restriction. The third way a fair housing violation can be proven is if the owner fails to "reasonably accommodate" members of a protected class. For instance, if an occupant develops a disability, the owner or landlord must attempt to reasonably accommodate that occupant's needs. Once a fair housing violation has been demonstrated, the burden shifts to the defendant to produce evidence that shows the defendant's conduct was for legitimate, nondiscriminatory purposes. If the owner can prove that, there is no fair housing violation.

Specifically, what do these two federal statutes prohibit, and what do they allow? The 1968 Fair Housing Law provides protection against the following acts if they discriminate against one or more of the *protected classes*:

1. Refusing to sell or rent to, deal with, or negotiate with any person.

2. Discriminating in the terms or conditions for buying or renting housing.

3. Discriminating by advertising that housing is available only to persons of a certain race, color, religion, sex, or national origin, those who are not handicapped, or adults only. This conduct violates the "preference" prohibition.

4. Denying that housing is available for inspection, sale, or rent when it really is available.

5. Denying or making different terms or conditions for home loans by commercial lenders.

6. Denying to anyone the use of or participation in any real estate services, such as brokers' organizations, multiple listing services, or other facilities related to the selling or renting of housing.

7. Steering or block busting.

steering

Practice of directing home seekers to particular neighborhoods based on race, color, religion, sex, national origin, handicapped, or adults-only status.

STEERING. **Steering** is the practice of directing home seekers to particular neighborhoods based on race, color, religion, sex, national origin, nonhandicapped, or adult-only housing. Steering includes efforts to exclude minority members from one area of a city as well as to direct them to minority or changing areas. Examples include showing only certain neighborhoods, slanting property descriptions, and downgrading neighborhoods. Steering is often subtle, sometimes no more than a word, phrase, or facial expression. Nonetheless, steering accounts for the bulk of the complaints filed against real estate licensees under the Fair Housing Act.

block busting

The illegal practice of inducing panic selling in a neighborhood for financial gain.

BLOCK BUSTING. **Block busting** is the illegal practice of inducing panic selling in a neighborhood for financial gain. Block busting typically starts when one person induces another to sell his property cheaply by stating that an impending change in the racial or religious composition of the neighborhood will cause property values to fall, school quality to decline, and crime to increase. The first home thus acquired is sold (at a markup) to a minority member. This event is used to reinforce fears that the neighborhood is indeed changing. The process quickly snowballs as residents panic and sell at progressively lower prices. The homes are then resold at higher prices to incoming residents.

Note that block busting is not limited to fears over people moving into a neighborhood. In a Virginia case, a real estate firm attempted to gain listings in a certain neighborhood by playing upon residents' fears regarding an upcoming expressway project.

PREFERENCE. An often overlooked issue in fair housing is a showing of **preferences**, or preferential treatment to a class of individuals. It is the opposite of traditional discrimination issues. For instance, if a mortgage broker chooses only to make loans to Spanish speaking individuals as a targeted market, he is discriminating against every other protected class. HUD has enforced claims against people who are targeting particular classes. Most of these cases, however have involved predatory lending practices where they charged a higher interest rate and loan fees. It seems to create a fine line, though. One may feel comfortable marketing to another minority because of the sharing of cultures and language, but it could violate the Fair Housing Act. One can never be too careful.

HOUSING COVERED BY THE 1968 FAIR HOUSING LAW. The 1968 Fair Housing Law applies to the following housing types:

1. Single-family houses owned by private individuals when: (1) a real estate broker or other person in the business of selling or renting dwellings is used, and/or (2) discriminatory advertising is used.

2. Single-family houses not owned by private individuals.

3. Single-family houses owned by a private individual who owns more than three such houses or who, in any two-year period, sells more than one in which the individual was not the most recent resident.

4. Multifamily dwellings of five or more units.

5. Multifamily dwellings containing four or fewer units, if the owner does not reside in one of the units.

ACTS NOT PROHIBITED BY THE 1968 FAIR HOUSING LAW. Not covered by the 1968 Fair Housing Law are the sale or rental of single-family houses owned by a private individual who owns three or fewer such single-family houses if: (1) a broker is not used, (2) discriminatory advertising is not used, and (3) no more than one house in which the owner was not the most recent resident is sold during any two-year period. Not covered by the 1968 act are rentals of rooms or units in owner-occupied multi-dwellings for two to four families, if discriminatory advertising is not used. The act also does not cover the sale, rental, or occupancy of dwellings that a religious organization owns or operates for other than a commercial purpose to persons of the same religion, if membership in that religion is not restricted on account of race, color, or national origin. It also does not cover the rental or occupancy of lodgings that a private club owns or operates for its members for other than a commercial purpose. Housing for the elderly may also allow discrimination in not permitting children or young adult occupants in the development or building, provided that the housing is primarily intended for the elderly, has minimum age requirements (55 or 62), and meets certain HUD guidelines.

Note, however, that the previously listed acts *not* prohibited by the 1968 Fair Housing Law *are* prohibited by the 1866 Civil Rights Act when discrimination based on race occurs in connection with such acts.

MOST RECENT AMENDMENTS. Understanding that one cannot discriminate on the basis of race, color, religion, national origin, and sex (gender) seems fundamental today. In 1988, the Civil Rights Act of 1968 was expanded to provide for housing for the handicapped, as well as for people with children under the age of 18. The act provides protection for any form of discrimination based on race, color, religion, national origin, sex, *familial status*, or *handicapped status*. The 1988 law's application is very broad, and needs to be discussed in more detail.

Handicapped   The 1988 amendment defines **handicapped** as follows:

1. Having a physical or mental impairment that substantially limits one or more major life activities.
2. Having a record of having such an impairment.
3. Being regarded as having such an impairment.

The act includes recovered mental patients, as well as those who are presently suffering from a mental handicap.

The legislation has definitely changed our attitudes about certain restrictions. It is assumed, for instance, that a blind person can live with a guide dog in a housing project that prohibits pets. The handicapped are also allowed to make reasonable modifications to existing units, as long as it is at the handicapped person's expense. The handicapped renter must also restore the unit to its original state upon termination of occupancy. The law also makes it unlawful for a landlord or owner to refuse to make reasonable accommodations, rules, policies, practices, or services when necessary to afford a handicapped person an equal opportunity to use and enjoy the dwelling. In addition, all new multi-family dwellings with four or more units must be constructed to allow access and use by handicapped persons. If the building has no elevators, only first floor units are covered by this provision. Doors and hallways in the buildings must be wide enough to accommodate wheelchairs. Light switches and other controls must be in convenient locations. Most rooms and spaces must be on an accessible route, and special accommodations such as grab bars in the bathrooms must be provided.

handicapped
Having a physical or mental impairment that substantially limits one or more life activities, or having a record of such impairment.

There are some exceptions under the handicapped person provision. The term *handicapped*, for instance, does not include current illegal use of or addiction to a controlled substance, but it *does* include recovering addicts (halfway houses). Handicapped status also does not include any person whose tenancy imposes a direct threat to the health, safety, and property of others.

Since the statute was enacted, cases have held that recovering drug addicts and alcoholics are handicapped, as are people infected with the HIV virus. Therefore, they cannot be discriminated against, and denial of housing as a result of this "handicap" is a violation of the Fair Housing Act. This may result in unusual situations where recovering drug addicts could be moving into a neighborhood, and the neighbors are prohibited from discriminating against them or denying them housing (by enforcing deed restrictions or zoning ordinances) because it would have a discriminatory effect on the handicapped.

familial status

One or more individuals under the age of 18 who are domiciled with a parent or other person having custody.

Familial Status   **Familial status** is defined as one or more individuals (who have not obtained the age of 18 years) being domiciled with a parent or another person having legal custody of such individual or individuals or the designee of such parent or other person having such custody, with the written permission of such parent or other person. These protections also apply to any person who is pregnant or is in the process of securing legal custody of any individual who has not obtained the age of 18 years.

The most significant effect of this amendment is that all homeowner association property, apartment projects, and condominiums now have to have facilities adapted for children and cannot discriminate against anyone on the basis of familial status when leasing, selling, or renting property.

There are specific exemptions to this portion of the act also. A building can qualify for an exemption if: (1) it provides housing under the state or federal program that the Secretary of Housing and Urban Development (HUD) determines is specifically designed and operated to assist elderly persons; (2) it provides housing intended for, and generally occupied only by, persons 62 years of age or older; or (3) it provides housing generally intended and operated for at least one person 55 years of age or older per unit and meets certain regulations that are adopted by the Secretary of HUD.

These amendments to the Fair Housing Law have a significant impact for all licensees attempting to sell, list, lease, or rent real estate. It is now unlawful to refuse to sell or rent or to refuse to negotiate the sale or rental of any property based on familial status or handicapped status. Printing and advertising cannot make any reference to preference based on handicapped or familial status. As stated previously, the landlord cannot deny the right of a handicapped tenant to make any changes in the physical structure of the building, provided that the tenant agrees to reinstate the building to its original form when he leaves.

It is safe to say that there are many more situations and circumstances that will occur that have not been specifically addressed by the statute. It is critically important that licensees recognize these two most recent prohibitions against discrimination and deem them as serious violations of an individual's civil rights, as are more traditional theories of race, color, religion, national origin, and sex.

FAIR HOUSING ENFORCEMENT. The penalties for violation of the act are severe. The first violation of the act results in a fine of not more than $75,000, and for subsequent violations, a fine of not more than $150,000. The fines are in addition to other civil damages, potential injunctions, reasonable attorney's fees, and costs.

Adherence to the 1968 act can be enforced in any of three ways by someone who feels discriminated against. The first is to file a written complaint with HUD in Washington,

DC. The second is to file court action directly in a U.S. District Court or state or local court. The third is to file a complaint with the U.S. Attorney General. If a complaint is filed with HUD, HUD may investigate to see if the law has been broken, may attempt to resolve the problem by conference, conciliation, or persuasion; may refer the matter to a state or local fair housing authority; or may recommend that the complaint be filed in court. If HUD finds that a Fair Housing violation has occurred, it will schedule a hearing before a HUD administrative law judge, where the defendant is given the opportunity to explain the justification for the discrimination charge. Either party, the complainant or the defendant, can cause the scheduled HUD administrative proceeding to be terminated, if they elect to have the matter litigated in federal court instead. HUD has a "complaints" section on its Web site, **http://www.hud.gov/complaints/housediscrim.cfm**. A person seeking enforcement of the 1866 act must file a suit in a federal court.

No matter which route is taken, the burden of proving illegal discrimination under the 1968 act is the responsibility of the person filing the complaint. If successful, the following remedies are available: (1) an injunction to stop the sale or rental of the property to someone else making it available to the complainant, (2) money for actual damages caused by the discrimination, (3) punitive damages, and (4) court costs. There are also criminal penalties for those who coerce, intimidate, threaten, or interfere with a person's buying, renting, or selling of housing.

AGENT'S DUTIES. A real estate agent's duties are to uphold the 1968 Fair Housing Law and the 1866 Civil Rights Act. If a property owner asks an agent to discriminate, the agent must refuse to accept the listing. An agent is in violation of fair housing laws by giving a minority buyer or seller less than favorable treatment or by ignoring him or referring him to an agent of the same minority. Violation also occurs when an agent fails to use best efforts, does not submit an offer because of race, color, religion, sex, national origin, physical handicap, or occupancy by children.

TESTERS. From time to time, a licensee may be approached by fair housing **testers**. These are individuals or organizations that respond to advertising and visit real estate offices to test for compliance with fair housing laws. The tester does not announce himself or herself as such or ask if the office follows fair housing practices. Rather, the tester plays the role of a person looking for housing to buy or rent and observes whether fair housing laws are being followed. If not followed, the tester lodges a complaint with the appropriate fair housing agency.

A person may also file a civil action in district court not later than the second year after the occurrence or the termination of an alleged discriminatory housing practice; or the breach of a conciliation agreement entered into with a state housing law, whichever occurs last; or to obtain relief of the breach or discriminatory housing practice. If the court finds a discriminatory practice has occurred or is about to occur, the court may award to the plaintiff actual and punitive damages, reasonable attorney's fees and court costs, and any permanent or temporary injunction.

STATE LAWS. What has been said so far has to do with federal housing laws. In addition, many states, counties, and cities have enacted their own fair housing laws. You will need to contact local fair housing authorities as these laws often go beyond the federal laws. For example, within some states it is illegal to discriminate on the basis of age, marital status, presence of children, physical handicap, sexual orientation, and welfare status. Within other states, an owner-occupant may discriminate only in his own single-family or two-family home, not the four-family building allowed in the 1968 act.

tester
An individual or organization that responds to advertising and visits real estate offices to test for compliance with fair housing laws.

The Americans with Disabilities Act

Americans with Disabilities Act (ADA)

A federal law giving disabled individuals the right of access to commercial facilities open to the public.

The **Americans with Disabilities Act (ADA)** deals primarily with commercial property. Generally stated, it provides access requirements and prohibits discrimination against people with disabilities in public accommodations, state and local government, transportation, telecommunications, and employment. Anyone who has had a physical or mental impairment, or who is "perceived" as having one that interferes with a "major life activity," is covered by the act.

The act specifically affects the real estate brokerage industry in that real estate licensees need to determine whether the product the licensee is selling, managing, or leasing is in compliance with the act. A licensee should always be cautioned, however, that the statute is very detailed, and there are a number of gray areas in the statute that still lack clear interpretation.

SCOPE

The antidiscrimination and the removal of barrier requirements of the ADA apply to "places of public accommodations," and the accessibility requirements of the ADA with respect to new construction and alterations apply to public accommodations and "commercial facilities."

"Places of public accommodations" encompasses 12 categories of retail and service businesses, including places of lodging; food and drink establishments; places of exhibitionary entertainment; places of public gathering; sales and rental establishments; services establishments such as law firms, accounting firms, and banks; public transportation stations; places of public display or collection; places of recreation; educational facilities; social service center establishments; and exercise clubs. It is presumed that this definition includes brokerage offices, even if they are located in private homes. "Commercial facility" is defined as a facility: (1) whose operations affect commerce, (2) that is intended for nonresidential use, and (3) that is not a facility expressly exempted from coverage under the Fair Housing Act of 1968.

The ADA contains a broad prohibition affecting the public accommodations and discrimination against those with disabilities by denying them the full and equal enjoyment of goods, services, facilities, privileges, advantages, and the accommodations of any place of public accommodation. Facilities need to be usable by those with disabilities.

All commercial facilities must also be accessible to the maximum extent feasible whenever alterations are being performed on the facility. Alteration is defined as any change that affects the usability of a facility. If the alterations are made to a lobby or work area of the public accommodation, a path of travel to the altered area and to the bathrooms, telephones, and drinking fountains serving that area must be made accessible to the extent that the added accessibility costs are not disproportionate to the overall cost of the original alteration. Disproportionate cost is defined for the purposes of the act as cost that exceeds 20% of the original alteration. The cost of alteration means all costs and renovating in particular proportion to the facility in a three-year period.

The act requires modifications to procedures so that disabled individuals are not excluded from regular programs. Places of public accommodations must make reasonable modifications to the policies and procedures in order to accommodate individuals with disabilities and not create restrictions that tend to screen out individuals with disabilities, such as requiring a person to produce a driver's license or not allowing more than one person in a clothes changing area when a disabled person needs the assistance of another. The act also requires auxiliary aids and services to ensure effective communication with individuals with hearing, vision, or speech impairments. These requirements include interpreters, listening headsets, television closed caption decoders, telecommunication devices for the deaf, video tech displays, and braille and large print materials.

There are several defenses and exclusions available under the act, but most are extremely narrow in scope. In addition, there are few court precedents to help us with interpretation of the ADA. Problems in compliance will occur. Examples: If a water fountain is placed low enough for someone in a wheelchair to use, what happens to the tall person who has difficulty in bending? Lowering a fire extinguisher for easier access to the person in the wheelchair also gives easier access to small children. Something that is childproof will also be inaccessible to someone with limited use of their hands.

Both the Department of Justice and private individuals may maintain a cause of action to enforce the ADA against commercial building owners. The Department may seek monetary damages or injunctive relief, but private individuals are entitled only to seek injunctive relief under the statute. Apparently, a tort claim may create a cause of action for monetary damages.

Equal Credit Opportunity Act

The **Equal Credit Opportunity Act (ECOA)** was originally passed to provide for equal credit for borrowers by making it unlawful to discriminate against an applicant for credit based on sex or marital status. In 1976, the act was amended to prohibit discrimination in any credit transaction based on race, color, religion, national origin, sex, marital status, age (not including minors), receipt of income from a public assistance program, and the good faith exercise of rights under the ECOA or other federal consumer protection laws.

Equal Credit Opportunity Act
Federal law that provides for equal credit to borrowers.

PROHIBITED REQUESTS

To effect this prohibition on discrimination, a creditor is prohibited from requiring certain information from the borrower:

1. Information concerning a spouse or former spouse, except when that spouse will be contractually obligated for repayment or if the spouse resides in a community property state.

2. Information regarding the applicant's marital status unless the credit requested is for an individual's unsecured account, or unless the applicant resides in a community property state and the community property is to be relied upon to repay the credit. Inquiries as to the applicant's marital status are limited, however, to categories of "married," "unmarried," and "separated." "Unmarried" includes single, divorced, and widowed persons and may be specified in the application.

3. Information concerning the source of an applicant's income without disclosing that information regarding alimony, child support, or separate maintenance is to be furnished only at the option of the applicant. The big exception to this rule is when the applicant expects to use any of those sources of income for repayment. If so, the lender may request this information.

4. Information regarding an applicant's birth control practices or any intentions concerning the bearing or rearing of children, although a lender still has the right to ask an applicant about the number and ages of any dependents or about dependent-related financial obligations.

5. Questions regarding race, color, religion, or national origin of the applicant.

There are minor exceptions when a real estate loan is involved. These exceptions are allowed in order to provide certain information that may be used by the federal government for the purposes of monitoring conformance with the Equal Credit Opportunity Act. When the information is requested, the lender is required to advise the applicants that the furnishing of the specific information is for purposes of monitoring the lender's compliance and is requested on a voluntary basis only. If the applicant does not wish to answer the questions, the lender simply notes the refusal on the application form. The refusal to give the information requested cannot be used in any way in considering whether credit is granted to the applicant. If the applicant agrees to provide the information on a voluntary basis, the following information can be furnished:

1. Race or national origin.
2. Sex, relating to gender only (not sexual preference).
3. Marital status (using the categories of married, unmarried, or separated).

When considering only race and national origin, the following categories can be used: American Indian or Alaskan Native, Asian or Pacific Islander, Black, White, Hispanic, or "other."

EVALUATING CREDIT APPLICATIONS

As previously stated, the lender cannot use information obtained from an applicant if that information might be considered to be discriminatory. Each applicant has to be evaluated on the same basic information as any other individual person. Lenders can't refuse credit based on individual category, such as newlyweds, recent divorcees, and so on. The lender's rules must be applied uniformly to all applicants. The areas in which there can be no discrimination have already been discussed (sex, marital status, race, color, religion, national origin, age, public assistance), but some of these areas need to be discussed in greater detail.

AGE. A lender is prohibited from taking an applicant's age into account in determining ability to repay. Neither can income from any public assistance program be taken into account. The only exception to this prohibition is minors, who lack contractual capacity and cannot enter into real estate transactions.

CHILDREN. As discussed in the previous sections on fair housing, the Equal Credit Opportunity Act has always provided that there can be no assumptions or statistics relating to the likelihood that a group of persons may bear children. During the initial years, lenders required nonpregnancy affidavits and other indications that a young, newly married couple would not endanger the income-producing capacity of the wife.

PART-TIME INCOME. Income from part-time employment or retirement income cannot be discounted because of the basis of its source. However, the creditor may still consider the amount and probability of continuance of such income.

ALIMONY AND CHILD SUPPORT. Alimony and child support and separate maintenance cannot be considered in evaluating a loan application unless the creditor determines that such payments are not likely to be made consistently. In such cases, the lender has the right to determine whether the applicant has the ability to compel payment and the creditworthiness of the party who is obligated to make such payments.

CREDIT HISTORY. The Equal Credit Opportunity Act requires a creditor to consider the separate record of the applicant. This prohibits the lender from tying the applicant's credit history to the past record of the spouse or former spouse.

IMMIGRATION RESIDENCY. A creditor may consider an applicant's immigration status and whether he or she is a permanent resident of the United States.

SEX. A lender may not ask about the sex of an applicant but may ask an applicant to designate a title on the application form (Ms., Miss, Mrs., or Mr.) if the form indicates the designation of the title is optional.

MARITAL STATUS. If an applicant applies for individual credit, the lender may not ask the applicant for marital status unless the applicant resides in a community property state or is relying on property located in community property state to repay the loan. Similarly, a lender may not seek information about a spouse or former spouse unless a spouse will be permitted to use the account, the spouse is contractually liable on the account, or the borrower is relying on the spouse's income as a basis for repayment of the loan.

CREDIT DENIAL

If an applicant is denied credit, the lender must give a written notice of decline, also referred to as "Notice of Adverse Action," to the applicant and advise the rejected applicant of the federal agency that administers compliance with the Equal Credit Opportunity Act for that particular loan transaction. The statement of specific reasons must give the precise reason or reasons for the denial of credit. There are suggested guidelines for giving reasons for credit denial, including the following:

1. unable to verify credit references;
2. temporary or irregular employment;
3. insufficient length of employment;
4. insufficient income;
5. excessive obligations;
6. inadequate collateral;
7. too short a period of residency;
8. delinquent credit obligation.

An application can also be declined for incompleteness.

PENALTIES

Failure to comply with the Equal Credit Opportunity Act or the accompanying federal regulations makes a creditor subject to a civil liability for damages limited to $10,000 in individual actions and the lesser of $500,000 or 1% of the creditor's net worth in class actions. The court may also award court costs and reasonable attorney's fees to an aggrieved applicant.

COPIES OF APPRAISAL REPORTS

A lender or loan broker must provide a copy of an appraisal report to an applicant for a loan to be secured by a lien on the dwelling. The report may be provided either routinely as a part of the lender's standard process or when the loan applicant requests a copy.

If the lender decides to provide the appraisal only upon request, it must notify the applicant in writing of the right to receive a copy of the appraisal report. The lender must promptly (generally within 30 calendar days) mail or deliver the copy of the appraisal report after he receives the borrower's request.

Community Reinvestment Act

Community Reinvestment Act

Federal statute encouraging federally regulated lenders to increase their participation in low-income areas.

The **Community Reinvestment Act (CRA)** expands the concept that regulated financial institutions must serve the needs of their communities. Its purpose is to provide credit for homeownership opportunities to underserved populations and commercial loans for small businesses. Whenever a financing institution regulated by the federal government applies for a charter, branch facility, office relocation, or acquisition of another financing institution, the record of the institution's help in meeting local credit needs must be one of the factors considered by the supervising agencies of the federal government. The supervising agencies include the Office of the Comptroller of the Currency; the Board of Governors of the Federal Reserve System, the Federal Deposit Insurance Corporation, and the Office of Thrift Supervision.

Federal regulators are required to evaluate each financial institution's actual performance in meeting the credit needs of its community, using a three-pronged test that includes lending, investment, and service tests to review an institution's performance. Some financial institutions may choose to adopt a strategic plan, which sets forth specific goals that must be obtained.

For larger institutions (more than $1 billion in assets), the lending, investment, and service tests are measured by home mortgage loan originations, small business and small firm loans, community development loans, and consumer loans. The investment test evaluates the extent to which an institution has been meeting community needs through qualified investment. A service test reviews the availability and responsiveness of an institution's system for delivering retail banking and community development of services. Smaller institutions are subject only to the lending test.

In addition, the retail institution must delineate an assessment area consisting of one or more metropolitan statistical areas or contiguous subdivisions, such as counties, cities, and towns, focusing on the location of where the lender has its main office, branches, and automatic teller machines.

CRA NOTICE

The institution must post, in the public lobby of its main office and in each branch office, a "Community Reinvestment Act" (CRA) notice, which informs consumers that they are entitled to certain information about the operations of the lender and its performance under the CRA, and which also informs the consumers of the schedules for the CRA examination and the availability of any federal regulatory report covered by the CRA.

It is very difficult to ascertain what impact the Community Reinvestment Act has on lending institutions and practices of lenders generally. Many areas of the statute are vague, and it is difficult for the federal regulators to establish hard-and-fast rules because of the variety of different needs the lending institutions generally serve in different communities. As with a lot of other federal legislation, it may take some time before the full impact of this act is felt.

Vocabulary Review

Match terms a–m with statements 1–13.

a. Americans with Disabilities Act (ADA)

b. Block busting

c. Community Reinvestment Act (CRA)

d. Equal Credit Opportunity Act

e. Fair Housing Law

f. Familial status

g. Fourteenth Amendment

h. Handicapped

i. Minority

j. Steering

k. Tester

l. Thirteenth Amendment

m. Title VIII

_____ 1. Applies to federal prohibitions under the Bill of Rights to the state.

_____ 2. Federal fair housing law under the Civil Rights Act of 1968.

_____ 3. One or more individuals being domiciled with a parent, or another person having legal custody of such individual.

_____ 4. Any group or member of a group that can be identified by race, color, religion, sex, or national origin.

_____ 5. The illegal practice of inducing panic selling in a neighborhood for financial gain.

_____ 6. The act of directing any group away from or to an integrated or minority neighborhood.

_____ 7. Having a physical or mental impairment that substantially limits one or more major life activities.

_____ 8. Law applying to single-family housing utilizing the services of a real estate broker.

_____ 9. The "badge of slavery" violates the constitutional amendment.

_____ 10. Federal statute requiring accessibility for commercial premises.

_____ 11. Federal statute prohibiting discrimination in lending practices.

_____ 12. Federal statute prohibiting discrimination in credit transactions.

_____ 13. An individual posing as a potential purchaser to determine whether discrimination exists in a real estate transaction.

Questions and Problems

1. Can you refuse to sell a home to a person because she is a lawyer?

2. What is the difference between prohibitions under the United States Constitution and prohibitions under the civil rights statutes?

3. What has your local lender done to comply with the Community Reinvestment Act?

4. Why would the federal statutes designate brokerage services as a method of enforcing fair housing?

5. Can I discriminate against white Anglo-Saxon Protestants?

6. Have you ever been discriminated against? Please explain.

7. Can I direct a potential home purchaser to a neighborhood that I feel is "safer"? Please note that behavior is more important than feelings.

Additional Readings

"Assisted Housing and Residential Segregation: The Role of Race and Ethnicity in the Siting of Assisted Housing Developments" by William M. Rohe et al. (*Journal of the American Planning Association*, Summer 2001, p. 279).

Doing the Right Thing: A Real Estate Practitioner's Guide to Ethical Decision Making, 4th ed. by Deborah H. Long (OnCourse Learning, 2008).

Ethics for the Real Estate Professional, 3rd ed. by Deborah H. Long (OnCourse Learning, 2008).

Fair Housing Handbook, 4th ed. (National Association of REALTORS®).

"HUD Secretary Cites Fair Housing in Wake of September Terrorist Attacks" (*Multi-Housing News*, November 2001, p.3).

"Let's Celebrate 34 Years of Fair Housing with Caution" by Nadeen Green (*Multi-Housing News*, April 2002, p. 13+).

"More on the Fair Housing Act" by Marianne M. Jennings (*Real Estate Law Journal*, Summer 2001, pp. 48–51).

CHAPTER 23

Condominiums, Cooperatives, PUDs, and Time-shares

This chapter covers methods of dividing land. The condominium declaration is covered in some detail. Other topics include management, maintenance fees, taxes, insurance, and financing. The advantages and disadvantages of condominium living are listed along with a list of things to check before buying. Other condo topics include a discussion of legislation, condo conversion, and physical appearance. Cooperative apartments, PUDs, and time-shares are also covered.

The idea of combining community living with community ownership is not new. Two thousand years ago, the Roman Senate passed condominium laws that permitted Roman citizens to own individual dwelling units in multiunit buildings. This form of ownership resulted because land was scarce and expensive in Rome. After the fall of the Roman Empire, condominium ownership was used in the walled cities of the Middle Ages. It was primarily a defensive measure, since residing outside the walls was dangerous because of roving bands of raiders. With the stabilization of governments after the Middle Ages, the condominium concept became dormant. Then in the early twentieth century, in response to land scarcity in cities, the idea was revived in western Europe. From there the concept spread to several Latin American countries and, in 1951, to Puerto Rico. Puerto Rican laws and experience in turn became the basis for passage by

LEARNING OBJECTIVES

After reading this chapter, you should be able to:

❬ Discuss the difference between condominiums, cooperatives, PUDs, and time-shares.

❬ Understand the creation and organization of a condominium regime.

❬ Understand the importance of homeowner's associations.

❬ Define and understand how cooperative housing differs from condominium housing.

❬ Discuss financing differences between condominiums and cooperatives.

❬ Understand the advantages and disadvantages of resort time-sharing.

KEY TERMS

Bylaws • CC&Rs • Common elements • Condominium • Cooperative • Limited common elements • Planned unit development (PUD) • Proprietary lease • Reserve

Congress in 1961 of Section 234 of the National Housing Act. Designed as a legal model that condominium developers could follow in order to obtain Federal Housing Administration (FHA) loan insurance, Section 234 also served as a model for state condominium laws now in effect across the United States.

The Desire for Land-Use Efficiency

Of the forces responsible for creating the need for condominiums, cooperatives, and Planned Unit Developments (PUDs), the most important are land scarcity in desirable areas, continuing escalation in construction costs, disenchantment with the work of maintaining the grounds around a house, and the desire to own rather than rent.

When constructing single-family houses on separate lots, a builder can usually average four to five houses per acre of land. In a growing number of cities, the sheer physical space necessary to continue building detached houses either does not exist or, if it does, it is a long distance from employment centers or is so expensive as to eliminate all but a small portion of the population from building there. As in ancient Roman times, the solution is to build more dwellings on the same parcel of land. Instead of four or five dwellings, build 25 or 100 on an acre of land. That way not only is the land more efficiently used, but the cost is divided among more owners. From the standpoint of construction costs, the builder does not have the miles of streets, sewers, or utility lines that would be necessary to reach every house in a subdivision. Furthermore, the facts that there are shared walls, that one dwelling unit's ceiling is often another's floor, and that one roof can cover many vertically stacked units can produce savings in construction materials and labor.

THE AMENITIES OF MULTIFAMILY LIVING

For some householders, the lure of "carefree living," wherein such chores as lawn mowing, watering, weeding, snow shoveling, and building maintenance are provided, is the major attraction. For others, it is the security often associated with clustered dwelling or the extensive recreational and social facilities that are not economically possible on a single-dwelling basis. It is commonplace to find swimming pools, recreation halls, tennis and volleyball courts, gymnasiums, and even social directors at some condominium, cooperative, and PUD projects.

A large rental apartment project can also produce the same advantages of land and construction economy and amenities. Nevertheless, we cannot overlook the preference of most American households to own rather than rent their dwellings. This preference is typically based on a desire for a savings program, observation of inflation in real estate prices, and advantageous income tax laws that allow owners, but not renters, to deduct property taxes and mortgage interest.

DIVIDING THE LAND OF AN ESTATE

Figure 23.1 illustrates the estate in land created by a condominium, cooperative, and planned unit development and compares each with the estate held by the owner of a house. Notice in Figure 23.1 that the ownership of house A extends from lot line B across to lot line C. Except where limited by zoning or other legal restrictions, the owner of house A has full control over and full right to use the land between the lot lines from the center of the earth to the limits of the sky. Within the law, the owner can choose how to use the land, what to build on it or add to it, what color to paint the house and garage, how many people and animals will live there, what type of

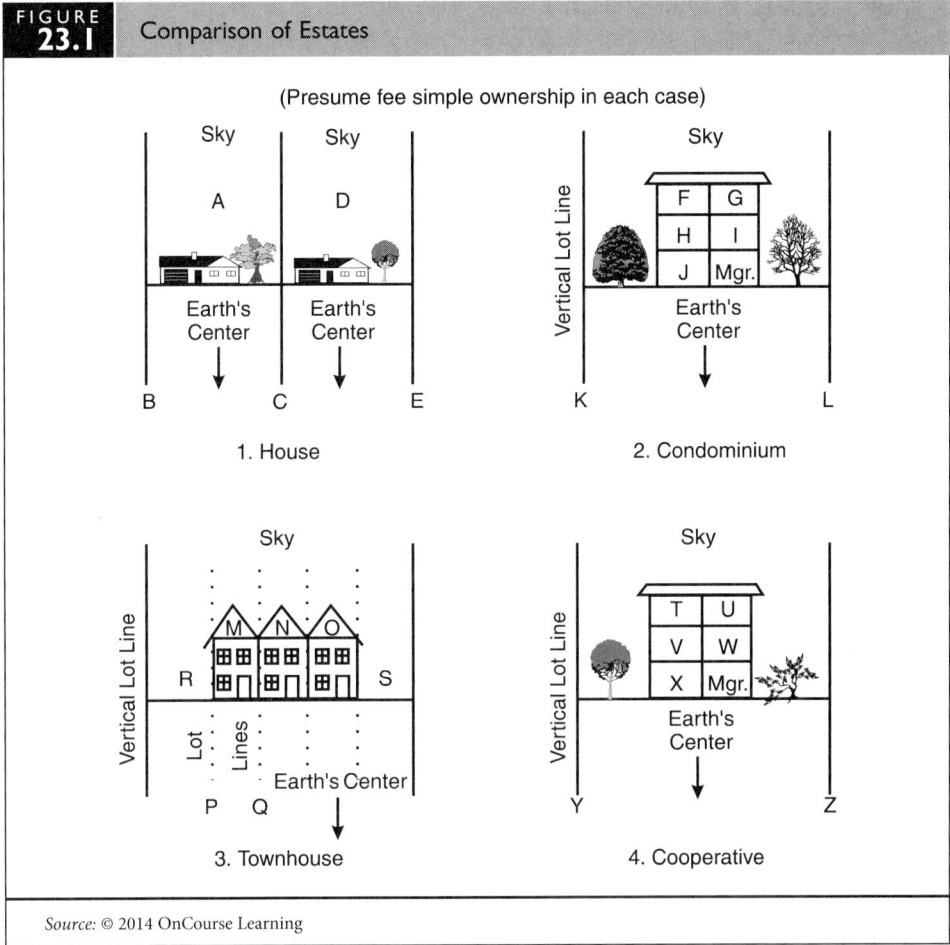

FIGURE 23.1   Comparison of Estates

(Presume fee simple ownership in each case)

1. House

2. Condominium

3. Townhouse

4. Cooperative

Source: © 2014 OnCourse Learning

landscaping to have, from whom to purchase property insurance, and so on. The owner of house D has the same control over the land between lot lines C and E.

The owner of A cannot dictate to a neighbor what color to paint the neighbor's house, what kind of shrubs and trees to grow, or from whom to buy hazard insurance, if any at all. (Occasionally, one will find deed restrictions in housing subdivisions that give the owners a limited amount of control over each other's land uses in the subdivision.)

Condominium

The first step in creating a **condominium** is for the state to pass laws that create the legal framework for condominium ownership. All states have passed them, and they are variously known as a state's horizontal property act, strata titles act, **condominium act**, or a similar name. They all follow the FHA model, adding each state's particular refinements. As the names suggest, these laws address the problem of subdividing the airspace over a given parcel of land. Prior to these acts, the legal framework that made it possible for people to own a cubicle of airspace plus an undivided interest in the shell of the building and the land under and around the building did not exist. Moreover, condominium acts had to be designed to be acceptable to lenders who would be asked to loan on condominiums, property tax authorities who would have to assess them, and income tax

condominium

Individual ownership of a space of air plus undivided ownership of the common elements.

authorities who would allow owners to deduct loan interest and property taxes. The lawmakers were successful, and today millions of people live in condominiums.

Physically, a condominium can take the shape of a two-story garden apartment building, a 40-story tower with several living units on each floor, row houses, clustered houses, or even detached houses sharing a single parcel of land. Condominiums are not restricted to residential uses. In recent years, a number of developers across the nation have built office buildings and sold individual suites to doctors, dentists, and lawyers. The same idea has been applied to shopping centers and industrial space. A condominium does not have to be a new building: Many existing apartment houses have been converted from rental status to condominium ownership with only a few physical changes to the building.

SEPARATE AND COMMON ELEMENTS

The distinguishing features of a condominium are its separate and common elements and its system of self-government. The separate elements are those areas in the condominium that are exclusively owned and used by the individual condominium owners, the individual dwelling units in the building. More precisely, the unit is the airspace occupied by a unit. This is the space lying between the interior surfaces of the unit walls and between the floor and the ceiling. Everything else is a common element in which each unit owner holds an undivided interest. Thus, the land and the shell of the building are **common elements** owned by all. Common elements include, for example, the manager's apartment, lobby, hallways, stairways, elevators, recreation areas, landscaping, and parking lot. Sometimes you will hear the term **limited common element**. This is a common element whose use is restricted to a specific unit owner. Examples are assigned parking stalls and individual storage units.

common elements

Those parts of a condominium that are owned by all the unit owners.

limited common elements

Common elements whose use is limited to certain owners.

OWNERS' ASSOCIATION

When a developer wants to create a condominium (either built from the ground up or the conversion of an existing building to condominium ownership), the developer prepares and records with the public recorder what is variously known as an enabling declaration, master deed, plan of condominium ownership, or **condominium subdivision**. This document, usually 50 to 150 pages long, converts a parcel of land held under a single deed into a number of individual separate property estates (the condominium units) and an estate composed of all the common elements. Survey maps are included to show the location of each condominium unit plus all the common elements.

The developer also creates a legal framework so that the unit owners can govern themselves. This is the condominium **owners' association** of which each unit purchaser automatically becomes a member. Although the association can be organized as a trust or unincorporated association, most often it will be organized as a corporation in order to provide the legal protections normally afforded by a corporation to its owners. Additionally, it will be organized as a not-for-profit so as to avoid income taxes on money collected from members. The main purpose of the owners' association is to control, regulate, and maintain the common elements for the overall welfare and benefit of its members. The owners' association is a mini-government by and for the condominium owners.

BYLAWS

bylaws

Rules that govern how an owners' association will be run.

The rules by which an owners' association operates are called its **bylaws**. They are prepared by the developer's attorney and recorded with the master deed. The bylaws provide the rules by which the association's board of directors is elected and set the standards by which the board must rule. The bylaws set forth how association dues (maintenance fees) will be established and collected; how contracts will be let for maintenance, management, and repair work; and how personnel will be hired.

CC&Rs

Finally, the developer must file a list of regulations by which anyone purchasing a unit in the condominium must abide. These are known as **covenants, conditions, and restrictions (CC&Rs)**. They tell a unit owner such things as whether personal items can be stored on balconies or driveways, what color the exterior of the living room drapes should be, to what extent an owner can alter the exterior of his unit, and whether an owner can install a satellite television dish on the roof. Additional regulations may be embodied in a set of **house rules**. Typically, these govern such things as when the swimming pool and other recreation facilities will be open for use and when quiet hours will be observed in the building.

CC&Rs
Covenants, conditions, and restrictions by which a property owner agrees to abide.

DEED

Each purchaser of a condominium unit receives a deed from the developer. The deed describes the location of the unit, both in terms of the unit number in the building and its surveyed airspace. The deed will also describe the common elements and state the percentage interest in the common elements that the grantee is receiving. The deed is recorded upon closing just like a deed to a house.

Upon selling, the owner has a new deed prepared that describes the unit and the common element interest and delivers it to the purchaser at closing. If the condominium is on leased land, the developer will deliver a lease (or sublease) to the unit buyer. Upon resale, that lease is assigned to the buyer.

VOTING RULES

Once the units in the building have been sold and the association turned over to the unit owners, the unit owners can change the rules. Generally, the bylaws require a three-fourths vote and the CC&Rs require a two-thirds vote by the association members for a change. House rules can be changed with a simple majority or, in some cases, by the board of directors without a vote of the association.

BOARD OF DIRECTORS

Condominium bylaws provide that a **board of directors** be elected by the association members. The board is authorized to administer the affairs of the condominium, including purchasing of hazard and liability insurance for the common elements, arranging for maintenance and repair of common elements, enforcing CC&Rs and house rules, assessing and collecting a sufficient amount of monthly homeowner fees and special assessments, and listening to complaints and suggestions from unit owners as to how the condominium should be run.

Board members are usually elected at the annual meeting of the association, are unit owners, and serve for one year. Typically there will be five to seven members on the board, and one will be elected as president, one as vice president, one as secretary, and one as treasurer. Meetings are held monthly unless added business requires more frequent meetings. Board meetings are usually open to all association members, who can then watch the proceedings and provide input. To help spread the work, the board will appoint committees on which owners are asked to serve. Examples are landscaping, architectural, security, clubhouse, and social committees. Directors and committee members are not usually paid for their time.

ANNUAL MEETINGS

Once a year the owners' association as a whole will meet for an **annual meeting**. Besides the election of board members for the following year, this is an opportunity for association members to vote on major issues such as changes in the CC&Rs and bylaws, monthly maintenance fee increases, special assessments, and any other matters the board feels should be put to a general ownership vote rather than handled at a board meeting. Owners also receive an annual report of the fiscal health of the association and other information pertinent to their ownership.

Condominium Management

Most condominium associations will employ a condominium **management company** to advise the board and take care of day-to-day tasks. The management company is usually responsible for finding, hiring, and paying gardeners, trash haulers, janitors, repair personnel, and a pool maintenance firm. The management company collects maintenance fees and special assessments from unit owners, accounts for condominium expenses, handles the payroll, and pays for contracted services.

If the association chooses to hire an on-site manager, that person is usually responsible for enforcing the house rules, handling complaints or problems regarding maintenance, making daily security checks, and supervising the swimming pool and recreation areas. The extent of his or her duties and responsibilities is set forth by the owners' association. The association should also retain the right to fire the resident manager and the management firm if their services are not satisfactory.

Maintenance Fees

The costs of maintaining the common elements in a condominium are allocated among the unit owners in accordance with percentages set forth in the master deed. These are called **maintenance fees** or **association dues** and are collected monthly. Failure to pay creates a lien against the delinquent owner's unit. The amount collected is based on the association's budget for the coming year. This is based on the board of directors' estimate of the cost of month-to-month maintenance, insurance, and legal and management services, plus reserves for expenses that do not occur monthly.

RESERVES

reserves

Money set aside for expenses that do not occur every month.

The importance of setting aside **reserves** each month is illustrated by the following example. Suppose it is estimated that the exterior of a 100-unit building will have to be painted every seven years and that the cost is expected to be $25,200. To avoid a special painting assessment of $252 per unit, the association instead collects $3 per month from each unit owner for 84 months. If the reserves are kept in an interest-bearing savings account as they should be, less than $3 per month would need to be collected.

Property Taxes and Insurance

Since condominium law recognizes each condominium dwelling unit as a separate legal ownership, property taxes are assessed on each unit separately. Property taxes are based on the assessed value of the unit, which is based on its market value. As a rule, it is not necessary for the taxing authority to assess and tax the common elements separately. The reason is that the market value of each unit reflects not only the value of the unit itself, but also the value of the fractional ownership in the common elements that accompany the unit.

The association is responsible for purchasing hazard and liability insurance covering the common elements. Each dwelling unit owner is responsible for purchasing hazard and liability insurance for the interior of his dwelling.

Thus, if a visitor slips on a banana peel in the lobby or in a hallway of the building, the association is responsible. If the accident occurs in an individual's unit, the unit owner is responsible. In a high-rise condominium, if the roof breaks during a heavy rainstorm and floods several apartments below, the association is responsible. If an apartment owner's dishwasher overflows and soaks the apartments below him, the owner is responsible. If patio furniture is stolen from the swimming pool area, the association is responsible. If patio furniture (or any personal property for that matter) is stolen from an individual's unit, that is the unit owner's responsibility. Policies designed for associations and policies designed for condominium owners are readily available from insurance companies.

If a condominium unit is being rented, the owner will want to have landlord insurance, and the tenant, for his own protection, will want a tenant's hazard and liability policy.

Condominium Financing

Because each condominium unit can be separately owned, each can be separately financed. Thus, a condominium purchaser can choose whether to borrow against her unit. If she borrows, she can choose a large or small down payment and a long or short amortization period. If she wants to repay early or refinance, that is her option too. Upon resale, the new buyer can elect to assume the loan, pay it off, or obtain new financing. In other words, while association bylaws, restrictions, and house rules may regulate the use of a unit, in no way does the association control how a unit may be financed.

Since each unit is a separate ownership, if a lender needs to foreclose against a delinquent borrower in the building, the remaining unit owners are not involved. They are neither responsible for the delinquent borrower's mortgage debt, nor are they parties to the foreclosure.

LOAN TERMS

Loan terms offered condominium buyers are quite similar to those offered on houses, although most lenders will require that at least 50% of the condominiums in the development be owner occupied. Typically, lenders will make conventional, uninsured loans for up to 80% of value. With private mortgage insurance, this can be raised to 90% or 95%. On FHA-approved buildings, the FHA offers insurance terms similar to those for detached dwellings. Financing can also be in the form of an installment contract or a seller carryback.

DEPOSIT PRACTICES

If a project is not already completed and ready for occupancy when it is offered for sale, it is common for the developer to require a substantial deposit. The best practice is to place this in an escrow account payable to the developer upon completion. Without this precaution, some developers will use deposits to help pay the expenses of construction while the building is being built. Unfortunately, if the deposits are spent by a developer who goes bankrupt before the project is completed, the buyer receives neither a finished unit nor the return of his deposit. If the deposits are held in escrow, the buyers do not receive a unit but they do get their deposits back.

CONDOMINIUM CONVERSIONS

During the late 1970s, the idea of condominium ownership became very popular in the United States. Builders constructed new condominiums at a rapid pace, but there were not enough to fill demand. Soon enterprising developers found that existing apartment buildings could be converted to condominiums and sold to the waiting public. Compared to new construction, a condominium conversion is often simpler, faster, and more profitable for the developer. The procedure involves finding an attractively built existing building that is well located and has good floor plans. The developer does a face-lift on the outside, adds more landscaping, paints the interior, and replaces carpets and appliances. The developer also files the necessary legal paperwork to convert the building and land into condominium units and common elements.

A potential problem area with condominium conversions, and one that a prospective buyer should be aware of, is that converted buildings are used buildings that were not intended as condominiums when built. As used buildings, there may be considerable deferred maintenance, and the building may have thermal insulation suitable to a time when energy costs were lower. If the building was originally built for rental purposes, sound-deadening insulation in the walls, floors, and ceilings may be inadequate. Fire protection between units may also be less than satisfactory. In contrast, newly built condominiums must meet current building code requirements regarding thermal and sound insulation, fire-wall construction, and so forth.

It is worth noting that not all condominium conversions are carried out by developers. Enterprising tenants have successfully converted their own buildings and saved considerable sums of money. It is not uncommon for the value of a building to double when it is converted to a condominium. Tenants who are willing to hire the legal, architectural, and construction help they need can create valuable condominium homes for themselves in the same building where they were previously renters.

Advantages of Condominium Living

Compared to detached dwellings, condominium living offers a number of advantages and some disadvantages. On the advantage side, instead of four or five detached dwellings on an acre of land, a condominium builder can place 25 or even 100 living units. This spreads the cost of the site among more dwellings, and the builder does not have the miles of streets, sewers, or utility lines that would be necessary to reach every house in a spread-out subdivision. Furthermore, the use of shared walls and foundations, meaning that one dwelling unit's ceiling is another's floor and that one roof can cover many vertically stacked units, can produce savings in construction materials and labor. In central city districts where a single square foot of vacant land can cost $100 or more, only a high-rise condominium can make housing units possible. In the suburbs, where land is cheaper, a condominium is often the difference between buying and renting for some people.

Disadvantages of Condominium Living

A major disadvantage of condominium living is the close proximity of one's neighbors and the extra level of government. In other words, buying into a condominium means buying into a group of people whose lifestyles may differ from yours and whose opinions as to how to run the association will differ from yours. By way of contrast, if you buy a single-family detached house on a lot, you will have (subject to zoning and legal restrictions) sole control over the use of it. You can choose to remodel or add on. You can choose what color to paint your house and garage, how many people and animals will live there, what type of landscaping to have, from whom to purchase property insurance, whether to rent it out or live in it, and so on. Your next-door neighbor will have the same rights over his land. You cannot dictate to him what color to paint his house, what kind of shrubs to grow, or from whom to buy hazard insurance if he buys it at all.

In a condominium, the owners have a considerable degree of control over each other in matters that affect the common good of the association. Moreover, certain decisions must be made as a group, such as what kinds of common element hazard and liability insurance to carry, how much to carry, and from whom to purchase it. If there is an outdoor swimming pool, a decision must be made as to which months it should be heated and how warm it should be kept. The group as a whole must decide on how the landscaping is to be maintained, who will do it, and how much should be spent. If there is to be security service, again there must be a group decision as to how much, when, and who should be hired. If a large truck runs into a unit on the other end of the building, it's an association problem because each owner has an undivided interest in the whole building.

All matters affecting the condominium must be brought to the attention of the board of directors, often by way of a committee. All committee and board positions are filled by volunteers from the association. Thus, owning a condominium is not entirely carefree, and there will be times when the board of directors will do things differently from what an individual owner would like. Another possibility is that there may be a lack of interested and talented people to serve as directors and on committees. Consequently, things that need to be done may be left undone, possibly posing a hazard to the association. Individual unit owners may be unaware of the management and maintenance requirements for a multimillion-dollar building and may have hired a management firm that knows (or does) even less.

Before Buying

If you are considering the purchase of a condominium unit, consider the previous points with care. Also look closely at the association's finances. The association may not have adequate reserves for upcoming maintenance work such as painting the building and putting on a new roof. If so, existing owners and new buyers will be in for a rude surprise in the form of a special assessment. Check the budget to see if it covers everything adequately and ask about lawsuits against the association that might drain its finances.

Although articles of incorporation, CC&Rs, and bylaws make boring reading, if you offer to buy a condominium unit, you should make the offer contingent on your reading and approving them. These are the rules you agree to live by, and it's better to read them before committing to buy than after. You may find prohibitions against your pet cat or dog or against renting your unit while you are temporarily transferred overseas. (At the closing, the seller must give you a current set of these documents along with the deed and keys to the unit. When you sell, you must give a current set to your buyer.)

Before buying, pay special attention to construction quality. Will ongoing maintenance be expensive? Is there deferred maintenance? Ask if the clubhouse and recreation facilities are owned by the association or by the developer who will continue to charge you for their use year after year. Is soundproofing between units adequate or will you hear your neighbor's piano, drums, and arguments? What is the owner-tenant mix? The most successful condominiums are predominantly owner occupied rather than renter occupied. This is because owners usually take more interest and care in their properties, and this in turn boosts resale values. The list of things to look for and ask about when buying into a condominium is longer than there is space here, and bookstores have good books that will help you. But before moving on, the following two thoughts apply to any purchase of a condominium, cooperative, planned unit development, or time-share. First, keep a balance between your heart and your head. It is easy to be enchanted to the point that no further investigation is made, perhaps knowing in advance it would sour the deal. Second, ask those who have already bought if they would buy again.

Cooperative Apartments

Now that you have just read about condominiums, take yourself back to the year 1900 in New York City. You've been renting an apartment unit on Manhattan for several years and would like to own it. Your neighbors in the building have expressed the same desire, but condominium legislation is more than half a century in the future. How would you and your neighbors accomplish this, given existing legal frameworks? Your answer is the corporate form of ownership, a form of multi-person ownership well established in America by that time. To carry out your collective desires, you form a not-for-profit corporation. Shares in the corporation are sold to the building's tenants, and the money is used as a down payment to buy the building. Title to the building is placed in the name of the corporation, and each shareholder receives from the corporation a lease to his apartment. Thus, the shareholders own the corporation, the corporation owns the building, and the corporation gives its shareholders leases to their apartments. Each month, each shareholder makes a payment to the corporation to enable it to make the required monthly payment on the debt against the building and to pay for maintenance and repairs. Government of the building is handled by a board of directors that meets monthly and at an annual meeting of all the shareholders.

This form of residential ownership, which can be found in significant numbers in New York City, Miami, Chicago, San Francisco, and Honolulu, is called a **cooperative**. The individual shareholders are called cooperators, and the lease that the corporation gives to a shareholder is called a **proprietary lease**.

When a cooperator wishes to sell, the cooperator does not sell his apartment but rather the shares of stock that carry with it a proprietary lease on that apartment. Although for all practical purposes the transaction looks like a sale of real estate, from a legal standpoint it is a sale of corporate stock. As such, the listing and selling forms that are used for houses and condominiums are not suitable, and special cooperative forms must be used.

cooperative

Land and building owned or leased by a corporation that, in turn, leases space to its shareholders.

proprietary lease

A lease issued by a cooperative corporation to its shareholders.

FINANCING

Financing a cooperative is different from financing a house or condominium. When a cooperative apartment building is first organized, the entire property is in the name of the cooperative corporation, and there is one mortgage loan on all of it. To illustrate, suppose a 10-unit building will cost the cooperators $1,000,000 and all the units are considered equal in desirability. A lender will finance 70% of the purchase if the cooperators raise the remaining 30%. This requires the cooperators to sell 10 shares of stock, each share for $30,000 and good for one apartment unit in the building. The lender provides the remaining $700,000 to complete the purchase, and the corporation gives the lender a note for $700,000 secured by a mortgage against the building. Suppose the monthly payments on this loan are $7,000; this means each month each cooperator must contribute $700 toward the mortgage plus money to maintain and operate the building, pay the property taxes on it, and keep it insured.

DEFAULT

What happens if one of the cooperators fails to make his monthly payment to the cooperative? For the cooperative to send the lender anything less than the required $7,000 per month puts the loan in default. This means the remaining cooperators must make up the difference. Meanwhile, they can seek voluntary reimbursement by the tardy cooperator, or, if that does not work, terminate him as a shareholder and resell the share to someone who will make the payments.

RESALE

What happens if a shareholder in good standing wants to sell her unit? Since the underlying mortgage is against the entire building, it is impossible to refinance a portion of the building. Only the whole building can be refinanced and that requires approval by the cooperators as a whole. Traditionally, this has forced the cooperator to sell her share for all cash or on an installment sale plan. This is a handicap where the value of the share has increased substantially due to property value increase and reduction of the building's mortgage loan. As a solution, at least two states, New York and California, have enacted legislation allowing state-regulated lenders to make loans using cooperative stock as collateral.

GOVERNMENT

A cooperative apartment is governed by its articles of incorporation, bylaws, CC&Rs, and house rules. The governing body is a board of directors elected by the cooperators. The board hires the services needed to maintain and operate the building just as in a condominium. Annual meetings are also held, just as in a condominium.

DIFFERENCES

Now that the condominium format is available, relatively few cooperatives are being organized. This is largely because in a condominium the individual apartment unit can be financed separately from the remainder of the building. Moreover, if one condominium unit owner fails to make loan payments, the remaining owners in the building are not responsible for that loan. The condominium unit owner also has the personal choice of whether to have no debt, a little debt, or a lot of debt against his unit. Unpaid property taxes are another potential difference. In a condominium, each unit is taxed separately, and nonpayment brings a property tax foreclosure sale against just the delinquent unit, not the entire building.

SIMILARITY

A similarity exists between condominiums and cooperatives with respect to the money collected each month for the general maintenance and upkeep of the building. In either case, nonpayment will bring action against the tardy owner by the association, and that can result in foreclosure of that owner. Income tax rules effectively allow the same homeowner deductions on cooperatives as on condominiums and houses. However, a strict set of rules must be followed because technically a cooperator does not own real estate, but owns shares of stock.

NEW LEGISLATION

Due to the financing difficulty and mutual liability potential associated with cooperatives, several states have enacted legislation that allows new cooperatives to be financed entirely by the sale of stock that in turn is pledged to a lender. This way the failure of one cooperator to make mortgage loan payments does not jeopardize the other coopera-tors. Also, a county assessor can assess each cooperator individually for property tax pur-poses if the board of directors so requests. This avoids joint liability. If you are considering the purchase of a cooperative, read the articles of incorporation, bylaws, CC&Rs, and house rules before buying. Some operate under old rules, some under new rules, some will have rules you will be comfortable with, and some will not.

Although the opening example in this section on cooperatives was one of tenants banding together to buy their building, cooperatives are also organized and sold by real estate developers. These can be existing buildings converted by developers to cooperative ownership and new buildings built by developers from the ground up. In either case, a prospective purchaser will find it worthwhile to reread earlier paragraphs in this chapter on deposit practices, conversions, advantages, disadvantages, and before buying.

Planned Unit Development

planned unit development (PUD)

Individually owned lots and houses with community ownership of common areas.

If you buy into a condominium, you get a dwelling unit as separate property plus an undivided interest in the land and other common elements. If you buy into a coopera-tive, you get stock in the corporation that owns the building and a lease on a particular apartment. If you buy into a **planned unit development (PUD)**, you get a house and lot as separate property plus ownership in a community association that owns the common areas. Common areas may be as minimal as a few green spaces in open areas between houses or as extensive as to also include parks, pools, clubhouse facilities, jogging trails, boat docks, horse trails, and a golf course.

Although you own your lot and house as separate property in a PUD, there will be CC&Rs to follow. The PUD developer will establish an initial set of CC&Rs, then turn them over to the association for enforcement. Thus, your lot and home are not quite all yours to do with as you please because your association can dictate what color you can paint the exterior of your home, what you can and cannot plant in your front yard, and how many people and pets can reside with you. As with condominiums and cooperatives, PUD CC&Rs are not meant to be burdensome for the sake of being burdensome, but rather to maintain the attractiveness and tranquility of the development, and in doing so keep home values up.

The dwellings in a planned unit development typically take the form of detached houses and houses that share a common wall, such as row houses, townhouses, and cluster houses. Because each owner owns his land, vertical stacking of homes is limited to one owner and housing densities to 8 or 10 units per acre. Even though this is twice the density of a typical detached house subdivision, by careful planning a developer can give each owner the feeling of more spaciousness. One way is by taking advantage of uneven terrain. If a parcel contains some flat land, some hilly land, some land covered with trees, and a running stream, the dwellings can be clustered on the land best suited for building and thus preserve the stream, woods, and steep slopes in their natural state. With a standard subdivision layout, the devel-oper would have to remove the groves of trees, fill in the stream, and terrace the slopes, and would still be able to provide homes for only half the number of families.

Resort Time-sharing

resort time-sharing

The exclusive use of a property for a specified number of days each year.

Resort time-sharing is a method of dividing up and selling a living unit at a vacation facility for specified lengths of time each year. The idea started in Europe in the 1960s, when groups of individuals would jointly purchase ski resort lodgings and summer vacation villas with each owner taking a week or two of exclusive occupancy. Resort developers quickly recognized the market potential of the idea, and, in 1969, the first resort time-share opened in the United States. Since then hotels, motels, condominiums, townhouses, lodges, villas, recreational vehicle parks, campgrounds, houseboats, and even cruise ships have been time-shared.

RIGHT-TO-USE

Nearly all time-shares fall into one of two legal formats. The first is the **right-to-use** format. This gives the buyer a contractual right to occupy a living unit at a resort property for one week a year for a specific term of 20 to 40 years. The cost for the entire period is paid in advance. At the end of the contract term all of the buyer's possessory rights terminate unless the contract contains a renewal clause or a right to buy. The developer creates these contracts by either buying or leasing a resort property and then selling 50 one-week-a-year right-to-use contracts on each living unit. (The other two weeks of the year are reserved for maintenance.) Approximately 30% of the time-share market is right-to-use.

FEE SIMPLE

The second format is **fee simple** ownership. Here, the time-share purchaser obtains a fee ownership in the unit purchased. The purchaser owns the property for one week a year in perpetuity, and the sale is handled like a sale of real estate. There will be a formal closing, a title policy, execution of a mortgage and note, and delivery of a recordable deed that conveys the time-share interest. A developer offers fee time-shares by either building or buying a resort property and then selling 50 one-week-a-year fee simple slices in each unit, with the remaining two weeks for maintenance. Approximately 70% of the time-share market is fee simple.

COSTS

The initial cost of a time-share week at a resort in the United States is around $14,200, depending on the quality and location of the resort, the time of year (low season or high season), and the form of ownership (right-to-use is usually less expensive). Additionally, there will be an annual maintenance fee of $140 to $280 per time-share week. Buyers can purchase two or more time-share weeks if they want a longer vacation. Some buyers purchase one week in the summer and one week in the winter.

BENEFITS

The appeal of time-sharing to developers is that a resort or condominium complex that can be bought and furnished for $100,000 per unit can be resold in 50 time-share slices at $14,800 each—that is, $740,000 a unit. The primary appeal of time-sharing to consumers is having a resort to go to every year at a prepaid price. This is particularly appealing during inflationary times, although the annual maintenance fee can change. There may be certain tax benefits if the time-share is financed and for property taxes paid on fee simple time-shares. There may also be appreciation of the time-share unit if it is in a particularly popular and well-run resort.

Then again, some or all of these benefits may not materialize. First, the lump sum paid for a time-share week does look cheaper than hotel bills year after year. However, the time-share must be paid for in full in advance (or financed at interest) whereas the hotel is paid as it is used each year. Also, there is a time-share maintenance fee of $380–$400 per annum that goes for clerk and maid service, linen laundry and replacement, structural maintenance and repairs, swimming pool service, hazard and liability insurance, reservations, collections and accounting services, general management, and so on.

Second, going to the same resort for the same week every year for the next 40 years may become wearisome. Yet, that is what a time-share buyer is agreeing to do. And, if the week goes vacant, the maintenance fee must still be paid. To offset this, two large resort exchange services and several smaller ones exist, and some of the larger time-share developers allow their buyers to exchange weeks among their various projects. There is a cost, however, to exchanging. There may be as many as three fees to pay: an initiation fee, an annual membership fee, and a fee when an exchange is made. These can amount to $100 or more for an exchange. Moreover, someone else with a time-share week they don't want that you do want at the right time of the year must also be in the exchange bank. Satisfaction is usually achieved in exchanging by being flexible in accepting an exchange. Note, too, if you own an off-season week at one resort, do not count on exchanging it for a peak-season vacation somewhere else. Exchange banks require members to accept periods of equal or lesser popularity.

Third, tax laws allow deductions for interest expense on time-shares that are financed and for property taxes on fee time-shares. Time-shares have occasionally been touted as tax shelter vehicles; however, that has already met the ire of the Internal Revenue Service.

Fourth, although there have been several reported instances of time-share appreciation, it is generally agreed in the time-share industry and by consumer groups that the primary reason to purchase a resort time-share is to obtain a vacation, not appreciation. In fact, a time-share industry rule-of-thumb is that one-third of the retail price of a time-share unit goes to marketing costs. This acts as a damper on time-share resale prices and even suggests that a buyer may be able to purchase a time-share on the resale market for less than from a developer.

COMMITMENT

Against the comfort of knowing that as a time-share owner one has a long-term commitment to use a resort, one also has a long-term commitment to its maintenance, repair, refurbishing, and management. This is similar to ownership in a condominium, except with ownership split among as many as 50 owners for each unit. Therefore, any one owner may not have a large enough stake to want to take an active part in overseeing the management. As a result, management falls to the developer who, having once sold out the project, may no longer have as much incentive to oversee things as carefully as it did during the sales period. The developer can turn the job over to a management firm, but who oversees them to make certain the time-share owners get good service at a fair price?

STATE REGULATIONS

There are 46 states that have adopted time-share regulations. Many of these follow the Model Time-share Act designed by the Association of Real Estate License Law Officials and endorsed by the National Association of REALTORS®. Much time-share legislation is in the form of consumer protection and disclosure (prospectus) requirements. Other legislation deals with how time-shares should be assessed for property taxation and what type of license a person employed to sell time-shares should hold, if any. Due to high-pressure sales techniques observed at some time-share sales offices, a number of states have enacted mandatory "cooling-off" periods of five days during which a buyer can rescind his contract. Because of multimillion-dollar consumer losses due to uncompleted time-share projects, the sale of the same time-share to more than one party, and money collected with deeds never sent, surety bonds and escrows are now required by some states. Meanwhile, any prospective time-share purchaser or salesperson would do well to take plenty of time in deciding, have all paperwork reviewed by an attorney before signing, and spend time talking to existing purchasers to ask if they would buy again.

Vocabulary Review

Match terms a–t with statements 1–20.

a. Annual meeting
b. Board of directors
c. Bylaws
d. Common elements
e. Condominium
f. Condominium act
g. Condominium subdivision
h. Condominium unit
i. Cooperative
j. Cooperator
k. Covenants, Conditions, and Restrictions (CC&Rs)
l. House rules
m. Maintenance fees
n. Management company
o. Owners' association
p. Planned unit development (PUD)
q. Proprietary lease
r. Reserves
s. Resort time-sharing
t. Right-to-use

_____ 1. Individual ownership of a space of air plus undivided ownership of the common elements.

_____ 2. Ownership by a corporation that in turn leases space to its shareholders.

_____ 3. Roof, stairs, elevator, lobby, and so on, in a condominium.

_____ 4. An organization composed of unit owners in which membership is automatic upon purchase of a unit.

_____ 5. Type of lease issued by a cooperative corporation to its shareholders.

_____ 6. A document that converts a parcel of land into a stratified subdivision; also called a master deed.

_____ 7. Rules that govern how the owners' association will be run.

_____ 8. A shareholder in a cooperative apartment.

_____ 9. Charges levied against unit owners to cover the costs of maintaining the common areas; also called association dues.

_____ 10. Form of community ownership where the houses and lots are privately owned but title to common areas is held by an owners' association.

_____ 11. State legislation that creates the legal framework for condominium subdivisions.

_____ 12. That portion of a condominium that is the exclusive property of an individual unit owner.

_____ 13. Regulations by which a condominium owner must abide.

_____ 14. Rules for the use of the swimming pool and recreation facilities would be found here.

_____ 15. A governing body elected by association members.

_____ 16. A once-a-year business meeting of the entire association membership.

_____ 17. Advises the board of directors; takes care of day-to-day tasks.

_____ 18. The exclusive use of a property for a specified number of days each year.

_____ 19. A contractual right to occupy a unit at a time-share resort.

_____ 20. Money set aside from the budget for expenses that do not occur every month.

Questions and Problems

1. Why are condominiums a popular alternative to single-family houses?

2. Who owns the land in a fee simple condominium project? In a cooperative?

3. What is the key difference between a proprietary lease in a cooperative and a landlord-tenant lease?

4. What is the purpose of the master deed in a condominium project?

5. Who owns the wall between two condominium units?

6. What are CC&Rs and what is their purpose?

7. What are maintenance fees? What happens if they are not paid?

8. If the owners' association carries hazard and liability insurance, why is it also advisable for each unit owner to purchase a hazard and liability policy?

9. Briefly explain the concept of right-to-use and fee simple time-sharing.

10. Briefly explain how title to land in a PUD is held.

Additional Readings

Condominium Development Guide, by Keith Romney and Brad Romney (Warren, Gorham, & Lamont, 1990). Legal, readable, practical, and detailed. This is the type of information one needs before developing a condominium. Contains procedures, analysis, and forms. Annual updates issued.

Developing Time-share and Vacation Ownership Properties by Diane R. Suchman (Urban Land Institute, 1999).

Drafting Documents for Condominiums, PUDs, and Golf Course Communities (American Law Institute, 1997). Audio cassette.

Income/Expense Analysis: Condos, Co-ops, PUDS (Institute for Real Estate Management, 1995). Updated annually.

"Managing Condos and Coops" (*National Real Estate Investor*, March 1, 2000, p. 14).

CHAPTER 24

Property Insurance

I f you own real estate, you take the risk that your property may be damaged due to fire or other catastrophe. Additionally, there is the possibility that someone may be injured while on your property and hold you responsible. Insurance to cover losses from either of these occurrences is available and is the topic of this chapter. Let's begin with property damage, then discuss public liability and homeowner insurance. We will conclude with new for old, flood insurance, policy cancellation, policy takeovers, and home buyer's insurance.

Property Damage

Fire insurance is the foundation of property damage policies. Historically, there have been a variety of solutions to the problem of fire damage. Two thousand years ago, a Roman named Crassus would bring his firefighters to the scene of a fire and quote a price for putting it out. If the owner refused, Crassus offered cash on the spot for the burning building, and, if accepted, sent in the firefighters to salvage as much as possible.

In colonial America, fire insurance groups were organized wherein payments by members to the group compensated for fire losses to members and subsidized volunteer firefighting companies. Each member received a plaque to display on the front of his building. Although the volunteer fire companies would answer all calls, they probably put more effort into saving houses displaying the plaque.

MODERN FIRE COVERAGE

A major step forward in fire insurance coverage was the enactment in 1886 by the New York legislature of a standardized fire policy. This policy, called the New York fire form, has been

LEARNING OBJECTIVES

After reading this chapter, you should be able to:

❬ Define the different types of insurance coverage and endorsements.

❬ Understand and discuss the basic forms for insurance coverage.

❬ Understand the difference between tenant's policy and a homeowner's policy.

❬ Discuss lender requirements involving insurance coverage.

❬ Discuss the difference between policy cancellation and policy takeovers.

KEY TERMS

All-risks policy • Broad form (HO-2) • Endorsement • Homeowner policy • Insurance premium • Insured • New for old • Old for old • Peril • Public liability revised twice, in 1918 and 1943, and today it serves as the foundation for nearly all property damage policies written in the United States. The 165 lines of court-tested language in the New York fire form cover the following: (1) loss by fire, (2) loss by lightning, and (3) losses sustained while removing property from an endangered premises. A person (called the **insured**) makes a payment (called an **insurance premium**) to an insurance company (called the **insurer**) and the company pays if a loss is suffered.

ENDORSEMENTS

Although fire is the single most important cause of property damage in the United States, a property owner is also exposed to other **perils** (also called **hazards** or **risks**). Examples are hail, tornado, earthquake, riot, windstorm, smoke damage, explosion, glass breakage, waterpipe leaks, vandalism, freezing, and building collapse. Coverage for each peril can be purchased with a separate policy or added to the fire form as an **endorsement**. An endorsement, also called a *rider* or *attachment*, is an agreement by the insurer to modify a basic policy. Usually this is to extend coverage to losses by perils not included in the basic policy.

Public Liability

Public liability (also called **personal liability**) is the financial responsibility one has toward others as a result of one's actions or failure to take action. For example, if you are trimming the limbs from a tall tree in your backyard and a limb falls on your neighbor's roof and damages it, you are liable to your neighbor for damages. If someone is injured on your property, that person may be able to successfully sue you for money damages.

Generally, you are liable when there exists a legal duty to exercise reasonable care and you fail to do so, thereby causing injury to an innocent party. Even though you did not intend for the limb to fall on your neighbor's roof or a house guest to slip on your newly waxed floor, you are not excused from liability. You can be held accountable, in money, for the amount of damage caused.

Homeowner Policies

For major commercial and industrial property owners and users, carefully identifying each risk exposure and then insuring for it is a logical and economic approach to purchasing insurance. But for the majority of homeowners, owners of small apartment and business properties, and their tenants, purchasing insurance piecemeal is a confusing process. As a result, package policies have been developed.

Of these, the best known and most widely used is the **homeowner policy**. It contains the coverage's deemed by insurance experts to be most useful to persons who own the home in which they live. Not only does this approach avoid overlaps and lessen the opportunity for gaps in coverage, but the cost is less than purchasing separate individual policies with the same total coverage. Moreover, homeowner policies also cover certain liability and property losses that occur away from the insured's premises. For renters there is a packaged tenant's policy. Let's take a closer look.

POLICY FORMATS

There are seven standardized home insurance policy forms in use in the United States. Five are designed for owners of single-family dwellings, one is for tenants, and one is for condominium owners. Each policy contains two sections. Section I deals with loss of or

---

insured
One who is covered by insurance.

insurance premium
The amount of money one must pay for insurance coverage.

peril
Hazard or risk.

endorsement
A policy modification; also called a rider or an attachment.

public liability
The financial responsibility one has toward others.

homeowner policy
A combined property and liability policy designed for residential use.

damage to the insured's property. Section II deals with liability of the insured and the insured's family. We will proceed in that order.

PROPERTIES COVERED

A homeowner policy covers your house, garage, and other structures on your lot such as a guest house or garden shed. If you are forced to live elsewhere while damage to your residence is being repaired, your homeowner policy will provide for additional living expenses. A homeowner policy also covers much of your personal property. This includes all household contents and other personal belongings that are used, owned, worn, or carried by you or your family, whether at home or somewhere else.

A homeowner policy does not cover structures on your property that are used for business purposes or rented or leased to others. A homeowner policy does not cover loss of or damage to automobiles, business property, or pets. Moreover, certain valuables such as jewels, furs, and stamp and coin collections may not be covered for full value without additional insurance.

PERILS COVERED

Basic form (HO-1) insures against the first 11 perils shown in Table 24.1. **Broad form (HO-2)** covers all 18 perils in Table 24.1. **Comprehensive form (HO-5)** is called an **all-risks policy** because it covers all perils except those listed in the policy. **Form HO-8** is designed for older homes. It covers the same perils as HO-1. Because it is usually difficult to duplicate an older home for anywhere close to its market value, Form HO-8 insures for actual cash value, not replacement cost. (Actual cash value and replacement cost will be explained momentarily.)

Excluded from all homeowner policies are loss or damage caused by flood, landslide, mud flow, tidal wave, earthquake, underground water, settling, cracking, war, and nuclear accident. Some of these can, however, be covered using riders or separate policies.

Special form (HO-3) is a combination form that provides HO-5 coverage on one's dwelling and private structures and HO-2 coverage on one's personal property. Forms HO-3 and HO-5 are the most popular of the four policies designed for single-family homes.

broad form (HO-2)
An insurance policy that covers a large number of named perils.

all-risks policy
All perils, except those excluded in writing, are covered.

TENANT'S POLICY

If you rent rather than own your residence, you would choose the **tenant's form (HO-4)**. This policy provides broad form coverage for personal property and reimbursement of any loss of use of rental property up to 20% of the personal property covered. The standard HO-4 rental policy provides no liability coverage automatically, so renters should make special arrangements for a general liability policy to get this coverage. The distinguishing feature in a tenant's policy is that it does not cover damage to the building.

CONDOMINIUM POLICY

In a condominium, the homeowners' association usually buys insurance covering all of the common elements. To cover personal property and any additions or alterations to the unit not insured by the association's policy, a **condominium unit owner's form (HO-6)** is available. It is always prudent to ensure that adequate coverage has been obtained by the association. Loss of assessment insurance will pay up to a stipulated

TABLE 24.1	Homeowner Policy Coverage: Perils Covered by Insurance	
Comprehensive (HO-5)	**Broad (HO-2)**	**Basic (HO-1)**
		1. Fire or lightning
		2. Losses sustained while removing property from an endangered premises
		3. Windstorm or hail
		4. Explosion
		5. Riot or civil commotion
		6. Aircraft
		7. Vehicles
		8. Smoke
		9. Vandalism and malicious mischief
		10. Theft
		11. Breakage of glass that is part of the building (no in HO-4)
	12. Falling objects	
	13. Weight of ice, snow, sleet	
	14. Collapse of building(s) or any part thereof	
	15. Sudden and accidental tearing asunder, cracking, burning, or bulging of a steam or hot water heating system or of appliances for heating water	
	16. Accidental discharge, leakage, or overflow of water or steam from within a plumbing, heating, or air-conditioning system or domestic appliance	
	17. Freezing of plumbing, heating, and air-conditioning systems and domestic appliances	
	18. Sudden and accidental injury from artificially generated currents to electrical appliances, devices, fixtures, and wiring	
All perils except flood, landslide, mud flow, tidal wave, earthquake, underground water, settling, cracking, war, and nuclear accident. (Check policy for a complete list of perils excluded.)		

Source: © 2014 OnCourse Learning

amount for assessments made against an insured by their association for both common element losses in liability suits filed against the association. This may also be a wise purchase.

REAL PROPERTY LOSS

In addition to the perils covered, there are also variations in homeowner's coverage. Dwelling coverage, or Coverage A under a homeowner's policy, indicates the maximum the insurance company will pay in the event of the total destruction of the property. The insurance company will not pay more than the amounts stipulated under Coverage A unless the policy includes a valuable rider referred to as an inflation guard endorsement. People should insure their homes for full replacement costs and add an inflation guard endorsement to their policies. Note that Coverage B provides for payment of 10% (of dwelling coverage) for other structures. Coverage C additionally provides for 50% of personal property, and Coverage D provides for 20% of Coverage A for loss of use. Note Table 24.2.

TABLE 24.2 Homeowner's Coverage				
	100% Dwelling	**10% of A** **Other Structures**	**50% of A** **Personal Property**	**20% of A** **Loss of Use**
	Coverage A	*Coverage B*	*Coverage C*	*Coverage D*
HO-1	Basic	Basic	Basic	Basic (10% of A)
HO-2	Broad	Broad	Broad	Broad
HO-3	All-Risk	All-Risk	Broad	All-Risk
HO-4 (For renters)	N/A	N/A	Broad (Basic coverage)	Broad (20% of C)
HO-5	All-Risk	All-Risk	All-Risk	All-Risk
HO-6 (For condo dwellers)	N/A	N/A	Broad	Broad (40% of C)
HO-8 (For properties not qualifying for HO-1, 2, 3, or 5)	Basic (ACV only)	Basic	Basic	Basic
HO-15 Converts broad to modified all risk				

Source: © 2014 OnCourse Learning

LIABILITY COVERAGE

Section II in all seven home insurance forms is a liability policy for you and all family members that live with you. This coverage is designed to protect you from a financially crippling claim or lawsuit. The falling limb and freshly waxed floor examples earlier in this chapter are events that would be covered by this coverage. If a liability claim arises, the insurance company will pay the legal costs of defending you as well as any damages up to the limits of the policy. Note that this section also provides you and your family with liability protection away from your premises. Thus, if you accidentally hit someone with a golf ball on a golf course or your child accidentally kicks a football through a neighbor's window, this part of the policy covers you. If you have a pet and it takes a bite out of a visitor to your home or out of a neighbor's leg while out for a walk, you are covered.

MEDICAL PAYMENTS

The cost of treating minor injuries for which you may be liable is paid by **medical payments coverage** found in home insurance policies. The main difference between this and liability coverage is that medical payments coverage provides payment regardless of who is at fault. However, it covers only relatively minor injuries, say $500 or $1,000. Major injuries would come under the liability coverage. The liability and medical payments coverage in a home insurance policy do not apply to your motor vehicles or your business pursuits. Those require separate policies. Additionally, your home insurance policy does not cover injuries to you or your family. Those must be insured separately.

ENDORSEMENTS

Any home policy can be endorsed for additional coverage. For example, **inflation guard** endorsements are available that automatically increase property damage coverage by 1½%, 2%, or 2½% per quarter, as selected by the insured. Another popular endorsement is **worker's compensation insurance**. This is designed to pay for injuries suffered by persons such as baby sitters and cleaning help who are employed by the insured to do work on the premises. If the property is to be rented out, tenant coverage can be added. Alternatively, a policy specifically designed for rental property can be purchased.

New for Old

A special problem in recovering from damage to a building is that although the building may not be new, any repairs are made new. For example, if a 20-year-old house burns to the ground, it is impossible to put back a used house, even though a used house is exactly what the insured lost. Thus, the question is whether insurance should pay for the full cost of fixing the damage, in effect, replace "new for old," or simply pay the actual cash value of the loss. **Actual cash value** is the new price minus accumulated depreciation and is, in effect, "**old for old**." Under "old for old," if the owner rebuilds, he pays the difference between actual cash value and the cost of the repairs. As this can be quite costly to the insured, the alternative is to purchase a policy that replaces "**new for old**."

For the owner of an apartment building, store, or other property operated on a business basis, obtaining "new for old" coverage is a matter of substituting the term *replacement cost* for *actual cash value* wherever it appears in the policy. Also, the policyholder must agree to carry coverage amounting to at least 80% of current replacement cost and to use the insurance proceeds to repair or replace the damaged property within a reasonable time.

Most homeowner policies provide that if the amount of insurance carried is 80% or more of the cost to replace the house today, the full cost of repair will be paid by the insurer, up to the face amount of the policy. If the face amount is less than 80% of replacement costs, the insured is entitled to the higher of (1) the actual cash value of the loss, or (2) the amount calculated as follows:

old for old

Policy pays only the depreciated cost.

new for old

Policy pays replacement cost.

$$\frac{\text{Insurance carried}}{\left(\begin{array}{c}\text{80\% of today's cost} \\ \text{to replace whole structure}\end{array}\right)} \times \left(\begin{array}{c}\text{Today's cost to} \\ \text{replace the} \\ \text{damaged portion}\end{array}\right) = \text{Recovery}$$

Lender Requirements

Real estate lenders such as savings and loans, banks, mortgage companies, etc., require that a borrower carry fire and extended coverage on the mortgaged structures. The reason, of course, is to protect the value of the security for the loan. The lender will be named on the policy along with the property owner, and any checks from the insurance company for damages will be made out to the borrower and the lender jointly. Note that the lender does not require liability and medical payments coverage as the lender is not concerned with that aspect of the borrower's exposure. Nonetheless, most borrowers will choose a homeowner policy that has Section I coverage satisfactory to the lender rather than fire and extended coverage only.

The borrower must have a policy that meets the lender's requirements before the loan is made and must keep the policy in force at all times while the loan is outstanding. Some lenders collect one-twelfth of the annual premium each month and forward the money to the insurer annually. Other lenders allow the homeowner to maintain the policy and each year mail proof of the policy to the lender. The lender on a condominium unit will require proof that the condominium association carries insurance on the common elements.

GUARANTEED REPLACEMENT COST

Because of the nearly constant increase in the cost of construction over the past several decades, lenders require either a replacement cost policy that guarantees adequate money to rebuild the entire structure at today's costs or coverage for the full amount of the loan. (The land is not insured as it is assumed it will survive any damage to the structures upon it.) The borrower, for peace of mind, will choose replacement cost coverage. This is especially true where the loan is less than the cost of replacement.

It is difficult to overemphasize the need for a policy review every one to three years. (The insurance agent will do this on request as part of the policy service.) Many a sad tale has been told by a homeowner who bought 20 years ago, has dutifully paid the insurance premium every year, has not revised the coverage to reflect current construction costs, and then has a major loss. Caution is also advised when a seller carries back financing or an individual buys mortgages as investments. If you fall into this category, make certain that any structures on the property serving as collateral are adequately insured so that if the structures are destroyed, there will be enough insurance money to fully pay you off. Also make certain you are named on the policy as a lender and that the borrower renews the policy each year.

Flood Insurance

In 1968, Congress created the National Flood Insurance Program. This program is a joint effort of the nation's insurance industry and the federal government to offer property owners coverage for losses to real and personal property resulting from the inundation of normally dry areas from the following: (1) the overflow of inland or tidal waters, (2) the unusual and rapid accumulation or runoff of surface waters, (3) mudslides resulting from accumulations of water on or under the ground, and (4) erosion losses caused by abnormal water runoff.

All mortgages in which the federal government is involved (including government-insured lenders and FHA, VA, FNMA, FHLMC, and GNMA loans) require either a certificate that the mortgaged property is not in a flood zone or a policy of **flood insurance**. Flood insurance is available through insurance agents. Earthquake insurance is also available from insurance agents. Lenders do not, as a rule, require borrowers to carry it. Nonetheless, it is enjoying some popularity in earthquake-prone regions such as California.

Landlord Policies

If you rent out part of your home to a tenant or if you buy a property (such as a house, condominium, apartment building, store, office, warehouse, or farm) and rent it out, make certain you purchase adequate property damage and liability coverage. If a loan is involved, the lender will require property damage coverage for the amount of the loan. But the lender is not concerned about the loan amount nor if someone is injured on your property and holds you liable. Landlord coverage can be obtained by endorsement to an existing homeowner policy or by purchasing a landlord package policy that combines property damage, liability, medical expenses, and loss of rents. The latter pays you what you would normally collect in rent when damage is severe enough that the tenant has to move out while repairs are made.

Note that if you buy vacant land and do not use it for business purposes and do not rent it out, most standard homeowner policies automatically include liability coverage on the land without additional cost or endorsement. You should, however, verify this with your insurance agent. In any event, do not fail to be adequately insured on any property you own. Reconstruction costs are expensive and liability suits more common and more expensive than in the past.

Policy Cancellation

A property damage or public liability policy can be canceled at any time by the insured. Since the policy is billed in advance, the insured is entitled to a refund for unused coverage. This refund is computed at short rates that are somewhat higher than a simple pro rata charge. For example, the holder of a one-year policy who cancels one-third of the way through the year is charged 44% of the one-year price, not 33⅓%.

The insurer also has the right to cancel a policy. However, unlike the policyholder who can cancel on immediate notice, the New York fire form requires the insurer to give the policyholder five-day notice. Also, the cost of the policy, and hence the refund of unused premium, must be calculated on a pro rata basis. For example, the insured would be charged one-half the annual premium for six months of coverage.

POLICY SUSPENSION

Certain acts of the policyholder will suspend coverage without the necessity of a written notice from the insurer. Suspension automatically occurs if the insured allows the hazard exposure to the insurer to increase beyond the risks normally associated with the type of property being insured, for example, converting a dwelling into a restaurant. Suspension also occurs if the insured building is left unoccupied for more than 60 days (30 days in some states) because unoccupied buildings are more attractive to thieves, vandals, and arsonists. If the condition causing the suspension is corrected (returning the restaurant to a dwelling or reoccupying the building) before a loss occurs, the policy becomes effective again.

Willful concealment or misrepresentation by the insured of any material fact or circumstance concerning the policy, the property, or the insured, either before or after a loss, will make the policy void. Thus, if a person operates a business in the basement of his house and conceals this from the insurer for fear of being charged more for insurance, the money he pays for insurance could be wasted.

Policy Takeovers

Oftentimes in a real estate transaction the buyer will ask to assume the seller's existing insurance policy for the property. This way the buyer avoids having to pay a full year's premium in advance and the seller benefits by avoiding a short-rate cancellation charge. To avoid a break in coverage, the insurer must accept the buyer as the new policyholder before the closing takes place. This is done with an endorsement issued by the insurer naming the buyer as the insured party. The reason for this requirement is that an insurance policy does not protect the property, but the insured's financial interest in the property. This is called an **insurable interest**.

Suppose the property is destroyed by fire immediately after the closing. Once title has passed, the seller no longer has an insurable interest in the property. If the insurance company has not endorsed the policy over to the buyer, the company is under no obligation to pay for the damage. If there is doubt that the endorsement to the buyer can be obtained in time for the closing, the buyer should purchase a new policy in his or her own name. Note that anyone holding a mortgage on an improved property has an insurable interest.

Home Buyer's Insurance

A long-standing concern of home buyers has been the possibility of finding structural or mechanical defects in a home after buying it. In new homes the builder can usually be held responsible for repairs, and many states require builders to give a one-year warranty. Additional protection is available from builders associated with the Home Owners Warranty Corporation (HOW). Under this program, during the first year the builder warrants against defects caused by faulty workmanship or materials and against major structural defects. During the second year the builder continues to warrant against major structural defects and against defects in wiring, piping, and ductwork. If the builder cannot or will not honor this warranty, the HOW program underwriter will do so. Then for eight more years, the underwriter directly insures the home buyer against major structural defects, less a $250 deductible.

In many cities the buyer, seller, or owner of a used house can purchase a home warranty policy for one to three years. Typically these policies cover the plumbing, electrical and heating systems, hot water heater, ductwork, air conditioning, and major appliances. The cost ranges from $250 to $400 per year. Some real estate brokers provide this with every home they sell as a way of encouraging people to buy. However, a warranty can also be purchased by the buyer, by the seller, or even by a person who does not plan to sell. Insurance plans vary by company and whether the buyer, seller, or owner is purchasing the coverage. Some plans require a pre-inspection, some do not. As a rule, the warranty company selects the repair firm, and there may be a service charge or deductible. Coverages, limitations, and exclusions in the contract must be read carefully.

Vocabulary Review

Match terms a–q with statements 1–17.

a. All-risks policy

b. Broad form (HO-2)

c. Endorsement

d. Flood insurance

e. Form HO-4

f. Form HO-6

g. Homeowner policy

h. Inflation guard

i. Insurable interest

j. Insurance premium

k. Insured

l. Medical payments

m. New for old

n. Old for old

o. Peril

p. Public liability

q. Worker's compensation insurance

_____ 1. Also called hazards or risks.

_____ 2. An endorsement that periodically increases insurance coverage.

_____ 3. Describes combined property and liability policies designed for residential owner-occupants.

_____ 4. Pays current cost of replacement less depreciation.

_____ 5. Pays cost of replacing damaged property at current prices.

_____ 6. Tenant's policy form.

_____ 7. Condominium unit owner's policy form.

_____ 8. The financial responsibility one has toward others.

_____ 9. The amount of money paid for insurance coverage.

_____ 10. Describes a policy that covers all perils, except those excluded in writing.

_____ 11. Insurance phrase for policies that cover a large number of named perils.

_____ 12. An agreement by the insurance company to extend coverage to perils not covered by the basic policy.

_____ 13. This would pay for damage from the overflow of inland or tidal waters.

_____ 14. A financial interest that can be insured.

_____ 15. Insurance coverage for injuries incurred by an employee on the job.

_____ 16. One who is covered by insurance.

_____ 17. Pays for the treatment of injuries without the need to determine fault.

Questions and Problems

1. What role does an endorsement or rider play in an insurance policy?

2. What is the purpose of liability insurance?

3. In a homeowner policy, what type of loss does Section I deal with? Section II?

4. How do all-risk insurance policies differ from broad form policies?

5. What does the phrase *new for old* refer to when talking about insurance policies that cover property damage?

6. Why will an insurer suspend coverage if a property is left vacant too long?

Additional Readings

Commercial Property Insurance & Risk Management, 7th ed. by Jerome Trupin et al. (Insurance Institute of America, 2003).

A Comprehensive Guide to Understanding Your Homeowner's Insurance by Gerald J. Curran (Edwin Mellen Press, 1996).

A Crisis of Homeowner's Insurance Availability in Disaster-Prone Areas: Congressional Hearing edited by Rick Lazio (DIANE, 2001).

Homeowners Analysis by George E. Krauss (Rough Notes Company, 1998).

H. R. 607—The Homeowners Insurance Protection Act: Congressional Hearing edited by James A. Leach (DIANE, 1999).

"Insuring Cooperatives and Condos" (*Mortgage and Real Estate Executive Report,* August 1, 1990, pp. 7–8).

"Insuring a Home for Flooding" by Jay Tomano (*The New York Times,* March 24, 2002, p. RE5).

"Is Your House Uninsurable? Insurers Are Now Refusing to Cover Homes with a History of Claims; Researching a Residence" by Jeff D. Opdyke et al. (*The Wall Street Journal,* May 23, 2002, p. D1).

The Lawyer's Guide to Insurance by Ben G. Baldwin, American Bar Association, 1999.

"Leases of Premises: Property Insurance Consideration" by Dwight E. Levick (*Real Estate Finance,* Fall 1991, pp. 77–86). Discusses rental insurance.

CHAPTER 25

Land-Use Control

land-use control

A broad term that describes any legal restriction that controls how a parcel of land may be used.

Land-use control is a broad term that describes any legal restriction that controls how a parcel of land may be used. Land-use controls can be divided into two broad categories: public controls and private controls. Examples of public controls are zoning, building codes, subdivision regulations, and master plans. Private controls come in the form of deed restrictions.

For further discussion, it should be noted that all methods of land-use control are coming under some level of scrutiny. The U.S. Supreme Court has recently held that land cannot be regulated such that it renders it totally valueless and has also held that any such regulation of one's private land must bear some "rough proportionality" to the benefit that the regulation gives to the public. There have also been a number of recent cases that have prohibited enforcement of certain zoning ordinances or deed restrictions because they result in discrimination under the Fair Housing Act (recall previous discussions on handicapped and familial status in Chapter 22), so the following discussion on land-use control must be tempered with the knowledge that these methods of land-use control are not absolute.

Zoning

Rudimentary forms of zoning can be traced back as far as medieval times when regulations prohibited certain activities from taking place within the town walls. In colonial America, cities and towns regulated the location of foul-smelling industries such as tallow rendering and leather tanning. In the late 1880s, Boston limited the heights of buildings, as did Baltimore, Indianapolis, and Washington, D.C. Between 1909 and 1915, Los Angeles adopted a complex series of land-use laws. However, credit for the first truly comprehensive and systematic zoning law goes to New York City in 1916. Three years in the making, it went beyond anything up to that time and set a basic pattern that has been followed and refined by American cities, towns, and counties ever since.

Zoning is based on the principle of use separation: some land uses are incompatible with others and should not be permitted in the same area. **Zoning laws** divide land into zones (districts) and within each zone regulate the purpose for which buildings may be constructed, the height and bulk of the buildings, the area of the lot that they may occupy, and the number of persons that they can accommodate. Through zoning, a community can protect existing land users from encroachment by undesirable uses and ensure that future land uses in the community will be compatible with one another. Zoning also can control development so that each parcel of land will be adequately serviced by streets, sanitary and storm sewers, schools, parks, and utilities.

The authority to control land use is derived from the basic police power of each state to protect the public health, safety, morals, and general welfare of its citizens. Through an enabling act passed by the state legislature, the authority to control land use is also given to individual towns, cities, and counties. These local government units then pass zoning ordinances that establish the boundaries of the various land-use zones and determine the type of development that will be permitted in each of them. By going to your local zoning office, you can learn how a parcel of land is zoned. By then consulting the zoning ordinance, you can see the permitted uses for the parcel.

ZONING SYMBOLS

For convenience, zones are identified by code abbreviations such as R (residential), C (commercial), I or M (industrial-manufacturing), and A (agriculture). Within general categories are subcategories: for example, single-family residences, two-family residences, low-rise apartments, and high-rise apartments. Similarly, there will usually be several subcategories of commercial ranging from small stores to shopping centers and several subcategories of manufacturing ranging from light, smoke-free to heavy industry.

Additionally, there can be found overlay zoning categories such as RPD (residential planned development) and PUD (planned unit development). These are designed to permit a mixture of land uses within a given parcel. For example, a 640-acre parcel may contain open spaces plus clusters of houses, townhouses, and apartments, and perhaps a neighborhood shopping center. Another combination zone is RO (residential-office), which allows apartment buildings alongside or on top of office buildings. This is a departure from typical zoning theories and a challenge for urban planners. Sometimes it makes good sense to have mixed uses in an urban area, and is often the product of **gentrification**, when new owners re-occupy and redevelop older neighborhoods.

Note that there is no uniformity to zoning classifications. A city may use *A* to designate apartments while the county uses *A* to designate agriculture. Similarly, one city may use *I* for industrial and another city may use *I* for institutional (hospitals and universities, for example).

LAND-USE RESTRICTIONS

Besides telling a landowner the use to which he may put his land, the zoning ordinance imposes additional rules. For example, land zoned for low-density apartments may require 1,500 square feet of land per living unit, a minimum of 600 square feet of living space per unit for 1 bedroom, 800 square feet for 2 bedrooms, and 1,000 square feet for

zoning laws

Public regulations that control the specific use of land.

3 bedrooms. The zoning ordinance may also contain a setback requirement that states that a building must be placed at least 25 feet back from the street, 10 feet from the sides of the lot, and 15 feet from the rear lot line. The ordinance may also limit the building's height to 2½ stories and require 2 parking spaces for each dwelling unit. As can be seen, traditional zoning usually encourages uniformity.

ENFORCEMENT

Zoning laws are enforced by virtue of the fact that in order to build, a person must obtain a building permit from his city or county government. Before a permit is issued, the proposed structure must conform with government-imposed structural standards and comply with the zoning on the land. If a landowner builds without a permit, he can be forced to tear down his building.

NONCONFORMING USE

When an existing structure does not conform with a new zoning law, it is "grandfathered-in" as a **nonconforming use**. Thus, the owner can continue to use the structure even though it does not conform to the new zoning. However, the owner is not permitted to enlarge or remodel the structure or to extend its life. When the structure is ultimately demolished, any new use of the land must be in accordance with the zoning law. If you are driving through a residential neighborhood and see an old store or service station that looks very much out of place, it is probably a nonconforming use that was allowed to stay because it was built before the current zoning on the property went into effect.

nonconforming use
An improvement that is inconsistent with current zoning regulations.

AMENDMENT

Once a zoning ordinance has been passed, it can be changed by **amendment** or a **rezoning application**. Thus, land previously zoned for agriculture may be changed to residential. Land along a city street that has become a major thoroughfare may change from residential to commercial. An amendment can be initiated by an owner of property in the area to be rezoned or by local government. Either way, notice of the proposed change must be given to all owners of property in and around the affected area, and a public hearing must be held so that property owners and the public at large may voice their opinions on the matter.

VARIANCE

A **variance** is an appeals procedure that allows an individual landowner to deviate from current zoning requirements for his parcel. Jurisdiction is given to a city's **Board of Adjustment** to overrule the zoning commission when hardships exist. For example, a variance might be granted to the owner of an odd-shaped lot to reduce the setback requirements slightly so that she can fit a building on it. Variances usually are granted where strict compliance with the zoning ordinance or code would cause undue hardship. A variance can also be used to change the permitted use of a parcel. However, the variance must not change the basic character of the neighborhood, and it must be consistent with the general objectives of zoning as they apply to that neighborhood.

variance
Allows an individual landowner to vary from zoning requirements.

CONDITIONAL-USE PERMIT

A **conditional-use permit** (sometimes referred to as a **specific use permit**) allows a land use that does not conform with existing zoning, provided the use is within the limitations that are specifically imposed by the city ordinance. A conditional-use permit is usually quite restrictive, and if the conditions of the permit are violated, the permit is no longer valid. For example, a neighborhood grocery store operating under a conditional-use permit can only be a neighborhood grocery. The structure cannot be used as an auto parts store.

SPOT ZONING

Spot zoning refers to the rezoning of a small area of land in an existing neighborhood. For example, a neighborhood convenience center (grocery, laundry, barbershop) might be allowed in a residential neighborhood provided it serves a useful purpose for neighborhood residents and is not a nuisance.

DOWNZONING

downzoning

Rezoning of land from a higher-density use to a lower-density use.

Downzoning means that land previously zoned for higher-density uses (or more active uses) is rezoned for lower-density uses (or less active uses). Examples are downzoning from high-rise commercial to low-rise commercial, apartment zoning to single-family, and single-family to agriculture. Although a landowner's property value may fall as a result of downzoning, there is no compensation to the landowner as there is no taking of land as with eminent domain.

TAKING

Taking is a concept wherein the municipality regulates the property to where it has no value or, in some cases, has no remaining economic value. The U.S. Supreme Court, in several cases, has determined that a municipality can regulate land use to where it becomes a "taking" and results in condemnation. In those instances, the municipality must pay the fair market value of the property to the landowner. In response to the U.S. Supreme Court's holdings, many individual states have passed laws limiting the right of the government to regulate or "take" property from a landowner, particularly if they are taking it to give to another private landowner for higher and better use (and higher values for tax purposes). One state even has legislation that allows for certain governmental entities to pay the landowner in the event the land is regulated to a less intense use, such that if the fair market value of the land is decreased by 25%, that governmental entity must pay the landowner for the reduction in value. This area of the law is clearly becoming more protective of the private landowner's rights.

BUFFER ZONE

A **buffer zone** is a strip of land that separates one land use from another. Thus, between a large shopping center and a neighborhood of single-family homes, there may be a row of garden apartments. Alternatively, between an industrial park and a residential subdivision, a developer may leave a strip of land in grass and trees rather than build homes immediately adjacent to the industrial buildings. Note that *buffer zone* is a generic term and not necessarily a zoning law category.

LEGALITY AND VALUE

A zoning law can be changed or struck down if it can be proved in court that it is unclear; discriminatory; unreasonable; not for the protection of the public health, safety, and general welfare; or not applied to all property in a similar manner.

Zoning alone does not create land value. For example, zoning 100 square miles of lonely desert or mountain land for stores and offices would not appreciably change its value. Value is created by the number of people who want to use a particular parcel of land for a specific purpose. To the extent that zoning channels that demand to certain parcels of land and away from others, zoning does have a powerful impact on property value.

Subdivision Regulations

Before a building lot can be sold, a subdivider must comply with government regulations concerning street construction, curbs, sidewalks, street lighting, fire hydrants, storm and sanitary sewers, grading and compacting of soil, water and utility lines, minimum lot size, and so on. In addition, the subdivider may be required to either set aside land for schools and parks or provide money so that land for that purpose may be purchased nearby. These are often referred to as **mapping or platting requirements**, and until the subdivider has complied with all state and local regulations, the subdivision will not be approved. Without approval, the plan cannot be recorded, which, in turn, means that the lots cannot be sold to the public. If the subdivider tries to sell lots without approval, he can be stopped by a government court order and, in some states, fined. Moreover, permits to build will be refused to lot owners, and anyone who bought from the subdivider is entitled to a refund.

Building Codes

Recognizing the need to protect public health and safety against slipshod construction practices, state and local governments have enacted **building codes**. These establish minimum acceptable material and construction standards for such things as structural load and stress, windows and ventilation, size and location of rooms, fire protection, exits, electrical installation, plumbing, heating, lighting, and so forth.

building codes
Local and state laws that set minimum construction standards.

Before a building permit is granted, the design of a proposed structure must meet the building-code requirements. During construction, local building department inspectors visit the construction site to make certain that the codes are being observed. Finally, when the building is completed, a **certificate of occupancy** is issued to the building owner to show that the structure meets the code. Without this certificate, the building cannot be legally occupied.

certificate of occupancy
A government-issued document that states a structure meets local zoning and building code requirements and is ready for use.

Traditionally, the establishment of building codes has been given by states to individual counties, cities, and towns. The result has been a lack of uniformity from one local government to the next, oftentimes adding unnecessary construction costs and occasionally leaving gaps in consumer protection. The trend today is toward statewide building codes that overcome these weaknesses and at the same time improve the uniformity of mortgage collateral for the secondary mortgage market.

Deed Restrictions

Although property owners tend to think of land-use controls as being strictly a product of government, it is possible to achieve land-use control through private means. In fact, Houston, Texas, operates without zoning and relies almost entirely upon private land-use controls to achieve a similar effect.

Private land-use controls take the form of *deed* and *lease restrictions*. In the United States it has long been recognized that the ownership of land includes the right to sell or lease it on whatever legally acceptable conditions the owner wishes, including the right to dictate to the buyer or lessee how he shall or shall not use it. For example, a developer can sell the lots in his subdivision subject to a restriction written into each deed that the land cannot be used for anything but a single-family residence containing at least 1,200 square feet of living area. The legal theory is that if the buyer or lessee agrees to the restrictions, he is bound by them. If they are not obeyed, any lot owner in the subdivision can obtain a court order to enforce compliance. Zoning restrictions are a governmental enforcement; therefore, they must be based on public health, safety, and welfare issues. Private deed restrictions, however, do not. Homeowners can agree to anything as long as it is legal, so they can regulate the use of properties with much greater specificity than zoning regulations can. The only limit to the number of restrictions that an owner may place on his land is economic. If there are too many restrictions, the landowner may find that no one wants the land.

restrictive covenants

Clauses placed in deeds and leases to control how future owners and lessees may or may not use the property.

Deed restrictions, also known as **restrictive covenants**, can be used to dictate such matters as the purpose of the structure to be built, architectural requirements, setbacks, size of the structure, and aesthetics. In neighborhoods with view lots, they are often used to limit the height to which trees may be permitted to grow. Deed restrictions cannot be used to discriminate on the basis of race, color, religion, sex, or national origin; if they do, those provisions of the restrictions are unenforceable are unenforceable.

Planning Ahead for Development

When a community first adopts a zoning ordinance, the usual procedure is to recognize existing land uses by zoning according to what already exists. Thus, a neighborhood that is already developed with houses is zoned for houses. Undeveloped land may be zoned for agriculture or may simply be left unzoned. As a community expands, undeveloped land is zoned for urban uses along a pattern that typically follows the availability of new roads, the aggressiveness of developers, and the willingness of landowners to sell. All too often this results in a hodgepodge of land-use districts, all conforming internally because of tightly enforced zoning, but with little or no relationship among them. This happens because they were created over a period of years without the aid of a long-range land-use plan that took a comprehensive view of the entire growth pattern of the city. Since uncoordinated land use can have a negative impact on both the quality of life and the economic vitality of a community, more attention is now being directed toward land-use master plans to guide the development of towns and cities, districts, coastlines, and even whole states.

MASTER PLAN

master plan

A comprehensive guide for the physical growth of a community.

To prepare a **master plan** (or **general plan** or **comprehensive plan**), a city or regional planning commission is usually created. The first step is a physical and economic survey of the area to be planned. The physical survey involves mapping existing roads, utility lines, developed land, and undeveloped land. The economic survey looks at the present and anticipated economic base of the region, its population, and its retail trade facilities. Together the two surveys provide the information upon which a master plan is built. The key is to view the region as a unified entity that provides its residents with jobs and housing as well as social, recreational, and cultural opportunities. In doing so, the master plan uses existing patterns of transportation and land use and directs future growth so as to achieve balanced development. For example, if agriculture is important to the area's economy, special attention is given to retaining the best soils for farming. Waterfront property may also receive special planning protection. Similarly, if houses in an older residential area of town are being converted to rooming houses and apartments, that transition can be encouraged by planning apartment usage for the area. In doing this, the master plan guides those who must make day-to-day decisions regarding zoning changes and gives the individual property owner a long-range idea of what his property may be used for in the future. There is only one problem with a master plan. Once the restrictions are in place, it may be very difficult to change them, even for a better use. For instance, if a subdivision has restrictions for one single-family residence per lot, but a new purchaser wants to build a bigger, better house on two lots with a five-car garage, this would be prohibited unless there was an amendment to the restrictions. Do you think you could get the lot owners to agree to this change? Probably not.

LONG-RUN CONTINUITY

To assure long-run continuity, a master plan should look at least 15 years into the future, but preferably 25 years or more. It must also include provisions for flexibility in the event that the city or region does not develop as expected, such as when population grows faster or slower than anticipated. Most importantly, the plan must provide for a balance between the economic and social functions of the community. For example, emphasizing culture and recreation, at the expense of adequate housing and the area's economic base, will result in the slow decay of the community because people will have to leave to find housing and jobs.

Precautions

Because zoning can greatly influence the value of a property, it is absolutely essential that when you purchase real estate you be aware of the zoning for the parcel. You will need to know what the zoning will allow and what it won't; whether the parcel is operating under a restrictive or temporary permit; and what the zoning and planning departments might allow on the property in the future. Where there is any uncertainty or where a zone change or variance will be necessary in order for you to use the property the way you want to, a conservative approach is to make the offer to buy contingent on obtaining planning and zoning approval before going to settlement.

If you are a real estate agent, you must stay abreast of zoning, planning, and building matters regarding the properties you list and sell. A particularly sensitive issue that occurs regularly is when a property listed for sale does not meet zoning and/or building code requirements. For example, suppose the current (or previous) owner of a house has converted the garage to a den or bedroom without obtaining building permits and without providing space for parking elsewhere on the parcel. Legally, this makes the property unmarketable. If you, as the agent, sell this property without telling the buyer about the lack of permits, you've given the buyer grounds to sue you, for misrepresentation, and the seller, for rescission. When faced with a situation like this, you should ask the seller to obtain the necessary permits. If the seller refuses, and the buyer still wants to buy, make the problem very clear to the buyer and have the buyer sign a statement indicating acceptance of title under these conditions. You can also refuse to accept the listing if it looks as though it will create more trouble than it's worth.

This issue may be particularly onerous for buyer's agents. One may recall that a buyer hires a real estate agent, in many cases, because they want to be sure that the property they are buying is zoned for the buyer's intended use. If the buyer acquires the property and finds out that the agent's information was incorrect, it may result in significant damages for the broker.

PROFESSIONALS

The point here is that the public has a right to expect real estate agents to be professionals in their field. Thus, the agent is expected to be fully aware of the permitted uses for a property and whether current uses comply. This is necessary to properly value the property for listing and to provide accurate information to prospective buyers. Even if the seller in the previous example was unaware of his zoning and building violations, it is the agent's responsibility to recognize the problem and inform the seller. An agent cannot take the position that if the seller didn't mention it, then the agent needn't worry about it, and if the buyer later complains, it's the seller's problem, not the agent's. Recent court decisions clearly indicate that the agent has a responsibility to inform the seller of a problem so that the seller cannot later complain to the agent, "You should have told me about that when I listed the property with you and certainly before I accepted the buyer's offer."

Environmental Impact Statements

environmental impact statement (EIS)

A report that contains information regarding the effect of a proposed project on the environment of an area.

The purpose of an **environmental impact statement (EIS)**, also called an **environmental impact report (EIR)**, is to gather into one document enough information about the effect of a proposed project on the total environment so that a neutral decision maker can judge the environmental benefits and costs of the project. For example, a city zoning commission considering a zone change can request an EIS that will show the expected impact of the change on such things as population density, automobile traffic, noise, air quality, water and sewage facilities, drainage, energy consumption, school enrollments, employment, public health and safety, recreation facilities, wildlife, and vegetation. The idea is that with this information at hand, better decisions regarding land uses can be made. When problems can be anticipated in advance, it is easier to make modifications or explore alternatives.

At the city and county levels, where the EIS requirement has the greatest effect on private development, the EIS usually accompanies the development application that is submitted to the planning or zoning commission. Where applicable, copies are also sent to affected school districts, water and sanitation districts, and highway and flood control departments. The EIS is then made available for public inspection as part of the hearing process on the development application. This gives concerned civic groups and the public at large an opportunity to voice their opinions regarding the anticipated benefits and costs of the proposed development. If the proposed development is partially or wholly funded by state or federal funds, then state or federal hearings are also held.

CONTENT OF AN EIS

Typically, an EIS will contain a description of present conditions at the proposed development site, plus information on the following five points: (1) the probable impact of the proposed project on the physical, economic, and social environment of the area; (2) any unavoidable adverse environmental effects; (3) any alternatives to the proposed project; (4) the short-term versus long-term effects of the proposed project on the environment; and (5) a listing of any irreversible commitment of resources if the project is implemented. For a government-initiated project, the EIS is prepared by a government agency, sometimes with the help of private consultants. In the case of a private development, it may be prepared by the developer, by a local government agency for a fee, or by a private firm specializing in the preparation of impact statements.

ENVIRONMENTAL LAWS

Since 1982, the number of environmental laws that have affected real estate development has expanded tremendously and has had a definite and profound effect on land-use control. In 1982, Congress passed a **Comprehensive Environmental Response, Compensation, and Liability Act** (commonly referred to as **CERCLA**) that imposed upon (1) the owners, (2) operators of facilities, and (3) any person who, at the time of disposal of any hazardous substance, owned or operated the facility at which such hazardous substances were disposed of, and any person who arranged for disposal, or (4) any persons who have accepted hazardous substances for transport to disposal or treatment sites, joint and several, 100% liability for damages resulting from that disposal. Subsequent legislation involved changes in the Clean Water Act that provide for a prohibition against storm water discharges.

Wetlands, once considered a source of neglected development and mosquitoes, have now been determined to help control flooding, filter out pollution, and provide habitats for fish and other wildlife. Wetlands regulations enforced by the U.S. Army Corps of Engineers include the assessment of administrative, civil, and/or criminal penalties. Wetlands are defined as "areas inundated or saturated by surface or groundwater at a frequency and duration sufficient to support, and that under normal circumstances do support, a prevalence of vegetation typically adapted for life in saturated soil conditions." The definition is broad, and its enforcement can vary, depending on the location, the country, and the developers' use of mitigation techniques to "bank" wetland areas while the developing others. The only way to be certain whether an area comes under the wetlands definition is to request the Corps to make an inspection and issue its own determination.

Federal statutes have been passed affecting asbestos, radon gas, lead-based paint, endangered species, and underground storage tanks. This has resulted in purchasers being required to exercise a level of "due diligence" in investigating sites prior to acquisition. A licensee should also note, and be particularly careful, that pertinent questions concerning environmental hazards may be directed to the broker and the broker may be on a "should have known" duty of care to know whether or not any of these incidents may have occurred.

The net result of all this federal legislation has resulted in **environmental site assessments**. Environmental site assessments have basically been divided into Phase I, Phase II, or Phase III Assessments. While none of these terms are specially defined by statute or common law, the consensus among environmental consultants seems to be that the principal elements of a Phase I Assessment include an on-site visual inspection of the property, interviews with owners and area residents as to the use and possession of the property, and review of historical aerial photographs and public records to determine past use and possession of the property. A Phase II Assessment typically involves sampling of the soil and water for the presence of hazardous substances. A Phase III Assessment involves further sampling and establishing limits of the contamination and developing a plan for remedial action and cleanup.

The horror stories involving environmental clean air pollution are legion. The liability is unlimited, while many of the concerns are real. Some areas of environmental legislation involve enormous expense with very little result. One can be assured this will remain a hot area of legislation, controversy, and federal legislation for the coming years.

The New EPA "All Appropriate Inquiry" Rule

In 2002, the Brownfields Revitalization and Environmental Restoration Act ("Brownfields Act") provided innocent landowner defense to CERCLA by defining the due diligence criteria that must be satisfied to provide an innocent landowner defense to CERCLA liability. The rule defining exactly what constitutes due diligence criteria was "all appropriate inquiries." Permanent standards were not published in November 2005 and became effective on November 1, 2006.

All appropriate inquiries, as defined under CERCLA Section 105(35)(B), must include the results of an inquiry conducted by an environmental professional within **one year prior** to the date of the acquisition of the subject property, which takes into account the following items:

1. interviews with past and present owners, operators, and occupants;
2. evaluations of historical sources of information;
3. searches for recorded environmental cleanup liens;
4. reviews of federal, tribal, state, and local government records; and
5. visual inspections of the facility and of adjoining properties;
6. the degree of the obviousness of the contamination and the ability to detect the contamination by appropriate investigation; and
7. commonly known or reasonably ascertainable information about the property.

Items (1), (3), (4), and (5) must be updated within the **180 days of and prior to the date** of acquisition of the property, and must also include a declaration made by an environmental professional.

New rules specifically require the hiring of an environmental professional, defined as a person who meets specific education and experience requirements necessary to render a professional judgment. The environmental professional must develop opinions and conclusions about releases or threatened releases of hazardous substances concerning the subject property sufficient to satisfy certain objective and performance standards. The inquiry should seek to reveal present and historical uses of the hazardous substances at the subject property and neighboring and adjoining properties, potentially harmful waste management and disposal practices, the presence of engineering and institutional controls, and current and past corrective actions and response actions and response activities undertaken to address past and ongoing releases of hazardous substances. They must also inquire as to the past uses of the subject property and past corrective actions associated with petroleum and petroleum products. How far back must they search? The environmental professional is entitled to rely on professional judgment as to how far back in time it is necessary to search these historical records to trace past uses of the property.

As the inquiry relates to federal, state, tribal, and local government records, the review includes searching for records in databases pertaining to nearby and adjoining properties as well as records concerning the subject property. There is no distance from the boundary that is specified by the rules, and may be modified and the judgment of the environmental professional to account for such factors as development and geological conditions. For commercial real estate brokers, this is a significant change. In many cases, there were pending sales that had to have second environmental inquiries because the contract wasn't closed by November 1, 2006; therefore, a new inquiry had to be maintained after November 1, 2006, to comply with the new rules.

There's an interesting question, what if the adjoining landowner won't allow inquiries? In these situations, the environmental professional may inspect the property by other means, including aerial imagery.

Windfalls and Wipeouts

Planning and zoning tend to provide **windfall gains** for the owners of land that has been authorized for development, while landowners who are prohibited from developing their land suffer financial **wipeouts**. This has been a major stumbling block to the orderly utilization of land in America. It is only natural that a landowner will want his land to be zoned for a use that will make it more valuable; however, not all land can be zoned for housing, stores, and offices. Some land must be reserved for agriculture and open spaces. If local and state governments embark upon bold land-planning programs, how will these financial inequities be resolved?

The past and current positions of government and of the courts is that if land-use restrictions are for the health, safety, and general welfare of the community at large, then under the rules of police power, the individual landowner is not compensated for any resulting loss in value. Only when there is an actual physical taking of land is the owner entitled to compensation under the rules of eminent domain. In today's environmentally conscious society, this often results in pitting the landowner who wants to develop his land against those who want to prevent development. For example, a government planning agency in one state stretched the limits of police power by denying an urban landowner a permit to build on his property and telling him he should grow flowers for the public's enjoyment. Many decisions like this could ultimately undermine planning efforts. Yet, government planning agencies do not have the money to buy all the land that they would like to see remain undeveloped.

Transferable Development Rights

The solution may come from some radical new thinking about land and the rights to use it. The new planning idea is to eliminate windfalls and wipeouts by creating **transferable development rights (TDRs)**. Previously, the right to develop a parcel of land could not be separated from the land itself. Now planners are exploring the idea of separating the two so that development rights can be transferred to land where greater density will not be objectionable. For example, suppose that within a given planning district there is an area of high-quality farmland that planners feel should be retained for agriculture and not be paved over with streets and covered with buildings. Also in the district is an area deemed more suitable for urban uses and hence an area where government will concentrate on constructing streets, schools, parks, waterlines, and other public facilities. To direct growth to the urban area, it is planned and zoned for urban uses. Meanwhile, areas designated for agriculture are forced to remain as farmland. Ordinarily, this would result in windfall gains for the owner of the urban land and a loss in land value for the owner of the farmland.

With the TDR concept in effect, owners of farmland are allowed to sell development rights to the owners of urban land. By purchasing development rights, the urban landowner is permitted to develop his land more intensely than otherwise permissible. This compensates the farmer for the prohibition against developing his land. For the TDR concept to work, there must be a comprehensive regional master plan.

TDRs could be traded on the open market like stocks and bonds. Alternatively, a government agency could pay cash for the value of rights lost. This would be financed by selling those rights to owners in districts to be developed.

WHERE USED

To date, Chicago and New York City have made use of TDRs for the purpose of protecting historical buildings not owned by the government. An owner who agrees not to tear down his building is given TDRs that can be sold to other nearby landowners. TDRs are also being used to protect open spaces, farm land, and environmentally sensitive land in parts of Pennsylvania, Virginia, Florida, Vermont, New Jersey, Maryland, and Puerto Rico. In a number of states the TDR concept is still being tested in court cases. It appears that much of the legal debate centers on the concept of separating the right to develop land from the land itself. The idea is new and has little legal precedence. But, for that matter, neither did zoning when it was new.

Vocabulary Review

Match terms a–n with statements 1–14.

a. Amendment
b. Buffer zone
c. Building codes
d. Certificate of occupancy
e. Downzoning
f. EIS or EIR
g. Land-use control
h. Mapping requirement
i. Master plan
j. Nonconforming use
k. Restrictive covenants
l. Spot zoning
m. Variance
n. Zoning laws

_____ 1. A broad term used to describe any legal restriction (such as zoning) that controls how a parcel of land may be used.

_____ 2. Public regulations that control the specific use of land.

_____ 3. An improvement that is inconsistent with current zoning regulations.

_____ 4. A comprehensive guide for a community's physical growth.

_____ 5. Clauses placed in deeds and leases to control how future owners and lessees may or may not use the property.

_____ 6. A government-issued document stating that a structure meets zoning and building code requirements and is ready for use.

_____ 7. A report that contains information regarding the effect of a proposed project on the environment.

_____ 8. Method used to change a zoning ordinance.

_____ 9. Allows an individual landowner to vary from a zoning ordinance without changing the ordinance.

_____ 10. The rezoning of a small area of land in an existing neighborhood.

_____ 11. Local and state laws that set minimum construction standards.

_____ 12. A strip of land that separates one land use from another.

_____ 13. Rezoning of land from a higher-density use to a lower-density use.

_____ 14. State and local regulations pertaining to subdivisions that a subdivider must meet before selling lots.

Questions and Problems

1. For land-use control to be successful, why is it necessary to consider the rights of individual property owners as well as the public as a whole?

2. Explain how a city obtains its power to control land use through zoning.

3. What is the purpose of a variance?

4. In your community, what are the letter/number designations for the following: high-rise apartments, low-rise apartments, single-family houses, stores, duplexes, and industrial sites?

5. What is the difference between master planning and zoning?

6. What is the purpose of an environmental impact statement?

7. How would the use of transferable development rights reduce windfalls and wipeouts for landowners?

8. Does any city or county in your state currently use transferable development rights? What have been the results?

Additional Readings

Zoning and Land-Use Controls by Patrick Rohan (Matthew Bender, updated annually). This 10-volume set of books on zoning law covers almost every aspect of zoning and land-use controls.

CHAPTER 26

Real Estate and the Economy

E arlier chapters of this book described real estate from the standpoints of what it is, how you convey it, how you finance it, how it is taxed, how you rent it, how you value it, how you insure it, and how you broker it. In this chapter we will look at the very important role of regional and national economics in giving value to real estate. In particular, this chapter will discuss the need for an economic base to support real estate values, short-run changes in housing demand when a new industry moves into town or an old one closes, long-run effects on housing demand caused by population and income changes, and the impact of federal tax, fiscal, and monetary policies. The chapter will conclude with a look at inflation, a review of the 1975–2012 period for real estate, the importance of watching the Federal Reserve, and an outlook for the future.

Economic Base

In order to survive, a city (or town or region) must export goods and services so that its residents may purchase goods and services not produced locally. To illustrate, Hollywood produces films for theaters and television stations across the country. Income from these films permits residents in Hollywood to purchase things not produced in Hollywood such as cars and trucks made in Detroit. The money Detroit receives is used to buy farm products. A farming region produces farm products in order to generate income with which to buy farm machinery, gasoline, fertilizer, clothing, and vacations. In turn, the economy of a resort area is kept alive with the money spent there by vacationers, and on and on.

economic base

The ability of a region to export goods and services to other regions and receive money in return.

base industry

An industry that produces goods or services for export from the region.

service industry

An industry that produces goods and services to sell to local residents.

The ability of a city or region to produce a commodity or service that can bring in money from outside its area is called its **economic base**. Industries that produce goods and services for export are called **base**, **export**, or **primary industries**. Thus, film making is a **base industry** for Hollywood, automobile manufacturing is a base industry for Detroit, and agriculture is a base industry in the Midwest. Producers of goods and services that are not exported are called **service**, **filler**, or **secondary industries**. This category includes local school systems, supermarkets, doctors, dentists, drugstores, and real estate agents.

EFFECT ON PROPERTY VALUES

Because land is immovable, the existence of base industries is *absolutely essential* to maintaining local real estate values. Unless a region or city exports, it will die economically, and the value of local real estate will fall. An extreme example of this can be found in the abandoned mining towns. Before the discovery of mineral riches, land was often worth but a few dollars an acre for grazing purposes. With the discovery of minerals and subsequent mine development, land that was suitable for townsites zoomed in value. A new and far richer economic base industry than grazing brought wealth and people into the area, and grazing land was suddenly in demand to be used for homesites, stores, and offices. Years later, when the mines played out and mineral wealth could no longer be exported from the area, outside money ceased to flow into the town. Miners were laid off and moved to other towns where jobs could be found. Without the miners' money, service industries folded and their employees left. The demand for real estate dropped and real estate prices fell, often all the way back to their value for grazing purposes.

Another scenario exists in these times of great political influence on the economy. Government interference can be very detrimental. Detroit, for instance, had a booming economy 60 years ago. Every major car manufacturer was there. When the local government starts taxing excessively and taking money out of any industry, it becomes less profitable. Note that the taxing authority does not produce anything for these companies, they only take away. Then the company's profits are lowered. The company moves to a more business oriented environment (another state, or even another country). What is the long term plan for Detroit? How can this trend be reversed?

VULNERABILITY

The extent to which regions and cities are vulnerable to changes in economic base depends on how many different kinds of base industries are present and the ability of those industries to consistently export their products. Thus, a city that relies on a single base industry is much more vulnerable than a city with a diversified group of base industries. For example, a city or town that has grown up around a military base suffers if that base is cut back in size or closed down. In the neighboring cities of Seattle and Tacoma, Washington, real estate prices are directly influenced by the rise and fall of airplane orders at the area's largest employer, Boeing Aircraft. Now that Boeing is leaving, another industry must expand or relocate to Seattle, or Seattle will suffer long-term downside effects. The economy of Detroit has been hurt by the change in consumer buying preferences to foreign-made cars, or cars made in nonunion factories. The steel-making region that spans Indiana, Ohio, Pennsylvania, and West Virginia has been adversely impacted by steel mill shutdowns due to better prices on steel from abroad. Towns that rely heavily on the lumber industry have seen their economies and real estate prices hurt by the drop in demand for lumber following the end of the last housing boom. The economies of farm communities and the prices of farm land are tied to the rise and fall of farm product prices.

Sometimes these events galvanize concerned citizens, property owners, and business people into action. Seattle and Tacoma have been busy attracting industries other than aircraft manufacturing so as to smooth out the ups and downs of the aircraft business. Oregon repealed its unitary tax on business firms and is actively courting electronics companies. Some steel mills have been bought by employees determined to keep them open and competitive with foreigners.

EMPLOYMENT MULTIPLIER

Just how important is a base industry job to a local economy? As a rule, for each additional person employed in a base industry, another two persons will be employed in local service industries. Thus, if an electronics firm moves into a community and creates 100 new base industry jobs, opportunities will be created for another 200 persons in jobs such as retail store clerks, restaurant services, gas station operators, gardeners, bankers, doctors, dentists, lawyers, police, firefighters, school teachers, and members of local government—to name only a few.

If you understand what is happening in local base industries, you can calculate the need for land and housing. For example, the 100 base industry jobs created by the electronics firm result in 200 service jobs, for a total of 300 new job opportunities in the community. If every three jobs require two households (more than one person working in some families) and each household averages 2.9 persons, then 300 jobs will provide income for 200 households containing a total of 580 persons. The ultimate effect of the 300 new jobs on local employment and housing demand will depend on what portion of the jobs can be filled from within the community and the extent of vacant housing. If the community is already operating at full employment and has no vacant housing to speak of, the addition of 100 base jobs will result in a demand for land, building materials, and labor necessary to provide 200 new housing units. From the standpoint of local government, 580 more people must be supplied with schools, parks, streets, libraries, water, sewage treatment, and police and fire protection. Unfortunately, the opposite is also true.

Short-run Demand for Housing

Economists agree on three factors that establish criteria for home sales: (1) job growth, (2) low interest rates, and (3) rising home prices. Job growth not only creates demand for new homes but also provides the opportunity to "move up" to better housing as new people are hired and/or as one's job improves. If an industry relocates to another area, the opposite happens. Low interest rates, particularly in the last few years, have enabled more people to qualify for home loans. Low interest rates can also raise prices on existing homes, since the buyer can afford to pay for a more expensive home. Increasing interest rates have the opposite effect. Another rule of thumb is the 6½ month rule. If a given market has 6½ months of new housing inventory, prices go flat or down, as there is more supply and less demand. If the housing inventory is less than 6½ months, prices increase, because demand outpaces supply.

There is no way to accurately anticipate housing market cycles, whether good or bad. However, the cycles never seem to last too long. But because it takes time to develop raw land into homes, offices, and stores, the supply of developed real estate cannot immediately respond to sudden changes in demand. As a result, price changes for developed real property can be rapid and dramatic over short periods of time.

SPECULATORS

It is important to know the cause of housing prices increasing, however. In a growing economy, there is more demand for housing as an investment. Investors with capital to invest have often looked to residential real estate as a hedge against inflation and as an additional source of income. When investors create a high demand, it often results in a "bubble" in housing prices. This **housing bubble** is an artificially high price in the market, as it is not a real increase in demand; it is investors who have created another market. When this market declines (there are no new investors or "greater fools"), it is a precipitous decline. Investors do not reflect a real market increase; they are mere speculators.

INCREASE IN DEMAND

To illustrate, suppose that in a given community there are presently 5,000 single-family houses and their average value is $182,000. A new industry (not speculative investors) moves into the community and increases the demand for houses by 100. Local builders, recognizing the new demand, set to work adding 100 houses to the available housing stock. However, it will take time to acquire land, file subdivision maps, acquire building permits, grade the land, and construct the houses. The entire process typically takes 10 to 36 months. Meanwhile the available supply of houses remains fixed. The result will be an increase in house prices as the newly arriving employees bid against each other for a place to live in the existing housing stock. The result is diagrammed in Figure 26.1. Demand Curve 1 represents the demand for houses at various prices before the new employees arrive. Supply and demand are in balance at $192,000 per house, as shown at A.

Next, the new industry moves in. The new employees added to the housing market produce Demand Curve 2. Prices rise owing to competition for the existing houses.

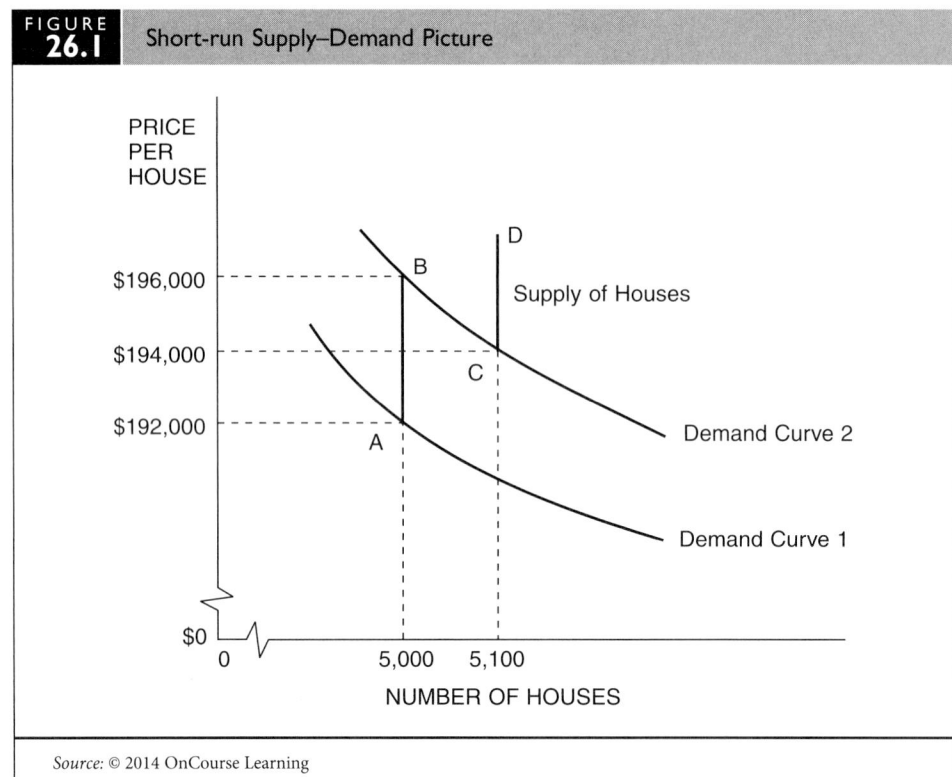

FIGURE 26.1 Short-run Supply–Demand Picture

Source: © 2014 OnCourse Learning

This increase literally rations the existing stock of 5,000 houses among 5,100 households. Prices rise until enough existing owners decide to sell and enough new buyers are priced out of the market. Once again, supply and demand are in balance, with 5,000 houses occupied by 5,000 families. This is point B, $196,000.

INCREASE IN SUPPLY

At last, the 100 new houses that were started in response to the new demand are completed and are on the market. At what price must these be offered in order to sell them all? It would appear that $196,000 is the answer, as that is what houses are now selling for. However, the supply–demand relationship in Figure 26.1 shows that only 5,000 houses are in demand at $196,000, not 5,100 houses. To find out at what price the additional 100 houses will be absorbed by the market, we must travel along Demand Curve 2 to 5,100 houses. At point C, the market will absorb 5,100 houses if they are priced at $194,000 each. Thus, a temporary glut of homes causes prices to be reduced slightly. This price softening applies to the builders of the 100 new houses and to the owners of the other 5,000 homes if they wish to sell during this temporary oversupply situation.

Aware of the oversupply of houses on the market, builders will react by halting building activity until those units are sold and demand starts pushing prices upward again to D at which time the process repeats itself. Over a period of years, the supply pattern for houses takes on a stair-step appearance as temporary shortages and temporary excesses alternate.

DECREASE IN DEMAND

Just as a short-run increase in demand can cause a quick run-up in prices, a short-run decrease in demand has the opposite effect because supply cannot be decreased as fast as demand falls. This situation is diagrammed in Figure 26.2, with supply and demand in

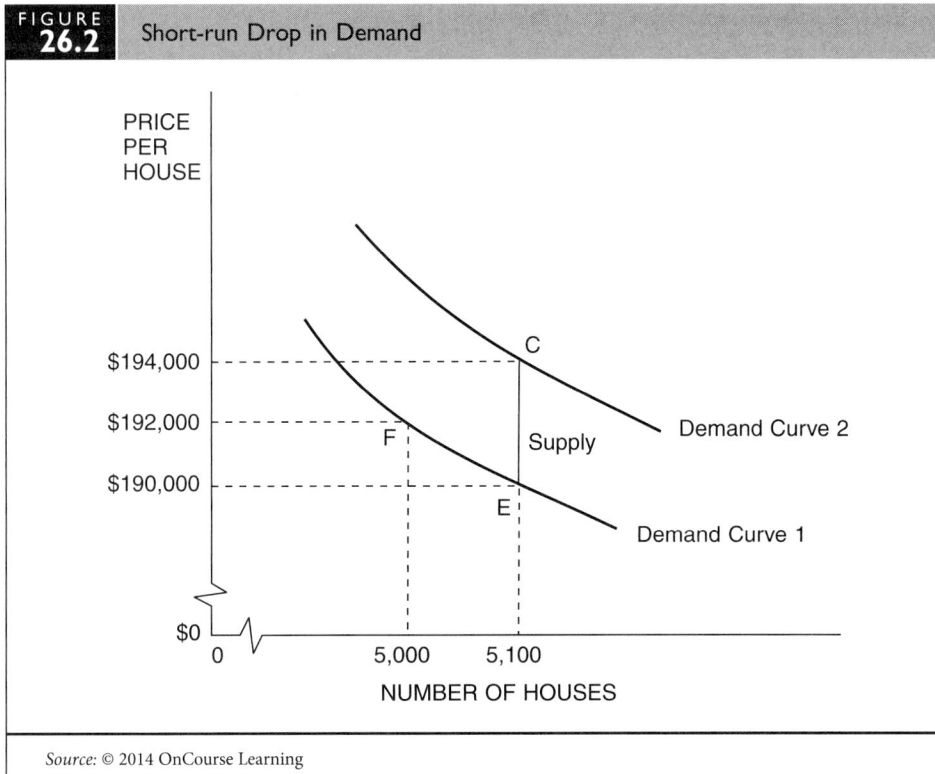

FIGURE 26.2 Short-run Drop in Demand

Source: © 2014 OnCourse Learning

balance at 5,100 houses at $194,000 each. Suppose there is an overnight cutback of jobs and, as a result, 100 homeowners decide to sell and move out of the community. This would cause demand to shift downward from Demand Curve 2 to Demand Curve 1. To sell 100 houses, it is necessary for prices to fall from $194,000 (point C) to $190,000 (point E). Without an increase in the economic base of the community, only a reduction in the supply of existing houses through demolition, disasters, and conversions to other uses will push prices back up along Demand Curve 1. If supply falls to 5,000 houses, prices will go to $192,000 (point F).

EFFECT OF INFLATION

The presence of inflation will cushion the drop in dollar values when demand shifts to Demand Curve 1 in Figure 26.2. Similarly, the drop in prices from B to C in Figure 26.1 will be milder in the presence of moderate inflation. In the presence of high inflation, prices may not drop, but actually rise. However, if you strip away the masking effect of inflation, Figures 26.1 and 26.2 accurately portray what actually happens when demand suddenly changes and supply cannot react fast enough. Although we have been talking in terms of houses, the same concept applies to vacant lots, apartment buildings, townhouses, condominiums, office buildings, factories, hotels and motels, store space, and so forth.

Long-run Demand for Housing

Future demand for housing in the United States can be seen by looking at the population in terms of age distribution and the ability of people to obtain income at various age levels. As shown in Figure 26.3, during the first 10 years of life, a person earns no income and is dependent on others, usually parents, for sustenance. During junior high school, high school, and college (if any), a person has part-time jobs but is usually still dependent on others for financial support.

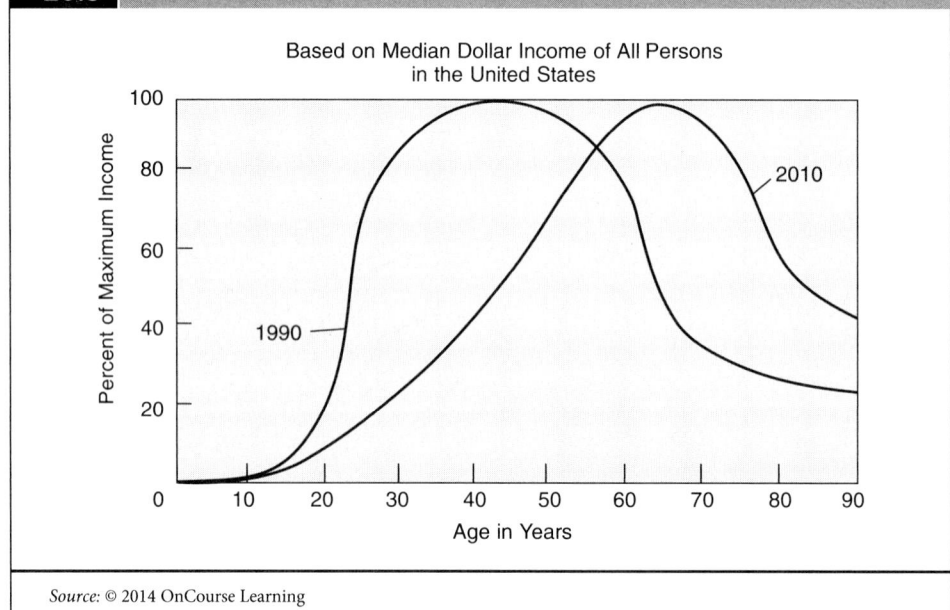

FIGURE 26.3   Lifetime Income Curve

Based on Median Dollar Income of All Persons in the United States

Source: © 2014 OnCourse Learning

Upon leaving school and entering the labor market on a full-time basis, a person's income rises quickly, reflecting increased productive capacity in society. As skills increase, income continues to rise rapidly. In another decade the rise stops increasing as rapidly, although it still advances. Then, somewhere between the ages of 40 and 60, depending on a person's skills and the usefulness of those skills in society, health, and/or the desire to slow down, the peak earning year occurs. For those with four years of college or the equivalent, this occurs around age 55. For the nation as a whole, it occurs in the mid-forties. People are working longer now (note Figure 26.3), so note the change in peak income for 1990–2010. The peak earning year is followed at first by mild decreases in income and then by more rapid decreases as retirement occurs.

BUYING PATTERN

With this earning pattern in mind, you can see the progression of housing demand. When a person is young and setting up a household for the first time, income is low and so are accumulated assets. Thus, housing that requires no equity investment at a minimum cost, that is, an inexpensive rental with no frills, is needed during the next decade, income increases and the household can increase the quality of its rental unit. At the same time, savings accumulate, which, coupled with the ability to make loan payments, enables the household to meet the down payment and loan requirements for a modest housing purchase. As the family grows and income increases, it can move to larger, more expensive quarters. Typically this occurs between the ages of 35 and 45. Another upward move in house size and price usually occurs between 45 and 55 when the family reaches its maximum income.

As the children move out and income peaks and then begins to recede, the household begins to consider a smaller and less expensive dwelling unit. The need for less expensive housing becomes even more compelling upon retirement and a further reduction in income. Retirement income typically is not sufficient to support the large home bought during the peak earning years. However, the household has an equity that it can now consolidate into a smaller residence that is fully or nearly fully paid for.

Age Distribution

With the previous pattern in mind, let's now turn our attention to Figure 26.4 where the population of the United States is graphed according to its age distribution. The lines labeled 1970, 1980, 1990, and 2000 are based on the U.S. census. The line labeled 2010 is very interesting. The older age group has increased. People are living longer!

They are also (1) holding on to their houses longer, or (2) moving into housing created specially for senior citizens. In either case, it increases the housing demand. With parents living considerably longer, a child will need to find other housing (or move in with Mom and Dad!). If the parents move into senior citizen housing, new housing must be built to accommodate the senior citizens. In both cases, the aging of America has created an increased demand for housing.

There are two peaks in the 1980 age distribution line. The smaller of the two, identified as [1], represents persons aged 50 to 60 years in 1980. These persons were born during the decade of the 1920s, a period of economic prosperity in most parts of the United States. Moving to the left, the dip at [2] represents children born during the economic depression that spanned the 1930s. By 1980, they were 40 to 50 years old. Moving again to the left, a substantial upward rise is encountered at [3]. This is the famed

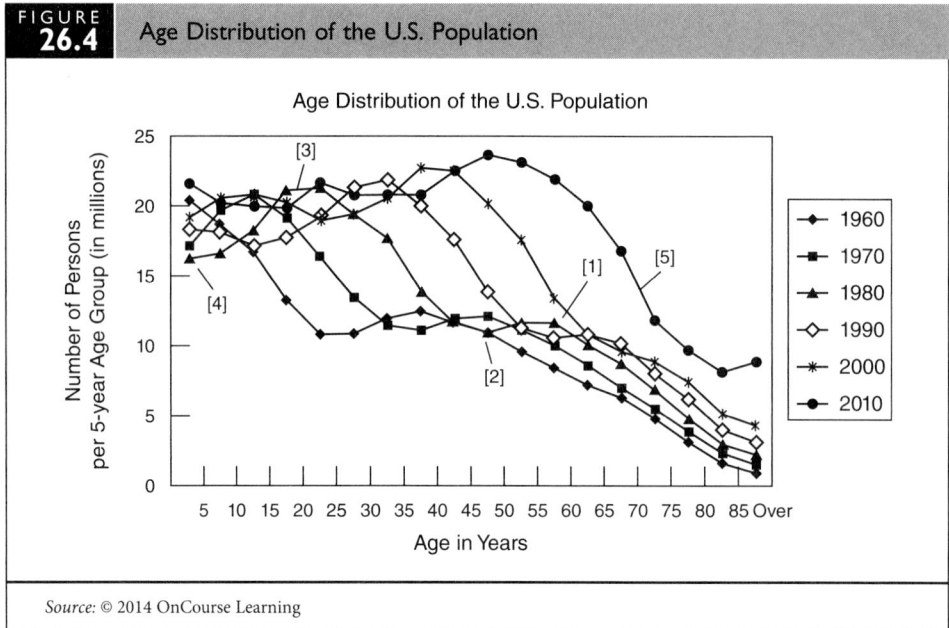

FIGURE **26.4** Age Distribution of the U.S. Population

Age Distribution of the U.S. Population

Source: © 2014 OnCourse Learning

World War II and postwar "baby boom." It started in 1946 and lasted until 1964. In 1960, the number of births per year began to decline and continued to decline in each subsequent year through 1978. This is shown at **[4]**.

HOUSING DEMAND

Of particular interest is the huge wave of demand from the baby boom that is working its way across Figure 26.4. How does this translate into housing demand? Beginning in the early 1960s, the United States experienced a growing demand for inexpensive rentals by persons under 25 years of age. By 1985, that demand peaked as all children born from 1940 to 1960 became 25 years or older. Between 1965 and 1975, the number of persons in the United States aged 25 through 34 increased by 9 million and resulted in the formation of 5 million households. Each household required a housing unit suitable to its income characteristics. By the year 2010, a total of 11 million people are above the age of 85, many still occupying their own homes.

MORE HOMEOWNERS

In addition to producing new households, the 1940–1960 children are climbing the income ladder and have more money to spend on housing. And, as they get older, they want to own, not rent. Government statistics show that 60% of all heads of households aged 35 through 44 are homeowners, and among those 45 through 54 years old, 75% are owners. (The percentages are even higher if there are children present.) Buying of more expensive homes will continue until the year 2015, at which time persons born in 1960 will reach the age of 55. Because personal income patterns have traditionally declined after that age, a retrenchment into more modest housing may then be observed, unless "fifty-five is the new forty" and people continue to actively work.

After 1985, the baby boomers have made fewer new purchases, except for "moving up" to bigger housing. Demand for housing by those in the peak new-home purchasing years has slowed somewhat as that population is now smaller in number than that of the baby boomers. Remember that we are living longer, so one can project that this demand may not decline as much if the baby boomers keep their homes longer.

OVER 65

Although the dominant factor in housing demand in the next several decades will be the maturing members of the 1940–1960 baby boom, we must not overlook the present steady growth in households over the age of 65 years. Households aged 65 and above have grown in numbers and, as may be seen at [5], did so until 1995. At that time there began a 10-year pause in growth because persons born during the decade of the 1930s reached the age of 65. Following that, the over-65 group will again grow in numbers as those born between 1940 and 1960 reach this age level. The housing demand created by these age groups may primarily be the result of their investments, pensions, social security income, public welfare, and assets accumulated earlier in life such as the family home, but a newer emerging health-conscious population may keep a much larger percentage of the labor force than may have been anticipated. The largest part of the growth in the elderly population is projected to occur between the years 2010 and 2050. A few years ago, everyone was predicting a massive shift in housing to retirement communities, smaller homes, and so on. In fact, the baby boomers are continuing to keep their homes for a number of reasons: (1) the cost of moving and discomfort of relocations; (2) when homes are paid for in the retirement years, it is often less expensive to stay in the existing house; (3) the retirees are very young and vibrant people and maintaining houses is not a burden for them; and (4) it's a great place to live when kids come back to visit!

When the children born after 1960 reach the age at which they want to have a residence of their own (usually 18 to 25 years of age), they will find large amounts of housing available as the persons born between 1946 and 1964 climb the lifetime income curve and upgrade their housing. The housing occupied by the 1946–1964 group has not been vacated. The United States experienced a virtual halt in new elementary school construction because of the drop in births after 1960. And this came after a 15-year-long frantic effort to build schoolrooms.

ANOTHER WAVE

Note that there is a new bubble for homeowners. Those born between 1976 and 1982 (generally referred to as Gen-Yers) outnumber the baby boomers by several million, these people are now moving into their prime home-buying years, so the demand for housing should remain strong. As they buy houses for the first time, more move up to a new house as their incomes continue to grow. While there is a number of Gen-Yers who continue to rent (probably to pay off college loans) a surprising number are already homeowners. Notwithstanding the existing housing market, it leads us to an unexpected conclusion. The housing market should remain strong and housing construction will expand as the huge number of Gen-Yers move into the marketplace. Note Figure 26.5. The National Center for Health Statistics has recently announced another "boom." Births in 2007 were at an all-time high. A third wave is coming!

Governmental Impact

Thus far we have talked about the requirement of an economic base to support local land values and the effect on housing demand by population age groups and income levels. Now let's look at the influence on real estate caused by the federal government's tax rules, laws, deficits, and monetary policies. The effects, as well as the history of

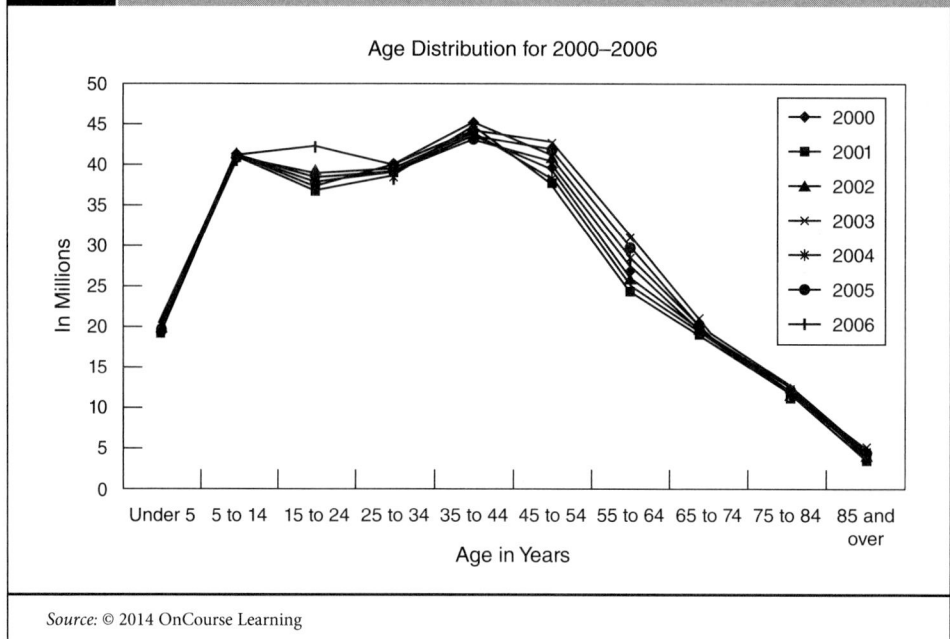

FIGURE 26.5   Age Distribution for 2000–2006

Source: © 2014 OnCourse Learning

governmental involvement in a capitalistic, free enterprise system, need a little more discussion.

TAX LAWS

Real estate has long been favored with special income tax treatment. For years, tax laws have allowed homeowners to deduct property taxes and mortgage loan interest when calculating state and federal taxes. To illustrate, for a person in a 28% tax bracket, a 4% interest rate costs, after taxes, only 2.88%. Similarly, property taxes of $1,500 per year cost, after taxes, only $1,080.

Owners of improved investment property can deduct costs of operating and maintaining the property plus depreciation on the improvements. For most investment properties owned between 1940 and 1980, depreciation expense was more of an accounting entry than a market reality. This was the result of rising real estate prices coupled with tax rules that allowed improvements to be depreciated over accounting lives shorter than their useful lives. Moreover, pre-1987 tax rules allowed depreciation to be accelerated, that is, taken sooner rather than later. Since depreciation is deductible at tax time and not repaid until years later when the property is sold, tax policies allowing short accounting lives and accelerated depreciation made real estate a very attractive investment.

1997 TAXPAYER RELIEF ACT AND 1986 TAX BILL

In the fall of 1986, a tax bill was passed by Congress and signed by the president that made drastic changes in the income tax treatment of real estate. The laws were revised with the 1997 Taxpayer Relief Act. (Details of these tax bills are in Chapters 15 and 27.) The 1986 law repealed the long-term capital gain exclusion, repealed accelerated depreciation on real estate, extended minimum depreciation periods from 19 years to 27½ years for residential and to 39 years for commercial property, and placed tight limits on real estate losses that could be deducted from other income. Each of these made real estate less attractive from a tax standpoint. And, since tax treatment is one of the deciding factors in buying investment real estate, these tax changes greatly influence what people can and will pay for a property. Most of the 1986 tax law changes fell upon real estate investors, with relatively few on homeowners. Of note in the 1986 tax bill is a tax credit allowed for the rehabilitation of old and historic structures. The intent of Congress is to induce people to renovate rather than tear down older structures. Also, there is a tax credit for those who will own and operate low-income rental housing.

The 1997 Taxpayer Relief Act reinstated capital gains and gave huge exclusions from income for sales of personal residences. This should greatly increase commercial real estate activity (to take advantage of lower tax rates) and allow homeowners to trade up or down without penalty, so residential sales are also positively affected.

FISCAL POLICY

Few home buyers can afford to pay all cash for a place to live; most must borrow. As a result, the housing industry is very sensitive to the price and availability of loan money. Not only does this affect contractors and construction workers, but also appliance and furniture manufacturers, lumber mills, cement factories, real estate appraisers, and real estate agents. Anyone connected with the manufacture, sale, or resale of housing is directly affected by the price and availability of mortgage loan money to home buyers. Low interest rates in recent years have resulted in booming home sales across the country. Many young home buyers have determined that it's as cheap or cheaper to buy a new home than to pay rent, with the tax benefits gained in equity appreciation and similar monthly payments. This, in turn, creates income for real estate agents, home builders, contractors, title companies, attorneys, interior decorators, and the like, stirring significant economic growth and prosperity.

The government, too, must borrow the money when it spends more than it earns. When it does, it competes with home buyers and businesses for available savings in the capital markets. Of these, government gets its needs filled first at whatever the interest cost. This is because if a government did not borrow, it would not have enough to pay its bills and would be bankrupt. This leaves home buyers and businesses to compete for what is left over. For the most part, state and local governments have learned to live within their budgets. The federal government has not. Defense spending and social spending in excess of income has produced federal deficits nearly every year since 1940. These were not terribly worrisome at first, but by the 1970s, financing the federal deficit was taking progressively larger and larger chunks of money out of the capital markets. By the middle of the 1980s, annual federal deficits were $200 billion and absorbing that much of the country's, and indeed the world's, capital. This borrowing continued to increase through the mid-1990s, but slowed significantly through the first quarter of 1998, and continued into a balanced budget through 2001. As a result, interest rates decreased. In view of this, it is generally agreed among economists that if the federal government lives within its means, interest rates will continue to decrease. Some administrations have attempted budget cuts, but Congress must approve them. As long as Congress perceives that there is voter support for federally supported projects, they are unwilling to cut back on spending. The deficit, then, continues because of the lack of congressional support to the contrary.

The federal government, unlike a homeowner, through its fiscal policy (its use of taxing and spending power to help influence the economy), establishes government programs and increases or decreases taxation to adjust its income. If the government increases taxes, it reduces private income and the consumer cannot spend as much (it lowers the consumer's disposal income). Therefore, the consumer's money cannot be spread throughout the economy. The economy, then, has to rely on the government infusion of money into the economy to create prosperity through government programs. This creates the constant political struggle over government's fiscal policy. The government, unlike homeowners and consumers, can change its income streams by passing new laws. History has shown us that keeping more money in consumers' pockets (through lower taxes) tends to lead to a more prosperous economy at the grassroots level. Higher taxes and government spending to stimulate the economy give Congress, not consumers, control of the outflow. This is why politics is at the root of the government's fiscal policy.

MONETARY POLICY

Federal Reserve Board

The governing board of the nation's central bank.

The **Federal Reserve Board**, through the Federal Reserve Banks, has the ability, through monetary policy, to create and destroy money. This is done by any of the following mechanisms: (1) open-market purchases and sales of Treasury securities, (2) changes in the discount rate charged to banks, and (3) changes in the reserve requirements of banks. We will omit a detailed explanation of each of these and go directly to the point: the Federal Reserve can create money. This is useful because in an economy that grows 3% a year, a 3% increase in the money supply is necessary to keep prices from falling. At the same time, however, there is the temptation to print more money than needed for economic growth because this new money can be used to buy back Treasury securities that were created to fund the federal deficit. The short-term result of such purchases is to drop interest rates, which benefits the government, businesses, and housing. Unfortunately, the longer-run effect (beyond two years) is more inflation as there is now more money in circulation without a corresponding increase in goods and services to buy, and the value of the dollar decreases.

When inflation is apparent, savers become wise and respond by buying equity assets such as real estate to hedge against further inflation and by raising the rate of interest they will accept to compensate for inflation. Thus, any benefits of creating extra money by the Federal Reserve are lost in the long term.

SECONDARY MORTGAGE MARKET

A very important influence on real estate activity and prices in the United States has been the secondary mortgage market. Before the 1970s, home loan money came mostly from savings and loans, mutual savings banks, commercial banks, and life insurance companies. This was a relatively limited source of money that tended to keep a lid on real estate prices. With the advent of the Federal National Mortgage Association, the Government National Mortgage Association, the Federal Home Loan Mortgage Corporation, and other secondary mortgage market operators raising additional funds through mortgage backed securities, previously untapped sources of loan money were now available to real estate borrowers. Individuals and pension funds that had avoided making mortgage loans because of the work involved could now invest with ease and a guarantee of safety. Additionally, the newly emerging private secondary market provides a place to sell a huge amount of mortgages that a lender does not want to hold until maturity. Much of the money raised in the secondary market has been used (and will continue to be used) to fund new homeowners as they buy housing.

Types of Inflation

In nearly all years since World War II, prices of consumer commodities and real estate have risen. Although inflation is currently not as pressing an issue as it was in the 1970s and 1980s, there are four concepts with which you should be familiar: cost-push inflation, demand-pull inflation, monetary inflation, and real-cost inflation.

COST-PUSH INFLATION

The increasing cost of inputs necessary to manufacture a product or offer a service results in what is called **cost-push inflation**. To illustrate, an automobile manufacturer increases the price of cars because labor and materials cost more. Similarly, a builder of new homes will include any increases in the prices of lumber, bricks, concrete, metal, construction labor, construction loans, and government permits. This creates the inevitable controversy: Does increasing wages force prices up, causing businesses to raise prices? Or do businesses, by raising prices, force the demand for higher wages? The economists are still arguing over a solution to these questions.

cost-push inflation
Higher prices due to increased costs of labor and supplies.

DEMAND-PULL INFLATION

When buyers bid against each other to buy something that has been offered for sale, **demand-pull inflation** results. For example, three buyers for a choice lot may bid $75,000, $76,000, and $77,000, respectively. Demand-pull inflation is basically the result of too much money chasing too few goods. Recently, the demand for corn has increased because we now use it for fuel additives. The farmers get higher offers for their product because more people are demanding it. A harder question may be: Does the increase in fuel prices create a cost-push inflation for the farmers' other products (eggs and milk)? This type of inflation usually has little to do with the actual cost of producing the particular goods or services being sought. Instead, it reflects what buyers feel they would have to pay elsewhere for the same thing.

demand-pull inflation
Higher prices due to buyers bidding against each other.

MONETARY INFLATION

Monetary inflation results from the creation of excessive amounts of money by government. The classic example of this was in Germany during the first five years after World War I. In an effort to provide money to solve all the war-torn country's problems at once, the German government created and spent money on a grand scale. However, there was no parallel increase in goods and services to be purchased with that money. The result was demand-pull inflation as millions of people with pockets and, later, wheelbarrows stuffed with newly printed currency fought to buy everything from bread and vegetables to real estate. Within a few years, prices rose on the order of 1 million percent before the printing presses were finally shut down.

To a lesser degree, monetary inflation is used today by many countries. Allowing the money supply to grow faster than the available supply of goods and services causes a temporary economic stimulus by placing more money in people's hands. But the ultimate result may be a reduction in the purchasing power of that money if the rate of monetary inflation exceeds increased supply of goods and services.

REAL-COST INFLATION

Real-cost inflation is inflation caused by the increased effort necessary to produce the same quantity of a good or service. For example, much easy-to-develop land has already been built upon, forcing developers to utilize more expensive land, or land that is more

real-cost inflation
Higher prices due to greater effort needed to produce the same product today versus several years ago.

expensive to bulldoze into usable lots. Another example is water service to new lots. Local water districts that once could supply the town's population from a few wells or a nearby lake or river must now travel many miles to find water. The additional cost of the water system and pumping charges must be added to the users' water bills.

1975–2012 Period

The period from 1975 through the 1990s has been one of the most dramatic in American economic history. In many areas, real estate prices doubled and tripled between 1975 and 1990. Inflation zoomed upward, interest rates reached record highs, and real estate was the favored investment. Then in the early 1990s, inflation fell dramatically, real estate prices stalled, and interest rates retreated. What the country witnessed was a combination of what's been discussed thus far in this chapter at work in the marketplace. Let's take a closer look at what happened then and what may happen in the future.

In 1975, members of the leading edge of the 1940–1960 baby boom were adults in the market ready for their first housing purchases. Simultaneously, the Equal Credit Opportunity Act made it easier to qualify for loans, and the secondary mortgage market was opening previously untapped sources of loan money. Added to this was the lack of new housing for sale because of a drop in housing starts in connection with a recession in 1974–1975.

As federal spending and money growth policies designed to end the recession took hold, interest rates fell, people regained jobs, and the mood of the country turned bullish. People began buying homes again and against a backdrop of limited supply quickly pulled prices upward. Rising prices usually dampen demand. But several other factors were involved that made buying real estate, and in particular buying homes, very attractive.

LOW REAL INTEREST

real
Inflation-adjusted.

The first factor was the low **real** (i.e., inflation-adjusted) cost of interest. Although interest rates for homes ranged from 8 to 10% between 1975 and 1978, inflation and home prices were rising faster. Thus, it made sense to borrow and buy real estate; in fact, the more the better. Since it was possible to buy with as little as 10% down, buyers were realizing enormous returns on their investments. Persons who received $60,000 for houses bought earlier for $40,000 were now making down payments on $80,000 houses. These sellers were taking their money into $110,000 houses while those sellers were buying $150,000 houses, and so on. From the late 1990s to the early "naughts" (2000–2004), the expansion of affordable housing programs (with little or no money down) brought us to a point where more people than ever before owned their own homes. Then we discovered the downside to this; predatory lending. Lenders often pushed loans on people to achieve the "American Dream" when the borrowers had no real ability to repay them.

TAX BENEFITS

As already noted, tax laws allow the deduction of interest in many situations. During the 1970s, wage increases of 10% per year and more were common. This pushed wage earners into higher tax brackets and made interest deductions even more valuable. Meanwhile, increases from appreciation were not taxable until the property sold and then received preferential long-term capital gains treatment. Thus, despite higher interest and higher home prices, as long as prices continued to rise substantially, real estate seemed to be an assured ticket to quick wealth.

REVERSAL/RECOVERY?

The boom came to a turning point in late 1979. Politically, high inflation (reaching at one point a rate of 18% per year) became a national political issue. There was still a high demand for housing by baby boomers. Interest rates for home loans reached the 16–17% range. The Federal Reserve policy changed from one of generous monetary growth to one of restrained monetary growth. Lenders made higher risk real estate loans (at high interest rates) and sometimes invested in real estate in an effort to keep pace with inflation. The lenders were in financial trouble.

In the 1980s, new, tight regulations by the federal government for high-risk loans resulted in fewer loans, regulated appraisals, and tighter credit standards. More importantly, fewer loans were being renewed because of the tighter lending requirements imposed by the new federal regulations. The existing loans had to be written down, and many lenders became insolvent. The initial effect was most severe in the southwestern states where the real property values had dropped, which then affected the loan-to-value ratios. By 1992, the Southwest was recovering, but the Northeast and Southern California were beginning to have similar difficulties. From 1996 to present (2007), there was unparalleled economic growth. The federal government has since kept a lower profile on regulations. The nation experienced low interest rates. This is partly because increased stability has resulted in availability of money, partly because of the increase in employment nationwide, the relatively few government controls, and more sources of investment capital being made available to first lien home loans because of the expanding private secondary market. Overall, this results in more people who can qualify for loans. In 2008, however, we've discovered how this lack of control resulted in huge defaults in home loans. We overlooked properly qualifying consumers for their loans, and gave in to the political pressure of the time to make "affordable loans" to those who couldn't afford to repay them.

LOOKING AHEAD

Expectations about inflation (or the lack of it) and interest rates lag the actual changes. At the midpoint of the 1980 decade, much of the home-buying public was unsure what to make of things. House prices, on average, essentially remained stable for the first half of the decade while interest rates were slow to drop. Many investors were left with high-priced properties that could not be sold except at below-market interest rates or below acquisition prices. More generous depreciation schedules offered by the 1981 tax act did help real estate's attractiveness, but investors and speculators remained unimpressed with housing and turned to office buildings, with depreciation being the carrot. However, even this carrot produced a problem as millions of square feet of office space built between 1981 and 1985 remained vacant at the end of the decade while someone was making the interest payments. The Tax Reform Act of 1986 made these investments even more unattractive into the late 1980s. There were fewer investors in the market, and many commercial properties were now selling for less than original construction cost. As the real estate market moved into the mid-1990s, supply still outpaced demand in most commercial markets. Prices were more dependent on quality, desirability, and cash flow, rather than federal economic indicators. The mid to late 1990s welcomed more relaxed tax laws, a booming economy, and a renewed seller's market in both commercial and residential markets throughout most of the country. The boom continued into the late 1990s, but the economy was beginning to show initial signs of weakness in the year 2000. Lower income tax and capital gains and tax rates put more disposable income into consumers' pockets in 2002, and we have seen a reversal of this weakness.

While the national unemployment rate was 5% in August 2008 (very low by historical standards), it was only 3.1% for high school graduates with some college, and for college graduates, age 25 and above, the unemployment rate was 1.8%. This is a clear indicator of the value of education.

By the end of 2008, unemployment began to increase dramatically and the government promoted "stimulus" packages (basically by printing money). It did very little to fuel economy in general. In addition, as the regulations were passed in an attempt to control some of the finance and mortgage markets, we passed additional regulations involving lending practices, off-shore drilling, and healthcare. But the economy remained sluggish. Can it improve under these conditions? At least one noted economist doesn't think so.[1] He notes the following problems: (1) complete uncertainty regarding the future cost of healthcare for business owners; (2) 2,000 pages of bank regulations that have yet to be written or enacted; (3) 13,000 pages of regulations of healthcare and healthcare insurance; (4) regulation of off-shore drilling; (5) regulation of oil-shale of deposits; (6) complete uncertainty about future income taxes; and (7) complete uncertainty about future capital gains rates. It seem axiomatic that when business owners have this much uncertainty they simply do nothing except to maximize profits. It's too risky to invest in growth in an uncertain environment.

OWNER-OCCUPANTS

The housing market is an owner-occupant market. The primary purpose in this market is to provide shelter and a place to live, more than investment potential. Owner-occupants receive the benefits of occupancy and the psychological value of owning their own homes. As such, they are less demanding of appreciation potential compared to investors who, sensing an unrewarding investment, will avoid it or sell out of it and go elsewhere with their capital. Thus, it appears that for the foreseeable future, success in new construction will go to those who appeal best to the owner-occupant's needs, tastes, and pocketbook. The 2000s have brought falling interest rates, and more creditworthy owner-occupants are able to qualify for loans and buy homes. This, along with the availability of money due to the rapid growth of money supplies for residential loans in the secondary market (not generally available for commercial loans), has especially helped the residential resale market and those owners who need to refinance existing loans. The issue, again, appears to be risk. The secondary market and loan pools rely on low-risk, qualified home buyers utilizing standard loan documentation. There is still less money available for the higher-risk, tougher credit, commercial markets. Some of those lenders that survived the loose lending practices of the early 1980s learned from their mistakes and now have much more conservative loan criteria. Other lenders pursuing aggressive loan programs, possibly predatory, are now out of their very short term businesses in 2010.

Watching the Fed

If you plan to develop or invest in real estate, it is very helpful to watch Federal Reserve statistics so as to better anticipate changes in interest rates. Although the marketplace is the ultimate decider of interest rates, the actions of the Federal Reserve Board can and do provide a powerful push on rates. For example, even though mortgage rates were already

---

[1] Mark Dotzour, Chief Economist. Texas A&M University, Mayes School of Business.

rising by 1978 as lenders tried to stay ahead of inflation, Federal Reserve action in 1979 and 1980 to slow money supply growth helped interest rates go higher. By 1989, the Board was carefully increasing the money supply in order to reduce interest rates and thus keep the U.S. economy from falling into another recession.

To understand the Federal Reserve Board, you need to know that the Board has four objectives for the American economy: (1) high employment, (2) stable prices, (3) steady growth in the nation's productive capacity, and (4) a stable foreign exchange value for the dollar. During a recession, employment and economic growth are of primary importance, and the Board adds extra money to the banking system as it did to pull out of the 1974–1975 recession. In the late 1970s, stable prices and a stable dollar were the prime concerns. This required a slowdown in the growth of the money supply, which the Board effected. By the end of 1984, inflation was down to 4% and the dollar was very strong. In 1985, the Board was gingerly touching the money accelerator to buoy a banking industry beleaguered by high interest rates, ward off recession, and take the edge off what many considered to be an overly strong dollar. The early 1990s saw the Fed drop the cost of money to member banks to a 20-year low, but lending regulations stemmed the potential inflation by requiring tighter credit standards. In the mid-1990s, the Fed began to raise interest rates again for a brief period in an effort to prevent an increase in inflation. It has since raised and lowered the rate again because of the nation's economics.

While there is no exact formula, when the Fed raises interest rates, employment growth slows, job creation slows, and the absorption of commercial real estate decreases. Alternatively, when the Fed cuts rates, employment generally rises. There is often a 12- to 18-month lag between the time the Fed initiates a change in interest rates and when the economy responds. The economy's response time to a rate hike is shorter than the response time for a rate cut. When rates are cut, the economy normally feels the impact about 34 months after the cut takes place. When rates are increased, however, the effect on the economy is shorter, generally about 16 months. Therefore, Fed cuts that began in September of 2011 will not have much effect on the U.S. economy until the summer of 2013. Note that the Federal rates have been very low for the last few years, but the economic outlook has not improved. It clearly shows that there's more at work here, perhaps it is other governmental policies that regulate too heavily or tax too much that stifle economic growth.

MONETARY BASE

Week-to-week changes in the results of Federal Reserve monetary policy can be found each Friday in *The Wall Street Journal* under "Federal Reserve Data." Of these, the most important is the **monetary base** figure. This shows the legal reserves of banks at the Federal Reserve plus cash in the hands of the public. If this grows faster than the real (i.e., inflation-adjusted) rate of growth of the country's gross domestic product (GDP), one can assume that the nation's money supply will soon be expanding at a greater rate than the real gross domestic product. This will cause interest rates to fall and economic growth to be stimulated. Two years down the road it may turn to inflation, depending on how the Fed deals with credit standards.

The Outlook

As this material is being written, there are two likely economic scenarios pending, and the federal deficit plays a leading role in both of them. The first scenario is that Congress

monetize the debt

The creation of money by the Federal Reserve to purchase Treasury securities.

will not balance its budget. This means the Federal Reserve Board must decide whether to expand the money supply in order to buy back the deficit—that is, **monetize the debt**. Failure to expand the money supply will allow interest rates to rise dramatically and cause a recession worse than the 1985–1986 recession, which was the worst since the 1930s. Yet creating money in excess of increases in goods and services will cause inflation and high interest costs, just as it did in the 1975–1979 period. To date, the Fed has managed to control the supply to maintain low inflation but has had difficulty dealing with the prospect of a recession.

The second scenario is that Congress will bring about a meaningful reduction in the size of the federal deficit. This would reduce the need of the U.S. Treasury to compete with businesses and home buyers for available loan funds. With less competition, interest rates will stay low and perhaps fall even lower. This will attract more loan funds as lenders become confident that rates won't soon be rising. Lower rates will reduce the federal deficit still further as interest paid on existing government debt gradually drops. The cost of this attractive scenario is overall fiscal belt tightening: recipients of government spending programs would have to receive less. Alternatively, Congress could continue to raise taxes to pay for its spending (as it did in 1993), or it could apply a combination of the two.

A PARALLEL

There is a very close parallel between the federal government's money problems and the money problems of a free-spending married couple that discovered credit cards. At first, the couple found that a credit card could help them buy a few things that their monthly paychecks would not have covered. But instead of repaying the credit card balance, more items were purchased until the limit on the card was reached. Flush with the pleasures of living beyond their monthly paychecks, another credit card was obtained. Purchases were made with it until it, too, reached its maximum. Now the first two credit card companies were demanding monthly payments, so a third credit card, this one with cash borrowing privileges, was obtained. This card was used to make payments on the previous two cards and buy still more on credit. Soon all three credit card companies wanted monthly repayments, so the couple took out a loan at the bank, mortgaging the appreciation in their house to do so. The buying continued and soon another loan was taken out with a finance company to make payments on the existing loans and buy more things. Then one day, there were simply no more places to borrow, yet the payments on all those loans kept coming due. The couple was advised by a credit counselor that they had two choices: declare bankruptcy or adopt an austerity budget and start repaying the loans. If you were in their shoes, which would you choose? If you were in the U.S. Congress, which would you choose for the country? Would you adopt an austere budget or would you look for one more lender to keep the deficits going a little while longer?

There is no lack of household formation potential in the United States. Additionally, there is a large stock of existing housing in the country plus the capacity to build 2 million new housing units every year. The main question will continue to be who gets what—that is, how housing will be distributed. Because real estate is so sensitive to the price and availability of loanable funds, the answer will continue to depend heavily on regulatory involvement of the government.

Vocabulary Review

Match terms a–j with statements 1–10.

a. Base industry
b. Cost-push inflation
c. Demand-pull inflation
d. Economic base
e. Federal Reserve Board
f. Monetary inflation
g. Monetize the debt
h. Real
i. Real-cost inflation
j. Service industry

_____ 1. An industry that produces goods or services for export from the region.

_____ 2. An industry that produces goods or services to sell to local residents.

_____ 3. The ability of a region to export goods and services to other regions.

_____ 4. Higher prices due to buyers bidding against each other.

_____ 5. Higher prices due to greater effort needed to produce the same product today.

_____ 6. Higher prices due to increased costs of labor and supplies.

_____ 7. Results from increasing the money supply faster than increases in goods and services to buy.

_____ 8. Governing board of the nation's central bank.

_____ 9. Inflation-adjusted.

_____10. The creation of money by the Federal Reserve to purchase Treasury securities.

Questions and Problems

1. List and rank in order of importance the base industries that support your community. How stable are they? Are any new ones coming? Are any existing ones leaving?

2. What would be the effect of a new industry creating 500 new jobs in your community? Is there sufficient vacant housing available? What would be the effect of a loss of 500 jobs?

3. Does the population age distribution of your community differ from the United States as a whole? How would this affect demand for housing in your area?

4. What was the effect of the Reagan years on inflation? What are the good points? The bad points?

5. What was the intent of government in passing the Equal Credit Opportunity Act?

6. Identify three specific examples of cost-push inflation that you have personally observed or read about during the past 12 months.

7. Did the years Bill Clinton was in office result in a marked change from the years George W. Bush was in office? Why or why not?

8. What are the economic goals of the Federal Reserve Board?

9. What are the advantage and the disadvantage of monetizing the federal debt?

10. If money supply grows slower than real gross national product, would the result be rising prices or falling prices?

Additional Readings

"Energy Efficiency Boosts Property Values: Seeing the Hidden Value of Energy-Efficient Properties" by Mark Jewell (*Energy User News*, April 2002, pp. 18+).

Essentials of Real Estate Economics, 6th ed. by Dennis J. McKenzie, Richard M. Betts and Carol A. Jensen (OnCourse Learning, 2011).

The Impact of Parks and Open Space on Property Values and the Property Tax Base by John L. Crompton (National Recreation & Park Association, 2000).

"Is It 'Discoloration' or Toxic Mold? (Health Hazards and Property Values, United States)" (*Mortgage Servicing News*, April 2002, p. 13).

Property and Values: Alternatives to Public and Private Ownership (Island Press, 2000).

Property Values by Funderberg (Farrar, Straus & Giroux, 2002).

CHAPTER 27

Investing in Real Estate

T here are more millionaires in the United States as a result of real estate investing than from any other source, including oil wells and computers. Moreover, real estate success and wealth have been and are available to people from all walks of life and all income levels. For most people thinking of making it big financially, real estate is at the top of the list. Considering that real estate provides 313 million people in the United States a place to sleep at night as well as approximately half that number a place to work during the day plus all other uses we make of real estate, you can begin to see why there are so many opportunities in real estate investing.

The keys to your personal success are time and your intelligence. There are some who say that luck plays the main role in real estate success and that it's all a matter of waiting for the right deal to come along. In reality, however, success results when opportunity and preparedness meet. As you become more knowledgeable as to what makes a good real estate investment and you apply your time looking for real estate opportunities, you will experience success.

It is impossible to do full justice to the topic of real estate investing in one chapter. There are, however, dozens of books entirely on the subject, many of which you can find at your local library and bookstore. This chapter will introduce you to some highlights of real estate investing. We'll begin with the investment benefits of real estate and then look at risks and rewards of various types of real estate, investment timing, investment strategies, and limited partnerships.

LEARNING OBJECTIVES

After reading this chapter, you should be able to:

‹ Define "appreciation," "mortgage reduction," and "cash flow."

‹ Discuss the concept of tax shelter.

‹ Understand the difference between passive investors and active investors as it relates to paying income tax.

‹ Define and calculate certain forms of depreciation.

‹ Define "equity building up."

‹ Understand the different types of property one can select for investment.

‹ Understand the concept of investment timing as it relates to good investment decision.

‹ Define "limited partnership" and discuss the concept of limited liability in real estate investments.

‹ Discuss and understand the need for the various disclosure laws as it relates to investments.

KEY TERMS

Appreciation • Cash flow • Cash-on-cash • Downside risk • Equity build-up • Investment strategy • Leverage • Limited partnership • Mortgage reduction • Negative cash flow • Prospectus • Straight-line depreciation • Tax shelter

Benefits of Real Estate Investing

The monetary benefits of investing in real estate come from cash flow, tax shelter, mortgage reduction, and appreciation.

Appreciation is the increase in property value that the owner hopes will occur while owning it. Enough appreciation can offset underestimated expenses, overestimated rents, and a rising adjustable rate loan. Without appreciation, a property must produce enough rental income to pay the operating expenses and loan interest, cover wear and obsolescence, and give the investor a decent return.

Mortgage reduction occurs when an investor uses a portion of a property's rental income to reduce the balance owing on the mortgage. At first, the reduction may be quite small because most of the loan payments might be applied to payments of interest rather than to the reduction of principal. But, eventually, the balance owing begins to fall at a more rapid rate. Some investors invest with the idea that if they hold a rental property for the entire life of the loan, the tenants will have paid for the property. This presumes the investor is patient and that the other elements of cash flow and income tax consequences are conducive to holding the property. Let's look at cash flow, tax shelter, depreciation, taxation of gains, and other real estate tax topics.

CASH FLOW

cash flow

The number of dollars remaining each year after collecting rents and paying operating expenses and mortgage payments.

Cash flow refers to the number of dollars remaining each year after you collect rents and pay operating expenses and mortgage payments. For example, suppose you own a small apartment building that generates $48,000 per year in rents. The operating expenses (including reserves) are $25,000 per year and mortgage payments are $20,000 per year. Given these facts, your cash flow picture is shown in Table 27.1.

The purpose of calculating cash flow is to show the cash-in-the-pocket effect of owning a particular property. In Table 27.1, $3,000 per year is going into your pocket. When money is flowing to you it is called a **positive cash flow**. If you must dip into your pocketbook to keep the property going, you have a **negative cash flow**. For example, if in Table 27.1 the mortgage payments were $25,000 per year, there would be a negative cash flow. A negative cash flow does not automatically mean a property is a poor investment. There may be mortgage reduction, tax benefits, and appreciation that more than offset this.

negative cash flow

When cash paid out exceeds cash received.

cash-on-cash

The cash flow produced by a property divided by the amount of cash necessary to purchase it.

Two terms that are related to cash flow are net spendable and cash-on-cash. **Net spendable** is the same thing as cash flow and refers to the amount of spendable income a property produces for its owner. **Cash-on-cash** is the cash flow (or net spendable) that a property produces in a given year divided by the amount of cash required to buy the property. For example, if a property has a cash flow of $5,000 per year and can be purchased with a $50,000 down payment (including closing costs), the cash-on-cash figure for that property is .1, or 10%. For many real estate investors, this is the heart of the investment decision, namely, "How much do I have to put down and how much will I have in my pocket at the end of each year?"

TABLE 27.1	Cash Flow Projections	
	Rent receipts for the year	$48,000
	Less operating expenses	25,000
	Less mortgage loan payments	20,000
	Equals cash flow	$ 3,000

Source: © 2014 OnCourse Learning

TAX SHELTER

Broadly defined, the term **tax shelter** describes any tax-deductible expense generated by an investment property. Examples most often utilized for real estate investment are interest, maintenance, insurance, property taxes, and depreciation. More narrowly defined, tax shelter refers only to *depreciation* (a noncash expense, discussed later in this chapter) that a taxpayer can report as a taxable deduction against other income.

The United States Congress has a decades-long history of tinkering with depreciation rules for income tax calculation. During the 1960s and 1970s, Congress wanted to encourage investment in real estate, especially residential real estate, and made income tax rules that allowed very generous treatment of depreciation expenses. Laws passed made it possible to deduct depreciation on property that was, in fact, appreciating in value. Moreover, tax laws made it possible to take a larger portion of depreciation early in the life of a building and less later. This produced paper losses for tax purposes that could offset income from one's job or from other investments. The tax benefits became so attractive that they were often a compelling force in choosing a property. In other words, not only did an investor look forward to the rents a property could produce, but also to the tax savings it would produce, as well as to mortgage reduction and anticipated appreciation. This, plus favorable tax status upon trade or sale, made real estate the hottest investment around.

The height of quick write-offs came with a 1981 federal tax law that permitted a building to be entirely depreciated in 15 years, no matter how old or new it was. This depreciation method was called the **Accelerated Cost Recovery System (ACRS)**. Then the tide started to change direction. Congress was concerned that real estate had become an immense tax loophole that needed tightening. In 1984, the depreciation period was lengthened to 18 years. In 1985, it went to 19 years and rules were added regarding below-market interest rates on seller financing (see Chapter 14). Then in the fall of 1986, a new Internal Revenue Code was passed by Congress that took away nearly all the extra tax benefits previously given to real estate. Now, Congress said, real estate investments would have to stand more on their economic merits, not on favorable tax treatment. Let's look at some of the important changes regarding taxation of real estate investments brought about by the Internal Revenue Code of 1986.

LOSS LIMITATIONS

There are now stricter limits on how much loss can be deducted from a person's other income. This is now a major consideration in whether to buy or sell or hold real estate as an investment and in choosing what types of real estate to own. Using our investment example, suppose that the $20,000 mortgage payment consists of $19,500 in interest (which is an expense for tax purposes) and $500 in loan reduction (which is not an expense for tax purposes). Suppose also that tax law allows $8,000 in depreciation on the property for the year. Even though there is a positive cash flow, the result is a taxable loss as shown in Table 27.2.

Under the pre-1987 tax rules, all of the operating expenses, the interest, and the depreciation were deductible against other income, with relatively little restriction. Under the 1987 rules, there are substantial restrictions, and a distinction is made between passive investors and active investors. If you are a **passive investor**, you can deduct your loss only against income from other passive investments. A passive investor is one who does not materially participate on a "regular, substantial, and continuous basis," for example, a limited partner.

If you are an **active investor** (for example, you manage the rentals you own), it is possible to use as much as $25,000 of your losses to offset your other income (such as

tax shelter

The income tax savings that an investment can produce for its owner.

TABLE 27.2	Taxable Loss	
	Rent receipts for the year	$48,000
	Less operating expenses	25,000
	Less interest on loan	19,500
	Less depreciation	8,000
	Equals taxable income	$ (4,500)*

*In accounting language, parentheses indicate a negative or minus amount.

Source: © 2014 OnCourse Learning

your job income). However, this only applies to taxpayers with up to $100,000 of adjusted gross income (as defined on one's annual IRS Form 1040). For those with higher adjusted gross incomes, the loss deduction is gradually reduced and is eliminated at $150,000 of adjusted gross income. This aspect of the tax law change had little effect on the middle-income person who owns a rental house or two, or a small apartment building, and has a hand in managing them. But, for persons with larger incomes who are affected by the new Internal Revenue Code, restructuring of investments and more investor participation is likely. For example, nonactive investors with passive losses look for properties with passive income, such as parking lots. Those who do not actively manage their real estate holdings may take a more active role so as to qualify as active investors. Loss-producing partnerships may be attractive acquisitions only for income-producing investors.

Congress recently created a new class of taxpayers who have the ability to offset their active income with passive losses. These are referred to as **eligible taxpayers**. Eligible taxpayers are individuals in closely held C corporations who must materially participate in rental real estate activities. To satisfy the eligibility requirements, individuals must (1) devote more than 50% of their personal services during the tax year to material participation in real property trades or businesses, and (2) perform more than 750 hours of material participation in real property trades or businesses.

Depreciation Calculation

straight-line depreciation

Depreciation in equal amounts each year over the life of the asset.

As noted several paragraphs earlier, under tax rules effective January 1, 1987, depreciation is to be straight-line. **Straight-line depreciation** is calculated by taking the total amount of anticipated depreciation and dividing by the number of years. For example, a building valued at $275,000 for depreciation purposes and depreciated over 27½ years using straight-line will have $10,000 in depreciation each year. (Note that only improvements are depreciable, land is not. Therefore, when buying investment real estate, it is necessary to subtract the value of the land from the purchase price before calculating depreciation.)

In contrast to straight-line depreciation, **accelerated depreciation** is any method of depreciation that allows depreciation at a rate faster than straight-line during the first several years of ownership. Although this is not allowed for real property placed in service starting January 1, 1987, it is retained for certain types of personal property used in business (such as a real estate agent's automobile) and for real property started under accelerated depreciation before 1987.

Passive losses (including depreciation) that are unusable in any given year can be carried forward from year to year and used later. Any losses carried forward into the year of sale can be deducted in full at that time. Be careful, though. Gain due to depreciation claimed or available in the past is "recaptured" by being taxed at 25% (15% in the lower tax bracket).

Capital Gains

You may recall from Chapter 15 that investment in and sale of capital assets are taxed at a much lower rate than regular income tax rates. This is a great incentive to buy, hold, and develop capital assets. You may recall that when capital assets are sold, it generates a lot of income for brokers, lawyers, and other service providers. They pay income tax at regular rates, which usually means more total income tax generated.

At-Risk Rules

Congress has enacted **at-risk rules** for investors. The issue was that an investor could invest $1, borrow $4 that did not require personal repayment, and take tax write-offs on the full $5. Congress passed rules that limited write-off to the amount actually invested plus **recourse financing**—that is, the investor is personally obligated to repay. Under the old rules, this applied to nearly every investment, except real estate. Under the new rules, it applies to real estate. But real estate sales nearly always require financing, and it is often **nonrecourse financing**—that is, there is no personal obligation, only the value of the property secures the debt. Therefore, Congress considers the amount at risk in real estate to be the sum of third-party financing (note that this does not include seller financing), recourse indebtedness, and cash.

Installment Sales

In the past, a seller of real estate who had a substantial gain might choose to sell on the *installment method* to spread out receipt of the gain and therefore the taxes on it. IRS rules limit the benefits of using installment sales. The wise seller will seek competent tax advice before agreeing to carry back a mortgage. Dealers in real property (developers) may not utilize the installment sales benefit.

Construction-Period Expenses

In past years, Congress has set various policies as to whether interest paid during construction could be taken as an immediate expense or had to be added to the cost of the building and amortized. Beginning January 1, 1987, the rule changed from amortization over 10 years to amortization over the depreciable life of the asset, even though the interest is an actual, paid expense during the construction period. This tax change is a disincentive for new construction.

Rehabilitation Tax Credits

In an effort to encourage individuals to rebuild older structures rather than tear them down or let them decay, Congress has had a policy of giving rehabilitation tax credits. Historic structures are allowed a credit of 20%. (This effectively means the federal government will pick up 20% of the cost of rehabilitating an historic structure.)

Nonhistoric structures constructed prior to 1935 receive a 10% tax credit. (The investor needs to have other income against which to claim the credit, and the passive loss rules apply.)

Low-Income Housing Credit

Whereas the 1987 tax law mostly tightened the rules on real estate, one area was loosened: low-income housing. A number of inducements such as tax-exempt bond financing, accelerated depreciation, and five-year amortization have been used in the past. The rules now allow a tax credit to owners of buildings that provide low-income rental housing. On new and newly rehabilitated housing, the credit is a maximum of 9% per year for 10 years. (Effectively, the government pays for most of the building.) On existing housing the credit is a maximum of 4% per year for 10 years.

Watch List

Historically, one thing has never changed. Tax law changes are occurring with increasing frequency and impact. In fact, one of the biggest risks in real estate in the mid-1980s was tax law changes. The values of land and buildings can, and do, go up and down with changes in tax rules. (This is in addition to the marketplace risks that an investor must take.) Therefore, it is of great importance that you stay abreast of tax law changes, impending tax law changes, and even swings in the mood of Congress toward real estate. As noted earlier in this chapter, the 1960s and 1970s saw exceptionally favorable treatment of real estate by the tax laws. In the 1980s, real estate had to stand on its own as an economic investment, which will continue unless Congress sees the need to encourage real estate investment. Keep this in mind as you continue to read this chapter. Also keep in mind that because approximately two out of three households in the United States own their homes, homeownership is likely to continue its favored tax status. Thus, as reported in Chapter 15, the tax rules have retained the personal deduction for home loan interest (although it has been limited, as discussed in Chapter 15), and the 1997 Taxpayer Relief Act greatly expanded tax benefits for homeowners by exempting profits from the sale of a personal residence (also discussed in Chapter 15). In 2009, we also eliminated classifying the lender's debt forgiveness as "income" under the Mortgage Forgiveness Debt Relief Act.

Equity Build-Up

An owner's *equity* in a property is defined as the market value of the property less all liens or other charges against the property. Thus, if you own a property worth $125,000 and owe $75,000, your equity is $50,000. If you own that property with your brother or sister, each with a one-half interest, your equity is $25,000 and his or her equity is $25,000.

equity build-up

The increase of one's equity in a property due to mortgage balance reduction and price appreciation.

Equity build-up is the change in your equity over a period of time. Suppose you purchase a small apartment building for $200,000, placing $60,000 down and borrowing the balance. Your beginning equity is your down payment of $60,000. If after five years you have paid the loan down to $120,000 and you can sell the property for $220,000, your equity is now $100,000. Since you started with $60,000, your equity build-up is $40,000, or 67%. Table 27.3 recaps this calculation.

TABLE 27.3 Calculating Equity Build-Up					
Equity at Time of Purchase		**Equity 5 Years Later**		**Equity Build-Up**	
Purchase price	$200,000	Market value	$220,000	Current equity	$100,000
Mortgage loan	–140,000	Less loan balance	–120,000	Less beginning equity	–60,000
Down payment (equity)	$ 60,000	Equals current equity	$100,000	Equals equity build-up	$ 40,000

Source: © 2014 OnCourse Learning

Leverage

Leverage is the impact that borrowed funds have on investment return. The purpose of borrowing is to earn more on the borrowed funds than the funds cost. For example, suppose you are an investor and you have $250,000 to invest in an apartment building. If you use all your money to buy a $250,000 building, there is zero leverage. If you use your $250,000 to buy a $500,000 building, there is 50% leverage. If you use your $250,000 to buy a $2,500,000 building, there is 90% leverage.

Whether to try leverage depends on whether the property can reasonably be expected to produce cash flow, tax benefits, mortgage reduction, and appreciation in excess of the cost of the borrowed funds. The decision also depends on your willingness to take risk. For example, the $250,000 building would have to fall to zero value before you lost all your money. Moreover, the building could experience a vacancy rate on the order of 60% and there would still be enough cash to meet out-of-pocket operating expenses. In other words, with zero leverage there is very little likelihood of a total financial wipe-out.

In contrast, if you buy the $2,500,000 building, a 10% drop in the property's value to $2,250,000 wipes out your entire equity. Moreover, even the slightest drop-off in occupancy from 95% down to 85% will cause great strain on your ability to meet mortgage loan payments and out-of-pocket operating expenses.

But, suppose apartment building values increase by 10%. If you had bought the $250,000 building with borrowed funds, it will now be worth $275,000, an increase of $25,000 on your investment of $250,000. Similarly, if you had bought the $2,500,000 building, it will now be worth $2,750,000, an increase of $250,000 on your investment of $250,000. As you can see, leverage can work both against you and for you. If the benefits from borrowing exceed the costs of borrowing, it is called **positive leverage**. If the borrowed funds cost more than they are producing, it is called **negative leverage**.

leverage
The impact that borrowed funds have on investment return.

Property Selection

The real estate market offers a wide selection of properties for investments, including vacant land; houses; condominiums; small, medium, and large apartment buildings; office buildings; retail and shopping centers; industrial property; and so forth. Selecting a suitable type of property is a matter of matching an investor's capital with his attitudes toward risk taking and the amount of time he is willing to spend on management. Let's begin by looking at the ownership of vacant land.

VACANT LAND

The major risk of owning vacant land as an investment is that one will have to wait too long for an increase in value. Vacant land produces little, if any, income, yet it consumes the investor's dollars in the form of interest, property taxes, insurance, and, eventually, selling costs. The rule of thumb is that the market value of vacant land must double every five years for the investor to break even. If this increase does not occur, the owner will have spent more on interest, insurance, property taxes, brokerage fees, and closing costs than is made on the price increase.

The key to successful land speculating is in outguessing the general public. If the public feels that development of a vacant parcel to a higher use is 10 years in the future, the market price will reflect the discounted cost at current interest rates and property taxes for that waiting period. If the land speculator buys at these prices, and the higher use occurs in five years, there is a good chance the purchase will be profitable. However, the speculator will lose money if the public expects the higher use to occur in five years and it actually takes 10 years.

Finally, land speculators expose themselves to an extra risk that owners of improved property can usually avoid. When it comes time to sell, unless buildings will immediately be placed upon the land by the purchaser, very few lenders will loan the purchaser money to buy the land. This may force the seller to accept the purchase price in the form of a down payment plus periodic payments for the balance. If the interest rate on the balance is below prevailing mortgage rates, as often happens in land sales, the seller is effectively subsidizing the buyer. Furthermore, if the payments are made over several years, the seller takes the risk that the money he receives will buy less because of inflation.

HOUSES AND CONDOMINIUMS

Houses and condominiums are the least expensive properties available in income-producing real estate and, as such, are within the financial reach of more prospective investors than apartment buildings, stores, or offices. Moreover, they can usually be purchased with lower down payments and interest rates because lenders feel that loans on houses and condominiums are less prone to default than those on larger buildings. With a small property, the investor can fall back upon salary and other income to meet loan payments in the event rents fall short. With larger properties, the lender knows he must rely more on the rental success of the property and less on the owner's other sources of income.

Houses and condominiums are usually overpriced in relation to the monthly rent they can generate. This is because their prices are influenced both by the value of the shelter they provide and the amenity value of homeownership. Thus, an investor must pay what prospective owner-occupants are willing to pay, yet when the property is rented, a tenant will pay only for the shelter value. However, when the investor sells, the sale price will be higher than would be justified by rents alone. What this means is that the investor can usually expect a negative cash flow during ownership. Consequently, there must be a substantial increase in property value to offset the monthly negative cash flow and give the investor a good return on investment.

Both single-family residences and condominiums can offer advantageous locations plus amenities, ensuring a good long-term investment. Condominiums may have more restrictions because of their obligation to abide by homeowners' associations' covenants (including highly restrictive rental policies), but, there are usually fewer management headaches, since the homeowners' association takes care of the exterior maintenance.

SMALL APARTMENT BUILDINGS

Because considerable appreciation must occur to make house and condominium investments profitable, many investors who start with these move to more income-oriented properties as their capital grows. Particularly popular with investors who have modest amounts of investment capital are duplexes (two units), triplexes (three units), and four-plexes (four units).

If it were necessary to hire professional management, such small buildings would be uneconomical to own. However, for most owners of two- to four-unit apartment buildings, management is on a do-it-yourself basis. Moreover, it is possible for the owner to live on the premises. This eliminates a cash outlay for management and allows the owner to reduce repair and maintenance expenses by handling them himself. Also, with the owner living on the property, tenants are encouraged to take better care of the premises and discouraged from moving out without paying their rent. Finally, the ownership of a residential rental property provides the owner with a wealth of experience and education in property management.

MEDIUM-SIZE BUILDINGS

Apartment buildings containing 5 to 24 units also present good investment opportunities for those with sufficient down payment. However, in addition to analyzing the building, rents, and neighborhood, thought must be given to the matter of property management before a purchase is made. An apartment building of this size is not large enough for a full-time manager; therefore, the owner must either do the job or hire a part-time manager to live on the property. An owner who does the job should be willing to live on the property and devote a substantial amount of time to management, maintenance, and upkeep activities. If a part-time manager is hired, the task is to find one who is knowledgeable and capable of maintaining property, showing vacant units, interviewing tenants, collecting rents on time, and handling landlord-tenant relations in accordance with local landlord-tenant laws. As the size of an apartment building increases, so does its efficiency. As a rule of thumb, when a building reaches 25 units, it will generate enough rent so that a full-time professional manager can be hired to live on the premises. With a live-in manager, the property owner need not reside on the property nor be involved in day-to-day management chores. This is very advantageous if the owner has another occupation where time is better spent.

LARGER APARTMENT BUILDINGS

As the number of apartment units increases, the cost of management per unit drops. Beyond 60 units, assistant managers can be hired. This makes it possible to have a representative of the owner on the premises more hours of the day to look after the investment and keep the tenants happy. Size also means it is possible to add recreational facilities and other amenities that are not possible on a small scale. The cost of having a swimming pool in a 10-unit building might add so much to apartment rents that they would be priced out of the market. The same pool in a 50- or 100-unit building would make relatively little difference in rent. As buildings reach 200 or more units in size, it becomes economical to add such things as a children's pool, gymnasium, game room, lounge, and a social director.

Since larger apartment buildings cost less to manage per unit and compete very effectively in the market for tenants, they tend to produce larger cash flows per invested dollar. However, errors in location selection, building design, and management policy are magnified as the building grows in size. Also, many lenders, particularly small- and medium-sized banks and savings associations, are simply not large enough to lend on big projects. Finally, the number of investors who can single-handedly invest a down payment of $500,000 or more is limited. This has caused the widespread growth of the limited partnership as a means of making the economies of large-scale ownership available to investors with as little as $2,000 to invest.

OFFICE BUILDINGS

Office buildings offer the prospective investor not only a higher rent per square foot of floor space than any of the investments discussed thus far, but also larger cash flows per dollar of property worth. This is because office buildings are costlier to build and operate than residential structures, and because they expose the owner to more risk.

The higher construction and operating costs of an office building reflect the amenities and services office users demand. To be competitive today, an office building must offer air-conditioning to all tenants on a room-by-room basis, thus adding to construction and operating costs. Office users also expect and pay for daily cleaning services, such as emptying wastebaskets, cleaning ashtrays, dusting, and vacuuming. Apartment dwellers neither expect these services nor pay for them.

One may note, however, that the need for office space has increased in the United States over the last several years because the U.S. economic base has shifted to a high percentage of service providers (lawyers, accountants, psychologists, etc.). Planned office developments often attract the service-related businesses because their client or customer base is interrelated. In addition, office building tenants are reluctant to leave their locations because of costs of relocating and moving, and they don't want to change their business address.

Tenant turnover is more expensive in an office building than in an apartment building because a change in office tenants usually requires more extensive remodeling. To offset this, building owners include the cost of remodeling in the tenant's rent. Another consideration is that it is not unusual for office space to remain vacant for long periods of time. Also, if a building is rented to a single tenant, a single vacancy means there is no income at all. To reduce tenant turnover, incentives such as lower rent may be offered if a tenant agrees to sign a longer lease, such as five years instead of one or two years. Care must be taken on longer leases, however, so that the owner does not become locked into a fixed monthly rent while operating costs escalate.

The risk in properly locating an office building is greater than with a residential property since office users are very particular about where they locate. If a residential building is not well located, the owner can usually drop rents a little and still fill the building. To do the same with an office building may require a much larger drop; then, even with the building full, it may not generate enough rent to pay the operating expenses and mortgage payments. Finally, the tax shelter benefits available from offices may not be as attractive as from comparably priced apartments. This is because compared to office buildings, residential properties tend to have a higher percentage of their value in depreciable improvements and less in nondepreciable land.

Investment Timing

The potential risks and rewards available from owning real estate depend to a great extent on the point in the life of a property at which an investment is made. Should one invest while a project is still an idea? Or is it better to wait until it is finished and fully rented? That depends on the risks one can afford and the potential rewards.

LAND PURCHASE

The riskiest point at which to invest in a project is when it is still an idea in someone's head. At this point, money is needed to purchase land. But beyond the cost of the land, there are many unknowns, including the geological suitability of the land to support buildings, the ability to obtain the needed zoning, the cost of construction, the availability of a loan, the rents the market will pay, how quickly the property will find tenants, the expenses of operating the property, and finally, the return the investor will obtain. Even though the investor may have a feasibility study that predicts success for the project, such a report is still only an educated guess. Therefore, the anticipated returns to an investor entering a project at this point must be high to offset the risks he takes. As the project clears such hurdles as zoning approval, obtaining construction cost bids, and finding a lender, it becomes less risky. Therefore, a person who invests after these hurdles are cleared would expect somewhat less potential reward. Nonetheless, the investor is buying into the project at a relatively low price; if it is successful, he will enjoy a developer's profit. Against this, he takes the risk that the project may stall along the way or that, once completed, it will lose money.

PROJECT COMPLETION

Another major milestone is reached when the project is completed and opens its doors for business. At this point, the finished cost of the building is known, and during the first 12 months of operations, the property owners learn what rents the market will pay, what level of occupancy will be achieved, and what actual operating expenses will be. As estimates are replaced with actual operating experience, the risk to the investor decreases. As a result, the investor entering at this stage receives a smaller dollar return on his investment, but is more certain of his return than if he had invested earlier.

FIRST DECADE

A building is new only once, and after its first year it begins to face competition from newer buildings. However, if an inflationary economy forces up the construction cost of newer buildings, existing buildings will be able to charge more rent. Furthermore, newer buildings may be forced to use less desirable sites. During the first 10 years, occupancy rates are stable, operating expenses are well established, tax benefits are good, and the building is relatively free of major repairs or replacements.

SECOND DECADE

As a building passes its tenth birthday, the costs and risks it presents to a prospective investor change. Before buying, he must ask whether the neighborhood is expected to remain desirable to tenants and whether the building's location will increase enough in value to offset wear and tear and obsolescence. A careful inspection must be made of the structure to determine whether poor construction quality will soon result in costly repairs. Also, the investor must be prepared for normal replacements and expenses such as new appliances, water heaters, and a fresh coat of paint. As a result, an investor buying a 10-year-old building will seek a larger return than the buyer of a younger building.

THIRD AND FOURTH DECADES

Larger returns are particularly important as a building reaches its twentieth year and major expense items such as a new roof, replacement of plumbing fixtures, repair of parking areas, and remodeling become necessary. As a building approaches and passes its thirtieth year, investors must consider carefully the remaining economic life of the property and whether rents permit a return on investment as well as a return of investment. Also, maintenance costs climb as a building becomes older, and decisions will be necessary regarding whether major restoration and remodeling should be undertaken. If it is, the cost must be recovered during the balance of the building's life. The alternative is to add little or no money to the building, a decision the surrounding neighborhood may already be forcing upon the property owner. Older properties may offer attractive tax benefits and may be a strong magnet to real estate investors who hope to find properties that can be fixed up for a profit. However, care must be taken not to overpay for this privilege.

BUILDING RECYCLING

More buildings are torn down than fall down, and this phase in a building's life also represents an investment opportunity. However, as with the first stage in the development cycle, raw land, the risks are high. In effect, when the decision is made to purchase a structure with the intention of demolishing it, the investor is counting on the value of the land being worth more in another use. That use may be a government-sponsored renewal program, or the investor may be accumulating adjoining properties with the ultimate intention of creating plottage value by demolishing the structures and joining the lots. Because the risks of capital loss in this phase are high, the potential returns should be too.

"Glitamad"

The acronym **GLITAMAD**, developed by Maury Selding and Richard Swesnik, is a helpful way to remember the various phases in the life cycle of improved real estate investments. (See Figure 27.1.)

investment strategy
A plan that balances returns available with risks that must be taken in order to enhance the investor's overall welfare.

Developing a Personal Investment Strategy

The objective in developing a personal investment strategy is to balance the returns available with the risks that must be taken so that the overall welfare of the investor is enhanced. To accomplish this, it is very helpful to look at lifetime income and consumption patterns.

FIGURE 27.1   "GLITAMAD"

G	=	Ground (the raw land stage)	Increasing risk, Increasing returns
L	=	Loan (long-term loan commitment)	
I	=	Interim (short-term loan and construction)	
T	=	Tenancy (building filled with tenants)	Least risk, Least returns
A	=	Absorption (second through tenth year)	
M	=	Maturity (eleventh through thirtieth year)	
A	=	Aging (more than 30 years)	
D	=	Demise (demolition, reuse of the land)	Increasing risk, Increasing returns

As the risk that an investor will suffer a loss increases, the expected returns must increase.

Adapted from Maury Selding and Richard H. Swesnik, *Real Estate Investment Strategy*, © 1970, John Wiley & Sons, Inc., New York.

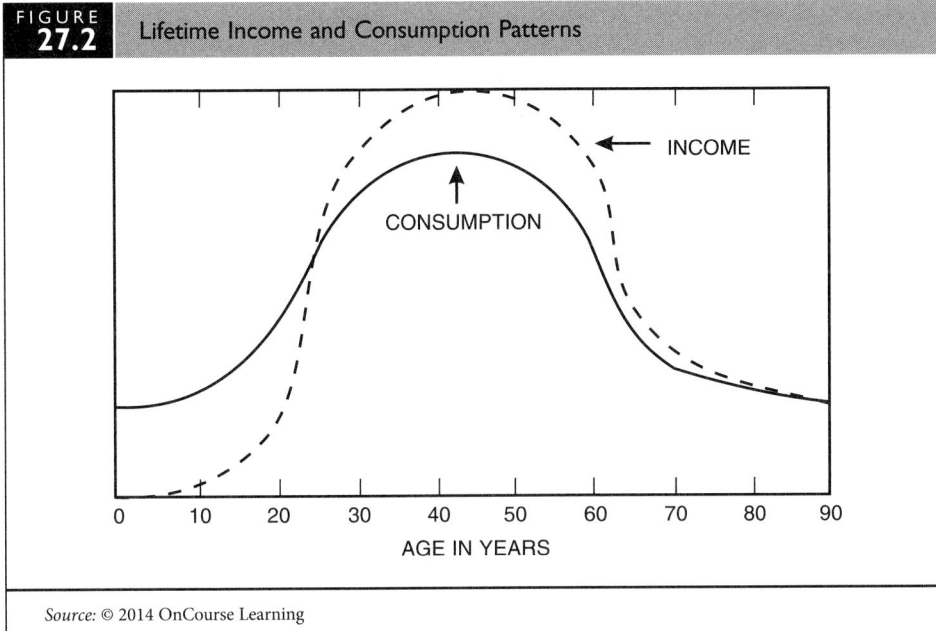

| FIGURE 27.2 | Lifetime Income and Consumption Patterns |

Source: © 2014 OnCourse Learning

In Figure 27.2 the broken line represents the income that a person can typically expect to receive at various ages during his or her life. It includes income from wages, pensions, and investments and is the same income curve that was discussed in Chapter 26. The solid line represents a person's lifetime consumption pattern. Taken together, the two lines show that during the first 20 to 25 years, consumption exceeds income. Then the situation reverses itself and income outpaces consumption. If one is planning an investment program, these are the years to carry it out.

RISK TAKING

Figure 27.2 shows that an investment opportunity offering a high risk of loss is better suited for a person under the age of 45. Then, even if the investment does turn sour, the investor still has a substantial amount of working life remaining to recover financially. An investor between 45 and 55 years of age should be somewhat more cautious in terms of risk taking, since there is less time to make a financial recovery if the need arises. Above the age of 55, high-risk investments are even less appropriate for the same reason. Therefore, as a person reaches 60 and 65, there should be a program of moving toward relatively risk-free investments, even though the returns will be smaller. Upon retirement, the investor can live off the investments he or she made when younger.

DEBT REPAYMENT

Mortgage debt commitments that require a portion of the investor's personal income should also be considered in light of one's position on the lifetime income and consumption curves. This is done to ascertain whether there will be sufficient income in the future to meet the loan payments. Not to consider the future may force a premature sale, perhaps in the midst of a very sluggish market at a distressed price. For the investor who has passed his income peak, financing with less debt and more equity means a higher probability that the properties will generate enough income to meet monthly loan payments. Also, with fewer dollars going to debt repayment, more can be kept by the investor for living expenses. By comparison, a relatively young investor may be handicapped by the lack of starting capital; however, he has the advantages of time and increasing income on his side.

The same points made here in connection with investments can also be applied to one's home. If a homeowner can purchase a home with a mortgage and then pay down the mortgage during those years in life when income substantially exceeds consumption, the home can be carried debt-free into retirement to provide a place to live without mortgage payments. The home then becomes an investment in every sense of the word.

Valuing an Investment

Chapter 18, "Real Estate Appraisal," discussed value from the standpoint of an appraiser or listing agent who uses current marketplace facts to estimate the value of a property. An investor's valuation problem is somewhat different. An investor knows the seller's asking price, can find information relating to the current income and expenses of a property, and can project future income based on these. Additionally, an investor will have information on how the property can be financed and will have some figure in mind as to how much appreciation to expect. From these, the investor calculates the anticipated return on investment. If this return is more appealing than alternative investments, the property is purchased. If not, no sale results. Figure 27.3 illustrates the different viewpoints of the appraiser and the investor.

You should note, however, that "return" has many different measurements and many different definitions. "A 7% return" can be calculated as a return on cash invested, a return on down payment, a return on down payment including closing costs, and to more sophisticated investors, a before-tax or after-tax return on their investment. An investor needs to know how to ask the right questions and how to evaluate the response to those questions.

Limited Partnerships

As discussed earlier in this chapter, large investment properties have a number of economic advantages over small ones. Yet the vast majority of investors in the United States do not have the capital to buy a large project single-handedly. Moreover, many persons who would like to own real estate do not do so because they wish to avoid the work and responsibilities of property management. As a result, the United States has witnessed the widespread use of limited partnerships for real estate investment. This popular form of investment offers investors the following advantages:

- Management of the property and financial affairs of the partnership by the general partner.

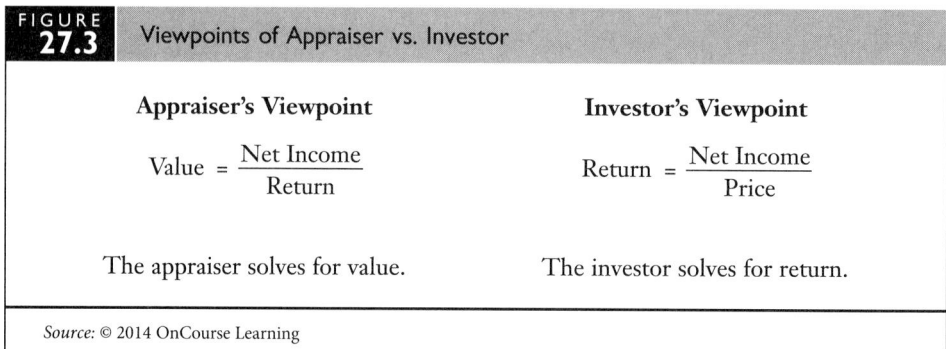

FIGURE 27.3   Viewpoints of Appraiser vs. Investor

Appraiser's Viewpoint	**Investor's Viewpoint**
$\text{Value} = \dfrac{\text{Net Income}}{\text{Return}}$	$\text{Return} = \dfrac{\text{Net Income}}{\text{Price}}$
The appraiser solves for value.	The investor solves for return.

Source: © 2014 OnCourse Learning

- Financial liability limited to the amount invested.
- The opportunity for a small investor to own a part of large projects and to diversify.

The organizers of a limited partnership are responsible for selecting properties, putting them into a financial package, and making it available to investors. As a rule, the organizers are the general partners and the investors are the limited partners. For their efforts in organizing the partnership, the general partners receive a cash fee from the limited partners and/or a promotional interest in the partnership.

PROPERTY PURCHASE METHODS

Property is purchased by one of two methods. The organizers can either buy properties first and then seek limited partners, or they can find limited partners first and then buy properties. The first approach is a **specific property offering**.

The second is a **blind pool**. The advantage of the specific property offering is that the prospective limited partner knows in advance precisely what properties will be owned. However, this approach requires the organizers either to find a seller who is willing to wait for a partnership to be formed or to buy the property in their own names using their own capital. If they use their own capital, the organizers risk the chance of financial loss if limited partners cannot be found.

The advantage of the blind pool is that the organizers do not buy until money has been raised from the limited partners. This requires less capital from the organizers and avoids the problem of holding property but not being able to find sufficient investors. Also, the organizers can negotiate better prices from sellers when they have cash in hand. However, if the organizers are poor judges of property, the investors may wind up owning property that they would not otherwise have purchased.

PROPERTY MANAGEMENT

Once property is purchased, the general partners are responsible for managing the property themselves or selecting a management firm to do the job. In addition, the general partners must maintain the accounting books and at least once a year remit to each investor his portion of the cash flow, an accounting of the partnership's performance for the year, and profit or loss data for income tax purposes. With regard to selling partnership property, the partnership agreement usually gives the limited partners the right to vote on when to sell, to whom to sell, and for how much. In practice, the general partners decide when to put the matter up to a vote, and the limited partners usually follow their advice.

FINANCIAL LIABILITY

The word *limited* in limited partnership refers to the limited financial liability of the limited partner. In a properly drawn agreement, limited partners cannot lose more than they have invested. By comparison, the general partners are legally liable for all the debts of the partnership, up to the full extent of their entire personal worth. Being a limited partner does not eliminate the possibility of being asked at a later date for more investment money if the properties in the partnership are not financially successful. When this happens, each limited partner must decide between adding more money in hopes the partnership will soon make a financial turnaround, or refusing to do so and being eliminated from the partnership. By way of comparison, an individual investor who buys real estate in his own name takes the risks of both the limited and general partner.

INVESTMENT DIVERSIFICATION

Investing with others can provide diversification. For example, a limited partnership of 200 members each contributing $5,000 would raise $1 million. This could be used as a down payment on one property worth $4 million or on four different properties priced at $1 million each. If the $4 million property is purchased, the entire success or failure of the partnership rides on that one property. With four $1 million properties, the failure of one can be balanced by the success of the others. Even greater diversification can be achieved by purchasing properties in different rental price ranges, in different parts of the same city, and in different cities in the country. Regarding income tax benefits, a very important advantage of the limited partnership is that it allows the investor to be taxed as though he is the sole owner of the property, because the partnership itself is not subject to taxation. All income and loss items, including any tax shelter generated by the property, are proportioned to each investor directly.

SERVICE FEES

The prospective investor should carefully look at the price the organizers are charging for their services. Is it adequate, but not excessive? To expect good performance from capable people, they must be compensated adequately, but to overpay reduces the returns from the investment that properly belong to those who provide the capital. When is the compensation to be paid? If management fees are paid in advance, there is less incentive for the organizers to provide quality management for the limited partners after the partnership is formed. The preferred arrangement is to pay for management services as they are received and for the limited partners to reserve the right to vote for new management. Similarly, it is preferable to base a substantial portion of the fee for organizing the partnership on the success of the investment. By giving the organizers a percentage of the partnership's profits instead of a fixed fee, the organizers have a direct stake in the success of the partnership.

PITFALLS

Although the limited partnership form of real estate ownership offers investors many advantages, experience has shown that there are numerous pitfalls that can separate investors from their money. Most importantly, a limited partner should recognize that the success or failure of a limited partnership depends on the organizers. Do they have a good record in selecting, organizing, and managing real estate investments in the past? Are they respected in the community for prompt and honest dealings? Will local banks and building suppliers offer them credit? What is their rating with credit bureaus? Are they permanent residents of the community in which they operate? Do the county court records show pending lawsuits or other legal complaints against them?

With reference to the properties in the partnership, are the income projections reasonable, and have adequate allowances been made for vacancies, maintenance, and management? Over optimism, sloppy income and expense projections, and outright shading of the truth will ultimately be costly to the investor. Unless there is absolute confidence in the promoters, one should personally visit the properties in the partnership and verify the rent schedules, vacancy levels, operating expenses, and physical condition of the improvements. Consideration should also be given to the partnership's **downside risk** (that is, the risk of losing one's money).

The careful investor will consult with a lawyer to make certain that the partnership agreement does limit liability to the amount invested and that the tax benefits will be as advertised. He will also want to know what to expect if the partnership suffers financial setbacks. Are the partnership's properties to be sold at a loss or at a foreclosure sale,

downside risk

The possibility that an investor will lose his money in an investment.

or do the general partners stand ready to provide the needed money? Will the limited partners be asked to contribute? The prospective investor should also investigate to see if the properties are overpriced. Far too many partnerships organized to date have placed so much emphasis on tax shelter benefits that the entire matter of whether the investment was economically feasible has been overlooked. Even to a taxpayer in the 28% tax bracket, a dollar wasted before taxes is still 72¢ wasted after taxes.

Finally, to receive maximum benefits from investment, the investor must be prepared to stay with the partnership until the properties are refinanced or sold. The resale market for limited partnership interests is almost nonexistent, and when a buyer is found, the price is usually below the proportional worth of the investor's interest in the partnership. Moreover, the partnership agreement may place restrictions on limited partners who want to sell their interests.

MASTER LIMITED PARTNERSHIPS

One major problem with limited partnerships has been that they are illiquid. Once an investor invests, the commitment is to stay in until the partnership dissolves, and this can be 5, 10, or even 15 or more years later. Until then, the limited partner can convert to cash only by selling to someone else or sometimes back to the partnership. This is usually done at a substantial discount to the value of the property in the partnership, assuming a sale can even be arranged. Into this need has come the **master limited partnership (MLP)**. MLPs are limited partnerships that can be traded on a stock exchange nearly as easily as corporate stock. Thus, an investor can buy into a partnership after it has been formed and sell out of it before it is dissolved. Meanwhile, the investor receives the available tax advantages of a limited partnership. However, if the underlying partnership is not well run, has poorly operating properties, or is uneconomic, simply making the partnership easily traded is no magic. MLPs do offer liquidity, but you must still carefully analyze the partnership's ability to perform before investing in it.

REAL ESTATE INVESTMENT TRUSTS

Real estate investments trusts were discussed in Chapter 4, but as an investment opportunity, it provides a lot of alternatives. They typically offer investors higher returns as well as liquidity. **Equity REITs** invest and own properties and their primary income is from rents. **Mortgage REITs** deal with investment and property mortgages. These REITs loan money to owners of real estate or purchase existing mortgages or mortgage-backed securities. Their revenues are generated by the return of interest on the mortgage loans. **Hybrid REITs** combine both investment strategies and invest in both properties and mortgages. Many REITs now specialize in one area of real estate, shopping malls or large apartment complexes, investing in them as a liquid dividend paying means of participating in the real estate market.

Disclosure Laws

Because investors are vulnerable to unsound investments and exploitation at the hands of limited partnership organizers, state and federal disclosure laws have been passed to protect them if the investment qualifies as a "security." Administered by the Securities & Exchange Commission at the federal level and by securities boards at the state level, these laws require organizers and sales staff to disclose all pertinent facts surrounding the partnership offering. Prospective investors must be told how much money the organizers wish to raise, what portion will go for promotional expenses and organizers' fees, what properties have been (or will be) purchased, from whom they were bought, and for how much. Also, prospective investors must be provided with a copy of the partnership agreement and given property income and expense records for past years. They must be told how long the partnership expects to hold its properties until selling, the partnership's policy on cash flow distribution, the right of limited partners to a voice in management, the names of those responsible for managing the partnership properties, and how profits (or losses) will be split when the properties are sold.

THE PROSPECTUS

The amount of disclosure detail required by state and federal laws varies with the number of properties and the partners' relationship. For a handful of friends forming a partnership among themselves, there would be little in the way of formal disclosure requirements. However, as the number of investors increases and the partnership is offered to investors across state lines, disclosure requirements increase dramatically. It is not unusual for a disclosure statement, called a **prospectus**, to be 50 to 100 pages long.

prospectus
A disclosure statement that describes an investment opportunity.

BLUE-SKY LAWS

The philosophy of disclosure laws is to make information available to prospective investors and let them make their own decisions. Thus, an investor is free to invest in an unsound investment so long as the facts are explained to him in advance. An alternative point of view is that many investors do not read or understand disclosure statements; therefore, it is the duty of government to pass on the economic soundness of an investment before it can be offered to the public. The result has been the passage of **blue-sky laws** in several states. The first of these was passed by the Kansas legislature in 1911 to protect purchasers from buying into dubious investment schemes that sold them nothing more than a piece of the blue sky. Other states have passed such laws and applied them to limited partnerships and other securities offered within their borders.

GOVERNMENTAL REGULATION

Another element of risk that has recently come to the forefront is governmental involvement. We have always had building permit requirements and the potential for zoning and changes to zoning. It has often been said that zoning is not truly land planning, but politics. There is always a risk of potential land use that responds to the whim of the city's planning and zoning commission and permitting authorities. There's a more detailed discussion of zoning in Chapter 25. Other risks involve the Americans with Disabilities Act (see Chapter 22). If an investor makes an acquisition and then determines that the building does not comply with the Americans with Disabilities Act, it can result in a massive expense to retrofit the building to bring it under compliance with the statute. Similar federal and local legislation creates similar risks under the Clean Water Act (wetlands designations), the Endangered Species Act (to protect flora and fauna indigenous to areas of appropriate hydrological conditions), and under federal legislation that regulates the dumping of hazardous waste products or establishes obligations for cleanup of the sites (see Chapter 25).

Most of the environmental issues are dealt with through a purchaser's prudent practice of hiring environmentalists to perform Phase I Environmental Studies and other pertinent investigations before acquiring the property. In today's business climate, investigating all the potential governmental use restrictions and mandates before acquiring the property is considered to be due diligence.

Effort and Courage

As the opening paragraph of this chapter suggested, you can become rich by investing in real estate. It should be pointed out, however, that success won't drop in your lap; it takes effort and courage. Good properties and good opportunities are always available, but you will look at many opportunities to find one good investment. You will also need to know which ones you don't want, and why. That is the part that takes effort. All investors need to know what a good opportunity looks like, and this book is a step in that direction. After you finish this text, start reading articles and books on real estate investing and take courses on the subject as well. But most importantly, get out and start looking at properties right away if you have not already done so. Begin to get a sense in the field for what you are learning from your books and classes. Always ask questions as you go along and demand straight, reasonable answers. After you've viewed several dozen properties and talked to appraisers, lenders, brokers, property managers, and others, you will begin to get a feel for the market—what's for sale, what a property can earn, how much mortgage money costs, and so on. As you do this, you will see everything you've learned in this book come to life.

As you continue, you will recognize what a good investment property looks like. At this point, your next big step is to muster the courage to acquire it. All the real estate investment education you've received will not translate into money in your pocket until you make an offer—until you put your money, reputation, and good judgment on the line. In light of today's twitter, Facebook, infomercials, and the like, you must understand that that there is no "get rich quick" formula, so don't expect one. There are a lot of con-men and fast, glib talkers in the real estate investment business. If the deal doesn't make sense, or there is no exit strategy in the event of a downturn in the economy, then it is probably not a good investment. If you have a good, informed investment strategy and the courage to take the risks, the rewards are certainly attainable.

Vocabulary Review

Match terms a–n with statements 1–14.

a. Accelerated depreciation

b. Active investor

c. At-risk rules

d. Blind pool

e. Cash flow

f. Cash-on-cash

g. Downside risk

h. Equity build-up

i. GLITAMAD

j. Leverage

k. Negative cash flow

l. Prospectus

m. Straight-line depreciation

n. Tax shelter

_____ 1. Number of dollars remaining each year after collecting rents and paying operating expenses and mortgage payments.

_____ 2. Requires the investor to dip into her own pocket.

_____ 3. Income tax savings that an investment can produce for its owner.

_____ 4. Results from mortgage balance reduction and price appreciation.

_____ 5. An acronym that refers to the various phases of the life cycle of an improved property.

_____ 6. A method of calculating depreciation that takes equal amounts of depreciation each year.

_____ 7. Any method of depreciation that achieves a faster rate of depreciation than the straight-line method.

_____ 8. A limited partnership wherein properties are purchased after the limited partners have invested their money.

_____ 9. The possibility that an investor will lose his money in an investment.

_____10. A disclosure statement that describes an investment opportunity.

_____11. The cash flow of a property divided by the amount of cash necessary to purchase it.

_____12. As defined by tax law, the amount an investor risks in an investment.

_____13. The impact that borrowed funds have on investment return.

_____14. An investor who takes an active role in property management, as defined by income tax law.

Questions and Problems

1. What monetary benefits do investors expect to receive by investing in real estate?

2. What is a tax-sheltered real estate investment?

3. What is the major risk that a speculator in vacant land takes?

4. What advantages and disadvantages do duplexes and triplexes offer to a prospective investor?

5. Is an investor better off investing in a project before it is built or after it is completed and occupied? Explain.

6. As a building grows older, why should an investor demand a higher return per dollar invested?

7. How does a person's age affect investment goals and the amount of investment risk that may be taken?

8. An investor is looking at a property that produces a net operating income of $22,000 per year. He expects the property to appreciate 50% in 10 years and plans to finance it with a 25-year, 11% interest, 75% loan-to-value loan. If the property is priced to produce an 18% return on the investor's equity, how much is the seller asking? (Use Table 18.5 in Chapter 18.)

9. Another investor looks at the property described in Problem 8, but feels it will appreciate only 25% in value. How much would she offer to pay the seller?

10. What advantages does the limited partnership form of ownership offer to real estate investors?

11. What can a prospective investor do to increase his chances of joining a limited partnership that will be successful?

Additional Readings

"Evaluating Master-planned Communities: What Every Investor Should Know" by David Chapman (*Real Estate Law Journal*, Winter 2000, pp. 223–226).

New Directions in Real Estate Finance and Investment: Maastricht-Cambridge Symposium 2000: A Special Issue of the Journal of Real Estate Finance and Economics (Kluwer Academic, 2002).

"Optimal Land Development Decisions" by Dennis R. Capozza (*Journal of Urban Economics*, January 2002, p. 123[20]).

Real Estate Investment, 7th ed. by John P. Wiedemer, Joseph E. Goeters and J. Edward Graham (OnCourse Learning, 2011).

"The Results Are In: New Forecasting Measure Just Stokes Debate (Method of Forecasting the Financial Performance of Real Estate Investment Trusts)" by Ray A. Smith (*The Wall Street Journal*, March 20, 2002, p. B10).

Construction Illustrations and Terminology

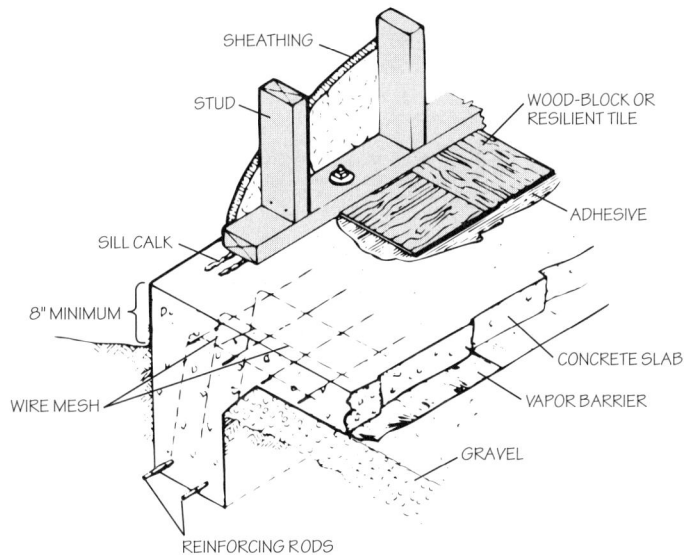

SHEATHING

STUD

WOOD-BLOCK OR
RESILIENT TILE

ADHESIVE

SILL CALK

8" MINIMUM

CONCRETE SLAB

WIRE MESH

VAPOR BARRIER

GRAVEL

REINFORCING RODS

| FIGURE A.2 | Basement Details |

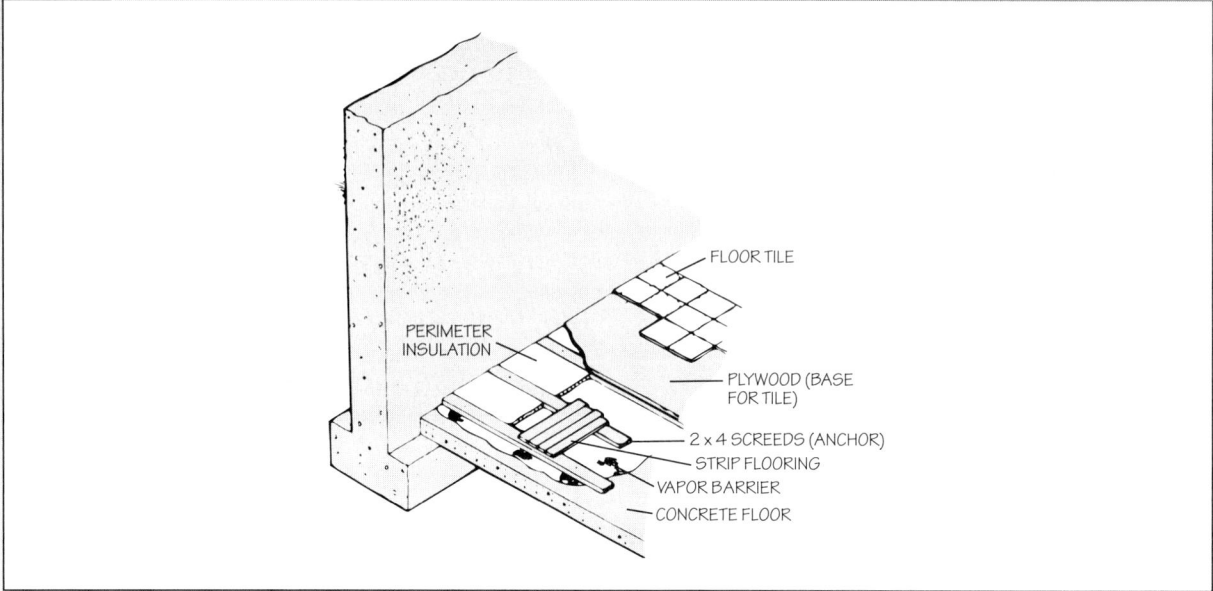

FLOOR TILE

PERIMETER
INSULATION

PLYWOOD (BASE
FOR TILE)

2 x 4 SCREEDS (ANCHOR)

STRIP FLOORING

VAPOR BARRIER

CONCRETE FLOOR

| FIGURE A.3 | Floor Framing |

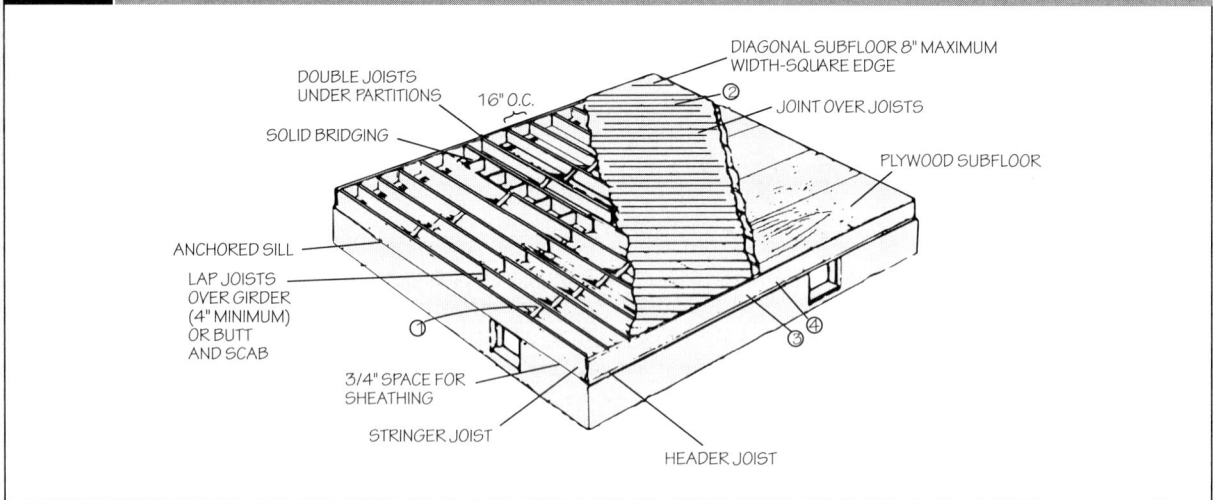

DIAGONAL SUBFLOOR 8" MAXIMUM
WIDTH-SQUARE EDGE

DOUBLE JOISTS
UNDER PARTITIONS

16" O.C.

JOINT OVER JOISTS

SOLID BRIDGING

PLYWOOD SUBFLOOR

ANCHORED SILL

LAP JOISTS
OVER GIRDER
(4" MINIMUM)
OR BUTT
AND SCAB

3/4" SPACE FOR
SHEATHING

STRINGER JOIST

HEADER JOIST

FIGURE A.4 Wall Framing Used with Platform Construction

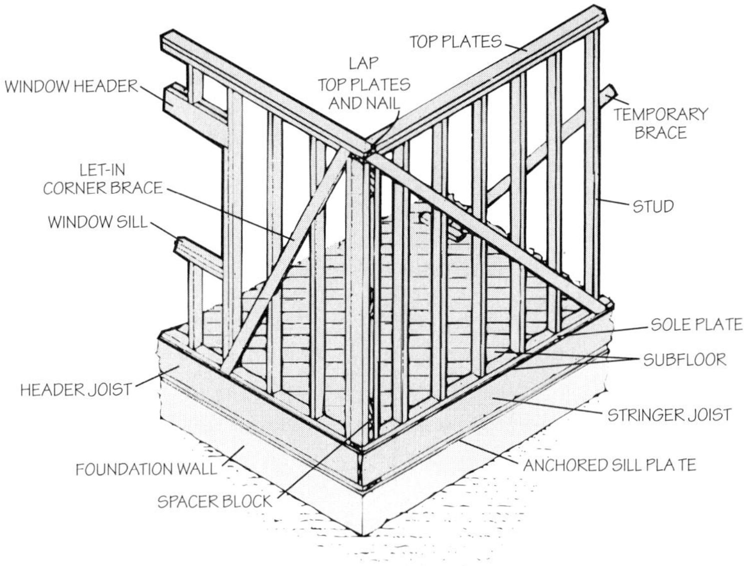
TOP PLATES
LAP
TOP PLATES
AND NAIL
WINDOW HEADER
TEMPORARY
BRACE
LET-IN
CORNER BRACE
STUD
WINDOW SILL
SOLE PLATE
SUBFLOOR
HEADER JOIST
STRINGER JOIST
FOUNDATION WALL
ANCHORED SILL PLATE
SPACER BLOCK

FIGURE A.5 Headers for Windows and Door Openings

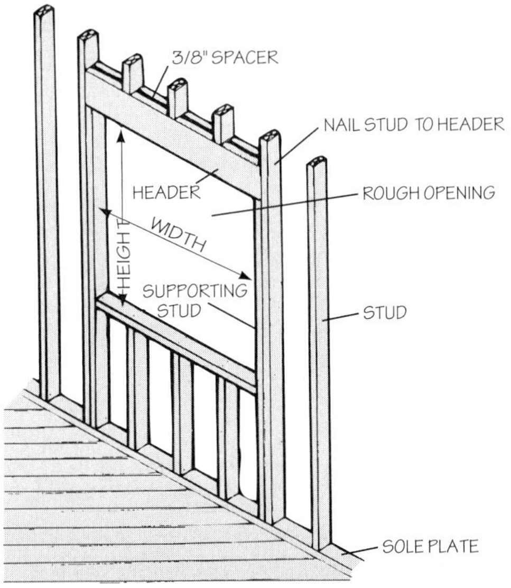
3/8" SPACER
NAIL STUD TO HEADER
HEADER
ROUGH OPENING
WIDTH
HEIGHT
SUPPORTING
STUD
STUD
SOLE PLATE

FIGURE A.6 — Vertical Application of Plywood or Structural Insulating Board Sheathing

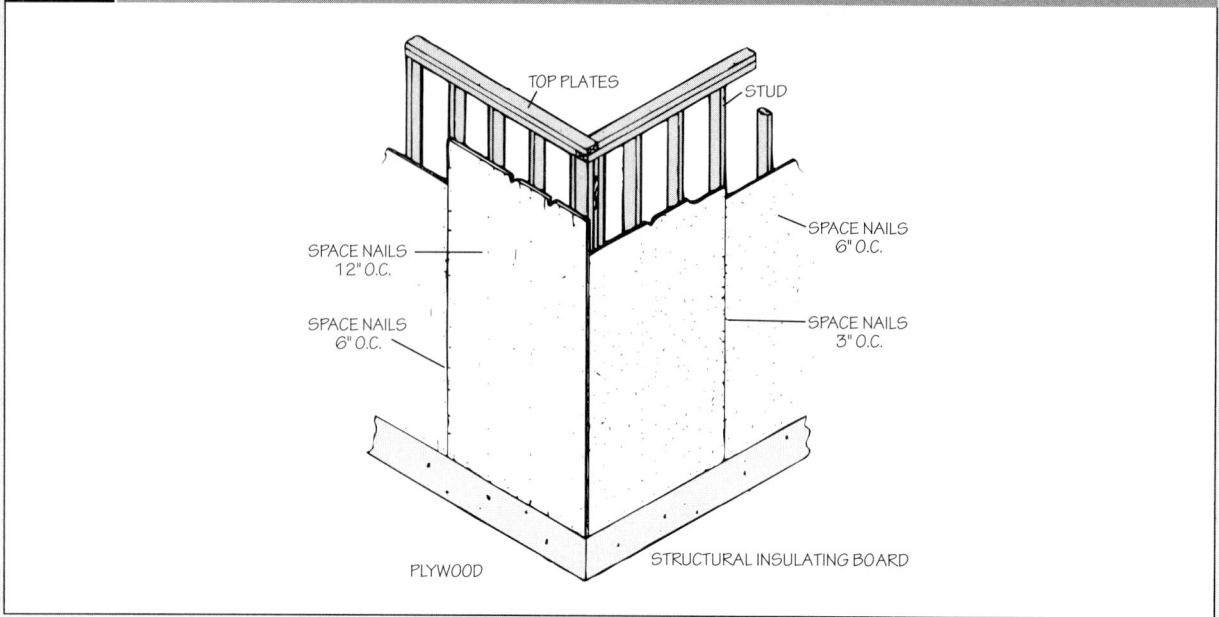

TOP PLATES

STUD

SPACE NAILS
6" O.C.

SPACE NAILS
12" O.C.

SPACE NAILS
3" O.C.

SPACE NAILS
6" O.C.

PLYWOOD

STRUCTURAL INSULATING BOARD

FIGURE A.7 — Exterior Siding

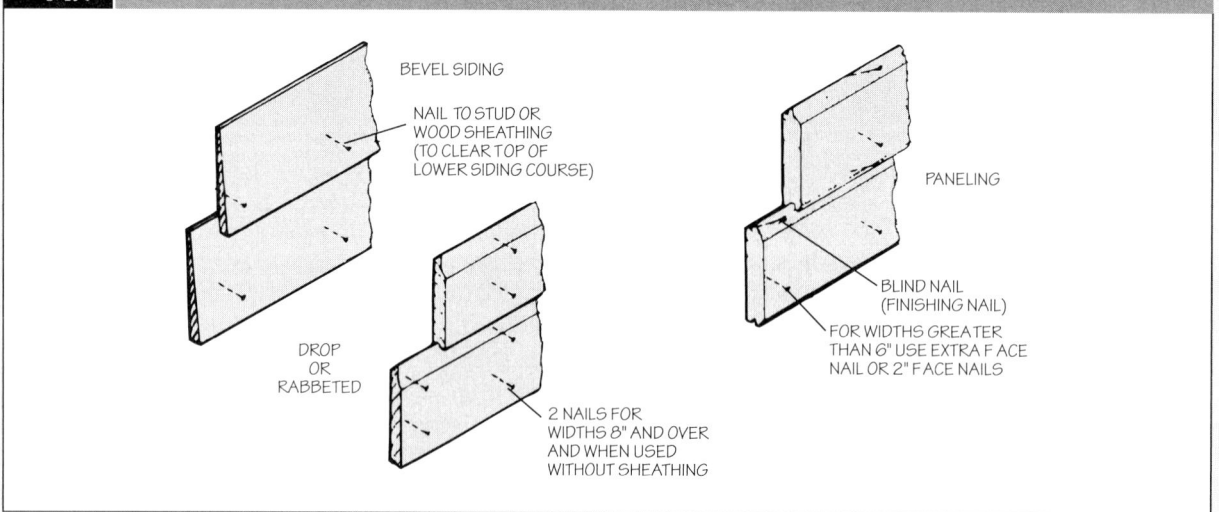

BEVEL SIDING

NAIL TO STUD OR
WOOD SHEATHING
(TO CLEAR TOP OF
LOWER SIDING COURSE)

PANELING

DROP
OR
RABBETED

BLIND NAIL
(FINISHING NAIL)

FOR WIDTHS GREATER
THAN 6" USE EXTRA FACE
NAIL OR 2" FACE NAILS

2 NAILS FOR
WIDTHS 8" AND OVER
AND WHEN USED
WITHOUT SHEATHING

FIGURE A.8   Vertical Board Siding

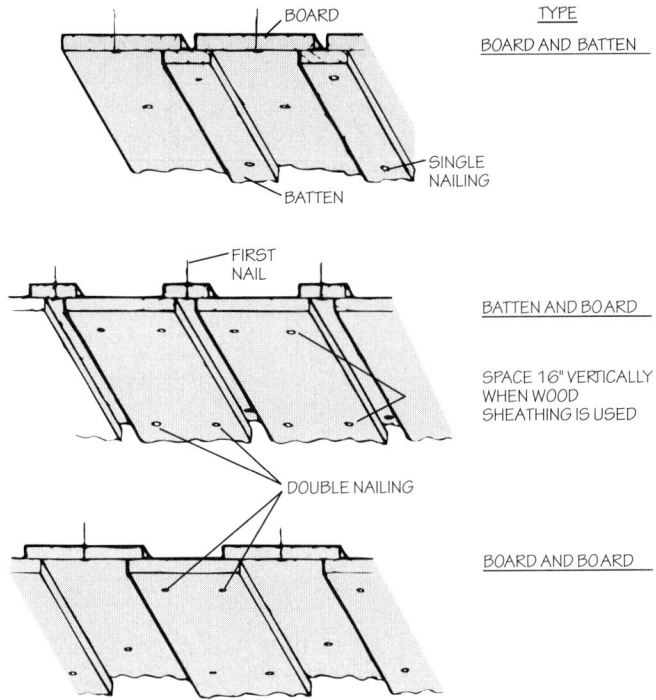

TYPE

BOARD AND BATTEN

BOARD

SINGLE NAILING

BATTEN

FIRST NAIL

BATTEN AND BOARD

SPACE 16" VERTICALLY WHEN WOOD SHEATHING IS USED

DOUBLE NAILING

BOARD AND BOARD

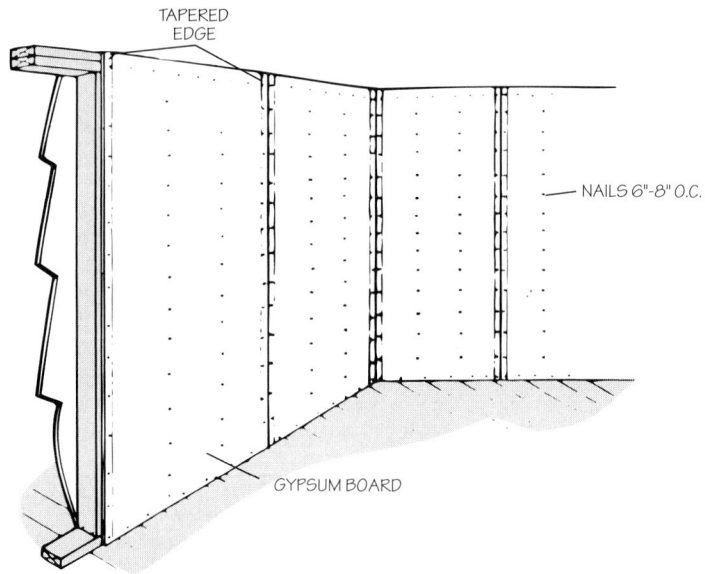

A

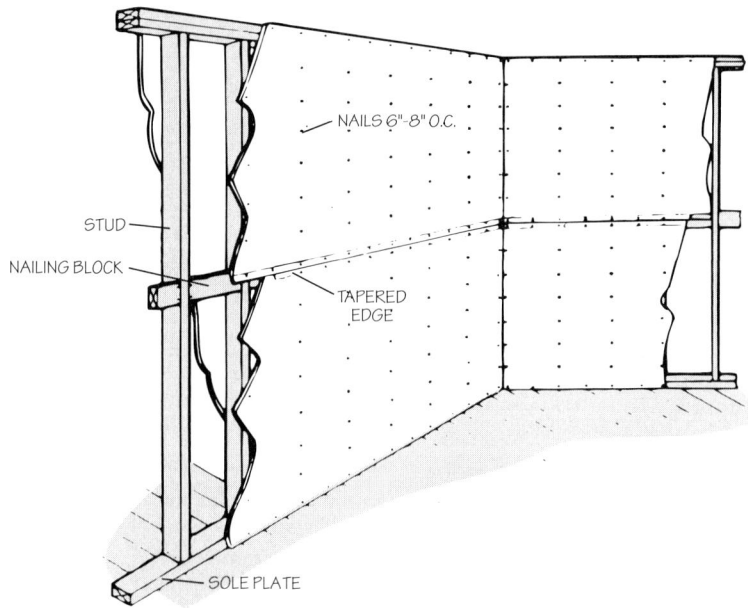

B

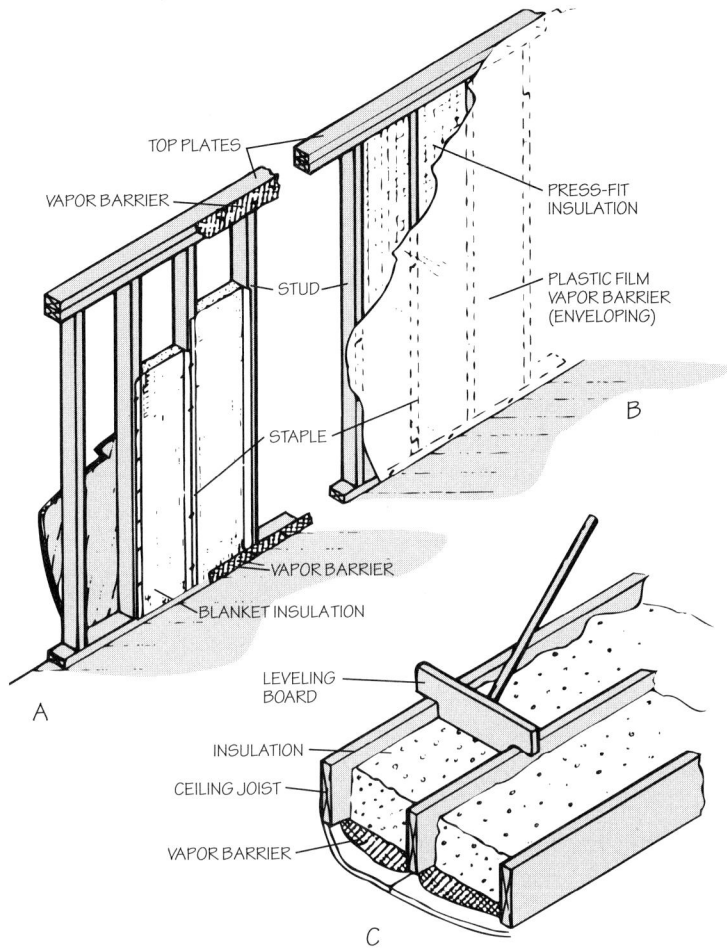

FIGURE A.10   Application of Insulation

TOP PLATES

VAPOR BARRIER

PRESS-FIT INSULATION

PLASTIC FILM VAPOR BARRIER (ENVELOPING)

STUD

B

STAPLE

VAPOR BARRIER

BLANKET INSULATION

A

LEVELING BOARD

INSULATION

CEILING JOIST

VAPOR BARRIER

C

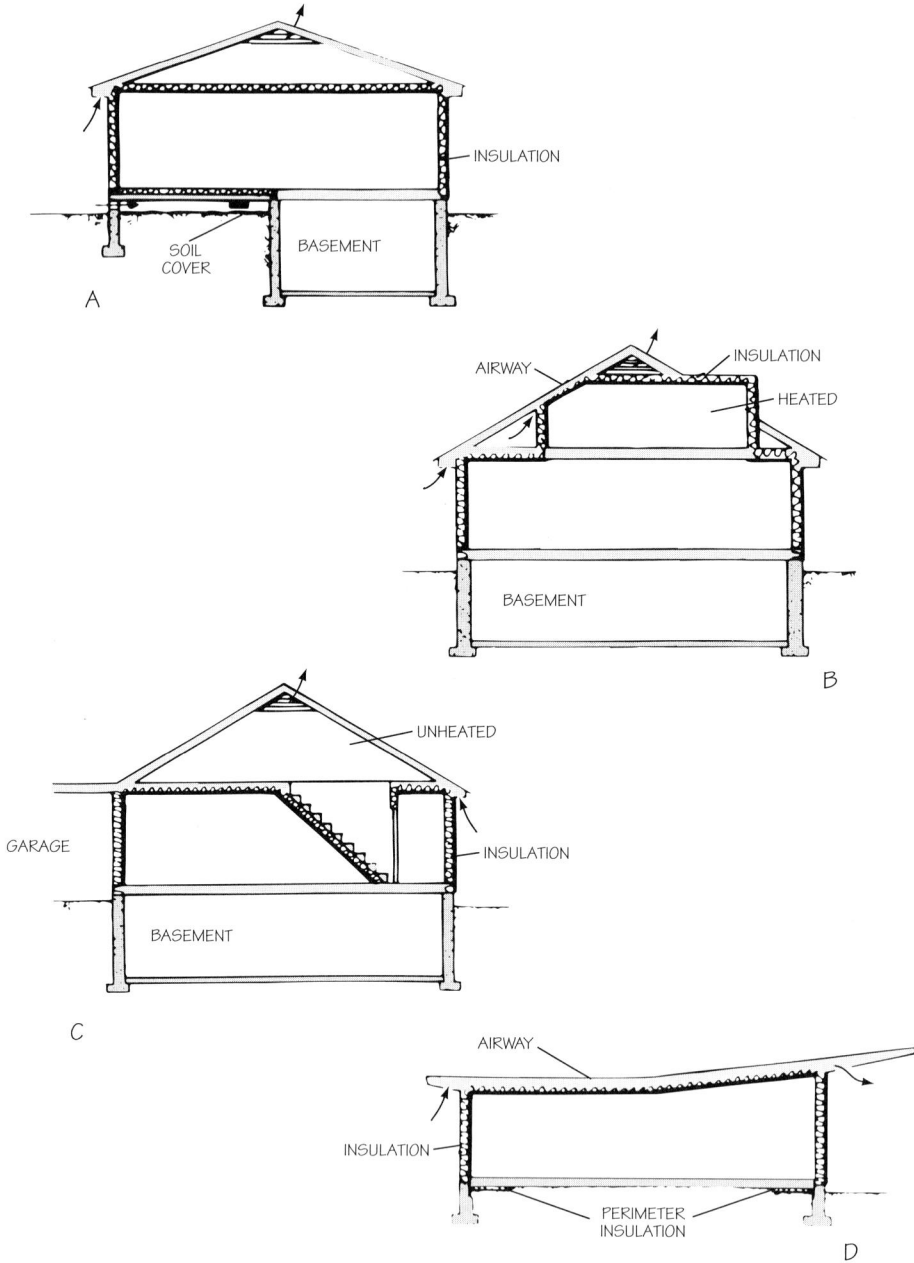

FIGURE A.11 Placement of Insulation

FIGURE A.12   Masonry Fireplace

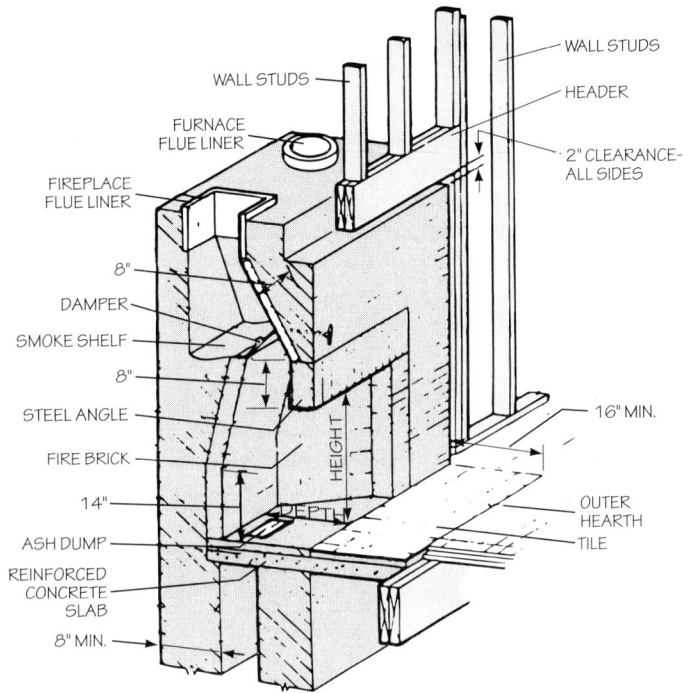

WALL STUDS
FURNACE FLUE LINER
FIREPLACE FLUE LINER
8"
DAMPER
SMOKE SHELF
8"
STEEL ANGLE
FIRE BRICK
14"
ASH DUMP
REINFORCED CONCRETE SLAB
8" MIN.
HEIGHT
DEPTH
WALL STUDS
HEADER
2" CLEARANCE-ALL SIDES
16" MIN.
OUTER HEARTH
TILE

FIGURE A.13   Stairway Details

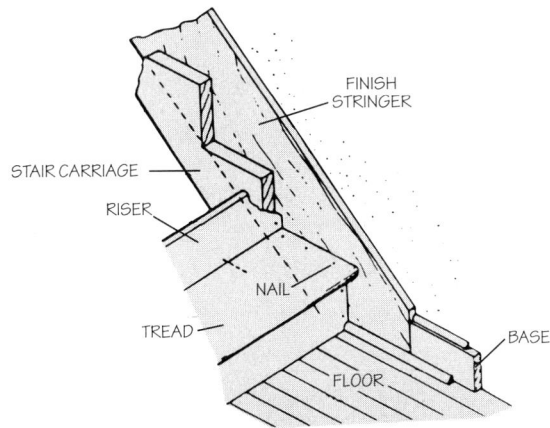

FINISH STRINGER
STAIR CARRIAGE
RISER
NAIL
TREAD
FLOOR
BASE

FIGURE A.14 Door Details

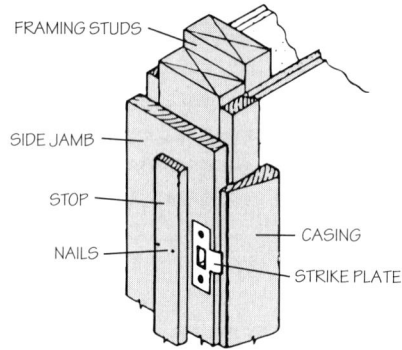

FRAMING STUDS
SIDE JAMB
STOP
NAILS
CASING
STRIKE PLATE

FIGURE A.15 Sound Insulation

WALL DETAIL	DESCRIPTION	STC RATING
16" 2 x 4	1/2" GYPSUM WALLBOARD	32
	5/8" GYPSUM WALLBOARD	37
2 x 4	5/8" GYPSUM WALLBOARD (DOUBLE LAYER EACH SIDE)	45
2 x 4 BETWEEN OR "WOVEN"	1/2" GYPSUM WALLBOARD 1-1/2" FIBROUS INSULATION	49
16" 2 x 4	RESILIENT CLIPS TO 3/8" GYPSUM BACKER BOARD 1/2" FIBERBOARD (LAMINATED) (EACH SIDE)	52

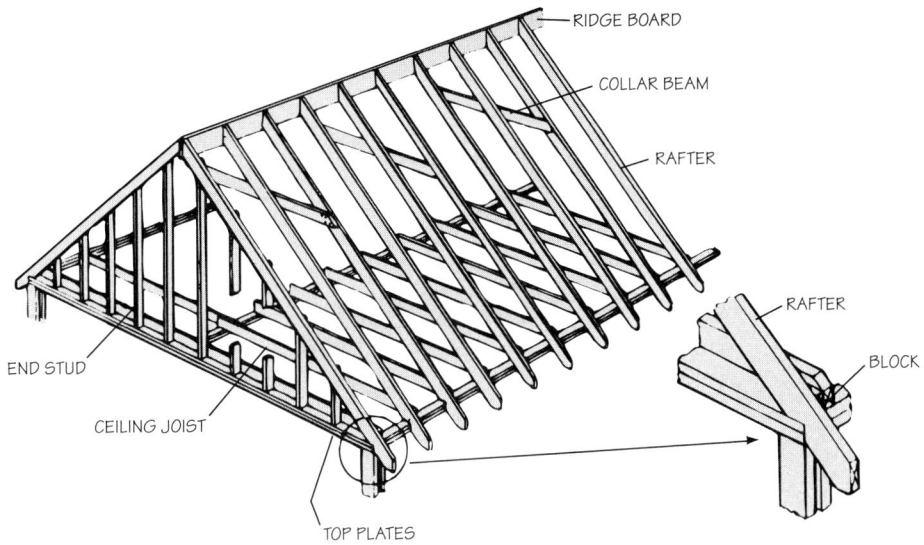

FIGURE A.16 Ceiling and Roof Framing

RIDGE BOARD
COLLAR BEAM
RAFTER
RAFTER
BLOCK
END STUD
CEILING JOIST
TOP PLATES

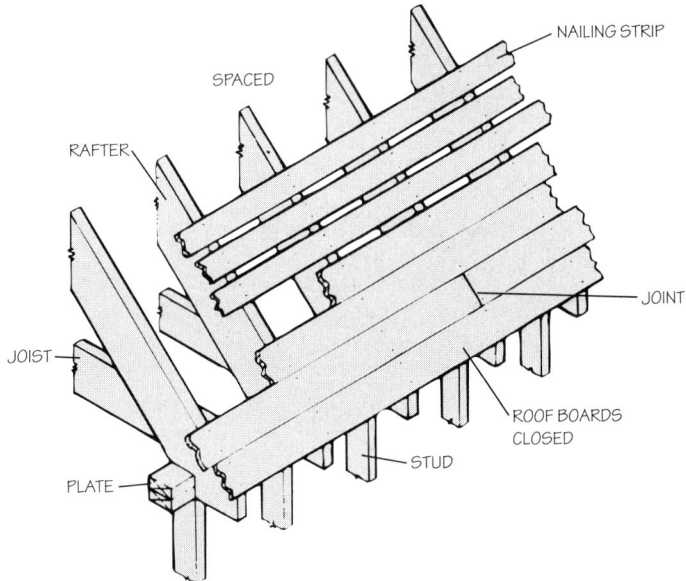

FIGURE A.17 Installation of Board Roof Sheathing, Showing Both Closed and Spaced Types

NAILING STRIP
SPACED
RAFTER
JOINT
JOIST
ROOF BOARDS CLOSED
STUD
PLATE

FIGURE A.18 Built-Up Roof

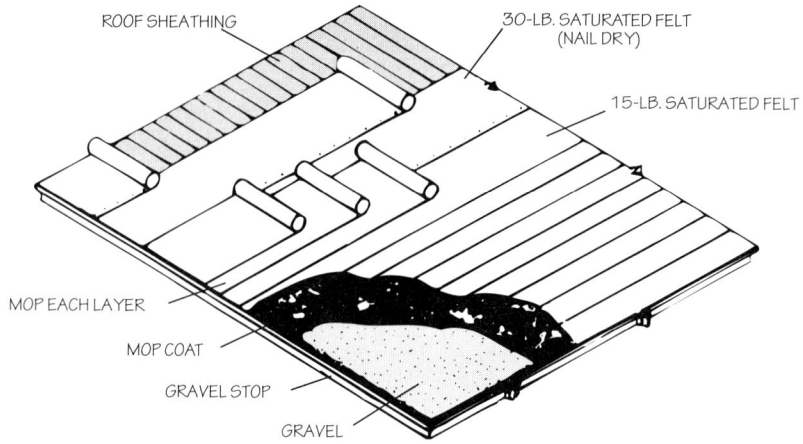

ROOF SHEATHING

30-LB. SATURATED FELT
(NAIL DRY)

15-LB. SATURATED FELT

MOP EACH LAYER

MOP COAT

GRAVEL STOP

GRAVEL

FIGURE A.19 Application of Asphalt Shingles

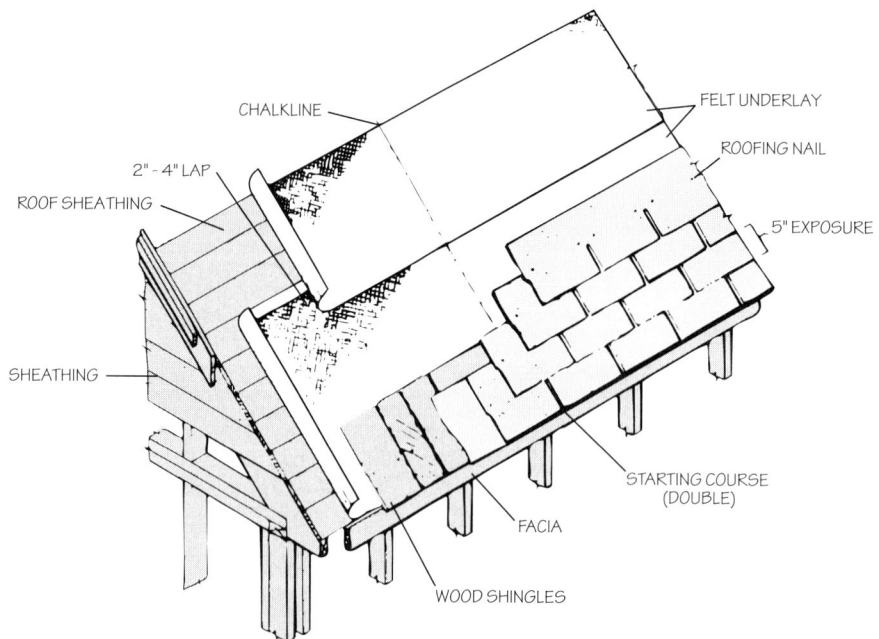

CHALKLINE

FELT UNDERLAY

ROOFING NAIL

2" - 4" LAP

ROOF SHEATHING

5" EXPOSURE

SHEATHING

STARTING COURSE
(DOUBLE)

FACIA

WOOD SHINGLES

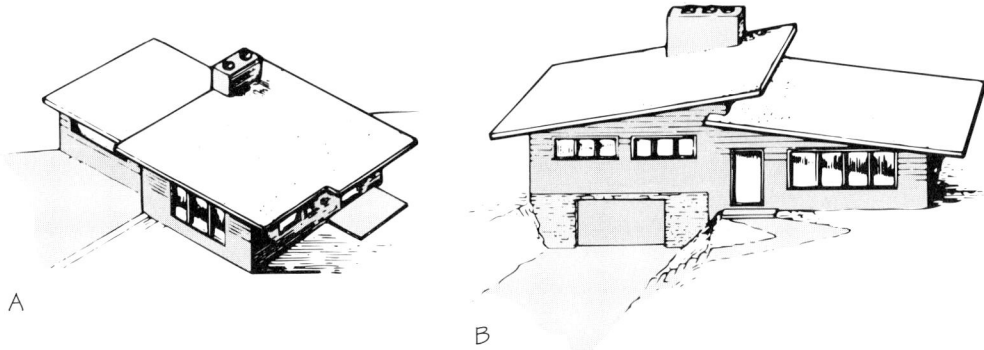

FIGURE A.20 Roofs Using Single Roof Construction

A

B

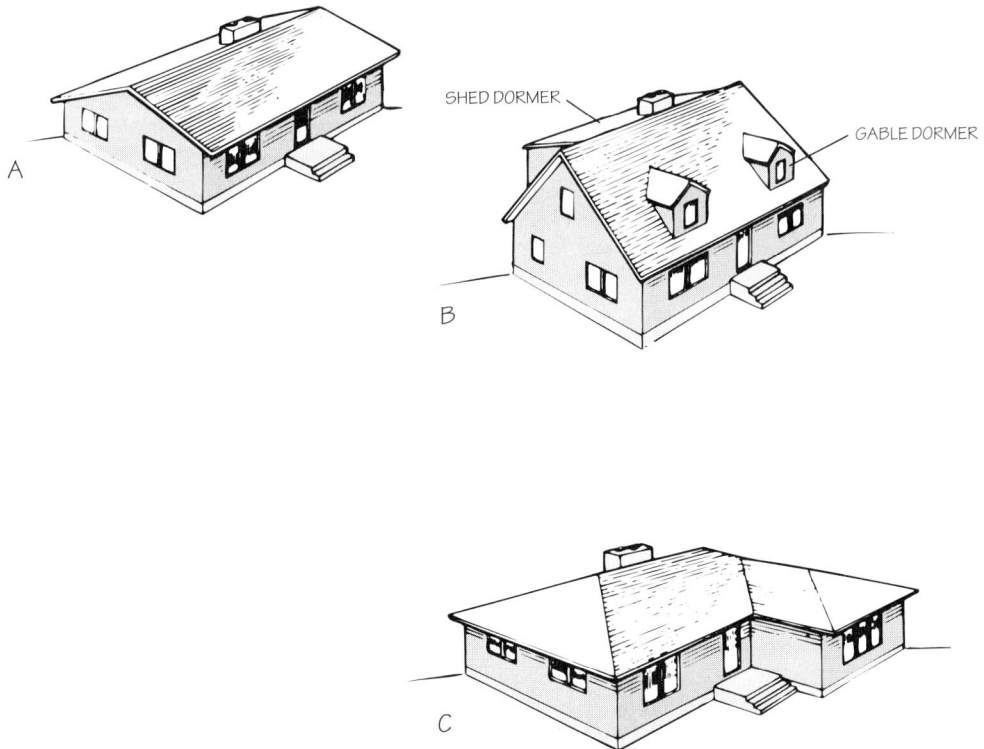

FIGURE A.21 Types of Pitched Roofs
A: Gable; B: Gable with Dormers; C: Hip

A

SHED DORMER

GABLE DORMER

B

C

APPENDIX **B**

Real Estate Math Review

Percent

Percent (%) means part per hundred. For example, 25% means 25 parts per hundred; 10% means 10 parts per hundred. Percentages are related to common and decimal fractions as follows:

5%	=	0.05	=	1/20
10%	=	0.10	=	1/10
25%	=	0.25	=	1/4
75%	=	0.75	=	3/4
99%	=	0.99	=	99/100

A percentage greater than 100% is greater than 1. For example:

110%	=	1.10	=	1-1/10
150%	=	1.50	=	1-1/2
200%	=	2.00	=	2
1,000%	=	10.0	=	10

To change a decimal fraction to a percentage, move the decimal point two places to the right and add the % sign. For example:

0.001	=	0.1%
0.01	=	1%
0.06	=	6%
0.35	=	35%
0.356	=	35.6%
1.15	=	115%

A percentage can be changed to a common fraction by writing it as hundredths and then reducing it to its lowest common denominator. For example:

20%	=	20/100	=	1/5
90%	=	90/100	=	9/10
225%	=	225/100	=	2-1/4

Adding and Subtracting Decimals

To add decimals, place the decimal points directly over one another. Then place the decimal point for the solution in the same column and add. For example:

$$
\begin{array}{r}
6.25 \\
1.10 \\
\underline{10.277} \\
17.627
\end{array}
$$

If you are working with percentages, there is no need to convert to decimal fractions; just line up the decimal points and add. For example:

$$
\begin{array}{r}
68.8\% \\
6.0\% \\
\underline{25.2\%} \\
100.0\%
\end{array}
$$

When subtracting, the same methods apply. For example:

$$
\begin{array}{rr}
1.00 & 100\% \\
\underline{-0.80} & \underline{-80\%} \\
0.20 & 20\%
\end{array}
$$

When there is a mixture of decimal fractions and percentages, first convert them all either to percentage or decimal fractions.

Multiplying and Dividing Decimals

Multiplying decimals is like multiplying whole numbers except that the decimal point must be correctly placed. This is done by counting the total number of places to the right of the decimal point in the numbers to be multiplied. Then round off the same number of places in the answer. The following examples illustrate this:

$$
\begin{array}{cccccc}
0.6 & 0.2 & 1.01 & 0.1 & 0.11 & 0.03 \\
\underline{\times\ 0.3} & \underline{\times\ 0.2} & \underline{\times\ \ 2} & \underline{\times\ \ 6} & \underline{\times\ \ 6} & \underline{\times\ 0.02} \\
0.18 & 0.04 & 2.02 & 0.6 & 0.66 & 0.0006
\end{array}
$$

When dividing, the process starts with properly placing the decimal point. A normal division then follows. When a decimal number is divided by a whole number, place the decimal point in the answer directly above the decimal point in the problem. For example:

$$
\begin{array}{cc}
1.03 & 0.033 \\
3\overline{)3.09} & 3\overline{)0.099}
\end{array}
$$

To divide by a decimal number, you must first change the divisor to a whole number. Then you must make a corresponding change in the dividend. This is done by simply moving both decimal points the same number of places to the right. For example, to divide 0.06 by 0.02, move the decimal point of each to the right two places.

$$
\begin{array}{lcl}
0.02\overline{)0.06} & \text{becomes} & 2\overline{)6} \\
0.5\overline{)3} & \text{becomes} & 5\overline{)30} \\
0.05\overline{)30} & \text{becomes} & 5\overline{)3,000}
\end{array}
$$

When multiplying or dividing with percentages, first convert them to decimal form. Thus, 6% of 200 is:

$$200$$
$$\underline{\times\ 0.06}$$
$$12.00$$

Problems Involving Rates

A simple way to solve rate problems is to think of

the word *is* as = (an equal sign).

the word *of* as × (a multiplication sign).

the word *per* as ÷ (a division sign).

For example:

"7% of $50,000 is $3,500"

translates:

"7% of $50,000 = $3,500"

Another formula for solving rate problems is: The Whole times the percentage Rate equals a Part, or, W × R = P.

What do you do if they give you the whole and the part and ask for the rate? Just use the simple circle formula:

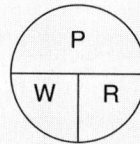

Insert the values that you are given in the circle. The position of the numbers will tell you whether to multiply or divide.

For example, you start with $4,000 (the Whole) and you end up with some percent of that number, like $360 (the Part). When you put $4,000 in for W, and $360 for P, you will notice that $360 is on top of $4,000, which means $360 is being divided by $4,000.

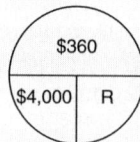

$$\frac{360}{4,000} = 0.09 \text{, so } 360 \text{ is } 9\% \text{ of } 4,000.$$

PROBLEM I

Beverly Broker sells a house for $60,000. Her share of the commission is to be 2.5% of the sales price. How much does she earn?

Her commission is 2.5% of $60,000

Her commission = 0.025 × $60,000

Her commission = $1,500

PROBLEM 2

Sam Salesman works in an office that will pay him 70% of the commission on each home he lists and sells. With a 6% commission, how much would he earn on a $50,000 sale?

His commission is 70% of 6% of $50,000

His commission = $0.70 \times 0.06 \times \$50,000$

His commission = $2,100

PROBLEM 3

Newt Newcomer wants to earn $21,000 during his first 12 months as a salesman. He feels he can average 3% on each sale. How much property must he sell?

3% of sales is $21,000

$0.0.3 \times sales = \$21,000$

sales = $\$21,000 \div 0.03$

sales = $700,000

Note: An equation will remain an equation as long as you make the same change on both sides of the equal sign. If you add the same number to both sides, it is still an equation. If you subtract the same amount from each side, it is still equal. If you multiply both sides by the same thing, it remains equal. If you divide both sides by the same thing, it remains equal.

PROBLEM 4

An apartment building nets the owners $12,000 per year on their investment of $100,000. What percent return are they receiving on their investment?

$12,000 is _____% of $100,000

$12,000 = _____% $\times$ $100,000

$$\frac{\$12,000}{\$100,000} = 12\%$$

PROBLEM 5

Smith wants to sell his property and have $47,000 after paying a 6% brokerage commission on the sales price. What price must Smith get?

$47,000 is 94% of selling price

$47,000 = $0.94 \times$ selling price

$$\frac{\$47,000}{0.94} = \text{selling price}$$

$50,000 = selling price

PROBLEM 6

Miller sold his home for $75,000, paid off an existing loan of $35,000, and paid closing costs of $500. The brokerage commission was 6% of the sales price. How much money did Miller receive?

amount = $75,000
less $4,500 (0.06 × $75,000)
less $35,000 (pay off)
less $500 (closing costs) yields
yields $35,000 to receive

PROBLEM 7

The assessed valuation of the Kelly home is $100,000. If the property tax rate is $6.00 per $100 of assessed valuation, what is the tax?

$$\text{The tax is } \frac{\$6.00}{\$100} \text{ of } \$100,000$$

$$\text{tax} = \frac{\$6.00}{\$100} \times \$100,000$$

$$\text{tax} = \$6,000$$

PROBLEM 8

Property in Clark County is assessed at 75% of market value. What should the assessed valuation of a $40,000 property be?

Assessed valuation is 75% of market value
Assessed valuation = 0.75 × $40,000
Assessed valuation = $30,000

PROBLEM 9

An insurance company charges $0.24 per $100 of coverage for a one-year fire insurance policy. How much would a $40,000 policy cost?

$$\text{Cost is } \frac{\$0.24}{\$100} \text{ of } \$40,000$$

$$\text{Cost} = \frac{\$0.24}{\$100} \times \$40,000$$

$$\text{Cost} = \$96$$

Area Measurement

The measurement of the distance from one point to another is called *linear* measurement. Usually this is along a straight line, but it can also be along a curved line. Distance is measured in inches, feet, yards, and miles. Less commonly used are chains (66 feet) and rods (16 and a half feet). Surface areas are measured in square feet, square yards, acres (43,560 square feet), and square miles. In the metric system, the standard unit of linear measurement is the meter (39.37 inches). Land area is measured in square meters and hectares. A hectare contains 10,000 square meters or 2.471 acres.

To determine the area of a square or rectangle, multiply its length times its width. The formula is:

Area = Length × Width
A   = L × W

PROBLEM 10

A parcel of land measures 660 feet by 330 feet. How many square feet is this?

Area = 660 feet × 330 feet

Area = 217,800 squre feet

How many acres does this parcel contain?

Acres = 217,800 ÷ 43,560

Acres = 5

If a buyer offers $42,500 for this parcel, how much is the offering per acre?

$42,500 ÷ 5 = $8,500

To determine the area of a right triangle, multiply one-half of the base times the height:

A = ½ × B × H   A = ½ × B × H
A = ½ × 25 × 50   A = ½ × 40 × 20
A = 625 square feet   A = 400 square feet

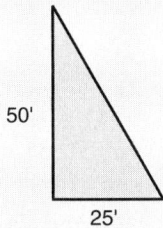

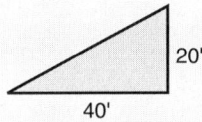

To determine the area of a circle, multiply 3.14 (p) times the square of the radius:

$A = \pi \times r^2$

$A = 3.14 \times 40^2$

$A = 3.14 \times 1{,}600$

$A = 5{,}024$ sq ft

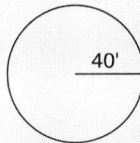

Note: Where the diameter of a circle is given, divide by two to get the radius.

To determine the area of composite figures, separate them into their various components. Thus:

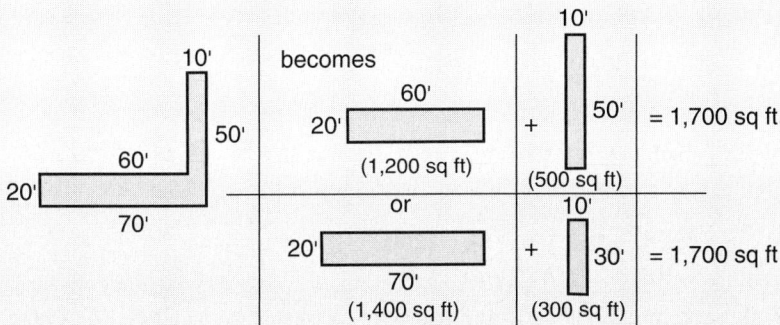

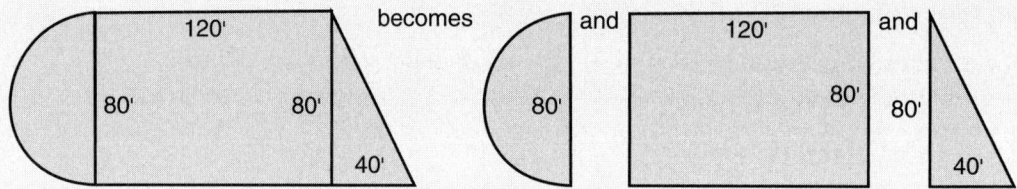

Volume Measurement

Volume is measured in cubic units. The formula is:

$$\text{Volume} = \text{Length} \times \text{Width} \times \text{Height}$$
$$V \qquad = L \times W \times H$$

For example, what is the volume of a room that is 10 ft by 15 ft with an 8 ft ceiling?

$$V = 10^{'} \times 15^{'} \times 8^{'}$$
$$V = 1{,}200 \text{ cu ft}$$

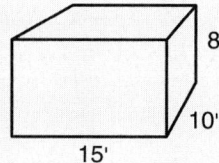

Caution: When solving area and volume problems, **make certain that all the units are the same**. For example, if a parcel of land is one-half mile long and 200 feet wide, convert one measurement so that both are expressed in the same unit; thus, the answer will be either in square feet or in square miles. There is no such area measurement as a mile-foot. If a building is 100 yards long by 100 feet wide by $16^{'}6^{''}$ high, convert to 300 ft by 100 ft by 16.5 before multiplying.

Ratios and Proportions

If the label on a 5-gallon can of paint says it will cover 2,000 square feet, how many gallons are necessary to cover 3,600 sq ft?

A problem like this can be solved two ways:

One way is to find out what area 1 gallon will cover. In this case 2,000 sq ft ÷ 5 gallons = 400 sq ft per gallon. Then divide 400 sq ft/gal into 3,600 sq ft and the result is 9 gallons.

The other method is to set up a proportion:

$$\frac{5 \text{ gal}}{2{,}000 \text{ sq ft}} = \frac{Y \text{ gal}}{3{,}600 \text{ sq ft}}$$

This reads, "5 gallons is to 2,000 sq ft as 'Y' gallons is to 3,600 sq ft." To solve for "Y," multiply both sides of the proportion by 3,600 sq ft. Thus:

$$\frac{5 \text{ gal} \times 3{,}600 \text{ sq ft}}{2{,}000 \text{ sq ft}} = Y \text{ gal}$$

Divide 2,000 sq ft into 3,600 sq ft and multiply the result by 5 gallons to get the answer.

Front-Foot Calculations

When land is sold on a front-foot basis, the price is the number of feet fronting on the street times the price per front foot.

Price = Front footage × Rate per front foot

Thus, a 50 ft × 150 ft lot priced at $1,000 per front foot would sell for $50,000. Note that in giving the dimensions of a lot, the first dimension given is the street frontage. The second dimension is the depth of the lot.

APPENDIX C

Interest and Present Value Tables

Compound Sum of Single Dollar

Year	2%	4%	6%	8%	10%	12%	14%	16%	18%	20%	22%	25%	30%	40%
1	1.020	1.040	1.060	1.080	1.100	1.120	1.140	1.160	1.180	1.200	1.220	1.250	1.300	1.400
2	1.040	1.082	1.124	1.166	1.210	1.254	1.300	1.346	1.392	1.440	1.488	1.563	1.690	1.960
3	1.061	1.125	1.191	1.260	1.331	1.405	1.482	1.561	1.643	1.728	1.816	1.953	2.197	2.744
4	1.082	1.170	1.262	1.360	1.464	1.574	1.689	1.811	1.939	2.074	2.215	2.441	2.856	3.842
5	1.104	1.217	1.338	1.469	1.611	1.762	1.925	2.100	2.288	2.488	2.703	3.052	3.713	5.378
6	1.126	1.265	1.419	1.587	1.772	1.974	2.195	2.436	2.700	2.986	3.297	3.851	4.827	7.530
7	1.149	1.316	1.504	1.714	1.949	2.211	2.502	2.826	3.185	3.583	4.023	4.768	6.275	10.541
8	1.172	1.369	1.594	1.851	2.144	2.476	2.853	3.278	3.759	4.300	4.908	5.960	8.157	14.758
9	1.195	1.423	1.689	1.999	2.358	2.773	3.252	3.803	4.435	5.160	5.987	7.451	10.604	20.661
10	1.219	1.480	1.791	2.159	2.594	3.106	3.707	4.411	5.234	6.192	7.305	9.313	13.786	28.925
11	1.243	1.539	1.898	2.332	2.853	3.479	4.226	5.117	6.176	7.430	8.912	11.642	17.921	40.496
12	1.268	1.601	2.012	2.518	3.138	3.896	4.818	5.936	7.288	8.916	10.872	14.552	23.298	56.694
13	1.294	1.665	2.133	2.720	3.452	4.363	5.492	6.886	8.599	10.699	13.264	18.190	30.287	79.371
14	1.319	1.732	2.261	2.937	3.797	4.887	6.261	7.988	10.147	12.839	16.182	22.737	39.373	
15	1.346	1.801	2.397	3.172	4.177	5.474	7.138	9.266	11.974	15.407	19.742	28.422	51.185	
16	1.373	1.873	2.540	3.426	4.595	6.130	8.137	10.748	14.129	18.488	24.085	35.527	66.541	
17	1.400	1.948	2.693	3.700	5.054	6.866	9.276	12.468	16.672	22.186	29.384	44.409	86.503	
18	1.428	2.026	2.854	3.996	5.560	7.690	10.575	14.462	19.673	26.623	35.849	55.511		
19	1.457	2.107	3.026	4.316	6.116	8.613	12.056	16.776	23.214	31.948	43.735	69.389		
20	1.486	2.191	3.207	4.661	6.727	9.646	13.743	19.461	27.393	38.337	53.357	86.736		
21	1.516	2.279	3.400	5.034	7.400	10.804	15.667	22.574	32.323	46.005	65.096			
22	1.546	2.370	3.603	5.437	8.140	12.100	17.861	26.186	38.142	55.206	79.417			
23	1.577	2.465	3.820	5.871	8.954	13.552	20.361	30.376	45.007	66.247	96.888			
24	1.608	2.563	4.049	6.341	9.850	15.179	23.212	35.236	53.108	79.497				
25	1.641	2.666	4.292	6.848	10.835	17.000	26.462	40.874	62.668	95.396				

Compound Sum of Annuity of $1

Year	2%	4%	6%	8%	10%	12%	14%	16%	18%	20%	22%	25%	30%	40%
1	1.020	1.000	1.000	1.000	1.000	1.000	1.000	1.000	1.000	1.000	1.000	1.000	1.000	1.000
2	2.020	2.040	2.060	2.080	2.100	2.120	2.140	2.160	2.180	2.200	2.220	2.250	2.300	2.400
3	3.060	3.122	3.184	3.246	3.310	3.374	3.440	3.506	3.572	3.640	3.708	3.813	3.990	4.360
4	4.121	4.246	4.375	4.506	4.641	4.779	4.921	5.066	5.215	5.368	5.524	5.766	6.187	7.104
5	5.204	5.416	5.637	5.867	6.105	6.353	6.610	6.877	7.154	7.442	7.740	8.207	9.043	10.846
6	6.308	6.633	6.975	7.336	7.716	8.115	8.535	8.977	9.442	9.930	10.442	11.259	12.756	16.324
7	7.434	7.898	8.394	8.923	9.487	10.089	10.730	11.414	12.141	12.916	13.740	15.073	17.583	23.853
8	8.583	9.214	9.897	10.637	11.436	12.300	13.233	14.240	15.327	16.499	17.762	19.842	23.858	34.395
9	9.754	10.583	11.491	12.488	13.579	14.776	16.085	17.518	19.086	20.799	22.670	25.802	32.015	49.153
10	10.949	12.006	13.181	14.487	15.937	17.549	19.337	21.321	23.521	25.959	28.657	33.253	42.619	69.814
11	12.168	13.486	14.971	16.645	18.531	20.655	23.044	25.733	28.755	32.150	35.962	42.566	56.405	98.739
12	13.412	15.026	16.870	18.977	21.384	24.133	27.271	30.850	34.931	39.580	44.873	54.208	74.326	
13	14.680	16.627	18.882	21.495	24.522	28.029	32.088	36.786	42.218	48.496	55.745	68.760	97.624	
14	15.973	18.292	21.015	24.215	27.975	32.393	37.581	43.672	50.818	59.196	69.009	86.949		
15	17.293	20.024	23.276	27.152	31.772	37.280	43.842	51.659	60.965	72.035	85.191			
16	18.639	21.824	25.672	30.324	35.949	42.753	50.980	60.925	72.938	87.442				
17	20.011	23.697	28.212	33.750	40.544	48.884	59.117	71.673	87.067					
18	21.412	25.645	30.905	37.450	45.599	55.750	68.393	84.141						
19	22.840	27.671	33.759	41.446	51.158	63.440	78.968	98.603						
20	24.297	29.778	36.785	45.762	57.274	72.052	91.024							
21	25.783	31.969	39.992	50.423	64.002	81.699								
22	27.298	34.248	43.392	55.457	71.402	92.502								
23	28.844	36.618	46.995	60.893	79.542									
24	30.421	39.083	50.815	66.765	88.496									
25	32.029	41.646	54.864	73.106	98.346									

Present Value of Single Dollar

Year	2%	4%	6%	8%	10%	12%	14%	16%	18%	20%	22%	24%	25%	30%	40%
1	0.980	0.962	0.943	0.926	0.909	0.893	0.877	0.862	0.847	0.833	0.820	0.806	0.800	0.769	0.714
2	0.961	0.925	0.890	0.857	0.826	0.797	0.769	0.743	0.718	0.694	0.672	0.650	0.640	0.592	0.510
3	0.942	0.889	0.840	0.794	0.751	0.712	0.675	0.641	0.609	0.579	0.551	0.524	0.512	0.455	0.364
4	0.924	0.855	0.792	0.735	0.683	0.636	0.592	0.552	0.516	0.482	0.451	0.423	0.410	0.350	0.260
5	0.906	0.822	0.747	0.681	0.621	0.567	0.519	0.476	0.437	0.402	0.370	0.341	0.328	0.269	0.186
6	0.888	0.790	0.705	0.630	0.564	0.507	0.456	0.410	0.370	0.335	0.303	0.275	0.262	0.207	0.133
7	0.871	0.760	0.665	0.583	0.513	0.452	0.400	0.354	0.314	0.279	0.249	0.222	0.210	0.159	0.095
8	0.853	0.731	0.627	0.540	0.467	0.404	0.351	0.305	0.266	0.233	0.204	0.179	0.168	0.123	0.068
9	0.837	0.703	0.592	0.500	0.424	0.361	0.308	0.263	0.225	0.194	0.167	0.144	0.134	0.094	0.048
10	0.820	0.676	0.558	0.463	0.386	0.322	0.270	0.227	0.191	0.162	0.137	0.116	0.107	0.073	0.035
11	0.804	0.650	0.527	0.429	0.350	0.287	0.237	0.195	0.162	0.135	0.112	0.094	0.086	0.056	0.025
12	0.788	0.625	0.497	0.397	0.319	0.257	0.208	0.168	0.137	0.112	0.092	0.076	0.069	0.043	0.018
13	0.773	0.601	0.469	0.368	0.290	0.229	0.182	0.145	0.116	0.093	0.075	0.061	0.055	0.033	0.013
14	0.758	0.577	0.442	0.340	0.263	0.205	0.160	0.125	0.099	0.078	0.062	0.049	0.044	0.025	0.009
15	0.743	0.555	0.417	0.315	0.239	0.183	0.140	0.108	0.084	0.065	0.051	0.040	0.035	0.020	0.006
16	0.728	0.534	0.394	0.292	0.218	0.163	0.123	0.093	0.071	0.054	0.042	0.032	0.028	0.015	0.005
17	0.714	0.513	0.371	0.270	0.198	0.146	0.108	0.080	0.060	0.045	0.034	0.026	0.023	0.012	0.003
18	0.700	0.494	0.350	0.250	0.180	0.130	0.095	0.069	0.051	0.038	0.028	0.021	0.018	0.009	0.002
19	0.686	0.475	0.331	0.232	0.164	0.116	0.083	0.060	0.043	0.031	0.023	0.017	0.014	0.007	0.002
20	0.673	0.456	0.312	0.215	0.149	0.104	0.073	0.051	0.037	0.026	0.019	0.014	0.012	0.005	0.001
25	0.610	0.375	0.233	0.146	0.092	0.059	0.038	0.024	0.016	0.010	0.007	0.005	0.004	0.001	
30	0.552	0.308	0.174	0.099	0.057	0.033	0.020	0.012	0.007	0.004	0.003	0.002	0.001		
40	0.453	0.208	0.097	0.046	0.022	0.011	0.005	0.003	0.001	0.001					
50	0.372	0.141	0.054	0.021	0.009	0.003	0.001	0.001							

Present Value of Annuity of $1

Year	2%	4%	6%	8%	10%	12%	14%	16%	18%	20%	22%	24%	25%	30%	40%
1	0.980	0.962	0.943	0.926	0.909	0.893	0.877	0.862	0.847	0.833	0.820	0.806	0.800	0.769	0.714
2	1.942	1.886	1.833	1.783	1.736	1.690	1.647	1.605	1.566	1.528	1.492	1.457	1.440	1.361	1.224
3	2.884	2.775	2.673	2.577	2.487	2.402	2.322	2.246	2.174	2.106	2.042	1.981	1.952	1.816	1.589
4	3.808	3.630	3.645	3.312	3.170	3.037	2.914	2.798	2.690	2.589	2.494	2.404	2.362	2.166	1.849
5	4.713	4.452	4.212	3.993	3.791	3.605	3.433	3.274	3.127	2.991	2.864	2.745	2.689	2.436	2.035
6	5.601	5.242	4.917	4.623	4.355	4.111	3.889	3.685	3.498	3.326	3.167	3.020	2.951	2.643	2.168
7	6.472	6.002	5.582	5.206	4.868	4.564	4.288	4.039	3.812	3.605	3.416	3.242	3.161	2.802	2.263
8	7.325	6.733	6.210	5.747	5.335	4.968	4.639	4.344	4.078	3.837	3.619	3.421	3.329	2.925	2.331
9	8.162	7.435	6.802	6.247	5.759	5.328	4.946	4.607	4.303	4.031	3.786	3.566	3.463	3.019	2.379
10	8.983	8.111	7.360	6.710	6.145	5.650	5.216	4.833	4.494	4.192	3.923	3.682	3.571	3.092	2.414
11	9.787	8.760	7.887	7.139	6.495	5.937	5.453	5.029	4.656	4.327	4.035	3.776	3.656	3.147	2.438
12	10.58	9.385	8.384	7.536	6.814	6.194	5.660	5.197	4.793	4.439	4.127	3.851	3.725	3.190	2.456
13	11.34	9.986	8.853	7.904	7.103	6.424	5.842	5.342	4.910	4.533	4.203	3.912	3.780	3.223	2.468
14	12.11	10.56	9.295	8.244	7.367	6.628	6.002	5.468	5.008	4.611	4.265	3.962	3.824	3.249	2.477
15	12.85	11.12	9.712	8.559	7.606	6.811	6.142	5.575	5.092	4.675	4.315	4.001	3.859	3.268	2.484
16	13.58	11.65	10.11	8.851	7.824	6.974	6.265	5.669	5.162	4.730	4.357	4.033	3.887	3.283	2.489
17	14.29	12.17	10.48	9.122	8.022	7.120	6.373	5.749	5.222	4.775	4.391	4.059	3.910	3.295	2.492
18	14.99	12.66	10.83	9.372	8.201	7.250	6.467	5.818	5.273	4.812	4.419	4.080	3.928	3.304	2.494
19	15.68	13.13	11.16	9.604	8.365	7.366	6.550	5.877	5.316	4.844	4.442	4.097	3.942	3.311	2.496
20	16.35	13.59	11.47	9.818	8.514	7.469	6.623	5.929	5.353	4.870	4.460	4.110	3.954	3.316	2.497
25	19.52	15.62	12.78	10.68	9.077	7.843	6.873	6.097	5.467	4.948	4.514	4.147	3.985	3.329	2.499
30	22.40	17.29	13.77	11.26	9.427	8.055	7.003	6.177	5.517	4.979	4.534	4.160	3.995	3.332	2.500
40	27.36	19.79	15.05	11.93	9.779	8.244	7.105	6.234	5.548	4.997	4.544	4.166	3.999	3.333	2.500
50	31.42	21.48	15.76	12.23	9.915	8.304	7.133	6.246	5.554	4.999	4.545	4.167	4.000	3.333	2.500

APPENDIX D

Measurement Conversion Table

Mile =
 5,280 feet
 1,760 yards
 320 rods
 80 chains
 =1.609 kilometers

Square mile =
 640 acres
 =2.590 sq kilometers

Acre =
 43,560 sq ft
 4,840 sq yds
 160 sq rods
 =4,047 sq meters

Rod =
 16.5 feet
 =5.029 meters

Chain =
 66 feet
 4 rods
 100 links
 =20.117 meters

Meter =
 39.37 inches
 =1,000 millimeters
 3.281 feet
 =100 centimeters
 1.094 yards
 =10 decimeters

Kilometer =
 0.6214 miles
 3,281 feet
 1,094 yards
 =1,000 meters

Square meter =
 10,765 sq ft
 1.196 sq yds
 =10,000 sq centimeters

Hectare =
 2.47 acres
 107,600 sq ft
 11,960 sq yds
 =10,000 sq meters

Square kilometer =
 0.3861 sq miles
 247 acres
 =1,000,000 sq meters

Kilogram =
 2.205 pounds
 =1,000 grams

Liter =
 1.052 quarts
 0.263 quarts
 =1,000 milliliters

Metric ton =
 2,205 pounds
 1.102 tons
 =1,000 kilograms

Answers to Chapter Questions and Problems

Chapter 2
Nature and Description of Real Estate

VOCABULARY REVIEW

a. 17	e. 20	i. 9	m. 16	q. 18	t. 14
b. 19	f. 15	j. 1	n. 8	r. 6	u. 2
c. 11	g. 21	k. 22	o. 12	s. 5	v. 3
d. 4	h. 10	l. 13	p. 7		

QUESTIONS AND PROBLEMS

1. Requires local answer.

2.

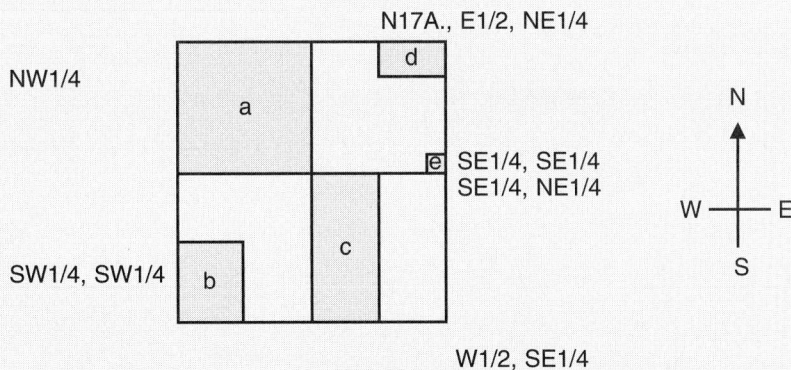

3. (a) 160 acres
    (b) 40 acres
    (c) 80 acres
    (d) 17 acres
    (e) 2½ acres

4. (a) NE¼
    (b) E½ of the SE¼
    (c) SW¼ of the NW¼
    (d) W½ of the SE¼ of the NW¼
    (e) NE¼ of the SE¼ of the NW¼

5.

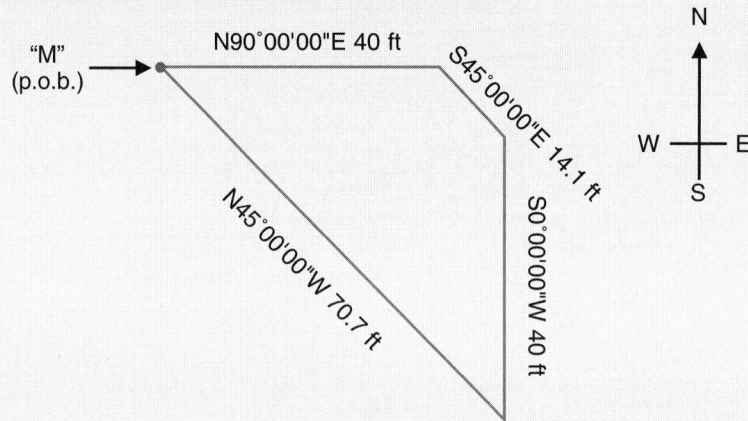

6. No. In the general public interest, laws have been passed that give aircraft the right to pass over land, provided they fly above certain altitudes.

7. The key to a door, although highly portable, is adapted to the door and as such is real property.

8. Requires individualized answer. However, as a general rule, anything that is permanently attached is real property and anything that is not attached is personal property.

9. Requires local answer.

10. Unless corrections are made (and they usually are), survey inaccuracies would result.

Chapter 3
Rights and Interests in Land

VOCABULARY REVIEW

a. 8	e. 13	i. 6	m. 21	q. 22	u. 24
b. 4	f. 20	j. 11	n. 10	r. 18	v. 17
c. 14	g. 7	k. 9	o. 12	s. 23	w. 15
d. 19	h. 5	l. 1	p. 2	t. 3	x. 16

QUESTIONS AND PROBLEMS

1. For a freehold estate to exist, there must be actual possession of the land (i.e., ownership) and the estate must be of unpredictable duration. Leasehold estates do not involve ownership of the land and are of determinate length. Freehold estate cases are tried under real property laws. Leasehold cases are tried under personal property laws.

2. An easement is created when a landowner fronting on a public byway deeds or leases a landlocked portion of his land to another person. This would be an easement by necessity. A second method is by prolonged use and is called an easement by prescription.

3. Requires local answer.

4. England, Spain, and France.

5. The holder of an easement coexists side by side with the landowner; that is, both may have a shared use of the land in question. The holder of a lease obtains exclusive right of occupancy and the landowner is excluded during the term of the lease.

6. An encumbrance is any impediment to clear title. Examples are lien, lease, easement, deed restriction, and encroachment.

7. Requires local answer. (Answers will likely center around zoning, building codes, general land planning, rent control, property taxation, eminent domain, and escheat.)

8. Requires local answer.

9. Requires local answer.

Chapter 4
Forms of Ownership

VOCABULARY REVIEW

a. 8	d. 10	g. 11	j. 4	m. 9	p. 6
b. 1	e. 5	h. 17	k. 13	n. 3	q. 7
c. 16	f. 12	i. 14	l. 15	o. 2	

QUESTIONS AND PROBLEMS

1. The key advantage of sole ownership is flexibility—the owner can make all decisions without approval of co-owners. The key disadvantages are responsibility and the high entry cost.

2. Undivided interest means that each co-owner has a right to use the entire property.

3. The four unities are

   Time: each must acquire ownership at the same moment.

   Title: all must acquire their interests from the same source.

   Interest: each owns an undivided whole of the property.

   Possession: all have the right to use the whole property.

4. Right of survivorship means that upon the death of a joint tenant, his interest in the property is extinguished and the remaining joint tenants are automatically left as the owners.

5. Requires local answer.

6. Requires local answer.

7. The three women would be considered to be tenants in common with each owning an undivided one-third interest.

8. No assumption can safely be made based on name only. Inquiry must be made into whether the land in question was separate or community property.

9. The key differences are in the financial liability of the limited partners, the limited management role of the limited partners, and the fact that limited partners are not found in a general partnership.

10. Real estate investment trusts (REITs) offer investors single taxation, built-in management, small minimum investment, and liquidity.

Chapter 5
Transferring Title

VOCABULARY REVIEW

a. 21	f. 7	k. 6	o. 24	s. 11	w. 25
b. 15	g. 14	l. 20	p. 4	t. 19	x. 2
c. 22	h. 16	m. 1	q. 3	u. 13	y. 8
d. 18	i. 5	n. 17	r. 12	v. 10	z. 26
e. 9	j. 23				

QUESTIONS AND PROBLEMS

1. Yes. The fact that a document is a deed depends on the wording it contains, not what it is labeled or not labeled.

2. Title passes upon delivery of the deed by the grantor to the grantee and its willing acceptance by the grantee.

3. The full covenant and warranty deed offers the grantee protection in the form of the grantor's assurances that he is the owner and possessor, that the grantee will not be disturbed after taking possession by someone else claiming ownership, that the title is not encumbered except as stated in the deed, and that the grantor will procure and deliver to the grantee any subsequent documents necessary to make good the title being conveyed.

4. Warranty deed. It provides the grantee with the maximum title protection available from a deed.

5. The hazards of preparing one's own deeds are that any errors made will cause confusion and may make the deed legally invalid. Preprinted deeds may not be suitable for the state where the land is located or for the grantor's purpose. An improperly prepared deed, once recorded, creates errors in the public records.

6. Dower right, curtesy right, community property right, mortgage right of redemption, tax lien, judgment lien, mechanic's lien, undivided interest held by another, inheritance rights, and easements are all examples of title clouds.

7. When a person dies without leaving a will, state law directs how that person's assets are to be distributed.

8. An executor is named by the deceased in the will to carry out its terms. In the absence of a will, the court appoints an administrator to settle the deceased's estate.

9. Requires local answer.

10. No. Occupancy on a rental basis is not hostile to the property owner, but rather, is by permission.

11. Requires local answer.

Chapter 6
Recordation, Abstracts, and Title Insurance

VOCABULARY REVIEW

a. 10	e. 2	i. 8	m. 19	q. 9	t. 21
b. 3	f. 6	j. 14	n. 11	r. 20	u. 17
c. 1	g. 18	k. 16	o. 5	s. 12	v. 22
d. 7	h. 13	l. 4	p. 15		

QUESTIONS AND PROBLEMS

1. Requires local answer.

2. Requires local answer.

3. By visibly occupying a parcel of land or by recording a document in the public records, a person gives constructive notice that he is claiming a right or interest in that parcel of land.

4. The grantor and grantee indexes are used to locate documents filed in the public recorder's office.

5. Although the bulk of the information necessary to conduct a title search can be found in the public recorder's office, it may also be necessary to inspect documents not kept there, for example, marriage records, judgment lien files, probate records, and the U.S. Tax Court.

6. A certificate of title issued by an attorney is his opinion of ownership, whereas a Torrens certificate of title shows ownership as determined by a court of law.

7. A title report shows the condition of title at a specific moment in time. An abstract provides a complete historical summary of all recorded documents affecting title. From this, an attorney renders an opinion as to the current condition of title.

8. The purpose of title insurance is to protect owners and lenders from monetary loss caused by errors in title report preparation and inaccuracies in the public records.

9. Although Williams did not record his deed, his occupancy of the house constitutes legal notice. The out-of-state investor, who probably felt safe because he bought a title insurance policy, apparently did not read the fine print, which, in most owner's policies, does not insure against facts, rights, interests, or claims that could be ascertained by an on-site inspection or by making inquiry of persons in possession. The out-of-state investor is the loser unless he can recover his money from Thorsen.

10. Requires local answer.

Chapter 7
Contract Law

VOCABULARY REVIEW

a. 12	f. 1	k. 11	o. 13	s. 18	w. 17
b. 20	g. 8	l. 3	p. 21	t. 9	x. 2
c. 14	h. 22	m. 16	q. 26	u. 15	y. 6
d. 4	i. 10	n. 5	r. 7	v. 24	z. 19
e. 23	j. 25				

QUESTIONS AND PROBLEMS

1. An expressed contract is the result of a written or oral agreement. An implied contract is one that is apparent from the actions of the parties involved. (Examples will vary with personal experiences.)

2. A legally valid contract requires (1) legally competent parties, (2) mutual agreement, (3) lawful objective, (4) sufficient consideration or cause, and (5) a writing when required by law.

3. A void contract has no legal effect on any party to the contract and may be ignored at the pleasure of any party to it. A voidable contract is a contract that is able to be voided by one of its parties.

4. Examples of legal incompetents include minors, insane persons, alcoholics, and felons. (Exceptions are possible in the latter two.)

5. An offer can be terminated by the passage of time and by withdrawal prior to its acceptance. Passage of time can be in the form of a fixed termination date for the offer or, lacking that, a reasonable amount of time to accept as fixed by a court of law.

6. Mistake as applied to contract law arises from ambiguity in negotiations and mistake of material fact.

7. Consideration is one of the legal requirements of a binding contract. The concept of one party doing something and receiving nothing in return is foreign to contract law. Examples are money, goods, services, and forbearance.

8. The parties to a legally unenforceable contract can still voluntarily carry out its terms. However, compliance could not be enforced by a court of law.

9. Alternatives include mutual rescission, assignment, novation, partial performance, money damages, unilateral rescission, specific performance suit, or liquidated damages.

10. His primary concern would be whether money damages would suitably restore his position or whether actual performance is necessary.

Chapter 8
Real Estate Sales Contracts

VOCABULARY REVIEW

a. 4	e. 18	h. 11	k. 14	n. 17	q. 13
b. 7	f. 5	i. 9	l. 16	o. 1	r. 8
c. 2	g. 3	j. 12	m. 15	p. 19	s. 10
d. 6					

QUESTIONS AND PROBLEMS

1. The purchase contract provides time to ascertain that the seller is capable of conveying title, time to arrange financing, and time to carry out the various terms and conditions of the contract.

2. Anything left to be "ironed out" later is an area for potential disagreement and possibly a lost deal. Moreover, the basic contract requirement of a meeting of the minds may be missing.

3. The advantages are convenience (the bulk of the contract is already written) and time (it is faster to fill out a form than construct a contract from scratch). The

disadvantages are that a preprinted contract may not adequately fit a given transaction and the blank spaces still leave room for errors.

4. A seller can accept an offer with or without a deposit. (An exception is that some court-ordered sales require a specified deposit.)

5. Most fixtures are considered by law to be a part of the land and therefore do not need separate mention. However, mention is made of any fixture that might be open to a difference of opinion.

6. If a seller is not under pressure to sell quickly and/or there are plenty of buyers in the marketplace, he can hold out for price and terms to his liking. If a buyer is aware of other buyers competing for the same property, he will act quickly and meet (or offer close to) the seller's price and terms. If the seller is in a rush to sell or is afraid that there are few buyers for his property in the market, he will negotiate terms more to the buyer's liking rather than risk not making the sale. If the buyer is aware of this, he can hold out for price and terms to his liking.

7. The advantages to the seller of holding title in an installment contract sale are that the seller still holds title in the event of the buyer's default and may be able to pledge the property as collateral for a loan.

8. Requires local answer.

9. The key advantages of trading are the tax-free exchange possibility and the need for little or no cash to complete the transaction. The disadvantages are in finding suitable trade property for all parties involved and in the fact that there are more transaction details in a trade (compared to a cash sale) that can go awry and ruin the trade.

10. A letter of intent is a mutual expression of interest to carry out some business objective. No firm, legal obligation is created.

Chapter 9
Mortgage and Note

VOCABULARY REVIEW

a. 26	f. 21	k. 3	o. 23	s. 17	w. 11
b. 9	g. 2	l. 22	p. 1	t. 24	x. 19
c. 13	h. 18	m. 4	q. 8	u. 7	y. 14
d. 6	i. 16	n. 15	r. 12	v. 25	z. 20
e. 10	j. 5				

QUESTIONS AND PROBLEMS

1. A prepayment privilege is to the advantage of the borrower. Without it the debt cannot be repaid ahead of schedule.

2. Lien theory sees a mortgage as creating only a lien against a property, whereas title theory sees a mortgage as conveying title to the lender subject to defeat by the borrower.

3. Strict foreclosure gives title to the lender, whereas foreclosure by sale requires that the foreclosed property be sold at public auction and the proceeds be used to repay the lender. (Part two requires local answer.)

4. The first mortgage is the senior mortgage while the second and third mortgages are classed as junior mortgages.

5. Requires local answer.

6. Requires local answer.

7. Requires local answer.

8. The obligor is the party making the obligation, that is, the borrower. The obligee is the party to whom the obligation is owed, that is, the lender.

9. The lender includes mortgage covenants pertaining to insurance, property taxes, and removal in order to protect the value of the collateral for the loan.

10. A certificate of reduction is prepared by the lender and shows how much remains to be paid on the loan. An estoppel certificate provides for a borrower's verification of the amount still owed and the rate of interest.

Chapter 10
Deed of Trust

VOCABULARY REVIEW

a. 11	c. 3	e. 8	g. 6	i. 9	k. 12
b. 7	d. 1	f. 10	h. 5	j. 4	l. 2

QUESTIONS AND PROBLEMS

1. The trustee's title lies dormant and there is no right of entry or use as long as the promissory note secured by the trust deed is not in default.

2. Under a deed of trust, the borrower gives the trustee title and gives the lender a promissory note. When the debt is paid, the lender instructs the trustee to reconvey title back to the borrower. With a mortgage, the lender acquires both the note and title (or lien rights) under the mortgage. Upon repayment, the lender releases the mortgage directly. In the event of default under a deed of trust, the trustee conducts the sale and delivers title to the buyer. With a mortgage, the lender is responsible for conducting the sale (if power of sale is present) or carrying out foreclosure proceedings.

3. A request for reconveyance is notification from the beneficiary to the trustee to reconvey (release) the trustee's title to the trustor.

4. The power of sale clause gives the trustee the right to foreclose the borrower's rights, sell the property, and convey title to a purchaser without having to go to court.

5. An assignment of rents clause gives the lender the right to operate the property and collect any rents or income generated by it if the borrower is delinquent.

6. In the automatic form, the trustee is not notified of his appointment as trustee and is usually unaware of it until called to perform in the event of default or to reconvey title when the note is paid. In the accepted form, the trustee agrees to his position as trustee at the time the deed of trust is prepared and signed.

7. Requires local answer.

Chapter 11
Lending Practices

VOCABULARY REVIEW

a. 6	c. 11	e. 10	g. 9	i. 5	k. 2
b. 7	d. 4	f. 8	h. 3	j. 1	

QUESTIONS AND PROBLEMS

1. The major risk is that when the balloon payment is due, the borrower will not have the cash to pay it and will not be able to find a lender to refinance it.

2. An amortized loan requires equal, periodic payments of principal and interest such that the loan balance owing will be zero at maturity. During the life of the loan, payments are first applied to interest owing and then to principal. As the balance owed is reduced, less of each monthly payment is taken for interest and more is applied to principal reduction until finally the loan is prepaid.

3. $65 \times \$9.91 = \$644.15$ per month

4. $\$800 \div \$9.53 \times \$1,000 + \$10,000 = \$93,945$

5. $\$800 \div \$8.05 \times \$1,000 + \$10,000 = \$109,379$

6. $\$902 \times 90 = \$81,180$

7. The Veterans Affairs (VA) offers a qualified veteran the opportunity of purchasing a home with no cash down payment.

8. A point is 1%. It is a method of expressing loan origination fees and discounts in connection with lending. Discount points are used to increase the effective rate of interest (yield) to the lender without changing the quoted interest rate.

Chapter 12
The Loan and the Consumer

VOCABULARY REVIEW

a. 1	b. 3	c. 6	d. 5	e. 2	f. 4

QUESTIONS AND PROBLEMS

1. As a rule, it is from the borrower's monthly income that monthly loan payments will be made. The assets, although substantial in size, may not be available for monthly payments.

2. The basic purpose of the Truth-in-Lending Act is to show the borrower how much he will be paying for credit in percentage terms and in total dollars.

3. No. The annual percentage rate calculation normally includes the interest rate in the note as part of the cost of the loan. Therefore, the annual percentage rate (APR) will be higher unless there are no other loan costs.

4. The Fair Credit Reporting Act controls accuracy and fairness for consumers in the granting of credit.

5. The right of rescission allows a borrower three days to back out of a transaction after executing the loan document. It is intended to eliminate loan sharking and high-pressure tactics in obtaining loans from consumers.

Chapter 13
Sources of Financing

VOCABULARY REVIEW

a. 9	c. 2	e. 4	g. 6	i. 3
b. 10	d. 5	f. 1	h. 8	j. 7

QUESTIONS AND PROBLEMS

1. A mortgage broker brings borrowers and lenders together. A mortgage banker makes loans and then resells them.

2. The main source of loan money in the secondary mortgage market is investors who buy mortgage-backed securities.

3. Loan servicing refers to the care and upkeep of a loan once it is made. This includes payment collection and accounting, handling defaults, borrower questions, loan payoff processing, and mortgage releasing.

4. Federal National Mortgage Association (FNMA) buys, by auction, mortgage loans. These purchases are financed by the sale of FNMA stock and bonds as well as the sale of these loans to investors. Government National Mortgage Association (GNMA) guarantees timely repayment of privately issued securities backed by pools of federally insured mortgages.

5. A loan dollar that is the result of real savings won't cause inflation. That is because the borrower is using goods and services the saver has foregone. But a fiat money dollar does not represent available goods and services; instead, it competes with real savings dollars and pushes prices up.

6. There is a large volume of investors who are willing to invest in the low-risk (mortgage-backed) notes, which makes more money available for home loans. It is a benefit for both the home mortgage borrower and the investor.

Chapter 14
Types of Financing

VOCABULARY REVIEW

a. 1	e. 13	h. 14	k. 7	n. 3	q. 6
b. 17	f. 16	i. 18	l. 15	o. 12	r. 4
c. 2	g. 9	j. 11	m. 5	p. 10	s. 19
d. 8					

QUESTIONS AND PROBLEMS

1. Adjustable rate loans share the risk of changing interest rates between the borrower and the lender. The lender feels more comfortable knowing the interest rate charged will change with the cost of money to the lender.

2. An adjustable rate mortgage is a loan on which the interest rate can be adjusted up or down as current interest rates change.

3. Rentals and leases are considered financing forms as they allow a person the use of something without having to first pay the full purchase price.

4. Above all, the investor should make certain that the realistic market value of the property is well in excess of the loans against it.

Chapter 15
Taxes and Assessments

VOCABULARY REVIEW

a. 10	d. 7	g. 14	j. 12	m. 16	o. 3
b. 2	e. 13	h. 9	k. 11	n. 8	p. 6
c. 4	f. 5	i. 15	l. 1		

QUESTIONS AND PROBLEMS

1. Sources of funds other than property taxes are subtracted from the district budget. The remainder is then divided by the total assessed valuation of property in the district to obtain the tax rate.

2. $960,000 divided by $120,000,000 equals 8 mills.

3. $40,000 times $0.008 equals $320.

4. $10,000 times $0.05 divided by $100 equals $5.

5. Requires local answer.

6. Requires local interpretation. However, the point is that the assessor does not set the tax rate. The assessor only applies it. If the complaint is in regard to assessment procedures, the assessment appeal process is taken. If it is in regard to the tax rate, then city, county, or state budget makers are responsible.

7. The greater the amount of tax-exempt property in a taxation district, the less taxable property is available to bear the burden of taxation.

8. Requires local answer.

9. $68,000 − $5,000 − ($21,000 + $2,000 + $5,000) = $35,000, none of which is subject to taxes.

10. Although their gain would be $5,000 ($68,000 − $5,000 − $58,000 = $5,000), none of it is subject to taxation, regardless of their ages.

11. Requires local answer.

Chapter 16
Title Closing and Escrow

VOCABULARY REVIEW

a. 15	d. 3	g. 2	j. 7	m. 5	o. 12
b. 11	e. 16	h. 9	k. 8	n. 1	p. 13
c. 14	f. 6	i. 10	l. 4		

QUESTIONS AND PROBLEMS

1. The key difference is that an escrow holder is a common agent of the parties to the transaction. This eliminates the need for each party to attend the closing and personally represent himself.

2. Escrow agent duties include preparation of escrow instructions, holding a buyer's earnest money, ordering a title search, obtaining title insurance, making prorations, loan payoffs, loan disbursement, deed and mortgage delivery, and handling papers and paperwork relative to the transaction.

3. The escrow agent is an agent of the buyer with respect to the buyer's role in the transaction and an agent of the seller with respect to the seller's role. The same holds true for the lender, title company, and so on. The escrow agent's duty is to treat all parties fairly and not to serve one party to the exclusion of the other.

4. $180 divided by 12 equals $15 per month or 50¢ per day. Using standard 30-day months and presuming the buyer is the owner commencing with the settlement date, there is 1 month and 26 days used, and there are 10 months and 4 days remaining. For this remaining coverage, the buyer pays the seller 10 times $15 plus 4 times $0.50 equals $152.00.

5. Daily rate equals $45,000 times 8% divided by 360 equals $10. The buyer is credited 11 days times $10 equals $110. The seller is debited the same amount.

6. **Buyer:**   **Seller:**

   Lender's title policy   conveyance tax

   loan appraisal fee   deed preparation

   mortgage recording   mortgage release

7. Without release papers, the buyer still has a vaguely defined liability to buy and the seller can still be required to sell.

Chapter 17
Real Estate Leases

VOCABULARY REVIEW

a. 19	f. 26	k. 2	o. 25	s. 14	w. 23
b. 4	g. 13	l. 1	p. 11	t. 24	x. 9
c. 18	h. 8	m. 6	q. 10	u. 22	y. 17
d. 21	i. 5	n. 16	r. 12	v. 7	z. 3
e. 20	j. 15				

QUESTIONS AND PROBLEMS

1. A lease assures a tenant space at the rent stated in the lease. But it also requires the tenant to pay for the total time leased. A month-to-month arrangement commits a tenant to one month at a time; however, it also commits the landlord for only one month at a time.

2. Requires local answer.

3. Requires local answer.

4. Contract rent is the amount of rent the tenant must pay the landlord. Economic rent is market value rent.

5. The tenant's basis would be that the premises is unfit to occupy as intended in the lease. The tenant's purpose is to either get the problem fixed or terminate the lease.

6. An option to renew is to the advantage of the lessee.

7. Requires local answer.

8. Questions asked will center on the prospective tenant's ability to pay the rent each month and willingness to abide by the lease contract. Names and addresses of the prospect's current employer and previous landlord would be requested and checked to verify information supplied by the tenant. A credit check would also be run.

Chapter 18
Real Estate Appraisal

VOCABULARY REVIEW

a. 7	f. 8	k. 18	o. 4	s. 9	w. 11
b. 16	g. 5	l. 24	p. 26	t. 15	x. 19
c. 23	h. 20	m. 17	q. 13	u. 2	y. 6
d. 12	i. 25	n. 21	r. 14	v. 3	z. 22
e. 1	j. 10				

QUESTIONS AND PROBLEMS

1. Enough comparables should be used to reasonably estimate market value but not so many as to involve more time and expense than is gained in added information. For a single-family house, three to five good comparables are usually adequate.

2. Asking prices are useful in that they set an upper limit on value. Offering prices are useful in that they set a lower limit on value.

3. Adjustments are made to the comparable properties. This is because it is impossible to adjust the value of something for which one does not yet know the value.

4. Using comparables that are not similar to the subject property with respect to zoning, neighborhood characteristics, size, or usefulness, requires adjustments that are likely to be very inaccurate or impossible to make.

5. Gross rent times gross rent multiplier equals indicated property value. The strength of this approach is in its simplicity. Its weakness is also in its simplicity as it overlooks anything other than gross rents.

6. The five steps are (1) estimate land value as though vacant, (2) estimate new construction cost of a similar building, (3) subtract estimated depreciation from construction cost to obtain (4) the indicated value of the structure, and (5) add this to the land value.

7. The income approach values a property based on its expected monetary returns in light of current rates of return being demanded by investors.

8. In the standard market comparison approach, a specific dollar adjustment is made for each item of difference between the comparables and the subject property. With competitive market analysis, adjustments are made in a generalized fashion in the minds of the agent and the seller. The competitive market analysis (CMA) approach

is usually preferred for listing homes for sale because there is less room for disagreement. The standard market approach is preferred for appraisal reports as it shows exactly how the appraiser valued the adjustments.

9. The principle of diminishing marginal returns warns against investing more than the capitalized value of the anticipated net returns.

10. All, under the new regulations, would require a formal appraisal report, although the departure provisions could be invoked.

11. The Appraisal Foundation was formed to establish regulations for the appraisal industry. It will raise standards for the appraisal industry.

Chapter 19
Licensing Laws and Professional Affiliation

VOCABULARY REVIEW

a. 6	e. 5	i. 1	m. 12	q. 20	u. 11
b. 21	f. 19	j. 15	n. 2	r. 9	v. 17
c. 14	g. 24	k. 16	o. 23	s. 10	w. 22
d. 18	h. 13	l. 4	p. 3	t. 8	x. 7

QUESTIONS AND PROBLEMS

1. In deciding on a compensation schedule for the salespersons, a broker must consider office overhead, employee retention, and the emphasis she wishes to place on listing versus selling.

2. Generally speaking, a real estate license is required when a person, who for compensation or the promise of compensation, lists or offers to list, sells or offers to sell, buys or offers to buy, negotiates or offers to negotiate, either directly or indirectly, for the purpose of bringing about a sale, purchase, option to purchase, exchange, auction, lease, or rental of, real estate. Some states also require that real estate appraisers, property managers, mortgage bankers, and rent collectors hold real estate licenses.

3. Early license laws were primarily aimed at protecting the public by qualifying license applicants based on their honesty, truthfulness, and good reputation. Real estate examinations and education requirements were added later.

4. Requires local answer.

5. Requires local answer.

6. Requires local answer.

7. Requires local answer.

8. Requires local answer.

9. The purpose of a bond requirement or a recovery fund is to have funds available that can be drawn upon in the event that a court judgment against a licensee, resulting from a license-related wrongdoing, is uncollectible.

10. The purpose of the National Association of REALTORS® is to promote the general welfare of the real estate industry by encouraging fair dealing among REALTORS® and the public, supporting legislation to protect property rights, offering education for members, and in general doing whatever is necessary to build the dignity, stability, and professionalization of the industry.

11. An employment contract will cover such matters as compensation, training, hours of work, company identification, fees and dues, expenses, use of an automobile, fringe benefits, independent contractor status, termination of employment, and general office policies and procedures.

12. You would want to consider location, compensation, broker's reputation, working hours, broker support, training opportunities, advertising policy, expense reimbursement, and fringe benefits.

Chapter 20
The Principal-Broker Relationship: Employment

VOCABULARY REVIEW

a. 8   c. 3   e. 9   g. 5   h. 1   i. 7
b. 4   d. 2   f. 6

QUESTIONS AND PROBLEMS

1. An exclusive right to sell listing protects the broker by entitling him to a commission no matter who sells the property. The exclusive agency listing puts the broker in competition with the owner by allowing the owner to find a buyer and owe no commission. The open listing adds other brokers to the competition as any number of brokers can have the listing simultaneously and the owner can still sell it himself and pay no commission.

2. A ready, willing, and able buyer is a buyer who is ready to buy at the seller's price and terms and who has the financial capacity to do so.

3. Listings are usually terminated with the completion of the agency objective, namely finding a buyer or a tenant. Lacking a buyer, termination usually results when the listing period expires. A listing can also be terminated if the broker fails to perform as agreed in the listing or if the broker and principal mutually agree to terminate.

4. The broker employed by the seller focuses on making the sale, marketing. The broker employed by the buyer focuses on obtaining the product to suit the buyer's needs and potential uses.

Chapter 21
The Principal-Broker Relationship: Agency

VOCABULARY REVIEW

a. 12   d. 5   g. 4   j. 15   l. 3   n. 2
b. 14   e. 10   h. 7   k. 8   m. 13   o. 11
c. 6   f. 9   i. 1

QUESTIONS AND PROBLEMS

1. **Faithful**: the broker must perform as promised in the listing contract and not depart from the principal's instructions.

Loyal: the broker owes his allegiance to the principal and as such works for the benefit of the principal. This means promoting and protecting the principal's best interests and keeping him informed of all matters that might affect the sale of the listed property.

2. Broker cooperation refers to the sharing of a single commission fee among the various brokers who brought about a sale. It is achieved by an agreement between the listing broker and the cooperating brokers.

3. The laws of agency refer to the legal responsibilities of a broker to his principal and vice versa.

4. An agency coupled with an interest exists when the agent holds an interest in the property he is representing.

5. The purpose of a property disclosure statement is to require that sellers of subdivisions provide prospective purchasers with information regarding the property they are being asked to buy; requires local answer.

6. Errors and omissions insurance are designed to defend and pay certain legal costs and judgments arising from business negligence suits.

7. Requires individual answer.

Chapter 22
Fair Housing, ADA, Equal Credit, and Community Reinvestment

VOCABULARY REVIEW

a. 10	d. 12	f. 3	h. 7	j. 6	l. 9
b. 5	e. 8	g. 1	i. 4	k. 13	m. 2
c. 11					

QUESTIONS AND PROBLEMS

1. Yes, lawyers are not a protected class of individuals, so long as this is the only reason you are not selling to her. Remember that if that lawyer is a minority member, she may have a discrimination suit on other grounds.

2. The U.S. Constitution deals primarily with fundamental rights: race, color, creed, national origin, and alienage. The statutes have expanded the coverage to sex and marital status, age, and handicapped discrimination theories.

3. Requires local answer but should include hosting of Community Reinvestment Act (CRA) disclosures and advertising in local community publications.

4. Brokerage services are regulated and monitored by every individual state through their various licensing laws. Brokers also have the most significant effect in marketing and sales of real estate throughout the country; therefore, the regulation of fair housing through brokers reaches more people faster and is easier to monitor in specific controls on every individual.

5. No, constitutional protections extend to white, Anglo-Saxon persons as they do to any other class, based on race, color, creed, national origin, or alienage.

6. Requires individual answer.

7. No, even if a real estate agent thinks that a neighborhood is safer, it may be perceived by the consumer that they are being "steered" for any number of other different reasons. It is best to always let the purchaser decide which neighborhoods they want to choose to avoid complications of steering and discrimination allegations.

Chapter 23
Condominiums, Cooperatives, PUDs, and Time-shares

VOCABULARY REVIEW

a. 16	e. 1	i. 2	l. 14	o. 4	r. 20
b. 15	f. 11	j. 8	m. 9	p. 10	s. 18
c. 7	g. 6	k. 13	n. 17	q. 5	t. 19
d. 3	h. 12				

QUESTIONS AND PROBLEMS

1. Condominiums are often cheaper to buy than a single-family house, are often better located, may offer better security and maintenance, and can be individually financed.

2. Each condominium unit owner holds an undivided interest in the land in a fee simple condominium project. The corporation owns the land in a cooperative.

3. A proprietary lease is a lease issued by a corporation to its stockholders. The lease "rent" is actually the stockholder's share of the cost of operating the building and repaying the debt against it. In a residential lease, the tenant pays for use of the premises, is not responsible for operating expenses or debt repayment, and does not have an ownership interest in the premises.

4. The master deed converts a given parcel of land into a condominium subdivision.

5. The wall between two condominium apartments belongs to the condominium owners as a group.

6. CC&Rs are the covenants, conditions, and restrictions by which a property owner agrees to abide. They are established for the harmony and well-being of the owners as a group.

7. Maintenance fees (association dues) pay for common operating costs and are spread among the unit owners. Failure to pay creates a lien against the delinquent owner's unit.

8. The owners' association hazard and liability policy covers only the common elements. To be protected against property loss and accident liability within a dwelling unit, the owner must have his own hazard and liability policy.

9. Right-to-use is a contractual right, whereas fee simple is ownership of real estate.

10. In a planned unit development (PUD), each owner holds title to the land occupied by his unit and is a member of an owners' association that holds title to the common areas.

Chapter 24
Property Insurance

VOCABULARY REVIEW

a. 10	d. 13	g. 3	j. 9	m. 5	p. 8
b. 11	e. 6	h. 2	k. 16	n. 4	q. 15
c. 12	f. 7	i. 14	l. 17	o. 1	

QUESTIONS AND PROBLEMS

1. An endorsement or rider is an agreement by the insurer to modify the coverage found in the basic policy.

2. Liability insurance is concerned with insuring against financial losses resulting from the responsibility of one person to another.

3. Section I in a home insurance policy covers loss of and damage to the insured's property. Section II deals with the liability of the insured.

4. All-risk insurance policies cover loss or damage resulting from any cause not excluded by the policy. A broad-form policy is one that covers a large number of perils that are specifically named in the policy.

5. "New for old" means that the insurer will pay for replacement at today's costs. Thus, although the property lost by the insured was used, he will receive a new replacement from the insurer.

6. Coverage is suspended on vacant buildings because they are more attractive to thieves, vandals, and arsonists than are occupied buildings.

Chapter 25
Land-Use Control

VOCABULARY REVIEW

a. 8	d. 6	g. 1	i. 4	k. 5	m. 9
b. 12	e. 13	h. 14	j. 3	l. 10	n. 2
c. 11	f. 7				

QUESTIONS AND PROBLEMS

1. The individual property owner does not consider his property to be a community resource. Thus, any substantial progress in land planning and control in the future must also consider the right of the individual to develop his land.

2. The authority of government to control land use is derived from the state's right of police power. Through enabling acts, this authority is passed on to the counties, cities, and towns in the state.

3. A variance allows an individual landowner to deviate from strict compliance with zoning requirements for his land. A variance must be consistent with the character

of the neighborhood and general objectives of zoning as they apply to that neighborhood.

4. Requires local answer.

5. A master plan takes a broad look at the entire land-use picture in a community, county, or region. The object is to view the area as a unified entity that provides its residents with jobs and housing as well as social, recreational, and cultural activities. In contrast, zoning laws tell a landowner specifically how a parcel of land may be used and what type and size structures may be placed on it.

6. The purpose of an environmental impact statement (EIS) is to gather information about the effect of a proposed project on the environment so that the anticipated environmental costs and benefits of the project may be considered along with the economic and humanitarian aspects.

7. Transferable development rights would equalize financial windfalls and wipeouts by requiring those whose land is approved for urban uses to purchase development rights from those whose land is prohibited from development.

8. Requires local answer.

Chapter 26
Real Estate and the Economy

VOCABULARY REVIEW

a. 1   c. 4   e. 8   g. 10   i. 5   j. 2
b. 6   d. 3   f. 7   h. 9

QUESTIONS AND PROBLEMS

1. Requires local answer.

2. Requires local answer.

3. Requires local answer.

4. The Reagan years slowed inflation and they lowered interest rates, making housing more affordable. They also resulted in a loss of jobs as the economy was restructured.

5. The purpose of the Equal Credit Opportunity Act is to require lenders to make credit available without regard to sex or marital status.

6. Requires individual answer.

7. Clinton attempted to avoid supply-side economics, but the effect did not produce a marked change.

8. The economic goals of the Federal Reserve Board are high employment, stable prices, steady growth, and a stable foreign exchange value for the dollar.

9. The advantage is that in the short-run interest rates can be pushed down, which gives the economy a boost. The disadvantage is that inflation will result.

10. Rising prices.

Chapter 27
Investing in Real Estate

VOCABULARY REVIEW

a. 7	d. 8	g. 9	i. 5	k. 2	m. 6
b. 14	e. 1	h. 4	j. 13	l. 10	n. 3
c. 12	f. 11				

QUESTIONS AND PROBLEMS

1. Investors in real estate look for cash flow, tax shelter, mortgage reduction, and appreciation.

2. A tax-sheltered investment is one where part or all of the return from a property is not subject to income taxes. The primary source is depreciation, which, although shown as an expense for calculating income taxes, is not an out-of-pocket (cash) expense.

3. The major risk of owning vacant land is having to wait too long for an increase in value. Another risk is that it may decrease in value. Taxes and carrying costs can also be high.

4. The advantages of duplexes and triplexes are that, compared to larger buildings, the investor's capital, management, and risk are on a smaller scale. These buildings are not, however, as efficient to manage, and rents are often relatively low per dollar of purchase price.

5. "Better off" must be considered in light of the investor's objectives and ability to take risks. The earlier one invests, the bigger the risks and potential rewards. By waiting, one can lower the risks and the rewards.

6. Higher returns are necessary in an older building to compensate for major replacement, repair, and refurbishing costs; for increasing maintenance expenses; for the risk that the neighborhood may decline in popularity; and for the building's limited remaining economic usefulness.

7. A person who has a number of high-income years remaining in life can more comfortably take risks as there is time to recover financially if losses should result. An older person without the time and energy to recover financially would seek to avoid risky investments.

8. $22,000 ÷ 0.10756 = $204,537. Round to $205,000.

9. $22,000 ÷ 0.11819 = $186,141. Round to $186,000.

10. Limited partnerships offer the investor the advantages of relatively small minimum investment, built-in property management, limited financial liability, the opportunity to diversify, and the same tax benefits as sole owners.

11. A careful investor will check out both the properties and the general partners. Do the general partners have a good record in selecting, organizing, and managing real estate investments? Are they honest and creditworthy? Are there lawsuits or other legal complaints against them? Regarding the properties, are the income and expense projections accurate and reasonable? Are the properties in sound physical and financial condition? Are they well located? Are they priced right? Are the tax benefits realistic? Is there financial responsibility or liability for the limited partner in the future? Is the limited partner willing and able to stay in the partnership for its full life span?

INDEX & GLOSSARY

Note: Page numbers referencing figures are italicized and followed by an "*f.*" Page numbers referencing tables are italicized and followed by a "*t.*" Also, boldfaced terms identify key terms from chapters.

B

Balloon loan: any loan in which the final payment is larger than the preceding payments, 186

Balloon payment: the name given to the final payment of a balloon loan, 186

Bare title, 195. *See* Naked title

Bargain and sale deed: a deed that contains no covenants but does imply that the grantor owns the property being conveyed, 78–79

Bargain broker, 396

Base industry: an industry that produces goods or services for export from the region, 474

Base line: a latitude line selected as a reference in the rectangular survey system, 19

Basic form (HO-1), 451

Basis: the price paid for property; used in calculating income taxes, 267–268

Bench mark: a reference point of known location and elevation, 17–18

Beneficial interest: a unit of ownership in a real estate investment trust, 66

Beneficiary: one for whose benefit a trust is created; the lender in a deed of trust arrangement, 65, 167

Beneficiary statement: a lienholder's statement as to the unpaid balance on a trust deed note, 276–277

Benefits, RESPA, 290

Bequest: personal property received under a will, 81

Bid the loan, 159

Bilateral contract: results when a promise is exchanged for a promise, 107–108

Bill of sale: a document that shows the transfer of personal property, 12

Binder: a short purchase contract used to secure a real estate transaction until a more formal contract can be signed, 131–132

Biweekly loan payment, 188

Blanket mortgage: a mortgage secured by two or more properties, 250

Blended-rate loan: a refinancing plan that combines the interest rate on an existing mortgage loan with current rates, 251–252

Blind pool: an investment pool wherein properties are purchased after investors have already invested their money, 507

Block busting: the illegal practice of inducing panic selling in a neighborhood for financial gain, 422

Blue-sky laws, 510

Board of directors, 437

Board of equalization: a governmental body that reviews property tax assessment procedures, 264

BOMI (Building Owners and Managers Institute), 317

Bonds, 231, 266–267, 361–362

Borrower analysis, 213–214

Borrowing short, 233

Boycotting: two or more people conspiring to restrain competition, 415

Branch offices, 359

Breach of contract: failure, without legal excuse, to perform as required by a contract, 116–118

Broad form (HO-2): an insurance policy that covers a large number of named perils, 451

Broad market: one wherein many buyers and many sellers are in the market at the same time, 348

Broker: a person or legal entity licensed to act independently in conducting a real estate brokerage business, 353
    bargain, 396
    compensation, 393–394
    cooperating, 407–410
    discount, 396
    flat-fee, 396
    obligations to principal, 401–404
    obligations to third parties, 404–406
    overview, 353
    protection of, 387–388
    sales staff, 407
    selection of, 407–365
    support, 364

Brokerage commission, 386–387

Budget, 261–262

Budget mortgage: feature loan payments that include principal, interest, taxes, and insurance (often called PITI), 186

Buffer zone: a strip of land that separates one land use from another, 462

Building codes: local and state laws that set minimum construction standards, 463

Building condition, 326

Building Owners and Managers Institute (BOMI): professional designation for property managers, 317

Building recycling, 504

Building societies, 228

Bundle of rights concept, 37

M